CONSERVATION AND MANAGEMENT OF ARCHAEOLOGICAL SITES

SPECIAL ISSUE: The 4th International Conference on Preserving Archaeological Remains *In Situ* (PARIS4): 23–26 May 2011, the National Museum of Denmark, Copenhagen
Guest Editors: David Gregory and Henning Matthiesen

VOLUME 14   NUMBERS 1–4   2012

CONTENTS

T0407697

CONSERVATION AND MGMT OF ARCH. SITES, Vol. 14 Nos 1–4, 2012, 1–6

EDITORIAL

The 4th International Conference on Preserving Archaeological Remains *In Situ* (PARIS4): 23–26 May 2011, the National Museum of Denmark, Copenhagen

DAVID GREGORY and HENNING MATTHIESEN

The advocacy of preserving archaeological sites *in situ* has been politically galvanized internationally and certainly within Europe through a number of conventions: the European Convention for the Protection of Archaeological Heritage 1969 (The London Convention), updated in 1992 as the Valetta Convention.[1] The treaty aims to protect the European archaeological heritage 'as a source of European collective memory and as an instrument for historical and scientific study. All remains and objects and any other traces of humankind from past times are considered elements of the archaeological heritage. The notion of archaeological heritage includes structures, constructions, groups of buildings, developed sites, moveable objects, monuments of other kinds as well as their context, whether situated on land or under water'. In particular, Articles 4ii and 5vii respectively seek the conservation and maintenance of archaeological heritage preferably *in situ* and to make provisions for *in situ* conservation, when feasible, in connection with building/development work. In terms of underwater archaeology, the Annex (General principles, Rule 1) of the international 2001 UNESCO Convention on the Protection of the Underwater Cultural Heritage[2] recommends that the protection of underwater cultural heritage through *in situ* preservation shall be considered as the first option.

It was the advent of the Valetta Treaty, increasingly backed up by national legislation that made preservation *in situ* the preferred option for dealing with archaeological evidence on sites being developed, that began to see concentrated efforts within Europe to investigate the feasibility and efficacy of *in situ* preservation. The results of much of this research have been presented in the international conferences that have collectively become known as the PARIS conferences (Preserving Archaeological Remains In Situ). The first and second conferences were organized and hosted by English Heritage and the Museum of London in the United Kingdom in 1996 (Corfield et al., 1998) and 2001 (Nixon, 2004), and the third by the Vrije University

   DOI 10.1179/1350503312Z.00000000042

in the Netherlands in 2006 (Kars and van Heeringen, 2008). The fourth conference was organized and hosted by the National Museum of Denmark in Copenhagen in 2011. The conference was made possible with grants and goodwill from the National Museum of Denmark, the Farumgaard Foundation, the National Cultural Heritage Agency of Denmark, English Heritage, the Viking Ship Museum in Denmark, the Danish Palaces and Properties Agency, and the Museum of Copenhagen. The conference attracted over a hundred participants. An interesting development for the conference was the geographic broadening of participants and the research presented, with delegates coming from Denmark, Sweden, Norway, the United Kingdom, Germany, the Netherlands, Belgium, Eire, Finland, France, Belgium, Italy, Portugal, Croatia, Turkey, USA, Australia, and New Zealand.

The key aim of the conference was to present and discuss the latest knowledge, yet focusing on long-term studies of degradation and monitoring of archaeological sites preserved *in situ* in urban, rural, and marine environments. One of the strengths of the PARIS conferences is their multidisciplinary nature bringing together scientists, heritage managers, and policy makers. Building on this, focus was given to presentations from both practitioners (scientists and archaeologists) and stakeholders (cultural resource managers) to cover the four following themes, taking into account the benefit of hindsight of almost twenty years' research.

1. Degradation of archaeological remains. Can we quantify the degradation rates and what rates are acceptable?
2. Monitoring and mitigation studies — with special focus on long-term projects. How and how long should sites be monitored?
3. Protocols standards and legislation for monitoring and management. Is it realistic to make multinational standards when the sites and national legislations are so variable?
4. Preserving archaeological remains *in situ*. Can we document the effectiveness of *in situ* preservation after nearly two decades of research?

The four themes were covered through a total of forty-six oral and poster presentations. Each theme was chaired by a practitioner and a stakeholder in order to try see 'both sides of the coin'. The conference was closed with a round table discussion, with panel members from the scientific committee. The full transcript of the round table is available on the conference home page[3] and key points have been included as part of our editorial.

Theme 1. Degradation of archaeological remains. Can we quantify degradation rates and what rates are acceptable?

This theme included twelve presentations at the conference (ten oral presentations and two posters) with nine papers in these proceedings. The papers represent different approaches to studying degradation and quantifying degradation rates. A literature-based approach using carbon budgets was presented by Durham et al. (wetlands in the UK). Field studies focusing on environmental monitoring and the state of preservation of archaeological material was presented by Martens et al. (urban deposits in Norway), and field studies of degradation processes were given by Ricci et al.

(underwater bioerosion of stone) and by Huismann (impact of piling and compression); however, these studies did not include estimates of actual degradation rates. Repeated visits to field sites using standardized documentation and monitoring was suggested by Heumüller (erosion of lake dwellings in Lake Constance). Model experiments were presented by several authors as a useful supplement for measuring degradation rates: microcosms in the laboratory were used by Gelbrich et al. (decay of wood), whereas modern replica samples were used in the field by Richards et al. (marine corrosion). By combining both model experiments, field monitoring, and descriptions of the archaeological objects Saheb et al. (corrosion of iron under anoxic conditions) studied corrosion mechanisms and estimated degradation rates that were validated by ground truthing. Overall, the presentations showed a whole range of different tools to study the degradation of archaeological remains, and also that it is necessary to combine several tools if degradation rates shall be estimated and validated. None of the presentations discussed what rates are acceptable.

The round table discussion on this theme was opened by Jim Williams from English Heritage and Mark Pollard from Oxford University. They pointed out that we already have many of the tools necessary to investigate degradation rates, and there are already a lot of data available from deterioration/preservation research and other research fields. However, we really need to ground truth the predictions from these tools and models. The question about 'what rates are acceptable' was discussed, but in general people were reluctant to give fixed limits as it depends on the sites in question. At this stage it is necessary to quantify, publish, and compare decay rates from a large number of different sites and different conditions in order to gain more experience with decay rates. We need to know what we can expect in the ideal and non-ideal situation before setting limits or goals.

Theme 2. Monitoring and mitigation studies — with special focus on long-term projects. How and how long should sites be monitored?

This theme included sixteen presentations (ten oral presentations and six posters) at the conference with fifteen papers in these proceedings. The case studies covered monitoring and mitigation strategies on a gamut of archaeological sites and environments. These ranged from: underwater sites (Richards, Pascoe, Petriaggi and Davidde, and Bjordal et al.); waterlogged rural sites (Jones and Bell, Lillie et al., Tjelldén et al., Dal Ri and Fruet); waterlogged urban sites (de Beer et al., Petersen and Bergersen), an arctic site (Hollesen et al.), the remains of built heritage sites (Goodburn Brown, Bai, De Mattia) and a complete country (de Lange et al.).

Many of the papers which discussed monitoring, especially those sites on land, discussed the variety of methods available for classifying and assessing the physical, chemical and biological environment. Aside from the description of the methods, it was also interesting to see progress in the interpretation and presentation of monitoring results. Of particular note was the development and use of models, modelling software, and geographical information systems (GIS) to come to grips with the great wealth of information modern dataloggers provide. This was highlighted particularly in the presentations by Bjordal et al. where GIS had been used to look at the spread of shipworm in the Baltic. De Beer et al. showed the hydrodynamic and geochemical modelling and 3D presentation of the conditions around the world heritage site of Bryggen in Bergen Norway. De Lange et al. showed the development of a predictive 3D model to assess the effects of compression of archaeological soils and sediments. This could be used to assess the likely effects of any building/development work around sites in the Netherlands. In the round table discussion, chaired by Jane Sidell, English Heritage, and Hans Huismann, the Dutch Cultural Heritage Agency, it was commented that perhaps the theme should have included not only how should we monitor but what should we monitor. This entails focusing upon what the aim of monitoring is: it may be purely intellectual archaeological questions; questions of establishing a baseline, monitoring the trend of decay, monitoring information loss. Petersen's and Bergersens paper on monitoring in Trondheim addressed this in part and showed the use of the Norwegian standard for monitoring (see Theme 3). The question of what to monitor was perfectly illustrated in Pascoe's paper concerning the monitoring of the wreck of the Sterling Castle in England, which was in part monitored using 3D marine geophysical techniques. This showed that the wreck was in a very dynamic environment being covered and uncovered due to sediment transport, with each episode leading to more loss of information both in terms of artefacts and archaeological context. Richards' and Patriaggi and Davidde's paper may offer some possible solutions to mitigation for the deteriorative processes in the marine environment as they discussed the *in situ* stabilization of the wreck of the *James Matthews* in Australia and the restoration and display of ancient underwater sites in Italy. On land, Goodburn Brown's and Bais paper discussed mitigation methods for re-buried and upstanding monuments on land.

The round table discussion also picked up on the consequences of monitoring and mitigation. The current editors have argued for a process-oriented approach to *in situ* preservation — what are the threats to a site, regardless of its environment, how can these be assessed and quantified (monitoring). Based on this baseline data, is the site safe or are mitigation measures required? However, if monitoring shows that the site is at risk of deterioration and mitigation methods are not the optimal solution, what happens then? How do we prioritize what should be preserved?

Theme 3. Protocols, standards, and legislation for monitoring and management. Is it realistic to make multinational standards when the sites and national legislations are so variable?

This theme included eight presentations (six oral presentations and two posters) at the conference with seven papers in these proceedings. The papers demonstrate the variability in monitoring and management in different countries. From Norway, Loska and Christensson presented a Norwegian Standard describing in detail how archaeological deposits shall be documented and monitored by standardized methods during and after development projects at urban sites. The methods included visual description, laboratory analyses and field monitoring with automated equipment. From the Netherlands, Os et al. suggested a simple method for assessing the burial environment based on visual observations during excavations. From Belgium, Goeminne described an organization that monitor the condition of the archaeological heritage, mainly based on visual observations, and from Turkey Kökten described how practical problems sometimes hinder a continued monitoring and maintenance of floor mosaics. From Croatia, Plēše described the management of a Roman site, however, without giving details on the monitoring. Overall the presentations represented a whole range of different approaches to monitoring — from detailed instrument based monitoring at individual sites, visual observations during excavation, to visual registration from the soil surface during systematic visits to a large number of sites — and all these approaches are probably needed in a standard monitoring scheme.

The round table discussion on this theme was opened by Jens Rytter from the Directorate of Cultural Heritage in Norway and Henk Kars from Vrije Universitet in Amsterdam. They pointed out that the standards need to be tested under different conditions, and to that end the Norwegian monitoring standard is currently being tested in England. As for international standards, Stub Johnsen from Denmark gave an overview of ongoing work to make CEN standards within the field of conservation, where he showed that the standardization procedure is relatively slow and it can be difficult to combine the needs in different countries. This was also emphasized in the round table discussion and overall it was concluded that the time is probably not ripe yet for making international standards for monitoring of *in situ* preserved archaeological sites — the national standards need to be implemented and their use evaluated first. It was suggested to work on 'guidelines for good practice' instead of rigid standards, as the latter are difficult to change when new knowledge has been gained.

Theme 4. Preserving archaeological remains *in situ* — can we document it works?

This theme included ten presentations (seven oral presentations and three posters) and all are presented in these proceedings. The majority of papers came from the UK (Sidell, Corfield, Brunning, Panter and Malim, and Williams), which may be understandable as systematic *in situ* preservation has been part of planning policy guides since the early 1990s. However, results of other long-term projects from Sweden (Godfrey and Bergstrand), Denmark (Gregory and Matthiesen) and the Netherlands (Huisman et al.) were also presented. Sidell's paper bodes well for *in situ* preservation, where sites that had been excavated up to 150 years ago, many of which were in good condition upon re-excavation in the recent past. The question of testing the efficacy of mitigation and monitoring methods also arose with the question of the Rose Theatre (Corfield), which was one of the first attempts to systematically monitor and rebury an urban site. The site has been continually monitored and is due to be re-excavated, so it will be interesting to see how the site has fared after twenty years. Brunning's, Panter and Malim's, and Williams' work brought together the pioneering work carried out in the UK over the past twenty years. Work on the Somerset levels, showed an excellent approach to systematic *in situ* preservation, particularly in terms of the efficacy of monitoring methods and also that in some areas it works and some areas it has not. This was reflected in the other papers from the UK and the Netherlands (Huisman et al.) and a general feeling was that monitoring methodology has improved significantly over the past twenty years. This was reflected in the round table discussion, chaired by Mike Corfield, former chief scientist for English Heritage, and Vicki Richards from the Western Australian Museum. However, both papers and the following discussion reflected that the aims and goals of *in situ* preservation should be better stated from the outset with thorough project planning, quality assurance and interdisciplinary involvement, and review of projects. It was also highlighted that the state of preservation of material on a site (both environmental and artefactual) should be a prerequisite when developing any *in situ* preservation strategy. One of the very interesting developments from previous PARIS conferences reflected in the aforementioned papers, and also by Godfrey and Bergstrand's paper, was the need for better understanding and communication between all parties involved with *in situ* preservation (archaeologists, conservators, planners, heritage, and other government agencies with responsibility for the natural environment) and a good dialogue should happen from the outset of a project. Furthermore, there should be other options available if monitoring and mitigation methods show that *in situ* preservation is not optimal. Only in this manner can we ensure that preservation *in situ* is a viable and realistic option.

To conclude, the PARIS4 conference has been successful in bringing together stakeholders and practitioners working with *in situ* preservation in a large number of countries. The presentations and discussions were of a high quality, and it was remarkable how the level of knowledge has developed since the first PARIS conference in 1996. The next PARIS conference will take place at Lake Constance in April 2015 — further details may be found on <www.archaeologie.tg.ch> in due course. Hopefully, the knowledge level will have increased even more by then — there is still work to be done: quantifying degradation rates, improving mitigation methods, developing guidelines for best practice, and documenting when *in situ* preservation is a realistic option and when it is not.

Notes

1 <http://conventions.coe.int/Treaty/en/Treaties/html/066.htm> and <http://conventions.coe.int/Treaty/en/Treaties/html/143.htm>

2 <http://www.unesco.org/new/en/culture/themes/underwater-cultural-heritage>

3 <http://natmus.dk/bevaringsafdelingen/forskning-analyse-og-raadgivning/kongresser/paris4>

Bibliography

Corfield, M., Hinton, P., Nixon, T., and Pollard, M. eds. 1998. *Preserving Archaeological Remains In Situ. Proceedings of the Conference of 1–3 April 1996*. London: Museum of London Archaeology Service.

Kars, H. and van Heeringen, R. M. eds. 2008. *Preserving Archaeological Remains In Situ: Proceedings of the 3rd Conference, 7–9 December 2006*. Amsterdam: Amsterdam: Institute for Geo and Bioarchaeology.

Nixon, T. ed. 2004. *Preserving Archaeological Remains In Situ? Proceedings of the 2nd Conference 12–14 September 2001*. London: Museum of London Archaeology Service.

CONSERVATION AND MGMT OF ARCH. SITES, Vol. 14 Nos 1–4, 2012, 7–15

Laboratory Experiments as Support for Development of *In Situ* Conservation Methods

JANA GELBRICH
German Maritime Museum, Germany

EV IRIS KRETSCHMAR
Federal Environment Agency, Germany

NORBERT LAMERSDORF
University of Goettingen, Germany

HOLGER MILITZ
University of Goettingen, Germany

Within the EU-Project BACPOLES (EVK4-CT-2001-00043) bacterial wood degradation could be simulated in laboratory experiments to investigate the living conditions of the up to now unknown bacteria consortia, named erosion bacteria (EB), which cause considerable decay on waterlogged archaeological wood. In these Microcosm (MC) experiments the role of oxygen and chemical composition of the sediment were investigated. Therefore, the microcosms were subjected to different gassing treatments and the free dissolved oxygen was measured in different depths of the microcosms by special oxygen sensors (optodes). In further experiments the chemical composition of the sediment was verified to investigate the influence of different nutrient concentrations to the degradation process by EB.

From the findings it can be concluded that bacterial wood decay can proceed without free oxygen present but that it is more intense if oxygen is available. A water flow like streams in the sea, simulated by vertical water circulation, seems to stimulate the degradation activity and the degradation of wood by EB seems to be a result of low nutrient levels in the surrounding area.

KEYWORDS waterlogged wood, erosion bacteria, decay simulation, microcosms, preservation strategies, *in situ* conservation

 DOI 10.1179/1350503312Z.0000000001

Introduction

Archaeological wood, stored in water-saturated conditions, must be well preserved as cultural heritage. The main enzymatic wood degraders in such near or completely anoxic conditions are erosion bacteria (EB) and up to now it has not been possible to prevent completely this kind of wood degradation in *in situ* or reburial conservations (Nyström Godfrey et. al., 2007).

For development of preservation strategies fundamental knowledge about the living conditions of the EB is needed. To gain new insights into the bacterial wood decay, the European project BACPOLES EVK4-CT-2001-00043 ('Preserving cultural heritage by preventing bacterial decay of wood foundation poles and archaeological sites') was initiated in 2002. The main two objectives of this project were, i) to determine environmental conditions which favour bacterial wood degradation, and ii) to develop environmental friendly preservation or conservation strategies against bacterial wood decay by laboratory experiments.

All previous investigations using pure cultures of isolated bacteria had failed to provide wood degradation. Therefore, the Microcosm experiments were conducted based on the simulation of living conditions using naturally occurring bacteria consortia (Kretschmar, 2007; Kretschmar et al., 2008a; Gelbrich, 2009; Gelbrich et al., 2010). Most of these results can be used directly as a basis for improvement of *in situ* or reburial conservation strategies, as will be presented in this paper.

Material and methods

Microcosm set up

To simulate bacterial wood degradation under laboratory conditions, naturally occurring bacteria consortia are necessary. The source medium of bacteria was sediment and ground water from a heavily decayed pine pile foundation site in the south of Amsterdam (NL), as well as already moderately infected pine sapwood sticks originating from a foundation pile extracted in Koog an de Zaan (NL). As microcosms, acrylic glass cylinders or glass jars were used and filled with original sediment. The already infected wood was placed in the middle. To stimulate decay, sound sapwood sticks were added, arranged in one or two layers in circles around the infected wood sample in the middle. All wood samples were completely submerged into the sediment and, finally, packed MCs were filled with ground water from the sediment sample site until the sediment column was overlaid by water for a completely water-saturated system. The MCs were incubated in the dark at 20°C.

Experimental design

To investigate the influence of available oxygen on the bacterial degradation process different gasses or gas mixtures were supplied in the overlaying water layer of the MCs. Four different treatments were used in this part of the experiment by using three different gas inflows — 1. Air (A — 21% vol. O_2), 2. Air + Oxygen (A+O — app. 50% vol. O_2), 3. Nitrogen (N_2- 0% vol. O_2) — and as fourth treatment the Air inflow was combined with a vertical circulation of the water (A+C) through the sediment column of the MCs as simulation of water current. The oxygen concentrations were measured in selected MCs with oxygen optodes (PreSense, Regensburg,

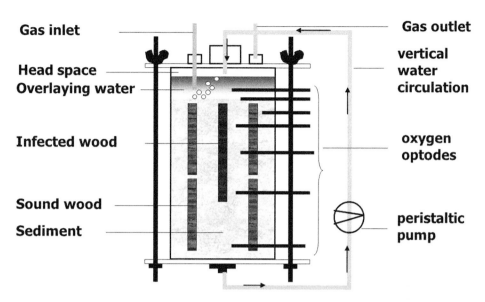

FIGURE 1 Microcosm scheme of the first experiment with gas supply, oxygen optodes, and water circulation.

Germany) during the experiment at different depth of the sediment column. A schematic of an MC of this experiment is shown in Figure 1. MCs were examined after 120, 150, 195, 350, and 400 days.

In a second experiment the treatment with air inflow into the overlaying water was used in a smaller experimental set up with glass jars (described in Kretschmar, 2007; Kretschmar et al., 2008a; Gelbrich, 2009) to investigate if the decay process was influenced by the chemical composition of the sediment or rather of the interstitial pore water of the sediment. Therefore, on the one side, the sediment (S) nutrient concentration was lowered by 'dilution' with silica sand (treatment M for mixture) or pure silica sand (SS). On the other side nitrate (S+N), ammonia (S+A), phosphorus (S+P), or sulphate (S+Su) were added to change the sediment composition. Table 1 shows the different chemical compositions of the sediments in the treatments. For each treatment and each control of the treatment, four replicates were used. For all MCs, the pH of the sediment was determined at the beginning and the end of the experiment after 155 days.

Microscopic investigations

For evaluation of bacterial wood degradation, light microscopy was used. Transverse and tangential sections of the samples were cut by hand using a razor blade and stained with either 1% w/v safranin in ethanol to highlight the micromorphology of the wood, or 0.1% w/v aniline blue in 50% lactic acid to stain fungal hyphae and bacteria. Polarized light was used to demonstrate the remains of crystalline cellulose. The microscopic examinations were conducted by one person only with unknown sample identities to ensure unbiased observations due to the evaluation of low intensities of bacterial degradation (details described in Gelbrich, 2009; Gelbrich et al., 2010).

Results and discussion

First experiment (influence of oxygen availability and water current)
In all treatments, bacterial wood attack was found at least after five months (150 days). Figure 2 shows the different decay intensities per treatment and incubation time. The first investigation periods were just to look if bacteria are active. Later the successful simulated bacteria attack had to be evaluated for which duplicates were investigated. The data does not allow a statistical evaluation, but some trends can be formulated.

In the first half of the experiment, bacteria colonized and opened up the wood. In this stage the decay intensity increased slightly with incubation time. From 195 days onwards the bacterial degradation seems to be stagnated or slowed down in all treatments except the circulated one. At the end of the experiment the three non-circulated treatments all showed comparable decay intensities independent of the gas supply. At all samplings the highest observed decay intensity was found in the circulated treatment. The bacterial degradation intensity increased clearly in this variant up to 400 days.

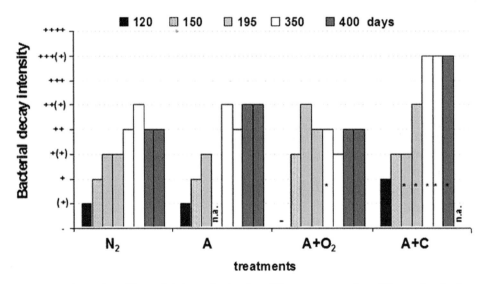

FIGURE 2   Intensity of bacterial decay in the four MC treatments after different incubation times (in days) (Gelbrich, 2009).
Key: n.a. = not analysed
* = additional soft rot decay
- no bacterial decay
TREATMENT abbreviations:
N_2 = Nitrogen inflow
A = Air inflow
$A+O_2$ = Air inflow enriched with oxygen
A+C = Air inflow combined with water circulation

The degree of wood degradation by bacteria was assigned after inspection of samples from different locations in the MCs. Some differences between the upper and the lower layer could be observed in all treatments. In these cases the degree of attack was always higher in the upper layer than in the lower one. Björdal et al. (2000) found a depth gradient in degree of bacterial wood degradation in archaeological poles and related it to small differences in oxygen concentration associated with the depth of burial in the ground.

During the experiment, the oxygen concentration in selected microcosms was measured with oxygen optodes (Kretschmar, 2007) for different depths. In the nitrogen treatment, no oxygen was detectable at any depth. For the other treatments, a steep gradient at the sediment-water interface was measured, ranging from oxygen concentrations corresponding to the solubility of oxygen in the overlaying water to zero at 1 to 2 cm depth in the sediment. The circulation of water in one treatment (A+C) resulted in oxygen being measured further down in the sediment. It is expected that, at the beginning of the experiment, easily degradable organic matter breakdown utilized oxygen and prevented deeper oxygen penetration into the sediment. Upon depletion of easily degradable substrate, the organic matter breakdown slowed down and less oxygen was needed in the upper sediment horizons. Oxygen was presumably transported via diffusion into deeper sediment layers and was measurable at one centimetre depth in the A+C treatment after approximately 100 days. After six months, oxygen was present even 12 cm deep in the sediment. This shows that oxygen penetrated deeper into the sediment during the experiment (Kretschmar et al., 2008a). From these findings it can be concluded, that bacterial wood decay can proceed without free oxygen present but it happens intensely if oxygen is available.

It has been observed that the differences in the degradation intensities between upper and lower layer decrease in the circulated treatment with incubation time, whereas in all other treatments the differences prevail (Gelbrich, 2009). Independent of possible oxygen transport, it can be assumed that exchanges of surrounding material, in general, support the bacterial wood degradation process. That would mean that environments with fluctuating conditions, leading to cycling of various elements, may lead to higher decay rates compared to environments with stable conditions. This is confirmed by Klaassen (2008), who investigated the water flow through wooden foundation piles: 'However, if wooden piles are enclosed in water-saturated soils with no water-pressure gradient along the piles and hence no water flow through the stem, bacterial wood degradation should be (almost) inactive'.

Second experiment (influence of chemical variation of sediment)

All observed decay was in the early initiation stage of wood degradation by bacteria. This is not surprising, given the short experimental duration of 155 days. Based on the aerated treatments with unchanged sediment, bacterial decay intensities of this second MC experiment were comparable with the degree of degradation of the first MC experiment after 150 days.

Treatments with pure sediment (S), silica sand (SS), or their mixture (M) show very slight bacterial wood decay in most of the samples. Furthermore, treatments in which either nitrate (KNO_3) or sulphur (K_2SO_4) was added to the sediment did not show any sign of attack after 155 days. However, in one single MC of the phosphorus

(K_3PO_4) and ammonium (NH_4Cl) added treatments some slight signs of bacterial attack were observed (see Table 1).

Bacterial wood decay intensity in this experiment appears to be highest at a sediment pH range from 7.9 to 8.4 in the treatments without chemical addition to the sediment (see Table 1). The 'optimal' pH range found in the experiment is supported by literature reports by Boutelje and Göransson (1975) which measured ground water pH values of 7.2–8.0 surrounding bacterial decayed wooden foundation piles in Stockholm. Ground water in contact with bacterial decayed archaeological wood and wooden foundation pilings showed a pH range of 7.0 to 8.5 (Huisman et al., 2008; Kretschmar et al., 2008b).

There are indications that a negative relationship exists between bacterial wood decay intensity and sediment nutrition, especially nitrogen concentration if it is presumed that sediment pH obscured, but did not totally govern bacterial wood decay intensity (see Table 1). This might indicate that in sediments with generally very low nutrition concentration, the C/N ratio of wood is still 'interesting' for the bacteria as

TABLE 1

CHEMICAL SEDIMENT COMPOSITION IN THE DIFFERENT TREATMENTS AT THE BEGINNING OF THE EXPERIMENT (TOTAL ELEMENT CONCENTRATIONS) AND SEDIMENT PH AT THE START AND THE END OF THE EXPERIMENT (DL = DETECTION LIMIT (N = 0.1 MG/G) (KRETSCHMAR ET AL., 2008A) AND INTENSITY OF BACTERIAL DECAY IN DIFFERENT TREATMENTS

Treatment	SS	M	S	S+A	S+N	S+P	S+Su
Addition of	-	-	-	NH_4Cl	KNO_3	K_3PO_4	K_2SO_4
pH start	5.4	8.4	8.3	7.4	8.2	10.1	8,2
pH end	8.0	8.0	7.9	6.7	8.9	9.3	8,5
C (mg/g)	0.0	2.2	4.2	4.6	4.3	3.9	4.1
P (mg/g)	0.07	0.11	0.16	0.19	0.18	0.48	0.14
S (mg/g)	0.17	0.21	0.25	0.38	0.42	0.20	0.45
N (mg/g)	<dl.	<dl.	0.11	0.62	0.96	0.12	0.12

Increasing sediment nitrogen condition $\longrightarrow$
Decreasing intensity of bacterial wood degradation $\longrightarrow$

	SS	M	S	S+A	S+N	S+P	S+Su
1	(+)	(+)	(+)	(+)	-	(+)	-
2	(+)	(+)	(+)	-	-	-	-
3	(+)	(+)	(+)	-	-	-	-
4	+	(+)	(+)	-	-	-	-

Key:
S = pure sediment
M = mixture from sediment and silica sand
SS = pure silica sand
S+A = sediment with ammonium addition
S+N = sediment and nitrate addition
S+P = phosphate addition
S+Su = sulphate addition
- no signs of bacterial wood decay found
(+) very slight decay
+ slight decay

a food source. Based on this it can be concluded — and was also confirmed by Gregory (1999), that wood surrounded by water-saturated sediment with low nitrogen content is more likely to be affected by bacterial wood decay than wood in sediments with medium to high nitrogen contents.

Conclusion

The performed investigations provided a starting point for understanding the ecology and physiology of erosion bacteria. All results presented are based on sandy sediments of a groundwater influenced sample site. In particular, better knowledge of the conditions suitable for causing attack on wood has been gained.

Concerning feasibility in *in situ* or reburial conservation projects, the most important results based on trends of the Microcosm experiments seem to be following:

- A distinguishable depth gradient of degree of bacterial wood degradation could be observed within about a 30 cm sediment column in the absence of any water currents.
- Clearly higher degradation intensity is to be expected in fluctuating conditions, e.g. caused by water currents.
- Bacterial wood degradation can proceed without free oxygen but the decay intensity seems to increase if oxygen is present.
- The contents of nutrients, especially of nitrogen of the wood's surroundings seem to have a crucial influence on the decay intensity by EB.

Further investigations, especially long-term experiments, are necessary to understand the complex interaction of bacterial wood degradation as a basis for best practice and environmental friendly conservation strategies to preserve archaeological waterlogged wood *in situ* as cultural heritage. Continuing research is needed which should combine laboratory and field experiments for different sediment and/or sample site types.

Preservations strategies based on addition of nutrients (nitrogen, phosphate and/or sulphate) are no realistic, environmental compatible methods in water-saturated environments. Nevertheless, the effect of these chemicals on the decay intensity is an important result concerning the ecology of wood degrading bacteria, which can be tested without restriction in such laboratory experiments.

Acknowledgement

We appreciate the financial support of the BACPOLES project from the European commission, which funded it under Key Action 4: City of tomorrow and cultural heritage (EVK4-CT-2001-00043), and we would like to thank all involved partners and staffs for data collection and interpretation.

Bibliography

Björdal, C., Daniel, G. and Nilsson, T. 2000. Depth of Burial, an Important Factor in Controlling Bacterial Decay of Waterlogged Archaeological Poles. *International Biodeterioration and Biodegradation*, 45: 15–26.

Boutelje, J. B. and Göransson, B. 1975. Decay in Wood Constructions Below the Ground Water Table. *Swedish Journal of Agricultural Research*, 5: 113–23.

Gelbrich, J. 2009. *Bacterial Wood Degradation — A Study of Chemical Changes in Wood and Growth Conditions of Bacteria*. Göttingen: Georg-August-University.

Gelbrich, J., Kretschmar, E. I., Militz, H., and Lamersdorf, N. 2010. Simulation and Investigation of Wood Degradation by Erosion Bacteria in Laboratory Experiments. *IRG/WP 10-20431. The International Research Group on Wood Protection*.

Gregory, D. 1999. Re-burial of Ship Timbers in the Marine Environment as a Method of In Situ Preservation. In: P. Hoffmann et al., eds. *Proceedings of the 7th ICOM-CC Working Group on Wet Organic Archaeological Materials Conference 1998*. Grenoble: France, pp. 78–84.

Huisman, D. J., Manders, M. R., Kretschmar, E. I., Klaassen, R., and Lamersdorf, N. 2008. Burial Conditions and Wood Degradation on Archaeological Sites in the Netherlands. *International Biodeterioration and Biodegradation*, 61(1): 33–44.

Klaassen, R. 2008. Bacterial Decay in Wooden Foundation Piles: Patterns and Causes — A Study on Historial Pile Foundations out of Pine, Spruce, Fir, and Oak in the Netherlands. *International Biodeterioration and Biodegradation*, 61(1): 45–60.

Kretschmar, E. I. 2007. *Anoxic Sediments and their Potential to Favour Bacterial Wood Decay*. Göttingen: Georg-August-University.

Kretschmar, E. I., Gelbrich, J., Militz, H. and Lamersdorf, N. 2008a. Studying Bacterial Wood Decay under Low Oxygen Conditions — Results of Microcosm Experiments. *International Biodeterioration and Biodegradation*, 61(1): 69–84.

Kretschmar, E. I., Huisman, D. J., and Lamersdorf, N. 2008b. Characterising Physicochemical Sediment Conditions at Selected Bacterial Decayed Wooden Pile Foundation Sites in the Netherlands, Germany, and Italy. *International Biodeterioration and Biodegradation*, 61(1): 117–25.

Nyström Godfrey, I., Bergstrand, T., Gjelstrup Björdal. C., Nilsson, T., Bohm, C., Christensson, E., Gregory, D., Peacock, E. E., Richards, V., and MacLeod, I. 2007. Reburial and Analyses of Archaeological Remains — The RAAR Project. Project Status and Cultural Heritage Management Implications Based on the First Preliminary Results. In: K. Straetkvern and D. J. Huisman, eds. *Proceedings of the 10th ICOM Group on Wet Organic Archaeological Materials Conference, Amsterdam*, pp. 169–96.

Notes on contributors

Dr Jana Gelbrich graduated in Forestry in 2001, received her PhD in 2009 in wood biology, research about bacterial wood degradation – chemical changes in wood as well as growth conditions of wood degrading bacteria. Currently she is working as researcher in conservation of waterlogged archaeological wood.

Correspondence to: Dr Jana Gelbrich, Head of Wood Conservation and Laboratory, German Maritime Museum, Hans-Scharoun-Platz 1, 27568 Bremerhaven, Germany. Email: gelbrich@dsm.museum

Dr Ev Kretschmar has a first education as environmental scientist and environmental engineer. PhD in landscape ecology, research about sediments characteristics at sites of bacterial wood decay. Currently she is working as ecotoxicologist in the field of environmental risk assessment of biocides. Research interests in the area of sustainable use of biocides and comparative assessment of biocidal products.

Correspondence to: Dr Ev Kretschmar. Email: ev_kretschmar@uba.de

Professor Dr Norbert Lamersdorf graduated in Forestry in 1983, received his PhD in 1988, and his 'venia legendi' for Soil Science and Forest Nutrition in 1999. He is involved in several national and international research projects. Since 2009 he has been the Deputy Head of the Department of Soil Science of Temperate and Boreal Ecosystems at the Faculty of Forest Sciences and Forest Ecology of the Göttingen University.

Correspondence to: Professor Dr Norbert Lamersdorf. Email: nlamers@gwdg.de

Professor Dr Holger Militz received his diploma Wood Science at University Hamburg in 1987. After thirteen years being in several functions in wood research in the Netherlands, since 2000 he is full professor in 'Wood Biology and Wood Products' at the University Göttingen, Germany.

Correspondence to: Professor Dr Holger Militz. Email: hmilitz@gwdg.de

CONSERVATION AND MGMT OF ARCH. SITES, Vol. 14 Nos 1–4, 2012, 16–27

An Analytical Methodology for the Study of the Corrosion of Ferrous Archaeological Remains in Soils

MANDANA SAHEB, DELPHINE NEFF, EDDY FOY, JEAN-PAUL GALLIEN
CEA/CNRS, France

PHILIPPE DILLMANN
CEA/CNRS and Institut de recherche sur les Archéomatériaux, CNRS, France

In the context of the cultural heritage, a methodology based on field and laboratory approaches is developed for studying the long-term corrosion of iron. Moreover it has been adapted to the study of archaeological artefacts buried in anoxic soils in the specific case of *in situ* preservation. The environmental parameters are determined on the archaeological sites and artefacts are collected and characterized using complementary multi-scale techniques. Moreover, laboratory experiments are performed to locate the reaction sites inside the corrosion layer and to identify its electronic properties. The results allow estimation of a low corrosion rate for iron buried in an anoxic soil (under 2 μm/year) and the proposal of a mechanism based on a decoupling of the anodic and the cathodic sites. Then a diagnosis of the alteration state of the samples is established.

KEYWORDS *in situ* preservation, anoxic water-saturated environment, iron corrosion

Introduction

The study of the long-term corrosion of iron is relevant in several fields of application. First, in the context of the preservation of cultural heritage, it is of importance to understand the corrosion of archaeological remains in order to diagnose their alteration state and to apply suitable treatments or storage conditions. Moreover, other more unusual domains of civil engineering are concerned by this issue. This is the case, for instance in the domain of nuclear waste management. Actually, in several countries including France it is envisaged to store or to dispose the radioactive

    DOI 10.1179/1350503312Z.0000000002

wastes in steel canisters in several environments, depending on their radioactivity level (e.g. soils, concrete, atmospheric environments, etc.). As the surrounding system has to be efficient for a period of time varying between several hundred to thousands of years, one needs to understand the corrosion behaviour of the steel materials (Clanfield et al., 2008). To this purpose, archaeological artefacts are studied because they provide long-term data that cannot be obtained on the basis of laboratory experiments.

In both domains (conservation of the cultural heritage and nuclear waste management) during the last decades, several studies have been carried out on the corrosion of ferrous artefacts. In some of them the corroding environment was not even taken into consideration (Accary and Haijtink, 1983), although it is a key parameter in the iron corrosion mechanism. Finer studies have been performed on waterlogged terrestrial sites including a characterization of the corrosion system composed of the environment and the archaeological artefacts (Fell, 1993; Fell and Ward, 1998; Sorensen and Gregory, 1998; Matthiesen, 2004; Matthiesen et al., 2001; 2003; 2004a; 2004b; Fell, 2005). However, these studies do not involve laboratory experiments aiming at understanding the instantaneous corrosion behaviour of the artefacts and the complex interactions driving the corrosion processes.

Consequently, a specific methodology has been developed in the LAPA (Laboratoire des Archéomatériaux et Prévision de l'Altération) (Neff et al., 2010) during the last years based on an integrated approach of the corrosion. This approach aims at understanding the behaviour of the archaeological remains at different time scales, in the long term (on the archaeological site) and in the short term (in the laboratory) (Figure 1). In the first step, the archaeological site is finely characterized with on-field measurements. Relevant parameters for iron corrosion are selected, such as redox potential, pH, dissolved oxygen concentration, and water chemistry. In parallel, metallic archaeological remains are selected and sampled. It has to be noted that in addition to the corrosion study of the sampled artefacts they are also submitted to detailed archaeometrical analyses (metallography, etc.) in order to detect any interesting information for historical issues. In the specific case of corrosion in anoxic

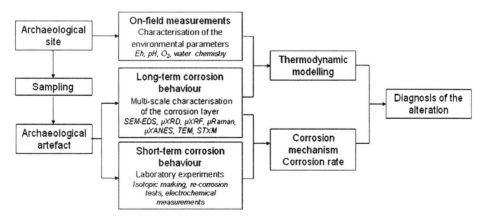

FIGURE 1   General approach used for the study of ferrous archaeological artefacts (from Neff et al., 2010).

environments, artefacts are stored in absolute ethanol to avoid any re-corroding after the excavation due to contact with air. Some of them are dedicated to a fine characterization of their corrosion layer in order to understand their behaviour during the long period they have been exposed to the archaeological site. They are studied on a transverse section to have a full overview, from the metallic substrate to the external part of the corrosion layer in contact with the environment (Neff et al., 2005). To this purpose, they are embedded into resin, cut and polished. Their characterization is performed using several complementary elemental and structural techniques at different scales, from mesoscopic to nanometric. Then the corrosion layers formed on the artefacts are compared to the thermodynamic modelling based on the environmental characterization. Other samples are dedicated to laboratory experiments aiming at understanding their instantaneous corrosion behaviour. The reactivity and the electronic properties of the phases in the corrosion layer can strongly influence the processes and the corrosion rate (Antony et al., 2007; Monnier et al., 2007; 2008; 2011). The location of the reaction sites inside the corrosion layer and its reactivity are studied using reaction marking (Vega et al., 2005; Chitty et al., 2008; Burger et al., 2011; Monnier et al., 2011) and electrochemical tests (Pons 2002; Monnier et al., 2007). The modelling of the *in situ* conditions on the one hand and the establishment of the corrosion rates and mechanisms on the other hand allow diagnosing the alteration state of the archaeological remains in order to improve the conservation strategy.

In the specific context of *in situ* preservation of archaeological artefacts, numerous sites correspond to anoxic and water-saturated environments (Matthiesen et al., 2004a; Fell, 2005). Consequently, we have decided here to give a complete overview of the methodology that has been followed to study the corrosion in this kind of environment. The analytical tools, the dedicated devices and the detailed operating modes have been presented in detail in previous articles (Saheb et al., 2010a; 2010b; 2011; 2012), and we chose to focus here only on the main results that have been obtained in order to propose a relevant corrosion mechanism. This kind of mechanism can be a helpful tool in the future for estimating the alteration state of the archaeological remains and for conservation diagnoses.

Characterization of the corrosion system

The environmental conditions

We have chosen to focus on a single archaeological site, in order to perform a fine and complete characterization of the environmental conditions. This site is the ancient iron-making of Glinet (Upper Normandy, France, sixteenth century) (Arribet-Deroin, 2001). It has been selected because part of its waterlogged zone contains numerous archaeological nails (Vega, 2004).

To characterize the environment, piezometers have been installed at several places near the excavation zones to collect porewater and perform *in situ* measurements (Saheb et al., 2010a). Three measurement campaigns have been carried out during one year, to follow the seasonal variations. The fine characterization of the porewater composition is presented in another article (Saheb et al., 2010a), only the main parameters are referred here. The water is a calco-carbonated electrolyte with a neutral to acidic pH. The presence of waste from the iron industry induces a high concentration of iron (up to 1.10^{-4} mol.L^{-1}). The dissolved oxygen concentration is under 0.3 ppm indicating reducing conditions. Moreover, the zones that are the most reducing on the site are located near the excavation zones.

The corrosion layer formed on the archaeological artefacts

As it is presented in Figure 2, three corrosion types formed on the 500-year-old archaeological artefacts are identified and, among them, two are considered as the main ones (Figure 2A and B) (Saheb et al., 2010c). All the corrosion patterns are composed of a mix of siderite ($FeCO_3$), chukanovite ($Fe_2(OH)_2CO_3$), magnetite (Fe_3O_4), and calcite ($CaCO_3$). The difference between the corrosion layer types lies in the arrangement of these phases. The first corrosion layer type (Figure 2A) contains an internal zone with ferrous carbonates and an outer magnetite border. In the second corrosion layer type (Figure 2B) magnetite is present in the ferrous carbonate matrix as islets of several 10 micrometers. For all these patterns, the distribution of the phases into the layer, their electronic properties and their possible connectivity with the metallic substrate can highly influence the corrosion mechanisms. For this reason laboratory experiments were performed in order to understand the corrosion mechanisms occurring on the samples.

Thermodynamic modelling

The characterization of the environmental conditions allows modelling of the thermodynamic equilibria in the porewater. Figure 3 presents the Pourbaix diagram

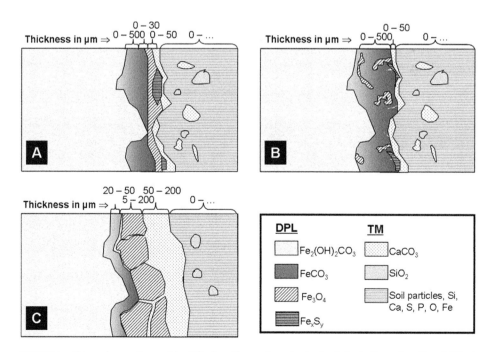

FIGURE 2   Corrosion patterns identified on the archaeological artefacts from the site of Glinet (Saheb et al., 2010c).

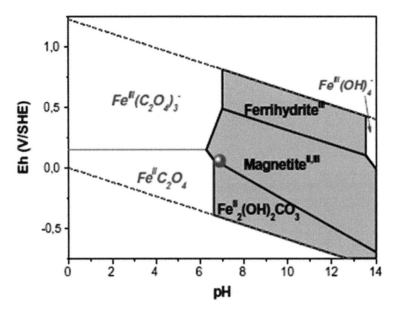

Pourbaix diagram established using the *in situ* conditions measured on the archaeological site of Glinet (Saheb et al., 2010a). The circle indicates the potential and pH values measured on the site.

(Eh-pH) established using the analyses of the porewater from the piezometers located near the excavation zones and is supposed to be the most representative of the initial reducing conditions.

The thermodynamically stable phases on the Eh-pH diagram (Figure 3) are compared to the corrosion products formed on the artefacts (Figure 2). Actually, the Eh-pH diagram indicates an equilibrium between magnetite Fe_3O_4 and chukanovite $Fe_2(OH)_2CO_3$. The stability of iron (II) carbonate species and magnetite is consistent with the mineralogical phases identified on the objects. Moreover, thermodynamic calculations show that the equilibrium is also close to the boundary between both iron carbonate phases (siderite and chukanovite). This can explain that both phases coexist in the corrosion layer. Lastly, the surrounding soil is mainly composed of calcite and quartz, which is also in good agreement with the modelled equilibria (Saheb et al., 2010a). The phase distribution in the layer could also be explained by local changes in the chemical composition of the corrosion layer porewater, depending on the species availability in the layer. This last parameter is linked on the one hand to the porosity of the corrosion layer and on the other hand to the corrosion processes that influence water chemistry.

The consistency between the environmental conditions and the corrosion layer formed on the archaeological artefacts ensures the reliability of the methodology used for the characterization of the corrosion system. Moreover, the measurements of the environmental parameters allowed laboratory re-corrosion experiments to be performed in a solution with a composition close to the one on the site.

Corrosion behaviour

Isotopic marking (Saheb et al., 2010b; 2012)
In an anoxic carbonated environment, the cathodic reaction is water reduction following equations (I), (II) and (III) depending on pH and carbonate concentrations:

$$2H^+ + 2e^- \rightarrow H_2 \tag{I}$$
$$2H_2CO_3 + 2e^- \rightarrow H_2 + 2HCO_3^- \tag{II}$$
$$2HCO_3^- + 2e^- \rightarrow H_2 + 2CO_3^{2-} \tag{III}$$

The products of these equations react with oxidized Fe^{2+} formed during the anodic process which leads to the precipitation of carbonated phases, such as siderite ($FeCO_3$) and chukanovite ($Fe_2(OH)_2CO_3$). The location of these phases inside the corrosion layer gives information on the mechanisms. For this reason, isotopic marking was performed and during this experiment deuterated water (D_2O) replaced H_2O. The experimental protocol is presented in Figure 4. After several months of treatment, samples exposed to a deuterated solution were transversely cut and the phases recently precipitated containing isotopes were detected and localized on the transverse section using a nuclear microprobe (NRA analyses).

Figure 5 presents the deuterium and iron maps on a sample that was exposed for 25 weeks to an anoxic deuterated carbonated environment. Near the metallic interface, Raman microspectroscopy revealed that the corrosion layer contains chukanovite $Fe_2(OH)_2CO_3$. Except for the thick crack of about 30 μm that appears dark on the optical microphotograph, no cracks or pores at a micrometric scale were seen inside the chukanovite zone (the thickness of the whole corrosion layer is of several hundred micrometers). This structural homogeneity of the sample consequently allows linking the deuterium signal variations observed on the deuterium mapping to a quantitative variation of this element in the corrosion layer. Figure 5 reveals that the entire corrosion layer contains deuterium which shows that the corrosion layer contains nanometric pores (not visible with the optical micrograph) and water can diffuse through it. Moreover, based on a normalization of the NRA signal (Saheb et al., 2012), a significant deuterium enrichment on the internal part of the

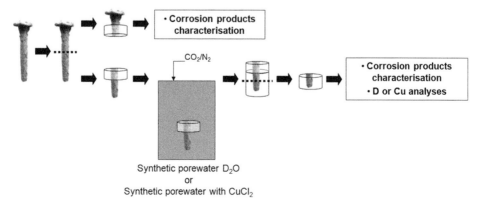

Synthetic porewater D_2O
or
Synthetic porewater with $CuCl_2$

FIGURE 4   Experimental protocol for the deuterium and copper reaction marking.

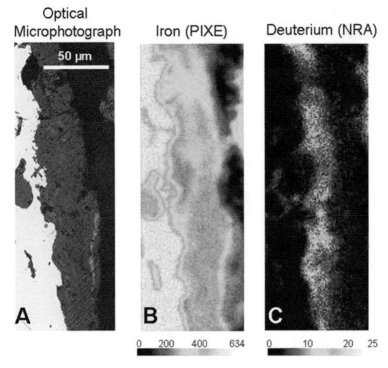

FIGURE 5   Optical microphotograph, iron and deuterium maps of a transverse section of a sample exposed to deuterated medium for six months (Saheb et al., 2012).

corrosion layer with a mean thickness between 16 and 28 μm (± 5 μm) is highlighted. In this zone, analyses using Raman microspectrometry (Saheb et al., 2010b) confirm the integration of deuterium in the corrosion products detected by NRA. Consequently, we propose that Fe^{2+} formed from the anodic process and DCO_3^- from the deuterated electrolyte precipitate near the metallic interface in the corrosion layer. Moreover, the deuterium quantification allows estimation of the corrosion rate which is lower than 2 μm/year. This result is consistent with the corrosion rate values estimated in the literature on iron corroding during a shorter period in an anoxic medium (Bataillon et al., 2001; Smart et al., 2002a; 2002b).

Copper marking (Saheb et al., 2011)

As the corrosion process involves an electron transfer between iron (the reduced element) and water (the oxidant), the electronic properties of the corrosion layer that is locater between both species need to be determined. Consequently, they are studied using reaction marking (Saheb et al., 2011). The redox couple that has been selected is the Cu(II)/Cu(0) couple. This marker has been chosen because its redox potential value is between the Fe(II)/Fe(0) couple and the Fe(III)/Fe(II) couple so that Cu(2+) can only react with Fe(0) to form Fe(II) and Cu(0). It is assumed that the electron consumption zones are the same in the reaction between iron and water and in the reaction between iron and copper. As a result, the reduction zones of Cu(II) into

Cu(0) are an indicator of the zones where electrons are available in the corrosion layer during the corrosion process. The methodology for the immersion in the copper containing solution is presented in Figure 4.

Figure 6 presents a cross section on a sample that was exposed to the solution containing cupric ions. On this microphotograph the metallic copper (red to orange zones) is located at the external part of the corrosion layer. Moreover other analyses have revealed that on the first and second corrosion patterns, copper marking determined that cupric ions can be reduced everywhere in the corrosion layer on the developed surface of the poral network leading to the formation of metallic copper. The specific enrichment on the external part is due to the fact that the copper source surrounds the archaeological artefact in the electrolyte. The reduction of copper inside the corrosion layer indicates that the electrons can diffuse through the corrosion layer and be consumed there. Consequently, the corrosion layer can conduct the electrons. This specific property has been attributed to the presence of the semi-conductive phase: magnetite (Cornell and Schwertmann, 2003: 664) as a thick layer connected to the metal (type 1 corrosion layer) or as islets inside the corrosion layer (type 2 corrosion layer). This result clearly demonstrates the possibility of a decoupling of the cathodic and anodic reaction during the corrosion process which strongly influences the corrosion mechanism.

Proposition of a corrosion mechanism

Based on the previous results, it is possible to estimate that the corrosion rate is lower than 2 µm/year (Saheb et al., 2010b; 2010c; 2012). This value is in the same range as the one estimated by several authors on iron corroding for a short period (at

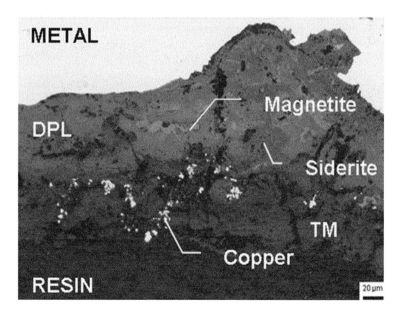

FIGURE 6   Optical microphotograph of a cross section of a sample exposed for two weeks to a cupric solution (Saheb et al., 2011).

most a few years) in an anoxic environment. Consequently, the presence of a thick corrosion layer does not seem to significantly influence the corrosion process. Based on literature studies on corrosion of iron in anoxic environments, the hypothesis is proposed that a nanometric non-porous layer of constant thickness, located at the metal/corrosion layer interface could control the corrosion rate since the beginning of the process and lead to a relative constant corrosion rate over the very long term (Saheb et al., 2012).

Taking into account these observations, a corrosion mechanism based on the hypothesis of the presence of a thick layer of carbonates is proposed (Figure 7). Its electronic properties allow the electrons to cross from the metallic interface to its external part. Moreover, this layer is porous and cracked so that the electrolyte can spread through it up to a few nanometres from the metallic interface. At this interface, the presence of a nanometric layer, already observed during short-term experiments in closed systems (Bataillon et al., 2001) could control the corrosion rate. Its dissolution leads to the formation of Fe(II); furthermore, its electronic properties allows the electrons to diffuse through it. The latter are consumed during the cathodic processes, which leads to the formation of HCO_3^-. In addition, carbonate ions precipitate with Fe(II) and form chukanovite $Fe_2(OH)_2CO_3$ at the interface with the nanometric layer.

Conclusion

Using the methodology developed on archaeological artefacts, it has been possible to estimate the corrosion rate (under 2 μm/year) and to propose a corrosion mechanism

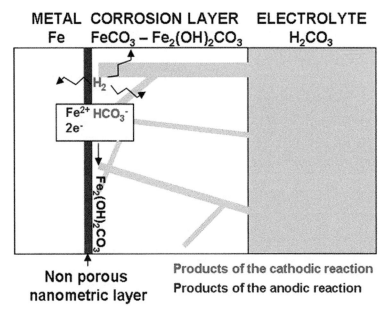

FIGURE 7   Diagram presenting a corrosion mechanism for the long-term corrosion of iron in anoxic soil (Saheb et al., 2012).

for ferrous archaeological remains evolving in an anoxic water-saturated environment. These results are of great importance in the context of the cultural heritage, because good preservation can only be achieved when the processes occurring in soils are understood.

We have also emphasized that even the local variations in the environmental conditions strongly influence the corrosion mechanism, because they can lead to different phase distribution in the corrosion layer with their specific electronic properties and reactivity. The next step in the study of the preservation of archaeological remains in soil would be to identify the influence of a strong perturbation of the environment, such as excavations leading to an oxidizing environment. To this purpose, similar to an aerated environment, the O_2 from the air is the oxidant and it would be relevant to perform re-corroding experiments in the laboratory using an $^{18}O_2$ labelled medium.

Acknowledgements

The authors would like to thank the ANDRA for its financial support. Moreover, we would like to thank Danielle Arribet-Deroin who provided the samples and the city of Compainville. This work has also been performed with the contribution of Pascal Berger, Christian Bataillon, Michael Descostes, Louis Raimbault, and Henning Matthiesen, the DiffAbs team of the synchrotron Soleil and the SUL-X team of the synchrotron ANKA.

Bibliography

Accary, A. and Haijtink, B. 1983. La paléométallurgie — Outil de prévision. Journées de paléométallurgie, Compiègne, Université de Technologie de Compiègne.

Antony, H., Perrin, S., Dillmann, P., Legrand, L. and Chaussé, A. 2007. Electrochemical Study of Indoor Atmospheric Corrosion Layers Formed on Ancient Iron Artefacts. Electrochimica Acta, 52(27): 7754–59.

Arribet-Deroin, D. 2001. Fondre le fer en gueuses au XVIe siècle. Le haut fourneau de Glinet en pays de Bray (Normandie). Archéologie. Paris: Paris I Sorbonne, p. 799.

Bataillon, C., Musy, C., and Roy, M. 2001. Corrosion des surconteneurs de déchets, cas d'un surconteneur en acier faiblement allié. J. Phys IV France, (11): 267–74.

Burger, E., Fénart, M., Perrin, S., Neff, D., and Dillmann P. 2011. Use of the Gold Markers Method to Predict the Mechanisms of Iron Atmospheric Corrosion. Corrosion Science, 53(6): 2122–30.

Chitty, W.-J., Berger P., Dillmann, P., and L'Hostis, V. 2008. Long-term Corrosion of Rebars Embedded in Aerial and Hydraulic Binders — Mechanisms and Crucial Physico-Chemical Parameters. Corrosion Science, 50: 2117–23.

Clanfield, A., Cattant F., Crusset, D., and Féron, D. 2008. Corrosion Issues in Nuclear Industry Today. Materials Today, 11(10): 32–37.

Cornell, R. and Schwertmann, U. 2003. The Iron Oxides — Structure, Properties, Occurrences and Uses. Weinheim, Wiley-VCH Verlag.

Fell, V. 1993. Examination of Four Iron Age Ferrous Hammer Heads from Bredon Hill (Hereford and Worcester), England. The Journal of the Historical Metallurgy Society, 27(2): 60–70.

Fell, V. 2005. Fiskerton: Scientific Analysis of Corrosion Layers on Archaeological Iron Artefacts and from Experimental Iron Samples Buried for up to 18 Months. Centre for Archaeology Report 65/2005.

Fell, V. and Ward, M. 1998. Iron Sulphides: Corrosion Products on Artifacts from Waterlogged Deposits. Metal 98 Conference on Metals Conservation, Draguignan-Figanières, France. James and James.

Matthiesen, H. 2004. In Situ Measurement of Soil pH. Journal of Archaeological Science, 31: 1373–81.

Matthiesen, H., Gregory, D., Jensen, P., and Sorensen, B. 2004a. Environmental Monitoring at a waterlogged Site with Weapon Sacrifices from the Danish Iron Age. I: Methodology and Results from Undisturbed Conditions. *Journal of Wetland Archaeology*, 4: 55–74.

Matthiesen, H., Gregory, D., Sorensen, B., Alstrom, T., and Jensen, P. 2001. Monitoring Methods in Mires and Meadows: Five Years of Studies at Nydam Mose, Denmark. *Preserving Archaeological Sites In Situ (PARIS2)*. London.

Matthiesen, H., Hilbert, L. R., Gregory, D., and Sorensen, B. 2004b. Long Term Corrosion of Iron at the Water-logged Site Nydam in Denmark: Studies of Environment, Archaeological Artefacts, and Modern Analogues. *Prediction of Long Term Corrosion Behaviour in Nuclear Waste Systems*. Nice.

Matthiesen, H., Hilbert, L. R., and Gregory, D. 2003. The Occurrence and Stability of Siderite as a Corrosion Product on Archaeological Iron from a Waterlogged Environment. *Studies in Conservation*, 48(3): 183–94.

Monnier, J., Bellot-Gurlet, L., Legrand, L., Dillmann, P., Reguer, S., Neff, D., and Guillot, I. 2007. The Long Term Indoor Atmospheric Corrosion of Iron: Rust Layer Characterisation and Electrochemical Study. *Metal07*. Amsterdam.

Monnier, J., Burger, E., Berger, P., Neff, D., Guillot, I., and Dillmann, P. 2011. Localisation of Oxygen Reduction Sites in the Case of Iron Long Term Atmospheric Corrosion. *Corrosion Science*, 53(8): 2468–73.

Monnier, J., Legrand, L., Bellot-Gurlet, L., Foy, E., Reguer, S., Rocca, E., Dillmann, P., Neff, D., Mirambet, F., Perrin, S., and Guillot, I.. 2008. Study of Archaeological Artefacts to Refine the Model of Iron Long-Term Indoor Atmospheric Corrosion. *Journal of Nuclear Materials*, 379: 105–11.

Neff, D., Dillmann, P., Bellot-Gurlet, L., and Béranger, G. 2005. Corrosion of Iron Archaeological Artefacts in Soil: Characterisation of the Corrosion System. *Corrosion Science*, 47: 515–35.

Neff, D., Saheb, M., Monnier, J., Perrin, S., Descostes, M., L'Hostis, V., Crusset, D., Millard, A., and Dillmann, P. 2010. A Review of the Archaeological Analogue Approaches to Predict the Long-Term Corrosion Behaviour of Carbon Steel Overpack and Reinforced Concrete Structures in the French Disposal Systems. *Journal of Nuclear Materials*, 402(2–3): 196–205.

Pons, E. 2002. *Corrosion à long terme du fer et des aciers non ou faiblement alliés dans les sols à dominante argileuse — Caractérisation Physico-chimique et étude électrochimique d'analogues archéologiques*. Compiègne: Université de Technologie de Compiègne, p. 239.

Saheb, M., Berger, P., Raimbault, L., Neff, D., and Dillmann, P. 2012. Investigation of Iron Long-Term Corrosion Mechanisms in Anoxic Media Using Deuterium Tracing. *Journal of Nuclear Materials*, 423(1–3): 61–66.

Saheb, M., Descostes, M., Neff, D., Matthiesen, H., Michelin, A., and Dillmann, P. 2010a. Iron Corrosion in an Anoxic Soil: Comparison Between Thermodynamic Modelling and Ferrous Archaeological Artefacts Characterised along with the Local In Situ Geochemical Conditions. *Applied Geochemistry*, 25(12): 1937–48.

Saheb, M., Neff, D., Bataillon, C., Foy, E., and Dillmann, P. 2011. Copper Tracing to Determine the Micrometric Electronic Properties of a Thick Ferrous Corrosion Layer Formed in an Anoxic Medium. *Corrosion Science*, 53(6): 2201–07.

Saheb, M., Neff, D., Bellot-Gurlet, L., and Dillmann, P. 2010b. Raman Study of a Deuterated Iron Hydroxycarbonate to Assess Long Term Corrosion Mechanisms in Anoxic Soils. *Journal of Raman Spectroscopy*, 42(5): 1100–08.

Saheb, M., Neff, D., Demory, J., Foy, E., and Dillmann P. 2010c. Characterisation of Corrosion Layers Formed on Ferrous Archaeological Artefacts Buried in Anoxic Media. *Corrosion Engineering, Science and Technology*, 45(5): 381–87.

Smart, N. R., Blackwood, D. J., and Werme, L. 2002a. Anaerobic Corrosion of Carbon Steel and Cast Iron in Artificial Groundwaters: Part 1 — Electochemical Aspects. *Corrosion*, 58(7): 547–59.

Smart, N. R., Blackwood, D. J., and Werme, L. 2002b. Anaerobic Corrosion of Carbon Steel and Cast Iron in Artificial Groundwaters: Part 2 — Gas Generation. *Corrosion*, 58(8): 627–37.

Sorensen, B. and Gregory, D. 1998. In Situ Preservation of Artifacts in Nydam Mose. *Metal 98 Conference on Metals Conservation, Draguignan-Figanières, France*. James and James.

Vega, E. 2004. Altération des objets ferreux archéologiques sur le site de Glinet (Seine-maritime, France, XVIe siècle). *Caractérisation des produits de corrosion et étude des mécanismes*. Belfort: Université de Technologie de Belfort Montbéliard, p. 127.

Vega, E., Berger, P., and Dillmann P. 2005. A Study of Transport Phenomena in the Corrosion Products of Ferrous Archaeological Artefacts Using 18O Tracing and Nuclear Microprobe Analysis. *Nuclear Instruments and Methods*, B 240: 554–58.

Notes on contributors

Mandana Saheb has a PhD in Materials Science from Paris Est University. She has been working on the corrosion of archaeological remains in anoxic soils, in the fields of cultural heritage preservation and nuclear waste management. She now has a post-doctoral position at the Laboratory of Archaeomaterials and Alteration Prediction in the French Atomic Energy Agency and the National Centre of Scientific Research.

Correspondence to: Mandana Saheb, SIS2M/LAPA, UMR 3299 CEA/CRNS, France. Email: mandana.saheb@cea.fr, mandana.saheb@lisa.u-pec.fr

Delphine Neff has a MSc/engineering degree in Material Science. She studied the long-term corrosion of iron during her PhD work and graduated from the Compiègne University in 2003. She obtained a research engineer position at the French Atomic Energy Agency where she pursues her research in the field of long term corrosion of iron in various conditions involving soils, marine environments, concrete, and the atmosphere.

Correspondence to: Delphine Neff, SIS2M/LAPA, UMR 3299 CEA/CRNS, France. Email: delphine.neff@cea.fr

Eddy Foy has a PhD in Solid State Physics and Crystallography from Centrale Paris School in 1999. He has been working on the physical properties of thin films, based on 3d transition metals, grown by MBE. He obtained a research engineer position at the French National Centre of Scientific Research (CNRS) in 2002, where he is in charge of the development of a X-ray generator for X-ray Diffraction and X-ray Fluorescence analyses of samples.

Correspondence to: Eddy Foy, SIS2M/LAPA, UMR 3299 CEA/CRNS, France. Email: eddy.foy@cea.fr

Jean-Paul Gallien has a PhD in radiochemistry in relation with the nuclear spent fuel cycle. He specializes in the microanalysis of trace elements using a light ion beam. He also worked on material behaviour under heavy ion irradiation. Since 2010, he has been in charge of corrosion experiments using stable light isotopes.

Correspondence to: Jean-Paul Gallien, SIS2M/LAPA, UMR 3299 CEA/CRNS, France. Email: jean-paul.gallien@cea.fr

Philippe Dillmann is Directeur de Recherche at the French Centre of Scientific Research (CNRS). He is a doctor and engineer in materials science and 'Habilité à Diriger des Recherches'. He conducts research into archaeometallurgy and archaeometry that deals with the understanding of manufacturing and trade routes of iron based artefacts in ancient societies and on long-term corrosion and conservation of archaeological iron artefacts. He is president of the Working Party 21 of the European Federation of Corrosion, dedicated to the study of corrosion of cultural heritage metals.

Correspondence to: Philippe Dillmann, SIS2M/LAPA, UMR 3299 CEA/CRNS, France. Email: philippe.dillmann@cea.fr

CONSERVATION AND MGMT OF ARCH. SITES, Vol. 14 Nos 1–4, 2012, 28–34

Some Aspects of the Bioerosion of Stone Artefact Found Underwater: Significant Case Studies

SANDRA RICCI and BARBARA DAVIDDE

Istituto Superiore per la Conservazione ed il Restauro, Rome, Italy

Within the framework of the project *Restoring Underwater* started in 2001, the ISCR Marine Biology sector with the ISCR Underwater Archaeology Operation Unit has begun a study of the deterioration of stone artefacts exposed to marine environments (Torre Astura – Nettuno; Baiae – Naples). These studies have allowed to better understanding the factor of degradation by biological, mineralogical, and petrographic analyses and to develop measures for the protection *in situ* of cultural heritage. Based on what was recorded, usually the bioerosion presents various degrees of gravity: limited and sporadic damage or very serious alterations. Depending on their chemical composition, the artefacts proved to be particularly susceptible to the action of corrosion exercised by perforating animal and plant organisms.

This phenomenon becomes more significant in the case in which the artefacts remain exposed and in the same position for a long period of time. It is possible to confirm that the combined action of attack from clionides (sponges) and bivalves can lead, over time, to the total destruction of portions of the artefact (macroboring). As well as these more macroscopic types of damage, there was evidence of the widespread presence of microscopic bioerosion (microboring), caused by autotrophic and heterotrophic microorganisms, visible only through SEM observations, which, despite not creating large chambers, progressively undermine the resistance of the stone and facilitate the development of other biodeteriogens. This paper will be focused on the characterization of the bioerosion observed on different artefacts: the roman statues discovered underwater in the Grotta Azzurra, Capri and in the Campi Flegrei area (Naples –Italy), and the marble sarcophagi that are still on the seabed of San Pietro in Bevagna (Taranto – Italy).

KEYWORDS bioerosion, microboring, pitting, *Cliona*, *Lithophaga*, *Plectonema terebrans*, Polydora

    DOI 10.1179/1350503312Z.0000000003

FIGURE 1 Statue of Neptune: detail of sponge pitting.
Museo Archeologico dei Campi Flegrei, Baia, Naples. Photograph by Roberto Petriaggi, ISCR

FIGURE 2   Statue of Cybele: detail of sponge pitting.
Museo Archeologico dei Campi Flegrei, Baia, Naples. Photograph by Roberto Petriaggi, ISCR

Bivalve molluscs play an essential role in the bioerosion processes creating cavities of various length and width, according to the shell or body size. The morphology and dimension of the perforations can be used for identification purposes in the absence of the shell.

Bivalve attacks were well represented by the Ulysses statue (white marble) of the Baiae Museum where about 20% of the artefact was lost (Figure 4). The most common species of bioeroding bivalves were *Lithophaga lithophaga* L., *Gastrochaena dubia* Pennant (found in several statues of Baiae Museum and in the sarcophagi of San Pietro in Bevagna), *Petricola lithophaga* Retzius, and *Coralliophaga lithophagella* Lamarck. *Lithophaga lithophaga* is cylindrical, lengthened, equivalve; the valves external surface is glossy with thin concentric and radial dark brown striations; the internal surface is pearly. This species colonizes calcareous rocky walls, particularly vertical ones, where it digs perforations similar to smooth channels. The animal does not use a mechanical action but it digs using chemical secretions. The chemical mechanism leading to limestone dissolution is triggered by a mucoprotein, secreted by some glands of the mantle, which can chelate calcium ions. *Gastrochaena dubia* secretes thin aragonite layers that can cover the eroded cavities' walls. Other aragonite deposits are always present and create tubular growths that protect and raise the siphons' exit level relatively to the substratum. On the surface, they appear hollow, with an eight-shaped section. In this way, *G. dubia* is able to avoid any occlusion of the inhaling and exhaling siphons which the animal uses to filter suspended food particle, and is therefore able to colonize horizontal substrata, even though affected by a high sedimentation rate.

A peculiar bioerosion form, visible as furrows with two parallel lines of incision, was observed on the bearded male Herma (white marble) and on the Pelagian Isis (grey marble) — Baiae Museum (Ricci et al., 2008b). This alteration was due to spionid polychaetes (Anellidae) of the genus *Polydora*. *Polydora* is an efficient bioeroder and it is commonly associated with calcareous substrates (corals, coralline

FIGURE 3   Statue of Poseidon recovered in the Grotta Azzurra, now exposed at the Casa Rossa Capri Island. Detail of the head showing bioerosion due to sponge and bivalves. *Photograph by Roberto Petriaggi, ISCR*

algae, bivalves, and gastropods). This Anellidae excavates U-shaped galleries in the substratum and removes calcium carbonate by two parallel arms. The boring processes can be summarized in three mechanisms: a chemical mechanism through the acid dissolution of the substrates; a mechanical mechanism where the organisms abrade the substrates; and a combined chemical and mechanical mechanism.

An important role in the bioerosion phenomena is played by endolithic eukariote and prokaryote micro-organisms which attack carbonate substrata and dig micro-galleries through biochemical dissolution due to the production of acidic or chelating substances. This type of bioerosion (microboring) was exclusively observed through SEM analyses (Zeiss EVO 60- under high vacuum conditions upon gold metallization). For taxonomic description of the bioerosion traces and for the identification of euendolithic microorganisms responsible of microboring, it used the embedding resin cast technique that allows one to obtain the casts of biological structures originally

FIGURE 4   Statue of Ulysses.
Museo Archeologico dei Campi Flegrei, Baia, Naples. (Photograph by Roberto Petriaggi, ISCR).

present in the galleries. Samples were impregnated with polyestere resin (SS — Styrene Styrol) and subsequently dissolved, producing so-called casts of the bioerosion patterns inside the carbonate. In our samples microboring usually appeared like galleries with sub-circular section, of variable length and 2–5 μm wide (Figure 5). The most common micro-euendoliths are *Ostreobium quekettii* (green alga), *Plectonema terebrans* and *Mastigocoleus testarum* (cyanobacteria), *Ostracoblabe implexa* and *Lithopythium gangliiforme* (fungi).

The study showed that the calcareous composition of the stone material is very important in the selection of the bioeroders. For example, the dolomitic nature of the sarcophagi of San Pietro in Bevagna strongly inhibited the development of most endolithic bivalves and sponge.

This bioerosion phenomenon becomes very significant when the artefacts remain exposed to the biological agents in the same position for a long period of time, and it was verified that the combined action of clionides and bivalves can lead, over time, to the destruction of large portions of the artefacts.

The conservation of the underwater artefacts *in situ* could be made by means of different kind of protection. For mosaic or *opus sectile* pavements can be used geotextile sheets and send bags or with geotexile mattresses. These devices have shown a good level of protection up to two years in the Baiae site and they are easy to remove for the diver visit and for the maintenance operations (Petriaggi and Mancinelli, 2004).

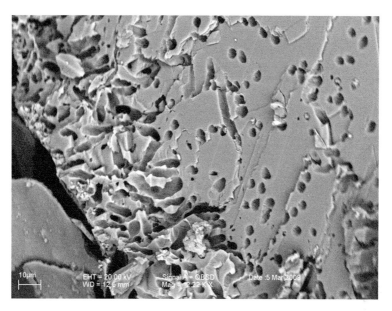

FIGURE 5   SEM image of microboring due to endolithic activity of microorganisms.
Photograph by Sandra Ricci, ISCR

Statues and other architectural artefacts well preserved (columns, capitals) are normally recovered and exposed in museums: their exposition *in situ* is not recommended and a good alternative is the exposition of copies. Also, in this case it is necessary to project a maintenance programme in order to monitoring and clean the copies periodically.

Reburial could be good practises for the *in situ* conservation if the artefacts should not remain visible. The case of San Pietro in Bevagna shows that the periodic and natural reburial by the sand well protected the marble sarcophagi by bioerosion and also by epilithic colonization.

According to our experiences, we can affirm that the choice of the protection is strictly related to several factors: dimensions and state of conservation of the artefact, environmental characteristics of the site (depth, type of seabed, currents, etc.), open to the public.

Bibliography

Davidde, B., Ricci, S., Poggi, D., and Bartolini, M. 2010. Marine Bioerosion of Stone Artefacts Preserved in the Museo archeologico dei campi Flegrei in the Castle of Baia (Naples). *Archaeologia Maritima Mediterranea*, 7: 75–115.

Petriaggi, R. and Mancinelli, R. 2004. An Experimental Conservation Treatment on the Mosaic Floor and Perimeter Walls of Room N. 1 of the So-Called 'Villa con ingresso a protiro' in the Underwater Archaeological Park of Baia (Naples), *Archaeologia Maritima Mediterranea*, 1: 109–26 [accessed 5 October 2012]. Available at: <www.libraweb.net>

Ricci, S., Priori, G. F., and Bartolini, M. 2008a. Bioerosione di pavimentazioni musive sommerse ad opera della spugna endolitica *Cliona celata*. *Bollettino ICR, Nuova serie*, 15: 7–18.

Ricci, S., Davidde, B., Bartolini, M., and Priori, G. F. 2008b. Bioerosion of Lapideous Objects Found in the Underwater Archaeological Site of Baia (Naples). *Archaeologia Maritima Mediterranea*, 6: 167–88.

Notes on contributors

Dr Sandra Ricci is Director of the Marine Biology Sector at the ISCR High Level School for Conservation and Restoration.

Correspondence to: Dr Sandra Ricci, Istituto Superiore per la Conservazione ed il Restauro (ISCR), Via di San Michele, 23. 00153 Rome, Italy. Email: sandra.ricci@ beniculturali.it

Dr Barbara Davidde is Director of the Underwater Archaeological Operations Unit and Adjunct professor of Underwater Archaeology at Università degli Studi Roma Tre (Rome, Italy).

Correspondence to: Dr Barbara Davidde, Istituto Superiore per la Conservazione ed il Restauro (ISCR), Via di San Michele, 23. 00153 Rome, Italy. Email: barbara. davidde@beniculturali.it

CONSERVATION AND MGMT OF ARCH. SITES, Vol. 14 Nos 1–4, 2012, 35–47

Reburial and Analyses of Archaeological Remains in the Marine Environment — Investigations into the Effects on Metals

VICKI RICHARDS

Department of Materials Conservation, Western Australian Museum, Australia

DAVID GREGORY

In-Situ Group, Conservation Department, Archaeology Section, National Museum of Denmark

IAN MACLEOD

Fremantle Museums and Maritime Heritage, Western Australian Museum, Australia

HENNING MATTHIESEN

In-Situ Group, Conservation Department, Archaeology Section, National Museum of Denmark

The treatment and long-term storage of recovered cultural material from underwater heritage sites is becoming less cost effective, and reburial of archaeological sites and the associated artefacts in the marine environment is becoming increasingly common practice in managing the submerged cultural resource. Following recent large-scale underwater archaeological excavations in Marstrand harbour, Sweden, the majority of recovered finds were reburied in defined trenches in the harbour sediment. Subsequently, the Studio of the Western Sweden Conservators in conjunction with the Bohus County Museum initiated a fifty-year research project to evaluate reburial as an appropriate method of preserving waterlogged archaeological artefacts in the long term. The research project, entitled 'Reburial and Analyses of Archaeological Remains', was launched in 2002 and consists of six sub-projects. The main aims of these sub-projects are to analyse the extent of deterioration of the most common material types found on underwater

    DOI 10.1179/1350503312Z.0000000004

archaeological sites, assess the stability of packing and marking materials used in archaeological documentation, and monitor the reburial environment.

The aim of the metals sub-project is to investigate the short- to long-term corrosion behaviour of metals buried in the marine environment by examining the deterioration of reburied and exposed modern metal coupons and eventually compare these results to the analysis of actual shipwreck artefacts. The environmental monitoring sub-project is designed to complement the other sub-projects by assessing the physico-chemical changes occurring in the reburial environment over time and the effect on the deterioration of the different reburied material types. In comparing the results obtained over the past seven years from both the metals and monitoring sub-projects, it should be possible to more accurately evaluate the effectiveness of reburial as a long-term *in situ* preservation strategy for metallic archaeological remains.

KEYWORDS *in situ* preservation, reburial, metals, marine environment, corrosion

Introduction

In 1997, land reclamation and construction works were proposed in Marstrand Harbour, on the west coast of Sweden. In 1998 and 1999, extensive marine archaeological excavations were carried out in the area that was to be affected. About 10,000 artefacts were recovered. However, based on a strict set of criteria, 10–15% of the collection was chosen for conservation and the remainder was to be reburied off site. Two reburial trenches were dug on the opposite side of the harbour, one for metals and the other for organics and silicates. The artefacts were labelled, packed, placed in the appropriate trench, and covered with at least 50 cm of sediment dredged from the immediate area.

With the exception of wood, the long-term effects of reburial on some of the other more common material types typically found on underwater cultural heritage sites, such as metals, ceramics, leather, bone, and so on has not been thoroughly investigated.

Therefore in 2001, the Reburial and Analyses of Archaeological Remains (RAAR) research project was initiated. One of the primary objectives of the project is to evaluate reburial as an alternative method for storing and preserving wet archaeological remains (Bergstrand et al., 2005).

The project is divided into six sub-projects coordinated by conservation specialists from Sweden, Denmark, Norway, and Australia. The aim of four of the six sub-projects is to analyse the extent of deterioration of the most common material types found on archaeological sites during long-term reburial. Another sub-project concentrates on assessing the stability of packing and marking materials used in archaeological documentation and the final sub-project involves monitoring chemical and physical changes occurring in the reburial environment over time.

In order to determine the long-term effects of reburial on the different material types, sufficient samples were buried to allow sampling to continue for 48 years.

The sample units were to be retrieved in the pre-determined order of 1, 2, 3, 6, 12, 24, and 48 years. Most sample units were buried in the organic/silicate trench in 2002, whereas the metal samples were buried in the metals trench in 2003. The final report for Phase 1 of the project (2003–05) was published in 2007 (Nyström Godfrey and Berstrand, 2007; Nyström Godfrey et al., 2009). However, since retrieval of the reburied samples is totally dependent on external funding, the six-year retrieval period was postponed to 2009 and as such the reburial period was extended to seven years for the samples reburied in 2002. The final report, including all detailed reports from each sub-project as appendices, was completed this year and is available on the project web site (Nyström Godfrey et al., 2011). However, this paper is a brief overview of the major results obtained from the environmental monitoring and the metal analyses after six years of reburial.

Environmental monitoring

Phase 2 aims

In 2006, after the completion of Phase 1, a seminar was organized where the coordinators of the sub-projects discussed their results. Following this seminar the following recommendations were made for Phase 2 of the environmental sub-project: develop a sediment core sampling technique whereby sediments deeper than 50 cm could be sampled to better understand the sulphate–sulphide system, which dominated the anoxic processes in the reburial sediments. Concerns had also been expressed by the metals and wood sub-projects that burial depths of 50 cm may not be sufficient to afford optimal protection of these materials. The second recommendation was to check that the environment in both trenches was still conducive to the preservation of the reburied artefacts.

Experimental

In April 2007 and September 2009, two sets of duplicate core samples were recovered from inside the organics and metals trenches and from an undisturbed area in close proximity. The first core was used to measure dissolved oxygen, sulphide, sulphate, and carbon dioxide content, redox potential and pH in the pore water at 5 cm intervals. The second core was used to measure the porosity, organic content, particle size distribution, and total iron content also at 5 cm depth intervals. More detailed descriptions of the sampling techniques and laboratory methods are presented in Nyström Godfrey et al. (2011).

Results

Pore water analyses

Results of the pore water analyses indicated that the conditions within the organic and metals reburial trenches were still sub-oxic to anoxic (dissolved oxygen contents = 0.30 – < 0.01 mg cu dm), strongly reducing in nature (redox potentials = -0.150 to -0.200 V vs NHE) with near neutral pH (pH = 7.00 – 7.50). Generally there was a decrease in sulphate content and a concomitant increase in sulphide concentration with increasing sediment depth (Figure 1), indicating that sulphate reduction remains

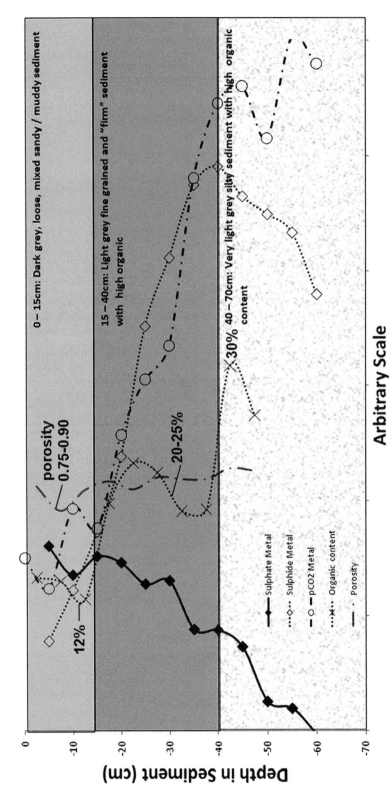

FIGURE 1   Results of pore water and sediment analyses in the metal trench in September 2009.

the dominant process occurring at the depths where the archaeological material is buried.

Sediment analyses

The graph shown in Figure 1 depicts some of the results from the pore water and sediment analyses of the 2009 metal trench core sample which were not dissimilar to the 2007 results. The metals trench sediment consists of porous (porosity ranging from 0.75–0.90), coarse to medium silts with a relatively high organic content. In the upper 15 cm of the core the organic content was about 12%, which increased to 20–25% in the 20–40 cm fraction, then increased again to about 30% in the 40–45 cm range. After 50 cm the organic content began to decrease. There were slower rates of sulphate reduction in the upper 40 cm of the metal trench sediments thereafter the sulphate was rapidly reduced. However, there was still some sulphate present in the deeper 50–55 cm fractions available for sulphate reducing bacteria. The carbon dioxide levels also indicate that there is significant microbial activity occurring at these deeper depths.

Metals sub-project

Aims

The main aim of the metals sub-project is to investigate the corrosion behaviour of modern metal coupons buried in the marine environment over time in order to evaluate the effectiveness of reburial as a long-term *in situ* preservation strategy for metallic archaeological remains.

Experimental

The samples units consisted of prefabricated proprietary metal coupons of known metal composition mounted utilizing high-density polyethylene (HDPE) materials. The copper alloy coupons tested were 99.9% copper, leaded (1.5–3.0%) yellow brass with 36–43% zinc and cast medium leaded (1%) zinc (3%) bronze with 10% tin typical of nineteenth-century marine bronzes. The ferrous alloy coupons consisted of cast iron with 3–3.6% carbon, mild steel with 0.14% Si as the modern equivalent to historic wrought iron and a standard low alloy copper (0.2%) steel coupon to provide reliable corrosion rate data. Each sample unit consisted of three sets of duplicate metal coupons mounted at three different depth intervals (totally exposed above the sediment, just below the sediment and buried 50 cm in the sediment) (Figure 2). The ferrous and copper alloys were mounted and buried separately to minimize galvanic and proximity corrosion.

One copper alloy and one ferrous alloy sample unit were recovered in 2009 (Figure 2). One of the duplicate coupons for each metal type was chemically stripped to remove the corrosion products and then weighed while the other coupon was left unstripped for analysis of the major corrosion products. Digital electron micrographs (SEM) and energy dispersive X-ray analyses (EDX) were collected as the primary data. More detailed descriptions of the sample preparation techniques and analytical methods are presented in Nyström Godfrey et al. (2011).

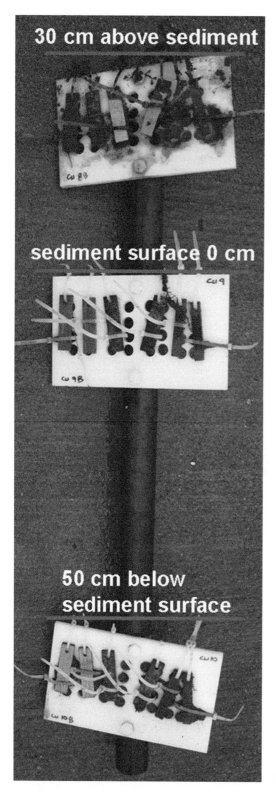

30 cm above sediment

sediment surface 0 cm

50 cm below
sediment surface

FIGURE 2   Copper alloy sample unit
immediately after recovery in 2009.

SEM/EDX analyses

Only the results from the SEM/EDX analyses of the buried coupons recovered from 50 cm below the sediment will be presented in this paper as this is the depth to which the archaeological materials are buried. However, in the final report (Nyström Godfrey et al., 2011) the analytical results obtained from all coupons recovered from the three different environments are discussed in detail and compared to the Phase 1 results.

Copper

The unstripped copper coupons showed a very uniform corrosion product matrix.

The main minerals identified were chalcocite (Cu_2S) and cuprite (Cu_2O) with a small amount of copper (I) chloride (CuCl). The stripped copper samples showed uniform anaerobic corrosion across the grain surfaces in combination with inter-granular corrosion along the grain boundaries due to the different electrochemical activity of the grain boundaries where micro-alloying impurities accumulate as compared to the bulk material.

On initial reburial, oxygen is introduced into the sediment and the normal aerobic corrosion mechanism will initially form cuprite on the copper coupon surface. How-ever, as the oxygen is consumed by oxidation reactions and biological activity, the environment will tend towards anaerobic conditions and the corrosion mechanism will change markedly. The redox potential of the interstitial water can fall below the hydrogen evolution potential and the main cathodic reaction in the metal corrosion process will be the reduction of water and not oxygen. This reaction is usually slow but the presence of facultative and anaerobic bacteria in the sediment can catalyse this reaction through use of their dehydrogenase enzymes. Sulphate reducing bacteria are especially important and utilize sulphate ions in the interstitial water of the sedi-ment and produce sulphide ions, which in turn react with the copper ions released by the anodic reaction and form insoluble copper sulphide precipitates, overlying the cuprite layer. The most common corrosion product found under these conditions is chalcocite (Cu_2S). Hence, the results of the SEM/EDX analysis were consistent with this corrosion mechanism.

Brass

General surface corrosion of the ($\alpha+\beta$) phases in the duplex brass produced a mixed copper-zinc sulphide layer and cuprite. Localized corrosion of the lead-rich phase at the grain boundaries of the β-zinc-rich phase resulted in topical concentrations of lead sulphide in these regions. The stripped coupon showed up slight surface enrichment of copper, which supports the fact that the dominant corrosion mechanism for duplex brass under anaerobic conditions is selective attack of the zinc-rich β phase and the lead which concentrates along the interdendritic boundaries between the β phase and the copper-rich α phase.

Bronze

The major corrosion products were copper-rich and tin-rich sulphides with some lead sulphides concentrated along the boundaries of the tin-rich ($\alpha + \delta$) eutectic phase. Complete stripping of the bronze coupons was difficult. However the residual phase was identified as 88% Cu and 4% Sn, which is consistent with it being the residual copper-rich α phase. This indicates the preferential corrosion of the copper-tin eutectoid phase and not corrosion of the copper-rich α phase, which is consistent with the anaerobic corrosion mechanism of bronzes.

Copper steel

The unstripped copper steel coupon showed a well-developed iron sulphide corrosion product layer incorporating sand and clay particles with some areas of very sulphur-rich deposits evidence of microbial corrosion. The stripped coupon showed uniform attack of the primary α ferrite grains of the metal. These results are typical for the corrosion of iron in an anaerobic sulphur-rich environment.

Cast iron

The unstripped coupon showed up a mixture of iron corrosion products that contained at least two different forms of iron sulphides along with adventitious sediment. The stripped coupon showed very extensive pitting corrosion of the ferrite phase leaving behind the residual carbon-rich phases. This increase in pitting corrosion of the ferrite α phase is likely to be due to microbial corrosion caused by sulphate reducing bacteria in the anaerobic sediment.

Mild steel

The unstripped mild steel coupon showed a very thick, uniform layer of iron sulphides. After stripping, the metal showed extreme pitting corrosion, extensive corrosion along the slag inclusion lines and also strong corrosion across the face of the α ferrite grains leading to a very rough surface topography. Again, this increase in pitting corrosion is typical of anaerobic microbial corrosion mechanisms in a sulphide-rich environment.

Normalized percentage weight loss

The results of the SEM/EDX analyses provided information regarding the primary corrosion mechanisms occurring on these coupons in the anaerobic sediments; however, it did not provide any empirical data that we could use to compare the extents of corrosion of the different coupons in this environment, therefore we used the weight loss data for comparative analysis. In order to directly compare the different sized coupons, the weight losses were normalized for the surface area of the coupons and then divided by the number of years of immersion to give a normalized percentage weight loss per year of immersion (Figure 3). This assumes that weight loss is linear over time, which may not be the case as the time of immersion increases. The weight loss data for the 2009 coupons that were exposed to the aerobic marine environment were also shown in Figure 3 so that the overall effect reburial has on the extent of corrosion is easier to discern. As expected the graph showed that there was a significant decrease in the extent of corrosion of all coupons when buried to depths of 50 cm in the Marstrand sediments.

Normalized corrosion rates

In order to better compare the weight loss data between the copper and iron based alloys the weight loss in grams normalized for the surface area was divided through

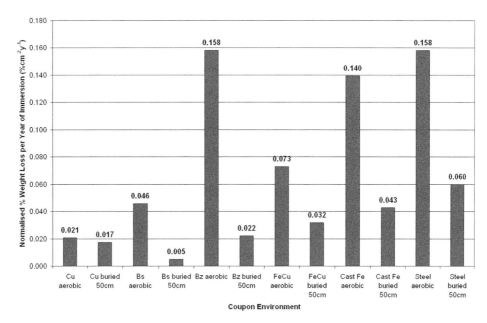

FIGURE 3   Normalized percentage weight loss per year of immersion for the 2009 metal coupons exposed to the aerobic marine environment and buried 50 cm under the sediment.

by the time of immersion and the density of the alloy to obtain a more standard corrosion rate in mm per year of immersion (Figure 4). Again from the graph it was obvious that corrosion rates of all coupons decreased significantly with reburial depths of 50 cm in these sediments.

Estimated years to total loss

Although the graphs shown in Figures 3 and 4 indicate that reburial to 50 cm does indeed decrease the overall extent and rates of corrosion of all metal coupons, they do not answer the question of how long can these different metal alloys realistically be buried at these depths before there is significant loss of the metal surfaces and therefore, important archaeological information? In order to estimate the years to total metal loss the normalized corrosion rates in mm per year and the initial thicknesses of the coupons were used in the calculations. However, since corrosion is not unidirectional and occurs on both sides of the coupon these results were then divided by a factor of 1.3, which takes into account the slower corrosion on the reverse sides of the coupons lying against the support plate where the dissolved oxygen concentration and total water movement is more limited and corrosion will be slower as compared to the exposed front surfaces (MacLeod, 2006; Russell et al., 2006). The resultant graph is shown in Figure 5. This calculation is obviously not ideal and the results are only ballpark estimations as we are assuming corrosion rates are linear over time which they are not but plots of corrosion rates versus time using a number of different mathematical functions gave a range of equations where the correlation coefficients of the lines of best fit were inconsistent. However, the results do provide some idea of the overall stability of the different metal alloys in this particular

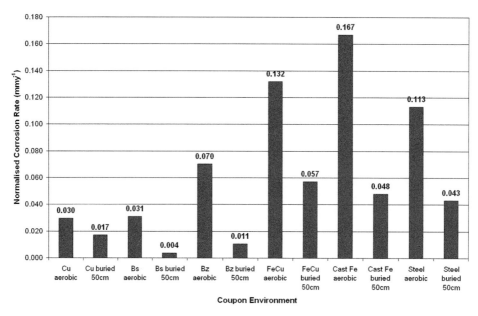

FIGURE 4   Normalized corrosion rates for the 2009 metal coupons exposed to the aerobic marine environment and buried 50 cm under the sediment.

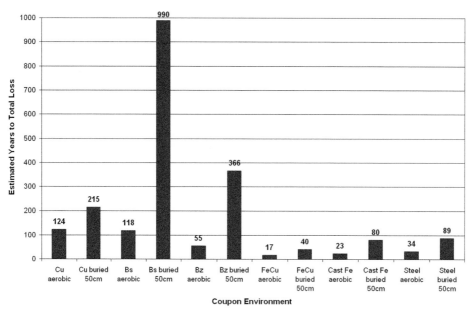

FIGURE 5   Estimated years to total loss for the 2009 metal coupons exposed to the aerobic marine environment and buried 50 cm under the sediment.

anaerobic environment in an easily understandable format. Taking into account the assumptions that have been made and the very large statistical variations in these calculated values it could be suggested that the extent of corrosion of all buried iron alloys would be excessive after fifty years and therefore they could not be recommended for reburial. On the other hand, reburial of the copper alloys might be feasible.

Conclusions

The effect of reburial at 50 cm on the extent of corrosion of the metal coupons after six years is summarized below.

- The major corrosion mechanisms occurring on the metal alloy coupons buried at 50 cm are consistent with the known anaerobic corrosion mechanisms for each alloy type.
- The extent of corrosion and the corrosion rates of all metal coupons decreased significantly with burial depths of 50 cm in the Marstrand sediments.
- It appears that reburial has the most positive effect on copper alloys and this would be primarily due to a combination of the biological toxicity of the copper and tin corrosion products and the more positive potentials of the copper and alloying metals.
- This positive effect is significantly reduced on ferrous alloys due to the fact that iron ions can be utilized by microbes and therefore, microbially induced corrosion can become more significant in controlling the corrosion rates than direct access to dissolved oxygen.
- Since sulphate reduction is the major process ongoing in the Marstrand sediments and the metals trench contains sulphate, albeit at low concentrations and significant quantities of organic matter, it is probable that sulphate reducing bacteria are causing the microbially induced corrosion of the buried ferrous alloy coupons.

Therefore, based on the 2009 results, copper alloys could be recommended for reburial in these types of sediments for a period of six years. It is probable that pure copper and brass alloy types may be buried for longer periods of time and at shallower depths; however, more information from the next phase of the experiment due in 2014 is required to support this inference. Conversely, ferrous alloys could not be recommended for reburial even in the medium term, based on their extensive degradation after six years and the significant increases in their corrosion rates since 2005. However, despite the concretion layers on the ferrous metal coupons being considerably better developed after six years, they are not yet totally encapsulating, making extrapolation to the corrosion behaviour of totally concreted archaeological ferrous artefacts difficult at this stage. Even after six years, it is still difficult to make any definitive statements regarding the longer term stability of these alloy types. It is of paramount importance therefore that this project continues to the next phase, so as much information as possible regarding the corrosion processes of these metal coupons can be obtained. This will allow us to establish whether or not the present conclusions are real indicators of the effects of the different microenvironments on long-term metal corrosion and whether reburial is indeed, an appropriate preservation strategy for maritime archaeological metals.

Bibliography

Bergstrand, T., Björdal, C. G., Bohm, C., Christenssen, E., Gregory, D., MacLeod, I. D., Nilsson, T., Nyström, I., Peacock, E. Richards, V. L., and Turner, G. 2005. Reburial as a Method of Preserving Archaeological Remains. A Presentation of the Marstrand Project. In: P. Hoffmann, K. Strætkvern, J. A. Spriggs, and D. Gregory, eds. *Proceedings of the 9th ICOM Group on Wet Organic Archaeological Materials Conference, Copenhagen, 7–11 June 2004*. Bremerhaven: The International Council of Museums, Committee for Conservation Working Group on Wet Organic Archaeological Materials, pp. 9–39.

MacLeod, I. D. 2006. Corrosion and Conservation Management of Iron Shipwrecks in Chuuk Lagoon, Federated States of Micronesia. *Conservation and Management of Archaeological Sites*, 7: 203–23.

Nyström Godfrey, I. and Bergstrand, T. eds. 2007. *Reburial and Analyses of Archaeological Remains — Studies on the Effect of Reburial on Archaeological Materials Performed in Marstrand, Sweden 2003–2005. The RAAR Project*. Udevalla, Sweden: Bohusläns Museum and Studio VästSvensk Konservering [accessed 10 October 2012]. Available at: <http://www9.vgregion.se/vastarvet/svk/reburial/index.htm>

Nyström Godfrey, I., Berstrand, T., Gjelstrup Björdal, C., Nilsson, T., Bohm, C., Christenssen, E., Gregory, D., Peacock, E. E., Richards, V., and MacLeod, I. D. 2009. Reburial and Analysis of Archaeological Remains — The RAAR Project. Project Status and Cultural Heritage Management Implications based on the First Preliminary Results. In: K. Straetkvern and D. J. Huisman, eds. *Proceedings of the 10th ICOM Group on Wet Organic Archaeological Materials Conference, Amsterdam, 10–15 September 2007*. Amersfoot: Rijksdienst voor Archeologie, Cultuurlandschap en Monumenten (RACM), pp. 169–96.

Nyström Godfrey, I., Bergstrand, T., and Petersson, H. eds. 2011. *Reburial and Analyses of Archaeological Remains — Phase II Results from the 4th Retrieval in 2009 from Marstrand, Sweden. The RAAR Project*. Udevalla, Sweden: Bohusläns Museum and Studio VästSvensk Konservering [accessed 10 October 2012]. Available at: <http://www9.vgregion.se/vastarvet/svk/reburial/index.htm>

Russell, M. A., Conlin, D. L., Murphy, L. E., Johnson, D. L., Wilson, B. M., and Carr, J. D. 2006. A Minimum-Impact Method for Measuring Corrosion Rate of Steel-Hulled Shipwrecks in Seawater. *The International Journal of Nautical Archaeology*, 35(2): 310–18.

Taylor, R. J. and MacLeod, I. D. 1985. Corrosion of Bronzes of Shipwrecks: A Comparison of Corrosion Rates Deduced from Shipwreck Material and from Electrochemical Methods. *Corrosion*, 41(2): 100–04.

Notes on contributors

Vicki Richards has a B.App.Sci. (Hons) (Curtin University) and a MPhil in chemistry (Murdoch University). She has been a Conservation Scientist in the Materials Conservation Department of the Western Australian Museum for the past twenty-four years. One of her primary research areas is investigating deterioration mechanisms of metals and organic materials on shipwreck sites and devising and implementing appropriate on-site management plans for the long-term *in situ* preservation of these sites.

Correspondence to: Vicki Richards, Department of Materials Conservation, Western Australian Museum, Shipwreck Galleries, 45–47 Cliff Street, Fremantle, WA 6160, Australia. Email: vicki.richards@museum.wa.gov.au

David Gregory worked for several years in the pharmaceutical industry as an analytical chemist. After that he obtained a BSc in archaeology (University of Leicester), MPhil in Maritime studies (St Andrews University), and PhD ('Formation processes in underwater archaeology: a study of the deterioration of archaeological materials in the marine environment', 1996) (University of Leicester). He is currently employed as a senior scientist at the National Museum of Denmark investigating methods of *in situ* preservation in waterlogged and underwater environments.

Correspondence to: David Gregory, In-Situ Group, Conservation Department, Archaeology Section, National Museum of Denmark, PO Box 260, Brede, DK-2800, Denmark. Email: david.john.gregory@natmus.dk

Ian MacLeod has a PhD and a Doctor of Philosophy from Melbourne University. He has been solving deterioration problems with shipwreck artefacts since 1978. He is passionately interested in the decay of glass, ceramics, wood, and metals. He was granted a Senior Fulbright Fellowship in 1993 and a Getty Conservation Institute fellowship in 2010 that allowed him to develop his research.

Correspondence to: Ian MacLeod, Western Australian Maritime Museum, Peter Hughes Drive, Victoria Quay, Fremantle, WA 6160, Australia. Email: ian.macleod@museum.wa.gov.au

Henning Matthiesen has a BSc in chemistry and mathematics, MSc in chemistry, and PhD in the biogeochemistry of marine sediments 1998 (University of Århus). He has worked as an analytical chemist in the industry. Since 2000 he has been employed as a senior researcher at the National Museum of Denmark. His main research areas are the *in situ* preservation of archaeological materials in wetlands and urban deposits.

Correspondence to: Henning Matthiesen, In-Situ Group, Conservation Department, Archaeology Section, National Museum of Denmark, PO Box 260, Brede, DK-2800, Denmark. Email: henning.matthiesen@natmus.dk

CONSERVATION AND MGMT OF ARCH. SITES, Vol. 14 Nos 1–4, 2012, 48–59

Erosion and Archaeological Heritage Protection in Lake Constance and Lake Zurich: The Interreg IV Project 'Erosion und Denkmalschutz am Bodensee und Zürichsee'

MARION HEUMÜLLER

Landesamt für Denkmalpflege, Regierungspräsidium Stuttgart, Germany

Lake Constance and Lake Zürich contain important archaeological cultural assets. Above all the so-called pile dwellings of the fifth to the first millennium BC are widespread in the shallow water areas of the lakes, and in 2011 a total of twenty of these sites were included into the inscription of 'Prehistoric Pile Dwellings around the Alps' on the UNESCO World Heritage List. However, construction in harbours and along the lakeshore, shipping traffic, and recreational facilities as well as erosion processes all considerably endanger the stability of the underwater cultural assets. Since the 1980s the authorities concerned with the preservation of archaeological heritage in Baden-Württemberg and the cantons of Thurgau and Zürich have developed working techniques for the preservation of these special underwater cultural assets. Numerous questions about the causes of erosion, the technical installation and the effectivity of protective measures against erosion and the ecological tolerance of such measures, however, remain open.

At this point the Interreg IV project 'Erosion and Archaeological Heritage Protection on Lake Constance and Lake Zürich', started in conjunction with various institutes concerned with lake research. Within the framework of this project the technical methods of mapping and surveillance of the site as a basis of an archaeological monitoring were refined and extended and measures for the integration of protection against erosion were intensified and checked. From the natural scientific point of view, the essential topics for a long-term reduction of anthropogenic-increased erosion are a reduction of ship-induced waves.

KEYWORDS pile-dwelling sites, erosion, protective installations, archaeological monitoring, erosion markers

© Taylor & Francis 2012   DOI 10.1179/1350503312Z.0000000005

Internationally renowned prehistoric sources

Pile dwellings from the prehistoric times are a particular phenomenon of the pre-Alpine region. In the Neolithic and Bronze Ages, and in isolated cases into the Iron Age, settlements were not only built on dry land but also in wetlands — in the shallow water zones of the larger and smaller lakes, on moorlands and less often on the floodplains of rivers. At these sites organic materials, in addition to the many other finds, remain preserved thanks to the ideal preservation conditions in the airtight and continuously waterlogged surroundings. Timber for construction, food remains, stockpiles, wooden tools, everyday objects and even pieces of clothing allow astonishingly vivid and multi-faceted insights into the lives of the people who established their villages there thousands of years ago.

Due to the diversity of the surviving materials the pile dwellings supply precise and detailed perceptions of the world of Europe's early farmers — their everyday lives, agriculture, animal husbandry and technological innovations. The possibilities of exact dating of the surviving wooden architectural elements using dendrochronology allow the history of the development of individual settlements to be traced and in ideal cases even the development of settlements in whole regions over a very long time span. The pile dwellings, therefore, constitute extraordinary archaeological sources for prehistoric settlements (Suter and Schlichtherle, 2009; Natter and Schlichtherle, 2011; Hafner et al., 2006).

Since June 2011, the prehistoric pile dwellings around the Alps have been accredited, by virtue of their unique preservation conditions, as UNESCO World Heritage Sites and inscribed on the list. In six Alpine countries, Switzerland, Germany, Austria, Slovenia, Italy, and France, 850 to 1000 wetland sites from between 5000 and 500 BC are registered (Figure 1). One hundred and eleven stations have been inscribed on the World Heritage List as representative for all the sites.

In addition to the pile dwellings other monuments remain conserved in the pre-Alpine lakes. Shipwreck remains can be found on the lakebeds and to some extent in the shallow water zones. Narrow areas of moorlands and the outflows of lakes were favoured places for crossings and it is here that the remains of crossings from the Neolithic Age to the Bronze Age are concentrated. Constructions from historical times still remain unresearched in the waters.

Dangers and strategies for the protection of underwater monuments

As long as organic materials always remain covered by water and sediment, the state of preservation, archaeologically speaking, is excellent in terms of tool marks and other archaeological information. The long-term maintenance of moorland and underwater monuments, however, is the cause of great concern as the conditions have deteriorated considerably in recent decades through agricultural usage, the drainage of wetlands and the growing pressures on resources along the lakeshores. In particular complex erosion processes increasingly threaten the lake dwellings on the shores of the pre-Alpine lakes. In the course of such erosion processes sand and lake marl sediment (Seekreide) are swept away from the shallow water zones and deposited in the deeper areas or at other shoreline sectors. A large number of pile dwellings have lost their protective covering and are being destroyed piece by piece. Many of the

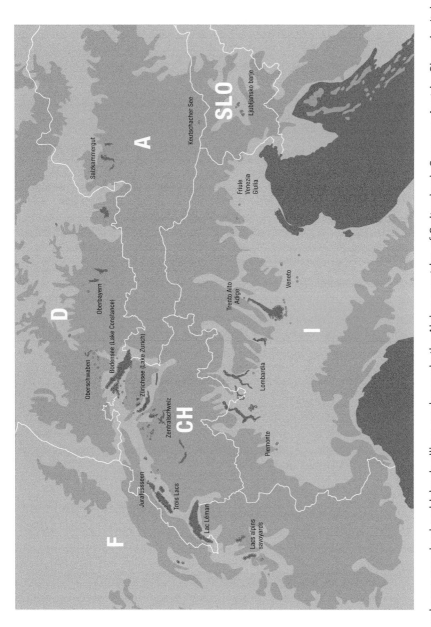

FIGURE 1   Around 1000 moorland and lake dwellings are known in the Alpine countries of Switzerland, Germany, Austria, Slovenia, Italy, and France. Of these, 111 have been inscribed on the UNESCO World Heritage List. Twenty-four of these can be found between Lake Constance and Lake Zürich. *Graphics: A. Mathis, AM Gestalten*

FIGURE 2   Sipplingen-Osthafen (D-Bodenseekreis): erosion rim in Sipplingen Bay. The waves continuously wash free new timber structures. Every year cultural layers disappear. *RPS/LAD, M. Kinsky*

sites, preserved for thousands of years in sediment under water, have in recent decades been totally or partially destroyed (Figure 2). The development of an effective protective strategy is thus an urgent necessity and an important task for the proper authorities.

Erosion on the shorelines of the lakes is caused by a number of different factors. Shipping traffic, shoreline constructions, and construction in the lakes all cause an increase in wave energy but also a reduction in protective aquatic plants, lower mean water levels, and an increase in certain waterfowl are further factors. The impact of individual factors, however, was until recently unknown. On Lake Constance and Lake Zürich a multi-disciplinary and transnational project was conceived in order to track the causes and the course of destructive erosion processes, to optimize and continue to develop protective measures for the pile dwellings, to introduce long-term measures for monitoring the lake dwellings while at the same time to inform the public about the importance of and the dangers to the pile dwellings. This was enabled within the framework of the Interreg IV programme 'Alpenrhein — Bodensee — Hochrhein' (ABH) sponsored by the European Union and the participating Swiss cantons within the programme region. The project 'Erosion and Archaeological Heritage Protection in Lake Constance and Lake Zurich' is supported jointly by the Landesamt für Denkmalpflege in the Regierungspräsidium Stuttgart, the Institut für Seenforschung, Baden-Württemberg, the Amt for Archaeology of the Canton of Thurgau, the Kantonsarchäologie Zürich, and the Vorarlberg Museum and carried out with the cooperation of the Limnologische Institut of the University of Constance and the Institute for Lake Research of the Eidgenössischen Technischen Hochschulen (EAWAG). In total 1.8 million Euros, including subsidies, have been made available from 2008 to 2011. The objective was to develop courses of action for the protection of pile dwellings and other underwater monuments.

The pile dwellings on Lake Constance and Lake Zurich are at the centre of the project. Between Lake Constance and Lake Zurich there are 192 known lake dwelling settlements, around 20 per cent of all known settlement sites. Most of them are found on the shore areas of the lakes. Only 1–5 per cent of them have been extensively researched. A far greater part of the sites are acutely threatened by erosion. A systematic excavation of all the threatened areas is impossible, particularly as excavations under water are very complex and costly and also not preferable as the scientific potential of the find site is lost. On numerous occasions threatened lake dwelling sites have been protected in conjunction with native conservation authorities. Thereby, as a rule, unnatural lakeshore constructions were removed and natural embankment slopes were restored by covering the shore sections in question with gravel (Schlichtherle, 2001: 128). Many sections of the shore, however, particularly those in the direct vicinity of towns or villages, have not yet been renatured or are unsuited to this. The excavation of such threatened sectors, including the follow-up costs, would be at least ten to fifteen times more expensive than a protective covering (Eberschweiler et al., 2006: 36).

For this reason protective installations have been introduced now for some twenty-five years, by the responsible bodies, for settlements that are particularly threatened by erosion. As one of the first measures under the auspices of the Landesdenkmalamtes Baden-Württemberg, (now the Landesamt für Denkmalpflege in the Regierungspräsidium Stuttgart) the lake dwelling in the bay of Wangen on the western shore of Lake Constance was completely sealed, in a number of stages between 1986 and 1995, by a 10,000 sq. m layer consisting of geotextile and gravel (Schlichtherle, 1996). Further gravel layers followed both on the German and Swiss shores of Lake Constance. Different variations (geotextile strips fixed to the lakebed, gravel coverings with complete or partial underlay of geotextiles, gravel covering without a geotextile underlay) were employed as protection against erosion. Most of the geotextiles used were made of synthetic materials and more unusually coconut matting. The depth of the gravel covering was on average 20–30 cm and was especially chosen so that the archaeological layers would not be damaged by the (Schlichtherle, 2001: 129; Brem et al., 2001: 21; Hafner and Schlichtherle, 2008: 112; Köninger and Schlichtherle, in press). In western Switzerland similar methods were used, particularly on Lake Bienne (Hafner, 2006). The application methods were continuously improved and a special floating vessel was developed in order to accomplish the task cheaply and efficiently.

Despite the evident success of the covering measures there are still a number of questions as to their durability and the best possible execution. The initial misgivings that the currents prevailing on the lakebed, for example during storms, could wash away the gravel layer leaving the geotextile exposed, proved unfounded (Hafner and Schlichtherle, 2008: 113). However, empirical data were missing as to the ideal application of the gravel mixture and the different geotextiles as well as the ecological implications of the covering. An important aspect of the Interreg IV project is, therefore, the monitoring of protective installations employed up to now and also their future development.

Four shore sections on the north and south shores of Lake Constance, off the villages of Unteruhldingen, Sipplingen, Litzelstetten, and Steckborn, each with distinctive erosion dynamics, were selected in order to develop new methods of effective protection against erosion. Surfaces were covered with different mixtures of gravel with differing stone sizes depending on the exposure of the shoreline area concerned in order to investigate how the gravel layers with varying thicknesses responded to the wash of the waves. A special boat designed and constructed for the purpose of transporting and depositing the gravel allowed individual loads of gravel to be deposited precisely to the last centimetre. This accuracy allowed a series of experiments with lattice structured gravel layers that are an important component of the Interreg IV project (Figure 3). As a variation on gravel coverings for entire areas, here over a total area of 3685 sq. m, only 5 m strips were covered with gravel. Between them were two larger rectangles of 32 × 26 m and five smaller squares of 7.5 × 7.5 m free of gravel. The aim was to find out whether the grids were any good as sediment traps and whether fine sediment was deposited in the inner, gravel-free areas after storms and thus whether a semi-natural protection against erosion could be established. If the experiment was a success then the amount of gravel required for coating areas of the lakebed could be greatly reduced leading to a considerable reduction in costs. Up until now on Lake Constance these measures have covered diverse areas of severely threatened lake dwellings and thus preserved archaeological resources for the future. They cover, at the moment, a total area of over 3 hectares (Figure 4).

Controls of the existing protective covering show that the gravel structures have largely remained *in situ*. A more detailed look, however, revealed something

FIGURE 3   Arial view of the lattice-structured gravel covering in Sipplingen Bay.
Photograph RPS/LAD, O. Braasch

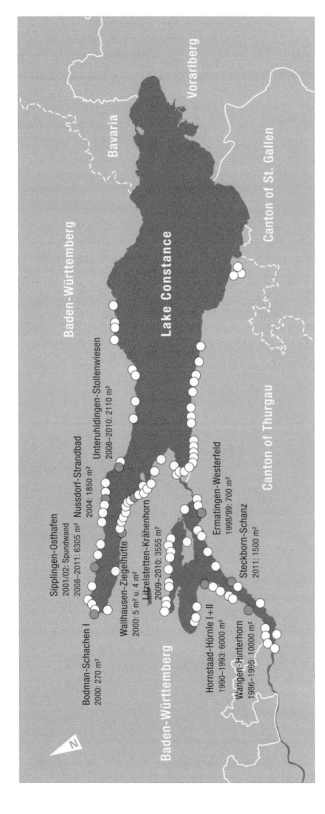

FIGURE 4   Protective measures against erosion for lake dwellings on Lake Constance as of 2011. White circles: the lake dwelling sites of Lake Constance; grey circles: lake dwellings with protective covering, representation of protected area in square metres.

Graphics: A. Mathis, AM Gestalten

unexpected. Swans combing through the cultural layers of the settlements for food have proven to be a previously underestimated destructive factor not only for the pile-dwelling settlements but also for the protective covering. When searching for food they are capable of digging holes in 25 cm thick layers of gravel. For this reason a higher proportion of coarser, larger pieces of gravel and the insertion of a geotextile underlay are important for durability of the protective covering.

The basic objective is an optimizing of erosion protection whilst at the same time blending in with the ecology of the shallow water zones and causing as little disruption as possible. This is why the accompanying ecological investigations documenting the repercussions of the measures on the lakebed as a biosphere were an important component of the Interreg IV project. They were conducted by the Arbeitsgruppe Bodenseeufer (AGBU). Sediment, fauna, and flora of the lakebed were extensively recorded and compared before and after the adoption of the protective measures. Additionally, unaffected reference areas were included in the studies. It would appear that the latticed structured gravel covering is ecologically more compatible than the blanket covering of individual sections (Ostendorp et al., in press). The effectiveness of the gravel covering, however, could not be tested within the framework of a three-year project and further observations are desirable both regarding the effectiveness of the gravel covering and the long-term development of the ecological circumstances.

Archaeological monitoring on Lake Zurich and Lake Constance

Another important objective of the project was to establish or rather extend the basis for a long-term, systematic monitoring system for the lake settlements. Since the beginnings of underwater archaeological research in the 1980s, divers have made observations that the appearance of individual sites has changed significantly. Settlement layers exposed on the lakebed and pile tips poking further out of the lakebed than previously point to sediment displacements. Although corresponding observations were mentioned in reports, initially they were not systematically quantified. In the 1990s wooden stakes, amongst other things, were placed at endangered stations in the canton of Zürich to monitor erosion. Here threatened areas, with cultural layers exposed on the lakebed, are often situated at the junction of the flat shallow water zones and the relatively steep slopes to the depths. In this situation sets of measuring stakes and floating lines have proven to be simple technical resources for monitoring erosion (Figure 5). To this end lines and measuring tapes were attached to the stakes above the lakebed. Monitoring is carried out by measuring the distance between the line and the lakebed and indicates the rate of erosion. Corresponding dives are conducted, as a general rule, every five years, but depending on the situation or the findings they can also be undertaken at shorter intervals. Almost a quarter of the stations on Lake Zürich are today furnished with equipment for monitoring erosion (Eberschweiler, in press; Scherer, T., pers. comm.).

On Lake Constance erosion markers have increasingly been installed only since the beginning of the Interreg IV project. Only 19 erosion markers existed at 14 stations until 2007. In the meantime 30 settlement areas — more than a third of all the known pile-dwelling sites on Lake Constance — have been supplied with 176 erosion markers and thus a representative cross-section is in place for a standard monitoring of pile dwellings on the lake.

FIGURE 5   Reference posts for monitoring erosion on Greifensee (Canton of Zürich). The tape measure and lines attached to the stake for monitoring purposes are easily recognizable. *Photograph Amt für Städtebau Zürich — Unterwasserarchäologie*

The erosion markers are placed by research divers in a number of alignments spread around the settlement areas and measured by GPS. Depending on the predetermined situation — deep or shallow water, close to the shore, strong or weak currents — different variations are deployed, for example oak stakes, PVC rods, and plastic or metal chains, and driven into the lakebed. In the following years the markers should be checked at regular intervals and readings taken. The aim is to establish tailored and durable reference points for the respective situations.

The erosion markers are, however, only a part of the monitoring process. Another important point is to establish whether archaeological occupation layers are exposed on the lakebed or embedded in sediment. For a systematic determination of the status of selected settlements, all the available archaeological, geological, topographical, sedimentological data and any information relevant to monument preservation are compiled and transferred to surface plans. Here a diversity of data sources becomes integrated. In the course of a project, a series of technical procedures were also tested, such as various echo sounding systems, terrain scans and bathymetric recordings, for the logging of erosion and accumulation processes. However, pinpoint accuracy in recording the lakebed, especially in the shallow water zones, has mostly proven to be problematic.

Ideally, as a result of archaeological monitoring, development prognoses can be made for individual sections of shore or threatened sites. If necessary, areas of lake settlements that are imminently endangered have to be selectively protected or rescue excavations have to be initiated. In any case further monitoring at regular intervals is needed.

Research into the causes and the progression of erosion

The natural scientific investigations into the causes and progression of erosion have been very extensive and used a variety of forms that included documentation of the lakebed using modern hydroacoustic procedures, analyses of sediment cores, long-term measurements of wave energy at selected stations, practical experiments on sediment transportation in the shallows, laboratory experiments on the erodibility of natural sediment, and the development of 2D and 3D models of sediment transportation in the shallows.

At this point the concluding book can only be referred to as it is due to be published in 2012 (Brem et al., in press). The most important factors for the energy input in the shallow water zones and the transformations on the lakebed resulting from this, are the wind and waves. Experiments by Hofmann et al. (in press), that there are clear differences between wind and the wash from shipping. Depending on the exposure of the site the energy input from the wash from shipping can amount to up to 50 per cent and thus has a large share in the continuous mobilization of fine particles (Hofmann et al., in press). A long-term objective has to be to reroute shipping traffic away from sensitive locations.

Raising the awareness of the public and the decision makers

A further aim of the project was to inform the public about the importance of and the dangers to pile dwellings in the form of an accompanying exhibition. The exhibition 'The Lake Recalls ... Underwater Archaeology and Lake Research', developed together within the project and implemented by the Voralberg Museum, has in the meantime been displayed in twenty-three communities in south-west Germany and Switzerland, and contributed to directly informing the public. In addition to being displayed in museums, the locations included selected authorities that are concerned with other aspects of the lakeshore, with foyers available with the corresponding space and frequented by the public. In this way not only were the broad public made aware but also the administrative and political decision makers were reached (Heumüller et al., in press).

Conclusions

The themes covered within the framework of the project represent an important basis for the future management of the UNESCO World Heritage Sites. The concluding book, due to be published in 2012 (Brem et al., in press), contains a series of related essays and case studies from a total of twenty-six authors. Particular value is placed on the formulation of courses of action. Various aspects of the tasks that have already begun, particularly the monitoring of the sites and the monitoring and development of new protective measures can be implemented as part of the accompanying measures for the UNESCO World Heritage.

Further information about the project can be found at: <http://www.der-see-erzaehlt. eu/> and <http://www.erosion-und-denkmalschutz-bodensee-zuerichsee.eu/>

Acknowledgements

Paper translated by Jamie McIntosh.

Bibliography

Brem, H., Eberschweiler, B., Grabher, G., Schlichtherle, H., and Schröder, G. eds. In press. *Erosion und Denk-malschutz am Bodensee und Zürichsee. Ein internationales Projekt im Rahmen des Interreg IV-Programms 'Alpenrhein-Bodensee-Hochrhein' zur Entwicklung von Handlungsoptionen zum Schutz des Kulturgutes unter Wasser*. Vorarlberg Museum Bregenz.

Brem, H., Schnyder, M., and Leuzinger, U. 2001. Archäologische Schutzmaßnahmen in den Seeufersiedlungen von Ermatingen TG — Westerfeld. *Jahrbuch der Schweizerischen Gesellschaft für Ur- und Frühgeschichte*, 84: 7–28.

Eberschweiler, B. In press. . . . hinterher ist man immer schlauer. Beobachtungen, Annahmen und erste Messungen am Zürichsee — eine Rückschau. In: Brem et al., in press.

Eberschweiler, B., Hafner, A. and Wolf. C. 2006. Unterwasserarchäologie in der Schweiz. Bilanz und Perspektiven aus den letzten 25 Jahren. In: A. Hafner, U. Niffeler, and U. Ruoff, eds. *Die Neue Sicht. Unterwasserarchäolo-gie und Geschichtsbild. Akten des 2. Internationalen Kongresses für Unterwasserarchäologie, Rüschlikon bei Zürich 21.–24.10.2004*, Antiqua, 40: 24–46.

Hafner, H. 2006. In situ preservation of submerged prehistoric settlements in lakes of the Alpine Region. Anti-erosion measures at sites in Lake Bienne, Switzerland. In: H. Kars and R. M. van Heeringen, eds. *Preserving Archaeological Remains In Situ. Proceedings of the 3rd Conference 7–9 Dezember*. Amsterdam/Institute for Geo and Bioarchaeology, VU University, pp. 245–51.

Hafner, A., Niffeler, U., and Ruoff, U. 2006. *Die Neue Sicht. Unterwasserarchäologie und Geschichtsbild. Akten des 2. Internationalen Kongresses für Unterwasserarchäologie, Rüschlikon bei Zürich 21.–24.10.2004*.

Hafner, A. and Schlichtherle, H. 2008. *Bedrohte Pfahlbauten. Gefährdete neolithische Siedlungsreste in Seen und Mooren rund um die Alpen*. Archäologie Bern/Archéologie bernoise, pp. 107–16.

Heumüller, M., Brem, H., Grabher, G., and Graf, M. In press. Der See erzählt . . . Unterwasserarchäologie & Seenforschung. Öffentlichkeitsarbeit im Rahmen des Interreg IV-Projektes 'Erosion und Denkmalschutz am Bodensee und Zürichsee'. In: Brem et al., in press.

Hofmann, H., Seibt, C., and Peeters, F. In press. Wellenexposition und Resuspensionspotential ausgewählter Untersuchungsgebiete am Bodensee: Messungen und Modellierung. In: Brem et al., in press.

Köninger, J. and Schlichtherle, H. In press. Schutzmaßnahmen für Pfahlbausiedlungen am baden-württembergischen Bodenseeufer — Verfahrenstechniken, Bestand, Erfahrungen und Ausblick. In: Brem et al., in press.

Natter, T. G. and Schlichtherle, H. 2011. *Time Travel? The Lake Recalls . . . Underwater Archaeology and Lake Research*. Vorarlberg Museum Bregenz.

Ostendorp, W., Dienst, M., Kramer, I., and Strang, I. In press. Ökologische Begleituntersuchungen an drei denk-malpflegerischen Erosionssicherungsmaßnahmen am deutschen und schweizerischen Bodenseeufer. In: Brem et al., in press.

Schlichtherle, H. 1996. Constitution de réserves archéologiques sur les sites de bord de lac et les tourbières de l'Allemagne du Sud-Ouest. In: D. Ramseyer and M.-J. Roulière-Lambert, eds. *Archéologie et erosion — 2. Zones humides en péril*. Lons-le-Saunier: Centre Jurassien du Patrimoine, pp. 25–34.

Schlichtherle, H. 2001. Schutz und Management archäologischer Denkmale im Bodensee und Federsee. In: Euro-pae Archaeologiae Consilium, eds. *The Heritage Management of Wetlands in Europe*. EAC occasional paper no 1. Brüssel/Exeter: EAC Secretariat/Centre for Wetland Research, pp. 125–32.

Suter, P. and Schlichtherle, H. 2009. *Pfahlbauten/Palafittes/Pile Dwellings. UNESCO Welterbe — Kandidatur Prähistorische Pfahlbauten rund um die Alpen*. Biel: Archäologischer Dienst Kanton Bern [accessed 8 October 2012]. PDF available at: <http://www.palafittes.org/de/service/informationsbroschuere/index.html>

Notes on contributor

Marion Heumüller studied Prehistory at Freiburg and Tübingen Universities. Her MA thesis on 'Trackways of the Federsee Wetlands' and a doctoral thesis on 'Jewellery of the Late Neolithic Lake Dwelling Hornstaad-Hörnle IA' were concerned with the themes of wetland and underwater archaeology. Since 1999 she has been a co-worker on various projects for the Baden-Württemberg State Office for the Preservation of Archaeological Monuments/Regional Council Stuttgart.

Correspondence to: Dr Marion Heumüller, Regierungspräsidium Stuttgart, Landesamt für Denkmalpflege, Fachbereich Feuchtbodenarchäologie, Fischersteig 9, 78343 Gaienhofen-Hemmenhofen, Germany. Email: marion.heumueller@rps.bwl.de

CONSERVATION AND MGMT OF ARCH. SITES, Vol. 14 Nos 1–4, 2012, 60–71

Deep Impact: What Happens When Archaeological Sites are Built on?

D. J. HUISMAN

Cultural Heritage Agency, Netherlands

Increasingly, developers and archaeologists search for ways to build on archaeological sites, while at the same time preserving the remains underneath. However, deciding which effects of construction on archaeological sites are acceptable and which are not is hampered by the lack of knowledge on the impacts of construction on archaeological sites. This paper provides an update on some of the effects of building on archaeological sites. Recent research had shown that displacement piles cause less disturbance in soft soils than previously thought. Moreover, replacement piles may be less benign that assumed up till now. Effects of loading on archaeological sites are described, and gaps in the knowledge on these effects are indicated. More research is needed in this field, especially on predicting soil disturbance and damage to weak materials. Impermeable surfaces and constructions on top of sites may affect the visibility of soil features due to decreased rainwater infiltration. Finally, a series of non-physical effects are mentioned that will have to be taken into account when deciding on allowing building on archaeological sites.

KEYWORDS construction, piling, loading, compression, deformation, burial environment

Introduction

One of the most well-known effects of the introduction of the Malta-convention is the obligation for developers to fund excavation of archaeological sites that they will disturb. The cost of excavating makes it appealing to find ways to preserve archaeological remains *in situ* while still developing and building on sites. Moreover, preservation *in situ* is the preferred option in the Malta convention. Increasingly, developers search for ways to build on archaeological sites while at the same time preserving the remains underneath (e.g. Davis et al., 2004). Some adverse effects on these archaeological sites are inevitable. It is up to archaeologists to decide to what extent such effects may be acceptable when evaluating construction plans that include *in situ* preservation. Deciding what effects are acceptable, and when excavations

 DOI 10.1179/1350503312Z.0000000006

(preservation *ex situ*) are necessary is difficult. This is not just because of the uncertainties of the archaeological remains present in an unexcavated site. A bigger problem is the lack of knowledge on the impacts of construction on archaeological sites.

A series of research projects have been initiated to give a better insight into the actual impact of some aspects of construction on the archaeological record. They include two projects researching the impact of piling on archaeological sites (Huisman et al., 2011b), a project on soil colour change (Huisman, 2007), and research on the vulnerability of carbonized remains under loading (Ngan-Tillard et al., forthcoming). These studies provide valuable information on the physical and chemical effects of construction. However, there is often little attention paid to the consequences of these effects of the value of the archaeological remains, including the future possibilities for research.

This paper presents an update to the present state of knowledge of the various ways in which building work affects archaeological sites. Special attention will be given to results of recent and ongoing research that will hopefully extend the possibilities for predicting future construction impacts. Areas where more research is needed are indicated, providing the basis for a tentative research agenda. This work is based on a project in which the Cultural Heritage Agency sought to provide decision makers with an up- to-date summary of how construction may impact archaeological sites and thus archaeological values (Huisman et al., 2011).

Building activities and their effects

Various activities that commonly form part of construction can influence the values of an archaeological site. They can be categorized as follows:

- Disturbance by digging
- Disturbance by piling
- Compression
- Degradation through changes in burial environment
- Soil colour change affecting visibility of soil features through changes in burial environment
- Non-physical effects like inaccessibility for monitoring and research.

For each of these categories, the effects on buried archaeological remains are different. Also, the level of knowledge on these effects and the availability of methods to predict them varies.

Disturbance by digging

The effects of digging on the archaeological record are clear and easily predicted. The effects are mixing of soil material and displacement and loss of context for artefacts, and so on. In principle, the dimensions of the area to be disturbed should also be clear, as it is indicated in the building plans. In practice, however, plans are often changed on the spot, and small-scale digging activities, for example for cables and pipes, are often left out of plans. This can result in unforeseen damage to the archaeological record.

Disturbance by piling

Introduction

Piling is often used in soft or unstable soils to transfer the load of a construction to deeper layers with better carrying capacity. The potential effects of piling on an archaeological site are well known. The archaeological record is lost in the volume taken up by the piles. Therefore, the loss of archaeological record is at least as large as the pile volume. In addition, the soil immediately surrounding the pile may be disturbed, compressed, or deformed down. The dimensions and type of damage of the disturbance outside of the pile volume is an unknown factor. Recent research has shown that the disturbed volume is up to an order of magnitude of three times the pile diameter (or 1.5 pile widths of the centre line of the pile) for driven piles (Williams et al., 2008). Displacement piles are often thought to cause no disturbance of the surrounding soil, except where they encounter obstructions, which can become caught in the auger flights and damage adjacent deposits (English Heritage, 2007: 12). This previous research has tested recently in the Netherlands and the results are reported on below.

Results of field test

In order to assess the impact of driven piles on archaeological sites in fine-grained sediments, we sampled three locations where piles had been driven through archaeological sites (Huisman et al., 2011b). A key element of this study was the use of micromorphological slides — thin sections of resin-impregnated blocks of undisturbed soil. Two of the locations were *terp* sites — artificially elevated settlements (dating from Iron Age to the Middle Ages in the former tidal area of the northern Netherlands). Both *terp* sites consisted of clayey soils, with variable stiffness. The third site was in the area of the Roman town and harbour of the city of 'Forum Hadriani' in present-day Voorburg. Here, a sequence of Neolithic peat, followed by sand and a clayey Roman harbour-fill with debris was present. On all three sites, concrete square piles had been driven through the archaeological layers. On the terp sites, sampling could be done prior to piling and after pile placement (Figure 1A). At Voorburg (Figure 1B), the piles dated from the 1950s so we have no pre-piling samples to study.

The micromorphological study showed that the disturbed zone around the pile in peat and clayey sediments in all three sites was very limited; some 7 cm from the pile surface in the most extreme cases, but most often 0 to 1.5 cm at the most (Figure 1C and D). These are remarkably small effects. The Voorburg sand layer, however, showed disturbance up to a distance of 1–1.5 m from the pile. This disturbance was mild, and consisted mostly of minor drawdown and small-scale (cm-scale) microtectonic features. Apart from that, there is evidence for increased pyrite formation directly next to the pile (Figure 1E). Based on these results, we now assume that the disturbed volume of driven piles in fine-grained soils is virtually identical to the pile volume. This study only investigated the effects on shallow depths. The effects may be larger at greater depths. The results of this study are corroborated by an inventory by the Gouda municipal archaeological service on the effects of piles on the archaeological record during the Koningshof excavations (Groenendijk, 2009). They

FIGURE 1   Micromorphological investigations on the impact of piling on archaeological layers (see also Huisman et al., 2011b).

A: Sampling at terp-site Kenwerd.

B: Sampling at Voorburg (Forum Hadriani). The stratigraphy shows a sequence from Neolithic peat at the base, a sand layer in the middle, and clay of the Roman harbour fill at the top.

C and D: Thin sections of samples taken directly next to a pile. In C, the soil mass has been compressed and deformed and now shows series of vertical clayey (shear?) planes. The left of the thin section is hardly affected, so the disturbed zone is estimated at 6–7 cm (Kenwerd; site A for position). D: The left of the sample shows some drawdown and sand liquefaction. Here, the disturbed zone is estimated at 1.5 cm (Groot-Wetsinge).

E: The sand layer from Voorburg (see B). The sand shows drawdown (white arrows) and small-scale microtectonic disturbances (e.g. black arrow). The black colouring in the peat (grey arrow) is caused by the precipitation of pyrite after the pile placement.

also concluded that the impact of driven piles — in this case mostly round wooden piles — was much smaller than expected.

New information from foundation engineers

While compiling the overview mentioned above (Huisman et al., 2011a), a discussion with foundation experts made it clear that replacement piles may have more influence on the surrounding soil material than assumed up till now in archaeological literature. When replacement piles are made by augering — and subsequently filling the resulting cavity with concrete — the augers' drag on the surrounding soil may cause disturbance and thus damage archaeological remains. This is especially the case if the soil contains stones or debris. Replacement piles that that are made by first placing a casing, subsequently excavating the soil material inside, and finally filling it with concrete seem at first glance to be ideal for limiting damage to archaeological sites. However, in practice groundwater levels inside the causing are often lowered to allow easier placement. This can result in displacement and mixing of soil material, especially sand, at the pile tip — which again may damage archaeological sites. This effect may be limited to deeper layers, and therefore not relevant for most archaeological sites. Moreover, removal of casings may also lead to sediment disturbance and therefore site damage. Unfortunately, we only have anecdotal evidence or experts' opinions of these effects. Documentation of cases where such effects could be observed would greatly increase our understanding, and help to make better founded decisions on whether or not to allow building projects on archaeological sites.

Compression

Compression occurs when the ground surface is loaded, for example with sand bodies from dykes, linear infrastructure, or simply with the weight of a construction. Potential adverse effects of compression on archaeological remains are deformation of layers — resulting in damage to stratigraphy or context — and damage to materials (including artefacts) (Figures 2 and 3).

One of the greatest problems in studying deformation is that there have been very few cases where such effects could be observed. This makes it difficult to properly assess the effects of compression on archaeological remains. Methods and models commonly used for predicting compression and deformation in civil engineering have limited predicting power, and commonly work on too large scales. Moreover, increasing the predictive power and level of detail of such models requires a huge increase in the amount of data on geotechnical properties of the subsurface layers and on the archaeology.

Lack of knowledge on the impact of loading and compression on archaeological sites is a major problem. In order to try and improve the situation, several initiatives have been started to try and observe the actual effects of loading on archaeological sites. One of these is a location (A4 Midden Delfland) where a 6 m sand embankment in a peat area will be removed, approximately forty years after it was constructed in order to make way for a tunnel. Prior to the new development, the impact of the mound on the archaeology will be studied.

With respect to damage to archaeological materials themselves by loading and compression, the amount of available knowledge is marginally bigger: there have

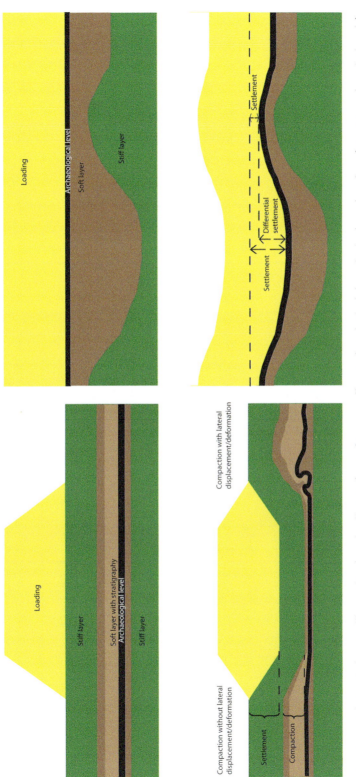

FIGURE 2   Schematic figures, illustrating, how loading at the surface can affect archaeological deposits in the subsurface (exaggerated vertical scale). Deformation due to differential compression and the difference between uniform and non-uniform loading is also demonstrated (after Huisman et al., 2011a).

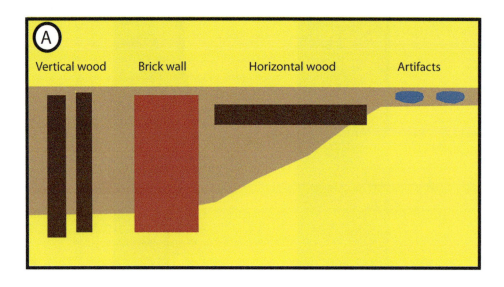

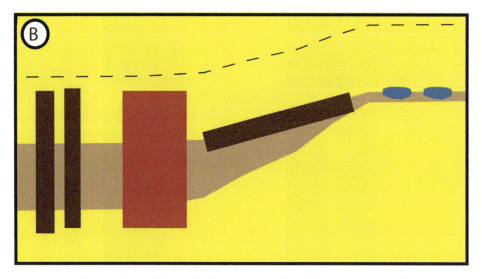

FIGURE 3   Schematic figure, illustrating how compression of heterogeneous soils with large, stiff artefacts can result in disturbance of the artefact-layer association (exaggerated vertical scale) (after Huisman et al., 2011a).

laboratory tests on the effects of loading on fragile model materials in sand, demonstrating that the effects under such conditions are small (e.g. Hyde, 2004; Sidell et al., 2004). Another pilot study investigated the effects of loading on carbonized and non-carbonized remains in soft clay and peat layers. This study indicated that loading on soft sediments may damage or destroy organic remains (van Kappel, 2004). At present, a series of tests are being executed at Delft Technical University to study the behaviour of carbonized grain embedded in soft sediments during loading and deformation (sheer). The results of these controlled experiments are expected soon.[1]

Changes in burial environment

Either deliberately or by accident, building projects often cause changes in the burial environment. The most common change is lowering of groundwater tables. The effects of such changes have been studied and described in many publications (see, e.g., the previous PARIS conference proceedings, and Huisman, 2009 for an overview). What makes building projects special, however, is that such changes are often temporary. Since knowledge on the speed of decay process is lacking, it is extremely hard to predict the damage to an archaeological site due to, for example, a few months or maybe a year of lowered groundwater tables. It is assumed that organic remains are degraded quickly. Slower processes, like metal corrosion, bioturbation, and acidification due to pyrite oxidation probably take several decades to cause serious damage and therefore may be less relevant in cases where changes in the burial environment are temporary.

As stated above, much is already known about the adverse effect of drying out of archaeological sites. It is less well known, however, that the opposite — increasingly wet conditions and a decrease in oxygen availability — can also have adverse effects. This is the case in many areas in the Netherlands, especially in alluvial clay soils. Here, the colour of soils underneath buildings and roads for example typically turns from brownish or brown-grey mottled to blue or blue-grey (see, e.g., Huisman, 2008; Figure 4). This so-called blue or grey discoloration occurs because the infiltrating of oxygen-rich rainwater is blocked. The ongoing supply of rainwater in the surrounding area forces water upwards from greater depths underneath the blockade. Moreover, the lack of vegetation results in lower evapotranspiration, causing increased moisture levels. Lack of oxygen results in the reduction of iron compounds like FeOOH and Fe_2O_3 — common minerals in oxygenated soils. This may, at first sight, seem a positive development, since organic and metal remains are better preserved in oxygen-poor conditions. However, as a result of this process, archaeological soil features (contexts) can become difficulty or even impossible to distinguish from the surrounding soil. When changes in the burial environment cause soil features to become invisible and make individual contexts indistinguishable from each other, the archaeological site loses a major part of its information value. This makes predicting under what conditions blue or grey discoloration occurs of great importance.

The chemical process of blue and grey discoloration itself can be understood easily from the behaviour of soil water underneath hard surfaces (Figure 5; Maas, 2001; Huisman et al., 2011a). Predicting under what conditions this occurs, however, is much harder. We assume that the chances of this type of discoloration to occur are larger:

- in fine-grained sediments
- if the reduction-oxidation boundary is close to the archaeological levels
- if the soil shows grey and yellowish to reddish mottling due to changing redox conditions (gley features).

If blue or grey discoloration occurs, problems with visibility of archaeological soil features are most likely:

- if the features have the same lithology as the surrounding soil
- if the features have low organic matter contents
- if the features contain few anthropogenic remains like charcoal and baked loam.

a

b

FIGURE 4   Field photographs (by author) of blue-grey colour change (Lent-Oosterhout), found underneath a demolished temporary school building.
A: The general brown to reddish brown soil colour has changed to blue-grey colours in the upper and lower horizons of the profile. Only the centre range still has more or less the original colour.
B: The former edge of the school building is still apparent from the colour change in the soil. Soil features in blue-grey areas like this one are often very difficult to distinguish from the surrounding soil mass — if at all.

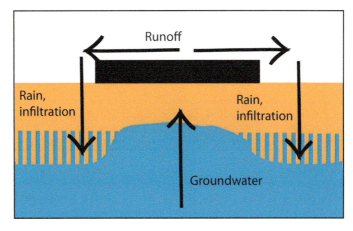

FIGURE 5   Schematic illustration, demonstrating how blue-grey colour change can occur underneath hard, impermeable surfaces like roads and buildings. Here, no oxygenated rainwater can infiltrate, but soil water is replenished from deeper, oxygen-poor groundwater (after Huisman et al., 2011a).

Non-physical effects like inaccessibility for monitoring and research
All effects described above directly affect the physical state of the burial environment of an archaeological site. Other effects can also be damaging, but are often over-looked. These effects include:

(1) Accessibility during the lifetime of the construction
An archaeological site may at first seem to be perfectly preserved underneath a building or road, but conditions may change. If the burial environment (unexpectedly) deteriorates, it may be impossible to ameliorate the situation or undertake a rescue-excavation due to the building on top. Moreover, one of the main reasons to preserve archaeological sites *in situ* is to make it possible to excavate it later. The option for excavating a site is blocked, however, as long as it is buried underneath a building.

(2) Accessibility after the lifetime of the construction
After a construction is removed, archaeological research may still be hampered, for example, by the presence of foundations. A dense network of piles may make it impossible to properly use a mechanical digger. Small numbers of widely spaced piles are therefore preferable in most cases preferable to larger numbers of densely spaced piles, even if the total disturbed volume becomes larger.

(3) Fragmentation of ownership
Large-scale archaeological sites (e.g. settlements, Roman villas, industrial complexes) can only be investigated properly if large areas can be opened up at once. Small excavation plots within such sites rarely yield much information. The process of stitching together dozens of small-scale excavation to make the overview of a large site is wrought with problems. This makes urban development of large-scale sites in rural areas potentially very damaging if the area is divided up into many relatively

small (house) plots with different owners. In the future it will never be possible to excavate more than one or two of such plots at the same time. A large-scale excavation will never be possible again.

Implications

The overview given above shows that damage to archaeological sites due to construction can be manifold. There can be physical disturbance, deformation, compression, fragmentation or decay of materials, fading of features, inaccessibility and fragmentation of ownership.

At present, we are often unable to predict the effects of a specific construction plan on an archaeological site. More research is needed to better understand and predict the effects of piling, loading, and changes in the burial environment.

Acknowledgements

I would like to thank two anonymous reviewers for their thorough and helpful comments on an earlier version of the manuscript.

Note

[1] Pers. comm., D. Ngan-Tillard, Delft University of Technology, Department of Applied Earth Science.

Bibliography

Davis, M. J., Gdaniec, K. L. A., Brice, M., and White, L. 2004. *Mitigation of Construction Impact on Archaeological Remains*. London: Museum of London Archaeological Service.

English Heritage 2007. *Piling and Archaeology. An English Heritage Guidance Note*. English Heritage: Swindon.

Groenendijk, M. 2009. *Archeologievriendelijk bouwen op de Koningshof te Gouda, Een evaluatie van de archeologievriendelijke aanpak*, Gouda: Gemeente Gouda.

Huisman, D. J. 2007. How Redox-Induced Soil Colour Changes Masks Soil Features; Cases from Alluvial Soils in the Netherlands. *Berichten van de Rijksdienst voor het Oudheidkundig Bodemonderzoek/Proceedings of the National Service for Archaeological Heritage in the Netherlands*, 46: 315–27.

Huisman, D. J., ed. 2009. *Degradation of Archaeological Remains*. Den Haag: SdU.

Huisman, D. J., Bouwmeester, J., de Lange, G., van der Linden, Th., Mauro, G., Ngan-Tillard, D., Groenendijk, M., de Ridder, T., van Rooijen, C., Roorda, I., Schmutzhart, D., and Stoevelaar, R. 2011a. *De invloed van bouwwerkzaamheden op archeologische vindplaatsen* [Online] [accessed 9 October 2012]. Available at: <http://www.cultureelerfgoed.nl/sites/default/files/u6/De%20invloed%20van%20bouwwerkzaamheden%20op%20archeologische%20vindplaatsen.pdf>.

Huisman, D. J., Müller, A., and van Doesburg, J. 2011b. Investigating the Impact of Concrete Driven Piles on the Archaeological Record Using Soil Micromorphology: Three Case Studies from the Netherlands. *Conservation and Management of Archaeological Sites*, 12(1): 8–30.

Hyde, A. 2004. Damage to Inclusions in Sand Subjected to One-Dimensional Compression. In: T. Nixon, ed., *Preserving Archaeological Remains In Situ? Proceedings of the 2nd Conference 12–14 September 2001*. London: Museum of London Archaeological Service, pp. 32–39.

Maas, K. 2001. Kwelvensters onder gebouwen en in het vrije veld. *Stromingen*, 7: 15–32.

Ngan-Tillard, D. J. M., van Dijk, N., van der Putte, E., Verwaal, W., Mulder, A., Huisman, D. J., and Braadbaart, F. forthcoming. Loss of Archaeological Value of Carbonized Seeds by Mechanical Loading in the Laboratory.

Sidell, E. J., Higuchi, T., Allison, R. J., and Long, A. J. 2004. The Response of Archaeological Sediments and Artefacts to Imposed Stress Regimes as a Consequence of Past, Present and Future Activity. In: T. Nixon, ed., *Preserving Archaeological Remains In Situ? Proceedings of the 2nd Conference 12–14 September 2001*. London: Museum of London Archaeological Service, pp. 42–49.

Van Kappel, K. 2004. Ondergedekt verleden, het effect van kunstmatige ophogingen op archeologische vindplaatsen in het noordelijke mariene gebied in Nederland. Unpublished MSc thesis, Wageningen University.

Williams, J., Hird, Ch., Emmet, K., Davies, G., and Rayner, T. 2008. Understanding Sub-Surface Impact of Driven Piles. In: H. Kars and R. M. van Heeringen, eds. *Preserving Archaeological Remains In Situ. Proceedings of the 3rd Conference, 7–9 December 2006, Geoarchaeological and Bioarchaeological Studies, 10*. Amsterdam: Vrije Universiteit, pp. 85–91.

Notes on contributor

Hans (D. J.) Huisman has an MSc in soil science and a PhD in geochemistry from Wageningen University. Since 2003, he has worked for the Cultural Heritage Agency of the Netherlands as senior researcher in soil science and degradation. He has undertaken a series of research projects on degradation of archaeological remains and the monitoring of archaeological sites, and has edited and co-authored a book on degradation of archaeological remains.

Correspondence to: D. J. Huisman, Cultural Heritage Agency, PO Box 3800 BP, Amersfoort, The Netherlands. Email: h.huisman@cultureelerfgoed.nl

CONSERVATION AND MGMT OF ARCH. SITES, Vol. 14 Nos 1–4, 2012, 72–84

Research on Conservation State and Preservation Conditions in Unsaturated Archaeological Deposits in Oslo

VIBEKE VANDRUP MARTENS

NIKU — Norwegian Institute for Cultural Heritage Research, Norway

CARL-EINAR AMUNDSEN and OVE BERGERSEN

Bioforsk — Norwegian Institute for Agricultural and Environmental Research, Norway

Archaeological, biological, and geochemical investigations of soil sample series from a section and five boreholes have been studied to evaluate the state of preservation at the time of investigation and the preservation conditions of urban archaeological deposits from medieval Oslo, Norway. Focus has been put on the most fragile deposits in the unsaturated and fluctuation zones. Even with limited investigations, it is possible to assess the archaeological conservation state and the preservation conditions. Further work should focus on interpreting measured results and on mitigation strategies.

KEYWORDS medieval, Norway, *in situ* preservation, unsaturated zone, fluctuation zone, saturated zone

Introduction

Over the last few years, a large number of augered boreholes have penetrated the archaeological deposits of the protected heritage site of the medieval town of Oslo, Norway, mostly as a result of large development projects. The archaeological observations and geochemical samples analysed from these investigations constitute the basic research material for evaluations of conservation state and preservation conditions. The data have been collected in collaboration between the Norwegian Institute for Cultural Heritage Research (NIKU) and Bioforsk. This paper presents the noted state of preservation of the archaeological deposits, groundwater levels, and assesses the conditions for continued *in situ* preservation. The question of *in situ* preservation is and has since the ratification of the Valletta treaty (Council of Europe, 1992) been a major concern to the Cultural Heritage Management authorities in Norway (cf.

DOI 10.1179/1350503312Z.0000000007

MD, 2010: 29–30), and is a prioritized area under the global challenges in the EU joint programme, 'Challenging Our Heritage'. International treaties and conventions are designed to protect the archaeological heritage as a source of the European collective memory and as an instrument for historical and scientific study. The Valletta treaty calls for preservation of the archaeological heritage *in situ*. To ensure that *in situ* preservation fulfils requirements of a sustainable strategy for archaeological remains, knowledge about the present state of preservation as well as the physical and chemical conditions for future preservation capacity is necessary. Urban archaeological deposits are very vulnerable to changes and degradation. Ultimately we seek to develop mitigation strategies that reduce the impact of human activities on archaeological deposits, and the Norwegian Directorate of Cultural Heritage has been instrumental in the development of tools to assess the state of preservation and conditions for continued *in situ* preservation, initiating two publications; The Monitoring Manual (RA and NIKU, 2008) and a Norwegian Standard (NS 9451, 2009) on sampling, monitoring, and assessing urban archaeological deposits. Much of this work is the result of research and mitigation strategies for the World Heritage Site of Bryggen in Bergen (see e.g. de Beer et al., 2008).

The Norwegian cultural heritage act protects listed monuments and demands that developers pay for the disturbance or destruction of archaeological remains (see also Petersén and Bergersen, in this volume). The law also opens up demands of sampling and monitoring sites, and even these demands must be financed by the developer.

Material

To demonstrate what is known so far about the present state of conservation and the conditions for preservation, sites have been chosen from two different parts and landscapes of the listed monument of medieval Oslo. Oslo was founded in the late tenth century AD on a peninsula deep within the Oslo fiord. Today, ruins of the Church of St Mary and the royal seat are still preserved, and an attempt has been made to recreate the medieval coastline (see Figure 1 between the points Sørenga and MB14). Other ruins of medieval churches, the cathedral, and the bishop's palace are preserved further NE, between Oslogate 6 and Arupsgate, and south of Oslogate 6. Archaeological deposits are preserved in varying thickness in the listed area, between 1 and 5.5 m. The two sites comprise four sample series from the NE part of medieval Oslo (one excavation section, Arupsgate, one dipwell, Oslogate 6) and five dipwells in the SW part of town (S7, Sørenga, MB6, MB9 and MB14, Figure 1). The SW part is the earliest settlement and original centre of the town, with the Church of St Mary and the royal seat. This area is very close to the medieval coastline, and not far from the modern one. The landscape is flat, originally marine deposits. Parts are grass covered, constituting a park with ruins and a reconstructed coastline. Other parts are covered with asphalt (industrial area). The archaeological deposits vary in thickness between 2.5 and 5.5 m. The NE landscape is on the outskirts of the medieval town. This area is on higher ground and on sloping terrain. Parts are grass covered, around medieval ruins or in areas of previous excavations, and the deposit thickness is 1.5–3 m.

In the street, Arupsgate archaeological excavations were carried out in 2007, when eighty-eight-year-old water pipelines needed renewal (Martens, 2010b). The street is

FIGURE 1   Aerial photograph of Oslo with boreholes and case sites marked.
'Kartgrunnlag Statens kartverk, Geovekst, kommuner'. © NIKU

asphalt covered, with a very dense layer of granite and alum shale supporting the road. The street slopes both towards W and N. Three sample series were taken from a section, one of them close to a large modern disturbance; a sewer manhole from the late 1980s which had been backfilled with sand. All the archaeological deposits were in the unsaturated zone, the groundwater level between 30 and 50 cm beneath the deepest deposits. However, most of the deposits had high water content, and the state of conservation was considered to be mostly good or excellent. One reason is almost certainly the sloping terrain and the relatively easy access to surface water from the nearby site of the ruins of the Church of the Holy Cross. After the new pipeline had been installed, the walls of the largest pit were covered with geotextile and a 20 cm thick layer of blue clay to protect the adjoining deposits from degradation. The rest of the pit was then back filled with sand and gravel around the new pipe. Clay plugs were also placed in some of the smaller pits to help keep water in the deposits on the higher ground.

At Oslogate 6, large archaeological excavations were carried out in 1987–89 as part of a development project. After the excavations, the development plans were abandoned, so the area was backfilled with compact clay-silt masses and covered with grass (RA, 1992; Wiberg, pers. comm.). Parts of the well-preserved medieval deposits were left still standing, and it is in these that a dipwell was installed as part of a research project concerning building on piles and preservation conditions (Bergersen et al., 2009). The augering prior to installation was done under archaeological supervision, the deposits were documented and evaluated, and geochemical samples were taken and analysed. The borehole was sealed with bentonite. This area also slants towards the west, and medieval ruins east of the site with grass-covered surroundings ensure that surface water may be filtered into the deposits.

As a part of that same project, the dipwell at Sørenga was installed (Bergersen et al., 2009), whereas the wells MB6, 9, 14 and S7 all were installed in connection with a large water pipe and sewage project called Midgardsormen (the Midgard serpent, see Johansen et al., 2009). All these are on flat terrain close to the sea, and after augering and installation of dipwells, bentonite was used in an attempt to seal the boreholes and secure the dipwells from direct surface water infiltration.

Methods

Archaeological documentation and evaluation

All deposits were described according to the Monitoring Manual (RA and NIKU, 2008), defining the composition and content of each layer, and the state of conservation was determined in accordance with Norwegian Standard (Table 1), separating the layers into the unsaturated (A), fluctuation (B), or saturated (C) zones, that is, above, partly in, or below groundwater level (and D, material later than 1900), and grading them from 0 (indefinable), 1 (lousy), 2 (poor), 3 (medium), and 4 (good) to 5 (excellent) (NS 9451, 2009: table 1; Martens, 2010a: table 8.1). To conduct this evaluation, studies were made of, for example, odour, colour, and organic content of each deposit.

Chemical analyses of samples

Soil samples from archaeological deposits were taken at various depths. All sampled deposits were subject to archaeological and chemical evaluations concerning both the state and conditions for preservation. In sections, the samples were taken using a hand auger with a cylinder diameter of 2.5 cm. The auger was horizontally driven into the profile and samples were taken from 20–50 cm within the deposits. At the augered boreholes for dipwells, all samples were taken from the auger immediately after archaeological cleansing and documentation. Soil samples were immediately packed in 500 ml zipper bags that were packed in additional zipper bags containing a sachet of Anaerocult A (VWR international). This ensures that the physical-chemical properties of the samples do not change significantly. All soil samples were analysed according to the Norwegian Standard S2 package (NS 9451: 2009 — see below for details on the analyses). Soil samples were stored at 4° C and opened in a nitrogen atmosphere in a glove box to keep anaerobic samples free from oxygen. All extractions of redox sensitive parameters were conducted in a nitrogen atmosphere.

TABLE 1

STATE OF PRESERVATION SCALE (SOPS). AFTER NORWEGIAN STANDARD (NS 9451, 2009) (TOP) AND CONCENTRATION LEVELS FOR ANALYSIS S2 PARAMETERS USED TO EVALUATE PRESERVATION CONDITIONS (BELOW)

Position related to ground water	Preservation scale					
	0	1 Lousy	2 Poor	3 Medium	4 Good	5 Excellent
Saturated	A0	A1	A2	A3	A4	A5
Fluctuation zone	B0	B1	B2	B3	B4	B5
Unsaturated	C0	C1	C2	C3	C4	C5
Material later than 1900	D0	D1	D2	D3	D4	D5

Nitrate NO_3^-	Ammonium NH_4^+	Sulphide S^{2-}	Iron (II) Fe^{2+}	Iron (III) Fe^{3+}	Redox conditions	Preservation
Low	Low	Low	Low	High	Oxidizing	Lousy
High	Low	Low	Low	High	Nitrate to oxidizing	Poor
High	Low	Low	High	Low	Nitrate to iron reducing	Medium
Low	Low	Low	High	Low	Ironreducing	Medium
High	High	High	Medium	Low	Nitrate to sulphatereducing	Good
Low	High	High	Medium	Low	Sulphatereducing	Good
Low	High	High	High	Low	Sulphatered. to methane prod.	Excellent

Reduced condition
Oxidized conditions

Dry matter (105° C overnight) followed by loss on ignition (550° C in twelve hours) were determined in the initial samples before redox sensitive parameters were analysed. pH and electric conductivity (Shirokova et al., 2000) was measured by mixing samples with deionizer water (ratio 1:5 by volume). The pH was measured after thirty minutes with a Ross electrode (Orion Instruments).

The soil samples were analysed for nitrate (NO_3^-), ammonium (NH_4^+), reduced (Fe^{2+}) and oxidized iron (Fe^{3+}) (Stookey, 1970), sulphate (SO_4^{2-}), (acid volatile) sulphide (S^{2-}) (Rickard and Morse, 2005). Nitrate (NO_3^-), ammonium (NH_4^+), and sulphate (SO_4^{2-}) were analysed at Eurofins Norsk Miljøanalyse AS. Ammonium represents the major reduced species of nitrogen in natural environments, while nitrate is the oxidized species. The ratio of molar concentrations of reduced and oxidized species can be used to assess the redox conditions in natural environments and addresses the predominant redox processes at a certain sampling point (Martens,

2010a: table 8.2). The scale of assessing and monitoring depositional stability and preservation conditions was performed after Norwegian Standard (NS 9451, 2009; table 1; Martens, 2010a: table 8.1).

Groundwater
At the sites with installed dipwells, dataloggers recorded groundwater level, temperature, and conductivity. These data were then compared to measured air temperatures and precipitation. During 2011, the sensors were replaced to include redox measurements.

Results

Archaeology
The samples from the NE part of town were almost all in the unsaturated zone (Figure 2). In Arupsgate, the state of conservation or preservation of the deposits was evaluated and graded between A1 (lousy) and A5 (excellent), with a clear majority of

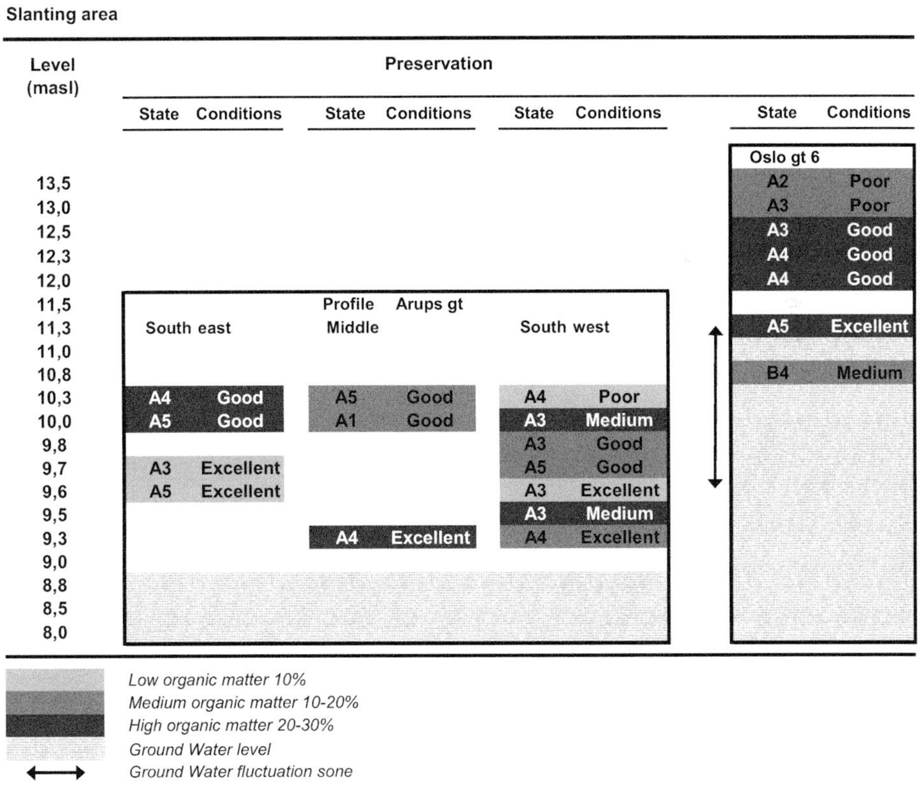

FIGURE 2 Comparing the state of preservation, preservation conditions, and scale of depositional stability in section at Arupsgate (left) and dipwell at Oslogate 6 (right) in the slanting area. The depth of the section and the well is marked in a box with groundwater level. The fluctuation zone is marked with arrow.

grades A3 to A5 (medium, good, excellent) and the overall impression was that the archaeological deposits in this area were very well preserved, with a high amount of organic finds. Even though the archaeological deposits were all clearly in the unsaturated zone, they had a high water content, which was probably partly due to heavy rains all summer, but mostly because of dense, undisturbed deposits. Otherwise, one could not have expected such a good state of conservation. This may be explained by the fact that the original water pipe had been put in a manually dug ditch which was then backfilled with the dug up deposits, thus minimizing the change of soil chemistry. Surprisingly, even the intrusion of the sewer manhole about twenty years ago does not seem to have altered the state of preservation, except in the case of wood immediately adjacent to it.

In Oslogate 6 much the same picture emerged (Figure 2). Most of the deposits were in the unsaturated zone and were graded A2 (poor, top layer) to A5. One deposits that was graded A4 turned out to be in the fluctuation zone, and should have been labelled B4. It is interesting to note that the conservation state was perceived as less good in this deposit than in the one above, which was permanently unsaturated. It would seem that the impact of the large excavation twenty years earlier was not as bad as one might have feared for the remaining deposits. The material used for back filling seems to have stabilized the whole area, as was intended.

In the area to the SW, a great difference in state of preservation was noted between the very well-preserved deposits at dipwell S7 and the bad ones at MB14 (Figure 3). Well S7 had some deposits in the unsaturated zone (graded A2, poor, to A4, good), a few in the fluctuation zone and most in the saturated zone, all deemed good and graded C4. Similarly, the Sørenga well had some deposits in the unsaturated zone, graded A4, and some in the saturated zone which were graded C5, excellent.

The Midgard serpent dipwell 6 had top soil in the unsaturated zone, but no samples were analysed from these deposits. In the fluctuation zone, the state of preservation was medium, graded B3, while the deposits below the groundwater table were medium to good, C3–C4. The deposits in MB9 were medium (A3) in the unsaturated and medium to good (C3–C4) in the saturated zone. In MB14, most of the deposits were in the unsaturated zone and graded lousy to medium (D1 to A3), and even the saturated deposits were poorly preserved (C2).

Geochemistry

During the augering of the dipwells (MB6, MB9, MB14, Sørenga, and Oslogate 6) soil samples were collected from some of the archaeological deposits. Preservation conditions and present state of preservation were determined (Johansen et al., 2009; RA and NIKU, 2008). Using data from the automatic monitoring of the groundwater level in the wells shows that thirteen samples were from the unsaturated zone, eight from deposits that are occasionally water saturated, and three samples from archaeological deposits being permanently water saturated (based upon groundwater fluctuations in the period May 2010–April 2011). The concentration level of reduced iron (FeII) was significantly ($p < 0.05$; Kruskal-Wallis Test) higher in the saturated and groundwater fluctuation zone compared to the unsaturated zone. There was also a clear tendency towards higher concentrations of ammonium and sulphide in the saturated zone compared to the unsaturated and groundwater fluctuation zones.

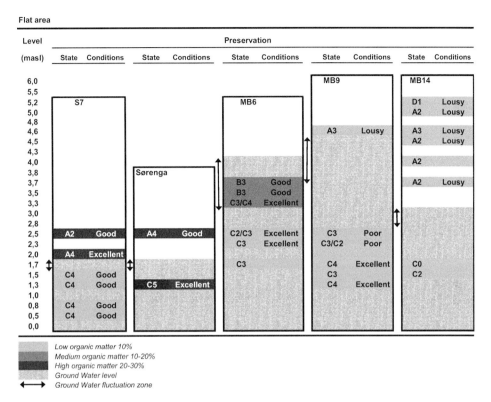

Flat area

FIGURE 3   Comparing the state of preservation, preservation conditions, and scale of depositional stability in different wells in the flat area. Each well depth is marked in boxes with groundwater level. The fluctuation zone is marked with arrows.

Nevertheless, sixteen of a total of nineteen samples analysed from archaeological deposits from the section and well in the slanting area show good to excellent preservation conditions. These samples were all from the unsaturated zone (Figure 2). These deposits also had a high content of organic matter. The same result was observed in the unsaturated deposits in the wells S7 and Sørenga placed closed to the sea level in the flat area (Figure 3). Samples analysed in the saturated zone from the flat area (wells 6 and, partly, 9) showed good to excellent preservation conditions. The wells 9 and 14 show low content of organic matter and lousy preservation conditions in the unsaturated zone (Figure 3).

Groundwater

The groundwater levels at wells MB9 and MB6 have the largest fluctuations and also the most rapid response on precipitation events (Figure 4A). The most likely explanation is that the archaeological deposits are covered by coarse material of crushed rock leading to rapid infiltration of rain or snowmelt. In both MB6 and MB9 the groundwater level reacts very rapidly to precipitation and snowmelt (from 21 March 2011) leading to an increase in the well within hours (Figure 4A). The well is located in an asphalt-covered area close to a large storage building. During precipitation events and

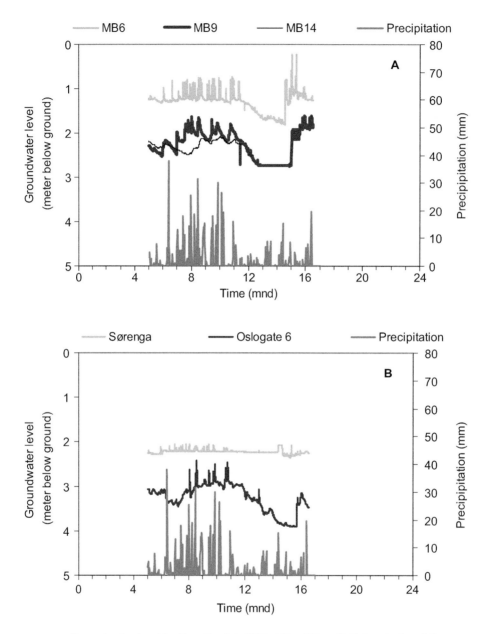

FIGURE 4   Groundwater level in dipwells at A: MB6, MB9, MB14, B: Oslogate 6 and Sørenga, Oslo, compared with precipitation in the period 13 May 2010–5 April 2011.

snowmelt large amounts of water are collected at these dense surfaces and drained to the groundwater through leak pipelines and cracks in the surface layer. Augering prior to installation of MB6 showed that the upper 1.2 m consisted of coarse filling materials, facilitating rapid penetration of water. Intense infiltration of surface water at particular spots close to the well and insufficient bentonite tightening around it may explain the fluctuation pattern in MB6.

During wintertime (air temperature below $0°$ C) the groundwater level decreases (Figure 5A). At Oslogate 6 the groundwater table was nearly 1 m lower in March 2011 than in August–November 2010 (Figure 4B). At the wells MB6 and 9, the decrease during winter was about 0.5 m (Figure 4A), at Sørenga none. Sørenga had the most stable groundwater level in the whole area (Figure 4B). Annual groundwater fluctuations seem to be smaller closer to the sea, probably stabilized by sea levels.

The temperature in the groundwater increases during spring and summer and peaks in August–September (Figure 5A). The temperature is $3.5°$ C higher at MB6 (most elevated groundwater) compared to MB9 and MB14 (lowest groundwater table). During high precipitation events temperature rises (during summer) or decreases (autumn) at MP6, confirming the rapid infiltration of rainwater in this well. Highest conductivity about 1.5 mS was observed in well MB14, while it was found between 0.8 and 0.5 mS in well MB9 and MB6 (Figure 5B).

Discussion

Implications for the in situ *preservation of archaeological deposits*
Automatic and continuous monitoring has shown that the fluctuations in groundwater level in these two parts of medieval Oslo vary considerably between sites. Some of the observed variations and fluctuations are natural and some are due to infrastructure changes. The monitoring results so far (appr. one year) show that a fluctuating groundwater table does not necessarily result in worse preservation conditions (Oslogt 6, Figure 2) and (S7, MB6; Figure 3). Dense soil types having high water-holding capacity (silt and clay) and high organic matter level, may contribute to good preservation conditions also in the unsaturated zone. Materials used for back-filling investigated areas should be dense and stable and have high water holding capacity, to ensure continued preservation of adjoining deposits. Areas with active degradation should be monitored, and more work should be put into mitigation strategies.

The logging of water levels at dipwell MB6 shows that large amounts of surface water may be transported rapidly to the groundwater in areas with 'cracked' dense ground covers, large buildings and coarse deposit materials. This may wash out archaeological remains and should be monitored. The monitoring data also indicate that coarse filling materials above archaeological remains may result in larger annual and short-term temperature fluctuations in the groundwater (Figure 3). Knowing that microbiological processes are often sensitive to temperature fluctuations, the significance of these fluctuations should be further investigated.

At MB9 the archaeological deposits in the fluctuating zone were poor to medium preserved (Figure 3; Johansen et al., 2009), but the preservation conditions are lousy, probably because of low content of organic matter. The deepest saturated layers were medium preserved but had excellent conditions for future preservation. In MB14 all deposits, even in the saturated zone, were badly to medium preserved. Low content of organic material in these deposits is the most likely explanation for the poor state of preservation and lousy preservation conditions. Since MB14 is placed in the cemetery right next to the St Mary church ruins, this result is most worrying and implies an immediate need for mitigation.

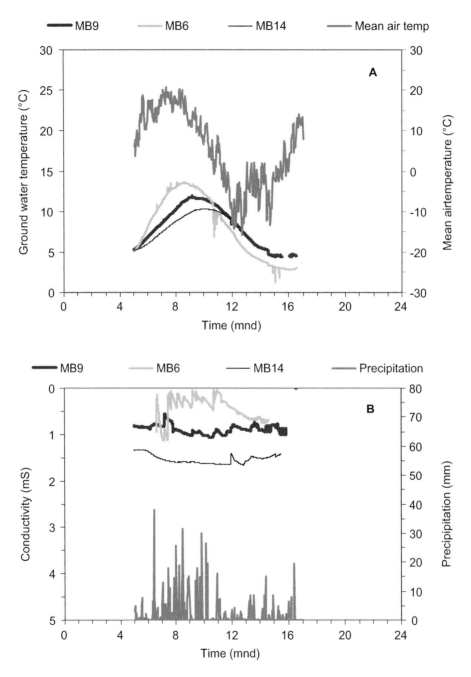

FIGURE 5   Temperature in groundwater at dipwells MB6, MB9 and MB14 compared with air temperature (A), conductivity compared with precipitation (B), Oslo in the period 13 May 2010–5 April 2011.

In the investigated area, hydrostatic pressure from the sea results in more stable/less fluctuating groundwater (short term and annually) and may have resulted in better preservation of archaeological deposits in areas close to the sea (e.g. Sørenga), both in the unsaturated and saturated zones.

Redox conditions measured from autumn of 2011 show good to excellent preservation conditions in groundwater from wells: MB9 (-430mV), MB6 (-330mV), Sørenga (-430mV) and Oslogt 6 (-356mV). In MB14 which contains archaeological deposits in the unsaturated zone redox values are around 10mV which may explain the lousy preservation conditions documented above.

Conclusion

Even with limited investigations as the above-described sites, it is possible to get a fairly detailed impression of both the archaeological state of preservation and the conditions for further *in situ* preservation of urban archaeological deposits. Monitoring of groundwater temperature, fluctuations and preferably also redox-conditions in archaeological deposits in Oslo should continue and prevail in the future and more efforts should be made to interpret results and evaluate the significance of these results for future mitigation. The ultimate goal should be to develop mitigation strategies that reduce the impact of human activities on archaeological deposits.

Bibliography

Bergersen, O., Hartnik, T., and Molaug, P. B. 2009. Bevaringstilstand og bevaringsforhold i kulturlag fra Oslogate 6 og Sørenga. *Rapport NIKU 7/2009.*

de Beer, H., Christensson, A., Jensen, J. A., and Matthiesen, H. 2008. Bryggen World Heritage Site: A Numerical Groundwater Model to Support Archaeological Preservation Strategies. In: H. Kars and R. M. Van Heeringen, eds. *Preserving Archaeological Remains In Situ: Proceedings of the 3rd Conference, 7–9 December 2006, Amsterdam.* Amsterdam: Institute for Geo and Bioarchaeology, pp. 95–100.

Johansen, L-M. B., Martens, V. V., Bergersen, O., and Hartnik, T. 2009. *Grunnundersøkelse i forbindelse med bygging av ny avløpsledning under Middelalderparken og Sørenga. Arkeologisk og jordfaglig undersøkelse i miljøbrønner.* Rapport NIKU 102/2009.

Martens, V. V. 2010a. Environmental Monitoring of Archaeological Deposits. In: S. Trow, V. Holyoak, and E. Byrnes, eds. *Heritage Management of Farmed and Forested Landscapes in Europe.* Budapest: EAC Occasional Papers 4, pp. 75–82.

Martens, V. V. 2010b. Arupsgate, Gamlebyen, Oslo. Arkeologisk undersøkelse og overvåking i forbindelse med utskiftning av vannledning. *Rapport NIKU 111/2010.* Oslo.

MD, 2010. Miljøverndepartementet Parliamentary Report 2010, *Miljøvernforvaltningens prioriterte forskningsbehov 2010–2015.* Oslo: Norwegian Ministry for the Environment.

NS 9451. 2009. *Norwegian Standard. Kulturminner. Krav til miljøovervåkelse og -undersøkelse av kulturlag.* Standard Norge.

Rickard, D. and Morse, J. W. 2005. Acid volatile sulphide (AVS). *Marine Chemistry,* 97: 141–97.

RA 1992. Årsberetning 1991 fra Riksantikvarens utgravningskontor for Oslo.

RA and NIKU. 2008. *The Monitoring Manual. Procedures and Guidelines for Monitoring, Recording and Preservation Management of Urban Archaeological Deposits.* Riksantikvaren and Norsk Institutt for Kulturminneforskning.

Shirokova, Y., Forkutsa, I., and Sharafutdinova, N. 2000. Use of Electrical Conductivity Instead of Soluble Salts for Soil Salinity Monitoring in Central Asia. *Irrigation and Drainage Systems,* 14: 199–205.

Stookey, L. L. 1970. Ferrozine — A New Spectrophotometric Reagent for Iron. *Analytical Chemistry,* 42: 779–81.

Notes on contributors

Vibeke Vandrup Martens finished an MA on medieval pottery in 1998 (Aarhus University). Worked as archaeologist in Denmark, Sweden, Finland (Aaland), and Norway. Has worked at the Norwegian Institute for Cultural Heritage Research since 2006, focusing on urban archaeology and preservation conditions in archaeological deposits.

Correspondence to: Vibeke Vandrup Martens, Norwegian Institute for Cultural Heritage Research, Storgata 2, PO Box 726 Sentrum, N-0105 Oslo, Norway. Email: vvm@niku.no

Carl-Einar Amundsen finished his PhD on soil buffer processes related to acid rain in 1993 (Norwegian University of Science and Technology). Since then his main work items have been mobility, leaching and toxicology of pollutants in soils (Norwegian Institute for Agricultural and Environmental Research).

Correspondence to: Carl-Einar Amundsen, Bioforsk Soil and Environment Division, Fredrik A Dahlsvei 20, N-1430 Ås, Norway. Email: Carl-einar.amundsen@bioforsk.no

Ove Bergersen finished a PhD (Dr Scient) in 'Molecular Genetics' in the Departments of Biochemistry and Animals Genetics, Norwegian College of Veterinary Medicine 1990. Main work as scientist at SINTEF 'Environmental microbiology' (e.g. degradation of oil, creosote, PCB, phthalates) to 2001 and 'Environmental microbiology and soil chemistry', the last ten years as a senior scientist at Norwegian Institute for Agricultural and Environmental Research.

Correspondence to: Ove Bergersen, Bioforsk Soil and Environment Division, Fredrik A Dahlsvei 20, N-1430 Ås, Norway. Email: ove.bergersen@bioforsk.no

CONSERVATION AND MGMT OF ARCH. SITES, Vol. 14 Nos 1–4, 2012, 85–98

Organic Loss in Drained Wetland Monuments: Managing the Carbon Footprint

BRIAN DURHAM
University of Oxford, UK

ROBERT VAN DE NOORT
University of Exeter, UK

VIBEKE VANDRUP MARTENS
Norwegian Institute for Cultural Heritage Research, Norway

MICHEL VORENHOUT
University of Amsterdam, Netherlands

The recent installation of land drains at Star Carr, Yorkshire, UK, has been linked with loss of preservation quality in this important Mesolithic buried landscape, challenging the PARIS principle. Historically captured organic carbon, including organic artefacts, is being converted to soluble organic compounds and less soluble carbon gases. At the same time sulphur and nitrogen compounds are oxidized to species that are chemically destructive of artefacts and ecofacts. Two of the carbon products, CO_2 and methane, are 'greenhouse gases' whose environmental impact can be costed in terms of carbon equivalents, which can be set against an assessment of the gain in agricultural productivity of the land arising from drainage, at Star Carr being the improved cereal crop. Wetland studies elsewhere suggest that such decay processes could be slowed by restoring the historic soil environment, and even reversed to create carbon capture, enabling the farmer to claim carbon credits.

KEYWORDS wetlands, organic preservation, peat-wastage, Holme post, jelly-bone, carbon footprint, water quality, preservation *in situ*

DOI 10.1179/1350503312Z.0000000008

Introduction

Carbon assay has not been centre-stage in this series of conferences on preservation *in situ* (PARIS), but as archaeologists we certainly recognize that our most informative materials are carbon-based, and are fragile. A quickening decay of such organic deposits will deliver an increasing dose of carbon into the Earth's atmosphere in its lowest energy form, CO_2. Here its property as a 'greenhouse gas' (GHG) will trap infra-red radiation and will thereby contribute to planetary warming, a positive feedback effect that is recognized as damaging (IPCC, 2007). The present paper therefore explores the extent to which the principle of PARIS, and the archaeologist's special understanding of decay in antler, bone, wood, and the organic matrix, may offer a fresh approach to managing the terrestrial segment of the carbon cycle, with potential benefits not only for heritage assets but for mitigating climate change, improving water quality, reducing flood risk and encouraging biodiversity (Figure 1).

The element carbon (atomic number 6) can share its four valency electrons with other carbon atoms and with a wide range of other elements to form branched chains of great complexity. Some chains can store energy by photosynthesis and release it again, and others can replicate such synthetic chains. This is the chemical basis of life, a process that has created stores of fossil fuel energy and that has also culminated in humanity learning to break free from subsistence livelihoods and to exploit that energy, releasing GHGs. Direct climate impacts attributed to this process include increased precipitation leading to flooding, the direct effect of which has been raised in the present series of conferences, together with the secondary effects from engineering designed to mitigate those impacts (Van den Berg et al., 2008). The present paper focuses on a mechanism that could benefit the study of global warming, complementing a parallel appraisal of archaeological concepts of palaeo-climate and human adaptation that could benefit future climate change adaptation (Van de Noort, 2011).

Given that archaeology routinely monitors up to ten variables in studying preservation on wetland sites, it is surprising that carbon fluxes have not been included (Matthiesen et al., 2004). One of us has argued that the 'containment' of such fluxes would encourage chemical changes that tend towards preservation, a case supported with examples of both waterlogged and non-waterlogged preservation (Durham, 2008). As a field management technique, full containment is seldom practicable — escape of carbon through gaseous and aquatic pathways will continue. Such carbon fluxes have however been measured for ecosystems, and we can borrow from those models (Luo and Zhou, 2006). We can also use data that we already collect as proxies for such carbon fluxes: loss of substance (mass) from artefact and ecofact families; loss from the supporting organic matrix; and vertical shrinkage of the deposit overall (wastage). Borrowed models and available proxies represent potentially seven information sources reviewed below.

For the present case study, Mesolithic material was found at Star Carr in the 1940s, and in 1949–51 Grahame Clark excavated in the area of greatest concentration (Clark, 1954; for location, see Figure 3 inset). Further excavation was done in the 1980s by Paul Mellars, who expressed concerns about deterioration after thirty-five years (Mellars and Dark, 1998). Milner et al. returned twenty years later and noted further deterioration following the installation of land drains *c.* 2000, and arable cropping

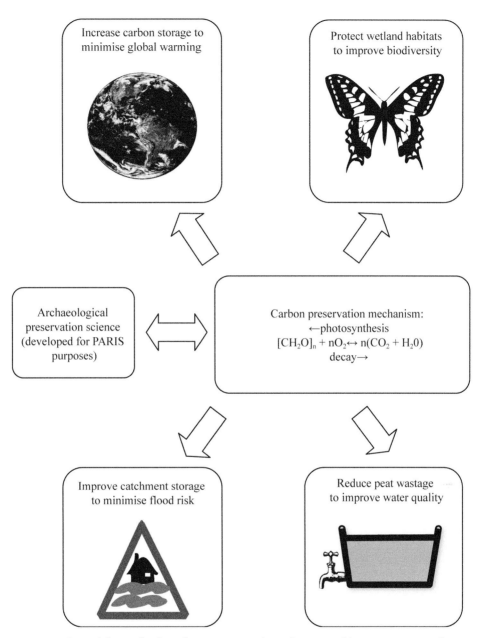

FIGURE 1   Potential contribution of peat preservation science to wider ecosystem services.

(Milner et al., 2011). Since that time English Heritage has commissioned reports from four UK universities. We are privileged to have access to some pre-publication material. The available information is presented here in relation to several issues raised above:

1. Can a provisional peat wastage curve be constructed for Star Carr, whether from levels, peat density, or artefact survival?

2. How does the Star Carr wastage compare with rates recorded elsewhere?
3. Is there evidence that the rate has changed since the installation of land drains?

Borrowed ecosystem models

Change in surface level of cultivated wetland (peat wastage) against time (Figure 2)

Peat wastage of the kind that is feared at Star Carr was familiar in the UK East Anglian fens from the seventeenth century. By 1848 the undrained wetland at Holme Fen near Peterborough was evidently a rarity in surviving to its original height, and in that year four oak piles were driven through the peat into the Oxford Clay at 6.7 m depth and left flush with the then ground surface. Two years later the top

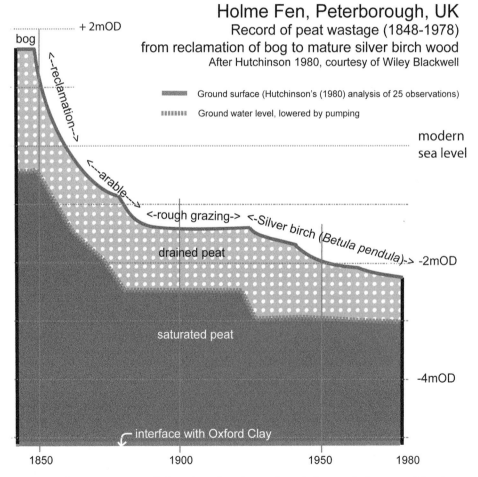

FIGURE 2   Peat wastage at Holme Fen, Peterborough, relative to drainage and land use (wastage and water table curves after Hutchinson, 1980).
Courtesy of Wiley Blackwell

3.5 m depth of one post was exposed by digging, cut off, and replaced with a cast iron column bolted onto to it, with an inscription at the top reading 'level of the ground in 1848' (Hutchinson, 1980). Changes in surface level were recorded relative to this iron post. They illustrate a stepped decay curve, the steps plausibly linked to ever deeper drainage pumping. Following reclamation the landscape was under arable farming for twenty-two years, followed by rough grazing and finally a silver birch wood, providing a range of landuse/drainage combinations for comparison with Star Carr (Figure 2).

Changes in GHG efflux from wetland against time

In the absence of gaseous and aquatic carbon monitoring for Star Carr we can look wider. The amount of carbon and nitrogen that is lost from or gained in a given site is called the net ecosystem exchange (NEE), which has been estimated from analysis of groundwater runoff and evolved gases at an ombrotrophic bog (Auchencorth Moss, Scotland) for the years 2007–08 (Dinsmore et al., 2010). In those years this catchment was a net sink for carbon. Only 4 per cent of annual NEE was returned to the atmosphere as GHGs (methane and nitrous oxide, percentage expressed as CO_2 equivalents). Some of the NEE was not stored in the system, 24 per cent leaving by the aquatic pathway as dissolved organic carbon, with a further 2 per cent embracing aquatic particulates, DIC and other GHGs combined.

The researchers note that these average figures will vary, and the total 26 per cent of exchange leaving via the aquatic path may not apply to a wasting peatland like Star Carr; but for our purposes we should note the finding that some aquatic path export is returned to the atmosphere as CO_2 effluxed from the catchment water-courses, and the researchers speculate that this process will continue in the bigger watercourses on the way to the sea (Dinsmore et al., 2010). For our purposes there-fore we are likely to be understating the GHG emissions if we assume that *c*. 26 per cent of the net ecosystem carbon exchange at Star Carr will leave the system via the water pathway, and this proportion will be of value in estimating the GHG budget at the Star Carr site (below).

Proxy values for carbon flux from Star Carr

Carbon-flux proxy derived from artefact/ecofact families recovered in successive excavation campaigns

Excavations at Star Carr in 2010 confirm the flattening of antler remains following complete demineralization, demonstrated by dimensional comparison between red deer antler recovered in excavations fifty-five years apart. Material from 1950 retained an average cylindrical cross-section typical of modern deer populations, while by 2005–06 similar examples had been compressed by an average 80 per cent (Milner et al., 2011). The same work reports the ignition-loss from 2006 antler samples, which if reconstructed as cylindrical cross sections might allow an estimate of carbon den-sity loss. Similar deterioration is also reported when comparing 2006 wood samples to those uncovered in previous excavations: decay of cellulose leaves only a lignin-rich skeleton, with values for lost wood substance (LWS) reported for willow, poplar and birch (Milner et al., 2011). Ignition-loss in association with such dimensional analysis therefore offers a possibility of proxy values for carbon flux in a case where material has been retrieved over successive excavation vintages (pers. comm., Ian Panter).

Carbon-flux proxy from loss of stratification of artefacts against time

The archaeological value of artefacts that are stratified within organic layers is not in doubt, for as long as the organic matter survives for the contextual meaning of the material to be interpreted. Degradation by decay processes will lead eventually to the collapse of the matrix, leaving the artefacts unstratified with loss of their contextual heritage information (Matthiesen, 2004; Martens, 2010; 2011). Contextual information is crucial for understanding a site and for letting the artefacts 'talk' about their past, and without it this dialogue will be lost (Martens, 2010; 2011). To measure the decay of stratification in a controlled way would require the recording of an extensive organic deposit comprising discrete layers of datable artefacts, on a site that could be re-measured in subsequent excavations. This is not a practicable vehicle for proxy estimate of carbon flux at Star Carr given the degree of decay since Clark's excavations, but it might have potential on other sites where long-term wastage is predicted, provided it was carefully planned at the outset.

Carbon-flux proxy from change in density of peat matrix against time

Core samples taken and stored carefully could be measured and weighed to establish density, with loss-on-ignition measured to establish any change in carbon matrix content. This sort of data may exist in relation to previous sampling at Star Carr. For present purposes this is relevant in confirming carbon content per unit volume of wasting peat. Lucas tabulated water content of a range of peat types against dry mass, giving values from 91 g water per litre of peat in sphagnum peat to 71 g/L in 'peat humus' (Lucas, 1982). For present purposes we will assume conservatively that the block samples from Star Carr were 80% water (pers. comm. Tim Burkinshaw; Nicky Milner), with a density of 1.07g/L (Lucas, 1982). Thus the mass of a 1 m³ block would be 1.07 t. The molecular structure of the bulk dry matter (cellulose) can be expressed as $(CH_2O)_n$, and where the end-product of wastage is gaseous carbon dioxide the process can be expressed as follows:

$$n (CH_2O) + n O_2 = n CO_2 + n H_2O$$

The implication for a typical annual wastage of cultivated peatland (see below) is expressed as a matrix in Table 1.

TABLE 1

MATRIX ILLUSTRATING TYPICAL PEATLAND CARBON CONTENT AND CARBON LOSS ON WASTAGE

Unit volumes	Mass of wet peat	% age water content	Mass of dry content (D)	Mass of elemental carbon content (= D x 12/30)	Mass of CO_2 assuming full oxidation and gaseous emission (= D x 44/30)
Per litre	1070 g	80%	214 g	85.6 g	314 g
Per m³	1070 kg	80%	214 kg	85.6 kg	314 kg
Per cm depth over 1 hectare	10.7 t	80%	2.14 t	0.856 t	3.14 t

Carbon-flux proxy from changes in ground level at Star Carr (Figures 3 and 4)

Without a counterpart of the 'Holme Post' against which to measure wastage, we need an assured datum at Star Carr. Clark publishes contours, but marks no absolute vertical datum on his drawn sections (Clark, 1954). English Heritage has commissioned a full analysis of all available data including LiDAR and a new laser survey (pers. comm., J. Heathcote). In anticipation of this we have reviewed available 2 m-resolution LiDAR data for February 2006 against a dataset twelve months earlier (Environment Agency), and against a laser survey from 2010 (courtesy *The Landscape Research Centre*, LRC). A difference of 0.17 m between the two LiDAR datasets falls outside a vertical error of +/- 15 cm quoted by the supplier. Comparison with the

Star Carr 2005 topography - surface hollows flanking R Hertford

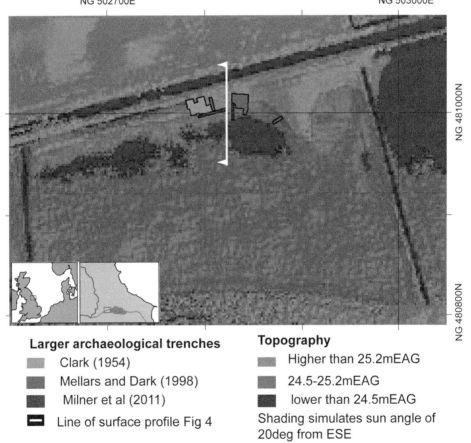

NG 502700E   NG 503000E

NG 481000N

NG 480800N

Larger archaeological trenches	Topography
Clark (1954)	Higher than 25.2mEAG
Mellars and Dark (1998)	24.5-25.2mEAG
Milner et al (2011)	lower than 24.5mEAG
Line of surface profile Fig 4	Shading simulates sun angle of 20deg from ESE

Topographical levels courtesy of Environment Agency Geomatics (EAG) (licence 20110421-1436/4096/li); subject to error +/- 150mm with respect to Ordnance Datum pending ground truthing.

FIGURE 3   Evidence for differential peat wastage flanking the artificial R Hertford at Star Carr, Yorkshire (site location inset).
Source LiDAR data courtesy of Environment Agency, Licence ref 20110421-1436/4096/li; analytical support courtesy of The Landscape Research Centre

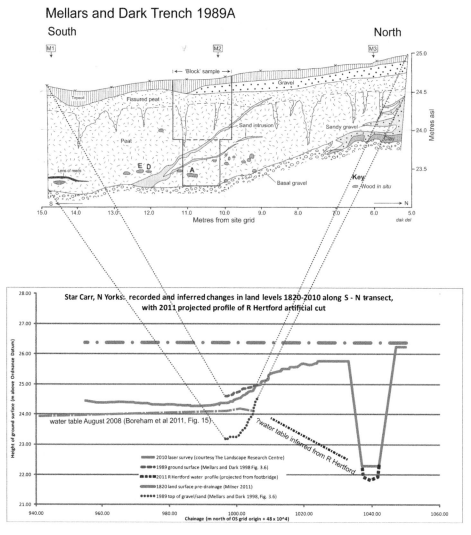

FIGURE 4   Sample transect at Star Carr, Yorkshire, illustrating wastage since 1989 in context of projected channel profile of the artificial R Hertford (Mellars and Dark, 1998: fig. 3.6
Courtesy of McDonald Institute, University of Cambridge

LRC laser survey suggests that the dataset of 2005 is closer to ground truth, and Figure 3 therefore presents this dataset using blue to simulate a winter flood at OD 24.5 m, revealing perceptible troughs flanking the River Hertford artificial cut.

A ground surface profile has been generated from the LRC laser data to compare with the 1986 profile (Figure 4). Mellars notes (pers. comm.) corroboration of this differential could come from re-opening trenches and measuring upwards from the interface between the organic deposits and the underlying gravel, which was crisp in his own excavations and would have been so in Clark's; this data may already be available from 2010 investigations (publication pending). Finally, a loss of 2 m depth in two centuries since the straightening of the River Hertford is estimated from the topography at Star Carr (Milner et al., 2011).

Potential future direct carbon flux monitoring at Star Carr?

For the missing carbon flux itself the equipment used by ecologists is relatively expensive, but a hand-held battery-powered CO_2 non-dispersive infrared (NDIR) spectrometer with humidity analyser is currently available from Duomo at around €200, requiring an air pump and filter to emulate the hand-held ground flux chamber measurements carried out by ecologists (Luo and Zhou, 2006).

Inference of above data review for carbon footprint at Star Carr

We have considered above seven data sources for inferring the carbon footprint of the Mesolithic site, and we need to derive figures for annual carbon exchange to compare with other environmental interests. The big item is the oxidation or hydrolysis of carbon compounds to more mobile gaseous and soluble derivatives, including gaseous methane and other GHGs expressed as their CO_2 equivalent in global warming effect. In estimating the *field* carbon footprint of 1 ha of agricultural peatland (i.e. ignoring the farmer's cultivation and transport carbon) we are hampered by absence of flux data from Star Carr for either the gaseous or aquatic pathways, but a specimen calculation would be as follows:

> 1 mm average depth vertical wastage of wet peat = 10 m³ per hectare;
> Assuming 80% water content (Table 1 above), these 10 m³ of wet peat = 2 m³ dryweight organic material $[CH_2O]_n$ weighing 2.14 tonnes;
> Of 2.14 tonnes dryweight, 26% is assumed in this case to leave the local system by the aquatic pathway without contributing to the atmospheric carbon footprint, leaving 1.58 tonnes to be oxidized to CO_2 (Dinsmore et al., 2010; Drewer et al., 2010);
> 1.58 tonnes dryweight organic matter converts to CO_2 in the molar proportion 44/30, giving 2.32 tonnes CO_2;
> Taking a 2005 average price for carbon as £47 +/-£24 per tonne (DECC 2009), 1 mm thickness of vertical wastage would be valued at €109.16, and pro rata for greater thickness.

Assuming peat wastage at Star Carr began with the construction of the artificial River Hertford around 1820 (above), an average wastage of around 10 mm per year seems to be provisionally corroborated by the levels presented in Figure 4, compared with average 19 mm during the Holme Post arable phase 1865–87 (Figure 2).

Thus we have a range of carbon footprint values for the Star Carr hectare in 2005:

1. Holme post arable model (19 mm p.a.) = €2074 p.a.;
2. Star Carr average arable and pasture (10 mm p.a.) = €1091 p.a.

For scale, one hectare of a high value crop on good UK land in 2005 would have fetched £608 (€700) (DEFRA, 2008).

Relationship between carbon flux and *in situ* preserving system at Star Carr

On the above argument a provisional rule of thumb can be made that, assuming a similar aqueous pathway to that at Auchencorth Moss (Dinsmore et al., 2010), an annual wastage of 10 mm depth would give carbon emissions exceeding the value of a wheat crop (ignoring cultivation and transport costs), with greater or lesser wastage pro rata.

Is this attributable solely to lowering of the water table? The organic archaeological levels were below groundwater in July 2008 (a time of year when water table might be expected to be low), and their medium-to-poor condition score suggests that wastage was occurring anyway (Boreham et al., 2011). If this is confirmed it would suggest that installing a groundwater bund around the site will have little effect alone, but other considerations need to be taken into account:

1. Hydrology: the present level of the River Hertford may be a variable, and may already be creating a drawdown effect on its surroundings (evidence the hollows in the field, above), which might particularly impact the lower face of the Mesolithic deposits (see Figures 3 and 4);

2. Preserving mechanism: if a mechanism that has preserved this material and its soil environment for nine millennia has been compromised, restoring it needs some general understanding of what that mechanism might have been, if only to inform the quartet of other environmental services, water quality, flood risk, carbon capture, and biodiversity;

3. Type of cultivation: a direct drilled cereal or hay crop may avoid ploughing episodes, while potatoes would be a worst case because of multiple ground disturbances, i.e. soil preparation, sowing, and harvesting (pers. comm., Tim Burkinshaw; Holyoak, 2010; Trow, 2010).

Arguments were presented at PARIS3 that built on the mechanism of organic decay and its antithesis, preservation. Pollard recognized that by comparison with an unstable isotope the half-life of an organic compound in the soil is likely to be much more influenced by its chemical environment, thus two basic rates, fast and slow, were speculated, with site-specific rate constants. It was suggested that measurement of CO_2 and methane should give a direct measure of the degradative process (Pollard, 2008). A complementary approach recognized that in thermodynamic terms decay is the norm, preservation is the exception, and thus sought to identify rate-limiting factors that might encourage preservation. The poisoning of decay organisms with biocides was argued to be counterproductive on the evidence that specialist soil flora tend in time to degrade most biocides, often into something even more unpleasant (Durham, 2004). However, there were two common factors independent of all such reservations, that is: the containment of the products of decay, which thereby slows the reaction to the point where it virtually stops; and the need for 'sacrificial' organic carbon, typically drip-fed from a wetland flora above. Because mass action has the status of a law in chemistry it will apply to organic deposits whether waterlogged or not, thereby providing common ground between the widest range of preserving systems (Durham, 2008).

The interpretation of the above for Star Carr, in advance of a more in-depth study by English Heritage (forthcoming) is provisionally as follows. The dipping of levels towards the artificial river at a point where it cuts a gravel ridge could mean that the organic deposits are exposed to oxygen-rich water from the bottom up, while the 2006 excavation showed, at least anecdotally, that the upper levels have unexpected degeneration of antler (Milner et al., 2011). Thus the preserving qualities of the deposit could be at risk from both above and below. Given that Clark used the term 'soft as leather' for some antler (Clark, 1954), it seems unlikely that the demineralization reported in the 2006 results would be entirely a result of installation of land drains some six years previously. If, however, the canalization of the River Hertford has since 1820 been progressively deepened as the local landscape has collapsed, a process of demineralization may have already started by 1950 when Clark first investigated the deposits, hence his terminology.

Options for minimizing the carbon footprint at Star Carr

With firm evidence of decay from above, and tentative from below, what options are open to minimize the carbon footprint at Star Carr? Taking, say, 1 ha of land out of cultivation and installing a groundwater bund would be an option, provided the bund totally enclosed the site including the river frontages, to the depth of an impervious moraine deposit (Clark, 1954). The loss of 1 ha crop production at 2005 prices, assuming a UK average yield of milling grain, would be £608 (€700). Taking it out of arable cultivation would appear to reduce carbon dioxide emissions, but encouraging instead a 'peat crop' might raise the risk of increased methane emissions, although this has been challenged elsewhere (Frolking and Roulet, 2007). In this connection it has been shown that deep-rooted vascular plants play an active role in both exporting methane (Saarnio et al., 1998) and in mechanical damage to artefacts from for instance horsetails (Matthiesen et al., 2004), indicating a need for surface treatment. Building on work in press, and without prejudice to future decisions by English Heritage as the authority responsible for its care, options might be listed as follows:

1. Do nothing (Milner et al., 2011);
2. Excavate selected parts (Milner et al., 2011);
3. Excavate selected parts and leave some preserved and monitored *in situ* (Vorenhout, 2012);
4. Bund only (ombrotrophic bog);
5. Bund and wind-pump minero/ombrotrophic bog;
6. Options 4 or 5 (above) plus measures to control deep roots and contain captured carbon.

Conclusions: protection of heritage by minimizing wetland carbon footprints

It has proved premature to reconstruct a peat wastage (= carbon footprint) curve for Star Carr, but we have seen evidence from elsewhere that typical values for annual peat wastage would make many agricultural crops uneconomic if costed at the market price for carbon. This may be exacerbated by impacts like the progressive lowering of farmland, loss of flood storage capacity, water quality, and biodiversity. The 2011 UK government claimed to be the 'greenest ever', and proposed to spend money on management of ecosystems to address these other environmental services (DEFRA, 2010). Jointly, and to a large extent individually, these aims will involve restoring and stabilizing water tables of wetlands to the extent that new carbon capture becomes possible. The 'containment' and 'drip-feed' principles of organic preservation have potential for ensuring that, once captured, carbon resources are managed with maximum efficiency. We cannot say that preservation fails until we have faithfully replicated the conditions of known success.

Acknowledgements

Our thanks to Steve Boreham, Tony Brown, Tim Burkinshaw, Neil Cape, Keri Dinsmore, Chris Durham, Keith Emerick, Jen Heathcote, Will Mayes, Nicky Milner, Ian Panter, Mike Plant, Dominic Powesland, Terhi Riutta, Gordon Turner-Walker.

Bibliography

Boreham, S., Conneller, C., Milner, N., Taylor, B., Needham, A., Boreham, J., and Rolfe, C. J. 2011. Geochemical Indicators of Preservation Status and Site Deterioration at Star Carr. *Journal of Archaeological Science*, 38: 2833–57.

Clark, J. D. G. 1954. *Excavations at Star Carr*. Cambridge: Cambridge University Press.

DECC, 2009. *Carbon Appraisal in UK Policy Appraisal: A Revised Approach*. London: DECC.

DEFRA, 2008. *Agriculture in the United Kingdom 2008*. London: DEFRA.

DEFRA, 2010. *Payments for Ecosystem Services: A Short Introduction*. London: DEFRA.

Dinsmore, K. J., Billett, M. F., Skiba, U. M., Rees, R. M., Drewer, J., and Helfter, C. 2010. Role of the Aquatic Pathway in the Carbon and Greenhouse Gas Budgets of a Peatland Catchment. *Global Change Biology*, 16: 2750–62.

Drewer, J., Lohila, A., Aurela, M., Laurila, T., Minkinnen, K., Penttila, T., Dinsmore, K. J., McKenzie, R., Helfter, C., Fletchard, C., Sutton, M. A., and Skiba, U. M. 2010. GHG and N-Budget Comparison of Two Peatland Sites: Comparison of Greenhouse Gas Fluxes and Nitrogen Budgets from an Ombotrophic Bog in Scotland and a Minerotrophic Sedge Fen in Finland. *European Journal of Soil Science*, 61: 640–50.

Durham, B. 2004. Cleaning Up: Protecting Deposits on Brownfield Sites under EIA. In: T. Nixon, ed. *Preserving Archaeological Remains In Situ? Proceedings of the 2nd Conference, 12–14 September 2001, London*. London: Museum of London Archaeology, pp. 239–48.

Durham, B. 2008. To Beguile the Time: Kinetic Factors in Modelling of Data from Organic Deposits. In: H. Kars and R. Van Heeringen, eds. *Preserving Archaeological Remains in Situ: Proceedings of the 3rd Conference, 7–9 December 2006, Amsterdam Vrije Universiteit, Amsterdam*. Amsterdam: Institute for Geo and Bioarchaeology, pp. 3–13.

Frolking, S. and Roulet, N. T. 2007. Holocene Radiative Forcing Impact of Northern Peatland Carbon Accumulation and Methane Emissions. *Global Change Biology*, 13: 1079–88.

Holyoak, V. 2010. Mitigation Impossible? Practical Approaches to Managing Archaeology in Arable Farming Systems. *EAC Occasional Paper*, 4: 135–40.

Hutchinson, J. N. 1980. The Record of Peat Wastage in the East Anglian Fenlands at Holme Post 1848–1978 AD. *Journal of Ecology*, 68: 229–49.

IPCC, 2007. *Climate Change 2007: The Physical Science Base*. Cambridge: IPCC.

Lucas, R. E. 1982. *Research Report No. 423 Organic Soils (Histosols): Formation, Distribution and Chemical Properties and Management for Crop Production*. Michigan State University (Crop Science).

Luo, Y. and Zhou, X. 2006. *Soil Respiration and the Environment*. Elsevier.

Martens, V. V. 2010. Environmental Monitoring of Archaeological Deposits. *EAC Occasional Paper*, 4: 75–82.

Martens, V. V. 2011. Environmental Monitoring and In Situ Preservation of Urban Archaeological Deposits. An Information Resource and a Preservation Challenge. *Suomen Keskiajan Arkeologian Seura — Sällskapet för Medeltidsarkeologi i Finland*, 2: 5–10.

Matthiesen, H. 2004. In-Situ Preservation and Monitoring of the Cultural Layers Below Bryggen. In: A. Christensson, ed. *Safeguarding Historic Waterfront Sites. Bryggen in Bergen as a Case Study*. Szcecin/Bergen: Stiftelsen Bryggen, pp. 71–75.

Matthiesen, H., Gregory, D., Sørensen, B., Alstrøm, T., and Jensen, P. 2004. Monitoring Methods in Mires and Meadows. In: T. Nixon, ed. *Preserving Archaeological Remains In Situ? Proceedings of the Conference, 12–14 September 2001, London*. London: Museum of London Archaeology, pp. 91–97.

Mellars, P. and Dark, P. 1998. *Star Carr in Context*. Cambridge: McDonald Institute for Quaternary Research.

Milner, N., Conneller, C., Elliott, B., Koon, H., Panter, I., Penkman, K., Taylor, B., and Taylor, M. 2011. From Riches to Rags: Organic Deterioration at Star Carr. *Journal of Archaeological Science*, 38: 2818–32.

Pollard, M. 2008. Prediction of Rates of Decay of Archaeological Organic Material using Soil Carbon Cycle Model. In: H. Kars and R. Van Heeringen, eds. *Preserving Archaeological Remains In Situ: Proceedings of the 3rd Conference, 7–9 December 2006, Amsterdam Vrije Universiteit, Amsterdam*. Amsterdam: Institute for Geo and Bioarchaeology, pp.

Saarnio SJ, J. A., Martikainen, P. J., and Silvola, J. 1998. Effects of Raised CO_2 on Potential CH_4 Production and Oxidation in, and CH_4 Emission from a Boreal Mire. *Journal of Ecology*, 86: 261–68.

Trow, S. 2010. Ripping Up History, Sordid Motives or Cultivating Solutions? Plough Damage and Archaeology: A Perspective from England. *EAC Occasional Paper*, 4: 129–35.

Van de Noort, R. 2011. Conceptualising Climate Change Archaeology. *Antiquity*, 85: 1039–48.

Van den Berg, M. M., Kars, H., Huisman, D. J., and van Heeringen, R. M. 2008. Climate Change, Water Management and the Preservation of Archaeological Sites. In: H. Kars and R. Van Heeringen, eds. *Preserving Archaeological Remains In Situ: Proceedings of the 3rd Conference, 7–9 December 2006, Amsterdam Vrije Universiteit, Amsterdam*. Amsterdam: Institute for Geo and Bioarchaeology, pp.

Vorenhout, M. 2012. In Situ Preservation and Monitoring with Particular Application to Star Carr, Yorkshire, UK. *Journal of Wetland Archaeology*, 11: 56–62.

Notes on contributors

Brian Durham is a 'deep-welly' field archaeologist with a special interest in the ecological relationship between human populations and their environment, which led him to develop UK curatorial guidelines for urban heritage. His first contribution to the PARIS movement ('Cleaning up', 2001 Conference) addressed the natural recycling of humanity's carbon-based detritus, while five years later ('To Beguile the Time', 2006 Conference) he developed a kinetic model of the storage of wetland carbon that doubled as a preserving system for artefacts and ecofacts. In retirement he has raised his eyes to the more challenging environment of the lower troposphere, and is monitoring rain and snowfall with the aim of understanding mechanisms that may have a cleansing effect on the atmosphere, not merely for volcanic residues but for human emissions of greenhouse gases.

Correspondence to: Brian Durham, Research Associate, Research Laboratory for Archaeology and the History of Art, University of Oxford, UK. Email: brian.durham@rlaha.ox.ac.uk

Robert Van De Noort is a landscape archaeologist with a particular interest in wetlands. His main field projects have been on the Humber Wetlands Project and the excavation of Sutton Common, an Iron Age 'marsh-fort' in South Yorkshire. His other research is focused on the archaeology of the North Sea, the sewn-plank boats of the Bronze Age, the impact of climate change on wetlands, and the perceptions of wetlands and the sea in the past and present. Recently, he has developed the concept of 'Climate Change Archaeology', which concerns the contribution of archaeological research to current climate change debates.

Vibeke Vandrup Martens is a medieval urban research archaeologist with special skills in environmental monitoring of archaeological deposits. She was educated in Lund and Aarhus and has work experience as an archaeologist from Denmark, Sweden, Finland and Norway. Since 2006 she has worked at NIKU, focusing on urban archaeology and preservation conditions in archaeological deposits. Current research projects concern preservation conditions particularly in the unsaturated zone, coupled with analyses of climate change and its impact on preservation, not only in urban contexts but also on medieval farm mounds in northern Norway ('In Situ Site Preservation in the Unsaturated Zone' and 'In-Situ Farms: Archaeological Deposits in a Changing Climate. In Situ Preservation of Farm Mounds in Northern Norway').

Michel Vorenhout is an ecologist with a special research interest in soil chemistry, preservation *in situ* of archaeological remains and monitoring of natural degradation processes. He is currently affiliated to the University of Amsterdam and runs his own company.

CONSERVATION AND MGMT OF ARCH. SITES, Vol. 14 Nos 1–4, 2012, 99–114

Changes in the Physico-Chemical and Microbial Nature of Wetlands from the Leaching of Chromated Copper Arsenate (CCA)-Treated Wood

T. G. Mercer
Keele University, UK

M. C. Lillie
University of Hull, UK

R. J. Smith
CgMs Consulting, UK

Microbial activities are responsible for reducing the harmful effects of pollutants in different burial environments. Within wetlands in particular, microorganisms play an important role in the transformation of heavy metals and metalloids via direct or indirect oxidation/reduction. In turn, these microbial transformations can lead to the detoxification of pollutant elements such as copper, chromium and arsenic that comprise CCA-treated wood.

CCA was the most commonly used wood preservative in the UK (up until its partial ban in 2004). CCA prolongs the service life of wood by making it resistant to microbiological attack. As such, it has been regularly used in the construction of platforms and boardwalks in wetlands. However, recent concerns over the impact of the chemical constituents of this treatment on both the environment and human health have prompted the introduction of legislation in order to ensure that this type of treated wood is disposed of in accordance with the relevant health and safety guidelines.

In light of this information, it is important to assess changes in the physico-chemical and microbial nature of wetlands associated with the leaching of CCA from wooden structures. The results will not only provide a greater scope for understanding the implications associated with the *in situ* preservation of the archaeological resource contained within these environments, but also highlight the potential ramifications for wetland ecosystem dynamics.

DOI 10.1179/1350503312Z.0000000009

KEYWORDS chromated copper arsenate, microbial activity, wetlands, leaching, heavy metal pollution

Introduction

CCA is a widely used wood preservative consisting of copper (Cu), chromium (Cr), and arsenic (As). The formulation acts as a strong biocide to inhibit the degradation of treated wood in various environments. However, during the treatment process, fixation is never 100 per cent complete and some unfixed preservative remains on the wood (Morrell, 2006). The most significant leaching risks associated with CCA occur during the application of the preservatives and whilst the wood is in service (WRAP, 2004). In-service treated wood can degrade over time due to biological, mechanical, and chemical degradation. CCA-treated wood is frequently in contact with soil, for example, in applications such as decking, fencing, and utility poles. Various studies have shown that release of the elements from CCA-treated wood can occur whilst in-service, causing significantly elevated levels of As, Cr, and Cu in the surrounding soil (Stilwell and Gorny, 1997) and impact on soil quality (Solo-Gabriele et al., 2003). Levels are usually highest at ground level and immediately adjacent to the structures, decreasing with depth and distance from the structures (Zagury et al., 2003).

CCA-treated wood is also commonly used for structures that are exposed to water (for example, jetties and walkways), in both marine and freshwater environments. The wood used in these environments tends to have higher levels of the preservative due to the severity of the exposure conditions. Higher leaching risks are associated with exposure to seawater and static systems (Lebow et al., 1999; Brown and Eaton, 2000) due to a higher ionic status and accumulation of the leached preservative. Furthermore, exposure to water has been shown to increase the mobility of the elements in the environment once leached under certain conditions (e.g. high pH, low Eh). CCA-treated wood is frequently used for viewing platforms and walkways in wetland settings and increasingly in reconstructed wetlands. The potential risks to sensitive wetland ecosystems resulting from leaching and, more particularly, for the *in situ* preservation of archaeological resources, is poorly understood and under-researched.

The release of the elements from CCA-treated wood can potentially contaminate soil and water resulting in toxic effects to animals, plants and/or whole ecosystems. The chemical constituents are not readily biodegradable and can accumulate in flora and fauna. Furthermore, exposure to arsenic and chromium can cause serious and wide-ranging human health issues. The objective of this study is to determine the concentrations of metal(loid)s leached out from CCA-treated wood. The role of physico-chemical soil conditions and micro-organisms in influencing the distribution, mobility, and speciation of the leachate will also be assessed. Finally, the potential ramifications of leaching will be evaluated for *in situ* preservation and wetland ecosystems.

Methods: lysimeter experiment

Field methods

A field lysimeter experiment was set up consisting of seventeen leaching trays exposed to natural conditions (University of Hull Botanic and Experimental Garden, Cottingham,

UK (Mercer and Frostick, 2012)). These were divided into seven trays containing topsoil with CCA-treated wood mulch and seven containing topsoil with untreated wood mulch. Wood blocks were chipped using a Jensen Industrial Chipper with the blank wood processed first to avoid contamination. Particle size reduction allowed for easier packing into the lysimeters and is representative of the varying wood particle sizes experienced in wood waste streams and also *in situ* were there may be weathering and degradation of the wood over time.

A further three monofills contained either soil, untreated wood mulch, or CCA-treated wood mulch. The trays measured 65 cm long, 35 cm wide, and 16.5 cm deep, and were placed on an untreated wooden frame with two holes at the base for drainage. The leachate was allowed to seep through the holes at the base and was transported along plastic tubing. This led to plastic collection containers with holes in the lid to allow leachate to drip through. The design of the leachate collection system prevented evaporation, overflow or external contamination of the leachate. Each of the soil and mulch lysimeters contained 20 L of well-mixed soil and 4.5 kg of surface mulch (Mercer et al., 2011).

The leaching study was set up on 9 May 2007 and ran for twenty-one weeks. Rainfall and temperature data were recorded onsite on an hourly basis with a Campbell Scientific^{TM} Mounted Weather Station. Leachate samples were collected after every major rainfall event. Soil samples were collected every three weeks from two CCA-treated wood and soil lysimeters, two untreated wood and soil lysimeters, and each monofill. Soil cores were taken using a trowel and placed in ziplock plastic bags. These were stored at 4° C until required for analysis.

Physico-chemical analyses

Soil samples were analysed for moisture content (MC), organic matter content (OM), particle size (PS), pH, redox, and total elemental concentrations for Cu, Cr, and As.

Measurements of soil moisture content were carried out gravimetrically following overnight oven drying at 105° C (Gardner and Black, 1965). Organic matter content analyses were calculated gravimetrically by weighing out oven-dried soil in replicate and placing in a furnace for 30 minutes at 850° C (Avery and Bascomb, 1974). Soil particle size analysis was measured using the techniques described by (Avery and Bascomb, 1974) and (Sheldrick et al., 1993). Size classes are differentiated using sieves and a settling procedure following removal of OM using heated hydrogen peroxide. Soil pH was measured with a Fisherbrand Hydrus^{TM} 300 pH probe in accordance with the manufacturers' instructions. The pH of the soil was measured using a soil-deionized water suspension as described by Rowell (1994). Soil samples were mixed with deionized water (ultrapure water with a resistivity of 18 Ωm cm^{-1}) (Pearson et al., 2007) and the pH electrode placed in the solution. Soil redox potential measurements were taken in the field using a handheld ExStik^{TM} ORP RE300. The redox data was corrected for variation in pH according to Cheetham (2004). Correction for standard hydrogen electrode (SHE) was not required as the probe was pre-calibrated. The samples were treated according to the manufacturer's instructions and the method of Janzen (1993).

Levels of Cu, Cr, and As were measured on field moist soils. Field moist soil was used as volatilization of arsenic during oven drying could result in underestimation.

Samples were acid digested using a pressurized microwave (Microwave Accelerated Reaction System MARS™ CEM Corporation, USA) to extract elements in the samples. Soil (2 g) was added to aqua regia (12 ml) (9 ml HCL to 3 ml HNO_3) (CEM, 2004). All acids used were SpA grade from Romil (Cambridge, UK). Acid blanks consisting of the same matrix type were included in the process. Blanks and spikes of Certified Reference Material (SpexCertiPrep, Middlesex) for soil were included in the process to ascertain spike recovery from the digestion process and cleanliness of the microwave vessels. Digested samples were then analysed using inductively coupled plasma–optical emission spectrometry (ICP-OES).

Statistical analyses

Statistical analyses were performed with SPSS™ (version 16) and Microsoft Excel (2007) with confidence levels of 95% ($p<0.05$) or 99% ($p<0.01$). A selection of standard statistical analyses and multivariate analyses were used on the data. Where ANOVA was used to compare more than two independent variables, for in text abbreviations, F refers to the F-ratio and the following brackets list the degrees of freedom for the effect of the model followed by the degrees of freedom for the residuals of the model. M refers to the mean values. Where data was non-parametric, the equivalent Kruskall-Wallis test was used. For in-text abbreviations, H refers to the Kruskall-Wallis test statistic and the degrees of freedom are included in the brackets that follow on. Mdn refers to the median values.

Soil physico-chemical results

Soil MC

The MC values in the leaching study were high over the experimental period due to the occurrence of heavy rainfall during this time. The trends observed appeared to be influenced by rainfall patterns with higher soil MC occurring on days 42 and 84 during periods of heavy rain and lower soil MC occurring on days 63 and 126 during days of no rainfall. There was also a lag effect in evidence where soil MC was high on days following heavy rain, for example day 84.

Significant differences were observed between those lysimeters containing CCA wood, those containing untreated wood and the soil monofill ($H(2) = 6.968$, $p < 0.05$). The MC of the soil in the monofill was found to be significantly lower ($Mdn = 34.31\%$) than the soil in the lysimeters containing untreated ($Mdn = 58.83\%$) and CCA-treated wood ($Mdn = 58.86\%$) ($U = 15.00$, $p < 0.05$ and $U = 17.00$, $p < 0.05$ respectively). Soil MC between the lysimeters containing untreated wood and CCA-treated wood were not significantly different.

The soil monofill fluctuated more than the lysimeters containing soil and wood. The results are to be expected since in the absence of a mulch layer, soil loses more moisture at a faster rate during dry periods (Othieno, 1980). Conversely, this soil wets up faster during wet periods. Therefore, in the wood-containing lysimeters, excess water was trapped within the soil following the periods of heavy rainfall and only escaped by slow percolation at the base of the lysimeter as evaporation at the surface was inhibited by the mulch. As such, MC levels in the lysimeters containing soil and wood remained high and fairly constant until the end of the study. This effect was

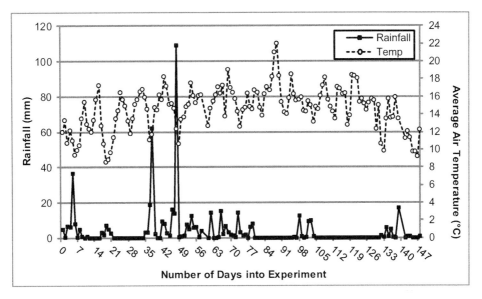

FIGURE 1   Rainfall and temperature data.

observed in the experiment where wood-containing lysimeters remained waterlogged throughout (Figure 1).

Soil OM

OM levels were found to range between 12% and 20%, with significant differences between the treatments ($F(2,30) = 8.659$, $p < 0.01$). The soil monofill ($M = 14\%$) had significantly lower soil OM levels than the lysimeters containing wood and soil (untreated wood and soil lysimeters, $M = 17.62\%$; CCA-treated wood + soil lysimeters, $M = 17.54\%$) ($p < 0.01$). There was no obvious or significant trend in soil organic matter content over time.

Soil redox

Redox levels generally decreased over time (all correlations significant $p < 0.05$) (Figure 2). During the period of heavy rainfall between day 1 and day 85, conditions in the soil of all lysimeters was moderately reducing (between +100mV to +400mV). Following this, the condition in the lysimeters containing the wood mulch became reducing (-100mV to +100mV) (Patrick and Mahaptra, 1968). This is explained by waterlogging following heavy rainfall. The conditions in the soil monofill lysimeters remained moderately reducing, supporting the assumption that the soil monofill lost more moisture at a faster rate than soil in the mixed lysimeters.

Soil pH

The pH condition of the soil remained neutral (Figure 3) although increased significantly over time in the soil monofill and CCA-treated wood and soil lysimeters ($p < 0.01$).

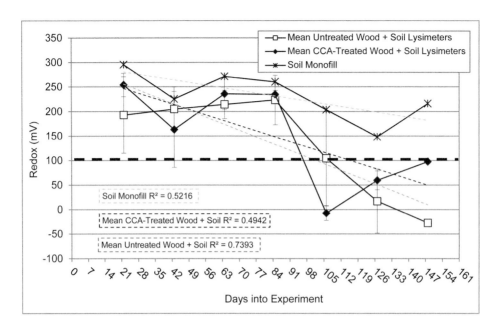

FIGURE 2   Soil redox (± 1 standard deviation). Thick dashed line denotes redox class boundary (< +100 are reducing conditions, +100 upwards are moderately reducing conditions).

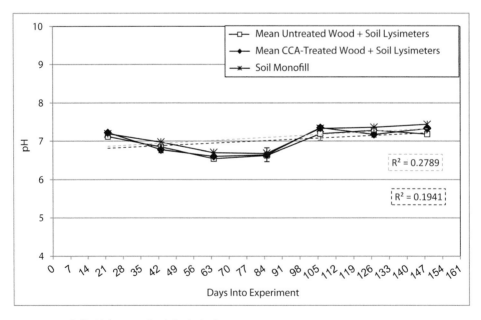

FIGURE 3   Soil pH (±1 standard deviation).

Concentrations of arsenic, chromium, and copper

Initial levels of arsenic, chromium, and copper were measured in wood and soil to gauge background levels in the study and for understanding the potential leaching properties of the wood, the fate of the elements within the soil and the influence of the leachant used. Arsenic, chromium, and copper analyses were carried out on the CCA-treated wood and the topsoil used in the study (Table 1).

The results over the experimental period are presented in Figure 4a–c. The metal(loid) levels in the soil were two orders of magnitude lower than in the wood. There was wide variation in the values in the CCA-treated wood and soil lysimeters resulting in large error bars. The variation suggests that the leaching from the CCA-treated wood may not be consistent over all the CCA-treated wood and soil lysimeters and metal(loid)s may be distributed unevenly in the soil both at the surface and with depth. Furthermore, as there were only two samples taken at each sample date, there were insufficient replicates to accurately assess variance between samples. Periods of variation also occur at times when there were high levels of rainfall. Levels of arsenic and chromium were significantly greater from lysimeters containing CCA-treated wood than soil in lysimeters containing untreated wood (arsenic $U = 45.00$, $p < 0.05$; chromium $U = 31.50$, $p < 0.01$). However, soil guideline values for arsenic at 32ppm (Environment Agency, 2009) and chromium at 130ppm (DEFRA, 2002) were not exceeded in any of the soil samples analysed. Conversely, in leachate samples, levels in the CCA-treated wood and soil and CCA wood monofill were frequently exceeding SGV and World Health Organisation drinking values at times by two to three orders of magnitude (Mercer and Frostick, 2012). This suggests that metals are released from the soil.

When comparing the proportions of the metal(loid) levels, significant differences were observed with the lysimeters containing untreated wood ($H(2) = 22.62$, $p < 0.01$) and CCA wood ($H(2) = 10.49$, $p < 0.01$). In the lysimeters containing untreated wood, levels of copper were highest followed by chromium and arsenic (As vs. Cr: $U = 19.00$, $p < 0.0167$; As vs Cu: $U = 14.00$, $p < 0.0167$, Cr vs. Cu: $U = 18.50$, $p < 0.0167$) (As<Cr<Cu). In the lysimeters containing CCA-treated wood, arsenic levels were significantly lower than copper ($U = 23.50$, $p < 0.0167$) whilst no significant differences were observed between chromium and copper ($U = 55.50$, $p < 0.071$) or chromium and arsenic ($U = 48.00$, $p < 0.06$).

Soil Eh/pH

Speciation analyses were not carried out on soil samples collected during the study due to time constraints. However, Eh/pH diagrams were used to predict the species that should be present under certain Eh and pH ranges in aqueous solutions at 25° C and 1 atmosphere (Stumm and Morgan, 1981).

The Eh/pH graph for arsenic (Figure 5) show that As (III) should dominate under reducing conditions and lower pH whilst As (V) is more stable under oxidizing

TABLE 1

TOTAL ELEMENTAL CONCENTRATIONS IN THE BACKGROUND SOIL AND WOOD SAMPLES
(± 1 STANDARD DEVIATION)

	Soil	CCA-treated Waste Wood
Arsenic	3.10 ± 0.7 ppm	5429.74 ± 1343.55 ppm
Chromium	10.76 ± 2.31 ppm	10647.95 ± 3345.23 ppm
Copper	24.24 ± 0.82 ppm	2920.74 ± 968.19 ppm

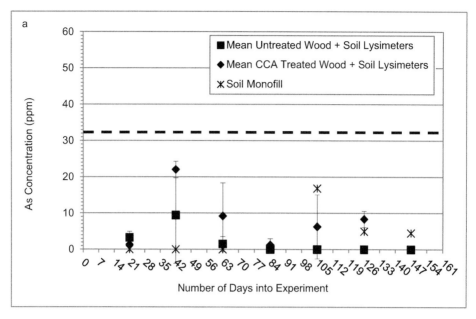

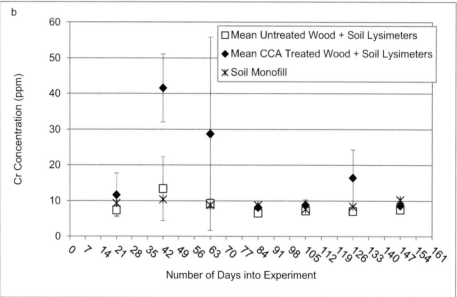

FIGURE 4   a) Concentration of arsenic in soil. Thick dashed line represents Soil Guideline Value (32 ppm); b) Concentration of chromium in soil. Values are well below the Soil Guideline Value (130ppm).

conditions and higher pH values. The soil Eh/pH suggests that redox and pH conditions in the soil would promote arsenic in the pentavalent form as $H_2AsO_4^-$ and $HAsO_4^{2-}$. Some of the soil Eh-pH data points sit near the boundary with As (III) where two species have equal activities (Cherry et al., 1979; Cullen and Reimer, 1989:

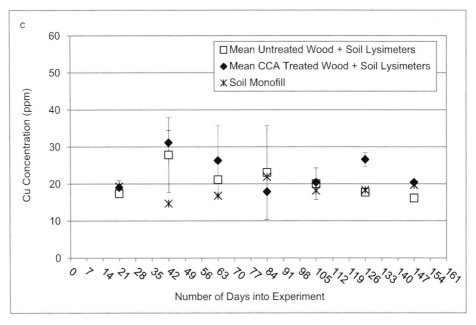

FIGURE 4   Continued. c) Concentration of copper in soil.

736). Therefore some of the data points near the boundary of As (V) and As (III) suggest the presence of more toxic, soluble and mobile As (III) species. The Eh/pH for chromium (Figure 6) shows that the expected species is Cr (III) as (Cr(OH)$_3$. The presence of chromium (VI) in the soil environment would be unusual as it is readily reduced to Cr (III) (Nico et al., 2006).

Discussion and conclusions

Influence of soil physico-chemical conditions on leaching
The soil moisture contents were closely related to the amount of leachant added to the lysimeters. Those lysimeters containing mulch were found to conserve soil moisture. CCA-treated wood in contact with wet soil loses more preservative than wood exposed to drier soil or to water alone (Cooper, 1994; Wang et al., 1998). Therefore, those CCA wood and soil containing lysimeters with higher soil moisture contents over longer periods were more conducive to leaching of CCA components due to prolonged leachant and wood contact.

   Soils with higher levels of organic matter and therefore organic acids have been shown to increase leaching of elements from CCA-treated wood (Balasoiu et al., 2001; Redman et al., 2002; Schultz et al., 2002; Kartal et al., 2007; Cooper and Ung, 2009). Humic and fulvic acids have been shown to be more effective leaching agents than inorganic acids and are highly effective at only 1% concentration (Crawford et al., 2002; Kartal et al., 2005). These acids alongside organic ligands found in soil can react with the CCA elements (in particular copper and chromium) to form chelate complexes (Warner and Solomon, 1990; Wang et al., 1998; Lebow and Foster, 2005).

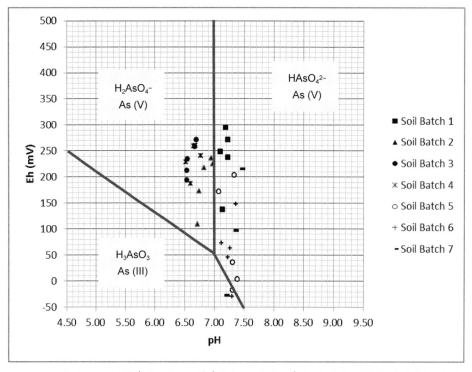

FIGURE 5   Soil arsenic Eh/pH values. Eh/pH boundaries (adapted from Solo-Gabriele et al., 2004).

This causes retention of Cr and Cu in the soil (Comfort, 1993). Arsenic mobility tends to increase with high organic matter content due to the high levels of dissolved organic compounds limiting its sorption onto soil (Redman et al., 2002; Dobran and Zagury, 2006).

The soil OM values found in the long- and short-term studies were between 12% and 28%. These levels are high compared to other CCA leaching studies (Gifford et al., 1997; Crawford et al., 2002; Lebow et al., 2006). At levels of only 5%, organic matter is an important predictor for loss of metal(loid)s (Crawford et al., 2002). Therefore, at much higher levels, leaching from wood will be facilitated and chromium and copper metals will be retained as complexes in the soil. Arsenic will become increasingly mobile. As such, arsenic concentrations in leachate are expected to be higher than chromium and copper.

Soil redox plays a major role in metal sorption and mobility. Generally, as conditions in the soil become more reducing, mobility of arsenic, chromium, and copper increases (Reddy and Patrick Jr, 1977; Masscheleyn et al., 1991; Guo et al., 1997; Maurice et al., 2007). Soil redox levels decreased from the moderately reducing class to the reducing class in all the mulch-containing lysimeters. The trends towards anaerobic conditions in the lysimeters is similar to those of Smith (2005) where redox conditions in saturated sediments became increasingly reducing over time. This was interpreted as sequential reduction where conditions become more reducing, the longer the period of saturation (Smith, 2005; Lillie and Smith, 2007; Smith and Lillie,

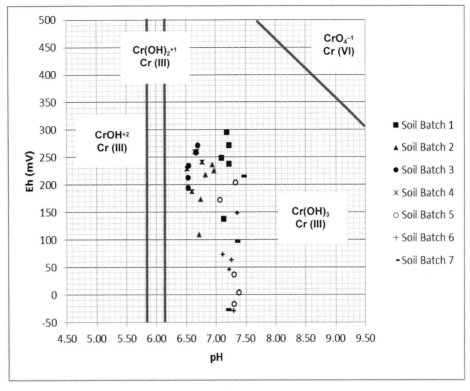

FIGURE 6   Soil chromium Eh/pH values. Eh/pH boundaries (adapted from Solo-Gabriele et al., 2004).

2007). In oxidized soil, oxygen acts as the only electron acceptor for organisms (Gregorich and Janzen, 1999). In saturated soils, the dissolved oxygen remaining in the soil is quickly depleted and other soil oxidants are used as electron acceptors by facultative anaerobes (Gregorich et al., 1999). The reductions of NO_3^-, Mn^{4+}, Fe^{3+}, SO_4^{2-}, and CO_2 occur sequentially causing a corresponding decrease in soil Eh (Leuders and Friedrich, 2000). At the reduced Eh values observed, it is most likely that Fe^{3+} or SO_4^{2-} reduction is taking place (Gregorich et al., 1999). In the CCA wood and soil lysimeters this would cause the elements to leach from the wood and remain readily dissolvable and mobile in the soil.

Implications of leaching in wetlands

This study has demonstrated that the physico-chemical conditions during the leaching experiment facilitated leaching of As, Cr, and Cu from CCA-treated wood. Furthermore, the more toxic and mobile species of As (III) were predicted in the soil samples based on Eh/pH data. The conditions influencing leaching were high soil MC, high levels of soil OM, anaerobic conditions and soil texture. Wetland soils by their very nature are hydric, resulting in anaerobic conditions (Mitsch and Gosselink, 2000). Soils can also be classed as mineral or organic depending on the percentage organic matter and vary over wide ranges, as do pH conditions. However, organic soils tend to have a lower pH particularly in peatlands arising from organic acids and lack of groundwater inflow (Mitsch and Gosselink, 2000). As such, it can be inferred that wetland hydric soils with high levels of organic matter will facilitate leaching. Furthermore, if soils have a high sand content, metal(loid)s are more likely to be increasingly mobile in the soil profile and pose a greater contamination risk.

Although concentrations of metal(loid)s were not high in the soil, levels were high in the leachate collected at the base of the lysimeters demonstrating that the metals were highly mobile in the soil profile (Mercer and Frostick, 2012). In constructed wetlands, metal oxides are reduced in the range of 100mV to -100mV (Marchand et al., 2010) as experienced in this study. These levels result in a release of dissolved metals. The pollutants have the potential to accumulate in surface waters, groundwater, substrates plants and animals within a wetland environment (Marchand et al., 2010; An et al., 2011).

Recent studies have looked at the leaching potential of CCA-treated wood in a wetland context. Lebow and Foster (2005) monitored soil, sediment, and water samples around the vicinity of a wetland boardwalk during construction and up to 60 months in service. They reported elevated levels of each preservative component to varying degrees over the time with leaching confined to the immediate area of the boardwalk. Levels were highest in month 60, suggesting continuous leaching and accumulation in both the underlying sediment and soil. Comfort (1993) also studied leaching over various ages of boardwalk in a variety of vegetation types over a wilderness area. Levels of copper and chromium were found to be elevated over background levels. These studies confirm that f CCA-treated wood structures leach in wetland contexts.

Microbial transformations and impacts on in situ archaeological remains

Microorganisms play an important role in the transformation of heavy metals and metalloids in wetlands through direct or indirect oxidation/reduction. Using arsenic as an example, As (III) may be oxidized to As (V), As (V) may be reduced to As (III), and the inorganic species may also be biomethylated to organic forms (Turpeinen et al., 1999). The detoxification mechanism is mediated through enzyme or respiratory chains and is related to arsenic resistance system gene (ars), arsenic respiratory reduction genes (arr), or arsenite oxidation genes (aox) (Stolz et al., 2006; Chang et al., 2010). Chang et al. (2010) reported on the detoxification of arsenic from As (III) to As (V) from arsenite oxidation gene isolated from soil sampled in natural and constructed wetlands. They found that aox genes could be involved in arsenic biogeochemical cycling and detoxification, although the ecological niches in constructed wetlands were different to natural wetlands due to factors such as the presence of man-made structures.

Recent studies have shown that changes to the burial environment and bacterial communities can impact on in situ preservation. Douterelo et al. (2010) documented soil microbial community response to different land-uses in English wetlands and the potential for these changes to impact on in situ preservation of archaeological remains. The wetland soil that was managed under an arable regime with elevated water levels had higher microbial metabolic activity and diversity than the wetlands with drier soil conditions, managed as pastureland. This suggests that waterlogged conditions (as experienced in this study) may not be sufficient for in situ preservation. Added to this, the impacts of heavy metals on wetland soil microbial communities is unclear. Although it would appear that the presence of heavy metals in soil may initially have an inhibiting effect on microbial degradation of organic remains such as bone (Müller et al., 2011), there are many other factors involved.

The introduction of anthropogenic structures and pollutants to the wetland environment may result in selective shifts of the microbial communities to those that are tolerant and/or resistant to the metal(loid)s. A study by Clausen (2000) identified twenty-eight metal-tolerant bacteria from eight soil environments with elevated levels of copper, chromium and arsenic arising from CCA. Metal-tolerant bacteria and fungi result from adaptation, environmental selection, and may be endemic. They also identified metal resistant isolates with the ability to remove copper, chromium, and arsenic (Clausen, 2000). Therefore, the original conditions that promote *in situ* preservation may be altered and therefore could increase the risk of biodeterioration of archaeological resources.

It is evident from the current study and similar wetland leaching studies that there is a very real leaching hazard from CCA-treated boardwalks and viewing platforms. These installations increase access of wetlands for research and appreciation by the general public and are therefore an important asset for the conservation of wetlands. However, there needs to be a balanced approach to the use of CCA-treated wood. It may be necessary to use less hazardous materials and, where this is not possible, the potential impacts need to be evaluated against the benefits of access. Further research into leaching and impacts on microbial communities and *in situ* preservation is required for an increased understanding of the processes involved.

Bibliography

An, J., Kin, J.-Y., Kim, K.-W., Park, J.-Y., Lee, J.-S., and Jang, M. 2011. Natural Attenuation of Arsenic in the Wetland System Around Abandoned Mining Area. *Environmental Geochemistry and Health*, 33: 71–80.

Balasoiu, C. F., Zagury, G. J., and Deschênes, L. 2001. Partitioning and Speciation of Chromium, Copper, and Arsenic in CCA-Contaminated Soils: Influence of Soil Composition. *The Science of The Total Environment*, 280: 239–55.

Brown, C. J. and Eaton, R. A. 2000. Leaching of Copper-Chrome-Arsenic (CCA) Wood Preservative in Sea Water. *Material und Organimen*, 33: 213–34.

CEM 2004. Mars Xpress Microwave Sample Preparation Note: XprAG-4: Wood Chips. CEM.

Chang, J.-S., Yoon, I.-H., Lee, J.-H., Kim, K.-R., An, J., and Kim, K.-W. 2010. Arsenic Detoxification Potential of *aox* Genes in Arsenite-Oxidizing Bacteria Isolated from Natural and Constructed Wetlands in the Republic of Korea. *Environmental Geochemistry and Health*, 32: 95–105.

Cheetham, J. L. 2004. An Assessment of the Potential for In Situ Preservation of Buried Organic Archaeological Remains at Sutton Common, South Yorkshire. Unpublished dissertation/thesis, University of Hull.

Cherry, J. A., Shaikh, A. U., Tallman, D. E., and Nicholson, R. V. 1979. Arsenic Species as an Indicator of Redox Conditions in Groundwater. *Contemporary Hydrogeology the George Burke Maxey Memorial Volume*, 43: 373–92.

Clausen, C. A. 2000. Isolating Metal-Tolerant Bacteria Capable of Removing Copper, Chromium, and Arsenic from Treated Wood. *Waste Management and Research*, 18: 264–68.

Comfort, M. 1993. *Environmental and Occupational Health Aspects of using CCA Treated Timber for Walking Track Construction in the Tasmanian Wilderness Heritage Area*. Hobart, Tasmania: Tasmanian Parks and Wildlife Service.

Cooper, P. A. 1994. Leaching of CCA: Is it a Problem? *Environmental Considerations in the Manufacture, Use and Disposal of Preservative-treated Wood*. Madison, WI: Forest Products Society, pp. 45–57.

Cooper, P. A. and Ung, Y. T. 2009. Component Leaching from CCA, ACQ and a Micronized Copper Quat (MCQ) System as Affected by Leaching Protocol. *International Research Group on Wood Preservation 40th Annual Meeting*. Beijing: International Research Group on Wood Protection.

Crawford, D., Fox, R., Kamden, P., Lebow, S., Nicholas, D., Pettry, D., Schultz, T., Sites, L., and Ziobro, R. 2002. Laboratory Studies of CCA-C Leaching: Influence of Wood and Soil Properties on Extent of Arsenic and Copper Depletion. *Proceedings International Research Group on Wood Preservation, 33rd Annual Meeting, 2002.* IRG/WP 02-50186.

Cullen, W. R. and Reimer, K. J. 1989. Arsenic Speciation in the Environment. *Chemical Reviews,* 89: 713–64.

DEFRA, 2002. *Soil Guideline Values for Chromium Contamination. R&D Publications.* Bristol: Environment Agency.

Dobran, S. and Zagury, G. R. J. 2006. Arsenic Speciation and Mobilization in CCA-Contaminated Soils: Influence of Organic Matter Content. *Science of the Total Environment,* 364: 239–50.

Douterelo, I., Goulder, R., and Lillie, M. 2010. Soil Microbial Community Response to Land-Management and Depth, Related to the Degradation of Organic Matter in English Wetlands: Implications for the In Situ Preservation of Archaeological Remains. *Applied Soil Ecology,* 44: 219–27.

Environment Agency, 2009. *Soil Guideline Values for Inorganic Arsenic in Soil.* Bristol: Environment Agency.

Gardner, W. H. and Black, C. A. 1965. Chapter 7: Water Content. In: C. A. Black, ed., *Methods of Soil Analysis Part 1: Physical and Mineralogical Properties, Including Statistics of Measurement and Sampling.* Madison, Wisconsin: American Society of Agronomy, pp. 82–127.

Gifford, J. S., Marvin, N. A., and Dare, P. H. 1997. Composition of Leachate from Field Lysimeters Containing CCA Treated Wood. *Proceedings of the 93rd Annual Meeting.* Selma, AL: American Wood Protection Association (AWPA) v. 93, pp. 426–40.

Gregorich, E. G. and Janzen, H. H. 1999. Section C: Soil Biology and Biochemistry. Chapter 3.2 Decomposition. In: M. E. Sumner, ed., *Handbook of Soil Science.* Boca Raton: CRC Press, C107–120.

Guo, T., Delaune, R. D., and Patrick, W. H. 1997. The Influence of Sediment Redox Chemistry on Chemically Active Forms of Arsenic, Cadmium, Chromium, and Zinc in Estuarine Sediment. *Environment International,* 23: 305–16.

Janzen, H. H. and Carter, M. R. 1993. Chapter 18: Soluble Salts. In: M. R. Carter and E. G. Gregorich, eds., *Soil Sampling and Methods of Analysis.* Boca Raton: Canadian Society of Soil Science, pp. 161–66.

Kartal, S. N., Hwang, W., and Imamura, Y. 2005. Effects of Hard Water, Sea Water and Humic Acid on the Release of CCA Components from Treated Wood. *Proceedings IRG Annual Meeting,* IRG/WP 05-50228.

Kartal, S. N., Hwang, W.-J., and Imamura, Y. 2007. Evaluation of Effect of Leaching Medium on the Release of Copper, Chromium, and Arsenic from Treated Wood. *Building and Environment,* 42: 1188–93.

Lebow, S. and Foster, D. 2005. Environmental Concentrations of Copper, Chromium, and Arsenic Released from a Chromated-Copper-Arsenate- (CCA-C-) Treated Wetland Boardwalk. *Forest Products Journal,* 55: 62–70.

Lebow, S. T., Foster, D. O., and Lebow, P. K. 1999. Release of Copper, Chromium and Arsenic from Treated Southern Pine Exposed in Seawater and Freshwater. *Forest Products Journal,* 49: 80–89.

Lebow, S. T., Cooper, P. A., Lebow, P. K., Townsed, T., and Solo-Gabriele, H. 2006. Chapter 5: Study Design Considerations in Evaluating Environmental Impacts. In: T. G. Townsend and H. Solo-Gabriele, eds, *Environmental Impacts of Treated Wood.* Boca Raton: Taylor & Francis, pp. 79–99.

Leuders, T. and Friedrich, M. 2000. Archael Population Dynamics during Sequential Reduction Processes in Rice Field Soil. *Applied and Environmental Microbiology,* 66: 2732–42.

Lillie, M. and Smith, R. 2007. The In Situ Preservation of Archaeological Remains: Using Lysimeters to Assess the Impacts of Saturation and Seasonality. *Journal of Archaeological Science,* 34: 1494–1504.

Marchand, L., Mench, M., Jacob, D. L., and Otte, M. L. 2010. Metal and Metalloid Removal in Constructed Wetlands, with Emphasis on the Importance of Plants and Standardized Measurements: A Review. *Environmental Pollution,* 158: 3447–61.

Masscheleyn, P. H., Delaune, R. D., and Patrick, W. H. 1991. Effect of Redox Potential and pH on Arsenic Speciation and Solubility in a Contaminated Soil. *Environmental Science and Technology,* 25: 1414–19.

Maurice, C., Lidelöw, S., Gustavsson, B., Lättström, A., Ragnvaldsson, D., Leffler, P., Lövgren, L., Tesfalidet, S., and Kumpiene, J. 2007. Techniques for the Stabilization and Assessment of Treated Copper-, Chromium-, and Arsenic-Contaminated Soil. *Ambio,* 36: 430–36.

Mercer, T. G., Frostick, L. E., and Walmsley, A. D. 2011. Recovering Incomplete Data using Statistical Multiple Imputations (SMI): A Case Study in Environmental Chemistry. *Talanta,* 85: 2599–2604.

Mercer, T. G. and Frostick, L. E. 2012. Leaching Characteristics of CCA-Treated Wood Waste: A UK Study. *Science of the Total Environment,* 427–28: 165–74.

Mitsch, W. J. and Gosselink, J. G. 2000. *Wetlands*. New York: Wiley.

Morrell, J. J. 2006. Chapter 1: Chromated Copper Arsenate as a Wood Preservative. In: T. G. Townsend and H. M. Solo-Gabriele, eds, *Environmental impacts of treated wood*. Boca Raton, Fla: CRC Taylor & Francis, pp. 5–18.

Müller, K., Chadefaux, C., Thomas, N., and Reiche, I. 2011. Microbial Attack of Archaeological Bones Versus High Concentrations of Heavy Metals in the Burial Environment. A Case Study of Animal Bones from a Mediaeval Copper Workshop in Paris. *Palaeogeography, Palaeoclimatology, Palaeoecology*, 310: 39–51.

Nico, P. S., Ruby, M. V., Lowney, Y. W., and Holm, S. E. 2006. Chemical Speciation and Bioaccessibility of Arsenic and Chromium in Chromated Copper Arsenate-Treated Wood and Soils. *Environmental Science & Technology*, 40: 402–08.

Othieno, C. O. 1980. Effects of Mulches on Soil Water Content and Water Status of Tea Plants in Kenya. *Experimental Agriculture*, 16: 295–302.

Patrick, W. H. and Mahaptra, I. C. 1968. Transformation and Availability to Rice of Nitrogen and Phosphorus in Waterlogged Soils. *Advances in Agronomy*, 20: 323–59.

Pearson, G. F., Greenway, G. M., Brima, E. I., and Haris, P. I. 2007. Rapid Arsenic Speciation using Ion Pair LC-ICPMS with a Monolithic Silica Column Reveals Increased Urinary DMA Excretion after Ingestion of Rice. *Journal of Analytical Atomic Spectrometry*, 22: 361–69.

Reddy, C. N. and Patrick Jr, W. H. 1977. Effect of Redox Potential on the Stability of Zinc and Copper Chelates in Flooded Soils. *Soil Science of America Journal*, 41: 729–32.

Redman, A. D., Macalady, D. L., and Ahmann, D. 2002. Natural Organic Matter Affects Arsenic Speciation and Sorption onto Hematite. *Environmental Science & Technology*, 36: 2889–96.

Rowell, D. L. 1994. *Soil Science Methods and Applications*. Harlow: Longman.

Schultz, T. P., Nicholas, D. D., and Pettry, D. E. 2002. Depletion of CCA-C from Ground-Contact Wood: Results from Two Field Sites with Significantly Different Soils. *Holzforschung*, 56: 125–29.

Sheldrick, B. H., Wang, C., and Carter, M. R. 1993. Chapter 47: Particle Size Distribution. In: M. R. Carter and E. G. Gregorich, eds, *Soil Sampling and Methods of Analysis*. Florida: Lewis Publishers (in association with the Canadian Society of Soil Science), pp. 713–26.

Smith, R. 2005. The Preservation and Degradation of Wood in Wetland Archaeological and Landfill Sites. Unpublished PhD thesis, University of Hull.

Smith, R. and Lillie, M. 2007. Using a Lysimeter Study to Assess the Parameters Responsible for Oak Wood Decay from Waterlogged Burial Environments and their Implication for the In Situ Preservation of Archaeological Remains. *International Biodeterioration & Biodegradation*, 60: 40–49.

Solo-Gabriele, H. M., Townsend, T. G., and Schert, J. 2003. Environmental Impact of CCA-Treated Wood: A Summary from Seven Years of Study Focusing on the US Florida Environment. *Proceedings IRG Annual Meeting*, IRG/WP 03-50205.

Solo-Gabriele, H., Khan, B., Townsend, T., Song, J., Jambeck, J., Dubey, B., Jang, Y., and Cai, Y. 2004. *Arsenic and Chromium Speciation of Leachates from CCA-Treated Wood: Final Report*. Gainesville, Florida: Florida Center for Solid and Hazardous Waste Management.

Solo-Gabriele, H. M., Townsend, T. G., and Schert, J. 2003. Environmental Impact of CCA-Treated Wood: A Summary from Seven Years of Study Focusing on the US Florida Environment. *IRGWP 34th Annual Meeting*. Brisbane: International Research Group on Wood Protection.

Stilwell, D. E. and Gorny, K. D. 1997. Contamination of Soil with Copper, Chromium and Arsenic Under Decks Built from Pressure Treated Wood. *Bulletin of Environmental Contamination and Toxicology*, 58: 22–29.

Stolz, J. F., Basu, P., Santini, J. M., and Oremland, R. S. 2006. Arsenic and Selenium in Microbial Metabolism. *Annual Review of Microbiology*, 60: 107–30.

Stumm, W. and Morgan, J. J. 1981. *Aquatic Chemistry: An Introduction Emphasizing Chemical Equilibria in Natural Waters*. Canada: John Wiley & Sons.

Turpeinen, R., Pantsar-Kallio, M., Häggblom, M., and Kairesalo, T. 1999. Influence of Microbes on the Mobilization, Toxicity and Biomethylation of Arsenic in Soil. *The Science of the Total Environment*, 236: 173–80.

Wang, J., Nicholas, D. D., Sites, L. S., and Pettry, D. E. 1998. Effect of Soil Chemistry and Physical Properties on Wood Preservative Leaching. *Proceedings IRG Annual Meeting*, IRG/WP 98-50111.

Warner, J. E. and Solomon, K. R. 1990. Acidity as a Factor in Leaching of Copper, Chromium and Arsenic from CCA-Treated Dimension Lumber. *Environmental Toxicology and Chemistry*, 9: 1331–37.

WRAP 2004. Treated Wood Waste: Assessment of the Waste Management Challenge — Summary Report. Oxon.

Zagury, G. J., Samson, R., and Deschenes, L. 2003. Occurrence of Metals in Soil and Ground Water Near Chromated Copper Arsenate-Treated Utility Poles. *Journal of Environmental Quality*, 32: 507–14.

Notes on contributors

Dr Theresa Mercer has research interests that span the environmental sciences, with a specific interest in contaminated land and waste management. She graduated from her PhD in 2010 at the Department of Geography, University of Hull. Her research investigated the environmental impacts from preservative treated wood waste in soil. This was followed by a post-doctoral research assistant role in the Department of Chemistry and the Centre for Adaptive Science and Sustainability at the University of Hull and academic tutoring at the University of Queensland, Australia. She held a lecturership in Environmental Science at Keele University during 2012, and is now a Research Fellow at Cranfield University.

Correspondence to: Dr Theresa Mercer, School of Physical and Geographical Sciences, Keele University, Staffordshire ST5 5BG, UK. Email: t.g.mercer@keele.ac.uk

Dr Malcolm Lillie has excavated and researched in wetlands for the past twenty-four years, beginning his career as a Fieldwork Supervisor on the Welsh side of the Severn Estuary, UK, excavating and surveying sites such as Goldcliff and Caldicot. He joined the English Heritage funded Humber Wetlands Project under the Directorship of Dr Steve Ellis at the University of Hull in 1994. In 2000 he joined the academic staff at Hull. He is currently a Reader in Prehistoric Archaeology and Wetland Science and Director of the Wetland Archaeology & Environments Research Centre at the University of Hull. He has an MSc and PhD from the University of Sheffield, the latter being supervised by Professor Marek Zvelebil.

Dr Robert Smith is a Director of CgMs Consulting. He has considerable experience in archaeological consultancy and provides specialist guidance and support in order to enable clients to better manage the heritage issues associated with their operations. He assists clients throughout the life cycle of each project, from the initial site acquisition, during the screening and scoping stages, through to the production of Environmental Assessments. Robert has particular experience of the renewable energy sector, as well as retail and other development projects. He routinely undertakes the design and implementation of desk studies, and the assessment/ determination of impact mitigation and management strategies, in order to fulfil the requirements of the planning process. Robert is a Chartered Environmentalist (CEnv), Chartered Geographer (CGeog), Chartered Scientist (CSci), Chartered Water and Environmental Manager (C.WEM), a Fellow of the Geographical Society (FRGS), a Member of the Institute of Field Archaeologists (MIfA), and a Member of the Institute of Water and Environmental Management (MCIWEM). He has a first degree in Physical Geography (University of Middlesex), and an MSc in Wetland Archaeological Science and Management and a PhD in Archaeological Science (both from the University of Hull).

CONSERVATION AND MGMT OF ARCH. SITES, Vol. 14 Nos 1–4, 2012, 115–25

In Situ Preservation of Wetland Heritage: Hydrological and Chemical Change in the Burial Environment of the Somerset Levels, UK

LOUISE JONES

Departments of Chemistry, Archaeology, and Geography and Environmental Science, University of Reading, UK

MARTIN BELL

Department of Archaeology, University of Reading, UK

In situ preservation is a core strategy for the conservation and management of waterlogged remains at wetland sites. Inorganic and organic remains can, however, quickly become degraded, or lost entirely, as a result of chemical or hydrological changes. Monitoring is therefore crucial in identifying baseline data for a site, the extent of spatial and or temporal variability, and in evaluating the potential impacts of these variables on current and future *in situ* preservation potential.

Since August 2009, monthly monitoring has taken place at the internationally important Iron Age site of Glastonbury Lake Village in the Somerset Levels, UK. A spatial, stratigraphic, and analytical approach to the analysis of sediment horizons and monitoring of groundwater chemistry, redox potential, water table depth and soil moisture (using TDR) was used to characterize the site.

Significant spatial and temporal variability has been identified, with results from water-table monitoring and some initial chemical analysis from Glastonbury presented here. It appears that during dry periods parts of this site are at risk from desiccation. Analysis of the chemical data, in addition to integrating the results from the other parameters, is ongoing, with the aim of clarifying the risk to the entire site.

KEYWORDS *in situ* preservation, monitoring, Glastonbury Lake Village, Sweet Track, water chemistry, hydrology

© Taylor & Francis 2012   DOI 10.1179/1350503312Z.00000000010

Introduction

The Somerset Levels have in the past seen extensive peat cutting and drainage which led to the discovery of a wealth of prehistoric wetland sites (Coles and Coles, 1986). Today large-scale peat cutting has ended, but what is not clear is whether what remains of the archaeological sites is still safe. Monitoring has been carried out recently at two sites, Glastonbury Lake Village, and a section of the Sweet Track located in a new extension to the Shapwick Heath National Nature Reserve. An interim report (Jones, 2010) outlines the overall project strategy and focuses on some preliminary results from the Sweet Track. This current paper is concerned solely with the initial results from the monitoring at Glastonbury Lake Village.

This work has involved monthly monitoring of variables including water table depth, redox potential, pH, and water chemistry, to look at spatial and temporal fluctuations, and assess the likely effects on the inorganic and organic remains. The work at Glastonbury Lake Village builds on the Monuments at Risk in Somerset's Peatlands (MARISP) project (Brunning et al., 2008), which in 2004 monitored thirteen sites including Glastonbury Lake Village, where three monitoring stations were installed. Although identified as the best-preserved site, hydrological analysis did indicate that the water table fell below the surface of the archaeological remains from April to October, leaving only lower deposits waterlogged. Although a zone of partial saturation may exist above the water table, nevertheless the upper section of the remains are at increased risk of desiccation and oxidation (Hogan, 2008). The water levels recorded at these monitoring stations in each of the three piezometers (installed at 65 cm, 115 cm, and 165 cm below the ground surface) were extremely consistent throughout the monitoring period, mirroring each other closely.

However, these data were from three monitoring locations all south of the site, outside the boundary of the palisade. Two of these locations were also outside the original excavated area. This raised questions as to how representative the results of the MARISP project are of the entire site, and also whether the hydrological regime is consistent between excavated and undisturbed areas. More extensive monitoring was required and, through discussion with English Heritage and Richard Brunning (Somerset County Council), this current project was developed.

The overall aims and objectives of this research have focused on identifying whether a spatial and stratigraphic approach to the analysis of soil/sediment horizons, and monitoring of groundwater chemistry, pH, redox potential, soil moisture, and water-table depth, can be used to characterize the sites more fully. An additional aim is to provide data to support strategies for the current and future *in situ* preservation of the inorganic and organic remains at the sites. The overall focus is on obtaining comprehensive baseline data and identifying whether there is variability in the parameters being monitored. This is in terms of

- spatially across each site
- within the profile at each monitoring point
- seasonally, i.e. over time.

As a result, this will enhance understanding of the burial environment and to what extent variability in the parameters being monitored impacts on *in situ* preservation potential in the short and long term. It is also anticipated that this research will be used to refine and focus future monitoring strategies at these sites as part of ongoing site management and conservation.

The archaeology of Glastonbury Lake Village

The Iron Age site of Glastonbury Lake Village is located north-west of Glastonbury, Somerset, and is characterized by the exceptional organic preservation of artefacts, structures, and palaeoenvironmental evidence. These were originally revealed during excavations in 1892–1907 by Bulleid and Gray (1911; 1917). The area excavated is shown in Figure 1. The site has been in the ownership of the Glastonbury Antiquarian Society since its discovery, therefore benefiting from management focused on site preservation.

The site was occupied between approximately 250 BC–50 BC and was originally constructed in a reed and sedge swamp, with areas of open water. A palisade of roundwood stakes (now slumped) formed the periphery of the lake village, within which the foundations were composed of layers of timber, brushwood, peat blocks, clay, stone and rushes (Brunning et al., 2008). There are ninety mounds within this palisade, each with superimposed clay floors and hearths (Coles and Coles, 1986).

Bulleid and Gray (1911; 1917) identified a diverse range of inorganic and organic artefact types including wood, antler, bone, glass, bronze, iron, lead, and pottery. Despite extensive excavations within the palisade and the removal of artefacts for analysis and conservation, much of the wood substructure, palisade, and some worked wood remains in situ; additional archaeological deposits are also likely to be outside this excavated area (Brunning, pers. comm.). This site is clearly very complex, with a large area excavated in sections between 1892–1907, several small-scale subsequent excavations, the reburial of artefacts, and a wide range of artefact types, all of which need to be considered when evaluating preservation potential.

Methodology

Utilizing a multidisciplinary approach, this project has combined analysis of the sediment context with monthly monitoring of environmental variables. These have included water-table depth; water chemistry using ICP-OES and anion chromatography; redox potential using in situ probes and data loggers (one of which was remote sensing); soil moisture analysis using Time Domain Reflectometry (TDR); water pH and conductivity. The remote sensing data logger has enabled the hourly monitoring of redox potential near the centre of the site, where artefacts including a ladder were reburied. These data are being related to hourly and daily rainfall totals (obtained from the Meteorological Office's Yeovilton weather station), as well as changes in water-table levels and soil moisture. This will clarify how rainfall affects these variables, and the rate of this impact, enhancing understanding of the burial environment in this important part of the site. The techniques selected reflect standard monitoring parameters used at many other sites both nationally and internationally, guidelines within the Archaeological Monitoring Standard (Smit et al., 2006), and a continuation of previous techniques used at both sites. The soil moisture analysis using Time Domain Reflectometry was requested by English Heritage to evaluate this technique as part of a monitoring strategy.

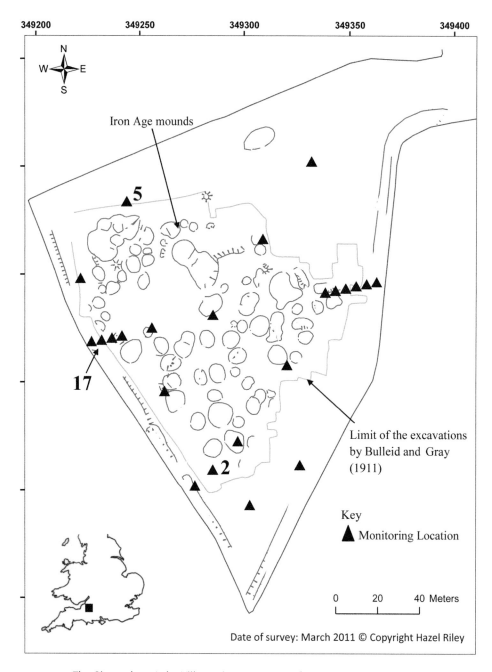

FIGURE 1   The Glastonbury Lake Village site, Somerset. The monitoring stations discussed in the text (Locations 2, 5, and 17) are highlighted (adapted from Hazel Riley, 2011).

Groundwater chemistry was a focus of monitoring because of its effects on the long-term preservation of artefacts through altering variables including redox potential, the stability of corrosion layers on inorganic artefacts, pH of the groundwater, and soil microbiology. In total, 925 groundwater samples were collected over fourteen months and analysed for sixteen key elements including calcium, chloride, nitrate, potassium, sodium, and sulphate.

At Glastonbury Lake Village the monitoring and coring strategy was based on a 30 m square grid system, designed to be both minimally invasive and target monitoring equipment according to key research questions. This was in order to examine the chemical, hydrological and sedimentological context at both large (field) and small (individual monitoring point) scale. In total, twenty-three locations were monitored monthly at Glastonbury (Figure 1) from August 2009 until November 2010, including the three stations monitored during the MARISP project. At each of the monitoring locations piezometers were installed at depths of 65 cm (upper), 115 cm (middle), and 165 cm (lower) beneath the ground surface. These enabled the monitoring of water-table depth using an automated depth meter, and the collection of samples for chemical analysis. Over this period a total of 1173 results were recorded for water-table depth at the site.

Results and discussion

This section discusses results from three monitoring locations at Glastonbury, with initial data from the hydrological investigations and some observations on the chemical analysis. The three monitoring locations are highlighted on Figure 1.

Location 17

The water levels recorded at location 17 are presented in Figure 2. A notable feature of these data are that in contrast to the MARISP data the levels recorded in all three piezometers differ each month throughout most of the monitoring project. For example, in April 2010 the water level recorded in the 65 cm piezometer was 4.07 m OD, at 115 cm the level was 3.65 m OD, and at 165 m OD the level was 4.19 m OD. Overall, at all of the monitoring locations during the course of the monitoring project, water levels in the 65 cm piezometer were recorded between 4.06 m and 4.43 m OD, in the 115 cm piezometer levels varied between 3.55 m and 4.22 m OD, whilst in the 165 cm piezometer the levels showed the greatest range, between 3.09 m and 4.16 m OD. There appears to be effectively two disconnects between the water levels, one between the upper and the middle level, and another between the middle and lower level.

During the sediment coring in 2009 a silty clay alluvial subsurface horizon with a topsoil layer developed above this was identified covering the entire site, including the mounds. The combined thickness of these units ranges from 34 cm to 94 cm, and is on average 55 cm thick. This potentially has important implications for the preservation of the peat and any organic remains it contains, as the peat is located below the alluvial horizon which may provide a protective barrier against surface desiccation. However, we also need to consider potential impacts of fluctuations in water-table depth, redox potential, pH, or variable water chemistry on preservation potential. The separation of the data points does, however, suggest the 65 cm piezometers are recording a different hydrological regime to the deeper piezometers and appears

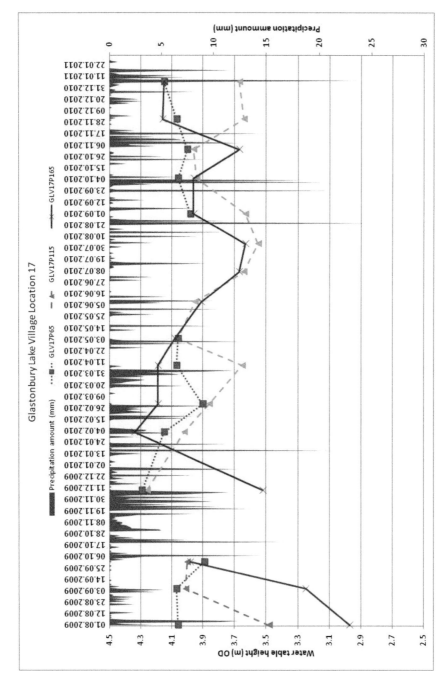

FIGURE 2   Water-table results for monitoring location 17, Glastonbury Lake Village. (Daily rainfall data; UK Met Office, MIDAS data. Yeovilton weather station.)

to indicate the presence of a transient, perched water table within this alluvial horizon.

Interestingly, the pattern of water movement at 165 cm, while in some months being similar to that at 115 cm, at other times there appears to be a lag in the response to rainfall events. During other months the pattern of water movement at 165 cm shows an opposite pattern, and appears to be antecedent, preceding the levels observed at 115 cm. Significantly, there is enormous variability at this depth and this appears to most likely represent the true water table. However, there is not a consistent pattern at this depth at each monitoring location. This suggests that the variability in water levels at 115 cm and 165 cm at each location (and importantly across the site) is influenced by a range of factors. These include

- whether each monitoring area has been excavated or left undisturbed
- whether it is adjacent to a drainage ditch either around the site or one of the superficial drains dug across the site
- the extent of peat humification
- the stratigraphy in terms of the peat type.

All of these factors impact on, and influence, hydraulic conductivity and hence the movement of water through the profile. It is, however, difficult to identify any one clear explanation for this variability and instead it appears likely that a combination of these factors can be used to explain why, in some areas of the site, there appears to be a more rapid response to rainfall, whereas at others there may be a negligible response, or a significant lag time.

Location 5

Monitoring location 5 is situated near the boundary of excavations in 1905/06 and later excavations by Avery in 1969 (unpublished). The hydrological data are plotted in Figure 3, and the following numbered observations relate to the numbers in Figure 3.

1)   At the start of the monitoring period the levels recorded in all three piezometers are different, reflecting the previously discussed two disconnects between the water levels.

2)   It was not possible to collect any data during November 2009 because that part of the site was under standing water. During this period the farmer made a series of superficial drains approximately 35–40 cm deep to remove surface water.

3)   Significantly, following this in December the water levels became consistent. This appears to suggest that by draining the water from this area the drains reconnected the water levels. This may explain why the water levels recorded at the three locations to the south of the site during the MARISP project are all so consistent. These are all located at the southern apex of the site, and near a main drainage ditch and a stream to the east, both of which appear to be controlling the water levels in this area.

4)   Further variability is observed at this point and it is unclear as to the cause of the water level fall at 165cm, however the levels mirror each other once again from May. This pattern of consistency from May onwards is almost universal across the site and appears to correspond with reduced rainfall totals.

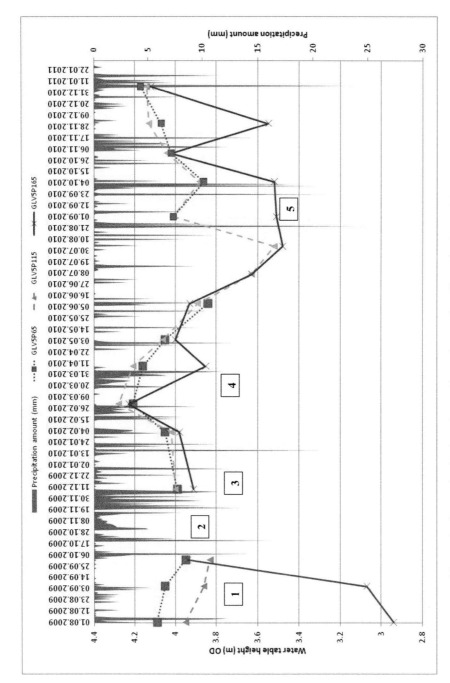

FIGURE 3   Water-table results for monitoring location 5, Glastonbury Lake Village. (Daily rainfall data; UK, MET Office, MIDAS data. Yeovilton weather station.)

5) Again the water levels are inconsistent here. This may reflect a slower response at 165 cm to this period of heavy rainfall events, due to slower recharge of water levels at this depth in comparison to 65 and 115 cm.

Location 2

In Figure 4 the data obtained for Station 2 in 2004 during the MARISP project are compared to those from 2010. It can be seen that the pattern of consistency in the water levels recorded at all three monitoring depths continued. Water levels fell below the top of the archaeological deposits (4.1 m OD) for seven months from April to October 2004, however during 2010 water levels fell 35 cm lower and were below the top of the archaeological remains for six months from May to October. The greater fall in water-table level appears to correspond with comparatively lower rainfall totals in 2010 compared to 2004.

Without any monitoring data for 2005–09 it is not possible to identify whether this reduction in water levels in 2010 represents an ongoing trend. With global warming and predictions for drier summers, the risk to the archaeological deposits is, however, likely to be exacerbated, highlighting the need for ongoing monitoring.

Chemical analysis

In terms of chemical analysis one initial observation is an increase in chloride concentrations with depth across a large part of the site. This is a good indicator of more brackish water. Interestingly, at the most southerly tip of the field (encompassing the three monitoring points in this area), there are variable chloride concentrations with depth with no clear pattern. Similarly, to the explanation for the more consistent water-level readings, this may reflect the close proximity of the surrounding drainage ditches which are both draining water from the site and being a source of groundwater to this area. The source of this more brackish water may be the estuarine silty clays underlying the site, or be older and from Jurassic evaporite deposits in the area. Whatever the source, the next stage of this project is to investigate what impact this has on preservation potential in terms of the inorganic and organic remains preserved at the site.

Conclusion

Glastonbury Lake Village is clearly a very complex site and it is only with such intensive and comprehensive monitoring that it has been possible to identify the differing hydrological regimes and spatial variability across the site. Integration of the datasets, in particular the water table, soil moisture, redox potential, and rainfall data, is continuing in order to develop a clearer understanding of the site. This is continuing in tandem with detailed chemical analysis, which provides an opportunity to examine the preservation potential of inorganic artefacts in more detail.

The data presented here suggests that the Glastonbury Lake Village site appears to be at risk of desiccation. As a result there is a clear need for ongoing monitoring to identify whether these trends continue. Small-scale test excavations should also be considered to determine the current preservation state of the artefacts and structures preserved *in situ*.

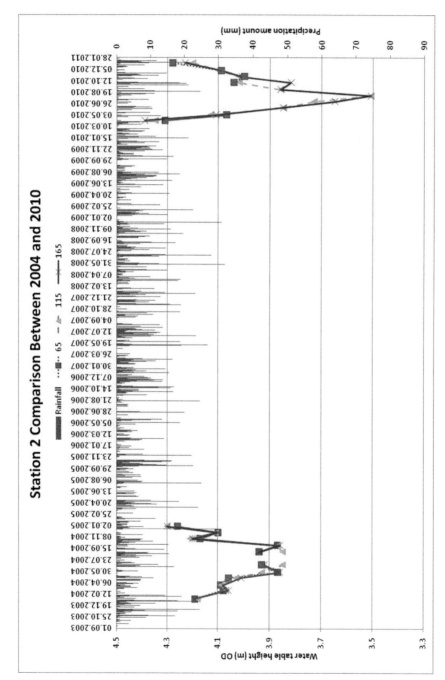

FIGURE 4   Water-table results for location 2 during 2004 and 2010. (Daily rainfall data; UK MET Office, MIDAS data. Yeovilton weather station.)

Acknowledgements

This project is funded by the AHRC and EPSRC (Science and Heritage Programme) with support from Somerset County Council and English Heritage. We acknowledge the advice of Professor J. R. L. Allen, Dr Matthew Almond, Dr Steve Robinson, Dr Stuart Black (University of Reading), Dr Richard Brunning (Somerset County Council), Dr Sebastian Payne and Vanessa Straker (English Heritage), and Glastonbury Antiquarian Society.

Bibliography

Brunning, R., Ramsey, C. B., Cameron, N., Cook, G., Davies, P., Gale, R., Groves, C., Hamilton, W. D., Hogan, D., Jones, J., Jones, M., Kenward, H., Kreiser, A., Locatelli, C., Marshall, P., Tinsley, H., and Tyres I. 2008. *Monuments at Risk in Somerset's Peatlands*. Draft Final Report August 2008. MARISP Project. Somerset County Council Heritage Service. Final Report 3191 MAIN.

Bulleid, A. and Gray, H. 1911 and 1917. *The Glastonbury Lake Village. Vols 1 and 2*. Glastonbury: The Glastonbury Antiquarian Society.

Coles, J. M. and Coles, B. 1986. *Sweet Track to Glastonbury*. London: Thames and Hudson.

Hogan, D. 2008. Monitoring of Burial Environment. In: R. Brunning, C. B. Ramsey, N. Cameron, G. Cook, P. Davies, R. Gale, C. Groves, W. D. Hamilton, D. Hogan, J. Jones, M. Jones, H. Kenward, A. Kreiser, C. Locatelli, P. Marshall, H. Tinsley, and I. Tyres, eds. *Monuments at Risk in Somerset's Peatlands*. Draft Final Report August 2008. MARISP Project. Somerset County Council Heritage Service. Final Report 3191 MAIN.

Jones, L. 2010. *In Situ* Preservation Research and Monitoring in the Somerset Levels: An Interim Report. *Archaeology in the Severn Estuary*, 20: 65–79

Smit, A., van Heeringen, R. M., and Theunissen, E. M. 2006. *Archaeological Monitoring Standard. Guidelines for the Non-Destructive Recording and Monitoring of the Physical Quality of Archaeological Sites and Monuments*. Amersfoort: Nederlandse Archeologische Rapporten 33.

Notes on contributors

Louise Jones has a BSc in Environmental Geology, completed in 2006, and an MSc in Geoarchaeology, completed in 2008, both from the University of Reading. She started her PhD research in 2008, also at the University of Reading, in the Departments of Archaeology, Chemistry, and Geography and Environmental Science. Her research project is focused on monitoring the *in situ* preservation of wetland heritage at two sites in the Somerset Levels. This is funded by the Science and Heritage Programme (AHRC/EPSRC), with additional support from English Heritage and Somerset County Council. A paper was published outlining the initial findings of this project (Jones, 2010).

Correspondence to: Louise Jones, Departments of Chemistry, Archaeology, and Geography and Environmental Science, University of Reading, Whiteknights, Reading, Berkshire RG6 6AB, UK. Email: L.A.Jones@pgr.reading.ac.uk

Martin Bell is Professor of Archaeological Science and Head of the Archaeology Department in the University of Reading. He teaches Geoarchaeology and Coastal and Maritime Archaeology and his research interests include experimental archaeology. Author of a number of books, including *Late Quaternary Environmental Change* (2005, with M. J. C. Walker), *Prehistoric Coastal Communities: The Mesolithic in Western Britain* (2007), and *Prehistoric Intertidal Archaeology* (with A. Caseldine and H. Neumann). He is a fellow of the British Academy and the Society of Antiquaries.

Correspondence to: Martin Bell, Department of Archaeology, University of Reading, UK. Email: m.g.bell@reading.ac.uk

CONSERVATION AND MGMT OF ARCH. SITES, Vol. 14 Nos 1–4, 2012, 126–49

Lowland Floodplain Responses to Extreme Flood Events: Long-Term Studies and Short-Term Microbial Community Response to Water Environment Impacts

Malcolm Lillie

Department of Geography, Environment and Earth Sciences, University of Hull, UK

Isabel Soler

Department of Civil & Structural Engineering, University of Sheffield, UK

Robert Smith

Wetland Archaeology & Environments Research Centre, University of Hull, UK

Targeted studies of waterlogged burial environments allow researchers to gain holistic insights into the physico-chemical and biological condition of wetlands that have the potential to contain organic remains of both anthropogenic and biogenic origin. Recent research has shown that microbial community diversity and functioning are intimately linked to physical and chemical parameters, such that environmental perturbations may have the potential to enhance the effectiveness of microbial communities in the degradation process. Our studies have shown that, as a consequence of the 2007 floods which impacted upon many British lowland rivers, a rapid microbial response to environmental perturbations can be demonstrated within the wetland deposits being monitored. As such, a quantification of the latent functionality of micro-organisms in a soil profile may be of fundamental importance for our understanding of potential *in situ* degradation processes; and, as a consequence, the likelihood for the biodegradation of sensitive archaeo-organic remains; a factor which is of primary importance for both ongoing and future mitigation strategies, and attempts at managing the cultural resource of wetlands.

This paper will present a consideration of the effectiveness of a long-term research project in a lowland wetland at Newington, Nottinghamshire,

    DOI 10.1179/1350503312Z.00000000011

England, studied between 2004 and 2008; and evaluate the efficacy of this study in relation to the significant impacts that occurred as a result of the severe floods in 2007. We conclude that the data generated after the floods necessitated a total re-evaluation of the first approximately two years of environmental monitoring, and that the impacts throughout the sediment profile continued for some time after the initial flood event. These observations potentially have far-reaching implications for future *in situ* monitoring as disruptions to weather patterns influence the various environmental impacts on the wetland resource.

KEYWORDS lowland floodplains, *in situ* preservation, monitoring, microbiology, sustainability

Introduction

This paper reports on a recent monitoring project aimed at assessing how a site needs to be monitored in order to assess the state of the burial environment, and how to establish whether a stable preserving environment is in place. The focus of this paper is an outline of the results of a multidisciplinary study of a lowland floodplain wetland located adjacent to the River Idle at Newington, near the town of Bawtry, Nottinghamshire, England (SK72109650) (Figure 1). This location was studied in an attempt to assess the potential impacts of de-watering on wetland deposits from aggregates extraction due to the potential for a 'halo' effect to emanate from the extraction area as a result of drawdown of the water table (as noted by French, 2004; 2009; French et al., 1999). The study was initiated due to the existence of a proven Late glacial to Holocene palaeoenvironmental record contained within up to 3 m of floodplain peats flanking the River Idle at this location. It was decided that the monitoring project would assess whether the extraction of aggregates adjacent to a floodplain containing 3 m of peat deposits could be shown to impact on the water table (*sensu* French, 2004; 2009), and also whether any changes in the burial environment could be identified over time. The palaeoenvironmental resource in the floodplain area included bog oaks, a number of which had been ploughed out in the past, and the floodplain peats themselves, whilst the archaeological potential of the area was highlighted by the presence of a Late Mesolithic-Neolithic flint scatter immediately adjacent to the floodplain area, beneath a later superficial peat deposit. In addition, crop marks of probable Romano-British date had been identified on the raised sand areas that flanked the floodplain in this location (Lakin and Howard, 2000).

Research undertaken since 1995 has shown that changes in saturation (e.g. water levels, total moisture content), pH, and redox potential can significantly effect *in situ* preservation potential in waterlogged environments (e.g. Caple and Dungworth, 1995; Caple et al., 1997; Hogan et al., 2002; Chapman and Cheetham, 2002; Cheetham, 2004; Corfield, 2007; Lillie, 2007; Lillie and Smith, 2007a; 2007b; 2008; Lillie et al., 2008). The range of degradation processes that occur as a result of the disruption of the anaerobic environment which usually characterizes a waterlogged burial environment are complex and difficult to quantify. In general, the assumption is that wetter is better, although this may well be an oversimplification.

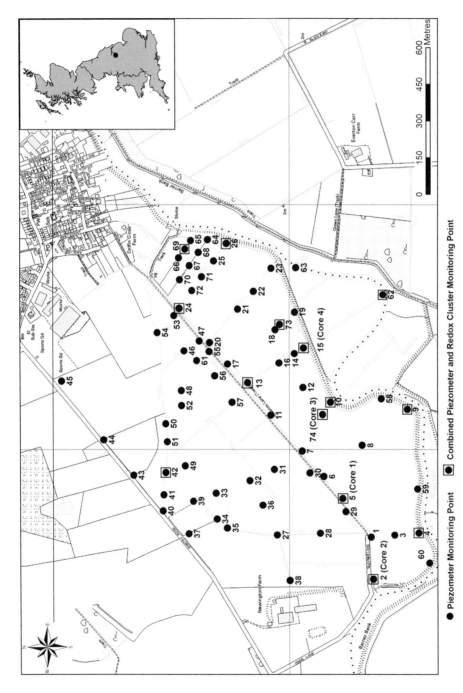

● Piezometer Monitoring Point   ◉ Combined Piezometer and Redox Cluster Monitoring Point

FIGURE 1   Location of the monitoring site and piezometer grid: Points 5 (Core 1) and 15 (Core 4) form the basis of the current study.

In order to reinforce the above observation this paper will outline the variability inherent in waterlogged burial environments through a consideration of a lowland floodplain wetland. As might be anticipated, when studying waterlogged burial environments each site will have its own specific context/s with a differing set of variables that have created the burial environment being studied. Factors such as geology, soil condition, hydrology, landscape history, and physical disruptions/anthropogenic impacts to the burial environment will all have influenced the environment as it has developed. The range of threats to the resource is diverse and has the potential to impact upon the waterlogged burial environment in a myriad of ways. Fundamentally, any disruption to the *in situ* conditions within the burial environment has the potential to promote biodegradation processes by both aerobic and anaerobic micro-organisms.

In this context there are a number of recent studies that have sought to characterize the microbiological component of waterlogged burial environments and their relationship to *in situ* preservation of waterlogged archaeological remains (e.g. Björdal et al., 1999; 2000; Blanchette, 2000; Helms et al., 2004; Jans et al., 2004; Kim et al., 1996; Klaassen, 2005). More recently, we have begun to investigate the nature of the soil microbial community with a view to assessing community diversity and functioning (Douterelo et al., 2009; 2010) so as to expand upon recent research into the microbial degradation of the archaeo-organic resource (e.g. Blanchette et al., 1990; Donaldson and Singh, 1990; Hedges, 1990; Kim, 1990; Blanchette and Hoffmann, 1994; Blanchette, 1995; Powell et al., 2001).

The study site

This study was initiated as a response to the threat of aggregates extraction in an area immediately to the north of the floodplain at Newington (Figure 1). The floodplain area itself is located on the north side of the River Idle as it follows a meandering north-easterly route past the town of Bawtry, up to the point where it joins the River Trent at West Stockwith. The study site lies in an area of subdued topography which ranges from between *c.* 2–3 m AOD (Above [UK] Ordnance Datum), rising to *c.* 6–8 m AOD to the north of the floodplain (SK72109650). The floodplain area, which lies to the south and east of Slaynes Lane (and which runs between boreholes 1 and 53 in Figure 1), comprises intensively farmed arable land. The landowner informed us of the addition of nitrates and agro-chemicals, during the preparation of the area for planting in May of 2007 (i.e. prior to the July 2007 floods in England). The flood waters were contaminated by effluent from adjacent pig and cattle farms, as the slurry pits of both were compromised during this event. In development terms this area will be converted to an open water wetland habitat after removal of the *c.* 3 m of floodplain peats and the subsequent quarrying of the underlying sands and gravels has ceased.

The floodplain peats vary in thickness, from a thin *c.* 0.3–0.5 m deposit to the north and west of Slaynes Lane up to *c.* 3 m of continuous peat to the south and west of Slaynes Lane, extending eastwards to the modern canalized course of the River Idle. The sands and gravels that underlie the floodplain exhibit an undulating topography, and a sand levee runs in a southwest to northeast direction between monitoring points 5 and 72 (Figure 1), resulting in a thinning of the floodplain peats in the areas immediately adjacent to Slaynes Lane.

The monitoring that was undertaken at Newington commenced with a detailed borehole and palaeoenvironmental study, followed by a general study of the hydrology of the catchment area, and a more detailed study of the physico-chemical parameters of the floodplain area using 72 piezometer clusters (Lillie et al., 2008). The piezometers comprise 1.0 m, 2.0 m, and 3.0 m long PVC tubes of 19 mm internal diameter. Attached to the buried end of the tube is a piezometer tip of 300 mm length, consisting of a perforated PVC tube containing a filter membrane designed to prevent contamination from surrounding soil. An acoustic sounder measured the level of the water table.

In addition to the hydrological survey, 14 redox clusters were located adjacent to a number of the piezometer monitoring points, and four locations in the floodplain were monitored with the addition of through-the-profile analysis (i.e. analysis at systematic depths from the ground surface down to a maximum of c. 3 m depth) of hydrology, redox, pH, temperature, and conventional microbiological methods (extracellular enzyme activity and ^{14}C-leucine assimilation) (Cores 1–4 in Figure 1).

Conventional microbiological methods

Prior to conventional microbiological analysis, 5 g wet weight of each soil sample was weighed and made up to 30 ml using 0.2 μm filtered, sterile, pure water. The slurry was transferred into a sterile polythene bag and homogenized in a stomacher (Colworth Lab Blender 400, A. J. Seward Ltd, London) for 5 min. Subsequently, the contents of the polythene bag were transferred into a 50 ml sterile glass beaker. 20 ml of 0.2 μm filtered, sterile, pure water are then used to rinse the remaining slurry from the bag. This produced a soil concentration of 100 g wet weight l^{-1}. In the current study the slurries were used to determine extracellular enzyme activity and ^{14}C-leucine assimilation. The extracellular enzyme activity assayed β-glucosidase, phosphatase, and leucine aminopeptidase activity through the profile.

We studied soil extracellular enzyme activities as these are primarily responsible for organic matter (OM) decomposition (Sinsabaugh et al., 1991; Tabatabai, 1994; Kang and Freeman, 1998; McLatchey and Reddy, 1998; Dick et al., 2000; Nannipieri et al., 2002). OM in wetlands is mainly comprised of complex polysaccharides such as cellulose and lignin which are broken down into simple monomers by extracellular enzyme activity (Sinsabaugh et al., 1991). Extracellular enzymes play an important role within soil ecology as they are involved in the cycling of nutrients, reflect microbial activity and act as indicators of physico-chemical change in soil (Burns, 1982). Microbial enzymatic activity is very sensitive to fluctuation in external factors (Bandick and Dick, 1999) and is an inexpensive and easy technique to employ; for this reason enzymatic assays have been widely used to study the effect of environmental change in soil (e.g. Nannipieri et al., 1990; Acosta Martinez et al., 2003; Trasar-Cepeda et al., 2008; Kolehmainen et al., 2009). The potential for enzyme synthesis is determined by the abundance and composition of the microbial community present in soil, as a consequence changes in microbial communities associated with environmental factors should be reflected in enzyme activity (Kandeler et al., 1996).

^{14}C-leucine assimilation was used to evaluate the effect of nutrient enrichment (nitrogen [N] and phosphorous [P]) in sediment suspensions from different depths. This method provides additional information regarding the activity of anaerobic bacteria as ^{14}C-leucine assimilation rate provides a measure of total bacterial activity with depth (Kirchman et al., 1985). Recent research (Douterelo et al., 2009) has confirmed this observation, and also suggested that greater levels of ^{14}C-leucine assimilation can occur during the warmer months and lower levels during the colder months, and also that leucine assimilation rates were higher under aerobic conditions than under anaerobic conditions. Furthermore, these authors also demonstrated a positive correlation between bacterial abundance and ^{14}C-leucine assimilation (Douterelo et al., 2009: 799).

Measurement of extracellular enzyme activities

Enzyme activities were estimated using a substrate containing fluorogenic 4-methyl-umbelliferone for phosphatase and β-D-glucosidase and 7-amido- 4-methylcoumarin for leucine aminopeptidase. For each of the enzyme assays, three replicates of 1 g wet wt l^{-1} for each soil sample were used and blank controls were prepared by boiling the samples for 5 min. Enzyme substrate was added to a final concentration of 200 μmol l^{-1} and samples were incubated in darkness for 5 h at 10° C. After incubation, the samples were centrifuged at 2225 RCF for 5 min and a 5 ml aliquot was then added to 0.4 ml of pH 10 borate buffer solution. The fluorescence intensity was measured using a fluorometer, which was fitted with an excitation filter 10-069 and an emission filter combination 10-059 and 10-061. The model-substrate concentration used in the assays represented a saturation concentration. As a consequence, the rate of substrate hydrolysis measured approximated to V_{max} (Brown and Goulder, 1996; see also Nannipieri et al., 1990; Hoppe, 1993; Goulder, 1990).

Evaluating ^{14}C-leucine assimilation

The current project evaluated the effect of nutrient enrichment (nitrogen [N] and phosphorous [P]) upon ^{14}C-leucine assimilation in soil suspensions from different depths. This method provides additional information regarding the activity of anaerobic bacteria.

Soil samples were homogenized into slurries as described in section 2.3. Leucine assimilation was assayed using the method of Ainsworth and Goulder (2000a; 2000b; also Goulder, 1991). ^{14}C-leucine solution (0.1 ml; c. 0.1μCi, L-[U-^{14}C] Leucine) was added to 10 ml of each of 3 replicates of 1.0 g l^{-1} soil suspension, in sterile universal bottles and to a blank with formalin 2% (w/v) and final concentration of leucine 32 nmol l^{-1} (Tulonen, 1993). Samples were incubated in darkness at 10° C for 5 h. At the end of the incubation period, 2 ml sub-samples were concentrated on 2.5 cm diameter cellulose acetate membrane filters (0.2 μm pore size). The filters were washed through with 5 ml of 0.2 μm filtered sdH$_2$O and were then transferred to scintillation vials which contained 10 ml of scintillation fluid. The radioactivity in the vials was assayed by liquid scintillation counting. The radioactivity of the ^{14}C-leucine solution that had been added to the incubation was determined by adding 10 μl of the ^{14}C-leucine solution to the scintillation vials containing 10 ml of scintillation fluid.

Results

The results of the analysis at Newington have shown that there are seasonal variations in floodplain hydrology (Lillie et al., 2008). At the wider catchment level of analysis however, the ground water table is suppressed due to over abstraction, which results in a perched water table within the floodplain peats due to drying out and mineralization of the organic matrix near the surface. In addition to the observations in relation to floodplain and catchment hydrology, it is apparent that, immediately prior to the June 2007 flood event (in May 2007) the water table throughout the floodplain area was very low, with significant water depths only being recorded in the area of the Site of Special Scientific Interest (SSSI) at this location (Figure 2) (although prior to this between February 2005 and February 2007, the opposite situation occurred) (Lillie et al., 2008).

Rainfall patterns were reducing from March onwards (Figs 4b and 5b), and desiccation cracks were visible in the floodplain area due to drying out of the superficial floodplain deposits. Even after the flood event the water table within the floodplain area was only elevated in those areas adjacent to the River Idle, and recharge of the floodplain peats progressed slowly. By November 2007 the floodplain peats were exhibiting a water deficit, being dryer in areas to the west of the floodplain than in May 2007 (Figure 3), and also dryer in the area of the SSSI when compared to the May monitoring. Lillie and Smith (2008: 58) recorded soil moisture contents of between 30–80 per cent in the upper 1m of the floodplain peats through the duration of the monitoring programme, with moisture content generally increasing with depth through-the-profile. However, values as low as 15–70 per cent were recorded at cores 2 and 4 in June and August of 2007, and in core 3 a marked reduction in moisture content occurs at depth, with a shift from moisture content values of $c.$ 80 per cent at 1 m depth being reversed to values of $c.$ 20–30 per cent at 1.75 m depth between June 2007 and January 2008.

Water-level measurements, redox potential values and conventional microbial results for Core 1 (Piezometer Point 5/Redox Cluster 3) (Figures 1 and 4)

We present the results of the analysis of cores 1 and 4 separately as the information generated for each core highlight the fact that at each location the specific *in situ* conditions indicate variability through-the-profile, both in terms of key soil parameters (e.g. hydrology, redox, pH, and temperature), reactions to changes in season water budgets and the reactions that occur as a result of the flood event. In addition, the data demonstrate that the variations in evidence in terms of physico-chemical parameters at each location produce a differing set of reactions in terms of the conventional microbiological analyses undertaken.

Water-level measurements

Figure 4a displays the piezometer measurements collected at 1 m, 2 m, and 3 m depths throughout the duration of the monitoring programme. Figure 4b presents the associated redox values at 0.1 m, 0.5 m, 1 m, and 2 m depths.

Throughout the duration of monitoring there is evidence for a general comparability between the piezometer measurements obtained at the lower depths (Figure 4a). These results suggest that the water level at this location is both rainfall fed and groundwater fed (i.e. there is a perched water table). Piezometers readings at this location indicate that the water level in the shallow piezometer (1 m depth) is

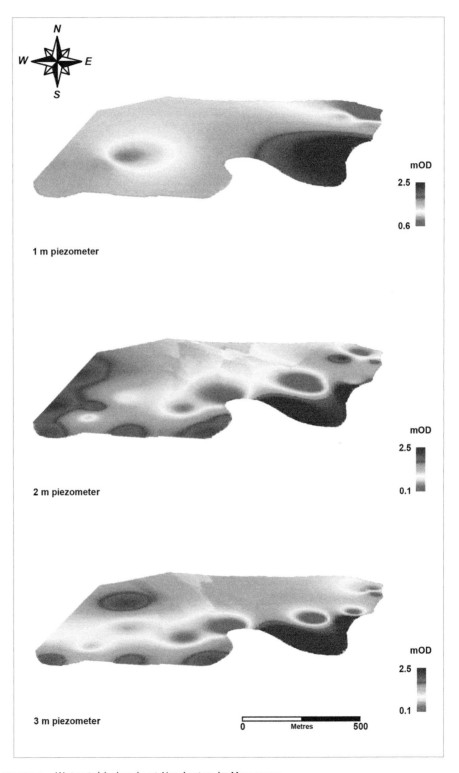

FIGURE 2   Water table levels at Newington in May 2007.

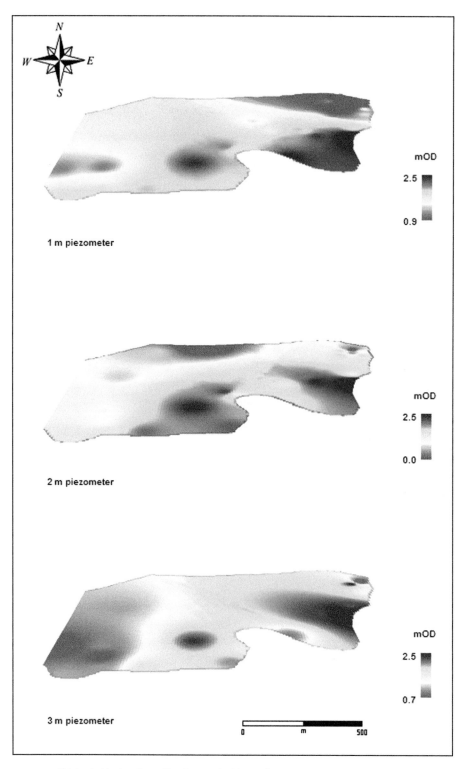

FIGURE 3   Water table levels at Newington in November 2007.

a

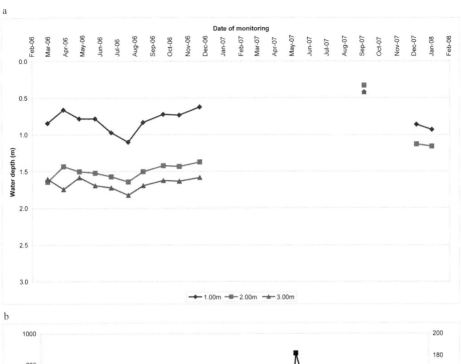

b

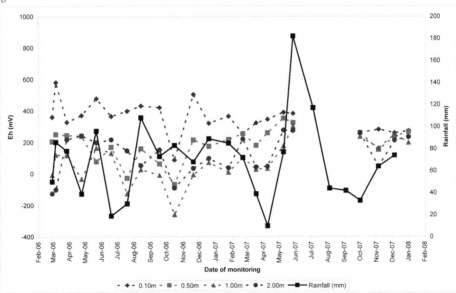

FIGURE 4   Water-level measurements, redox potential values, and conventional microbiological results from Core 1 over the duration of the monitoring programme.

c

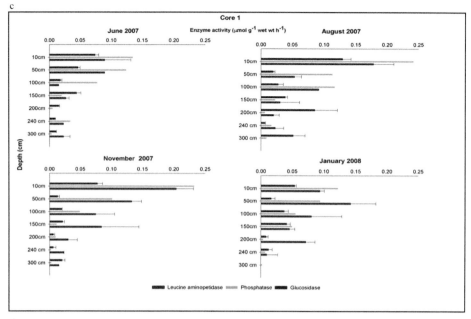

d

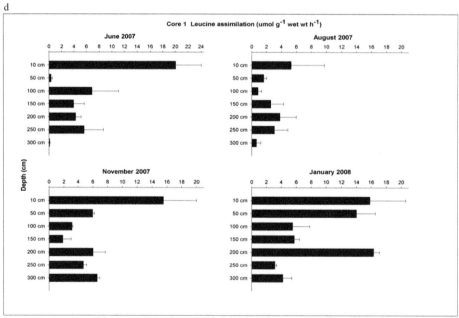

FIGURE 4   Continued.

generally between *c.* 0.6 m and 1.1 m below the ground surface throughout the dura-tion of monitoring. The water level in the 2 m piezometer is between *c.* 1.4 m and 1.7 m below the ground level; and the water level in the 3 m piezometer is between *c.* 1.6 m and 1.8 m below ground level. This suggests that the floodplain has a perched, shallow, superficial water table that is divorced from the ground water table for the majority of the year. There are however two exceptions to this general trend; these are discussed in greater detail below.

Note:
- Due to vandalism on site there are no readings available for the period January–June 2007. Replacement piezometers were installed in June 2007, one week before the subsequent flood event. As a consequence of standing water on-site following the flood event, it was only possible to obtain readings for the monitoring visit in September 2007.
- The last two monitoring visits made to site (December 2007 and January 2008) indicated that there was a re-establishment of similar conditions prior to the flood. (Further destruction of the deepest piezometer point [by 4x4 vehicles] prevented the collection of data at this depth during the last two months of monitoring.)

Redox potential values

The standard classification used to define the redox status of soils originated from the research by Patrick and Mahapatra (1968) who assessed well-drained and waterlogged sediments during studies of rice production. This research determined that values >+400 mV indicate oxidized conditions, values between +100 mV to +400 mV are indicative of moderately reducing conditions, values between −100 mV to +100 mV highlight reduced conditions and values between −300 mV to −100 mV indicate highly reduced conditions.

The corresponding redox values obtained throughout the monitoring programme (Figure 3b) indicate that there are differences in the oxidizing/reducing nature of the floodplain peats at this location. These differences can be seen in the peat profile. Although the majority of the redox values obtained from the surface of the peats (0.10 m depth) vary between +600 mV (indicating oxidized conditions) and +300 mV (which are indicative of moderately reduced conditions), the redox values collected from the remaining three depths (0.5 m, 1 m, and 2 m) are generally lower. The majority of the values fall between +350mV (indicating moderately reducing condi-tions) and −250 mV (indicative of highly reducing conditions). These results suggest that while there is no water input from Slaynes Lane ditch into the peats at 0.1 m depth, there appears to be a degree of water ingress, resulting in sustained saturation, at 0.5 m, 1 m, and 2 m depths. Whilst the ditch receives water from the pumping activities associated with the aggregates extraction at this location the water at depth is probably stagnant, and it maintains the saturation of the deposits adjacent to it.

No seasonal trends are evident in the redox values obtained from 0.5 m, 1 m, and 2 m depths. However, seasonality is evident in the redox values collected from 0.1 m depth, with the summer months generally producing higher redox values and the winter months producing lower redox values.

The gap in the data between the June and September of 2007 is associated with the flood event (June 2007), and the subsequent standing water on site at this location.

(The height of the piezometer tips above the ground surface [*c.* 0.15 m] enabled water readings to be obtained, even though it was not possible to collect redox potential values.)

The redox values obtained from October 2007 until the end of the monitoring programme are similar to those collected prior to the flood event. An exception to this pattern is the redox values at 0.1 m depth which display lower values commensurate with the readings obtained from the remaining three depths. These findings suggest that the upper 10 cm of the peat profile is experiencing moderately reducing conditions. The three different extracellular enzyme and ^{14}C-leucine assimilation studies were undertaken in order to assess bacterial activity throughout the peat profiles at both of the cores studied.

Extracellular enzyme activity

Figure 4c shows the extracellular enzyme activity at different depth intervals between June 2007 and January 2008. Enzyme activity tended to decrease with depth throughout the sediment profile. There were, however, anomalous peaks recorded in the deeper strata; e.g. leucine aminopeptidase at 100 cm depth and glucosidase at 250 cm and 300 cm depths, in August 2007; and leucine aminopeptidase at 200 cm depth in January 2008.

Greater enzyme activity was recorded in August and November of 2007, particularly in the upper 50 cm of the sediment profile. It is suggested that the flood event in June 2007 (followed by standing water on the surface at this location for several months thereafter) is responsible for the changes in enzyme activity at/near the surface of the peat deposit. Levels of measured enzyme activity at both depths decrease in January of 2008, and are comparable to the enzyme activity in June 2007, that is, immediately before the flood event.

In general, the highest level of enzyme activity was produced by phosphatase throughout the peat profile in August and November of 2007 (i.e. after the June flood event). The highest levels of activity in the remaining sampling periods (June 2007 and January 2008) were indicated by leucine aminopeptidase.

^{14}C-leucine assimilation

Figure 4d shows the ^{14}C-leucine assimilation at different depth intervals. In general, throughout the duration of monitoring, ^{14}C-leucine assimilation rates were higher in the upper 10 cm of the sediment profile than at greater depth. An exception to this pattern is the ^{14}C-leucine at 200 cm depth in the January of 2008.

Throughout the rest of the sediment profile, ^{14}C-leucine assimilation rates remain similar between monitoring periods. There are however exceptions to this patterning; at 50 cm and 300 cm depths in June 2007, at 150 cm depth in November 2007 and at 200 cm depth in January 2008. Furthermore, the flooding event of June 2007 appears to have a marked impact on ^{14}C-leucine assimilation rates in the upper 50 cm of the sediment profile during August of 2007. However, the ^{14}C-leucine assimilation measurements obtained from the November 2007 sampling indicates values comparable to the June 2007 and January 2008 monitoring periods. The highest ^{14}C-leucine assimilation rate over the monitoring period was observed in June 2007 at 10 cm depth (*c.* 20 µmol g^{-1} h^{-1}).

As has been noted in our previous work (Douterelo et al., 2009; 2010), low ^{14}C-leucine assimilation rates in the deeper horizons of the soil profile might indicate that most bacteria are inactive or have very slow metabolic rates (Hopkins, 1998; Welch and Thomas, 1998; D'Hondt et al., 2002). The variations in ^{14}C assimilation occurring through-the-profile at Core 1 indicates that the bacterial communities are inhibited in their activity as a direct result of the flood event, but that this reduced activity is relatively short-lived, with a resumption to pre-flood levels of activity (and at certain depths increases in activity) occurring by November of 2007. In addition, differential reactions are in evidence as at depths of 50 cm and 300 cm in Core 1 the post flood ^{14}C-leucine assimilation rates are greater than those in evidence prior to the flood.

Water-level measurements, redox potential values and conventional microbial results for Core 4 (Piezometer point 15/Redox cluster 6) (Figures 1 and 5)

Water-level measurements

Figure 5a presents the piezometer measurements collected at 1 m and 2 m depths throughout the duration of the monitoring programme in Core 4. Figure 5b presents the associated redox values at 0.1 m, 0.5 m, 1 m, and 2 m depths.

There is only limited data available from the 1 m piezometer throughout the duration of the monitoring. The lack of data from the 1 m piezometer prior to the flood event indicates that the water level in the peats was consistently below this depth (as confirmed during sampling) from the outset of the programme, until the time of the 2007 flooding.

There is some evidence for seasonal variability in the water-level data obtained from the 2 m piezometer at this location prior to the flood. The lack of data available between July and October 2006 clearly indicates that the water table has fallen below 2 m below the surface of the floodplain at this location across the summer of 2006. Water levels then rise consistently through the winter of 2006 and through until February 2007 (Lillie et al., 2008). The reductions in water levels through until April 2007 mirror the rainfall data for this period (Figure 5b).

In general, the results from this location indicate that the water depth in the peats is consistently at or c. 2 m below the ground surface. The elevated water levels in evidence across the winter of 2006–07 reflect sustained rainfall patterning from September 2006 through until February 2007.

Following the flood event (June 2007) water-level readings at both depths decreased gradually from near the surface of the peats to c. 0.6 m (as displayed in the 1 m piezometer) and c. 0.75 m depths (as displayed in the 2 m piezometer). However, further monitoring at this location would have been necessary in order to identify any significant trends in the data after the end of the monitoring programme.

Redox potential values

The corresponding redox values (Figure 5b) indicate that there is a general separation of values in relation to the depth of the peats at this location. The redox values obtained at 0.1 m depth between the onset of monitoring (February 2006) and the flood event (June 2007) (with the exception of the readings obtained between

February and April 2006) generally indicate that the peats are oxidizing (+650 mV to +350 mV), and that redox reactions correspond to the rainfall patterning in evidence (especially between July 2006 and June 2007). In contrast to this, the majority of the redox values (with the exception of May–June 2006) obtained from 0.50 m depth indicates that the peat is displaying moderately reducing conditions (between +400 mV and +100 mV).

The redox values obtained at 1 m depth between the onset of monitoring and the flood event display variable patterning; with fluctuations in readings indicating moderately reducing conditions (i.e. +400 m to +100 mV) between May 2006 and March 2007, which contrast with the oxidizing conditions (>+400 mV) occurring between February–April 2006 and April–June 2007. Contrasting redox values are also displayed at 2 m depth between February 2006 and June 2007. During this period redox values vary from *c*. +300 mV (indicating moderately reducing conditions) to *c*. −175 mV (indicative of highly reduced conditions).

The variable patterning at 1 m and 2 m depths suggests that there is a general decrease in redox values throughout the profile of the peats at this location, ranging from oxidizing conditions which are present at the surface of the peat, to highly reducing conditions which are experienced at 2 m depth. The low level of water at this location (to a depth of >1.7 m below the surface of the floodplain for the majority of this period), suggests that separate rainfall events may be responsible for the variation in redox values displayed at the three upper depths within the peat profile (i.e. those above 1.7–2 m), with some suggestion that more stable conditions persist around the 2 m boundary.

There is a lacuna of redox data between the June and October of 2007 due to standing water on-site from the flood event (June 2007). The redox values obtained from November 2007 up until the end of the monitoring programme indicate that moderately reducing conditions are evident throughout the profile. The similarity in redox values during this period has not been identified previously in the monitoring results, and this might suggest that the slow infiltration of flood waters into the peats (over a period of five months) has created similar conditions throughout the soil profile.

Extracellular enzyme activity

Figure 5c shows the extracellular enzyme activity at different depth intervals. Data for the three assayed enzyme activities showed a general increase in phosphatase in the upper 50 cm of the sediment profile, which was followed by a decrease thereafter to the base of the peats. Enzyme activity which was displayed by leucine aminopeptidase and glucosidase also decreased with an increase in sediment depth.

There is, however, a notable exception to the decline of leucine aminopeptidase and glucosidase with depth. In the November of 2007, high levels of leucine aminopeptidase were recorded throughout the sediment profile. However, it is not possible to suggest reasons for this anomaly without further enzyme activity measurements being obtained in the future.

[14]C-leucine assimilation

Figure 5d shows the ^{14}C-leucine assimilation rates at different depth intervals. There is a significant difference between the June 2007 monitoring period and the other

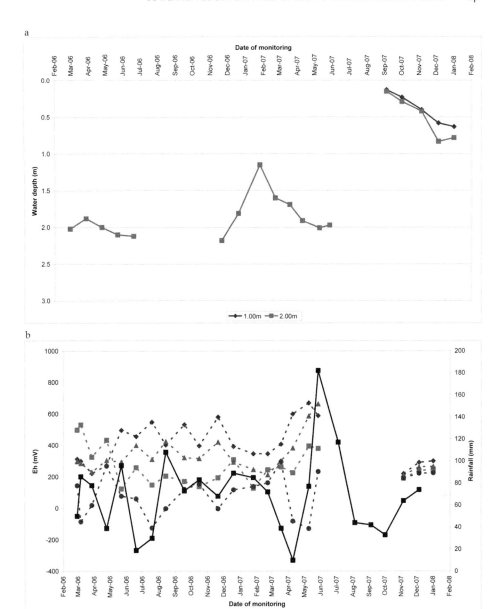

FIGURE 5   Water-level measurements, redox potential values, and conventional microbiological results from Core 4 over the duration of the monitoring programme.

c

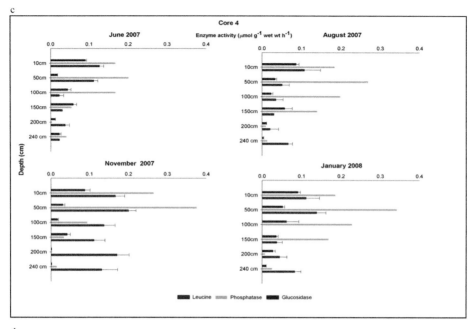

d

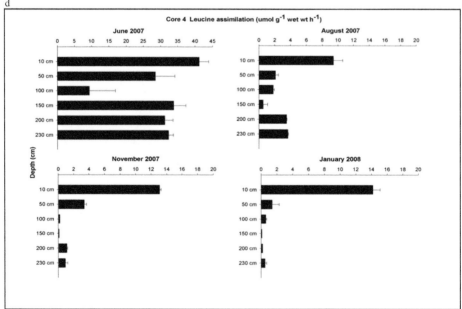

FIGURE 5   Continued.

three monitoring periods (August and November 2007, and January 2008). ^{14}C-leucine assimilation rates throughout the peat profile are very high prior to the flood, suggesting high levels of bacterial activity when compared to that in evidence after the flood (-with the exception of the values at 10 cm depths). The highest rates occurred at the surface of the peat (*c.* 41 μmol g^{-1} h^{-1}).

The ^{14}C-leucine assimilation rates obtained throughout the peat profile for the remaining three monitoring periods after the flood (with the exception of the surface samples) exhibit values, obtained from the November 2007 and January 2008 monitoring periods, which indicate that there are relatively low levels of ^{14}C-leucine assimilation below 10 cm depth. The data suggest that these levels may be indicating that the burial environment has been compromised to the point where microbial activity is being suppressed.

Discussion and conclusions

The analyses undertaken at Newington have sought to establish the questions which need to be asked when undertaking a monitoring project that extend beyond 'simply' trying to determine how and how long a site should be monitored. When attempting to characterize a location such as a river floodplain, fundamentals such as site context, catchment hydrology, sedimentology, the nature of the archaeo-environmental resource, and the material preserved within in, external and internal variables, and longer term environmental perturbations in an everchanging and unpredictable climate can all be implicated in whether a stable preserving environment is in place, and whether a site is potentially sustainable into the future. At Newington, the entire project has sought to assess the majority of these parameters. However, as outlined above, long-term dewatering at the catchment level, and the 2007 flood event, combine to produce differing responses in the burial environment, with these responses being dependent on the prevailing *in situ* conditions at cores 1 and 4.

The positive aspect of the study is that, perhaps with the obvious exception of extreme weather events, many of the variables discussed throughout this paper can be assessed, evaluated and accounted for in a systematic and established manner (e.g. French, 2009). However, it should be stressed that such an assessment requires a multidisciplinary approach to the study of the site, its environmental context and its landscape context. French (2009: 62) has noted this, pointing out that 'every site's landscape dynamics contribute to its individual hydrological setting, each case is different and requires tailored monitoring programmes to protect the archaeological and palaeo-environmental record from the adverse effects of water abstraction associated with development schemes'.

We would reinforce this observation, but modify it with the inclusion of the caveat that it is not simply the adverse effects of a development scheme that impact upon the archaeo- and environmental resource; you can have too little water (as occurs in the catchment at Newington due to over abstraction), but equally you can have too much water, or even the wrong type of water (!), as highlighted by the impacts witnessed at Newington as a result of the 2007 floods. In addition, the input of nitrates during arable farming practices at this location in May 2007, is considered to contribute to the high rate of ^{14}C-leucine assimilation shown in the upper levels of the peat profile. Furthermore, whilst French reports that the reinstatement of the ground water table, pH, conductivity, redox and dissolved oxygen values in the ground water system at Over, Cambridgeshire had ostensibly been restored to pre-extraction levels, there is no way to assess how the microbial communities had responded to the environmental perturbations at this site, or as French notes 'manifestation of any organic degradation *was* not [. . .] proven by "appropriate" analysis, *but* there was sufficient time for degradation to occur' (2009: 73).

This situation is exacerbated at sites such as Newington as, whilst we were able to demonstrate (variably) enhanced/reduced and/or compromised microbial activity prior to the 2007 floods (Lillie and Smith, 2008: 97) and identify changes in activity after the flood event, it was not possible to continue our monitoring through until equilibrium with the pre-flood activity was established. As such we have proven that microbiological activity occurs differentially at cores 1 and 4 as a result of the 2007 floods, but we could not monitor the activity for its full duration. However, as noted above, the extracellular enzyme activities do provide an indication of organic matter (OM) decomposition, and play an important role within soil ecology as they are involved in the cycling of nutrients, reflect microbial activity and act as indicators of physico-chemical change in soil. The ^{14}C leucine assimilation analysis was aimed at providing additional information regarding the activity of anaerobic bacteria as ^{14}C-leucine assimilation rates provide a measure of total bacterial activity with depth (Kirchman et al., 1985). As such, the results demonstrate that microbial activity is occurring to significant depths within the floodplain peats, and that the flood event causes differential disruptions in the rate and duration of activity depending on the location that is studied.

Following on from the observations made by French (2009: 73), we would add that although our study was able to identify variations in microbial activity, it was not possible to determine just how much organic degradation occurred as a result of changes in the burial environment at Newington. Nevertheless, long-term sustainability must be in doubt as re-establishment of the physico-chemical values prior to the flood was not determined during the monitoring programme. Even if this had been established however, the *in situ* conditions at Newington were presumably already compromised prior to aggregates extraction due to long term over abstraction in the catchment, as the presence of a perched water table would suggest, with the specific *in situ* context at Newington varying depending on which part of the floodplain was being monitored. As the results of the extracellular enzyme activity and ^{14}C-leucine assimilation studies at Newington have shown, the flood event results in considerable variations in the response of the bacterial communities through the profile between cores 1 and 4. Increases in microbial activity through-the-profile at Newington clearly indicate the potential for increased organic matter decomposition; conversely, reduced microbial activity will offer the potential to inhibit organic matter decomposition. Identification of the factors responsible for increases/reductions in microbial activity may provide the potential to control these variables in the future.

However, in light of the above observations, we believe that the current study highlights a fundamental flaw in longer-term monitoring projects as, in this instance, funding ceased before the monitoring of the post-flood burial environment was completed, thereby leaving numerous questions unanswered.

In situ studies must be designed to account for the specific detail of each site's environmental and archaeological context, and whilst there are a number of parameters that can be assessed to ensure that valuable and informative insights into the burial environment can be obtained, the duration of monitoring will be dependent upon the nature of the impacts and the re-establishment of pre-impact conditions at a site. We would argue that the addition of the assessment of microbial community functioning to 'standard' baseline parameters such as moisture content, pH, redox potential and temperature (amongst others), enhances our ability to reliably determine the nature and duration of impacts, but in the case of Newington a longer-term study was required. French's work at Over comprised a total of fifty-two months of monitoring and many parameters were re-established to the pre-impact state. However, long-term *in situ* sustainability could still be questioned despite this exceptional study (in a British context at least), as the microbial component variable of the burial environment remains an unknown.

Finally, it is now apparent that we must take a pro-active approach to the potential impacts of future climate change scenarios in addition to immediate threats such as aggregates extraction, water abstraction, and development or 'restoration' impacts if we ever hope to achieve the nirvana of sustainable *in situ* preservation in waterlogged burial environments.

Acknowledgements

The authors would like to thank our funders, English Heritage and MIRO, for the help and assistance that they gave during the project, and we would especially like to thank Ian Panter (formerly English Heritage) for all the help and support we received whilst he oversaw this project. The extraction company, Hansons (now Heidelberg Cement in the UK) provided a considerable amount of help with the project, both in terms of access to the site, and access to their own hydrological data for the Newington area. Finally, numerous colleagues helped with the earlier stages of the project, provided advice and information on the equipment used in the monitoring and gave opinions on the project as it developed, and the two reviewers of this paper pointed out a number of flaws in our attempts at summarizing the vast quantity of data that we generated during the project, our thanks are extended to you all. As usual, any errors are our own.

Bibliography

Acosta-Martinez, V., Zobeck, T. M., Gill, T. E., and Kennedy, A. C. 2003. Enzyme Activities and Microbial Community Structure in Semiarid Agricultural Soils. *Biology and Fertility of Soils*, 38: 216–27.

Ainsworth, A. M. and Goulder, R. 2000a. Epilithic and Planktonic Leucine Aminopeptidase Activity and Leucine Assimilation Along the River Tweed, Scottish Borders. *Sciences of the Total Environment*, 251/252: 83–93.

Ainsworth, A. M. and Goulder, R. 2000b. The Effects of Sewage-Works Effluent on Riverine Extracellular Aminopeptidase Activity and Microbial Leucine Assimilation. *Water Research*, 34: 2551–57.

Bandick, A. K. and Dick, R. P. 1999. Field Management Effects on Soil Enzyme Activities. *Soil Biology and Biochemistry*, 31: 1471–79.

Björdal, C. G., Nilsson, T., and Daniel. G. 1999. Microbial Decay of Waterlogged Archaeological Wood Found in Sweden: Applicable to Archaeology and Conservation. *International Biodeterioration and Biodegradation*, 43: 63–73.

Björdal, C. G., Daniel, G., and Nilsson, T. 2000. Depth of Burial, an Important Factor in controlling Bacterial Decay of Waterlogged Archaeological Poles. *International Biodeterioration and Biogradation*, 45: 15–26.

Blanchette, R. A. 1995. Biodeterioration of Archaeological Wood. *Biodeterioration Abstracts*, 9(2): 113–27.

Blanchette, R. A. 2000. A Review of Microbial Deterioration Found in Archaeological Wood from Different Environments. *International Biodeterioration and Biodegradation*, 46: 189–204.

Blanchette, R. A. and Hoffmann, P. 1994. Degradation Processes in Waterlogged Archaeological Wood. In: P. Hoffmann, ed. *Proceedings of the 5th ICOM Group on Wet Organic Archaeological Materials Conference, Portland, Maine 1993*. International Council of Museums, Committee for Conservation. Bremerhaven, Germany: Druckerei Ditzen GmbH & Co. KG, pp. 111–23.

Blanchette, R. A., Nilsson, T., Daniel, G., and Abad, A. 1990. Biological Degradation of Wood. Archaeological Wood Properties, Chemistry, and Preservation. Developed from a symposium sponsored by the Cellulose Paper and Textile Division at the 196th National Meeting of the American Chemical Society, Los Angeles, California, September 25–September 30, 1988. *Advances in Chemistry Series*, 225: 141–74.

Brown, S. E. and Goulder, R. 1996. Extracellular Enzyme Activity in Trout-Farm Effluents and a Recipient River. *Aquaculture Research*, 27: 895–901.

Burns, R. G. 1982. Enzyme Activity in Soil: Location and Possible Role in Microbial Ecology. *Soil Biology and Biochemistry*, 14: 423–27.

Caple, C. and Dungworth, D. 1995 Investigations into Waterlogged Burial Environments. In: A. Sinclair, E. Slater, and J. Goaulett, eds. *Archaeological Sciences 1995: Proceedings of a Conference on the Application of Scientific Techniques to the Study of Archaeology*, Oxbow Monograph, Oxford, pp. 233–40.

Caple, C., Dungworth, D., and Clogg, P. 1997. Results of the Characterisation of the Anoxic Waterlogged Environments which Preserve Archaeological Organic Materials. In: P. Hoffmann, P. Daley, T. Grant, J. A. Spriggs, eds. *Proceedings of the ICOM Group on Wet Organic Materials Conference, York 1996*. International Council of Museums, Committee for Conservation. Bremerhaven, Germany: Druckerei Ditzen GmbH & Co. KG, pp. 5–71.

Chapman, H. P. and Cheetham, J. L. 2002. Monitoring and Modelling Saturation as a Proxy Indicator for *In Situ* Preservation of Wetlands – a GIS-Based Approach. *Journal of Archaeological Science*, 29: 277–89.

Cheetham, J. L. 2004. An Assessment of the Potential for In Situ Preservation of Buried Organic Archaeological Remains at Sutton Common, South Yorkshire. Unpublished PhD thesis, University of Hull, Hull.

Corfield, M. 2007. Wetland Science. In: M. C. Lillie, S. Ellis, eds. *Wetland Archaeology and Environments: Regional Issues, Global Perspectives*. Oxford: Oxbow, pp. 143–55.

D'Hondt, S., Rutherford, S. and Spivack, A. J. 2002. Metabolic Activity of Subsurface Life in Deep-Sea Sediments. *Science*, 295: 2067–70.

Dick, W. A., Cheng, L., and Wang. P. 2000. Soil Acid Alkaline Phosphatase Activity as pH Adjustment Indicators. *Soil Biology and Biochemistry*, 32: 1915–19.

Donaldson, L. A. and Singh, A. P. 1990. Ultrastructure of Terminalia Wood from an Ancient Polynesian Canoe. *International Association of Wood Anatomists Bulletin*, NS 11: 195–202.

Douterelo Soler, I., Goulder, R., and Lillie, M. C. 2009. Response of the Microbial Community to Water Table Variation and Nutrient Addition and its Implication for In Situ Preservation of Organic Archaeological Remains in Wetlands Soils. *International Biodeterioration and Biodegradation*, 63: 795–805.

Douterelo Soler, I., Goulder, R., and Lillie, M. C. 2010. Soil Microbial Community Response to Land-Management and Depth, Related to the Degradation of Organic Matter in English Wetlands: Implications for the In Situ Preservation of Archaeological Remains. *Applied Soil Ecology*, 44: 219–27.

French, C. 2004. Hydrological Monitoring of an Alluviated Landscape in the Lower Great Ouse Valley at Over, Cambridgeshire: Results of the Gravel Extraction Phase. *Environmental Archaeology*, 9: 1–12.

French, C. 2009. Hydrological Monitoring of an Alleviated Landscape in the Lower Great Ouse Valley at Over, Cambridgeshire: The Quarry Restoration Phase. *Environmental Archaeology*, 14(1): 62–75.

French, C., Davis, M. and Heathcote, J. 1999. Hydrological Monitoring of an Alluviated Landscape in the Lower Great Ouse Valley, Cambridgeshire. *Environmental Archaeology*, 4: 41–56.

Goulder, R. 1990. Extracellular Enzyme Activities Associated with Epiphytic Microbiota on Submerged Stems of the Reed Pragmites Australis. *FEMS Microbiology Ecology*, 73: 323–30.

Goulder, R. 1991. Metabolic Activity of Freshwater Bacteria. *Scientific Progress*, 75: 73–91.

Hedges, J. I. 1990. The Chemistry of Archaeological Wood. In: R. J. Barbour and R. M. Rowell, eds. *Archaeological Wood Properties, Chemistry, and Preservation. Developed from a symposium sponsored by the Cellulose Paper and Textile Division at the 196th National Meeting of the American Chemical Society, Los Angeles, California, September 25–September 30, 1988. Advances in Chemistry Series*, 225: 111–40.

Helms, A. C., Martiny, A. C., Hofman-Bang, J., Ahring, B. K., and Kilstrup, M. 2004. Identification of Bacterial Cultures from Archaeological Wood using Molecular Biological Techniques. *International Biodeterioration and Biodegradation*, 53: 79–88.

Hogan, D. V., Simpson, P., Jones, A. M., and Maltby, E. 2002. Development of a Protocol for the Reburial of Organic Archaeological Remains. In: P. Hoffmann, J. A. Spriggs, T. Grant, C. Cook, and A. Recht, eds. *Proceedings of the 8th ICOM on Wet Organic Archaeological Materials Conference, Stockholm 2001. International Council of Museums, Committee for Conservation*. Bremerhaven, Germany: Druckerei Ditzen GmbH & Co. KG, pp. 187–207.

Hopkins, D. W., 1998. The Biology of the Burial Environment. In: M. Corfield, P. Hinton, and M. Pollard, eds. *Preserving Archaeological Remains 'in situ'. Proceedings of the Conference of 1st–3rd April 1996*. London: Museum of London Archaeological Service, pp. 73–86.

Hoppe, H. G. 1993. Use of Fluorogenic Model Substrates for Extracellular Enzyme Activity (EEA) Measurement of Bacteria. In: P. F. Kemp, E. B. Sherr, and J. J. Cole, eds. *Handbook of Methods in Aquatic Microbial Ecology*. Boca Raton: Lewis Publishers, pp. 423–31.

Jans, M. M. E., Nielsen-Marsh, C. M., Smith, C. I., Collins, M. J. and Kars, H. 2004. Characterisation of Microbial Attack on Archaeological Bone. *Journal of Archaeological Science*, 31: 87–95.

Kandeler, E., Kampichler, C., and Horak, O. 1996. Influence of Heavy Metals on the Functional Diversity of Soil Communities. *Biology and Fertility of Soils*, 23: 299–306.

Kang, H. and Freeman, C. 1999. Phosphatase and Arylsulphatase Activities in Wetland Soils: Annual Variation and Controlling Factors. *Soil Biology and Biochemistry*, 31: 449–54.

Kim, Y. S. 1990. Chemical Characteristics of Waterlogged Archaeological Wood. *Holzforschung*, 44: 169–72.

Kim, Y. S., Singh, A. P., and Nilsson, T. 1996. Bacteria as Important Degraders in Waterlogged Archaeological Woods. *Holzforschung*, 50: 389–92.

Klaassen, R. 2005. *Preserving Cultural Heritage by Preventing Bacterial Decay of Wood in Foundation Poles and Archaeological Sites*. Final Report No. EVK4-CT-2001-0043, Wageningen, the Netherlands.

Kolehmainen, R. E., Korpela, J. P., Münster, U., Puhakka, J. A. and Tuovinen, O. H. 2009. Extracellular Enzyme Activities and Nutrient Availability During Artificial Groundwater Recharge. *Water Research*, 43: 405–16.

Lakin, M. and Howard, A. 2000. Newington Quarry Environmental Statement: Archaeological Assessment & Stage 1 – Evaluation Project Design. (2nd draft.) Durham: NAA unpublished report.

Lillie, M. C. 2007. In Situ Preservation: Geo-Archaeological Perspectives on an Archaeological Nirvana, In: M. C. Lillie and S. Ellis, eds. *Wetland Archaeology & Environments: Regional Issues, Global Perspectives*. Oxford: Oxbow Books, pp. 156–72.

Lillie, M. C. and Smith, R. J. 2007a. The In Situ Preservation of Archaeological Remains: Using Lysimeters to Assess the Impacts of Saturation and Seasonality. *Journal of Archaeological Science*, 34: 1494–1504.

Lillie, M. C. and Smith, R. J. 2007b. Understanding Water Table Dynamics and their Influence on the Buried Archaeological Resource in Relation to Aggregate Extraction Sites. Unpublished Report (March 2007 [2 vols]), Wetland Archaeology and Environments Research Centre, University of Hull, Hull.

Lillie, M. C. and Smith, R. J. 2008. Understanding Waterlogged Burial Environments: The Impacts of Aggregates Extraction and De-Watering on the Buried Archaeological Resource. Unpublished Report (February 2008), Wetland Archaeology and Environments Research Centre, University of Hull, Hull.

Lillie, M. C., Smith, R. J., Wallace, G., Davison, R., and Garrick, H. 2008. Wetland Archaeology, Water Tables and Lowland River Systems: Assessing Aggregate Extraction, In Situ Preservation and Sustainability. In: H. Kars and R. M. van Heeringen, eds. *Preserving Archaeological Remains In Situ: Proceedings of the 3rd Conference 7–9 December 2006, Amsterdam*. Geoarchaeological and Bioarchaeological Studies 10, pp. 151–62.

McLatchey, G. P. and Reddy, K. R. 1998. Wetlands and Aquatic Processes: Regulation of Organic Matter Decomposition and Nutrient Release in a Wetland Soil. *Journal of Environmental Quality*, 27: 1268–74.

Nannipieri, P., Grego, S., and Ceccanti, B. 1990. Ecological Significance of the Biological Activity in Soil. In: J. M. Bollas, ed. *Soil Biochemistry*, 6. New York: Marcel Dekker Inc., pp. 293–355.

Nannipieri, P., Kandeler, E., and Ruggiero, P. 2002. Enzyme Activities and Microbiological and Biochemical Processes in Soil. In: R. G. Burns and R. P. Dick, eds. *Enzymes in the Environment: Activity, Ecology and Applications*. New York: Dekker, p. 13.

Patrick, W. H. and Mahapatra, I. C. 1968. Transformation and Availability to Rice of Nitrogen and Phosphorous in Waterlogged Soils. *Advances in Agronomy*, 20: 323–59.

Powell, K. L., Pedley, S., Daniel, G., and Corfield, M. 2001. Ultrastructural Observations of Microbial Succession and Decay of Wood Buried at a Bronze Age Archaeological Site. *International Biodeterioration and Biodegradation*, 47: 165–73.

Sinsabaugh, R. L., Antibus, R. K., and Linkins, A. E. 1991. An Enzymic Approach to the Analysis of Microbial Activity During Plant Litter Decomposition. *Agriculture, Ecosystems and Environment*, 34: 43–54.

Tabatabai, M. A. 1994, Soil Enzymes. In: R. W. Weaver, J. S. Angle, and P. S. Bottomley, eds. *Methods of Soil Analysis: Microbiological and Biochemical Properties. Part 2*. Soil Sciences Society of America Ser. 5, Madison, Wisconsin, pp. 775–833.

Trasar-Cepeda, C., Leiros, M. C., and Gil-Sotres, F. 2008. Hydrolytic Enzyme Activities in Agricultural and Forest Soils. Some Implications for their Use as Indicators of Soil Quality. *Soil Biology and Biochemistry*, 40: 2146–55.

Tulonen, T. 1993. Bacterial Production in a Mesohumic Lake Estimated from 14C Leucine Incorporation Rate. *Microbial Ecology*, 26: 201–17.

Welch, J. and Thomas, S. 1998. Groundwater Modelling of Waterlogged Archaeological Deposits. In: M. Corfield, P. Hinton, T. Nixon, and M. Pollard, eds. *Preserving Archaeological Remains in situ. Proceedings of the Conference 1st–3rd April 1996, Bradford*, pp. 16–20.

Notes on contributors

Dr Malcolm Lillie has excavated and researched in wetlands for the past twenty-four years, beginning his career as a Fieldwork Supervisor on the Welsh side of the Severn Estuary, UK, excavating and surveying sites such as Goldcliff and Caldicot. He joined the English Heritage funded Humber Wetlands Project under the Directorship of Dr Steve Ellis at the University of Hull in 1994. In 2000 he joined the academic staff at Hull. He is currently a Reader in Prehistoric Archaeology and Wetland Science and Director of the Wetland Archaeology & Environments Research Centre at the University of Hull. He has an MSc and PhD from the University of Sheffield, the latter being supervised by Professor Marek Zvelebil.

Correspondence to: Dr Malcolm Lillie, Department of Geography, University of Hull, Hull HU6 7RX, UK. Email: m.c.lillie@hull.ac.uk

Isabel Soler is a member of Water Group (PWG), which is based in the Department of Civil and Structural Engineering at the University of Sheffield, UK. Prior to joining the PWG Isabel worked as a microbiologist at the Department of Biological Sciences, University of Warwick. Isabel obtained her PhD from the University of Hull, Department of Geography in 2007 and subsequently joined the Wetland Archaeology & Environments Research Centre as a Research Assistant on Phase 2 of the Newington project until January 2008. She is currently working on the Pipe Dreams Project investigating the microbial ecology of drinking water distribution systems, a project which aims to develop our understanding of the role of microbial biofilms inside water distribution systems.

Correspondence to: Isabel Soler, Department of Civil & Structural Engineering, University of Sheffield S1 3JD, UK.

Dr Robert Smith is a Director of CgMs Consulting. He has considerable experience in archaeological consultancy and provides specialist guidance and support in order to enable clients to better manage the heritage issues associated with their operations. He assists clients throughout the life cycle of each project, from the initial site acquisition, during the screening and scoping stages, through to the production of Environmental Assessments. Robert has particular experience of the renewable energy sector, as well as retail and other development projects. He routinely undertakes the design and implementation of desk studies, and the assessment/determination of impact mitigation and management strategies, in order to fulfil the requirements of the planning process. Robert is a Chartered Environmentalist (CEnv), Chartered Geographer (CGeog), Chartered Scientist (CSci), Chartered Water and Environmental Manager (CWEM), a Fellow of the Geographical Society (FRGS), a Member of the Institute of Field Archaeologists (MIfA) and a Member of the Institute of Water and Environmental Management (MCIWEM). He has a first degree in Physical Geography (University of Middlesex), and an MSc in Wetland Archaeological Science and Management and a PhD in Archaeological Science (both from the University of Hull).

Correspondence to: Dr Robert Smith, Wetland Archaeology & Environments Research Centre, Department of Geography, University of Hull, Hull HU6 7RX, UK.

CONSERVATION AND MGMT OF ARCH. SITES, Vol. 14 Nos 1–4, 2012, 150–58

Preservation Status and Priorities for *In Situ* Monitoring of the Weapon Sacrifice in Illerup Ådal, Denmark

ANNA K. E. TJELLDÉN
Moesgaard Museum, Denmark

SØREN M. KRISTIANSEN
Aarhus University, Denmark

KNUD B. BOTFELDT
The Royal Danish Academy of Fine Arts, School of Conservation, Denmark

Excavations of the southern part of a very rich sacrificial bog in Illerup Ådal, Denmark between 1950 and 1985 recovered approximately 15,000 Iron Age artefacts. At the time, 60 per cent of the area was left unexcavated and thousands of objects are now preserved *in situ*, but the present preservation status has not been investigated for approximately twenty-five years. Extensive *in situ* monitoring was carried out for one year in order to present a prioritized plan for further monitoring of the unexcavated areas, producing documentation of groundwater table variations, water quality and vegetation in the area. Results show that the remaining artefacts are generally well preserved in a waterlogged and anaerobic environment. However, in the north-eastern part of the bog, the groundwater table is too low even in a year when net precipitation and hydrological conditions were near normal. In the centre of the bog elevated salt concentrations have been measured in the groundwater.

KEYWORDS Iron Age, bog, monitoring, waterlogging, anaerobic environments, Denmark

Introduction

The European Convention on the preservation of archaeological heritage (European Council, 1992) declares the need for implementing measures that secure preservation and maintenance of archaeological artefacts *in situ*. Due to this declaration, a number

DOI 10.1179/1350503312Z.00000000012

of *in situ* monitoring projects have been carried out by the National Museum of Denmark (Gregory et al., 2002; Matthiesen, 2004). Experiences from these studies were implemented at the Danish sacrificial bog in Illerup Ådal, Jutland, a site that holds one of the largest and best-preserved Iron Age weapon sacrifices ever found in Northern Europe.

The sacrificed war material in Illerup Ådal dates back to AD 200–500, and excavations of *c*. 40 per cent of the sacrificial area have hitherto revealed approximately 15,000 artefacts. The artefacts from Illerup are generally very well preserved (Ilkjær, 2000) due to the anaerobic and near neutral environment of the lake and bog sediment containing the sacrifice. Shields, swords, lances, and spears are practically fully preserved, but protein-rich organic materials such as woollen textiles and equestrian equipment made of leather have deteriorated in the burial environment. Such objects are found as partly mineralized fragments only.

In situ preservation requires environmental conditions that are non-aggressive for the buried artefacts. For example, a groundwater level below or very near to the depth of artefact burial is very harmful to *in situ* preserved metal, since excess amounts of oxygen quickly oxidize metal surfaces and accelerate the deterioration of organic objects caused by micro-organisms. If water is drained from the organic materials the deteriorated parts can collapse. Plants may also pose a threat to weapon sacrifices in sacrificial bogs, as the roots of plants such as the horsetails (*Equisetum* sp.) or willows reach several metres down into strongly anoxic sediment and can pierce through organic artefacts (Gregory et al., 2002).

The aim was to monitor current preservation conditions at the unexcavated areas of Illerup Ådal in order to evaluate the primary parameters for future *in situ* investigations and to identify present and possible future threats to the *in situ* preserved weapon sacrifice.

Materials and methods

Site description
Illerup Ådal is situated in central Jutland, Denmark (Figure 1). Parts of the sacrificial bog, approximately 60,000 m², have been left unexcavated for future research, and several thousand objects are expected to be found still *in situ* (Figure 1). Today the excavated area is covered by several small ponds, while a meadow for grazing and bogs cover the unexcavated areas. Groundwater table and environmental conditions have not been monitored since the site was restored after the archaeological excavations ended in 1985. The artefacts are found at depths varying from 1 to 3 m in lake deposited gyttja.

Environmental monitoring
The estimation of threats and primary monitoring parameters in Illerup Ådal rely on environmental measurements of the water table, analysis of water quality and assessment of vegetation in the area. In October 2009, the northern part of the sacrificial bog was surveyed and the groundwater table was monitored using a grid of nine wells with PE tubing with perforated intakes slightly deeper (1.5–3 m b.s.) than the artefact layer. Groundwater levels were measured manually twice a month from November 2008 to November 2009.

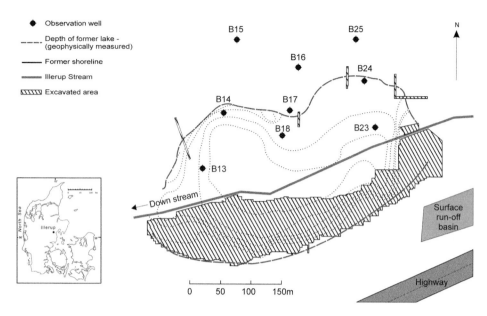

FIGURE 1   Map of the former lake basin at Illerup, Denmark. Positions of the wells are shown. The Illerup stream runs through the sacrificial bog from north-east towards south-west. The inserted map shows the location of Illerup Ådal in Denmark. (Partly redrawn from Ilkjær, 2000.)

The water quality was measured *in situ* on 28 November 2008 using a flow-through cell, with in-line measurement of pH, electrical conductivity, and redox potential. It was only possible to install an in-line pump (for the abstraction of non-oxidized samples) to three out of nine wells. Due to the very low yield of all wells, in-line flow-through cell readings were carried out every ½ minute until no more water was obtainable, and the last recorded value was noted.

The low yields caused relative high redox potentials and presence of NH_4^+ suggesting chemical non-equilibrium of the water samples, and redox sensitive parameters are hence likely to be more reduced due to partial oxidation during sampling. Dissolved Fe data are not reported of the same reason as precipitation was observed during sampling.

Water samples for laboratory analysis were withdrawn on 3 December 2008 from wells B13, B17, and B23, along with water from the Illerup stream and the surface water run-off basin. Groundwater samples were collected in acid-rinsed glass bottles, ensuring that as little atmospheric air as possible entered. An extra sample from the run-off basin was taken on 9 January 2009 to investigate the impact of de-icing road salt used nearby. Water samples were stored at 3°C and 0.45µm filtered prior to analysis. Concentrations of major cations (NH_4^+, Na^+, K^+, Ca^{2+}, and Mg^{2+}) and anions (NO_3^-, SO_4^{2-}, PO_4^{3-}, and Cl^-) were measured.

The vegetation in the unexcavated areas was recorded in October 2009 by an experienced botanist.

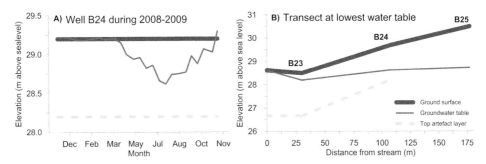

FIGURE 2   Groundwater table fluctuations at well B24 from November 2008 to November 2009 are shown in Figure 2A; while 2B shows a cross-section through the northern part of the sacrificial bog at the time of the lowest water table (19 July 1 2009). The y-axis refers to a Danish vertical reference system, i.e. m a.s.l. (DNN).

Results

Measurements of the groundwater table show that the artefacts were below the groundwater table between November 2008 and November 2009. Figure 2 shows the lowest groundwater level in relation to the artefact layer during the period. For example, at B24 the artefacts are situated approximately 100 cm below the surface; the minimum groundwater table was 42 cm above the artefacts and the upper >60 cm thick layer of peat was exposed to atmospheric oxygen during the driest summer month. In the summer of 2009, the other wells had >64 cm between the minimum groundwater level and the expected depth of the artefacts.

Water chemistry from the four wells reflected a neutral peat soil with a pH of approximately 6.5–6.8 buffered by the gyttja layer rich in carbonate-consisting shells. The excavation in 1975–85 documented precipitation of vivianite (iron phosphate), which only occurs in a highly reducing environment. The water analysis from 2008 supported this as it produced a very high content of reduced compounds (Tables 1 and 2). The artefacts therefore lie in an anaerobic, reduced, and high pH environment. The Cl concentration in the surface water run-off basin was 150 mg/l in December 2008 but measurements in January 2009 revealed up to 650 mg/l.

No Horsetails (either *Equisetum palustre* or *Equisetum fluviátile* L.) were found at the northern part of the sacrificial bog in Illerup Ådal. However, a larger group of grey willow (*Salix cinerea* L.) grow right on top of the sacrificial bog, covering an area of 2–400 m².

TABLE 1

GROUNDWATER CHEMISTRY MEASURED IN SITU AT THE DEPTHS OF ARTEFACT BURIAL IN ILLERUP ÅDAL

Site	Redox potential [mV]	Oxygen [mg/l]	pH	Conductivity [µS/cm]	Temperature [Celcius]
Well B13	181	0.95	6.54	424	8.5
Well B17	243	3.52	6.82	218	7.0
Well B23	185	0.80	6.56	220	6.2

TABLE 2

MAJOR IONS IN THE GROUNDWATER AT THE DEPTHS OF ARTEFACT BURIAL IN ILLERUP ÅDAL

Parameter Site	Ca^{2+} mg/l	Cl^- mg/l	K^+ mg/l	Mg^{2+} mg/l	Na^+ mg/l	NH_4^+ mg/l	NO^{3-} mg/l	PO_4^{3-} mg/l	SO_4^{2-} mg/l
Illerup stream	82.2	59	3.7	5.92	31.3	146	10.5	115	40.6
Well B23	165	41.2	2.8	12.3	28.3	47.6	1.0	54	1.8
Well B13	179	110	3.7	13.6	72.4	44.2	<1	47.8	<1
Well B17	158	39.9	0.9	5.62	17.2	5.26	3.3	146	2.1
Surface water run-off basin	38.8	150	5.6	2.74	90.6	1.09	3.3	158	14.1

*n.d. denotes not determined.

Discussion

Critical low groundwater levels

In Illerup Ådal, the most critical measurements in relation to the upper layer of the artefacts were measured in the northeastern part of the bog. The lowest measured water table was on 19 July 2009 when the water table at B24 was only *c.* 40 cm above the depth of the artefacts. At well B17 a relatively low water table was also measured on 5 July; just 64 cm above the artefacts. A thick unsaturated zone with atmospheric air circulation may cause a slow but steady mineralization of the peat and hence a continuous subsidence of the surface can be expected. Estimates based on a review made by Fanger (1990) on Danish and international experiences suggest a 0.5–1 cm loss of terrain height per year due to mineralization in such geological settings. This is likely to take place in most of the north-eastern part of the area, but this has not been documented yet.

The winter of 2008 had below average rainfall and April 2009 was also dry. However, the summer and autumn of 2009 were unusually wet, and seen as a whole the measured period had a small surplus of precipitation relative to the Danish Metrological normal (1961–90) (Frich et al., 1998). Although Illerup received more rainfall than average, a month long summer drought caused the groundwater table to drop to less than 50 cm above the artefacts. Detailed investigations in another Danish sacrificial bog at Åmosen, with comparable environmental settings, showed that when the groundwater is <20cm above the artefacts, measureable deteriorations of the organic matter were observed (Matthiesen and Jensen, 2005). Considering the increase in degradation rates of repeated dry-wet cycles (Hopkins, 2004; Williams et al., 2008) this suggests that the groundwater table of the sacrificial bog in Illerup Ådal is too low in the north-eastern part. Future subsidence due to mineralization will enhance this problem.

Chemical preservation status

The measured level of ammonium in Illerup is high, while nitrate levels are below the detection limit, generally suggesting a reduced environment at the burial depth of the artefacts. High concentrations of dissolved Fe^{2+} were observed during sampling which only occurs in a reduced environment. The O_2 contents of 0.80 and 0.95 mg/l were probably caused by the pumping and do not reflect the actual oxygen content at depth.

In contrast, the measured redox potentials in the groundwater are surprisingly high (average of 203 mV). However, the redox potential is measured after only 1½–2½ minutes of water flow which is too little time to gain a plausible reading from the electrodes, thus reflecting the true groundwater quality. An *in situ* measurement of the redox potential in these bog sediments with very low hydraulic conductivity would most likely give a more reliable result.

The groundwater composition of well B13 differs from the two other analysed wells by an increased electrical conductivity (respectively c. 220 vs. 424 µS/cm). The reason for this is the elevated sodium chloride content. As long as the artefacts are preserved in a waterlogged environment they are not threatened by chloride ions. However, if the objects are to be excavated and subsequently conserved, the presence of chlorides presents a problem for the preservation of metals and ceramics (Selwyn, 2004; Madsen, 1994), wood (McLeod et al., 1993) and artefacts of bone, antler, and teeth (Jørgensen and Botfeldt, 1986). Chloride contents in the surface water run-off basin upstream showed a high content of 150 to 650 mg/l during the winter 2008/09 when de-icing road salt is applied (data not shown). The large content of chloride in the basin and in well B13 could correlate with the highway salting southeast of the sacrificial bog. However, as the Illerup stream is situated between B13 and the run-off basin this might not be the case, and the elevated chloride content of B13 could be due to infiltrating river water enriched in salt from previous de-icing episodes up-stream. This observation is supported by the fact that the groundwater table in the sacrificial bog is lower than the stream during some of the year (see Figure 2) and that the stream thereby regulates the groundwater table of the northern part of the bog.

During excavations in the 1970–80s pH was measured in the surface water and the archaeologists came to the conclusion that pH *in situ* was 8–8.5. They found that the artefacts were enclosed in organic rich lake sediments full of carbonate mussels from the prehistoric freshwater lake, thus producing a basic environment. If the organic-rich lake sediment is oxidized due to drainage or archaeological excavation, the sediment will adjust itself to equilibrium between calcium carbonate and the CO_2 pressure of soil air. The resulting pH value is approximately 8. However, in an anaerobic soil environment with strongly elevated CO_2 partial pressures (10–100 times ambient air concentrations) carbonates may buffer the bog sediment to a pH between 6 and 7 only (Matthiesen, 2004). The pH measurements in Illerup carried out in 1975–85 were on oxidized soil water and the result was therefore alkalinic. Today well B17 has slightly raised oxygen content (3.5 mg/l), while the highest pH value (6.82) is found here. This indicates de-gassing of CO_2 because of stagnated water in the well. The pH values of the *in situ* environment indicate a neutral environment around pH 6.5–6.8 in the sacrificial bog, suggesting *in situ* decomposition at a microscale. Kinetic processes are however likely to be extremely slow due to a buffering effect of the calciumcarbonate rich water surrounding the artefacts. Given the uncertainties regarding *in situ* H^+ due to oxidation during measurements, it is of great importance to measure pH a.o. parameters *in situ* in future investigations (Caple, 2004).

Threats from deep-rooted vegetation

The grey willows (S. *cinerea*) situated on top of parts of the sacrificial bog area are deep rooted when growing in wet, but still unsaturated soils while the root growth of Salix species are halted within a few weeks after fully flooding occurs (Jackson et al., 1997; Talbot et al., 1987). The lake sediment in the sacrificial bog had very low hydraulic conductivity (cf. low yields) meaning that the soil is very impermeable, and thus lowering of groundwater tables only slowly will affect subsoils. However, the existence of Salix species could be very problematic in relation to *in situ* buried artefacts if the sediment overlying the burial depth is not permanently fully waterlogged.

Conclusion

The presented preliminary *in situ* investigations of the northern part of the sacrificial bog in Illerup show a generally positive image of the preservation conditions for the remaining weapon sacrifice. However there are circumstances that could harm the artefacts, now or in the future (Figure 3).

A critical low groundwater table was measured in the north-eastern part of the sacrificial bog and it is recommended that the water table is raised here to prevent any risk of oxidation. An area of grey willow grows right on top of the sacrificial bog thus endangering the archaeological artefacts, particularly those made of organic material, and it is recommended that the shrubs are cleared. Measurements of the water quality showed that the water in well B13 was enriched in Cl, which is probably caused by seepage of de-icing salts from the surface water of up-stream run-off

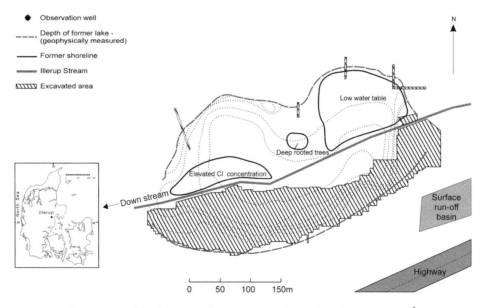

FIGURE 3   Current, possible threats to the unexcavated sacrificial bog in Illerup Ådal. (Partly redrawn from Ilkjær, 2000.)

basins. It is recommended that future monitoring focuses on possible changes of the chloride content in the wells located near the stream.

Future monitoring

Recommendations for future monitoring of *in situ* preservation of the artefacts in Illerup Ådal are as follows:

1) A longer period of monitoring encompassing effects of extreme weather conditions such as a long, dry summer.
2) More targeted monitoring concentrated on the artefact layer throughout the northern part of the bog.
3) Further *in situ* measurements of soil chemistry and monitoring of the ground-water table by data loggers.
4) Studies of current speed and type of deterioration by introducing test materials in the artefact layer.
5) Biannual monitoring of the vegetation to combat any invading deep-rooted plants.

Acknowledgements

We would like to thank Jørgen Ilkjær for answering many questions regarding the excavation in 1975–85 and for assisting with slides, reports, and geological maps of the sacrificial bog. We greatly acknowledge Henning Matthiesen, Hans Huisman, Rune H. Kristiansen, and Bent Aaby for their time and assistance with various aspects of the study. Also skilled technical help from Ruth S. Nielsen and Lars Thomsen is acknowledged. We would like to thank the Royal Danish Academy of Fine Arts, School of Conservation in Copenhagen, the Fondation Idella, and the Augustinus Fonden for financial support. Finally, for the comments of the two anonymous reviewers, whose comments help improve the article.

Bibliography

Aaby, B. 2010. Discussion on plants in relation to in situ preservation. (Personal communication, 18 February 2010).

Caple, C., 2004. Towards a Benign Reburial Context: The Chemistry of the Burial Environment. *Conservation and Management of Archaeological Sites*, 6(3 and 4): 155–65.

European Council, 1992. Article 4 §ii, Council of Europe 1992.

Fanger, K., 1990. Sætning af organiske jorder efter dræning. Master thesis 1990, Royal Veterinary and Agricultural University of Denmark, 136 pp.

Frich, P., Rosenørn, S., Madsen, H., and Jensen, J.J . 1997. Observed Precipitation in Denmark, 1961–90. Danish Metrological Institute, Technical report 97–8. 40 pp.

Gregory, D., Matthiesen, H. and Bjørdal, C. 2002. *In Situ* Preservation of Artefacts in Nydam Mose: Studies into Environmental Monitoring and the Deterioration of Wooden Artefacts. *Proceedings of the 8th ICOM Group on Wet Organic Archaeological Materials Conference*. Stockholm, 11–15 June, pp. 213–23.

Hopkins, D. W., 2004. Relevance of Soil Biology and Fertility Research to Archaeological Preservation by Reburial. *Conservation and Management of Archaeological Sites*, 6(3 and 4): 167–75.

Ilkjær, J., 2000. *Illerup Ådal — et arkæologisk tryllespejl. Jysk Arkæologisk Selskab 2000*, Moesgård Museum. Aarhus: Aarhus University, pp. 1–151.

Jackson, M. B. and Attwood, P. A. 1997. Roots of willow (*Salix viminalis* L.) Show Marked Tolerance to Oxygen Shortage in Flooded Soils and in Solution Culture. *Plant and Soil*, 187: 37–45.

Jørgensen, G. and Botfeldt, K. B. 1986. *Knogler, tak, tænder, skaller og hornmaterialer. Struktur, nedbrydning og konservering*. Copenhagen: The Royal Danish Academy of Fine Arts, School of Conservation, 88 p.

Madsen, H. B. 1994. *Handbook of Field Conservation*. The Royal Danish Academy of Fine Arts, School of Conservation, BB. Copenhagen: Grafik, 124 pp.

Matthiesen, H. 2004. *In Situ* Measurement of Soil pH. *Journal of Archaeological Science*, 31: 1373–81.

Matthiesen, H. and Jensen, P. 2005. Bevaring i Åmosen — hvor vådt er vådt nok?. In: *Kultuarv i Naturpark Åmosen-Tissø*. Special-Trykkeriet Viborg, 2005, pp. 43–52.

McLeod, I. D., Mardikian, P., and Richards, V. L. 1993. Observations on the Extraction of Iron and Chloride from Composite Materials. *Proceedings of the 5th ICOM Group on Wet Organic Archaeological Materials Conference*. Portland/Maine, 1993, pp. 199–209.

Selwyn, L. S. 2004. Overview of Archaeological Iron: The Corrosion Problem, Key Factors Affecting Treatment, and Gaps in Current Knowledge. *Proceedings of Metal*. National Museum of Australia, 4–8 October 2004, pp. 294–306.

Talbot, J. R., Etherington, J. R., and Bryant, J. A. 1987. Comparative Studies of Plant Growth and Distribution in Relation to Waterlogging. XII. Growth, Photosynthetic Capacity and Ion Uptake in *Salix caprea* and *C. cinerea* spp. *Oliefolia*. *New Phytologist*, 105: 563–74.

Williams, J., Fell, V., Graham, K., Simpson, P., Collins, M., Koon, H., and Griffin, R. 2008. Re-watering of the Iron Age Causeway at Fiskerton, England. In: H. Kars and R. M. van Heeringen, eds. *Preserving Archaeological Remains* In Situ. *Proceedings of the 3rd Conference 7–9 December 2006, Amsterdam*. *Geoarchaeological and Bioarchaeological Studies*, 10: 181–97.

Notes on contributors

Anna K. E. Tjelldén is an object conservator with focus on *in situ* preservation. She is employed at the Department of Conservation and Environmental Archaeology at Moesgård Museum, Denmark.

Correspondence to: Anna K. E. Tjelldén, The Department of Conservation and Environmental Archaeology, Moesgaard Museum, Moesgaard Allé 20, 8270 Højbjerg, Denmark. Email: moesat@hum.au.dk

Søren M. Kristiansen is associate professor at the Department of Earth Sciences, University of Aarhus, and focuses on geochemistry of groundwater, soils, and sediments.

Knud B. Botfeldt is a lecturer in archaeological and natural history conservation at the Royal Danish Academy of Fine Arts, School of Conservation.

CONSERVATION AND MGMT OF ARCH. SITES, Vol. 14 Nos 1–4, 2012, 159–68

The Future Preservation of a Permanently Frozen Kitchen Midden in Western Greenland

Jørgen Hollesen, Jan Bruun Jensen, Henning Matthiesen

National Museum of Denmark, Denmark

Bo Elberling

Department of Geography and Geology, University of Copenhagen, Denmark and UNIS, The University Centre in Svalbard, Norway

Hans Lange

Greenland National Museum and Archives, Greenland

Morten Meldgaard

Natural History Museum of Denmark, University of Copenhagen, Denmark

Archaeological materials may be extraordinarily well preserved in Arctic areas, where permanently frozen conditions in the ground slow down the decay of materials such as wood, bone, flesh, hair, and DNA. However, the mean annual air temperature in the Arctic is expected to increase by between 2.5 to 7.5° C by the end of the twenty-first century. This may have a significant warming effect on the soil and could lead to permafrost thaw and degradation of currently frozen archaeological remains. Here we present a four-year monitoring and research project taking place at Qajaa in the Disko Bay area in West Greenland. Qajaa is a large kitchen midden, containing frozen remains from 4000 years of inhabitation, from when the first Palaeo-Eskimos entered Greenland, until the site was abandoned in the eighteenth century. The purpose of the project is to investigate current preservation conditions through field and laboratory measurements and to evaluate possible threats to the future preservation.

Preliminary results show that the archaeological material at Qajaa is still very well preserved, but some microbial decay is observed in the exposed wooden artefacts that thaw every summer. Maximum temperatures are above 0° C in the upper 40–50 cm of the midden and between 0 and −2° C

    DOI 10.1179/1350503312Z.00000000013

down to 3 m depth. Thereby the permafrost may be vulnerable to quite small increases in air temperatures. Laboratory measurements show that the decay of the archaeological wood in the midden is temperature-dependent, with rates increasing 11–12% every time the soil temperature increases 1° C. Moreover, the soil organic material produces heat when decomposed, which could have an additional warming effect on the midden. At the moment the water or ice content within the midden is high, limiting the subsurface oxygen availability. Threats to the future preservation are related to further thawing followed by drainage, increased oxygen availability, microbial decay of the organic material, and heat production.

KEYWORDS Palaeo-Eskimo, midden, preservation, permafrost, Greenland

Introduction

Most Palaeo-Eskimo sites in Greenland lack well-preserved organic artefacts because organic materials such as wood, fat and skin quickly decompose in the presence of oxygen and above zero temperatures. However, at a few archaeological kitchen middens a combination of high disposal rates and favourable hydrological conditions have caused the permafrost to move up into the deposited material fast enough to preserve the organic material. At these sites important organic archaeological materials are found that may hold the information needed to provide insight to the earliest documented human expansion into Greenland by the Palaeo-Eskimo Saqqaq culture. This was recently shown by Rasmussen et al. (2010) who used a 4000-year-old hair from a permanently frozen kitchen midden at Qeqertasussuk in Western Greenland to extract the complete human genome of a Saqqaq man.

Temperatures are currently rising in Greenland and Global Climate Models predict an increase in the Arctic mean annual air temperature of between 2.5 to 7.5° C by the end of the twenty-first century (Chapman and Walsh, 2007). Even a small increase in the air temperature may have a great influence on the thermal state of permafrost (Romanovsky et al., 2007; Hollesen et al., 2011a) and hence the future preservation of the archaeological kitchen middens may be threatened. One of the sites that are at risk is the Qajaa kitchen midden at the Ilulissat Ice Fjord in western Greenland. With 250 cm of organic archaeological layers embedded in the permafrost, this is considered the best-preserved site for Saqqaq and Dorset culture in all of Greenland. The site was last subject to investigations in 1982 and since then the mean annual air temperature has increased by more than 2° C (Carstensen and Jørgensen, 2011). The question is whether the state of preservation has changed during the last twenty-eight years and whether future climatic changes may cause the Qajaa kitchen midden to thaw and decay.

In this paper we present a four-year monitoring and research project at the Qajaa kitchen midden that aims to investigate the current preservation conditions through field and laboratory measurements and to evaluate possible threats to the future preservation.

Study site

The Qajaa kitchen midden is situated 18 km south-east of Ilulissat at the Ilulissat Icefjord in the western central part of Greenland (Figure 1). The annual mean temperature in Ilulissat is −4.5 ± 1.7° C (1974 to 2004) and the annual amount of precipitation is 266 mm (1961 to 1984) (Carstensen and Jørgensen, 2011).

The kitchen midden has been known at least since 1871 when the first Palaeo-Eskimo artefacts were collected (Meldgaard, 1983). The midden primarily consists of peat but also contains rocks from fireplaces, bones from animals, and anthropogenic materials such as tools. The midden is up to 300 cm thick and consists of at least four layers representing three individual periods of settlement in the area (Figure 2). The first 120 cm thick layer from the bottom represents the Saqqaq people who lived year-round at the site from around 2000–1000 BC, followed by 20–30 cm peat without evidence of human activity (1000–400 BC). This layer may represent a colder and wetter period of time, which is overlaid by a 2–30 cm thick layer representing the hunters of the Dorset people living in the area from about 400–200 BC. The uppermost archaeological layer (in some places up to 1 m thick) has been dated to represent the last immigration of Eskimos to Greenland (the Thule People) who inhabited the site from 1200–1750 AD. The kitchen midden is in most places covered by a sand layer of about 20 cm.

Methods

Field measurements

Fieldwork was conducted in August 2009 and 2010. A meteorological station was placed at the top of the kitchen midden (Figure 1), logging air temperature and relative humidity (Campbell Scientific, 215 Temperature probe), wind speed and wind direction (Campbell Scientific, 05103-5 wind monitor), and snow depth (Campbell Scientific, SR50 Sonic Ranging Sensor). A hole was drilled at the top of the kitchen midden down to a depth of 340 cm. Temperature sensors (Campbell Scientific T-107 sensors) were installed at 0, 7, 16, 32, 50, 120, 170, 220, 270, 320 cm depth. Moreover, soil water content, thermal conductivity, and heat capacity sensors were installed at 7, 16, 20, and 32 cm depth using Theta Probe, Soil Moisture Sensors (ML2x, Delta-T Devices Ltd, Cambridge, UK), and Specific Heat Sensors (East 30 Sensors). All of the sensors were connected to a Campbell Scientific Cr1000 datalogger programmed to log every three hours.

Oxygen concentrations were measured during the field campaigns at different depths in the soil using the oxygen optode technique (Glud et al., 2000) with calibrated oxygen sensor foils (SF-PSt3-NAU-YOP) and a fibre optic meter (Fibox3LCD) from Pre-Sens.

Depth specific soil samples were taken from the drilling core. Moreover, wooden artefacts were collected in order to investigate the current state of preservation. During the archaeological investigations in 1982 several soil profiles were made that could still be found in 2009. Artefacts were collected from the profiles to represent different environmental conditions such as frozen/thawed and wet/dry.

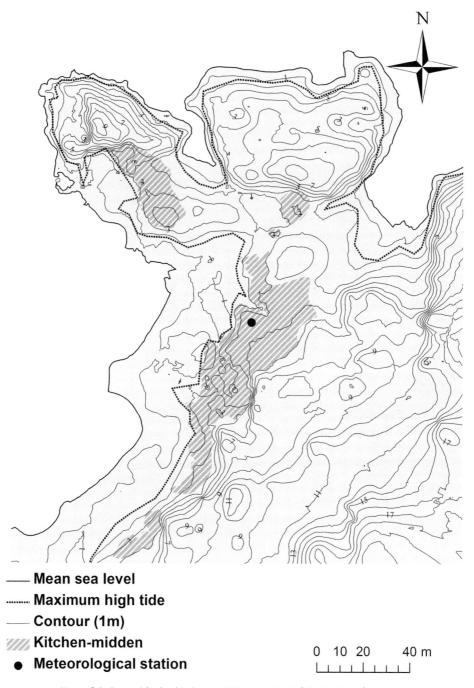

Mean sea level
.... Maximum high tide
—— Contour (1m)
▨▨ Kitchen-midden
● Meteorological station

0 10 20   40 m

FIGURE 1   Map of Qajaa, with the kitchen midden outlined (shaded area).

FIGURE 2   The Qajaa kitchen midden contains thick layers of refuse that represents three individual periods of settlement during the last 4000 years. The archaeological layer representing the Thule People is very limited on this picture.
Photograph by Jesper Stub Johnsen

Laboratory experiments

The oxygen consumption rates were measured in wood samples from the Saqqaq layers at o, 5, 10, 15, and 20° C to investigate the temperature dependency of the decay. Two permafrozen samples (sample 1 and 2) and one unfrozen sample (sample 3) were used. Measurements were made in three replicates of each sample according to Matthiesen (2007). In short: 3–5 g samples of wood were transferred to 12.1 ml glass vials, the samples were flushed with atmospheric air and the vials closed with an airtight lid. The oxygen consumption was subsequently measured by monitoring the decrease of headspace O_2 concentrations over time by using oxygen optodes from PreSens (www.presens.de).

Heat production from the decomposition of the soil organic bulk material was measured calorimetrically under aerobic conditions at 15° C for ten permafrost samples (< 2 mm). Samples from the following depth intervals were included: 40–46 cm, 56–62 cm, 76–86 cm, 100–16 cm, 136–48 cm, 168–90 cm, 192–94 cm, 226–38 cm,

267–80 cm, and 323–38 cm. Measurements were made using a thermal-activity monitor (type 2277, Thermometric, Sweden, or C3-analysentechnik, Germany) equipped with ampoule cylinders (4 ml twin, type 2277-201, and 20 ml twin, type 2230) and measured according to Elberling et al. (2000). Glass ampoules containing 10 g of soil were freely drained and exposed to air for 2 days before inserted in the measurement cylinders. After thermal equilibration (within 12 h), the heat output was recorded.

In order to identify macroscopic damages the collected wooden artefacts were first visually inspected and then the density (oven-dry mass/swollen volume) was measured in order to determine the degree of degradation. Optical and scanning electron microscopic imaging (SEM) was used to identify microscopic damages of the wood tissue.

Results and discussion

The mean air temperature during the observation period (26 August 2010–19 July 2011) is −4.9° C with a temperature variation from 10.6° C to −23.0° C (Figure 3a). The mean soil temperatures vary from −3.1° C at the surface to −2.1° C in the deepest layers (−320 cm depth). The temperature variation at the surface is somewhat lower than in the air (6° C to −15° C) which is mainly due to surface evaporation lowering temperatures during the summer and a surface snow cover increasing

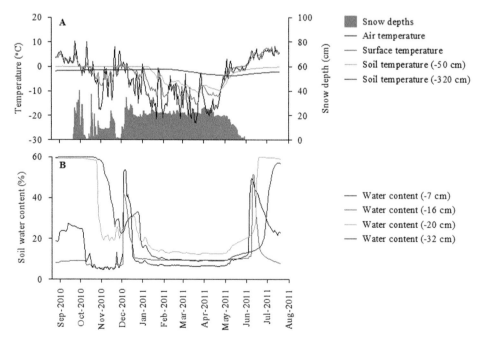

FIGURE 3   (A) The lines show measured air and soil temperatures in the Qajaa kitchen midden and the bars show measured snow depths. (B) Measured soil water contents in upper layers of the kitchen midden. NB. The low water contents seen during the winter period are due to freezing.

temperatures during the winter. The temperature variation decreases further with depth and is only −1.2 to −3.8° C in the deepest part of the midden. Only the upper 50 cm of the kitchen midden thaw every summer and the midden is permanently frozen below (Figure 3a). As seen in Figure 3a and b, the freezing of the soil is significantly delayed by a mild period in December where snow melt and water infiltration causes the upper layers of the soil to thaw. Thereby the soil is first completely frozen in the beginning of January. Such a thaw event may result in the formation of a thick ice layer that may change insulating effect of snow and act as an impermeable layer that can prevent cold winds from penetrating the midden. The soil remains frozen until the beginning of June where above zero air and surface temperature initiates snow melt and soil thaw. During the snow melt period in the beginning of June the whole soil profile gets water saturated but this only lasts for a couple of weeks in the upper 15–20 cm (Figure 3b). Thereafter, the upper 15–20 cm of kitchen midden remains relatively dry during the summer whereas the midden remains water saturated from 20 cm and below. These results are in good agreement with measurements of oxygen that show 90 to 100 per cent oxygen saturation in the dry upper part of the midden and almost no oxygen in the water saturated parts or in the deeper, frozen parts. The decrease in water content seen during the autumn is due to freezing and thus has no influence on the oxygen content in the kitchen midden. As the vast majority of the archaeological layers are located in the permanently frozen and water saturated part of the kitchen midden the current preservation conditions are considered to be good. This is confirmed by the investigations of the collected wooden artefacts which show that the permanently frozen artefacts are in excellent conditions (Matthiesen et al., in press).

Laboratory investigations confirm that soil temperatures and water content play a very important role in relation to the preservation of the organic archaeological materials found at Qajaa. Investigations of decay patterns show that wood which have been submitted to freeze/thaw the last twenty-seven years are significantly more decayed than the permafrozen wooden artefacts (Matthiesen et al., in press).

Investigations of oxygen consumption rates show that the oxygen consumption in the wood samples increases exponentially with temperature (Figure 4). The temperature dependency is often expressed using the Q_{10} value — which is the proportional change in rates given a 10° C change in temperature:

$$Q_{10} = \left(\frac{R_2}{R_1}\right)^{\left(\frac{10}{T_2-T_1}\right)}$$

(eq. 1)

where R_1 and R_2 are the reaction rates at temperatures T_1 and T_2.

In the temperature interval from 0 to 20° C Q_{10} values from 2.7 to 3.4 were found for the exponential fits. The percentage change in decomposition rates (D_x) due to a change in temperature can then be calculated as:

$$D_x = \left(Q_{10}^{\left(\frac{T_2-T_1}{10}\right)} - 1\right) * 100\%$$

(eq. 2)

Thereby, a temperature increase of 1° C could increase decomposition rates of the wooden material by 11–12%, a 5° C increase by 65–85% and a 10° C increase by 170–240%. The temperature dependency was measured in samples with *in situ* water

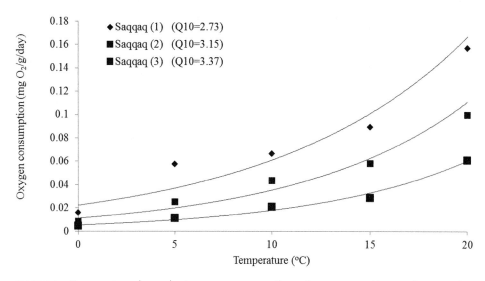

FIGURE 4   Temperature dependent oxygen consumption rates measured in wooden samples taken from the Saqqaq layers. Samples 1 and 2 were taken from permafrozen layers and sample 3 from soil layers that thaw during the summer.

contents. As discussed above, the future preservation of the archaeological materials will depend on a combination of soil temperatures and soil water contents. Consequently, to fully understand the sensitivity of the materials to future changes the oxygen consumption should be measured not only at different temperatures but also at different water contents.

Ground warming and decomposition of organic material may also produce heat, which can impose a positive feedback on soil temperatures leading to further soil thaw and decomposition of organic materials (Khvorostyanov et al., 2008). Measurements of heat production rates show an average heat production at 15° C of 18 μW/g dry soil which is twenty times higher than what have been measured in a natural permafrost soil (Hollesen et al., 2011a) and ten times higher than what have been measured in Arctic coal mine waste (Elberling et al., 2007; Hollesen et al., 2011b). The results therefore suggest that heat production from the decaying organic layers could become very important as a positive feedback mechanism (additional warming) if the kitchen midden starts to thaw and particularly if thawing occurs in combination with drainage.

Although the current preservation conditions at Qajaa are considered good, preliminary results indicate that the future preservation of the kitchen midden may be threatened by soil thaw.

The permafrost is surprisingly warm at the moment with annual mean temperatures in the deepest layers of the kitchen midden (220–320 cm) varying from −2.2 to −2.1° C. Considering that air temperatures are expected to increase with 2.5 to 7.5° C by the end of the twenty-first century (Chapman and Walsh, 2007) the upper layers of the permafrost are in great risk of thawing. At the moment only the upper 50 cm of the soil thaws every summer, but the thickness of this 'active layer' will increase if air temperatures increase. Investigations from Zackenberg in central North-east

Greenland show that an increase in the mean annual air temperature of 1° C from 1996 to 2007 caused the active layer to increase by more than 1 cm per year (Hollesen et al., 2011a). The important Dorset and Saqqaq layers are found at 110 cm depth and below and hence the preservation of these layers will only be threatened if the thickness of the active layer exceeds this depth. Moreover, if the archaeological layers thaw, the preservation of the organic material will depend on whether the layers remain water saturated or not. A simple analytical model investigation (Elberling et al., 2011) indicates that maximum thawing depth at Qajaa will increase by 10–30 cm the next seventy years depending on the degree of climate change, thus, the important Dorset and Saqqaq layers do not seem directly threatened by thawing. However, this model was not based on meteorological data from Qajaa and it did not include temporal trends in precipitation and soil water content or the effect of heat production from the decomposition of organic layers. Considering the high soil temperatures and heat production rates presented in this study, future preservation conditions can only be fully evaluated by including site-specific data from Qajaa.

Conclusion and future investigations

Preliminary results show that archaeological materials in the Qajaa kitchen midden are very well preserved because permafrost and a high water and ice content limit decay processes. However, current mean annual soil temperatures of −2° C questions whether or not the permafrost will survive the predicted increase in air temperatures of 2.5 to 7.5° C. Investigations of wooden artefacts show that summer thaw and draining cause microbial decay. Laboratory measurements show that the decay of the wooden artefacts in the midden could increase by 12 per cent every time the soil temperature increases with 1° C and hence even small changes in soil temperature may have a great effect on the preservation. Moreover, the decaying soil organic material produces heat that may increase soil temperatures and thereby increase decay rates even more. However, decay rates and heat production will only increase if the soil drains and the availability of oxygen increases. The exact sensitivity of the decay rates to soil water content is still unknown. Future investigations will focus on performing measurements of decay rates at different water contents on samples from both the soil bulk material and from the different archaeological artefacts. Additionally, factors such as air temperature, precipitation rates, snow, vegetation, and topography will be investigated to fully evaluate the future risk of permafrost thaw and draining. This will be done by using a numerical heat and water flow model.

Bibliography

Carstensen, L. S and Jørgensen, B. V. 2011. Weather and Climate Data from Greenland 1958-2010 Danish Meteorological Institute. Technical Report No. 11-10.

Chapman, W. L. and Walsh, J. E. 2007. Simulations of Arctic Temperature and Pressure by Global Coupled Models. *Journal of Climate*, 20: 609–32.

Elberling, B., Matthiesen, H., Jørgensen, C. J., Hansen, B., Grønnow, B., Meldgaard, M., Andresen, C. and Khan, C. 2011. Paleo-Eskimo Kitchen Midden Preservation in Permafrost under Future Climate Conditions at Qajaa, West Greenland. *Journal of Archaeological Science*, 38(6): 1331–39.

Elberling, B., Sondergaard, J., Jensen, L. A., Schmidt, L. B., Hansen, B. U., Asmund, G., Balic-Zunic, T., Hollesen, J., Hansson, S., Jansson, P. E., and Friborg, T. 2007. Arctic Vegetation Damage by Winter-Generated Coal Mining Pollution Released upon Thawing. *Environmental Science & Technology*, 41: 2407–13.

Elberling, B., Schippers, A., and Sand, W. 2000. Bacterial and Chemical Oxidation of Pyritic Mine Tailings at Low Temperatures. *Journal of Contaminant Hydrology*, 41: 225–38.

Glud, R. N., Gundersen, J. K., and Ramsing, N. B. 2000. Electrochemical and Optical Oxygen Microsensors for In Situ Measurements. In: J. Buffle and G. Horvai, eds. *In Situ Monitoring of Aquatic Systems; Chemical Analysis and Speciation*. Chichester: Wiley, p. 19.

Hollesen, J., Elberling, B., and Jansson, P. E. 2011a. Future Active Layer Dynamics and CO_2 Production from Thawing Permafrost Layers in Northeast Greenland. *Global Change Biology*, 17: 911–26. doi: 10.1111/j.1365-2486.2010.02256.x

Hollesen, J., Elberling, B., and Jansson, P. E. 2011b. Modelling Temperature-Dependent Heat Production over Decades in High-Arctic Coal Waste Rock Piles. *Cold Regions Science and Technology*, 65: 258–68.

Khvorostyanov, D. V., Krinner, G., Ciais, P., Heimann, M., and Zimov, S. A. 2008. Vulnerability of Permafrost Carbon to Global Warming. Part I: Model Description and Role of Heat Generated by Organic Matter Decomposition. *Tellus Series B-Chemical and Physical Meteorology*, 60: 250–64.

Matthiesen, H., Jensen, J. B., Gregory, D., Hollesen, J., and Elberling, B. In press. Degradation of Archaeological Wood under Freezing and Thawing Conditions — Effects of Permafrost and Climate Change, submitted to *Archaeometry*.

Matthiesen, H. 2007. A Novel Method to Determine Oxidation Rates of Heritage Materials In Vitro and In Situ. *Studies in Conservation*, 52: 271–80.

Meldgaard, J. 1983. Qajaa, en køkkenmødding i dybfrost. *Feltrapport fra arbejdsmarken i Grønland*. National-museets Arbejdsmark, pp. 83–86 (in Danish).

Rasmussen, M., Li, Y., Lindgreen S., Pedersen, J. S., Albrechtsen, A., Moltke, I., Metspalu, M., Metspalu, E., Kivisild, T., Gupta, R., dos Santos, M. B. Q., Nielsen, K., Gilbert, M. T. P., Wang, Y., Raghavan, M., Campos, P. F., Kamp, H. M., Wilson, A. S., Gledhill, A., Tridico, S., Bunce, M., Lorenzen, E. D., Binladen, J., Guo, X., Zhao, J., Zhang, X., Zhang, H., Li, Z., Chen, M., Orlando, L., Kristiansen, K., Bak, M., Tommerup, N., Bendixen, C., Pierre, T. L., Grønnow, B., Meldgaard, M., Andreasen, C., Fedorova, S. A., Osipova, L. P., Higham, T. F. G., Ramsey, C. B., Hansen, T. V. O., Nielsen, F. C., Crawford, M. H., Brunak, S., Sicheritz-Pontén, T., Villems, R., Nielsen, R., Krogh, A., Wang, J., and Willerslev, E. 2010. Ancient Human Genome Sequence of an Extinct Palaeo-Eskimo. *Nature*, 463: 757–62.

Romanovsky, V. E., Sazonova, T. S., Balobaev, V. T., Shender, N. I., and Sergueev, D. O. 2007. Past and Recent Changes in Air and Permafrost Temperatures in Eastern Siberia. *Global and Planetary Change*, 56: 399–413.

Notes on contributors

Jørgen Hollesen is a researcher at the National Museum of Denmark, where he works with the *in situ* preservation of archaeological remains. His research is focused on urban deposits and arctic sites.

Correspondence to: Jørgen Hollesen. Email: Joergen.Hollesen@natmus.dk

Jan Bruun Jensen is a conservator at the National Museum of Denmark, where he works with conservation of waterlogged organic archaeological material.

Henning Matthiesen is a senior researcher at the National Museum of Denmark, where he works with the *in situ* preservation of archaeological remains. His research is focused on wetlands, urban deposits, and permafrozen sites.

Bo Elberling is Professor at the Department of Geography and Geology, University of Copenhagen, and is leader of the research centre CENPERM. His research is focused on permafrost dynamics in relation decomposition of organic material and release of greenhouse gases.

Hans Lange is a curator at the National Museum of Greenland.

Morten Meldgaard is Director of the Natural History Museum of Denmark and is a specialist in arctic zoology and quaternary studies.

In Situ Preservation and Monitoring of the *James Matthews* Shipwreck Site

Vicki Richards

Department of Materials Conservation, Western Australian Museum, Australia

Over the past few decades, the archaeological community has been moving away from the more traditional methods of excavation and recovery of underwater cultural heritage towards a less intrusive management approach, essentially involving the preservation of sites *in situ*. This trend has been politically galvanized in Article 2, point 5 of the Convention on the Protection of the Underwater Cultural Heritage (UNESCO, 2001), which states that 'The preservation in-situ of underwater cultural heritage shall be considered as the first option before allowing or engaging in any activities directed at this heritage'. Over the years, a number of different remediation strategies have been utilized in order to protect underwater cultural heritage sites *in situ*, and most of the techniques or combinations thereof involve reburial of sites. Reburial may be an appropriate means of stabilizing and decreasing the deterioration rate of a site, however, there needs to be a holistic approach to the study of the environment, before and after reburial, to gain a full understanding of the changes that are occurring on the site and determine the effectiveness of the technique.

In early 2000, the *James Matthews*, a copper-sheathed, wooden-hulled vessel wrecked in 1841 south of Fremantle, Western Australia, was identified as being under considerable threat from increased site exposure due to a combination of natural near-shore sedimentary processes and industrial activity in the immediate area. An extensive on-site conservation survey was carried out to establish the state of preservation of the wreck and provide information regarding the physico-chemical and biological nature of the environment prior to the implementation of any mitigation strategy. In 2003 it was confirmed that further exposure of the site was occurring and devising a management plan was of paramount importance.

Since this time a number of different reburial techniques have been trialled on the site and these include sand bags of differing material composition, polymeric shade cloth, artificial sea grass mats made from polyvinyl chloride bunting, and the use of interlocking medium density polyethylene 'crash barrier' units in a cofferdam arrangement to confine deposited sand.

DOI 10.1179/1350503312Z.00000000014

The geological, physico-chemical, and microbiological changes in the burial environments have been monitored over this time. Furthermore, the broader scale, near-shore sedimentary processes affecting the site are being assessed in order to establish the reasons behind the continuing sediment loss. *In situ* preservation of the iron fittings by cathodic protection has also been included in these field trials. In this paper the results from these experiments will be summarized. This information will be used to finalize the design of the full-scale *in situ* preservation strategy for the site and assist in establishing a post-reburial monitoring programme that will measure the success of the adopted remediation technique.

KEYWORDS *in situ* preservation, reburial, shipwrecks, marine environment, monitoring, sediment

Introduction

Reburial of maritime archaeological sites is becoming increasingly more common in managing and preserving our underwater cultural resource for future generations. The first serious attempts were made in the late 1970s where shipwrecks excavated in the Netherlands' polders were reburied on land below the ground water table (De Jong, 1979; 1981; Eenkhoorn et al., 1980). Since that time, some of the techniques used have ranged from the relatively simple (depositing extra layers of sediment and/or sandbags on a site) to the more complicated (techniques that promote natural accretion of sediment on a site and the construction of artificial mounds in several layers) (Manders et al., 2008). Some examples of past, more successful reburial projects using combinations of the aforementioned techniques were the controlled reburial of the Basque whaler, *San Juan*, in Red Bay, Labrador, 1984 (Stewart et al., 1995), the seasonal reburial and stabilization with Terram 4000 of a fifteenth–sixteenth-century wreck in Zakynthos harbour, Greece in the early 1980s (Pournou et al., 1999), the extensive sandbagging of the BZN 3 site in the Wadden Sea in the mid-1980s (Maarleveld, 1988), the use of proprietary seagrass matting on the *William Salthouse*, Victoria, Australia in 1989 (Harvey, 1996; Hosty, 1988), and the *in situ* preservation of the Danish warship, *Stora Sofia*, in Gothenberg, Sweden, 2002 (Bergstrand, 2002) and the Darsser Cog in Mecklenburg Vorpommern, Germany, 2003 (MoSS, 2001).

Reburial may be an appropriate means of stabilizing and decreasing the overall deterioration rate of an archaeological site; however, there is often little, if any subsequent monitoring to determine the effectiveness of the applied technique. A holistic approach to the study of the pre- and post-reburial environment is necessary to gain a full understanding of the changes occurring in the local environment and the associated deterioration of the archaeological material. This in turn will allow accurate assessment of the adopted mitigation strategy on the long-term preservation of the site.

Notably, a few of the more recent reburial projects have included very extensive on-site environmental monitoring programmes as an integral part of their overall *in situ* management plans. Some excellent examples were the European Commission-funded projects, Preserving Cultural Heritage by Preventing Bacterial Decay of Wood in Foundation Piles and Archaeological Sites (Bacpoles) (Bacpoles, 2002; Klassen, 2005) and Monitoring, Safeguarding and Visualizing North-European Shipwreck Sites (MoSS) (Cederlund, 2004; MoSS, 2001), the ongoing Scandinavian funded Reburial and Analysis of Archaeological Remains project (RAAR) (Bergstrand et al., 2005; Godfrey et al., 2004; Nyström-Godfrey and Bergstrand, 2007; Nyström Godfrey et al., 2011) and the Western Australian Museum funded *James Matthews* project (Richards, 2001; 2003).

The *James Matthews* project began in 2000 and one important aspect of the project has been the collaboration between coastal engineers, microbiologists, wood technologists, chemists, corrosion scientists, conservators, and maritime archaeologists contributing to the overall success of the project to date. This paper will present a brief historical overview of the project, highlighting the major conclusions obtained from the results of the reburial experiments since 2000 and the remediation strategies proposed for the wreck site including a post-reburial monitoring programme. However, over the past eleven years a number of scientific papers have been published by the author presenting, in much greater detail, the results of the initial conservation survey and the environmental monitoring and the success of the different reburial experiments currently being trialled on the shipwreck site (Godfrey et al., 2004; 2005; Heldtberg et al., 2004; Richards, 2011; Richards et al., 2009; Winton and Richards, 2005).

Background

The *James Matthews* was a relatively small copper-sheathed, wooden-hulled ship, constructed in France in the late 1700s. During the 1830s, registered as the *Don Francisco*, it operated in the illegal slave trade between Africa and the West Indies until it was captured by the British in 1837. At that time captured slave ships were usually destroyed, but this vessel was sold, re-registered, and taken into general trading as the *James Matthews*.

In 1841 the ship sailed for the Swan River colony in Fremantle, Western Australia, but one day after arrival a violent storm struck the port and the vessel was wrecked on 22 July 1841. The wreck site is about 12 km south of Fremantle and lies about 100 m off shore in 2 m of water. The *James Matthews* was discovered in 1973 and is protected by the Historic Shipwrecks Act 1976 (Australian Government 2012). The Western Australian Museum is the delegated state authority and has the legislative responsibility for the protection and management of sites in Western Australia covered by this Act. The *James Matthews* has been identified as historically and archaeologically important not only because of its significance to the early colonial history of Western Australia but because the near-complete starboard side of this vessel remains intact. As most of these types of vessels were destroyed under the anti-slave legislation of the time, it is one of the world's best-preserved examples of a nineteenth-century purpose-built illegal slaving ship.

On discovery, the site was extensively covered with seagrass meadows and very little of the wreck was visible above the sediment. Four seasons of excavation were carried out by the Western Australian Museum between 1974 and 1977 (Baker and

Henderson, 1979). All loose artefacts were recovered and stabilized by standard con-servation treatments appropriate for each material type. At the completion of each excavation period the exposed vessel remains were reburied by backfilling with the original overburden, but some of the higher profile features, such as the windlass and iron deck knees, were not reburied to their original burial depths leading to consider-able deterioration over time. Despite this oversight, the site appeared to be relatively stable and remained buried for many years. However, in early 2000 it was observed that the edges of the wooden vessel and timbers at the stern and bow were exposed and severely degraded by marine borers. Therefore, devising an appropriate *in situ* management plan to significantly reduce the continued deterioration of this historic shipwreck site is of paramount importance.

Conservation survey

In July 2000 a comprehensive on-site conservation survey was conducted involving a limited excavation of the site, which consisted of dredging six 2 cu m test trenches (TT) at various positions on the site. The survey included a full corrosion survey of the exposed iron fittings, measuring the extent of deterioration of the structural timbers in each test trench and physico-chemical and microbiological analyses of the surrounding sediments. The results of the survey showed that all exposed iron fea-tures were actively corroding (Heldtberg et al., 2004) and the wooden vessel remains were extensively degraded to a depth of 30 cm; therefore, remediation of the wreck site was required (Godfrey et al., 2005; Richards, 2001; 2003). In addition, the results from the sediment analyses provided important baseline information on the nature of the environment prior to the implementation of any reburial strategy (Godfrey et al., 2005).

Coastal processes study

Concurrent to the on-site conservation survey another study was conducted by the project coastal engineer examining the broader scale sedimentary processes affecting the site. It was concluded that the local coastal and sedimentary changes caused by groyne construction and commercial shell dredging for cement manufacture had altered the natural longshore processes and the net effect was sediment mobilization away from the immediate area resulting in an overall reduction in sand coverage over the site. More importantly, it was unlikely that significant sediment accumulation would occur naturally in the future (Winton and Richards, 2005).

Subsequent visits to the site at irregular intervals from 2001 to 2004 confirmed the results of the coastal processes study. It was observed that the site was becoming increasingly more exposed every year. Obviously some form of remediation was of paramount importance to alleviate or at least reduce the major physico-chemical and biological degradative forces acting on this site.

Experimental remediation strategies and monitoring

Realistically it was going to be impossible to achieve the 1973 pre-excavation depths of burial (2–3 m), but from past and present research into *in situ* preservation and from the results of both the conservation survey and the coastal processes study, any proposed remediation strategy had to maintain sediment coverage of at least 50 cm over the entire site. This was especially important around the periphery of the site where the extent of hull exposure was most extensive. More importantly, this depth of sand coverage had to be maintained in the long-term and the chosen technique could not adversely affect the wreck material and/or the local micro-environment.

Sediment level monitoring

Since 2006 the broad scale sediment levels in a 200 sq m area around the site have been monitored using both total station measurements and contour plots of water depth. The results indicate that the sediment in the local area is now relatively stable except for normal seasonal changes that do not seem to have a significant effect on the sediment coverage on the immediate wreck site. Therefore, it appears that the rapid rate of sediment loss that was observed on-site up until 2004 has decreased significantly and the site is relatively stable for the moment. This has positive implications for any full-scale remediation strategy implemented in the future.

Cathodic protection

In 2001 zinc anodes were attached to the windlass and the iron deck knees to lower the corrosion rates through cathodic protection. The anodes are replaced when exhausted, every one to three years, dependent on the surface area of the structural iron feature being protected. The use of the anodes was effective, however, there was some concern regarding the environmental impact of the zinc corrosion products. Analysis of the sediments indicated that high concentrations of zinc were localized to the seabed immediately under the anodes and the ecotoxicological assessment indicated that it was in a form that would not have a detrimental effect on the local marine biota (Heldtberg et al., 2004).

Sand bags

Since large sections of the site were exposed and severely degraded (Godfrey et al., 2005; Richards, 2001), in 2001 these areas were covered with about 500 cotton sand bags to temporarily stabilize the site while more long-term preservation options were investigated. Unfortunately, the sand bags totally disintegrated after six months and in 2003 the remediated areas were only covered with a very thin layer of sand. By 2004 the timbers were exposed again confirming the results of the coastal processes study and the extent of degradation of the timbers had increased markedly from 2000 (Richards et al., 2009). Therefore, all exposed areas were re-covered with UV stabilized, polyethylene reinforced sand bags. Although the polymeric sand bags were an improvement on the cotton sand bags, deterioration of the timbers continued (Richards, 2011; Richards et al., 2009). Hence, the traditional sandbagging method could not be recommended for the medium to long-term preservation of this wreck site.

Cofferdam solution

Another strategy considered was dumping sand on the site and then stabilizing the burial mound with geotextile fabrics or polymeric matting. The problem with this option is as the dumped sand hits the seabed it is laterally dispersed and the depth of coverage is significantly reduced. Therefore in order to gain full coverage of greater than 50 cm over the entire site, especially at the periphery where exposure is extensive (> 30 cm), the reburial area would need to be significantly larger than the actual wreck itself (25 m length × 7 m wide).

It was obvious that that some form of cofferdam surrounding the site was required to confine the deposited sand and minimize the reburial area and sediment mobilization in the long-term. Cofferdams are usually constructed from timber, which would deteriorate rapidly in this marine environment or steel plate, which would corrode and could adversely affect the delicate balance of the wreck ecosystem. In late 2002, Winton and Richards (2005) proposed the use of chemically and environmentally inert, interlocking medium density polyethylene 'crash barrier' units (2 m length; 1 m height) (Figure 1). This innovative approach would utilize approximately eighty of these units, interlocked into a ring-like arrangement using a pin and hinge system, around the periphery of the wreck site, filled with sand to the required depth (~1 m in total) and covered with geotextile and polymeric sand bags to minimize sediment loss during storm activity.

In 2003, a field trial of the 'test square' was initiated on the *Omeo*, a site subjected to more wave loading, in order to assess the logistics of deployment, stability of the structure, the effect on the local seabed topography and sediment movement within the barrier arrangement. After two years this approach, with some modifications, had

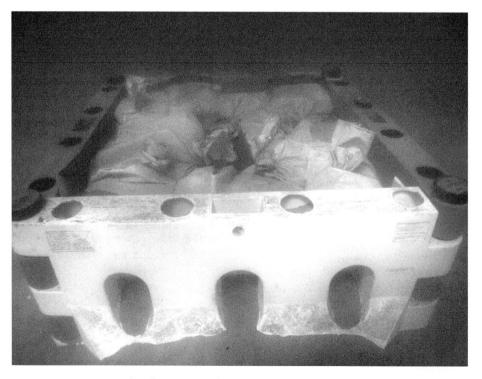

FIGURE 1   Test square (2 m² × 1 m deep) on the *James Matthews* site three months after deployment.
Photograph by Carpenter

shown the concept to be effective (Winton and Richards, 2005). Therefore, in 2005 another 'test square' was placed adjacent to the *James Matthews* wreck site and it remains stable after six years (Richards, 2011; Richards et al., 2009). Since deployment the usual sediment and seabed response have been monitored within and around the test square with changes in the micro-environment (i.e. dissolved oxygen, redox potential, pH, total sulphide, nutrient levels, biological activity) of the sediment inside the test square also monitored at regular intervals (Richards et al., 2009).

Sediment trapping experiments

Despite the success of the test squares, it was envisaged that there may be some potential problems with filling the cofferdam surrounding the *James Matthews* with 250 cu m of sand. Therefore it was decided to trial some simpler and significantly cheaper techniques utilizing different types of mats that would hopefully trap sediment and accretion would occur naturally without recourse to dredging or dumping huge volumes of sand on the site (Manders et al., 2008).

One mat was manufactured from polyvinylchloride bunting anchored with cable ties to plastic garden trellis to simulate natural seagrass leaves. Another mat was made of 50 per cent UV blocking shade cloth with a mesh size of 1000 microns as the average sediment size on the site was 700 microns. Small fishing buoys were attached to the shade cloth mat so the material would stay suspended in the water column and not sink when it became covered in algae during the summer months. Some problems were encountered on deployment, but after a few adjustments the mats were placed adjacent to the site in 2005 using UV stabilized polymeric sand bags to anchor the mats to the seabed.

After only three months, there was extensive algal growth on the fronds of the seagrass mat and by 2009 they had totally collapsed and lay flush with the seabed. In addition, there was an appreciable amount of dead seagrass trapped under the mat and extensive scouring had occurred beneath the mat (Figure 2).

After only one month, despite the use of the fishing buoys, the weight of the algal growth on the shade cloth had caused the mat to sink to the seabed and some toe scouring had occurred in some places around the periphery of the mat. However, after two years the toe scouring had ceased and the mat was completely filled to its maximum capacity, which was about 1.5 m above the seabed and by 2010 sediment had begun building up around the edges of the mat (Figure 3).

A sediment monitoring programme similar to that being used to measure changes in the micro-environment in the test square sediment has also been implemented for these mats (Richards et al., 2009).

Sediment analysis results

Sediment core samples were collected from under each mat (30 cm in length) and within the test square (60 cm in length) for microbiological and physico-chemical analyses via wet chemical techniques. Baseline sediment core samples (60 cm in length) were also collected for comparative assessment. The sediment fractions were analysed for particle size distribution, total sulphur, and extractable organic matter (EOM) content and the pore waters for pH, sulphide, sulphate, total sulphur, and nutrients (ammoniacal nitrogen (NH_3), nitrate nitrogen (NO_3^-), total nitrogen, soluble reactive phosphorus, total phosphorus).

FIGURE 2   The artificial seagrass mat (4 m length; 3 m width) after five years on-site.
Photograph by Carpenter

The scientific reasoning behind the microbiological analyses of the sediment samples was to identify the different fungi and bacteria present at different depths in the reburial sediments in order to better understand the synergistic relationship between sediment chemistry and microbial activity and possibly, in the future, their effects on reburied wreck materials. A brief synopsis of the major results of these analyses, with the exception of the sediment under the seagrass mat as it was unsuccessful in accumulating sediment, will be presented below, but an extensive analysis and interpretation of all data is published in Richards et al. (2009).

The results indicated that the accreted sediment under the shade cloth mat and the deposited sediment in the test square were stable with moderately well-sorted medium-grained calcareous sediments with relatively low water contents and near neutral pHs, which would be conducive to preserving wreck material. Alternatively, the reburial sediments were not very reducing in nature, indicated by low levels of total sulphides and high levels of sulphates in the sediment cores, and this may have a detrimental effect on the deterioration rates of organics and metals buried via these remediation methods. In addition, the redeposited sediments contained significant stores of organic matter and nutrients and a wide range of micro-organisms were identified, but there was little difference when compared to those present in the baseline sediments. More importantly, where there were high levels of organic matter, there were high levels of nutrients and this would increase biological activity in those areas which, in turn, may increase degradation rates of timbers and the corrosion of iron.

FIGURE 3   The shade cloth mat (4 m length; 3 m width; 1.5 m height) after five years on-site.
Photograph by Carpenter

Sacrificial samples

In order to ascertain whether these high levels of organic matter and nutrients in the reburial sediments would in fact, increase the deterioration of wood and iron in these areas, the next phase of the experiment, which will be initiated in early 2012, will involve inserting modern sacrificial wood (white oak and pine) and iron (cast iron and mild steel) samples at different levels in the existing shade cloth mat mound and test square. Again, the same microbiological and physico-chemical analyses will be carried out but in addition, the extent of deterioration of the sacrificial samples will be analysed over time. Another shade cloth mat will also be deployed, but the samples will already be in place so deterioration rates can be monitored during and after sediment accretion (Godfrey et al., 2005; Richards, 2011; Richards et al. 2009).

Proposed full-scale *in situ* preservation management plan

From the results of our experiments and analyses the crash barrier cofferdam technique appears to be the best solution for the *in situ* preservation of the *James Matthews* site. A diagrammatic representation of this proposal is shown in Figure 4. Some of the exposed areas of the site are about 30 cm above the original seabed, so the depth of sand within the cofferdam would have to be at least 80 cm so filling to a height of 1 m would allow for some settling of the dredged/dumped sediment. At

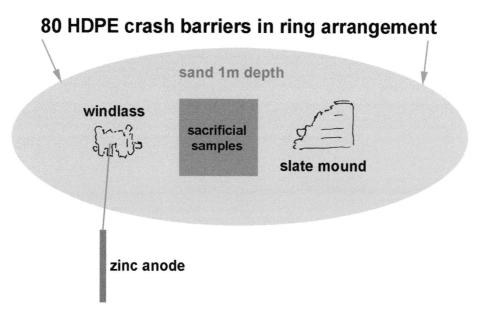

FIGURE 4 Diagrammatic representation of the crash barrier cofferdam remediation technique.

this height only the top of the windlass and the slate mound would be exposed. A zinc anode would be attached to the exposed section of the windlass to decrease the corrosion rate. Sacrificial wood and iron samples would be placed within the confines of the cofferdam to recover at regular intervals in order to measure the success of the crash barrier method. The sediment would be monitored at regular intervals for any change in the micro-environment, which may adversely affect the reburied wreck remains.

However, in the current economic environment this will probably not be possible in the near future so it may be more economically viable to cover the entire site with sections of shade cloth (Figure 5). It would be very difficult to cover the windlass and some of the higher profile deck knees so they would again be cathodically protected with zinc anodes. Similar to the cofferdam reburial plan, analysis of sacrificial samples and sediments would occur at regular intervals to monitor the success of this reburial strategy. Some very exposed sections of the wreck site have already been reburied and covered with shade cloth, however we have had significant problems with toe scouring occurring around the edges of some of the mats. Therefore, the crash barrier cofferdam reburial technique is the preferred remediation strategy for the long-term *in situ* preservation of the *James Matthews* site.

Conclusion

It is difficult to predict the effect a particular reburial environment may have on the deterioration of different archaeological material types as there are many synergistic, symbiotic, and opposing processes occurring within the redeposited sediment column and at this point in time, their inter-relationships remain unclear. However, some recommendations can be made based on these research results.

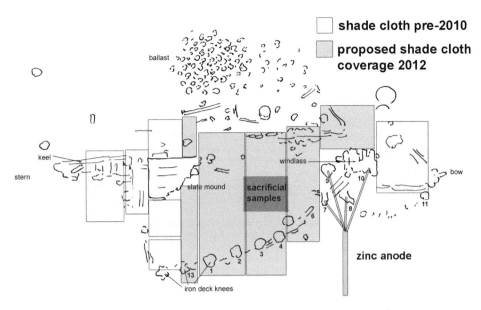

shade cloth pre-2010

proposed shade cloth coverage 2012

ballast

keel

stern

slate mound

windlass

sacrificial samples

bow

zinc anode

iron deck knees

FIGURE 5   Diagrammatic representation of the shade cloth remediation technique.

Canvas sand bags are totally unsuitable even as an interim remediation strategy, but polymeric sand bags may be used for short-term preservation of a wreck site.

The use of artificial seagrass mats could not be recommended as a means of stabilizing the *James Matthews* wreck site. On the other hand, the shade cloth mats were quite successful in trapping sediment. Correct orientation of the shade cloth is very important in order to gain maximum sediment coverage (> 60 cm) over the exposed sections of the shipwreck. This may prove difficult in some areas and therefore, the use of the road crash barriers remains the preferred reburial option. However, considerable funds are required to establish this management strategy and, therefore, research will continue into the shade cloth sediment trapping technique as it is a relatively inexpensive alternative to the road crash barrier containment method.

Despite the many questions and uncertainties that surround reburial of archaeological sites and the associated artefacts, reburial is likely to play an increasingly important role in the *in situ* preservation of underwater cultural heritage. Hence, more research projects that include extensive monitoring programmes need to be initiated in order to provide information that will ultimately lead to a better understanding of the associated advantages and disadvantages of this technique.

Acknowledgements

The author would like to thank every staff member from the Department of Materials Conservation and the Department of Maritime Archaeology, Western Australian Museum who have been involved in this project from its inception. However, the author would especially like to acknowledge Jon Carpenter, Senior Conservator, Materials Conservation Department, Western Australian Museum, Michael McCarthy, Senior Maritime Archaeologist, Department of Maritime Archaeology, Western

Australian Museum and David Gregory, Senior Scientist, Conservation Department of the National Museum of Denmark, whom without their unwavering support this important project would not have been possible.

Bibliography

Australian Government. 2012. *Historic Shipwrecks Act 1976*. Canberra: Attorney-General's Department [accessed 10 October 2012]. Available at: <http://www.comlaw.gov.au/Details/C2012C00174>.

Bacpoles. 2002. *Preserving Cultural Heritage by Preventing Bacterial Decay of Wood in Foundation Piles and Archaeological Sites*. Netherlands: SHR Timber Research [accessed 10 October 2012]. Available at: <http://www.bacpoles.nl>.

Baker, P. and Henderson, G. 1979. *James Matthews* Excavation. A Second Interim Report. *The International Journal of Archaeology*, 8: 225–44.

Bergstrand, T. 2002. In-Situ Preservation and Re-Burial. In: P. Hoffmann, J. A. Spriggs, T. Grant, C. Cook, and A. Recht, eds. *Proceedings of the 8th ICOM Group on Wet Organic Archaeological Materials Conference, Stockholm 11–15 June 2001*. Bremerhaven: International Council of Museums (ICOM), Committee for Conservation, Working Group on Wet Organic Archaeological Materials, pp. 155–66.

Bergstrand, T., Björdal, C. G., Bohm, C., Christenssen, E., Gregory, D., MacLeod, I. D., Nilsson, T., Nyström, I., Peacock, E., Richards, V. L., and Turner, G. 2005. Reburial as a Method of Preserving Archaeological Remains. A Presentation of the Marstrand Project. In: P. Hoffmann, K. Strætkvern, J. A. Spriggs, and D. Gregory, eds. *Proceedings of the 9th ICOM Group on Wet Organic Archaeological Materials Conference, Copenhagen, 7–11 June 2004*. Bremerhaven: The International Council of Museums, Committee for Conservation Working Group on Wet Organic Archaeological Materials, pp. 9–39.

Cederlund, C. ed. 2004. *Monitoring, Safeguarding and Visualizing North-European Shipwreck Sites, Final Report*. Helsinki: The National Board of Antiquities.

De Jong, J. 1979. Protection and Conservation of Shipwrecks. In: M. Grail, ed. *Medieval Ships and Harbours*. BAR International Series 68. Oxford: British Archaeological Reports.

De Jong, J. 1981. The Deterioration of Waterlogged Wood and its Protection in Soil. In: H. de Vries-Zuiderbaan, ed. *Conservation of Waterlogged Wood: International Symposium on the Conservation of Large Objects of Waterlogged Wood, Netherlands, 1981*. The Hague: Netherlands National Commission for UNESCO, pp. 57–68.

Eenkhoorn, W., de Jong, J., and Wevers, A. 1980. Beschermen van scheepsresten in de polders. *De Houtwereld*, 33(17): 19–25.

Godfrey, I. M., Gregory, D., Nyström, I., and Richards, V. 2004. In-Situ Preservation of Archaeological Materials and Sites Underwater. In: F. Maniscalco, ed. *Mediterraneum*. Italy: Massa Editore, pp. 343–51.

Godfrey, I. M., Reed, E., Richards, V. L., West, N. F., and Winton, T. 2005. The *James Matthews* Shipwreck — Conservation Survey and In-Situ Stabilisation. In: P. Hoffmann, K. Strætkvern, J. A. Spriggs, and D. Gregory, eds. *Proceedings of the 9th ICOM Group on Wet Organic Archaeological Materials Conference, Copenhagen, 2004*. Bremerhaven: The International Council of Museums, Committee for Conservation Working Group on Wet Organic Archaeological Materials, pp. 40–76.

Harvey, P. 1996. A Review of the Stabilisation Works on the Wreck of the *William Salthouse* in Port Philip Bay. *Bulletin of the Australasian Institute for Maritime Archaeology*, 20(2): 1–8.

Heldtberg, M., MacLeod, I., and Richards, V. 2004. Corrosion and Cathodic Protection of Iron in Seawater: A Case Study of the *James Matthews* (1841). In: J. Ashton and D. Hallam, eds. *Metal 04: Proceedings of the International Conference on Metals Conservation, Canberra, 4–8 October 2004*. Canberra: National Museum of Australia, pp. 75–87.

Hosty, K. 1988. Bagging the *William Salthouse*: Site Stabilization Work on the *William Salthouse*. *Bulletin of the Australasian Institute of Maritime Archaeology*, 12(2): 13–16.

Klaassen, R. ed. 2005. *Preserving Cultural Heritage by Preventing Bacterial Decay of Wood in Foundation Piles and Archaeological Sites, Final report EVK4-CT-2001-00043*. Netherlands: SHR Timber Research.

Maarleveld, Th. J. 1988. Texel-Burgzand III: Een scheepswrak met bewapening. In: W. A. van Es, H. Sarfatij, and P. J. Woltering, eds. *Archeologie in Nederland*. Amersfoort, pp. 189–91.

Manders, M., Gregory, D., and Richards, V. 2008. The In-Situ Preservation of Archaeological Sites Underwater. An Evaluation of Some Techniques. In: E. May, M. Jones, and J. Mitchell, eds. *Proceedings of the 2nd Heritage, Microbiology and Science, Microbes, Monuments and Maritime Materials Conference, 28 June–1 July 2005, Portsmouth, UK.* London: RSC Publishing, pp. 179–203.

MoSS. 2001. *Monitoring, Safeguarding and Visualizing North-European Shipwreck Sites.* Helsinki: The National Board of Antiquities/The Section of Maritime Archaeology [accessed 10 October 2012]. Available at: <http://www.nba.fi/INTERNAT/MoSS>.

Nyström Godfrey, I. and Bergstrand, T. eds. 2007. *Reburial and Analyses of Archaeological Remains — Studies on the Effect of Reburial on Archaeological Materials Performed in Marstrand, Sweden 2003–2005. The RAAR Project.* Udevalla, Sweden: Bohusläns Museum and Studio VästSvensk Konservering.

Nyström Godfrey, I., Bergstrand, T., and Petersson, H. eds. 2011. *Reburial and Analyses of Archaeological Remains — Phase II Results from the 4th Retrieval in 2009 from Marstrand, Sweden. The RAAR project.* Udevalla, Sweden: Bohusläns Museum and Studio VästSvensk Konservering.

Pournou, A., Jones, A. M., and Moss, S. T. 1999. *In-Situ* Protection of the Zakynthos Wreck. In: C. Bonnet-Diconne, X. Hiron, Q. K. Tran, and P. Hoffmann, eds. *Proceedings of the 7th ICOM-CC Working Group on Wet Organic Archaeological Materials Conference, Grenoble, France 1998.* France: The International Council of Museums (ICOM), Committee for Conservation, Working Group on Wet Organic Archaeological Materials, pp. 58–64.

Richards, V. L. 2001. James Matthews (1841). Conservation Pre-Disturbance Survey Report. Unpublished report. Department of Materials Conservation, Western Australian Museum, Fremantle, pp. 1–37.

Richards, V. L. 2003. James Matthews (1841) Reburial Project. Conservation Research Design, August 2003. Unpublished report. Department of Materials Conservation, Western Australian Museum, Fremantle, pp. 1–33.

Richards, V. 2011. In-Situ Preservation and Reburial of the ex-Slave Ship, *James Matthews. AICCM Bulletin,* 32: 33–43.

Richards, V., Godfrey, I., Blanchette, R., Held, B., Gregory, D., and Reed, E. 2009. In-Situ Monitoring and Stabilisation of the *James Matthews* site. In: K. Straetkvern and D. J. Huisman, eds. *Proceedings of the 10th ICOM Group on Wet Organic Archaeological Materials Conference, Amsterdam, 10–15 September 2007.* Amersfoort: Rijksdienst voor Archeologie, Cultuurlandschap en Monumenten (RACM), pp. 113–60.

Stewart, J., Murdock, L. D., and Waddell, P. 1995. Reburial of the Red Bay Wreck as a Form of Preservation and Protection of the Historic Resource. *Mat. Res. Soc. Symp. Proc.,* 352: 791–805.

UNESCO. 2001. *Convention on the Protection of the Underwater Cultural Heritage.* Paris: UNESCO.

Winton, T. and Richards, V. 2005. In-Situ Containment of Sediment for Shipwreck Reburial Projects. In: P. Hoffmann, K. Strætkvern, J. A. Spriggs, and D. Gregory, eds. *Proceedings of the 9th ICOM Group on Wet Organic Archaeological Materials Conference, Copenhagen, 7–11 June 2004.* Bremerhaven: The International Council of Museums, Committee for Conservation Working Group on Wet Organic Archaeological Materials, pp. 77–89.

Notes on contributor

Vicki Richards has a B.App.Sci (Hons) (Curtin University) and an MPhil in Chemistry (Murdoch University). She has been a Conservation Scientist in the Materials Conservation Department of the Western Australian Museum for the past twenty-four years. One of her primary research areas is investigating deterioration mechanisms of metals and organic materials on shipwreck sites and devising and implementing appropriate on-site management plans for the long-term *in situ* preservation of these sites.

Correspondence to: Vicki Richards, Department of Materials Conservation, Western Australian Museum, Shipwreck Galleries, 45–47 Cliff St, Fremantle, WA 6160, Australia. Email: vicki.richards@museum.wa.gov.au

CONSERVATION AND MGMT OF ARCH. SITES, Vol. 14 Nos 1–4, 2012, 182–92

Samuel Pepys's Navy Preserved *In Situ?*

DANIEL PASCOE

Seadive Organization, UK

This paper will focus on the wreck of the *Stirling Castle*, which was one of four ships of the line to perish on the Goodwin Sands during the Great Storm of 27 November 1703. The Goodwin Sands lies off the south-east coast of Kent between Dover and Ramsgate. These sands are famously known as the 'Ship Swallower'. This paper will discuss what has been learnt from the site's investigations, the heritage management issues of preservation *in situ*, and offer a strategy for the future management of the site.

KEYWORDS Goodwin Sands, *Stirling Castle*, Restoration Navy, heritage at risk, licensing

Introduction

For all that are interested in maritime archaeology and the development of the Royal Navy, it is indeed fortunate that there are many examples of the Restoration Navy wrecked in easily accessible areas within British coastal waters (Hepper, 1994). Such examples are the designated wrecks of the *Stirling Castle, Northumberland, Restoration, Anne, Coronation*, the Royal Yacht *Mary*, and the *Dartmouth* (Fenwick et al., 1998). For archaeologists and historians there is a wonderful opportunity to study the remains of these ships and learn so much about shipboard society, culture, and technological developments.

Of these wrecks, *the Stirling Castle, Northumberland, Restoration, Anne*, and the *Coronation* were part of Samuel Pepys's rapid shipbuilding programme of 1677. This was the largest and most ambitious building programme of its time, constructing thirty ships consisting of twenty Third Rates, nine Second Rates, and one First Rate (Fox, 1980: 154). Pepys and Charles II created a series of reforming measures to create uniformity, and professionalism in the Navy (Knighton, 2003: 113). Pepys did this by reforming the Officers Corps (Knighton, 2003: 113) and standardizing the ordnance while Charles insisted on the standardization of the masts, spars rigging, and fittings on all of the ships. This was the first steps in the control of naval architecture by the naval administration (McElvogue, 2008: 35). This occurred to create a permanent and professional Navy that could protect all the maritime needs of the nation (Marcus, 1961: 175).

DOI 10.1179/1350503312Z.00000000015

This paper will focus on the wreck of the *Stirling Castle* which was one of four ships of the line to perish on the Goodwin Sands during the Great Storm of 27 November 1703. The other three were the *Northumberland*, *Restoration*, and the *Mary*. These are the most preserved ships of the Restoration Navy, but none more so than the *Stirling Castle*. The Goodwin Sands lies off the south-east coast of Kent between Dover and Ramsgate. These sands are famously known as the 'Ship Swallower'. The remains of the ship are not only of high historical and archaeological importance, but they hold the potential for the development of methodological approaches to the protection of wrecks that are threatened by natural erosion (English Heritage, 2007: 5). This paper will discuss what has been learnt from the site's investigations, the heritage management issues of preservation *in situ* and offer a strategy for the future management of the site.

The *Stirling Castle*

The *Stirling Castle* was a Third Rate man of war of seventy guns constructed at Deptford in 1679 by John Shish (Winfield, 2009: 66). During her service the *Stirling Castle* had experienced defeat at the Battle of Beachy Head in 1690 and victory at the famous battle of Barfleur in 1692; the Trafalgar of the Restoration Navy. In 1699 the ship was rebuilt but was not recommissioned until 1701. Within two years of her recommission she was wrecked with the loss of many hands on the Goodwin Sands during the Great Storm (Hamblyn, 2005).

Discovery, designation, and reburial

After 265 years the *Stirling Castle* was finally discovered in 1979 by the Underwater Research Group of the Isle of Thanet Archaeological Unit (Perkins, 1980: 3). The description of what the divers found amazed the world of underwater archaeology. The sands had shifted revealing a relatively complete seventeenth-century man of war resting upright and proud on the seabed with guns still mounted on their carriages on the gundeck (Lapthorne,1986). The *Stirling Castle* had sailed once more into our midst as the sands of the Goodwins had shifted, gifting us a unique opportunity to travel back in time.

The ship was well preserved up to the lower gundeck with areas of collapsed main deck above. The quarter deck and poop deck were missing, although fragments were lying amongst the remains of the collapsed main deck. The bowsprit was detached lying on the seabed and much of the stern structure above the rudder had gone and large quantities of material were scattered on the seabed all around the wreck (Perkins, 1980: 5).

During the 1979 season many artefacts were recovered, including navigational instruments, personal possessions of the officers and men, numerous rigging elements, and small arms (Lyons, 1980: 339–42). A pewter plate was amongst the early finds with the initial 'JJ' recognized as belonging to John Johnson, the Captain of the *Stirling Castle* and therefore positively identifying the ship (Perkins, 1980: 7). Many of these artefacts were extremely vulnerable whilst exposed and had they been left on the seabed these artefacts would not have survived. The extent of the survival of the ship and its contents meant the *Stirling Castle* was an obvious candidate for designation and was protected under the 1973 Protection of Wrecks Act. Despite designation, the ship was still vulnerable to highly degrading processes of biological and physical decay. Limited time, funds, knowledge and calls for the ship's conservation were only relieved by the reburial of the ship a year later. By 1981 the other three naval ships of the Great Storm, the *Northumberland, Restoration* and possibly the *Mary* were discovered and designated (Perkins, 1980: 8). The remains of the *Stirling Castle* were purchased from the Ministry of Defence by the Thanet Archaeological Society. All artefacts recovered from the site are owned and under the curatorial control of the Society.

The Stirling Castle *re-emerges*

In 1998 the *Stirling Castle* re-emerged once more. The whole of the port stern was exposed from the keel up to the lower gundeck, including a gun pointing through one of the gunports (Bates et al., 2007: 61). By this time the site had a licensee who was appointed by the Secretary of State for Culture, Media and Sport to carryout licensed archaeological investigations on the site. The Licensee, Robert Peacock, with the help from members of the Seadive Organization, a charitable trust, began to record the site in earnest. Conditions on the site and Goodwins were and are, in general, far from favourable. Visibility is very poor, tides are strong and the depth of sand on the site can change daily. The combination of all of these makes recording the site extremely challenging.

The constant movement of sand exposing and covering different areas of the wreck changed the appearance of the site on a daily basis. The migration of sand away from the wreck and the weight of sand within caused the sides of the ship to bulge and collapse outwards (Figures 1 and 2). As the sides of the ship began to collapse, fragile artefacts from the interior of the ship became exposed, such as the ship's log reel (Figure 3). This was a unique artefact that had not been discovered from a wreck of this period. However, due to the licensing regime this artefact was not allowed to be removed from the seabed. A surface recovery licence had to be applied for before artefacts could be raised. Within days of the log reel being exposed it was lost to the tide. A surface recovery licence was not granted for the site until the year 2000, a year after the log reel and many other artefacts were first exposed. Unfortunately this delay meant valuable information and artefacts of enormous importance to our maritime heritage and history were lost or irreversibly damaged.

Planning and mapping the site

As soon as the *Stirling Castle* was exposed, the ship's aging process increased rapidly. The seabed and the sea around the site are highly dynamic due to the shifting sands and strong tides. The mobility of the sands has been demonstrated by the results numerous geophysical surveys on the site funded by English Heritage (EH) (Dix et al., 2009). Exposed structure and artefacts also become immediately vulnerable to marine boring organisms. So what at first appeared to be an archaeologists and divers dream shipwreck soon turned into a heritage management nightmare. Time was then of the essence to record and rescue information rapidly before it was lost.

Robert Peacock and his team have been recording the site since 1998, producing site plans and elevations with assistance from the Government appointed archaeological diving contractors, the Archaeological Diving Unit of the University of

FIGURE 1   View of the underside of the hull at the stern in 1998, revealing the complete loss of the supporting sands beneath the stern of the ship.
Photograph Bob Peacock

FIGURE 2   Diver sketch of the stern port quarter before collapse. It illustrates the extent of the preserved hull at the stern of the ship in July 1999.
Photograph Ted Westhead

FIGURE 3   The exposed log reel before loss.
Photograph Bob Peacock

St Andrews (ADU) from 1998–2002 and Wessex Archaeology from 2003–present. However, it has been an almost impossible task to keep up with the rate of environmental change. Fortunately, this was realized and geophysical methodologies were used to compliment the diver investigations. In 2005 the University of St Andrews under took a three-year project, the Rapid Archaeological Site Surveying and Evaluation (RASSE) administered by EH and funded through the Aggregates Levy Sustainability Fund (ALSF) (Bates et al., 2005; 2007; 2011). In 2008 and 2009 English Heritage continued with geophysical investigations by contracting Wessex Archaeology to carryout geophysical surveys as well as diver inspections on the site (Wessex Archaeology, 2009a; 2009b; 2010).

These surveys were able to record the changes in the surrounding seabed and monitor the changes occurring to the site due to its exposure. Geophysics has been a useful tool to produce a rapid record of the site which has also identified features for divers to investigate and record in more detail. Geophysical and diver survey combined with a good photographic record has been the only way to keep up with

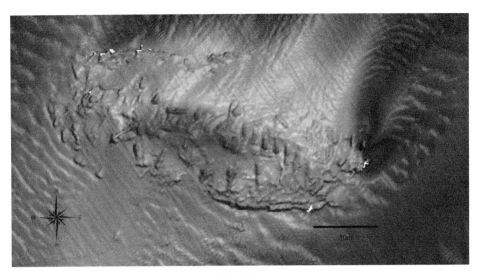

FIGURE 4   2006 multibeam image of site identifying key features such as guns and anchor. *Photograph ADU of the University of St Andrews, 2006*

the rapid physical changes due to the site dynamics. However, this is by no means claiming to have achieved a total record or to have saved parts of the ship from loss. The results of the surveys observed increases in sediment levels over the site between 2005 and 2006 (Bates et al., 2007: 107) but it has not been able to predict whether these levels are unlikely to rise sufficiently to completely cover the site and therefore protect it. At present both structure and artefacts remain exposed and at risk.

Unfortunately, Robert Peacock, despite his best efforts, has had to watch helplessly while the ship degrades *in situ*. The stern of the vessel, which was complete up to the top of the rudder, has almost completely collapsed along with the port quarter (Peacock 2006; 2007a; 2007b; 2008; 2009). Despite the loss of much of the stern structure and contents within the interior of this part of the ship, some important artefacts have been rescued.

Recovery of artefacts at risk

During the season of 2000 the port quarter had collapsed revealing a cannon complete with carriage and associated blocks and tackle. With the port quarter gone the gun was not only exposed but in danger of falling out of the wreck onto the seabed below (Peacock, pers. comm.). If left, this would be a lost opportunity to study not only the ordnance of the ship but the equipment that was essential in its operation. There was, therefore, a unique chance to enhance the knowledge of naval ordnance and associated equipment. It was decided that the threat was too great, and by the end of the season the decision was taken to raise the gun (Figure 5). After the recovery of the gun funding was sourced for the gun's conservation and for detailed recording and sampling by an archaeologist working along side the Licensee (McElvogue, 2008: 37).

FIGURE 5   The Rupertino cannon being lowered into the holding tank at Ramsgate to desalinate before conservation.
Photograph Bob Peacock

Investigations of the gun have revealed it is a unique Rupertino demi-cannon (McElvogue, 2008: 43). Although found on the broadside, this gun was one of two stern chases (McElvogue, forthcoming b). Each would be moved to the stern ports if required. Analysis of the gun has revealed a special type of casting process which has highlighted the new sciences that were being used at this time instigated by the newly formed Royal Society in London (McElvogue, 2008: 42). The Rupertino is the only one of its size, though there are at least twelve others of different bore sizes in Britain and the West Indies. This gun is also extremely important as it was complete with all its associated gun furniture: blocks and tackle, breaching ropes, carriage, and even things not found in the historical record, such as a wooden platter used as a match holder (McElvogue, 2008: 39). Rope was also found around the muzzle of the gun, suggesting it was secured against the side of the ship during the storm (McElvogue, 2008: 42).

Since the gun was raised it has been put on public display at Ramsgate Maritime Museum and the recording and research of the gun has been published (McElvogue, 2008) with further publications on their way (McElvogue, forthcoming a and b). The rescue, recording, and display of one of the *Stirling Castle's* guns has been extremely worthwhile greatly adding to the knowledge of naval ordnance on board a late seventeenth-century/early eighteenth-century warship. Only through recovery and detailed recording in a controlled environment was it possible to gain so much information from this gun.

How has site management progressed?

Up to March 2003 the Secretary of State, the heritage bodies of the dissolved Administrations, and the Advisory Committee on Historic Wreck Sites (ACHWS) were assisted by a team of contracted diving archaeologists, the ADU.[1] Following March 2003 EH took over the administration of the contract following the National Heritage Act (2002). This Act extended EH's remit to include ancient monuments in, on, or under the seabed to the 12 mile limit around England (Roberts et al., 2002). EH contracted Wessex Archaeology (WA) to visit designated sites to report on their condition and stability. Since gaining responsibility of the *Stirling Castle* in 2002, English Heritage has prioritized its investigations.

When the *Stirling Castle* re-emerged from the sands UK maritime archaeology was not prepared. In the intervening period between 1980 and 1998 nothing had really been done to plan for the ship's re-emergence. Within a very short period of becoming exposed it was quickly realized by the Licensee that diver fieldwork could not keep up with the rate at which the site was degrading. Either the site should be reburied or, at the very least, artefacts at high risk should be rescued. Sadly, it took two years to make a decision to issue a surface recovery licence, by which time hugely significant material had been lost. This delay to issue the site with a surface recovery licence was a grave misjudgement. This highlighted the limitations of preservation *in situ* without a proactive mitigation strategy. The absolute minimum requirement for such an exposed site in a highly dynamic environment is a surface recovery licence to enable the rescue of artefacts at high risk. Recovered material can be stored in passive storage in a controlled environment while funding is sourced for conservation.

The realization that the site was degrading faster than the site could be physically recorded led firstly to a surface recovery licence. With the lack of funding for a large-scale excavation and conservation programme, the second and short-term solution appeared to be the rapid recording of the site through high-resolution geophysical survey methods. This resulted in numerous geophysical surveys on the site between 2002 and 2009 (Bates et al., 2007; Wessex Archaeology, 2009a; 2010; Dix et al., 2009). This has produced a rapid record of the site, which has recognized the changes occurring over time and it has also identified archaeological features for interpretation. From this it has been possible to identify changes not only to the ship but also the surrounding seabed, and better inform when the ship may be exposed or naturally reburied again. This should be key for the future management of the site.

In 2007 EH published a Conservation Statement and Management Plan (CSMP) for the *Stirling Castle*, which utilized all the knowledge gained from the site since its discovery. The CSMP realizes through the sheer magnitude of the archaeological remains of the *Stirling Castle* that managing the entire hull is no longer appropriate and that selected areas for stabilization is considered a better management option (English Heritage, 2007: 14). The plan also realized the need to consolidate existing archival and artefactual material from the site and disseminate this information through academic publications and public information boards. Thus, by securing what already exists from the site and through stabilizing the most at risk parts of the ship one can preserve aspects of the ship for the future.

As a result of the *Stirling Castle* it has been realized that sites in highly dynamic environments cannot be ignored and that a proactive approach must be taken. This has been applied to the designated sites of the Swash Channel wreck, *Hazardous*, *Northumberland*, and *Colossus*. These sites are all at high risk and thus were issued with surface recovery licences. Within the last three years comprehensive research agendas have been developed for these sites and as a result excavation licences have been issued.

Sadly, for the *Stirling Castle* the reaction and response to the ship's exposure and deterioration was several years overdue and despite the CSMP some of the most important objectives have yet to be fulfilled, such as stabilizing and preserving the remains of the stern *in situ* (English Heritage, 2007: 20).

Future management for the *Stirling Castle*

The *Stirling Castle* is a significant and internationally important seventeenth-century warship. However, when it was most needed it was never given the archaeological attention that it deserved. The result has been the considerable loss of structure and content of the ship. The collapse of exposed and unsupported structure and the encroaching sands is allowing the ship to reach an equilibrium with the surrounding seabed. Despite this both structure and artefacts still remain exposed and at risk in all areas of the site (Wessex Archaeology, 2009a).

With the improved stability of the site new management priorities have evolved; shifting from saving archaeology to dealing with a backlog of records. EH commissioned the Hampshire and Wight Trust for Maritime Archaeology (HWTMA) to work alongside the Licensee to consolidate previous work to produce an archive of the site that all can access (English Heritage, 2007). This will aid future site management for when the site becomes exposed again and assist in formulating a new research led strategy for when the time is right to excavate. In the meantime exposed and vulnerable parts of the ship should be stabilized or recovered as prioritized in the CSMP (English Heritage, 2007). This can be achieved by working alongside the Licensee to identify the areas and artefacts of the ship most at risk. Recovered material can be kept in passive storage facilities until funding is sourced. The recording of the objects while in storage can be utilized by trainees of archaeology such as members of the Nautical Archaeology Society (NAS) or other local interest groups supervised by professional archaeologists. This not only preserves parts of the *Stirling Castle* through recording but proactively disseminates the history and story of the ship to a wider audience through active participation.

Should the *Stirling Castle* re-emerge again and remain untouched it will continue to deteriorate and eventually disappear. The *Stirling Castle* and others like it in similar seabed dynamics cannot realistically be preserved *in situ*. Information of enormous importance to British maritime culture and heritage will be lost unless such vulnerable wreck sites are developed through research led excavation and recovery in an archaeologically responsible manner. Lessons have been learned from the *Stirling Castle* and vulnerable sites such as the Swash Channel wreck, *Hazardous*, *Northumberland*, and *Colossus* are now being investigated through research-led excavations and surface recovery.

Acknowledgements

I would like to thank Robert Peacock, the Licensee for the Great Storm wrecks, and Dr Douglas McElvogue, the site archaeologist for the *Stirling Castle*, for all their assistance and knowledge of the sites.

Note

1 <http://www.english-heritage.org.uk/professional/ advice/our-planning-role/consent/protected-wreck- sites/contract-for-archaeological-services/> [accessed 10 October 2012].

Bibliography

Bates, R., Dean, M., Lawrence, M., Robertson, P., and Tempera, F. 2005. Innovative Approaches to Rapid Archaeological Site Surveying and Evaluation (RASSE) Year One Report. Unpublished ALSF report for English Heritage, University of St Andrews.

Bates, R., Dean, M., Lawrence, M., Robertson, P., Tempera, F., and Laird, S. 2007. Innovative Approaches to Rapid Archaeological Site Surveying and Evaluation (RASSE) Final Report. Unpublished ALSF report for English Heritage, University of St Andrews.

Bates, C. R., Lawrence, M., Dean, M., and Robertson, P. 2011. Geophysical Methods for Wreck Monitoring: The Rapid Archaeological Site Survey and Evaluation (RASSE) Programme. *International Journal of Nautical Archaeology*, 40.2: 404–16.

Dix, J., Lambkin, D., and Rangecroft, T. 2009. Modelling Sediment Mobility. *MACCHU Report 2*. Rotterdam: Educom BV.

English Heritage, 2007. *Stirling Castle: Conservation & Management Plan*. Available at: <http://www.english-heritage.org.uk/content/imported-docs/p-t/mgmtplan-stirlingcastlevfinal.pdf>. [Accessed 15 August 2012].

Fenwick, V. and Gale, A. 1998. *Historic Shipwrecks Discovered, Protected and Investigated*. Stroud: Tempus.

Fox, F. L. 1980. *Great Ships: The Battle Fleet of King Charles II*. London: Conway Maritime Press.

Hamblyn, R. 2005 ed. *Daniel Defoe, The Storm*. London: Penguin.

Hepper, D. J. 1994. *British Warship Losses in the Age of Sail, 1650–1859*. Rotherfield, East Sussex: Jean Boudroit.

Knighton, C.S. 2003. *Pepys and the Navy*. Stroud: Sutton.

Lapthorne, W.H. 1986. Secrets of the World's Greatest Ocean Graveyard. *The Searcher*, 7: 12–14.

Lyon, D. J. 1980. The Goodwins Wreck. *International Journal of Nautical Archaeology and Underwater Exploration*, 9(4): 339–50.

McElvogue, D. 2008. The *Stirling Castle* Prince Rupert patient demi-cannon. *Ordnance Society Journal*, 20: 35–46.

McElvogue, D. forthcoming a. *The Naval Gun Carriage of the Restoration Navy. An Example from the Stirling Castle*.

McElvogue, D. forthcoming b. *Supply and Demand in the Restoration Navy; Stirling Castle's Rupertino*.

Marcus, G. J. 1961. *A Naval History of England. The Formative Centuries*. London: Whitefriars Press.

Peacock, B. 2006. Licensee Report to ACHWS. Unpublished report.

Peacock, B. 2007a. Licensee Report to ACHWS. Unpublished report.

Peacock, B. 2007b. A Survey on the Stirling Castle Wreck in 1703. Unpublished dissertation.

Peacock, B. 2008. Survey Report for the 2008 Season on the Sites of 'Stirling Castle', 'Northumberland' and 'Restoration'. Unpublished licensee report to ACHWS.

Peacock, B. 2009. Survey Report for the 2009 Season on the Sites of 'Stirling Castle', 'Northumberland' and 'Restoration'. Unpublished licensee report to ACHWS.

Perkins, D. R. J. 1980. *The Great Storm Wrecks*. East Kent Maritime Trust.

Roberts, P. and Trow, S. 2002. Taking to the Water: English Heritage's Initial Policy for the Management of Maritime Archaeology in England. Unpublished report: English Heritage.

Wessex Archaeology, 2009a. South East of England Designated Wrecks: Marine Geophysical Surveys. Unpublished report, ref. 69951.01.

Wessex Archaeology, 2009b. Stirling Castle, Designated Assessment: Archaeological Report. Unpublished report, ref. 53111.03000.

Wessex Archaeology, 2010. East of England Designated Wrecks: Marine Geophysical Surveys. Unpublished report, ref. 71770.01.

Winfield, R. 2009. British Warships in the Age of Sail, 1603–1715: Design, Construction, Careers and Fates. Barnsley, Yorkshire: Seaforth.

Notes on contributor

Daniel Pascoe is a marine archaeologist with a special interest in the Great Storm wrecks on the Goodwin Sands. He is a member of the Seadive Organization, who are a charitable trust concerned with the protection and recording of shipwrecks on the Goodwin Sands.

Correspondence to: Daniel Pascoe, 44 Methuen Road, Southsea PO4 9HH, UK. Email: danielpascoe23@hotmail.com

CONSERVATION AND MGMT OF ARCH. SITES, Vol. 14 Nos 1–4, 2012, 193–200

The ISCR Project 'Restoring Underwater': An Evaluation of the Results After Ten Years

ROBERTO PETRIAGGI
Editor of Archaeologia Maritima Mediterranea, Italy

BARBARA DAVIDDE
Istituto Superiore per la Conservazione ed il Restauro (ISCR), Italy

The project 'Restoring Underwater' launched and conducted by the Underwater Archaeology Operations Unit of the Istituto Superiore per la Conservazione ed il Restauro (ISCR, Rome, Italy) is aimed at the study and the experimentation of instruments, materials, methodologies, and techniques for the restoration, conservation, and *in situ* display of ancient submerged artefacts. The project commenced in 2001 with the restoration of the *vivaria* of the Roman villa of Torre Astura (Nettuno, Rome), since 2003 the main subject of researches has been the submerged archaeological site of Baiae (Naples, Italy), where, over the years, the restoration of sectors of certain buildings in the protected marine area has been carried out: the *Villa con ingresso a Protiro*, the *Villa dei Pisoni*, the *Via Herculanea*, and the *Building with porticoed courtyard* near *Portus Iulius*. In 2007, in 2009, and in 2010 three new archaeological targets have been added to the research: a group of nine cast iron cannons discovered offshore the coast of the Marettimo Island (Sicily, Italy), the Roman wreck carrying a load of sarcophagi discovered off the coast of San Pietro in Bevagna (Taranto, Italy), and the traditional fishing boat recently discovered off the cost of Martana Island (Bolsena Lake, Italy).

The purpose of this paper is to sum up the work in progress and the results of these ten years of the project. The paper will shows as the conservation and museum display *in situ* of underwater heritage must not just be considered an opportune choice but may in itself provide a strong stimulus for experimenting new materials and technologies as well as representing a factor in the socio-economic development of the communities concerned, as shown by the example of Baiae.

© Taylor & Francis 2012   DOI 10.1179/1350503312Z.00000000016

KEYWORDS underwater *in situ* conservation, cathodic protection, underwater archaeological parks, Baiae, Torre Astura, San Pietro in Bevagna wreck, Marettimo Island

The project 'Restoring Underwater', launched and conducted by ISCR, is aimed at the study and the experimentation of instruments, materials, methods, and techniques for the *in situ* restoration, conservation, and display of cultural heritage, in accordance with the Convention on the Protection of the Underwater Cultural Heritage, Unesco (Paris, 2 November 2001). The project commenced in 2001 with the restoration of the *vivaria* of the Roman villa of Torre Astura (Nettuno-Rome). Still well preserved (150 × 120 m) and divided into geometric sectors, the ruins of the fish farm lie in the sea rising up from a depth of about 2 m in front of the archaeological structures of the villa. Since 2003 the main subject of research has been the submerged archaeological site of Baiae (Naples), the famous seaside town much prized in antiquity for its temperate climate, beautiful setting, and the properties of its mineral waters which have been exploited since the second century BC. It was the most popular resort of Roman Aristocracy and the Imperial Family up to the end of the third century AD, when the bradyseisme caused the beginning of the submersion of the city. Now the remains of the city lie underwater along up to a distance of 400–500 m far from the modern shoreline. Here, over the years, the restoration of sectors of several buildings has been carried out: the *Villa con ingresso a Protiro*, the *Villa dei Pisoni* (Figure 1) (Petriaggi and Mancinelli, 2004; Petriaggi, 2005), a sector of the so called *Via Herculanea* and the *Building with porticoed courtyard* near *Portus Iulius* (Figures 2 and 3) (Petriaggi and Davidde, 2005; 2007; 2008). In 2007, 2009, and 2010 three new targets have been added to the research programme: nine cast iron cannons discovered off the coast of Marettimo Island (Trapani) (Bartuli et al., 2008), the roman wreck carrying a load of sarcophagi off the coast of San Pietro in Bevagna (Taranto) (Petriaggi and Davidde, 2010), and the traditional fishing boat recently discovered off the coast of Martana Island (Bolsena Lake, Viterbo).

The possibility to test the effects of different conservation and restoration methods on different materials in various environmental contexts has allowed us to assess and classify the effects of the different degradation agents and to especially understand the importance of ordinary maintenance. Therefore, due to the varying nature and degree of degradation of the individual items we had to develop a target strategy for each different methodological approach. Unfortunately, the problems of aggressive attack by underwater organisms, together with the difficulties of working in a liquid medium, were constant factors that needed to be addressed.

At Torre Astura we initially decided to tackle the biological colonization by adding a biocide in the mortar dough, but later this practice was abandoned because of environmental ethics.

In Baiae our efforts have therefore focused on physical rather than chemical biological control, by covering the mosaic floors more susceptible to degradation with geotextile sheets or mattresses stuffed with suitable material (small grains of gravel). The mortars used for the restoration of the masonry structures and for the mosaic

FIGURE 1   Baia (Naples). Wall of the *viridarium* of the Villa dei Pisoni. Particular of the semi-column after restoration. *Photograph by authors*

floors were also the subject of our experimentation. In fact, the materials used in the early restorations (Albaria ® injection mortar, and Albaria ® structural bedding mortar, supplied by M.A.C. S.p.a. Treviso, Italy) although at the beginning showed excellent hardening properties, showed some leaks over the years in some localized spots, chiefly due to interference from environmental or human factors at the time of the consolidation phases. As a result, we changed the initial products with others that have so far proved very effective, despite any interference (Volteco Microlime Gel ®). Above all, in order to remove the biological agents that attacked the ancient structures, we carried out a careful cleaning, by mechanical removal, using instruments normally employed above ground for this procedure (axes, hammers, chisels and metal spatulas and so on). A pneumatic micro-grinder was also used on an experimental basis to reach a refined cleaning (Figure 4).

The filling of the upper masonry surfaces has been carried out using supply sacks made of a plasticized fabric or by means of a 'regulator/injector' to distribute the mortar under pressure that was built specifically to be used underwater, for filling lacunae and deep cracks.[1]

FIGURE 2   Portus Iulius (Naples). Building with porticoed courtyard. A detail of one of the
brick columns after restoration.
Photograph by authors

FIGURE 3   Portus Iulius (Naples). Building with porticoed courtyard after restoration.
Photograph by authors

FIGURE 4   Baia (Naples). Villa dei Pisoni. A restorer removes the biological incrustations using a pneumatic micro-grinder.
Photograph by authors

Furthermore, following the experience gained in North Europe and Australia, we have applied a sacrificial anode to limit the effects of electrochemical corrosion and conserve *in situ* the iron cannons lying in the depths of Marettimo Island in the Mediterranean. In previous experiments, a metal bow, bearing two lateral pins that pierced the concretion, was applied to the cannon. These pins were connected to the electrical cable leading to the anode of sacrifice (Bartuli et al., 2008). Later, since 2008, a new method, less invasive, with a single perforation of the concretions, allows us to work without the metal bow, with aesthetically better effects. We make a hole about 2 cm in diameter in the concretion, in hidden parts that were not otherwise accessible with arches, until reaching the metal. Then we insert a rubber cylinder and, within this, a threaded pin connected to the anode (Figures 5 and 6). At this point the rubber cylinder, crossed by the pin, expands by screwing a nut, resulting in the isolation of the pin from the concretions and from the marine environment.

Finally, the study of appropriate ways to present to the public the underwater archaeological remains, has led us to test illustrative panels encased in stainless steel boxes at the site of the wreck of San Pietro in Bevagna (Figure 7) (Petriaggi and Davidde, 2010), and a band reinforced plexiglass and polycarbonate system for impact protection, for the fishing boat wreck located off the coast of Martana Island.

FIGURE 5   Marettimo Island. On the left the threaded pin applied to the cannon.

FIGURE 6   Marettimo Island On the left the threaded pin applied to the cannon and connected to the anode (in the centre of the picture).

FIGURE 7   Wreck of San Pietro in Bevagna (Taranto). A diver reading the illustrative panel encased in stainless steel box.
Photograph by authors

After ten years, the project 'Restoring Underwater' demonstrates that the conservation and museum display *in situ* of underwater heritage must not just be considered an appropriate choice, but may in itself provide a strong stimulus for experimenting new materials and technologies, as well as representing an important factor in the socio-economic development of the communities involved.

Notes

[1] This tool was designed by R. Petriaggi and manufactured by G. Santinelli (Fluimac S.r.l.).

[2] <www.libraweb.net> [accessed 5 October 2012].

Bibliography

Bartuli, C., Petriaggi, R., Davidde, B., Palmisano, E., and Lino, G. 2008. *In situ* Conservation by Cathodic Protection of Cast Iron Findings in Marine Environment. In: *9th International Conference on Non-Destructive Investigations and Microanalysis for the Diagnostics and Conservation of Cultural and Environmental Heritage of Art 2008 Jerusalem, 25–30 May 2008, Jerusalem* [accessed 5 October 2012]. Available at: <http://www.ndt.net/search/docs.php3?DocGroup=-1&date=-1&language=-1&Country=-1&KeywordID=-1&MainSource=65&instID=-1&SearchDocs=bartuli&restrict=authors&searchmode=AND&OrderBy=session&admin=&rpp=20&rppoffset=0&menu=docs.php3>.

Petriaggi, R. and Mancinelli, R. 2004. An Experimental Conservation Treatment on the Mosaic Floor and Perimeter Walls of Room n. 1 of the So-Called «Villa con ingresso a protiro» in the Underwater Archaeological Park of Baia (Naples). *Archaeologia Maritima Mediterranea*, 1: 109–26. Available at: <www.libraweb.net>.

Petriaggi, R. 2005. Nuove esperienze di restauro conservativo nel Parco Sommerso di Baia. *Archaeologia Maritima Mediterranea*, 2: 135–47.

Petriaggi, R. and Davidde, B. 2005. The Analytical Data Card of Underwater Archaeological Finds (SAMAS) for Diagnosing the Deterioration. *Archaeologia Maritima Mediterranea*, 2: 161–70.

Petriaggi, R. and Davidde, B. 2007. Restaurare sott'acqua: cinque anni di sperimentazione del NIAS-ICR. *Bollettino dell'Istituto Centrale per il Restauro, nuova serie*, 14: 127–41.

Petriaggi, R. and Davidde, B. 2008. Restauration subaquatique: le bilan de cinq années de travaux expérimentaux de l'Institut Central pour la Restauration. In: E. Bréaud, ed. *IVèmes Rencontres Internationales Monaco et la Méditerranée, Monaco 22–24 Mars 2007*. Monaco: Association Monégasque pur la Connaissance des Arts, pp. 105–16.

Petriaggi, R. and Davidde, B. 2010. The Sarcophagi from the Wreck of San Pietro in Bevagna (TA): The Subject of New Works by the Istituto Superiore per la Conservazione ed il Restauro. *Archaeologia Maritima Mediterranea*, 7: 131–37.

Notes on contributors

Dr Roberto Petriaggi is editor of *Archaeologia Maritima Mediterranea. An International Journal on Underwater Archaeology*,[2] and was former Adjunct Professor of Underwater Archaeology at Università degli Studi Roma Tre (Rome, Italy). He was also the former Director of the Underwater Archaeological Operations Unit, Istituto Superiore per la Conservazione ed il Restauro (ISCR).

Correspondence to: Dr Roberto Petriaggi. Email: r.petriaggi@tiscali.it

Dr Barbara Davidde is Director of the Underwater Archaeological Operations Unit, Istituto Superiore per la Conservazione ed il Restauro (ISCR), Rome, Italy, and Adjunct Professor of Underwater Archaeology, Università degli Studi Roma Tre, Rome, Italy.

Correspondence to: Dr Barbara Davidde. Email: barbara.davidde@beniculturali.it

CONSERVATION AND MGMT OF ARCH. SITES, Vol. 14 Nos 1–4, 2012, 201–14

Strategies for Protection of Wooden Underwater Cultural Heritage in the Baltic Sea Against Marine Borers. The EU Project 'WreckProtect'

CHARLOTTE GJELSTRUP BJÖRDAL
University of Gothenburg, Sweden
Responsible author and coordinator of WreckProtect

DAVID GREGORY
National Museum of Denmark, Denmark

MARTIJN MANDERS
RCE, Netherlands

ZYAD AL-HAMDANI
GEUS, Denmark

CHRISTIN APPELQVIST and JON HAVERHAND
University of Gothenburg, Sweden

JÖRGEN DENCKER
The Viking Ship Museum, Roskilde, Denmark

Marine borers constitute a great danger to historical shipwreck in marine environments as they are able to decompose wood material in just a few years. Recently, there have been indications that the marine borer *Teredo navalis* is spreading into the brackish Baltic sea, where thousands of invaluable historical wrecks for centuries have had unique preservation conditions. The WreckProtect project was a coordination and support action funded by the European Commission within the 7th Framework Program. The main objective of the project was to develop tools for predicting the spread of marine borers into the Baltic and to evaluate methods for *in situ* protection of the historical wreck and submerged settlements. This paper gives a summary final report of the project and an overview of results.

© Taylor & Francis 2012   DOI 10.1179/1350503312Z.00000000017

KEYWORDS WreckProtect, shipwreck, Baltic Sea, decay, *in situ* protection, GIS modelling, *Teredo navalis*

Introduction

Today the Baltic Sea is a unique resource for marine archaeology. The low salinity (5–10 practical salinity units (PSU)) of the water has excluded aggressive marine borers, and historical shipwrecks can be found intact both above and beneath the seabed. The Vasa ship, the number one tourist attraction of Stockholm, Sweden, is an example of the unique preservation conditions in the Baltic Sea (Figure 1). It is estimated that around 100,000 shipwrecks are present in the Baltic today and at least 6000 are of high archaeological importance (Olsson, 2006). The nine countries that surround the Baltic — Denmark, Sweden, Germany, Poland, Finland, Estonia, Latvia, Lithuania and Russia — discover new wrecks each year and consequently the number of wrecks is still rising.

Salvaging each unique wreck is not a realistic option; in the first instance, due to the tremendous costs for conservation, excavation, storage, and exhibition. Consequently, *in situ* preservation has become more and more common and accepted as a long-term preservation method. It is also recommended as a first choice option by the

FIGURE 1   The warship Vasa displayed at the Vasa museum in Stockholm, Sweden.
© *Lindman, Vasamuseum*

2001 UNESCO convention for the Protection of the Submerged Cultural Heritage which should be followed by all nations (UNESCO, 2001)

New information and observations have indicated that *Teredo navalis* is spreading into the southern parts of the Baltic Sea (Manders and Luth, 2004). The aggressive marine borers, with a worm-like appearance, are able to decompose wood constructions in a few years (Figure 2). This spread is possibly an effect of global climatic change and the worst case scenario would be a massive loss of unique archaeological shipwrecks and submerged wooden settlements or other wooden constructions in the Baltic.

The WreckProtect project started in May 2009 and ended in April 2011. The full title of the project was 'Strategies for the protection of shipwrecks in the Baltic Sea against forthcoming attack by wood degrading marine borers. A synthesis and

FIGURE 2 Heavy attack by *Teredo navalis*. The mollusc penetrates and digests the wood material forming up to 1 cm wide tunnels. *Photograph C. Björdal*

information project based on the effects of climatic changes'. It was financed mainly by the European Commission within the 7th framework programme, Theme Environment, and was a cross-disciplinary project involving scientists within geophysics, marine biology, marine archaeology, wood decay, and conservation. The consortia consisted of six partners from three countries, the Netherlands, Denmark, and Sweden, and was coordinated by SP technical research institute of Sweden. All work within the project was based on present knowledge and was carried out by careful literature studies in each field of interest. The accumulated knowledge was synthesized and evaluated and used in a cross-disciplinary context (Björdal and Gregory, in press; Gregory and Björdal, in press).

This paper will give the reader a short final report on the project and highlight the most important results.[1]

Summary description of the project objectives

The main scientific objectives were:

- To provide cultural resource managers, archaeologists, and conservators responsible for the long-term preservation of cultural heritage with tools for assessing and predicting the future spread of wood degrading organisms, especially *Teredo navalis*, which can rapidly attack underwater wooden objects and constructions.
- Recommend practical methods for protection of shipwrecks and historical settlements *in situ*, in order to prevent/delay their decay.
- To develop two user-friendly practical guidelines for prediction of risk zones and *in situ* protection of cultural heritage.

Project plan

The project was divided into five work packages, where the three scientific work packages are found in Table 1. The remaining two work packages (WP) were focused on management and dissemination of the project. This paper will give an overview of the scientific work only.

During the first year of the project, work was concentrated to WP 1 and WP 2.

WP 1: Coordinating present biological and environmental data

The aim was to synthesize environmental data from the Baltic Sea in order to produce a simple model that is able to predict the growth of the marine borer, *Teredo navalis*, in brackish waters.

TABLE 1

THE THREE SCIENTIFIC WORKPACKAGES OF WRECKPROTECT

Work packages (WP)	Title
WP 1	Coordinating present biological and environmental data
WP 2	Review of methods for protection of historical wreck and settlements in marine environments
WP 3	Strategy and tools for protection of cultural heritage

The environmental data sets used for this work included information from a relatively wide period of time; 1980–2008 for the hind cast data sets, and 2009–20 for the predicted data sets. The key environmental parameters that determine the species' distribution are salinity, temperature, oxygen, and ocean currents. Hydrographical datasets were obtained from the DHI company[2] and transferred into a GIS model. The spatial resolution of data for the model was 3and 9 nautical miles for the western and eastern Baltic respectively with average weekly measurements being obtained for both hind case and predicted data sets. The data were divided into two sets where one is the sea surface layer representing the larval habitat, and the other represents the adult habitat in the bottom layer. The Model Builder, one of the ESRI's ArcGIS extensions (www.esri.com), was used in this project. A step-by-step guide to model building is presented in the coming sections. Three models were built: one to merge the environmental data sets, a second to extract the spatial extent per year of particular merging scenarios, and the third to find the number of times a scenario will appear in a specific month over the investigated period of time (Frequency of Occurrence) of when situations are favourable for reproduction and growth of shipworm. To facilitate this, a full literature survey was conducted to elucidate the ecological criteria of *Teredo navalis* and point out which environmental parameters are important for survival and reproduction.

Although microbial decay was not included in the model, a comprehensive literature survey was conducted on these degraders to give a full picture of the biological degraders of wood in the marine environment.

Finally, a tool for the prediction of potential decay areas of *Teredo navalis* was synthesized. A very large amount of data was restructured and reformatted to a GIS (Geographical Information System) compatible format and a database was built for housing the data and restructuring them. The data was then loaded to the GIS program 'ArcGIS' for processing. Intense cross-disciplinary discussions were conducted and aimed specifically to categorize the environmental parameters into ecologically relevant classes. These classes were used in the GIS Geoprocessing program for delineating and predicting areas where forthcoming spread and attack of *Teredo navali*s are most likely to take place, that is, 'Hot Spots'. A verification of the model was based on known outbreaks of the *Teredo navalis* in the Baltic Sea region.

WP 2: Review of methods for protection of historical wreck and settlements in marine environments

An extensive literature review on methods for protection of shipwreck *in situ* was carried out. This included experimental studies and methods carried out and tested by conservators and marine archaeologists, as well as experiences from coastal engineering and the offshore industry when protecting wooden constructions such as piles or harbour constructions in marine environments. Additionally, a review of 'historical' literature, primarily from the Netherlands in the 1700s, was accomplished. The aims of all the literature reviews were to see what methods could be applicable to the *in situ* protection of shipwreck and other wooden archaeological artefacts.

As a result of the literature reviews, researchers from the aforementioned fields were invited to participate in a seminar to shed light on the results of the literature review and also highlight potential methods which had possibly not been covered in the literature review.

WP 3: Strategy and tools for protection of cultural heritage

In WP 3, two guidelines were produced. These were based on previous work carried out in WP 1 and WP 2 respectively, and aimed to be practical tools for stakeholder, managers and conservators working with protection of wooden underwater cultural heritage. It was the intention that both should be readily understandable and straightforward for use in practice. The first guideline was instructions on how to use the GIS model (produced in WP 1) as a tool for detection and prediction the spread of *Teredo navalis* in the Baltic Sea. It also included important background information on the Baltic Sea and *Teredo navalis*. The second guideline (based on WP 2) provided managers responsible for the protection of underwater cultural heritage with information and methods on how sites can be protected, the advantages and disadvantages of these protection measures, the threats, and cost benefit analyses.

Summary of main results achieved

WP 1: Coordinating present biological and environmental data

- A comprehensive study was presented on marine borers *Teredo navalis* (Figure 3a (Nair and Saraswarthy, 1971) and 3b), their ecology, biology, and their classification criteria with respect to the environmental parameters in their habitat. These parameters, summarized in Table 2, included salinity, temperature, dissolved oxygen, and current. Each parameter was studied and a numerical measure was established for its influence on the marine borer productivity and survivability both as adult and larvae.
- A full literature review for the historical documentation of shipworm attack and outbreaks, dating back from the present (2009) to the 1870s, in Danish territorial waters was carried out. Outbreaks of shipworm have occurred throughout the past 100 years or more in Danish territorial waters and the southern Baltic — it is not just a recent phenomenon. Recent reports from 1990 to 2009 state that these attacks appear to be worsening or are unprecedented. Outbreaks of *Teredo navalis* along the Baltic coast of Germany have been a reoccurring event since at least 1872, with records in almost each decade since then. Also in Danish waters large outbreaks have been seen in periods (1924–26, 1932–35, 1937–1941, 1947–50, 1955–60). In the 1970s and 1980s there was a dearth of literature relating to attacks, but in the 1990s problems seemed to start again.
- A full study on the microbial degraders was completed, giving an overview on the situation of microbial degradation by fungi and bacteria taking place in the Baltic Sea today. It was found that soft rot fungi and bacteria degrade the surface and interior layer of timbers in all types of saline, brackish, or fresh water environments (Björdal, in press). Where marine borers are absent, like in most part of the Baltic, these fungi and bacteria are the most important wood degraders in a long-term prospective, both above and beneath sediment.
- A model was built in ModelBuilder ArcGIS geoprocessing program for processing and combining the modelled environmental parameters. This model was used as a platform for additional models. The total spatial extent of a given

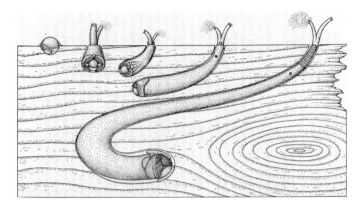

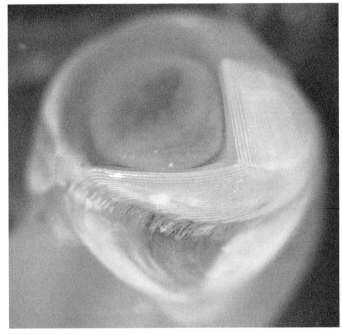

FIGURE 3   *Teredo navalis.*
FIGURE 3a   Life-cycle of *T. navalis* (Nair and Saraswarthy, 1971).
FIGURE 3b   Shell and muscular foot (ø 5mm) of an adult *T. Navalis.*
Photograph C. Appelqvist

combination scenario over an entire year was calculated and presented in separate maps for each year. The model reconstructed the situation from 1980–2008, and subsequently predicted different scenarios for the future 2009–20. It was evident that the areas of risk zones fluctuated between years, but no significant extension of the geographical zone of spread could be observed (Figure 4a and b). However, the model showed a prolongation of the infestation season, as water temperatures during October will in future be warmer (Figure 5a and b). Thus, there will be a risk for an increased total number of larvae during a season, which gives a higher risk of growth and hence attack by *T. navalis*.

- The model was verified by information from known locations with and without attacks on test panels during the time periods of the model in the south western part of the Baltic Sea and from records in modern and historical archives
- To conclude, an increased number of larvae could be expected in the Baltic Sea, but not a spread into new areas.

Table 2

ENVIRONMENTAL PARAMETERS FOR THE SURVIVAL OF SHIPWORM LARVAE AND ADULTS

Larvae Class	1	2	3
Temperature (°C)	< 7 lethal	7–12 survival	> 12 development possible
Salinity (PSU)	< 5 lethal	5–8 survival	> 8 metamorphosis possible
Oxygen (mg O$_2$/l)	< 1 lethal 24 hr	1–4 effect on physiology	> 4 healthy condition
Currents (m/s)	< 0.1 (<120 km/2wks)	0.1–0.2 (120–240 km/2wks)	> 0.2 (>240 km/2 wks)
Adults Class	1	2	3
Temperature (°C)	< - 2 lethal	-2–11 survival	> 11 reproduction possible
Salinity (PSU)	< 4 lethal	4–8 survival	> 8 reproduction possible
Oxygen (mg O$_2$/l)	< 1 lethal 4 wks	1–4 effect on physiology	> 4 healthy condition

WP 2: Review of methods for protection of historical wreck and settlements in marine environments

- The literature review examined over 1000 articles, reports, and books. Summarily, many of the historical methods, although fascinating, were not applicable to *in situ* preservation of archaeological finds against shipworm. Likewise modern methods used by the wood industry are not applicable as they include simply using different materials to wood or impregnation with toxic chemicals unsuitable for marine archaeological purposes. The most successful and applicable methods appear to be physical barriers which either prevent the shipworm attacking the wood or making the environment unfavourable for their growth. These methods have included covering with plastic materials and geotextiles or creating an artificial burial mound over a wreck with sand bags or other means which utilize the natural transport of sediment within the water column around a site (Figure 6).

WP 3: Strategy and tools for protection of cultural heritage
Two guidelines were produced:

Guideline for prediction of decay by shipworm in the Baltic Sea[3]
A user-friendly guideline with information and instructions on how to predict the spread of *Teredo navalis* was written. A translation of data (scientific) was disseminated to the stakeholders such as policymakers, managers of cultural heritage, and a larger public. As the guidelines involve the use of a GIS-model, additional information directed to persons familiar with GIS modelling was provided. General information on the biological degraders in the Baltic Sea was given with a main focus on the growth and reproduction of *Teredo navalis*. With help of this tool and information, it is now possible to identify areas in the Baltic Sea where *Teredo navalis* could be active. When WreckProtect GIS Map is combined with national GIS maps with

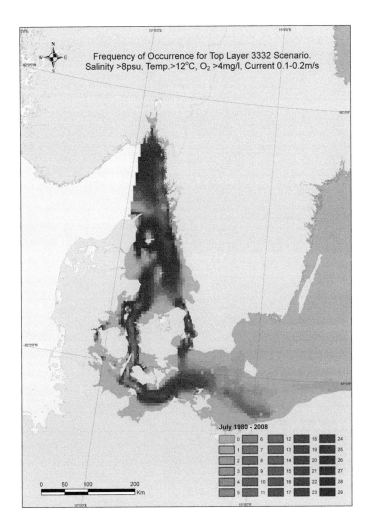

FIGURE 4   Spread of *Teredo navalis*. Top layer/larvae: No significant difference in spread into the Baltic Sea of *Teredo navalis* in the hind cast GIS map of July 1989–2009 (Figure 4a), compared to predicted spread July 2009–20 (Figure 4 b).

positions of historical wrecks, stakeholders in countries surrounding the Baltic Sea will be able to identify wrecks in risk zones and take the necessary precautions.

Guideline for the protection of wrecks including cost-benefit analysis[4]
Instructions on how to protect submerged wooden cultural heritage against deteriorating factors. This means not only the *Teredo navalis*, but also, for example, abrasion and human factors. The protection methods for in situ preservation are explained carefully with instructions, illustrating photos, tips, and suggested reading.

A cost-benefit analysis on *in situ* versus *ex situ* (excavation) is included and examples show very clearly that a full excavation, conservation, and exhibition of a larger shipwreck is very expensive and could be estimated roughly as 700 times as costly compared to *in situ* protection.

The guideline should be a tool for managers responsible for the protection of underwater cultural heritage to make decisions on whether sites can be protected,

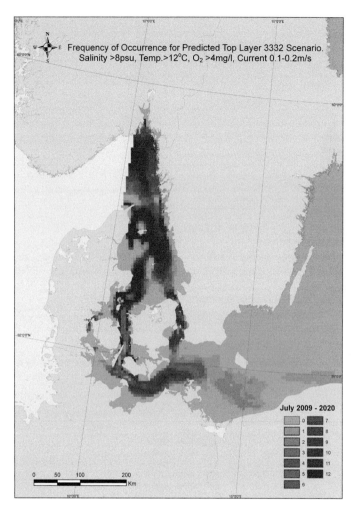

FIGURE 4b

how they can be protected, the advantages and disadvantages and the costs of these actions compared to *ex situ* conservation. The methods are applicable to hulls that are partly embedded in the sediments, which include wrecks in all waters such as the Mediterranean and the Baltic Sea.

Conclusion

The outcome of WreckProtect has provided stakeholders, managers, marine archaeologists, and conservators in Europe, that are responsible for long-term preservation of cultural heritage, with new tools for tracking environmental changes that endanger the long term preservation of historical shipwreck, as well as offer methods for *in situ* protection based on the most cost efficient choice. By using the guidelines, sites and unique historical shipwreck which are at threat from marine borers can be identified and prioritized for protection and saved for future generations.

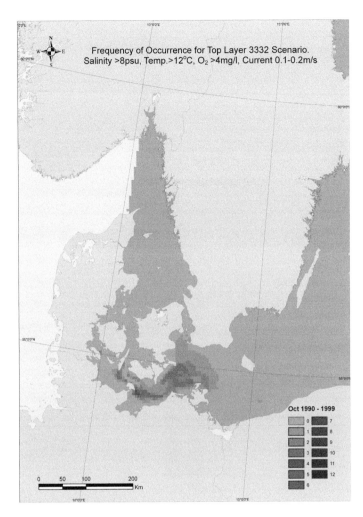

FIGURE 5   Occurrence of *Teredo navalis* in October. Top layer/ larvae. Frequency of occurrence in October 1990–99 (Figure 5a) is less frequent than the spread and frequency of occurrence of *Teredo navalis* found for the future period (Figure 5b). Frequency of occurrence of *Teredo navalis* in October month 2009–20 is based on future climate data, and shows a more frequent occurrence and wider spread in October, due to the warmer waters.

The awareness of shipwreck as vulnerable and important cultural heritage objects has been highlighted and the processes that endanger the long-term preservation have been enlightened. Scientific papers and conference proceedings, as well as a monograph dedicated to the topic, are important end products of the project that will be available for an international forum. WreckProtect has pointed out a need for further research within this multidisciplinary area and it is hoped that the project can inspire and encourage continued work dedicated to the long-term preservation of historical shipwreck *in situ*.

Acknowledgement

The work leading to these results has received funding from the European Community's seventh Framework programme (FP7/2007–2013, Environment) under grant agreement no. 226225. The European Commission 7th framework programme, Environment, is gratefully acknowledged for promoting this cross-disciplinary area of research.

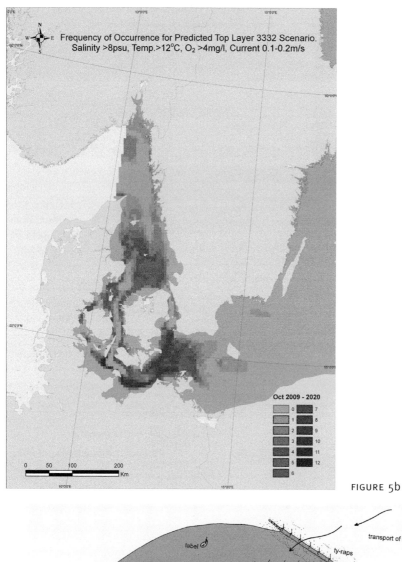

FIGURE 5b

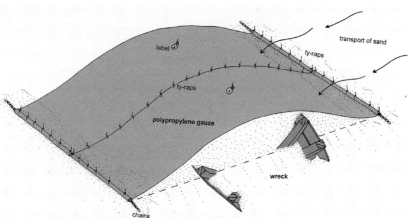

FIGURE 6   A method using sediment transport and a porous net to cover a wreck with sediment and preventing attack by shipworm.
Drawing by M. Manders, RCE

Notes

[1] For detailed information on results, we recommend the guidelines on <www.wreckprotect.eu> and the project monograph (Björdal and Gregory, 2012).

[2] <www.dhigroup.com>.

[3] The Guideline for prediction of decay is freely available as a PDF download from <www.wreckprotect. eu>. User-friendly maps can be downloaded for use in database/GIS systems from <www.wreckprotect. eu>. For those who do not have their own systems, MACHU GIS (Managing Cultural Heritage Underwater, a European Project under the Culture 2000 programme 2006–09) is available for (restricted) use at <www.machuproject.eu>.

[4] The guideline is available, including the cost benefit analysis, from <www.wreckprotect.eu>.

Bibliography

Björdal, C. and Gregory, D. In press. Wreckprotect — A European Project to Protect Historical Wooden Shipwrecks Against Shipworm Attack in the Baltic Sea. *Ars Nautica*, 2009. Dubrovnic.

Björdal, C. G. In press. Evaluation of Microbial Degradation of Shipwrecks in the Baltic Sea. *International Biodeterioration & Biodegradation*. In press.

Björdal, C. G. and Gregory, D. eds. 2012. *Wreckprotect. Decay And Protection of Wooden Archaeological Shipwrecks*. London: Archaeopress.

Gregory, D. and Björdal, C. G. In press. Wreckprotect — A European Project to Protect Wooden Historical Shipwreck Against Attack by Shipworm in the Baltic Sea. *Icom Woam Conference, 2010 Greenville, USA*. In press.

Manders, M. and Luth, F. 2004. Safeguarding. *Moss Project Final Report*.

Nair, N. B. and Saraswarthy, M. 1971. The Biology of Wood-Boring Teredinid Molluscs. *Advances In Marine Biology*, 9: 335–509.

Olsson, A. 2006. The Rutilus Project. Strategies for a Sustainable Development of the Underwater Cultural Heritage in the Baltic Sea Region. *The Swedish Maritime Museums*. Stockholm.

Unesco. 2001. *Unesco Convention On The Protection Of Underwater Cultural Heritage* [Online] [accessed 10 October 2012]. Available at: <http://www.unesco.org/culture/underwater/infokit_en/>.

Wreckprotect Home Page: <http://www.wreckprotect.eu> [accessed 10 October 2012].

Notes on contributors

Charlotte Gjelstrup Björdal gained a BSc in conservation from the Royal Academy of Arts, Copenhagen, 1986, specializing in conservation of waterlogged archaeological wood. In 2000 she defended her doctoral thesis 'Waterlogged Archaeological Wood — Biodegradation and its Implication for Conservation', at the Dept of Wood Science, Swedish University of Agricultural Sciences. During the last fifteen years her research has focused on microbial degradation processes of archaeological wood in marine and terrestrial environments; *in situ* preservation, decay processes, and reburial techniques for shipwrecks and other historical constructions are ongoing research topics. Currently she is the director of the Conservation Program at the Dept of Conservation, University of Gothenburg, Sweden.

Correspondence to: Charlotte Gjelstrup Björdal, University of Gothenburg, Dept of Conservation, Box 130, SE-405 30 Gothenburg, Sweden. Email: charlotte.bjordal@conservation.gu.se

David Gregory worked for several years in the pharmaceutical industry as an analytical chemist. After that he obtained a BSc in archaeology (University of Leicester), MPhil in Maritime studies (St Andrews University), and PhD ('Formation processes in underwater archaeology: a study of the deterioration of archaeological materials in the marine environment', 1996 (University of Leicester). He is currently employed as a senior scientist at the National Museum of Denmark investigating methods of *in situ* preservation in waterlogged and underwater environments.

Correspondence to: David Gregory, National Museum of Denmark, Conservation Department, I.C. Modewegs Vej, Brede, Kongens Lyngby, DK-2800, Denmark. Email: david.john.gregory@natmus.dk

CONSERVATION AND MGMT OF ARCH. SITES, Vol. 14 Nos 1–4, 2012, 215–27

Quantification and Visualization of *In Situ* Degradation at the World Heritage Site Bryggen in Bergen, Norway

JOHANNES DE BEER
Geological Survey of Norway (NGU), Norway

HENNING MATTHIESEN
National Museum of Denmark, Denmark

ANN CHRISTENSSON
Directorate for Cultural Heritage, Norway

Environmental monitoring at the World Heritage Site of Bryggen in Bergen, Norway, has shown damaging settling rates caused by degradation of underlying archaeological deposits. Measurements of piezometric head, oxygen, and soil moisture content, as well as chemical analyses of water and soil samples are key elements of the environmental monitoring.

Groundwater monitoring and geochemical analyses reveal a complex and dynamic flow through the natural and anthropogenic stratigraphy. The preservation conditions within the organic archaeological deposits are strongly correlated with oxygen and soil moisture content, that are controlled by the groundwater flow conditions at the site. To quantify decay rates, it is thus essential to understand the wider hydrogeological context of the site. This paper presents recent advancements in quantifying decay rates in the saturated zone at Bryggen. The paper also shows that 3D geo-archaeological modelling can contribute to preservation management by visually combining results of geological, archaeological, geochemical, and hydrological investigations. This opens up for improved multidisciplinary understanding of preservation potential, thereby contributing to an improved protection of archaeological deposits *in situ*.

KEYWORDS *in situ* preservation, groundwater, geochemistry, modelling, monitoring, visualization

© Taylor & Francis 2012   DOI 10.1179/1350503312Z.00000000018

Introduction

Protective management of archaeological sites *in situ* requires knowledge of the state of preservation and understanding of ongoing degradation processes, preferably on a quantitative scale. The preservation potential of organic archaeological deposits is strongly dependent on hydrological conditions, and it is thus necessary for any archaeological site to be placed within the context of its wider natural environment (Holden et al., 2006; 2009). The aim of this paper is to present recent advancements in quantifying degradation rates at Bryggen in Bergen, and presentation of multidisciplinary subsurface data through 3D framework modelling.

The Bryggen site dates back to the eleventh century. The current buildings date from 1702, but the underlying archaeological deposits cover the entire span of Bryggen's history. The archaeological deposits and artefacts add up to a thickness exceeding 8 m in places, with ten or more separate building phases often built on top of another. The oldest structures were built on the former sandy beach. A 'typical' sequence consists of layers with high organic content interspersed with fire layers, the latter being the remains of many fires in medieval and later times. The total system comprising Bryggen, including underground archaeological remains plus sixty-one buildings, that is, from the underlying bedrock to the rooftops, is considered a single cultural monument (for details of the history of Bryggen, see Christensson et al., 2004).

The hydrogeological situation of the site is characterized by its position along the Vågen harbour, just beneath a mountain slope. The regional groundwater level is topographically induced with regional groundwater flow towards the harbour. The regional piezometric levels (water levels in dipwells) depend on the amount of precipitation, the infiltration capacity and the hydraulic characteristics of bedrock and sediments (de Beer, 2008). At the site and near surroundings, local effects disturb the regional flow pattern, influencing groundwater levels, soil moisture content, and chemistry within the archaeological remains (de Beer and Matthiesen, 2008) (Figure 1).

Today's policy for Bryggen is not to excavate, but to leave as much of the archaeological deposits as possible for future generations, in line with national and European policy (Malta Convention, 1992; Norwegian Ministry of the Environment, 2005; 2008). This implies ensuring the survival of all the evidence preserved in the archaeological deposits through the maintenance of the physical, chemical, and hydrological conditions that resulted in its preservation.

Environmental monitoring at Bryggen

Standard for environmental monitoring of archaeological deposits

The experiences with monitoring methods and procedures at Bryggen and other sites in Bergen were first introduced in the Finnegården Project in 1983 (Myrvoll et al., 1983). Myrvoll describes it as 'the basis for the excavations has been stratigraphy based on depositional activities' (Myrvoll, 1991). The documentation method was thus introduced in Bergen in 1983, by the Polish archaeologist Andrzej Golembnik. The experiences with monitoring and documentation methods and procedures at

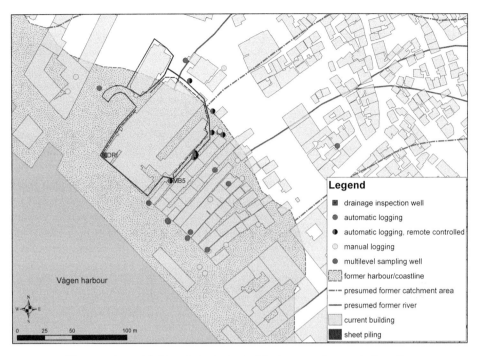

FIGURE 1   Site overview with historic hydrological features and current dipwells.

Bergen have been described in the Monitoring Manual (Riksantikvaren/NIKU, 2007). The manual's methods and procedures were formalized in a Norwegian Standard for environmental monitoring of archaeological deposits in 2009 (Standard Norge, 2009). The standard stipulates various requirements concerning monitoring and investigation of all kinds of archaeological deposits. One of the major advancements of the monitoring standard is the state of preservation scale (SOPS), for archaeological layer recording, classifying each documented sample in a preservation category. The SOPS is intended to be an (ideally) absolute scale that allows the state of preservation to be assessed and compared both over time and between locations. The state of preservation scale is presented in Table 1.

TABLE 1

STATE OF PRESERVATION SCALE (STANDARD NORGE, 2009)

Position in relation to groundwater level	Degree of preservation					
	0 null-value	1 lousy	2 poor	3 medium	4 good	5 excellent
Unsaturated zone (A)	A0	A1	A2	A3	A4	A5
Seasonally saturated zone (B)	B0	B1	B2	B3	B4	B5
Saturated zone (C)	C0	C1	C2	C3	C4	C5
Fill, later than ca. 1900 AD	D0	D1	D2	D3	D4	D5

Documentation of archaeological deposits according to the state of preservation scale gives a more or less objective static picture of the current quality of the archaeological deposits. However, it does not tell us if decay processes have stopped or still are ongoing. Assessment of ongoing decay requires knowledge about the conditions of the burial environment with respect to its external effect on the decay processes and rates. Environmental monitoring provides this knowledge through geotechnical, hydrological, and geochemical methods of analysis. The environmental preservation conditions are determined by a combination of physical, chemical, and hydrological parameters, but are also dependent on the constituents of the archaeological deposits themselves. It is not possible to assess the preservation conditions of any archaeological site using a standard set of monitoring parameters, though some environmental parameters, such as oxygen, have a clearly more detrimental effect on archaeological deposits than others. At Bryggen, we have tried to assess the preservation conditions by an expert judgement of multiple environmental parameters, and translating the results into different categories of preservation conditions, similar to the categories shown in Table 1 (Standard Norge, 2009). The categorization of preservation states and preservation conditions in boreholes or profiles can then be visualized side-by-side for comparison, giving an indication of current or historic decay. A first attempt to quantify the current decay rate in the saturated zone is presented in this paper.

Environmental monitoring results

The environmental monitoring at Bryggen is focused on chemistry and quantity of groundwater and soil moisture, as well as terrain and building movements. Monitoring consists of logging of piezometric head and temperature, oxygen in selected dipwells, soil moisture content and oxygen in the unsaturated zone, electric conductivity in selected dipwells, sampling and chemical analyses from all (38) dipwells, and measurement of settling rates of the terrain and buildings. Selection of dipwells for oxygen, electric conductivity is done based on archaeological documentation from the borehole drillings, spatial distribution, and hydrological conditions. The monitoring parameters for the burial environment are assessed with respect to the archaeological documentation from drillings and excavations.

The results of the environmental monitoring have been described in detail elsewhere (Matthiesen et al., 2008; Matthiesen, 2008; De Beer and Matthiesen, 2008). It has been found that preservation conditions vary considerably within the study area, from excellent to very bad, as well as intermediate zones with less ideal preservation conditions, and some initial, very rough, estimates of decay rates in the different areas were given at the PARISIII conference in 2006 (Matthiesen et al., 2008). Correlation between chemical species in the groundwater has shown that, although the deposits are very heterogeneous, the groundwater chemistry and therefore preservation conditions are not completely random across the site (Matthiesen, 2008). The hydrological conditions have been described based on continuous logging of piezometric head. The groundwater level and flow within the archaeological deposits are highly correlated with the average observed tidal fluctuation in the Vågen harbour, and only indirectly by direct precipitation. The piezometric head below the archaeological deposits is largely controlled by the drainage system below the neighbouring hotel (De Beer and Matthiesen, 2008). Monitoring of the piezometric head during a controlled temporary increase of the drainage level in 2010 has confirmed these correlations (De Beer, 2010). Figure 2 shows the drainage level in a drainage inspection well (red line, left axis) at the southern corner of the hotel, which was artificially increased by an overflow pipe on 18 November 2010. The overflow pipe was again removed on 23 November 2010, returning the system to its original drainage level, about sea level. The drainage inspection well is connected via the storm water runoff system to the harbour. This results in short peaks (inflow) in the drainage system during high tides, sometimes blocked by pumping in the connected storm water runoff system. The blue line shows the groundwater level variations in a dipwell at the heritage site, on the outside of the sheet piling that surrounds the drained area (MB5). The inspection well and dipwell are indicated in Figure 1. The groundwater level shows a positive correlation with the controlled drainage level change.

During the controlled test, there was no precipitation. Groundwater levels are corrected for barometric pressure variations. However, effects from barometric efficiency (Acworth and Brain, 2008) in some (semi-)confined dipwells may also result in a positive correlation and can therefore not be excluded a-priori from the analysis. MB5 is not confined, and has no significant barometric efficiency effects. Positive correlations of groundwater level responses to the drainage level change in other dipwells without significant barometric efficiency, as well as the general flow pattern,

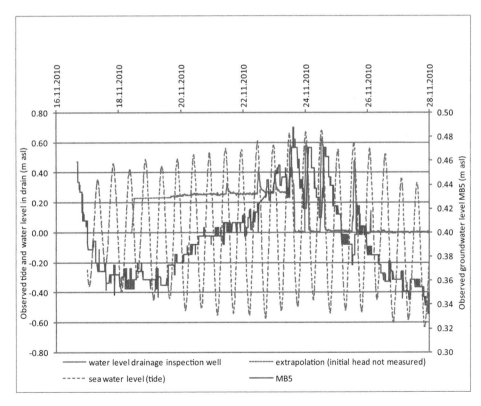

FIGURE 2 Monitoring of water level in drainage inspection well below the hotel and in dipwell MB5 at the adjacent heritage site.

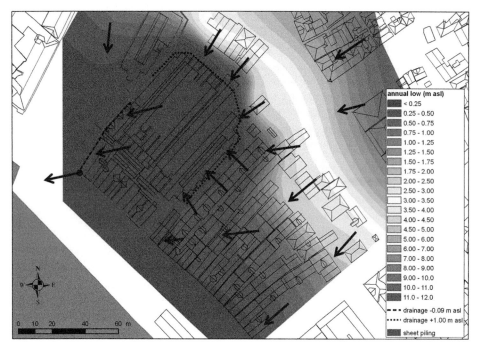

FIGURE 3   Groundwater flow pattern.

support the hypothesis that the drainage level directly influences the groundwater level in the cultural deposits. Barometric efficiency effects are not further discussed in this article.

Settling rates are described in Jensen and Stordal (2004) and Jensen (2010). The monitoring shows an uneven settling rate of up to 8 mm per year, where highest settling rates coincide with lowest groundwater levels.

Quantification of degradation

Flow modelling

In order to better understand and quantify the water balance and to identify factors influencing the groundwater conditions at Bryggen, numerical groundwater flow modelling has been used in conjunction with environmental monitoring. The goal of numerical modelling has been to obtain a predictive tool for temporal and spatial changes in hydraulic head, phreatic groundwater levels and flow rates, and thereby identify zones that may be or become at risk for *in situ* decay (De Beer and Matthiesen, 2008). The numerical groundwater flow model (De Beer, 2008) was constructed in Feflow® 5.3 and has provided us with increased understanding of the hydrogeological system of the site, as well as given feedback to adjustment of the environmental monitoring system and vice versa. It also has, to a certain extent, resulted in delineation of areas that are or may become at risk for increased degradation. This model does, however, not include geochemical processes, such as oxidation of organic material. Ultimately, a more quantitative approach would be to extend the groundwater model with geochemical processes and monitoring data, resulting in a predictive tool for quantify chemical changes in the groundwater that control preservation conditions. A first attempt towards this more quantitative approach through geochemical modelling is presented here.

Hydrogeochemical modelling

An initial one-dimensional hydrogeochemical model has been made in the program PHREEQC that is designed to make aqueous geochemical calculations (available as freeware from the US Geological Survey homepage). A brief and general description of modelling work is presented here, the full model is described in a preliminary report by Matthiesen (2009), which will be re-worked and presented in a forthcoming paper.

The main purpose of the hydrogeochemical modelling is to evaluate the decay rates for organic material at Bryggen. Decay takes place through different oxidation and reduction processes involving organic material, including oxygen-, nitrate-, manganese-, iron-, and sulphate-reduction as well as fermentation and methanogenesis. A secondary purpose is to use hydrochemical modelling to get a better overview and understanding of the groundwater formation processes at the site. Groundwater was sampled from all dipwells in May 2008 and analysed for pH, alkalinity, oxygen, sodium, potassium, calcium, magnesium, iron, manganese, ammonium, chloride, sulphate, sulphide, nitrate, phosphate, and methane (the analyses are described in detail in Matthiesen, 2008). Soil samples from the installation of each dipwell have been analysed for their content of dry matter, organic matter, chloride, and pH, and some samples for the content of nitrogen, phosphorus, and different sulphur species.

Hydrogeochemical model setup

The hydrogeochemical model focuses on the description of organic material in the soil and the decay of this material through different redox reactions. An organic content of 26 per cent (weight to dry weight) and a dry matter content of 42 per cent are used to describe the soil in the model, based on the median results from analysis of more than 100 soil samples from Bryggen. The organic material is conceptualized in the model as $CH_2ON_{0.05}P_{0.005}K_{0.02}$, where the content of N is taken as the median C:N ratio measured in soil samples from Bryggen, and the content of P and K is taken from typical contents in organic matter such as manure, grass, and wood (Appelo and Postma, 2005: table 2.5). In the very organic soil at Bryggen, the oxidation rate will to a high degree be controlled by the supply of oxidants, rather than the supply or reactivity of the organic material. The rate of the different redox processes for each oxidant is therefore expressed through equations of the type:

$$rate = k \cdot \frac{[oxidant]}{(K + [oxidant])}. \tag{1}$$

As long as there is sufficient of the oxidant available, the rate will be approximately k, but the rate decreases when the oxidant approaches the half saturation coefficient,

K, and becomes zero when there is no more of the oxidant available. For different species, both measured reduction rates and rates from the literature are used (Franken et al., 2009). The rate for methanogenesis is given as a constant (rate = k) within the range measured by Beer et al. (2008). In the kinetic expression in the model these different rates are then added to a 'total decay rate' for organic material. Calcite, assumed to stem from lime production or seashells in the deposits, is included as an equilibrium phase and serves as a Ca-source and pH buffer. A gas-phase consisting of $CH_4(g)$ and $CO_2(g)$ is added, where the total pressure increases with 0.1 atm per metre depth. Monitoring has shown a high partial pressure for methane, with maximum values that increase more or less linearly with depth. This may indicate an upward transport of methane by diffusion and/or by bubbles (Beer et al., 2008).

As an example the model is used for modelling the groundwater chemistry in the central part of Bryggen, where there are relatively stagnant conditions and where we expect the lowest decay rates at Bryggen. The cultural deposits are approximately 8 m thick here, which in the model are divided into 16 compartments of ½ m thickness each containing the different soil components described above. The model is based on a downwards groundwater flow, where (rain)water is added to the top of the deposits, and interacts with the different soil components on its way down, according to the kinetic expressions and thermodynamic equilibria described above. A groundwater flow rate of 0.1 m/year is used, which is derived from calibration of the groundwater flow model based on the monitoring of piezometric heads at different levels in and below the archaeological deposits. No *in situ* measurements of the permeability of the archaeological deposits have been done, which makes the rate uncertain, particularly in view of the heterogeneity of the deposits. The initial solution in the model is pure water, and the system is flushed with oxidized rainwater consistent with water sampled from a monitoring well (MB5) in June 2005 (Matthiesen, 2008).

Modelling results

The transport model was run until a steady state had been obtained. The main fitting parameter was the rate for methanogenesis. This relatively simple model gives a reasonable approximation of the groundwater chemistry (Figure 4), indicating that the composition of the groundwater controls and/or is controlled by the decay of organic material.

There is a good correspondence between the modelled and measured results for alkalinity, ammonium, and K concentrations, indicating that decay of organic material with composition $CH_2ON_{0.05}P_{0.005}K_{0.02}$ may explain the occurrence of these species in the groundwater. The modelled P concentrations seem slightly too low, indicating an additional P source in the deposits, such as for instance bone or release of adsorbed P. The addition of a gas-phase with increasing pressure with depth in the model gives a good fit of the measured methane and carbon dioxide partial pressures, indicating that they are controlled by bubble formation at some depths. The use of calcite as Ca source gives a reasonable fit of Ca (not shown) and pH. Work is still ongoing to extent the model to fit other parameters from the groundwater analysis, such as for instance sodium and chloride that may be strongly influenced by input from seawater.

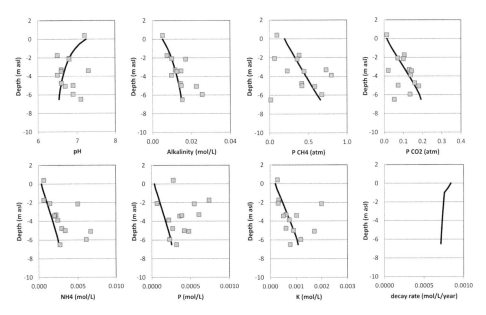

FIGURE 4   Results from hydrogeochemical modelling, focusing on species that are directly influenced by the decay of organic matter. Black lines show the output of the model, and squares show actual concentrations measured in groundwater samples from the central area of Bryggen in May 2008.

There is a strong correlation between ammonium, potassium, and alkalinity in the groundwater samples at Bryggen. This correlation has been discussed in an earlier paper (Matthiesen, 2008), where it was suggested that the correlation could be due to degradation of organic material with a relatively stable composition. This suggestion is supported by the results from the hydrogeochemical model.

One of the most important outputs of the model is an estimate of the total decay rate for the organic material in the deposits (lower right in Figure 4). A decay rate of less than 0.001 mol/L/year (0.001 mol organic material pr L of soil water) is estimated by the present model. The average amount of organic matter in the deposits at Bryggen is 6.5 mol/L, so if we — just for illustration — assumed a constant decay rate, it would take thousands of years before half the organic material was gone in this area of Bryggen. Decay rates cannot be measured directly in the groundwater or soil, and hence there are no measured values (squares) in the graph.

However, the uncertainty of this estimated decay rate must also be emphasized, as it is extremely dependent on the water flow through the system. If the groundwater flow was for instance 1 m/year instead of 0.1 m/year, an equally good fit of the groundwater data may be obtained by increasing the rate of methanogenesis by a factor 10. In that case the model would give a decay rate of the organic matter of 0.006 mol/L/year, which means that half of the deposits could disappear in only 500 years. To find the real decay rate it is thus crucial that we verify the estimate of the groundwater flow rate and/or get a direct measure of the methane release rate.

In some areas at Bryggen the decay is significantly faster due to increased water flow, and in other areas due to drainage. Work is ongoing to try to estimate the decay rates in these areas as well, in order to prioritize the mitigation work at the site.

Visualization of multidisciplinary subsurface data

Framework modelling

The complexity of the site, and the large amounts of documentation, monitoring, and modelling data, have called for an easy-to-use visualization and modelling system of the underground in three dimensions. A portrayal of multidisciplinary data from archaeological, geochemical, and hydrological monitoring and modelling within an interrogative 3D subsurface modelling framework of the site and its wider surroundings, contributes to a more holistic evaluation and better risk assessment. An initial framework model of the underground has been constructed using proprietary software GSI3D (Hinze et al., 1999; Kessler and Mathers, 2004; Mathers and Kessler, 2010). The model construction and its geoscientific outputs are described in De Beer et al. (2011; 2012). An example output from Bryggen is shown in Figure 5.

The strength of geological, or geo-archaeological, framework modelling is the opportunity to visualize data of archaeological deposits, hydrogeological features and other attributes within a framework of geological and anthropogenic deposits of the site and its surroundings. In the framework model, it is possible to visualize intra-formational information, such as the state of preservation categories, together with other attributes in borehole logs, sections and in a 3D environment. This offers a holistic assessment of complex multidisciplinary data that in an understandable and attractive way, a necessity for a sustainable management of the subsurface (De Beer, 2011).

Future developments

The initial framework modelling work at Bryggen is currently being followed up by a systematic digitization and interpretation of archaeological, geological, and hydrogeological information in four medieval cities in Norway, integrated through the use of GSI3D. In the near future, these registrations are to be part of the national database for environmental monitoring of archaeological sites.

The use of 3D models would be greatly increased if intra-formational data, such as the state of preservation or the hydraulic conductivity, could be presented more statistically, by using voxels (volume pixel) in the three-dimensional space, attributed with correlated data from documented registrations at boreholes and/or excavations. In geosciences, pure probabilistic voxel models are already being produced, and it is only a matter of time before combinations with geo-archaeological framework models will be in place.

Conclusion

It has been possible to make models that reflect the groundwater flow conditions and chemistry at the centre of Bryggen relatively well. They show that, even though the deposits are very heterogeneous, the groundwater chemistry is not 'random'.

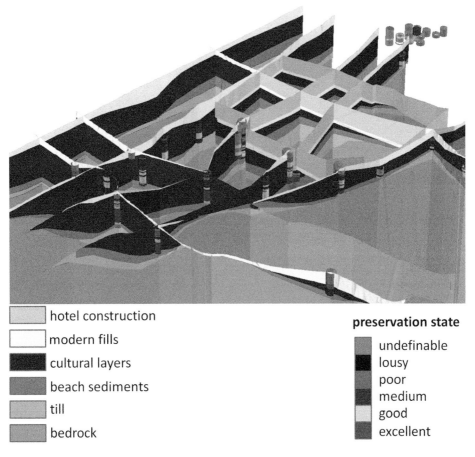

hotel construction
modern fills
cultural layers
beach sediments
till
bedrock

preservation state

undefinable
lousy
poor
medium
good
excellent

FIGURE 5   3D visualization of underground and documented preservation states from archaeological observations from auger drillings (a colour version of this figure is available from the author).

Environmental monitoring and modelling have given good, partly quantitative, insight into groundwater formation processes and verified that the groundwater composition to a large extent is determined by the decay of organic material. The models resulted in some estimates of the decay rate for the organic archaeological material at the site. However, it has also been shown that these decay rates are extremely dependent on the water flow set for the models. In order to verify the decay rates it will be necessary to get better estimates of the groundwater flow rate, and to couple the hydrogeochemical modelling more closely to the dynamic hydrological model that has been made for Bryggen.

Developments in three dimensional geological and anthropogenic framework modelling show that 3D subsurface modelling methodology offers a more holistic assessment of complex multidisciplinary data, in an understandable and attractive way. This multidisciplinary assessment is necessary for a future sustainable management of the subsurface, certainly in areas with subsurface archaeological deposits.

Acknowledgements

The monitoring work at Bryggen is financed by the Directorate for Cultural Heritage in Norway, Riksantikvaren. This paper is part of a research programme on groundwater and cultural heritage. Contributions and comments of two anonymous reviewers are highly appreciated.

Bibliography

Acworth, R. I. and Brain, T. 2008. Calculation of Barometric Efficiency in Shallow Piezometers using Water Levels, Atmospheric and Earth Tide Data. *Hydrogeology Journal*, 16: 1469–81.

Appelo, C. A. J and Postma, D. 2005. *Geochemistry, Groundwater and Pollution*. Leiden: A. A.Balkema.

Beer, J., Lee, K., Whiticar, M., and Blodau, C. 2008. Geochemical Controls on Anaerobic Organic Matter Decomposition in a Northern Peatland. *Limnology and Oceanography*, 53: 1393–1407.

Christensson, A., Paszkowski, Z., Spriggs, J. A., and Verhoef, L. eds. 2004. *Safeguarding Historic Waterfront Sites. Bryggen in Bergen as a Case Study*. 1st edn. Bergen, Norway: Stiftelsen Bryggen and Polytechnika Szczecinska.

De Beer, J. 2008. Statusrapport grunnvannsovervåking og hydrogeologisk modellering ved Bryggen i Bergen. NGU report 2008.069.

De Beer, J. and Matthiesen, H. 2008. Groundwater Monitoring and Modelling from an Archaeological Perspective: Possibilities and Challenges. *NGU Special Publication*, 11: 67–81.

De Beer, J., Price, S. J., and Ford, J. R. 2012. 3D Modelling of Geological and Anthropogenic Deposits at the World Heritage Site of Bryggen in Bergen, Norway. *Quaternary International*, 251: 107–16.

De Beer, J. 2011. GSI3D; A Significant Contribution to the Digital Revolution in Geo-Archaeology. *GSI3D Research Consortium Newsletter*, 1(4) [online] [accessed 6 January 2012]. Available at: <http://www.gsi3d. org/downloads/ConsortiumNewsletterJune2011.pdf>.

Franken, G., Postma, D., Duijnisveld, W. H. M., Böttcher, J., and Molson, J. 2009. Acid Groundwater in an Anoxic Aquifer: Reactive Transport Modelling of Buffering Processes. *Applied Geochemistry*, 24: 890–99.

Hinze, C., Sobisch, H., and Voss, H. 1999. Spatial Modelling in Geology and its Practical Use. *Fortschritte Der Geoinformatik = Progress in Geoinformatics*, 51–60.

Holden, J., West, L. J., Howard, A. J., Maxfield, E., Panter, I., and Oxley, J. 2006. Hydrological Controls of In Situ Preservation of Waterlogged Archaeological Deposits. *Earth-Science Reviews*, 78: 59–83.

Holden, J., Howard, A. J., West, L. J., Maxfield, E., Panter, I., and Oxley, J. 2009. A Critical Review of Hydrological Data Collection for Assessing Preservation Risk for Urban Waterlogged Archaeology: A Case Study from the City of York, UK. *Journal of Environmental Management*, 90: 3197–3204.

Jensen, J. A. and Stordal, A. D. 2004. Miljøovervåkningsprosjekt Bugården — Bryggen i Bergen FoU-prosjekt. Grunnundersøkelser og setningsmålinger. Bergen, Norway: Multiconsult report 400962-1.

Jensen, J. A., Stordal, A. D., and Systad, H. 2010. *Setningsmålinger på Bryggen i Bergen. Setninger og horisontalbevegelser til 2009*. Bergen, Norway: Multiconsult report 610694-5, 3 March 2010.

Kessler, H. and Mathers S. J. 2004. Maps to Models. *Geoscientist*, 14: 4–6.

Malta Convention, 1992. The European Convention About Protection of the *Archaeological Heritage*. European Treaty Series No. 143. Valetta: Council of Europe.

Mathers, S. J. and Kessler, H. 2010. *GSI3D — Version 2.6. User Manual*. British Geological Survey Open report OR/10/007.

Matthiesen, H., Dunlop, R., Jensen, J. A., De Beer, J., and Christensson, A. 2008. Monitoring of Preservation Conditions and Evaluation of Decay Rates of Urban Deposits — Results from the First Five Years of Monitoring at Bryggen in Bergen. In: H. Kars and R. H. Van Heeringen, eds. Proceedings from the Conference Preserving Archaeological Remains In Situ 3, Amsterdam. *Geoarchaeological and Bioarchaeological Studies*, 10: 163–74.

Matthiesen, H. 2008. Detailed Chemical Analysis of Groundwater as a Tool for Monitoring Urban Archaeological Deposits: Results from Bryggen in Bergen. *Journal of Archaeological Science*, 35: 1378–88.

Matthiesen, H. 2009. Modelling Decay of Organic Archaeological Deposits Beneath Bryggen in Bergen, Norway. Unpublished report, Department of Conservation, National Museum of Denmark.

Myrvoll, S. 1991. Forvaltningsstyrt forskning? Byundersøkelser i Bergen 1979. *Nytt fra Utgravningskontoret i Bergen (N.U.B)*, 1: 69–84.

Myrvoll, S., Golembnik, A., and Dunlop, R. 1983. *The Finnegården Project*. Manuskript. Bergen, Riksantikvarens urgravningskontor.

Norwegian Ministry of the Environment, 2005. St.meld. nr. 16 (2004–05). *Leve med kulturminner* [accessed 6 January 2012]. Available at: <http://www.regjeringen.no/Rpub/STM/20042005/016/PDFS/STM200420050016000DDDPDFS.pdf>.

Norwegian Ministry of the Environment, 2008. The Government's Environmental Policy and the State of the Environment in Norway. Excerpts in English: Report. No. 26 (2006–07) to the Storting [accessed 6 January 2012]. Available at: <http://www.regjeringen.no/pages/2094393/PDFS/STM200620070026000EN_PDFS.pdf>.

Riksantikvaren and NIKU, 2007. The Monitoring Manual. Procedures & Guidelines for the Monitoring, Recording and Preservation/Management of Urban Archaeological Deposits [accessed 6 January 2012]. Available at: <http://www.riksantikvaren.no/filestore/Veileder_komp.pdf>.

Standard Norge, 2009. Kulturminner. Krav til miljøovervåking og -undersøkelse av kulturlag. NS 9451:2009. Lysaker, Norway [accessed 20 November 2012]. Available at: <http://brage.bibsys.no/riksant/bitstream/URN:NBN:no-bibsys_brage_30947/1/Requirements_eng_versjon_Norwegian_National_Standard_2012.pdf>.

USGS homepage with the software PHREEQC [online] [accessed 9 August 2011]. Available at: <http://wwwbrr.cr.usgs.gov/projects/GWC_coupled/phreeqc/>.

Notes on contributors

Johannes de Beer is hydrogeologist and team leader for Groundwater and Urban Geology at the Geological Survey of Norway in Trondheim. He has many years' experience in urban groundwater management and modelling. His current research is focused on hydrogeological site characterization and risk-assessment of organic cultural deposits in urban areas.

Correspondence to: Johannes de Beer, Geological Survey of Norway (NGU), Leiv Eirikssons vei 39, PO Box 6315 Sluppen, 7491 Trondheim, Norway. Email: hans.debeer@ngu.no

Henning Matthiesen is senior researcher at the National Museum of Denmark. His research focuses on *in situ* preservation of archaeological remains. He has a background in chemistry and environmental monitoring.

Correspondence to: Henning Matthiesen, National Museum of Denmark, IC Modewegsvej 1, 2800 Kgs. Lyngby, Denmark.

Ann Christensson is senior advisor at the Directorate for Cultural Heritage in Norway and has a background in archaeology from the University of Bergen. She wrote her theses on material from excavations in Bergen, amongst them several from Bryggen and the surrounding area. She has for the last ten years been leading the monitoring programme for the archaeological deposits in Project Bryggen.

Correspondence to: Ann Christensson, Directorate for Cultural Heritage, Dronningensgate 13, Pb. 8196 Dep., 0034 Oslo, Norway.

CONSERVATION AND MGMT OF ARCH. SITES, Vol. 14 Nos 1–4, 2012, 228–38

An Assessment of the Status and Condition of Archaeological Remains Preserved *In Situ* in the Medieval Town of Trondheim Based on Archeochemical Investigations Conducted During the Period 2007–2010

ANNA PETERSÉN

Norwegian Institute for Cultural Heritage Research (NIKU), Norway

OVE BERGERSEN

Norwegian Institute for Agricultural and Environmental Research (Bioforsk), Norway

In recent years systematic archeochemical investigations in the medieval town of Trondheim have provided the heritage management authorities with a rich and complex set of data concerning the status and condition of the cultural deposits in the anthropogenic material. The collected data raises important questions for the long-time management of *in situ* preservation for archaeological material in non-saturated zones. In this paper we present the standardized scientific methods used in these archeochemical investigations. We examine the results from several sites in the town and discuss the challenges facing modern heritage management in its efforts to protect a complex body of archaeological material in the non-saturated zone. We show that sediments with a thickness of 1–2 m have low levels of moisture and organic matter, and most of the inorganic parameters analysed are found in oxidized form with low preservations. The 2–3 m thick anthropogenic sediments showed better preservation conditions.

KEYWORDS archaeology, *in situ* preservation, inorganic chemistry, redox conditions, cultural deposits, organic material

© Taylor & Francis 2012   DOI 10.1179/1350503312Z.00000000019

Introduction

Norway has one of the more extensive and coherent legislative systems for protecting and safeguarding Cultural Heritage. For example, archaeological monuments and sites of all known and identified types older than 1536 are automatically protected (Act of 9 June 1978 No.50 Concerning the Cultural Heritage, ref. § 4). Eight medieval towns are defined as coherent archaeological sites and they form by far the nation's largest automatically protected Cultural Heritage, both in area and volume.

Sites and monuments from medieval time up to 1537 are managed by the Directorate for Cultural Heritage (Riksantikvaren). The Directorate is the principal decision-making body and recommends the archaeological strategy for sites and areas affected by development plans. In the medieval towns, developers are required to use less intrusive foundation techniques (such as piling) in order to protect as much as possible of the remaining archaeological material. In accordance with the national policy of protection and mitigation, physical preservation of archaeological features (*in situ* preservation) is preferred in favour of scientific recording of archaeological features prior to their destruction (preservation by record).

National standards for recording of preservation status of anthropogenic sediments

Since 2007 a standardized interdisciplinary method combining archaeological evaluation with chemical analysis of soil samples has been used to record existing condition and preservation status for anthropogenic sediments in the urban environment. The standard (approved in 2009), came about as a result of the Ministry of Environment's work on coordinating environmental data, Norsk Standard 9451 (NS 9451:2009). The method has uniform status and is applied in all archeochemical investigations in the medieval towns of Norway.

NIKU, the Norwegian Institute for Cultural Heritage Research (founded in 1994), conducts archaeological work in the medieval towns on behalf of the Directorate for Cultural Heritage. In archaeological investigations focusing on preservation status and where soil-chemical analyses are required, NIKU collaborates with the Norwegian Institute for Agricultural and Environmental Research (Bioforsk).

In recent years archeochemical investigations in the medieval towns of Norway such as Oslo, Tønsberg, Bergen, and Trondheim have provided the heritage management authorities with a complex set of data concerning the status and condition of the medieval deposits (Petersén and Martens, 2011). The collected data raise important questions for the long-term management of *in situ* preservation for archaeological material in saturated and unsaturated zones (Martens, 2010). In this paper we will focus exclusively on preservation conditions in Trondheim, where all the archaeological remains fall within the unsaturated zone. Our analysis reviews the information provided in a number of reports from local archeochemical investigations conducted between 2007 and 2010. These reports provide a comprehensive and detailed empirical basis for the analysis and the conclusions we have drawn. Finally, we conclude with a discussion of the challenges facing modern heritage management in its efforts to protect a complex body of archaeological material in the unsaturated zone.

Materials and methods

Assessing preservation status and measuring preservation conditions

The empirical data forming the basis of our study come from sediment samples which have all been treated according to the detailed specification regarding both site and laboratory work described in the standard (NS 9451:2009). All sampled sediments are subject to archaeological and chemical assessments which provide information on the preservation status of the archaeological deposits and the below-ground (sediment) conditions. Both types of evidence are required as part of the standard. The evaluation of the degree of preservation for each specific soil sample are summarized in scales, one for status of the archaeological deposits, and one for chemical conditions (i.e. pH, redox, etc). The scales follow the same gradient for each assessment, from 1 to 5: 1(lousy), 2 (poor), 3 (medium), 4 (good), 5 (excellent) (NIKU and RA, 2008; NS 9451:2009). The scale for preservation status also records the sediment ground-water level. In the chemical analysis the concentration, levels, and relationship between reduced and oxidized species dictates preservation status on the scale of 1 to 5 (Table 1).

In the laboratory sediment samples were stored at 4° C and opened in a nitrogen atmosphere in a glove box to keep anaerobic samples free of oxygen. All extractions of redox sensitive parameters were done in this chamber. The samples were analysed for nitrate (NO_3-), ammonium (NH_4+), reduced iron (Fe_2+), and oxidized iron (Fe_3+) (Stookey, 1970), sulphate (SO_42-), (acid volatile) sulphide (S_2-) (Rickard and Morse, 2005). Nitrate (NO_3-), ammonium (NH_4+), and sulphate (SO_42-) were analysed at Eurofins, Norsk Miljøanalyse AS. Ammonium represents the major reduced species of nitrogen in natural environments, while nitrate is the oxidized species. The ratio of molar concentrations of reduced and oxidized species can be used to assess the redox conditions in natural environments and can be used to investigate the predominant redox processes of any given sampling point.

TABLE 1

CONCENTRATION LEVELS FOR PARAMETERS USED TO EVALUATE PRESERVATION CONDITIONS

Nitrate	Ammonium	Sulphide	Iron (II)	Iron (III)	Redox conditions	Preservation
NO_3^-	NH_4^+	S^{2-}	Fe^{2+}	Fe^{3+}		
Low	Low	Low	Low	High	Oxidizing	Lousy
High	Low	Low	Low	High	Nitrate to oxidizing	Poor
High	Low	Low	High	Low	Nitrate to iron reducing	Medium
Low	Low	Low	High	Low	Ironreducing	Medium
High	High	High	Medium	Low	Nitrate to sulphatereducing	Good
Low	High	High	Medium	Low	Sulphatereducing	Good
Low	High	High	High	Low	Sulphatered. to methan prod.	Excellent

Reduced condition

Oxidized condition

Dry matter (105° C over night) followed by loss on ignition (550° C in 12 hours) was determined in the initial samples. pH and electric conductivity (Shirokova et al., 2000) was measured by mixing samples with deionized water (ratio 1:5 by volume). The pH was measured after 30 minutes with a Ross electrode (Orion Instruments).

Material for our study has been retrieved from four investigated archaeological sites in Trondheim. The sites are unevenly distributed, as the localities are the result of development plans and not test-areas selected for research projects. Even though the sites are randomly dispersed within the medieval area, they can be categorized according to thickness of the anthropogenic material (Figure 1). Two of the sites (sites 1 and 2) lie in areas with a thickness of 3–4 m, and two lie in areas with a thickness of 1–2 m (sites 3 and 4). We present the data and discuss our results using these two categories of sediment thickness for comparison. Additionally, we have used site 1, which has sediments 3–4 m thick, to investigate differences in reduced parameters at different depths of the sediments.

Materials

Site 1. Schultz gate 8. A total of 23 samples were collected and analysed from three sections and two bore-holes (Petersén, 2008; Bergersen and Hartnik, 2008).

Site 2. Søndre gate 5–11: A total of 15 samples were collected and analysed from six boreholes (Petersén 2007a; Bergersen and Hartnik, 2007b).

Site 3. Vår Frue gate 1–3. A total of 18 samples were collected and analysed from two sections in an investigation in 2010 (Bergersen and Petersén 2010) and from six boreholes in 2009 (Bergersen and Petersén, 2009).

Site 4. Kjøpmannsgt 36–38: A total of 12 samples were collected and analysed from one section (Petersén 2007b; Bergersen and Hartnik, 2007a).

Results and discussion

Natural topography and character of anthropogenic sediments in medieval Trondheim

Trondheim in Mid-Norway is located on a river plain by the mouth of the river Nid where it enters the Trondheim Fiord. The Nidarneset Plain is made up of well-drained alluvial sands and gravels and these natural sediments have a thickness of 75–125 m above the bedrock. The groundwater level lies several metres below the top of the natural sediments. The automatically protected zone which corresponds with the historic parts of Trondheim covers approximately 560 ha. The thickness of anthropogenic sediments in the medieval area of Trondheim varies from less than 0.5 m up to 4 m. The average depth is between 1 and 2 m. Areas with maximum depth of 2–3 m are confined to a few parts that correspond well with the intensively used residential areas of the medieval settlement where habitation has been continuous from early medieval time (Figure 1). The main source of construction material recorded in the archaeological remains consists of wood. Habitation waste from the residential areas also contains a fair amount of wood and other visible organic components and these types of material add volume to the sediments. The differentiated nature of activities and functions present in the urban environment can be seen in the thickness and composition of the anthropogenic sediments. Areas used for industrial

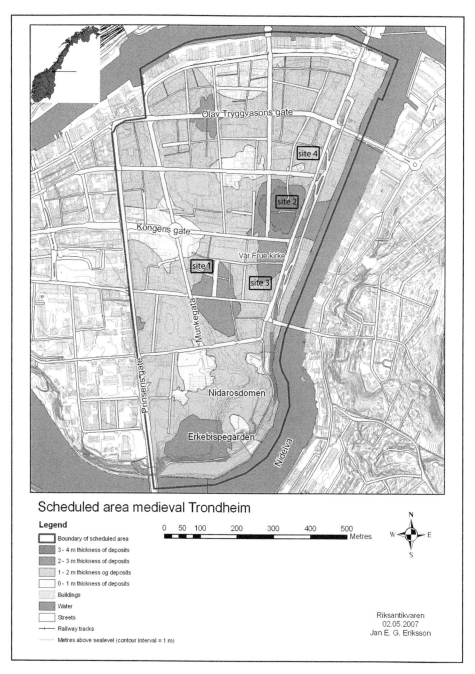

FIGURE 1 Estimated depth of anthropogenic deposits within the medieval town of Trondheim.

Map by Jan E. G. Eriksson, Riksantikvaren

activities, farming, or that have periods of less intensive use, normally produce thinner and less organic sediments compared to residential areas. As can be seen in Figure 1, the areas with sediment thickness of 1–2 m covers a more extensive area than the areas with sediments thicker than 2 m, and this can partly be explained in terms of use of space in the medieval town.

Preservation conditions

Results from the chemical analysis of samples from sites of varying thickness were found to be significantly (p<0.05) different from each other. Comparison of organic matter content and moisture (measured in %) show distinct difference relating to sediment thickness. Figure 2a and 3a show that both moisture and organic matter were found to be higher in the thicker sediments. Most of the samples analysed from the thicker sediments contain organic matter in the range 20–50 per cent (Figure 2a), while the deposits with 1–2 m thickness contain organic matter between 10 and 20 per cent (Figure 3a). The pH values were also found to be higher in the thinner sediment samples compared to the 2–3 m thick deposits, where values from the samples were more neutral (Figure 2b and 3b). The concentration of reduced iron (Fe^{2+}), ammonium (NH_4^+), and sulphide (S^{2-}) was significantly (p<0.05) higher in the

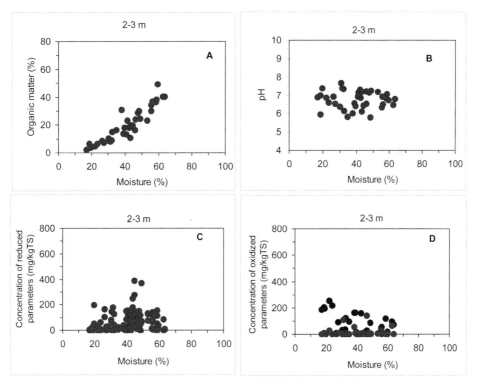

FIGURE 2   Chemical parameters mg/kg dry matter (TS) analysed from medieval deposits at sites 1 and 2 with thickness 2–3 m. A: Organic matter against water content, B: pH against water content, C: Concentration of reduced parameters (NH_4^+, H_2S, Fe^{2+}) against water content, and D: Concentration of oxidized parameters (NO_3, Fe^{3+}) against water content.

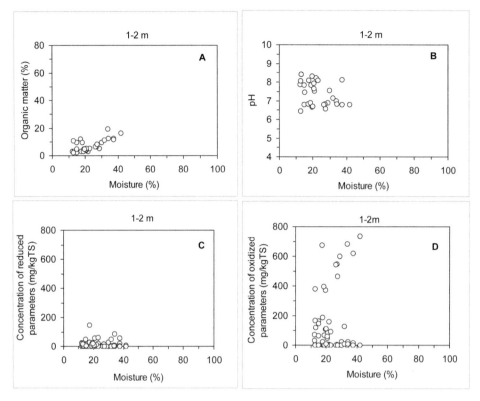

FIGURE 3   Chemical parameters mg/kg dry matter (TS) analysed from medieval deposits sites 3 and 4 with thickness 1–2 m. A: Organic matter against water content, B: pH against water content, C: Concentration of reduced parameters (NH_{4+}, H_2S, Fe^{2+}) against water content, and D: Concentration of oxidized parameters (NO_3, Fe^{3+}) against water content.

samples analysed from sediments of 2–3 m thickness compared to the sediments of 1–2 m thickness (Figure 2c and 3c). In addition, the concentration of oxidized iron (Fe^{3+}) and nitrate (NO_3^-) were significantly ($p<0.05$) higher in the samples from the sediments of 1–2 m thickness (Figure 3d). Oxidized iron (Fe^{3+}) and nitrate (NO_3^-) were found to be variable in the thicker sediments (Figure 2d).

Archaeological background and results from analysis of reduced parameters from site 1. Schultz gate 8

In the medieval town the area of site 1 lies at the western fringe of the inhabited area, between two medieval streets, south-east of the Church of St Mary (Figure 1).

Archaeological results from an excavation carried out in 1985 provided evidence of approximately 200 years of continuous habitation from the early twelfth to the fourteenth century, structured in several separate building phases interspersed with fire debris and organic-rich sediments. The excavation recovered a large and varied assortment of finds from different materials, both organic and inorganic. The condition of timber and wood was described as being very good, although the excavation did not involve any specific recording of condition and preservation status for the organic material. However, site photographs support written comments and show construction elements like floorings with well-preserved planks and surfaces.

The investigation of sections in 2007 did not lead to the retrieval of finds of any kind, but the sediments had a fairly high proportion of visible organic components and separate levels of wood constructions could be seen. These sediments were compact and botanical components like nutshells, twigs, and moss were present together with fish and animal bones. Even though the evaluation of the preservation status concluded with, at best, medium value (3), the archaeological remains were fairly intact and the sediments still easy to interpret.

A comparison was made with results from the analysis of reduced parameters from sediment samples in one of the investigated sections, in order to spot possible variations in the sediments at different depths. The results have therefore been structured in relation to depth measured from the modern surface in three intervals 1) uppermost, from surface down to 0.5 m, 2) middle from 0.5–1.6 m and, 3) lowermost from 1.6 to approximately 2 m. Figure 4 shows clearly that samples taken in the middle of the sediments (approximately 1 m) are characterized by stable chemical conditions. Samples from these middle sediments contained higher amounts of reduced parameters than the uppermost and lowermost samples. The lowermost sediments in fact show a surprisingly low amount of reduced parameters, comparable to the amounts recorded in the uppermost levels, where infiltration of oxygen can be expected.

Conclusion

The Trondheim study has revealed significant differences in preservation conditions measured by chemical parameters between sediments of different thickness. Results show that sediments with a thickness of 1–2 m have low levels of moisture and organic matter, and most of the inorganic parameters analysed are found in oxidized form. The 2–3 m thick anthropogenic sediments have better preservation conditions. The levels of moisture and organic matter are significantly higher in the thicker sediments and pH levels are more stable and closer to neutral. These compact sediments (which consisted of wooden structures and sediments with a high amount of organic components, especially cellulose) often contain high amounts of both nitrate and ammonium. These types of sediments seem to have a self-preserving character and surrounding deposits might also benefit from this effect.

Our analysis of reduced parameters in sediments with a fairly high amount of organic material shows that oxygen penetration occurs in both the uppermost and lowermost depths, leaving the middle parts unaffected. In this case it would appear that the presence of porous sediments in upper and lower levels of the archaeological material seems to facilitate the penetration of oxygen both from above and below, either by means of air or water or both. This is an interesting, if worrying, observation since oxygen penetration is of importance for heritage management in the assessment of mitigation initiatives of *in situ* preservation.

Final comments

The character of urban life in the medieval towns of Norway is broadly comparable. However, the topographic conditions for Trondheim differ from those of the other

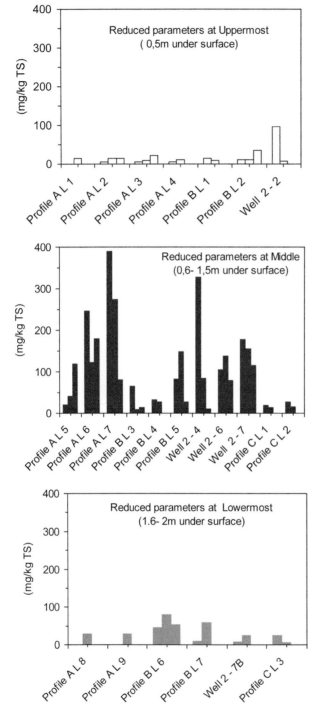

FIGURE 4   Contents of reduced parameters mg/kg dry matter (TS) measured in samples from anthropogenic sediments at site 1 at different levels. Uppermost: (0.5 m), middle (0.6–1.5 m), and lowermost (1.6–2 m) below the surface. Reduced parameters include analysis of NH_{4+}, H_2S, and Fe^{2+}.

medieval towns (notably Bergen, Oslo, and Tønsberg), and the protected, historic part of Trondheim is unique in containing archaeological remains which lie completely in an unsaturated environment. The results of our study provide grounds for concern. The data recorded at sites with anthropogenic sediments between 1–2 m in thickness show that preservation conditions are unstable and therefore vulnerable and sensitive to environmental changes, both chemical and mechanical.

On the basis of our results, it is suggested that *in situ* preservation and mitigation strategies designed to protect archaeological remains in the unsaturated zone of medieval Trondheim should to be evaluated and assessed from case to case at a local level, rather than in accordance with generally applied guidelines set by the management authorities' national *in situ* protection plan. This is particularly relevant in instances were such guidelines stipulate that sediments may be preserved *in situ* beneath newly constructed buildings for an unspecified time. Deficiencies in our current level of knowledge mean that we do not fully understand the long-term impacts on *in situ* archaeological remains preserved beneath newly erected buildings. If environmental monitoring of such sealed anthropogenic sediments indicates their deterioration and that future mitigation strategies are necessary, these might be technically impossible to implement in practice due to these sediments' inaccessibility, thereby in effect rendering them, unprotected and exposed to an uncertain fate.

Bibliography

Bergersen, O. and Hartnik, T. 2007a. Bevaringsforhold i kulturlag ved Kjøpmannsgt 36–38, Trondheim. Jordfaglig vurdering av miljøforhold på bakgrunn av laboratorieanalyser. *Bioforsk Rapport*, 2(88).

Bergersen, O. and Hartnik, T. 2007b. Bevaringsforhold i kulturlag ved Petter Egges Plass TA 200710, Trondheim. Jordfaglig vurdering av miljøforhold på bakgrunn av laboratorieanalyser. *Bioforsk Rapport*, 2(103).

Bergersen, O. and Hartnik, T. 2008. Tilstandsvurdering av kulturlag i Schultz gata — Trondheim. *Bioforsk Rapport*, 3(7).

Bergersen, O. and Petersén, A. 2009. Tilstandsundersøkelse med grunnboring for analyse av bevaringsforhold og bevaringstilstand for kulturlag. Gerhard Schønings Skole, Vår Frue gt. 1–3, Trondheim. NIKU (211) and Bioforsk RAPPORT 4(116).

Bergersen, O. and Petersén, A. 2010. Supplerende forundersøkelse med tilstandsanalyse av bevaringsforhold i forbindelse med nybygg i Thora Storm vgs. Vår Frue gt. 1–3, Trondheim TA 2010/15. NIKU (137) and Bioforsk RAPPORT 4(116).

Martens, V.V. 2010. Environmental Monitoring of Archaeological Deposits. In: S. Trow, V. Holyoak, and E. Byrnes, eds. EAC occasional paper no. 4. Budapest, pp. 75–82.

NIKU and RA. 2008. *The Monitoring Manual. Procedures and Guidelines for Monitoring, Recording, and Preservation Management of Urban Archaeological Deposits.*

NS 9451: 2010. Norwegian Standard 2009: Cultural Property. Requirements on Environmental Monitoring and Investigation of Archaeological Deposits.

Petersén, A. 2007a. Søndre gate 5–11, Dronningen gate 1B, Petter Egges Plass, Trondheim kommune, Sør-Trøndelag fylkeskommune. Rapport Arkeologiske utgravninger Trondheim TA 2007/10.

Petersén, A. 2007b. Kjøpmannsgata 36–38(Gnr 401/258), Trondheim kommune, Sør-Trøndelag fylkeskommune. Rapport Arkeologiske utgravninger Trondheim TA 2007/07, Trondheim 65/2007.

Petersén, A. 2008. Kvartalet Schultz gate- Munkhaugveita-Munkegata-Presidentveita (Gnr 400/102,129), Trondheim kommune, Sør-Trøndelag. Rapport Arkeologiske utgravninger Trondheim TA 2007/24.

Petersén, A. and Martens, V. V. 2011. Sammenstilling av miljøovervåkingsundersøkelser frem til 2010 i middelalderbyene Tønsberg, Trondheim og Oslo. *NIKU Oppdragsrapport*, 55.

Rickard, D. and Morse, J. W. 2005. Acid Volatile Sulfide (AVS). *Marine Chemistry*, 97: 141–97.

Shirokova, Y., Forkutsa, I., and Sharafutdinova, N. 2000. Use of Electrical Conductivity instead of Soluble Salts for Soil Salinity Monitoring in Central Asia. *Irrigation and Drainage Systems*, 14: 199–205.

Stookey, L. L. 1970. Ferrozine — A New Spectrophotometric Reagent for Iron. *Analytical Chemistry*, 42: 779–81.

Notes on contributors

Anna Helena Petersén studied archaeology at Uppsala and Lund University and graduated in 1988. She has worked as an archaeologist since 1990, and has worked for NIKU since 1994. She has conducted several large-scale excavations in Trondheim. At present she works with issues relating to preservation conditions for archaeological deposits both in Trondheim and other medieval towns of Norway.

Correspondence to: Anna H. Petersén, Archaeologist, Norwegian Institute for Cultural Heritage Research, NIKU, Kjøpmannsgata 25, N-7013 Trondheim. Email: anna.petersen@niku.no

Ove Bergersen finished a PhD (Dr Scient) in 'Molecular Genetics' in the Departments of Biochemistry and Animals genetics, Norwegian College of Veterinary Medicine in 1990. Main work as scientist at SINTEF 'Environmental microbiology' (e.g. degradation of oil, creosote, PCB, phthalates) to 2001 and 'Environmental microbiology and soil chemistry', the last ten years as a senior scientist at Norwegian Institute for Agricultural and Environmental Research.

Correspondence to: Ove Bergersen, Senior Researcher, Bioforsk Soil and Environment Division, Fredrik A Dahlsvei 20, N-1430 Ås, Norway. Email: ove.bergersen@bioforsk.no

CONSERVATION AND MGMT OF ARCH. SITES, Vol. 14 Nos 1–4, 2012, 239–48

Preserving Archaeological Remains *In Situ*: Three Case Studies in Trentino, Italy

CRISTINA DAL RÌ, SUSANNA FRUET, PAOLO BELLINTANI, NICOLETTA PISU

Soprintendenza per i beni librari archivistici e archeologici, Provincia Autonoma di Trento

NICOLA MACCHIONI, BENEDETTO PIZZO, CHIARA CAPRETTI

CNR IVALSA Istituto per la Valorizzazione del Legno e delle specie Arboree

The paper presents the results of the restoration and conservation work which has been carried out in three archaeological areas in the Autonomous Province of Trento. The areas, which have been opened to the public for more than ten years, are the open-air archaeological site of Monte S. Martino, Roman *Tridentum* (an underground site under the historical city centre of Trento), and Fiavé (a pile dwelling site in a peat bog). These areas present very different environmental characteristics and have therefore required different interventions according to their specific situation.

In order to reduce maintenance and extraordinary costs, appropriate conservation of the archaeological remains is required. This consists of methodologies of conservation according to the characteristics of the environment; continuous monitoring systems and indirect preventive intervention; and annual maintenance planning.

KEYWORDS archaeological sites, public access, conservation, maintenance, waterlogged wood

Introduction

The Soprintendenza per i Beni librari archivistici e archeologici (Archaeological Heritage Office) of the Autonomous Province of Trento, according to the Italian law, is in charge of the protection, conservation, and enhancement of the archaeological heritage. Among the fifteen archaeological sites open to the public we have chosen three examples. Each of them needs different conservation approaches.

   DOI 10.1179/1350503312Z.00000000020

1. The paper presents the history of the restoration work carried out since the 1980s until today in the open-air site of Monte S. Martino. We have analysed and observed the mechanical resistance of the materials used in the last thirty years, considering their relation with the climate conditions and the fact that the remains have no roof covering.

2. In the case of the Roman *Tridentum*, we have taken into consideration a restored area which is located in a protected underground space, where we have carried out preventive intervention measures in order to prevent biological decline. These measures consisted of integrated temperature, light, and humidity monitoring system.

3. The pile dwelling site of Fiavé, which has been recently included in the UNESCO Heritage List, is particularly interesting as far as the conservation of the piles in wet land is concerned.

We have analysed the state of conservation of the poles and the wooden remains in the water *in situ* since the 1970s thanks to a research programme carried out with the CNR-IVALSA (National Research Centre) of Sesto Fiorentino (Firenze, Italia). The aim of this project is to identify the best conservation methodologies in order to be able to show them in the upcoming archaeological pile dwelling park of Fiavé.

Open-air archaeological site: Monte S. Martino

Cristina Dal Rì and Nicoletta Pisu

The Monte S. Martino area is situated above the village of Campi di Riva del Garda at an altitude of 850 m a.s.l. to the north of Lake Garda, in a very important position from a strategic and logistical point of view.

Archaeological investigations took place starting from the 1970s, leading to identification of an important Roman Age sanctuary dating back to between the first century BC and the fourth century AD (55×30 m) (Figure 1).

In 1996 new excavations were begun, at annual intervals, establishing the existence of a previous settlement and a cult site dating back to the Iron Age, a sanctuary dating back to the first–fourth century AD and a settlement, probably military, dating back to the fifth–sixth century AD. This was followed by construction of the small church of S. Martino and subsequent use of the terraces and plateaus of Monte San Martino for agricultural purposes.

In the early 1980s the area was made into an open-air site, without the construction of any roof covering. The climate is characterized by hot summers and cold winters marked by snow and temperatures regularly going below freezing point (average annual temperatures range from $-5°$ C to $+ 25°$ C but no measurements of the parameters have been made). According to the methods of the time, restoration work was carried out by a construction company which reinforced the walls with cement mortar, also reconstructing the last row of stones.

Excessive restoration intervention is not accepted any more from an archaeological point of view. Cement mortars are not reversible and cause efflorescence and deposits of crystals of salt on the archaeological remains.

FIGURE 1   Site of Monte S. Martino. Area of the Roman sanctuary.
Photograph Archivio Soprintendenza per i beni librari, archivistici e archeologici Provincia Autonoma di Trento

Following the renewed excavations at the end of the 1990s, the problem of consolidating the new archaeological remains presented itself. According to the modern concept of restoration, we decided not to use any more cement-based mortars. Instead we used a reversible material similar to the ancient lime-based mortar. Premixed mortars based on hydraulic lime and sand (Fen-X Tassullo, Trento, Italia) were initially used. However, these were not considered satisfactory in terms of colour and particle size, but even in the long term they proved to be resistant to low temperatures and frost.

In order to improve the aesthetical aspect mortars made with local lime and sand, sifted and mixed on site were used. The results were aesthetically satisfying, however in these climatic conditions and without any roof covering the mortar disintegrated very rapidly (in a wintertime) (Figure 2).

FIGURE 2   Site of Monte S. Martino. Detail of the decay of the sand and lime based mortar on the walls after winter.
Photograph Archivio Soprintendenza per i beni librari, archivistici e archeo-logici Provincia Autonoma di Trento

In the last few years a general programme concerning restoration and excavation work started again. Interventions were carried out in 2010 and 2011 by Diego Malvestio. Scavi e restauri archeologici, Concordia Sagittaria (Venezia, Italia).

In the light of this experience, a compromise has been found, making it possible to satisfy deontological and aesthetic canons and resist freezing-thawing: the solution adopted by us was to insert a very small percentage (about 0.02 or 0.03) of white lime cement (Aquila Bianca Portland B LL 32.2R) into the mixture. The mortar which has been used to fix the upper part of the walls was further strengthened with cement in order to reinforce the most critical point where water stagnation and freezing can occur.

We also noticed that a better and most durable result can be obtained by cleaning out properly earth, pebbles, and ancient mortar from the gap between bricks. In the last years, in order to enhance the strength and resistance of walls, lime-based mortar (Albaria TM injection BASF) was also injected at depth until return.

These procedures avoid the mortar crumbling and the rapid growth of vegetation and weeds.

It is indispensable to check the state of conservation of the works annually and to carry out regular maintenance procedures, such as the filling of cracks and removal of plants, with relative biocide treatments.

Archaeological site: the Roman city of Tridentum

Cristina Dal Rì and Susanna Fruet

Following restoration work on the Teatro Sociale in Trento (1990–2000) archaeological excavations were carried out bringing to light part of the ancient Roman city of *Tridentum* (first century BC–sixth century AD) under the current level of the theatre. This extensive area is made up of public spaces and private areas: dwellings with floors decorated with mosaics, a long stretch of the eastern city walls, and an extensive section of street paved with large slabs of local red stone. Below the street, various ducts belonging to an extensive system of sewers were brought to light.

Restoration work was carried out in the 1990s and included all archaeological remains: walls, sewers realized in bricks and other parts in terracotta, mosaics, and slabs of red limestone. Methodologies and materials used have been chosen according to the principles of reversibility and compatibility with ancient materials. As far as walls are concerned, Lafarge lime-based mortars, slaked lime, sand, and diluted acrylic resin (Primal AC33, Bresciani, Milano, Italia) were used. Stone strengthening was carried out by using ethyl silicate (RC70 e RC80 — Rhodorsil — Rhodia Siliconi Italia).

The archaeological area was opened to the public in 2001 and offers a wide range of activities: educational initiatives, meetings, conferences, exhibitions, and performances (Figure 3). Ten years after the site was opened up to the public, the state of

FIGURE 3   The Roman city of *Tridentum*.
Photograph Archivio Soprintendenza per i beni librari, archivistici e archeologici Provincia Autonoma di Trento

'health' of the area can be considered to be good, thanks to heating system for the winter and air-conditioning in summer.

There are no particular problems in terms of conservation apart from those linked to the dust deposits from all the structures within the area and at the same time structural stability checks of such structures, growth of micro-organisms, or phenomena of biological colonization, located above all in the sewers, which are sealed by glass and house a number of lights.

Ordinary maintenance of the site, which takes place every two years, contributes significantly to conserving the archaeological structures properly and also allows monitoring.

The procedures are carried out with the assistance of vacuum cleaners and brushes for cleaning surfaces and removing superficial deposits, whereas for the mosaic and street paving slabs cleaning takes place using water spray and gentle sponging; a protective and strengthening ethyl silicate (RC80 — Rhodorsil — Rhodia Siliconi Italia) coating has been applied to the red limestone paving slabs of the street. At the same time structural stability checks of such structures, with renovation of mortar joints and securing of loose stones is carried out.

To deal with this problem, a number of direct and indirect measures have been taken, such as:

- Substitution of incandescent light bulbs with low energy consumption light bulbs,
- Substitution of some glass covering panels with metal grids, in order to assist ventilation of the duct,
- localized treatment with broad spectrum biocides (Biotin R — CTS, Vicenza, Italia).

To date this intervention would seem to have resolved the problem. Maintenance was last carried out in 2009 by Ambra Conservazione e Restauro (Milano, Italia).

Archaeological site in a wetland area: the lake dwelling at Fiavè

Cristina Dal Rì, Paolo Bellintani, Nicola Macchioni, Benedetto Pizzo, and Chiara Capretti

The Fiavè peat bog (formerly Lake Carera) is situated in the south-west of Trentino at an altitude of 646 m a.s.l., 10 km north of Lake Garda.

Excavation works carried out between 1969 and 1975 by Renato Perini allowed to identify seven anthropization zones and various lake dwellings dating back between the fourth and second millennium BC. In zone 2 a pile-dwelling settlement has been identified (about 1800–1500 BC in the last phase of the Early Bronze Age–beginning of the Middle Bronze Age). The settlement is characterized by piles up to 9–10 m long (829 piles in 475 m² excavation area).

In the nearby zone 1 (about 1500–1350 BC — the last phase of the Middle Bronze Age) an elaborate system of 'grid' foundations and a stockade along the eastern side of the village has been conserved (Figure 4). Following the excavations in the 1970s, the piles, in spruce, larch, silver fir, and Scots pine, have remained *in situ* in very different conditions as compared to those originally experienced: partially or totally

FIGURE 4   Fiavè. Pile dwellings: zones 1 and 2 excavation works by R. Perini 1969–75.
Photograph Archivio Soprintendenza per i beni librari, archivistici e archeologici Provincia Autonoma di Trento and by permission of the CNR-IVALSA (National Research Council of Italy)

immersed in the groundwater, representing the main tourist attraction in the area. After the latest interventions of excavation and research, dated back to 1994, many organisms have settled permanently on both the submerged parts of the poles and on those emerging: algae, molluscs were anchored to the posts, and other organisms, like plants (herbs and willows), were rooted on the heads of the poles emerging from water. In 2009 a cleaning intervention was made in the lake basin and the emerged parts of the poles have been cleaned by the vegetation from the tops and root systems.

In order to determine the degree of deterioration a cooperation with the National Research Council of Italy CNR-IVALSA (Firenze Italia) was started, also considering the plan of the creation of an archaeological park.

In summer 2010 the water table in the zone 1 was lowered. Following this intervention we have been able to survey the wooden remains of the settlements dated to the Late Neolithic (Fiavè 1 *c.* 3800–3600 BC), to the Middle Bronze Age and to the Late Bronze Age (Fiavè 6 and 7 *c.* 1500–1200 BC), which are situated on a small morainic hill in the centre of the lake and the wooden remains of the cross-linked structure (Fiavè 6).

On these remains a new georeferenced topographic survey was carried out. We also took 101 samples from 81 wooden artefacts. The samples, crossing the piles completely at several points, were taken using a 'Pressler borer'[1] (Figure 5). There were considerable problems in extracting the core sample from parts underwater (poor state of conservation, sucker effect, etc.).

The following tests were undertaken on these samples:

- anatomical (micromorphological) characterization, by optical and Scanning Electron Microscope (SEM Philps XL 20) to evaluate the state of preservation of the cell walls and to trace the type of organisms that caused the decay;
- chemical characterization, to measure the residual percentage of extractives, holocellulose, lignin, and ashes. Spectroscopic techniques will also allow evaluating more in detail the distribution of the chemical components from the surface to the depth of the artefacts. More specifically, this kind of test will be carried out also on a quantitative basis, after a preliminary calibration procedure, thus to handle very limited amounts of material. Tests will be performed on a Alpha Bruker Optics instruments equipped with an ATR (*Attenuated Total Reflectance*) device, which allow taking measurements directly on samples, without any preliminary modification;
- physical characterization to measure the decay through the measurement and calculation of the densities and the Maximum Water Content (MWC, %).

It should be underlined that there are no analytical references to the state of preservation at the time of finding.

On the basis of visual evaluation and state of the core samples extracted, first impressions regarding the state of preservation are not good: there is a seriously deteriorated outer layer which has provided support and food for various categories of plant and animal organisms. Inside the piles, it has been possible to note the activity of organisms living in wetland environments, feeding on decomposing plant debris. Indeed, the parts of the wood immersed in the sediment only apparently look like fresh wood, whereas the material has actually lost a substantial part of its organic consistency.

The data are still being processed. The results will be used to verify whether the *in situ* conservation of structural timber is feasible or not, in order to make the archaeological structures enjoyable by the public through the realization of the 'Park of the pile dwellings', or whether other solutions should be considered, and probably

FIGURE 5   Sample of pile-dwelling pole taken using a 'Pressler borer'.
Photograph by CNR-IVALSA

start a new study for the reburial of at least part of the poles. At present, no evidences of other similar experiences or processes of reburial carried out on wood preserved in peat bogs have been found in literature. Moreover, it is also interesting that wood material has been preserved in water for around the last thirty years, instead of in peat bog like in previous thousands of years. Therefore, the data that will be collected on the wooden elements of Fiavè will represent an important milestone in detecting the effect of an eventual reburial, or alternatively of an eventual exhibition, on the future state of preservations of artefacts.

Note

1   Sampling was carried out by CNR, CORA — Ricerche archeologiche, BRAIDOSUB.

Bibliography

Bellintani, P., Dal Rì, C., Macchioni, N., Pizzo, B., Capretti, C., De Gasperi, N., and Moranti, N. 2011. Dopo 40 anni. Diagnostica sui pali delle aree di scavo Perini e ipotesi di lavoro per la conservazione delle palafitte di Fiavè. Unpublished paper for: International Conference 'Pile-dwellings: Investigations, Conservation, Enhancement', Desenzano del Garda, 6–8 October.

Capretti, C., Macchioni, N., Pizzo, B., Galotta, G., Giachi, G., and Giampaola, D. 2008. The Characterisation of Waterlogged Archaeological Wood: The Three Roman Ships Found in Naples. *Archaeometry*, 50(5): 855–76.

Ciurletti, G. 2000. Trento romana. Archeologia e urbanistica. In: *Storia del Trentino, L'età romana, Volume I*. Istituto Trentino di Cultura, Trento, pp. 287–346.

Ciurletti, G. ed. 2007. *Fra il Garda e le Alpi di Ledro Monte S. Martino il luogo di culto (ricerche e scavi 1969–1979)*. Giunta della Provincia Autonoma di Trento, Soprintendenza per i beni Archeologici, Trento.

Dal Rì, C., Bellintani, P., Macchioni, N., Pizzo, B., and Capretti, C. 2011. Preliminary Studies for the Conservation of Wooden Poles of the Pile Dwelling in Fiavè (North East, Italy). International Conference IKUWA 4 'Managing the Underwater Cultural Heritage'. Zadar (Croatia), 29 September–2 October.[Online] Available at: <http://www.ikuwa4.com.>.

Marzatico, F. 2003. Aspetti della storia delle ricerche nella torbiera di Fiavè. In: P. Bellintani and L. Moser, eds. *Archeologie sperimenatali. Metodologie ed esperienze fra verifica, riproduzione, comunicazione e simulazione*. Provincia Autonoma di Trento, Servizio Beni Culturali, Ufficio Beni Archeologici, Trento, pp. 171–80.

Perini, R. 1984. *Scavi archeologici nella zona palafitticola di Fiavè–Carera, Parte I, campagne 1969–1976. Situazione dei depositi e dei resti strutturali*. Patrimonio storico artistico del Trentino, 8, Provincia Autonoma di Trento, Servizio Beni Culturali, Trento.

Pulga, S. 1999. Climatologia nella conservazione di scavi archeologici coperti. In: C. Dal Ri and S. Fruet, eds. *Climatologia applicata alla conservazione dei beni archeologici e storico artistici, Incontri di restauro 2*. Provincia Autonoma di Trento, Servizio Beni Culturali, Trento, pp. 88–125.

Pedeli, C.and Pulga S. 2002. *Pratiche conservative sullo scavo archeologico, principi e metodi*. MIC (Museo Internazionale delle Ceramiche in Faenza), Firenze.

Notes on contributors

Cristina Dal Rì, conservator-restorer, at the Archaeological Heritage Office of the Autonomous Province of Trento. She is in charge of the conservation restoration of all kind of archaeological remains and of the archaeological areas. Her specialization area is the conservation of wet organic materials.

Contact: Cristina Dal Rì, Soprintendenza per i beni librari archivistici e archeologici, Provincia Autonoma di Trento, Laboratorio di restauro, Via Aosta 1, 38122 Trento, Italia. Email: cristina.dalri@provincia.tn.it

Susanna Fruet, conservator-restorer, at the Archaeological Heritage Office of the Autonomous Province of Trento. She is in charge of the conservation restoration of all kind of archaeological remains and of the archaeological areas. Her specialization area is the conservation of metal materials.

Contact: Susanna Fruet, Soprintendenza per i beni librari archivistici e archeologici, Provincia Autonoma di Trento, Laboratorio di restauro, Via Aosta 1, 38122 Trento, Italia. Email: susanna.fruet@provincia.tn.it

Paolo Bellintani, PhD, graduated in Paletnology, and is archaeologist at the Archaeological Heritage Office of the Autonomous Province of Trento, he is in charge of the archaeological pile-dwelling site, museum, and park of Fiavé.

Contact: Paolo Bellintani, Soprintendenza per i beni librari archivistici e archeologici, Provincia Autonoma di Trento, Via Aosta 1, 38122 Trento, Italia. Email: paolo.bellintani@provincia.tn.it

Nicoletta Pisu, PhD, graduated in Medieval Archaeology, and is archaeologist at the Archaeological Heritage Office of the Autonomous Province of Trento. She is in charge of the excavation and restoration works on the archaeological site of Monte S. Martino.

Contact: Nicoletta Pisu, Soprintendenza per i beni librari archivistici e archeologici, Provincia Autonoma di Trento, Via Aosta 1, 38122 Trento, Italia. Email: nicoletta.pisu@provincia.tn.it

Nicola Macchioni, PhD, graduated in Forest Science and is currently Researcher at CNR-IVALSA, where he is coordinator of the Wood Conservation Department. He is also in charge of the 'Laboratory of Wood Anatomy'. He developed a large experience in diagnosis applied to the wooden Cultural Heritage, from timber structures to wood statues, including archaeological wood.

Contact: Nicola Macchioni, CNR-IVALSA Istituto per la Valorizzazione del Legno e delle specie Arboree, Via Madonna del Piano 10, 50019 Sesto Fiorentino, Firenze, Italia. Email: macchioni@ivalsa.cnr.it

Benedetto Pizzo, PhD, graduated in Chemical Engineering and is currently Researcher at CNR-IVALSA, where he is in charge of the 'Laboratory of Chemistry of Wood and Wood Products'. He developed a large experience in the characterization of wood artifacts belonging to the Cultural Heritage and of the materials used for restoration. He matured a specific experience in the characterization and in the conservation of waterlogged archaeological wood.

Contact: Benedetto Pizzo, CNR-IVALSA Istituto per la Valorizzazione del Legno e delle specie Arboree, Via Madonna del Piano 10, 50019 Sesto Fiorentino, Firenze, Italia. Email: pizzo@ivalsa.cnr.it

Chiara Capretti, PhD, graduated in Forest Science and is currently Researcher at CNR-IVALSA. She developed a broad experience on microscopy applied to archaeological wooden artifacts and more generally on the diagnosis of waterlogged wood.

Contact: Chiara Capretti, CNR-IVALSA Istituto per la Valorizzazione del Legno e delle specie Arboree, Via Madonna del Piano 10, 50019 Sesto Fiorentino, Firenze, Italia. Email: capretti@ivalsa.cnr.it

CONSERVATION AND MGMT OF ARCH. SITES, Vol. 14 Nos 1–4, 2012, 249–62

Preservation *In Situ* for Tourism: An Early Christian Monastic Complex on Sir Bani Yas Island, Western Abu Dhabi, UAE

DANA GOODBURN-BROWN
Head of Conservation, Sir Bani Yas Monastery Project, UAE

KIRSTY NORMAN
Centre for Applied Archaeology, Institute of Archaeology, University College London, UK

JOSEPH ELDERS
Archaeological Director, Sir Bani Yas Monastery Project, UAE

ELIZABETH POPESCU
Field Director, Sir Bani Yas Monastery Project, UAE

This paper reports on the conservation measures taken to protect and display the remains of a pre-Islamic Christian monastic complex on Sir Bani Yas Island, Abu Dhabi, UAE, and the reasoning behind the decisions. The excavated areas of the site are now partly sheltered, and partly reburied. Observations are made on the effectiveness of the shelter building, and the reburial system used between 1996 and 2010, and on the measures currently being used to preserve plaster floors and faced standing walls in aggressive environmental conditions. Work has been carried out to find ways to make the site as legible as possible while also conserving it. Methods of site monitoring are also discussed.

KEYWORDS reburial, wall capping, shelters, lime mortar, sustainable conservation, Gulf tourism

Introduction

On the island of Sir Bani Yas, just off the southern part of the coast of Abu Dhabi, a programme is currently being developed in order to preserve the remains of a

                    DOI 10.1179/1350503312Z.00000000021

remarkable early Christian church and monastic complex. The island is believed to have been settled around 600 AD by a community of thirty to forty monks of the Church of the East ('Nestorian Church'). There are documentary references to Christian activity in the Gulf region from the fourth–twelfth centuries AD, but until recent investigations in the northern Gulf, in Kuwait, on the Iranian coast, and also at Jubayl in the Eastern Province of Saudi Arabia, there was little archaeological evidence to support this.

The Sir Bani Yas site is one of the best dated and most complete sites of this type, and, as such, the church and site are of exceptional, international importance for the understanding of the development and decline of settlement and Christianity in the region.

Excavation and plans for development

The site was initially excavated between 1993 and 1996 by the Abu Dhabi Islands Archaeological Survey (ADIAS) under the patronage of Sheikh Zayed, the founder of the UAE (ADIAS, n.d.). At that time, Sheikh Zayed used Sir Bani Yas Island as a retreat, and the island underwent intensive tree planting, and was developed as a wildlife sanctuary.

The monastery site was then reburied until 2009, when Sheikh Mohammed bin Zayed the Crown Prince of Abu Dhabi ordered excavations to resume under the aegis of the Abu Dhabi Tourism Development and Investment Company (TDIC). TDIC are now developing the island as a resort, and the site was re-opened for public viewing in December 2010 (Figure 1).

FIGURE 1   Tourists and guide at the site while archaeological team works.
© *Tourism Development and Investment Company*

It is planned that the monastery will be part of a new heritage trail, as part of the range of nature, history, and sport activities for visitors to the island. For this reason, TDIC are interested in not only opening up the previously excavated areas, but are considering having the site fully excavated. This presents some real challenges in terms of conservation, but the involvement of a major development organization also raises the possibility of serious and much-needed research into site conservation.

In the Gulf region, there are very few examples of shelter buildings, and none that we knew of where the building's effectiveness had been assessed. Yet the common use of relatively soft building materials (coralstone, mudbrick, plaster) and the extreme climate makes the conservation of exposed archaeology particularly difficult without using sheltering.

Previous attempts at conservation have often suffered due to lack of maintenance.[1] This project hopes to develop regular monitoring and maintenance of the monument and aims to both document and assess the performance of conservation work, and of the shelter building, in order to build up experience which will be of use for conservation in the region.

Environmental conditions on Sir Bani Yas

One of the main challenges for the conservation of exposed archaeological sites in the Gulf is the aggressive climate.

Rainfall

Whereas there is very little rain for most of the year, torrential rain can fall during the winter and spring: March 2010 saw one of the heaviest rainstorms seen in Abu Dhabi for some years when 40 mm of rain fell in one rainstorm of several hours. Torrential rain will quickly erode and gully earthen structures, soft mortars, and soft sand and coral stones.

Humidity/drying

Mean monthly humidity in Abu Dhabi ranges from 23 per cent to 89 per cent over the year. However, there is extreme fluctuation within every month of the year, and even within 24-hour cycles. Very heavy dew has been noted on the site, drenching surfaces and then drying off quickly as the sun rises.

Wind/windblown sand

Maximum wind speeds for the months of February to December range from 41–59 km per hour, but in January these can reach 86 km per hour. Windblown sand is a major factor with regard to erosion of exposed archaeology. The wind also carries salt: the monastery is less than a mile from the sea.

Plant roots and growth

Since the 1960s, vast numbers of trees and shrubs have been planted in rows across much of the island, which had been almost barren. An irrigation system of water pipes which feed each tree was laid at the same time (current irrigation is at a level of 8 million gallons a day of desalinated water). Smaller shrubs are also scattered around the site, and are increasingly naturalizing and becoming established (Figure 2).

FIGURE 2   Sir Bani Yas Island: setting of the monastery.

Character and condition of the monument

The church is in the middle of a large courtyard, and the complete plan has survived (Figure 3). Archaeological survey has shown that around the courtyard, on each side, were ranges of rooms, and presumed to be the monastic living quarters. The buildings are composed of local limestone, coralstone, and mud mortar walls, standing up to 1 m high in places. Several rooms have gypsum plaster floors and wall renders (Figure 4).

General condition statement

Surviving walls have extensive cracking, areas of loose mortar, and vulnerable under-cuts. Floor levels and types vary around the monument, and some were cut through during the earlier archaeological excavation work. Some surviving plaster surfaces are hard and compact, but fine networks of roots were noticed within the wall structures and plaster layers, on close inspection. These roots have caused some spalling of stone and plaster and/or complete disruption of isolated areas.

The church: walls

Before the site had been identified, several large holes were dug through the archaeology in order to plant trees or shrubs, and preparatory clearing of the site by bulldozer levelled the remains of the walls to a relatively uniform height. Some lengths

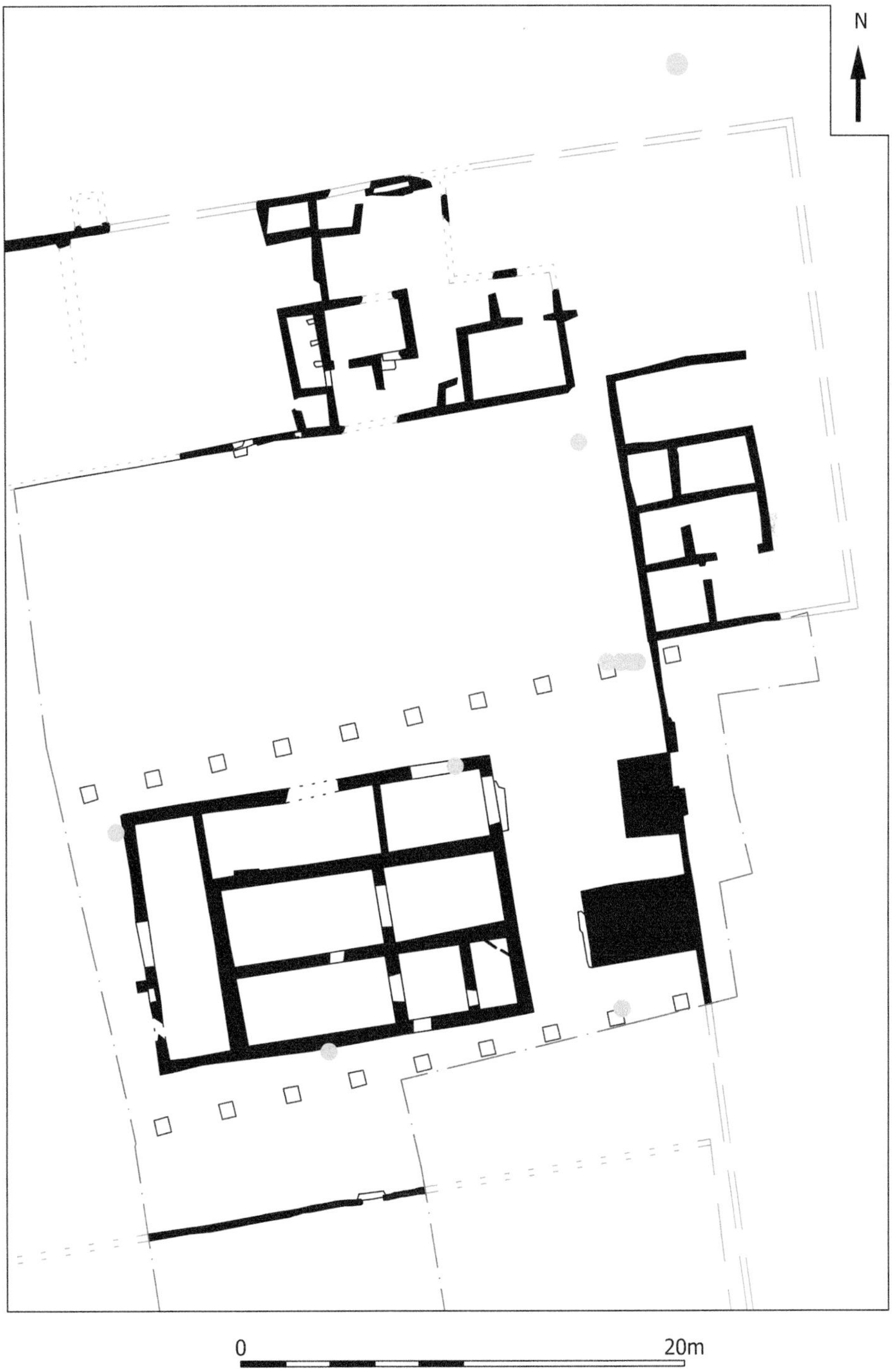

N

0   20m

Location of conservation test blocks. Scale 1:250.

FIGURE 3   Site plan of the church and monastic buildings, plus locations of ten monitoring blocks.

FIGURE 4   Condition of wall plaster before stabilising with lime mortar in one of the rooms of the church.

of wall and some areas of plaster flooring are therefore now missing, although the remaining walls are generally in remarkably sound condition.

The walls of the church are composed of a mixture of materials, including:

- a material called, colloquially, 'beach rock': a natural mixture of finely crushed and compacted coral, shell, and sand. It is therefore composed largely of carbonates, with some silicate
- 'coralstone': ancient coral
- a layered sandstone with fairly fine particles of sand
- a grittier sandstone with small particles of shell
- an almost black tabular flint, used traditionally near the tops of walls, and sometimes as a low course to impede rising damp.

The mortar varies in composition. Most of it appears to be similar to the gypsum-rich analysis sample described below. In places, a greenish mud mortar has been used, which is prone to shrinkage and cracking.

The church: plaster

The plaster varies considerably in thickness, and different layers and perhaps periods of application can be seen. In the main, the surface layer of the plaster is fine, smooth, and white, but in some areas the wall plaster is coarser, and more sand-coloured: floors are all white plaster.

Materials: vulnerability

Apart from the flint, once excavated, all of these materials are vulnerable to erosion by salts and the wet-dry cycle, wind, sand, and especially rain. It is noticeable that the exposed tops of the walls are 'sugary', with tiny particles which eroded off them after the site was rained on in the short period between re-excavation, and covered with a temporary shelter. In the two seasons we have been observing the site, however, we have not seen evidence of salts crystallizing within or on the surfaces of the monument. This may change now that the site is permanently exposed, and the situation will be monitored.

Materials: analysis

Samples of the mortar and plaster from the church were provided, and these were sent for analysis at Greenwich University by Dr Ian Slipper. This was done in order to understand the sources of the building material, and also to be able to choose a material for conservation purposes which would be sufficiently differentiated that it would not cause confusion later if samples of mortar or plaster are analysed. The mortar sample provided proved to have a high proportion of gypsum (calcium sulfate dihydrate $CaSO_4 \cdot 2H_2O$) compared to the plaster; the latter contained more calcite ($CaCo3$). The proportion of gypsum used generally is unsurprising, as there are large deposits on the islands in this area.

Observations on the previous reburial system

A large area of the north side of the site, known to the archaeological team as the 'Abbot's quarters', was excavated in the mid-1990s and subsequently backfilled. Since then the tops of some walls have become exposed by wind, and the exposed geotextile covering has decayed in the sun and adhered to the tops of walls in places. Roots were observed to have grown along the open weave synthetic geotextile surface in some areas, as reported on other reburied sites (Roby, 2010; Neguer, 2004). The exposure of the wall tops means that they are eroding, and there is a danger that unwary visitors may walk on them.

The area was re-excavated, and the below-surface remains of the church and Abbot's quarters appeared to have survived almost unchanged from their condition in 1990s, based on general photographs, but with some areas of plaster loosened due to fine root growth.

Conservation measures

Fencing

Cutting down on wind erosion was a priority for this site. An *arish* (reed) fence has been placed around what would have been the original external perimeter of the courtyard complex. This has the added advantage of providing some spatial sense of the size of the original buildings.

Observations	Proposals
General protection from wind and windblown sand good; but thin in places.	Fence to be maintained, worn areas to be repaired, and whole doubled in thickness.

The temporary shelter structure

As it had been decided that the remains of the church are to be on open display, a shelter building was constructed over this area of the site by TDIC in early 2009. This was designed by TDIC's engineers. The shelter is a lightweight open-sided structure of 10 cm square powder-coated steel pillars set into 1 m deep concrete blocks, and smaller upper struts built to withstand the considerable winds that Sir Bani Yas experiences. Holes for the blocks were dug under archaeological supervision. The gabled roof is covered with a tightly stretched tan-coloured fabric, waterproofed on the underside. The shelter building is simple, relatively unobtrusive, and the tan colour of the fabric and the powder coating blend well in the landscape

The principal aim of the structure was to provide shelter from violent winter rains, and in this it has succeeded. Evidence of the beginnings of damage that can be caused by rain could be seen on the site, where one earlier rainstorm had caused mud mortars exposed on the tops of walls to start to develop spider cracks, and white runnels of dilute plaster to flow down walls.

Slight flapping of roofing fabric seems to have the unexpected benefit of discouraging birds from settling in the eaves, and dropping guano and nesting detritus on the site, which had been a concern.

Observations	Proposals
General protection from rain good, but some condensation from metal beams and edge dripping a problem (Figure 5).	Beams to be wrapped with hemp rope to act as a buffer and absorb moisture. Guttering and water capture/drainage to be installed. Better ventilation (to prevent a build-up of heat in the eaves and resulting condensation), and a more robust structure to be considered for a more permanent solution. Ongoing monitoring.

Stabilization of plaster walls

Loose areas of wall plaster, cracks, and undercuts were filled with a mortar based on lime putty, a thixotropic non-hydraulic lime primarily composed of calcium hydroxide $CA(OH)_2$ for the following reasons:

- differentiation of materials from the original largely gypsum-based mortar
- good workability, with a much slower setting time than gypsum
- better 'breathability' than gypsum plaster.

Experiments were carried out to establish the most appropriate mix of lime and filler to replicate the colour and texture of the plaster reasonably closely and provide long-term physical support, and local yellow 'plasterer's sand' was found to be a good choice.

The following two mixes were found to work well:

'Conservation mortar mix': (for fills, and supporting undercuts) 1 part lime putty: 3 parts dry washed yellow 'plasterer's' or site sand, by volume.
'Liquid mix' (for use in re-adhering loose pieces of plaster/stones): 1:1 lime putty: washed yellow sand and water.

Lime putty had not been found to be available in the UAE, and was brought as hold luggage from the UK, but, as it was being used mainly in a 1:3 mix, a 10 kg tub went a long way.

FIGURE 5   Temporary shelter with lines of water from rain and condensation drips.

Observations	Proposals
Preliminary results have been good.	Monitoring is needed over the next 5–10 years to establish the success of the method.

Reburial of the Abbot's quarters and lower floor levels in the church

Reasons for reburial

Having re-excavated part of the Abbot's quarters in order to examine their condition, replace decaying geotextile, and discuss the development of the site with TDIC, it was decided that, until more informed choices could be made about a long-term shelter building, they should be reburied (Demas, 2004). Reburial of some of the more deeply excavated parts of the church was also necessary to level the site up to make it more 'readable' to the visitor.

Methodology for reburial

1. 'Containment walls' were constructed with dry stones from the site, to replace missing wall sections (see below: Presenting the site).
2. Approx. 2 cm of sifted site sand was used as the first layer of fill for each room.

3. A layer of geotextile (HPS2 from Geofabircs Ltd, UK) was put down as a filter/marker layer (Kavazanjian, 2004; Cooke, 2007). For walls outside the shelter, the geotextile carried up the wall surfaces, and over the uncapped walls, taking care to have some sand fill between the geotextile and wall surfaces.
4. Sifted site sand was added to nearly complete the fill.
5. All rooms with plaster floors had a final fill consisting of washed white gravel. This gravel was applied tight up to the geotextile wall coverings and heaped slightly along each wall edge. Sand was used to cover the geotextile over the tops of Abbot's quarters' walls.

Observations	Proposals
The site is much more legible to the visitor.	In future years it may be necessary to lift the gravel in order to remove sand which has drifted in.

Plant growth

Irrigation and larger trees close to the site have been removed. Plants growing on the archaeological structures have been and will continue to be removed. Low ground-cover plants on unexcavated areas of the site are allowed to grow for the moment, as they contribute to holding down the sand.

Observations	Proposals
The site is clearly visible, and safe from root growth.	Plants growing on the archaeological structures should be removed on a regular basis by a designated archaeologist or conservator.

Maintenance and monitoring

The site is casually monitored by island staff. Biennial visits of the archaeological and conservation team, however, provide intensive monitoring and maintenance during the present programme of development.

Wind and windborne sand-erosion monitoring blocks

In March 2011, cement blocks with a layer of mortar applied to them were placed in several locations around the site (both inside and outside the boundary fencing). These have been created in order to monitor the effects of wind and windborne sand on surfaces of the monument by mimicking their properties in these sacrificial surfaces. One series tests the juxtapositions of hard ('conservation mortar mix') and soft (hard mix + sand, 1:1) fill mixtures on a flat surface, and the other consists of stepped (2–10 mm in 2 mm steps) surfaces of hard and soft mortars (Figure 6).

Observations	Proposals
The erosion monitoring blocks will give an indication of how well the site is being protected from wind.	This information should feed into any design for a permanent shelter building.
Monitoring of the site needs to be carried out in a systematic and regular fashion.	Staff on the island should be trained and encouraged to take over this work.

FIGURE 6   Profile of mortared cement monitoring block. Top surface has a 3:1 (sand:lime) layer applied in 2 cm incremental steps.

Presenting the site

Missing areas of wall

Several areas of the walls of the church are missing, having been removed when tree pits were dug across the site. These gaps made the building harder to 'read' for the average visitor.

They were filled by creating 'containment walls', constructed with larger site stones and faced with 'conservation mortar mix' plus sand (1:1).

Missing floors, or areas of floor

During excavation, parts of the floors of the church had had to be removed during investigation of the stratigraphy of the site. The resulting lower levels were filled with clean sand in November 2009 after re-excavation to protect the archaeological layers below, and to provide a base on which to lay a heavier aggregate which would then hold down the sand fill. This was intended as far as possible to blend in with the site, while also clearly indicating the areas where floors are missing.

Wall capping

The reburial of the Abbot's quarters was necessary for conservation reasons. However, it was potentially going to hide from visitors the area of the site which gives the best sense of the scale of the outer courtyard buildings. As an experiment therefore, in the 2010 season, one wall was capped with lime mortar and stones in the method described by Severson (2010). Using this method allows an area of the site to be almost completely backfilled, but to have the wall lines still visible.

Stones used were sourced from the site (loose on the surface and from site spoil). A thick layer of 'conservation mortar mix' + 10% by volume pozzolan was applied as mortar to secure the stones, and then a layer of 'conservation mortar' without pozzolan was applied as a sacrificial top coat.

The experiment worked well apart from some slight surface cracks, although it was found that the required wetting of the wall and continued dampening for seven days in order to facilitate proper setting of the mortar caused some loosening of the plaster facings. Therefore, it was decided to create 'floating' wall caps for the remaining wall. These were made from dry stone without the securing layer of mortar, with gaps plugged with damp sand and/or a sand and conservation mortar mix (1:1) as described above. Some walls had geotextile under the dry stone wall caps, some not, as further experimentation. Damp sand was laid on top of the walls as a bed for the stone wall caps, which were constructed slightly wider than the walls themselves, so that water would be shed into the fill rather than run down the wall surfaces.

Delineation of rooms and courtyards in reburied areas

Different colours of gravel and other fill have been used to indicate what is buried below: white gravel illustrates where there are plaster floors, sandy gravel taken from the site represents where courtyards exist, and black gravel is used to represent an area of burning (Figure 7).

FIGURE 7   Visitor walkways, reburied Abbot's quarters, and church under the shelter.

Observations	Proposals
Preliminary results have been good. Floating wall caps less damaging to original walls and plaster facings.	Monitoring is needed over the next 5–10 years to establish the success of the method. Soft sand and mortar facings will need re-application following extensive rain and/or wind erosion.

Wall facings

One of the dry stone walls (at the southern boundary, facing the tourist viewing platform) was faced with 'conservation mortar' + 10% pozzolan mix. A pozzolan additive was chosen as it creates a harder surface, more resilient to erosion (Proudfoot and Severson, 2010). This facing was applied primarily for aesthetic and site interpretation reasons, as this section of wall had a decorative finish surviving and it was felt important to improve the visibility of this.

Visitor information

Site display panels illustrate and explain the floor plans for the site, and laminated information sheets on both the archaeological significance and conservation measures have been produced and supplied to the island's tour guides.

It is hoped that, as plans for a visitor centre on the island progress, the project will be able to contribute information not only about the history of the site, but about its conservation.

Conclusion

Work at Sir Bani Yas has just begun: there will be continued monitoring, possible new discoveries, and further conservation work on the monument, and all these will be made public to visitors on the island. It is hoped that monitoring of the conservation work and associated experiments being carried out will contribute to an understanding of how to manage archaeological sites in the wider Gulf area.

The conservation work thus far has been well received by island tourists, and will help to ensure that the fragile but rich and diverse heritage of the area remains as publicly available as possible.

Acknowledgements

We would like to thank Sheikh Mohammed bin Zayed and TDIC for their support for this conservation project. We would also like to thank Peter Hellyer for his project leadership and contributions to this work. Archaeological staff Sarah Bates and John Percival and Conservation Assistants Katrina Redman, Daniela Boos Pedrosa, and Marie Le Saux contributed to the success of the preservation efforts. The dry stone walling skills were provided by TDIC workers Yogandra Khanal, Bhuwan Karki, and Humaun Kabir.

Note

[1] A summary of the project and conservation work can be viewed online at: <http://www.youtube.com/watch?v=GyaTeoCmuLM>.

Bibliography

ADIAS, n.d. [accessed 2 August 2011] Available at: <http://www.adias-uae.com/sirbaniyas.html>

Cooke, L. 2007. The Archaeologist's Challenge or Despair: Reburial at Merv, Turkmenistan. *Conservation and Management of Archaeological Sites*, 9(2): 97–112.

Demas, M. 2004. 'Site unseen': The Case for Reburial of Archaeological Sites. *Conservation and Management of Archaeological Sites*, 6: 137–54.

Kavazanjian, Jr, E. 2004. The uSe of Geosynthetics for Archaeological Site Reburial, *Conservation and Management of Archaeological Sites*, 6: 377–93.

Neguer J. 2004. Reburial and Protective Covering of Ancient Mosaic Pavements, *Conservation and Management of Archaeological Sites*, 6: 247–58.

Proudfoot, T. and Severson, K. 2010. Stabilization of Walls with Lime-Mortar Capping. In: C. Rozeik, A. Roy, and D. Saunders, eds. *Conservation and the Eastern Mediterranean*. London: The International Institute for Conservation of Historic and Artistic Works, pp. 201–06.

Roby, T., Alberti, L., and Ben Abed, A. 2010. A Preliminary Assessment of Mosaic Reburials in Tunisia. In: C. Rozeik, A. Roy, and D. Saunders, eds. *Conservation and the Eastern Mediterranean*. London: The International Institute for Conservation of Historic and Artistic Works, pp. 207–13.

Notes on contributors

Dana Goodburn-Brown MSc ACR is an accredited archaeological conservator and founding director of AMTeC Coop Ltd and CSI: Sittingbourne. She has worked on developer-funded archaeological conservation projects for most of her thirty-year career, and instigated the first PARIS conference, when working at the Museum of London 1987–97. Her work on international projects include Zeugma, South-East Turkey; Chersonesos, Crimea, Ukraine; Baharia, Egypt; and Upper Sabina Tiberina, Italy. She recently obtained an MSc in Sustainable Heritage from UCL.

Correspondence to: Dana Goodburn-Brown, The Cottage, Tonge Corner, Sittingbourne, Kent ME9 9BA, UK. Email: danagb@msn.com

Kirsty Norman worked as an archaeological conservator for twenty-five years, at the British Museum and then mainly in the Arabian Gulf and Turkey. She took an MA in heritage management at the Institute of Archaeology UCL in London in 2004, and worked on a series of World Heritage-based projects for the Centre for Applied Archaeology at UCL. She continues to work as a Principal Consultant for the CAA, and is also an Honorary Lecturer at the Institute.

Dr Joseph Elders MA PhD FSA is an archaeologist and architectural historian who specializes in the study of churches and monasteries. He has directed excavations in the UK, Germany, and the UAE, and since 1999 is responsible for archaeological matters relating to the Church of England's 13,000 medieval churches, as well as compiling reports on churches at risk, compiling Conservation Management Plans, and giving advice on major development projects aimed at enhancing heritage assets for public appreciation. He has been Archaeological Director of the excavations at the Sir Bani Yas monastery sites since 1993.

Elizabeth Popescu began her career as a field archaeologist at the Museum of London and moved into post-excavation analysis and publication. She has excavated extensively in the UK and in Italy, Bulgaria, Romania, Syria, and the UAE. She is currently the Post-Excavation and Publications Manager at Oxford Archaeology East.

CONSERVATION AND MGMT OF ARCH. SITES, Vol. 14 Nos 1–4, 2012, 263–72

Issues *of In Situ* Conservation at Jinsha, People's Republic of China

Lu Bai

Chengdu Museum, China and University College London, UK

Shuang-Lin Zhou

Department of Archaeology and Museology, Peking University, China

The archaeological site of Jinsha, in Sichuan Province, China, was excavated in 2001, revealing extensive evidence of a substantial 3000 years old settlement. The site was subsequently sheltered and in 2007 an on-site museum was constructed. The shelter's performance, in terms of environmental control, public interpretation and site management, is assessed. The need for more scientific research on site material science is highlighted.

KEYWORDS prehistory, Jinsha, China, Shelters, *in situ* conservation

Background

The conservation and presentation of archaeological sites has become fashionable in the People's Republic of China. Since the promulgation by the State Administration of Cultural Heritage (SACH) of a revised Law on the *Protection of Cultural Relics* in 2002 (NPCSC, 2002), and in 2009 the *National Archaeological Park Administration Measures* (SACH, 2010), it has been made clear that the social and economic benefits of archaeological sites needs to be recognized in archaeological site management and local development (China ICOMOS, 2004; Shan, 2010: 50–51). As a result, a large number of Chinese archaeological site managers sensed the real benefits of becoming a 'National Archaeological Park': as a result, in 2010, twenty-three archaeological sites applied for designation. To achieve this recognition, sites must undertake appropriate actions on conservation management.

As one of the earliest National Archaeological Parks in China, Jinsha, in Sichuan Province, has become one of the prototypes of archaeological site conservation in China. However, the conservation of Jinsha is far from satisfactory: in part this is due to the lack of a tradition of research into site conservation techniques in China, and in part due to the emphasis on the conservation of portable artefacts excavated at Jinsha. Among the small number of scientific papers on site conservation most concentrate on interventions rather than preventative conservation (Zhou and Pan,

DOI 10.1179/1350503312Z.00000000022

2004: 52–55; Zhou and Yuan, 2004: 50–52; Zhou et al., 2005: 567–70; Zhou et al., 2008: 954–62), while some paper concentrates on the deterioration caused by environmental factors (Zhou, 2003: 78–83), or environmental monitoring (Wang and Yan, 2010: 391–95; Zhang et al., 2010: 104–08).

The lack of research on the conservation of archaeological sites attracted the attention of SACH in 2006, which launched a research project entitled *Research and development in the key technique of site conservation — the research*. The preliminary research report was completed in 2009 (SACH, 2009), but the conservation of archaeological sites is still regarded as difficult. In addition, conservation treatment cannot be executed without considering other factors, such as public interpretation and the visitor experience. There needs to be a balance between technical conservation and site presentation (Merriman, 2004: 1–18; Aslan, 2008: 70). Unfortunately, in China technical conservation has often been sacrificed to provide the quality of presentation.

In 2007, Peking University (PKU) collaborated with Jinsha On-site Museum regarding the conservation of the Jinsha site. The scientific data presented in this paper comes from that collaboration. The aim of this paper is: first, to introduce the conservation at Jinsha, which is seen as the epitome of the present conservation of archaeological sites in China, and secondly, to analyse the site conditions and suggest strategies for improvement.

The site

Jinsha site is one of the most significant and famous archaeological sites in China. It is located in Chengdu, the Capital of Sichuan Province, and represents the distinct and impressive ancient Shu culture, dating from *c.* 1000 BCE. A unique bronze statue tradition, and large numbers of gold, ivory, and jade objects attracted public attention after its discovery in 2001. Jinsha is both a *Major Site Protected at the National Level* and on the *World Cultural Heritage Tentative List*. The sunbird gold foil found there has become the symbol of China's cultural heritage (SACH, 2005).

Jinsha was excavated by the Chengdu Institute of Archaeology in 2002. The archaeological remains lie within the modern urban area (Figure 1), extending over an area of 5 sq. km. The majority of the area, after excavation, has been covered by urban development. However, an on-site museum established in 2007 and covering 6 hectares includes the most important sanctuary. The museum is responsible for the daily maintenance, surveillance, and security of the site, while the conservation department of Chengdu Museum is in charge of scientific studies and the conservation treatment of the site. According to China's law, governments at various levels have the responsibility to fund the conservation of cultural heritage.

The sanctuary remains at Jinsha are displayed in an on-site museum hall (Figure 2), with transparent glass curtain wall and roof which stops the penetration of ultraviolent light. The archaeological excavation grids have been left in place, as have numerous organic and inorganic archaeological objects (Figure 3); the latter is problematic in terms of long-term conservation. The museum planned to have on-going archaeological excavations, in order to attract visitors, but this has not happened because the archaeological remains are finite and site managers feared the diminution of site attraction.

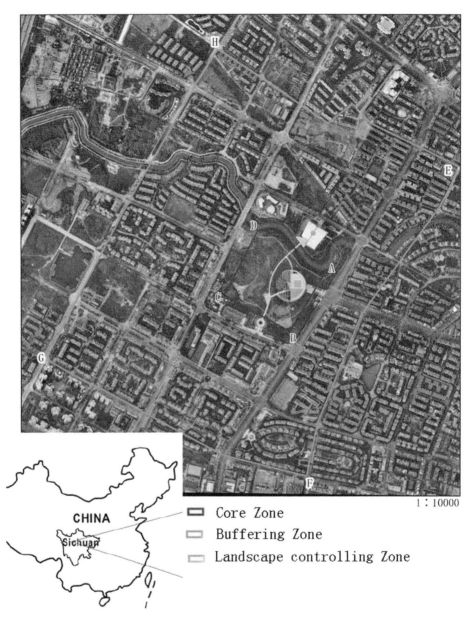

CHINA

Sichuan

□ Core Zone
□ Buffering Zone
□ Landscape controlling Zone

1 : 10000

FIGURE 1   Aerial photograph of Jinsha site (annotated by Yuan-Xiang Zhao and reproduced by permission of the Chengdu Institute of Archaeology).

Diagnosis of site conditions

There was a lack of conservation investigation at Jinsha until 2007, when PKU began both fieldwork and laboratory testing. Through literature reviews, field observation, and interviewing, the condition of the site was recorded. Laboratory analyses of soil samples, along with environmental monitoring, were used to explore the causes of

FIGURE 2   The site enclosed by a glass hall.

FIGURE 3   Ivory and antler objects on the surface of the site.

deterioration. However, the results of the conservation investigation were unsatisfactory, and the data collected is far from complete and systematic.

Site conditions

The Jinsha region has a hot and humid environment, where relative humidity hovers around 80 per cent, average annual rainfall fluctuates between 800 and 1000 mm, and the average annual temperature is 16°. This environment encourages the growth of flora and invertebrates. Although the site has been sheltered since the time of archaeological excavation in 2002, mosses and cracks have emerged. Despite the site being enclosed by a new site hall in 2007, the environment is still unstable and problematic, due to the design of the protective structure: the transparent curtain walls and roof allow sunshine to penetrate into the hall and the controllable glass panels on the roof provide ventilation but also access to birds and raindrops.

The most obvious pathologies on the site are cracks and mosses. Surface cracking, with polygonal patterns, only penetrates a few cm, which is decided by the materials and their structures (Velde, 1999: 101–24; Li and Zhang, 2010: 466–75; Tang *et al.*, 2011: 69–77). Cracks have been measured periodically since 2008, and the result shows that the cracks have not grown. The mosses were also periodically investigated. They are observed to have formed in the dim and humid corners of the site and the retained archaeological earth baulks have promoted the growth of mosses. In addition, there is a daily water sprinkling on the site (inherited from excavators' working routine) which dramatically increases the soil moisture and humidity. Observations also suggest that summer and early autumn are the optimum time for moss growth on the site.

As mentioned before, there are a large number of artefacts exposed on the surface of the site (Figure 3) which are seriously impacted by the environment: these include both organic (such as antlers, ivories, bones, and tusks) and inorganic objects (such as jades and silicified wood). The organic objects are deteriorating rapidly, although different types show different symptoms: tusks and antlers demonstrate powdering of outer surface, the reason for which is unknown as yet. With ivories, surface fracturing is critical, due to the variance of expansion volume between different layers within the objects.

Environment monitoring of the site

There was no quantitative environmental monitoring until 2007, when environmental sensors were installed by PKU. The environment data collected included air temperature and relative humidity (Figure 4). From this data we can conclude that the inner environment reflects changes in the outdoor climate. It seems that the air-conditioning in the site hall has little impact on the stabilization of site environment. Even today, the site environment fluctuates dramatically. This unstable environment influences both the growth of mosses and the activity of invertebrates: when temperature and humidity is high in summer and early autumn, the microbiological activities increase.

Laboratory soil test

PKU have also undertaken laboratory tests of soil samples from Jinsha, exploring soil composition and plasticity, which helps to explain the appearance of cracks on the site.

The XRD analysis of Jinsha soil sample (Table 1) shows that quartz, feldspar and illite account for the majority of soil mineral. The high content of illite suggests the

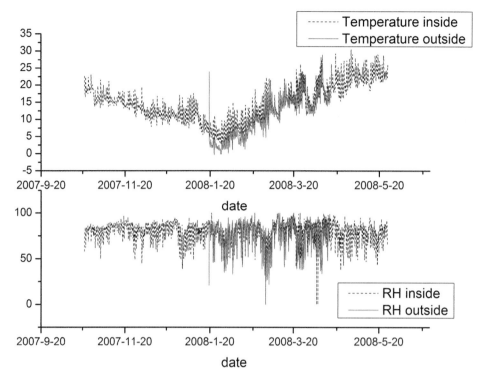

FIGURE 4   In situ environmental monitoring, inside and outside the hall, for a period of 8 months from the end of 2007 to mid–2008.

cause of cracks: as a mineral with low expansion and plasticity (Warren, 1999: 47), during phases of shrinkage due to the loss of soil water, illite can bring about fissures easily. Experimentation with the soil indicated that the liquid limit of Jinsha soil is 37.18 and the plastic limit is 21.65. However, the low plastic index, which is 15, indicates poor plasticity due to the high illite content. Scanning Electronic Microscope (SEM) images (Figure 5) show the micro-structure of Jinsha soil, which has low porosity and high density. As a result, the strength of soil is high; this may be the reason why, once cracks emerge, they are stable.

The causes of deterioration at Jinsha

In conclusion, the main cause for deterioration is the lack of adequate preventive conservation. The temperature and humidity in the site hall fluctuates according to the outside climate, promoting the growth of mosses and invertebrates, as well as the deterioration of artefacts. The other factor promoting deterioration is the nature of

TABLE 1

SOIL MINERAL IDENTIFICATION AND SEMI-QUANTITATIVE MEASUREMENT OF JINSHA SAMPLES

Soil Mineral	Quartz	Albite	Microcline	Clay Mineral				Amphibole
				Chlorite	Illite	Kaonilite	Smectite	
	36%	27%	5%	7%	20%	2%	3%	<1%

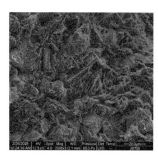

FIGURE 5   SEM images of Jinsha soil sample, amplified 500 times (left), 1000 times (middle) and 2000 times (right).

the soil itself: although cracks occur due to the changes in the burial environment, the nature of the soil undoubtedly intensify the severity.

Conservation of Jinsha

Jinsha Museum and Chengdu Museum have collaborated to undertake measures on site preservation since 2007.

The first action was the removal of mosses from the surface of the site. There was no precedent in China as to how to treat this microbiological event, so the first step was to test different biocides to select the most effective. The criteria for selection included: to be harmless to environment, visitors and artefacts; to be broad-spectrum and highly efficient; to be water-soluble. The biocide also needed to be cost-effective. Since 2007 we experimented with *methylparaben, butylparaben, mortox, DMDM hydantoin, germall*, and *triclosan* for moss control and removal. Sample squares were marked with tape (Figure 6) and each square was sprinkled with a different chemical, in the same concentration and volume. Periodic observation demonstrated that the most effective biocide was *germall*. In the summer of 2009, *germall* was used on a large scale to remove the mosses at Jinsha, in a 5 per cent concentration: 40 ml of *gemall* in an aqueous solution was enough for an area of 1 sq. m. One week after the use of the biocide, the mosses turn yellow and die. However, the disadvantage of using biocides is that the moss revives one month after sprinkling, which requires the repeated periodical use of the biocide and, as yet, we do not know whether *germall* has any potential chemical reaction with the organic artefacts.

There was no treatment of the cracks until 2011 when Jinsha Museum and Chengdu Museum had decided to put Jinsha forward for the World Heritage list. Although the cracks are stable, they spoiled the site aesthetically. The Jinzhou Conservation Centre documented the appearance of the cracks before filling the cracks with fine sand. It is planned that the incongruent colour, between the original surface and the sand, will be resolved by colouration (Figure 7). The project is currently underway and will be finished in 2012.

Discussion

As discussed above, the conservation work at Jinsha archaeological site is not perfect. As one of the most important archaeological sites in China, Jinsha has received

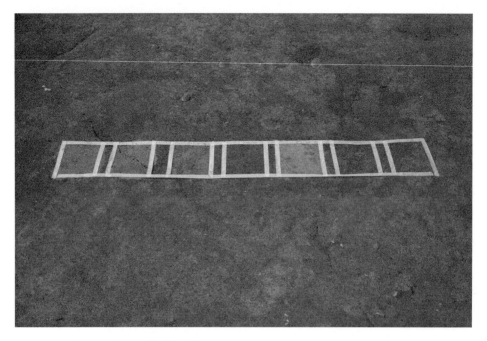

FIGURE 6   The experiment for biocide selection.

FIGURE 7   The site surface after infilling of cracks with sand.

considerable attention from the government and the public, so it is important to discuss which elements are responsible for this.

1) It is evident that the lack of preventive conservation measures has necessitated costly conservation work. The design of site hall did not sufficiently address the potential damage of micro-environment. The failure of environmental control is due to the lack of adequate communication with conservators and conservation scientists.

2) Site managers tend to think visitor satisfaction is the primary work for the site museum. In their mind, since the cracks and mosses have not led to complaints, there is no need to change the current situation.

3) With regard to the objects on site, site managers fear that removing them will diminish the fascination of the site. As a result, current deterioration is deemed to be tolerable.

4) There is a lack of public interest in conservation. What really attract visitors' attention are the activities on site, even the common daily water sprinkling: visitors associate it to the exciting and often supernatural adventure depicted on the mass media (Ascherson, 2004: 145–58). Vivid pictures and stories are what visitors care about. For example, visitors are glad to be told that the stone slave figures were being devoured by the stone tiger.

Scientific research on archaeological site conservation is insufficient. Although the preservation and display of sites is increasingly common, scientific research on the material of archaeological sites is still very rare.

Conclusion

The value of archaeological sites is understood and accepted both by academic scholars and the public in China. However, conservation research on site materials is under-developed. Jinsha, one of most significant Bronze Age archaeological sites in the whole of China, whose story can largely describe current trends in cultural heritage conservation in China, is an excellent case-study.

The site suffers deterioration, mainly due to the unsatisfactory micro-environment and the managers' lack of motivation to change the current situation. The lack of environmental control has to be compensated for by the costly and iterative conservation measures. So far, the site is stable, but there need further research on the long-term implications.

Bibliography

Ascherson, N. 2004. Archaeology and the British Media. In: Merriman, N. ed. *Public Archaeology*. London and New York: Routledge, pp. 145–58.

Aslan, Z. 2008. The Design of Protective Structures for the Conservation and Presentation of Archaeological Sites. Unpublished PhD thesis, University of London.

China ICOMOS 2004. *Principles for the Conservation of Heritage Sites in China*. Los Angeles: The Getty Conservation Institute.

International Centre for the Study of the Preservation and the Restoration of Cultural Property & Rijksuniversiteit te Gent, Faculty of Greek Archaeology. 1986. *Preventive Measures during Excavation and Site Protection: Conference Ghent, 6–8 November 1985 = Mesures préventives en cours de fouilles et protection du site: Gand, 6–8 novembre 1985*. Rome: ICCROM.

Li, J. H. and Zhang, L. M. 2010. Geometric Parameters and REV of a Crack Network in Soil. *Computers and Geotechnics*, 37: 466–75.

Merriman, N. 2004. Introduction: Diversity and Dissonance in Public Archaeology. In: Merriman, N. ed. *Public Archaeology*. London and New York: Routledge, pp. 1–18.

NPCSC. 2002. The Law of the People's Republic of China on Protection of Cultural Relics [online]. Beijing: China Cultural Heritage Information and Consulting Centre [accessed 28 October 2002]. Available at: <http://www.cchmi.com/tabid/129/InfoID/457/Default.aspx>.

SACH. 2005. Proclamation for Initiate the Symbol of China Cultural Heritage [online]. Beijing [accessed 16 August 2005]. Available at: <http://www.sach.gov.cn/tabid/312/InfoID/6845/Default.aspx>.

SACH. 2009. Research and Development in the Key Technique of Site Conservation — The Research. Unpublished research report for SACH, Dunhuang Academy.

SACH. 2010. National Archaeological Sites Administration Measures (Trial) [online]. Beijing [accessed 6 January 2010]. Available at: <http://www.sach.gov.cn/tabid/314/InfoID/22762/Default.aspx>.

Shan, J.-x. 2010. For the Bright Future of Archaeological Sites Conservation. *China Cultural Heritage*, 50–51.

Tang, C.-S., Shi, B., Liu, C., Suo, W.-B., and Gao, L. 2011. Experimental Characterization of Shrinkage and Desiccation Cracking in Thin Clay Layer. *Applied Clay Science*, 52: 69–77.

Velde, B. 1999. Structure of Surface Cracks in Soil and Muds. *Geoderma*, 93: 101–24.

Wang, J. and Yan, Z.-f. 2010. Test Analysis of the Winter Thermal Environment in the Earthen Heritage Site Museum. In: China Association of Architectural Physics, School of Architecture Southeast University, National Key Laboratory for Conservation of Urban Heritage & International Centre for Urban Engineering Southeast University, *Building Environment-Science & Technology Nanjing, China, 2010 (2010, BEST-CN)*. Nanjing: Southeast University Press, pp. 391–95.

Warren, J. 1999. *Conservation of Earth Structures*. Oxford and Boston: Butterworth-Heinemann.

Zhang, B.-j., Zhou, H., and Wang, X. d. 2010. Quantitative Discrimination of Humid Environment: A Case Study of Hangzhou Liangzhu Sites. *Dunhuang Research*, 2010(6): 104–08.

Zhou, H., Zhang, B.-j., Chen, G.-q., Zhang, H.-y., Zeng, Y.-y., Guo, q.-l., Li, Z.-x., and Wang, X.-d. 2008. Study on Consolidation and Conservation of Historical Earthen Sites in Moisture Circumstances Conservation of Tangshan Site In Situ. *Rock and Soil Mechanics*, 29: 954–62.

Zhou, S.-L. 2003. Introduction on Anti-Deterioration of Archaeological Sites. *Cultural Relics of Central China*, pp. 78–83.

Zhou, S.-l. and Pan, X.-l. 2004. Research on the Consolidation Ability of Non-Aqueous Dispersion to Sandy Soil Archaeological Sites. *Science of Conservation and Archaeology*, 16: 52–55.

.Zhou, S.-l., Wang, X.-y., Hu, Y., and Huang, K.-z. 2005. Selection of strengthening medium for archaelogical site of Hongshan Culture at Niuheliang, Liaoning Province. *Chinese Journal of Geotechnical Engineering*, 27: 567–70.

Zhou, S.-l. and Yuan, S.-x. 2004. Silicone Modified Non-Aqueous Dispersion of acrylic Latex: Its Preparation and Test on its Ability of Anti-Weathering on Earthen Archaeological Sites. *Science of Conservation and Archaeology*, 16: 50–52.

Notes on contributors

Lu Bai obtained his Master degree for conservation of cultural heritage at Peking University, Beijing, China in 2008 and is a curator of Chengdu Museum since then. Since 2010, he is a PhD candidate of UCL in the conservation and management of archaeological sites. His academic interests are cultural resources management, and the scientific conservation of earth, brick, and stone monuments and sites.

Correspondence to: Lu Bai, Chengdu Museum, 18 Shierqiao Road, Chengdu, China. Email: lu.bai.09@ucl.ac.uk

Shuang-Lin Zhou. Correspondence to: Shuang-Lin Zhou, Department of Archaeology and Museology, Peking University, 5 Yiheyuan Road, Beijing, China. Email: zhousl@pku.edu.cn

CONSERVATION AND MGMT OF ARCH. SITES, Vol. 14 Nos 1–4, 2012, 273–83

Integrated Design of Conservation of the Archaeological Heritage

Daniela De Mattia

Polytechnic University of Bari, Italy

This article aims to establish a connection between (a) the identification of heritage and measures for its protection, and (b) the collection and dissemination of scientific information, as set out in the Treaty of Valletta. This is illustrated through research conducted at the Asklepieion of Kos, which led to an *anastylosis* project on the Roman temple, within a wider project to re-organize the entire area of the sanctuary. The paper highlights the development of the project, including traditional methods of direct survey (manual and digital), a database of the three-dimension models of the single architectural elements of the temple, and a CAD/CAM model of the reconstruction project.

KEYWORDS architectural research, protection, *anastylosis*, 3D database, CAD/CAM modelling

Introduction: The Valletta Treaty[1] and the Aims of the Project

During a period of the research on Bauforschung,[2] I analysed case studies at Pergamum and the Asklepieion of Kos (De Mattia, 2009), in order to explore the conservation of the archaeological heritage *in situ*, in particular in relation to monumental complexes. This article draws upon that work and offers an example of integrated conservation, as applied to a monumental complex, the Asklepieion of Kos. It highlights the importance of integrating architectural design and restoration in archaeological areas. Reviewing some points from the Valletta Treaty, the paper explores the themes of authenticity, the legibility of settlement systems and architectural composition, and the conservation of architecture.

I draw attention to two articles of the Treaty:

To preserve the archaeological heritage and guarantee the scientific significance of archaeological research work, each Party undertakes:

to ensure that archaeological excavations and prospecting are undertaken in a scientific manner and provided that:

non-destructive methods of investigation are applied wherever possible;

    DOI 10.1179/1350503312Z.00000000023

the elements of the archaeological heritage are not uncovered or left exposed during or after excavation without provision being made for their proper preservation, conservation and management.

(Article 3)

Each Party undertakes to implement measures for the physical protection of the archaeological heritage, making provision, as circumstances demand:

for the acquisition or protection by other appropriate means by the authorities of areas intended to constitute archaeological reserves;

for the conservation and maintenance of the archaeological heritage, preferably *in situ*;

for appropriate storage places for archaeological remains which have been removed from their original location.

(Article 4)

The main aim of the Asklepieion of Kos project was to propose conservation and *anastylosis in situ*, where the original architectural elements permit this kind of intervention, along with the creation of digital databases and CAD/CAM models, to enable the documentation and exhibition of the most fragile fragments and to assist in the understanding of architectural organisms in their entirety. In particular, for the reconstruction project of the Roman temple, the application of CAD/CAM technologies allowed the creation of scale models of the reconstruction, in accordance with studies performed with high-precision digital instruments. These scale models were used to assist the conservation projects and to enrich the museum exhibitions, allowing a comprehensive understanding of the architectural organism and its relationship with its context.

The Valletta Treaty stated that the 'integrated conservation of the archaeological heritage' should 'ensure well-balanced strategies for the protection, conservation and enhancement of sites of archaeological interest'. Thus the Asklepieion of Kos project aimed to coordinate strategies and techniques of conservation, integrating the methods of analysis and intervention: from archaeological survey to the study of the architectural composition and settlement systems; from cataloguing to the digital database; from drawing to 3D modelling; from reconstruction to the creation of material models for the museum.

Article 5 of the Treaty also stated that 'the opening of archaeological sites to the public, especially any structural arrangements necessary for the reception of large numbers of visitors, does not adversely affect the archaeological and scientific character of such sites and their surroundings'. This project highlights these issues, especially in relation to the opening of archaeological sites, consisting of monumental complexes, to the public. Three key issues were identified: access, the 'enclosure', and paths. These played a role in the design, allowing visitors to observe the architecture according to the viewing points established by Hellenistic and Romans designers. We created two itineraries, one for general visitors to the site and one for the educational tours. These aimed to make the site accessible and 'readable', and to enable the visitor to understand the original concept of the Hellenistic and Roman architectural composition that shaped the monumental complex.

Brief history of the restorations at the Asklepieion of Kos

There are a number of links in the conservation and restoration works between Kos and Pergamon. The architect-archaeologist (*Bauforscher*[3]) Paul Schazmann graphically reconstructed the Asklepieion of Kos with Herzog (Herzog and Schazmann, 1932). In 1908 Schazmann had excavated and surveyed the Gymnasia of Pergamum, in collaboration with Wilhelm Dörpfeld (Schazmann, 1923), and created a reconstruction model of the site, and the research methods developed in Pergamum were used at both sites until the first half of the twentieth century. In addition, the architect Mario Paolini worked in Kos (1902–54) and then with W. Radt and K. Nohlen on the Traianeum of Pergamum. During this period, attention at both sites turned to the reconstruction of the Roman temples erected within the Hellenistic layouts, highlighting the privileged position originally chosen by the Romans (Figure 1). The two cities also shared the need to consolidate the retaining walls of the artificial terraces and to conceal the partition walls of pre-Roman structures.

The differences between the approaches to classical architecture in the early twentieth century and today lies in distinction between an architectural-planning approach and an architectural-archaeological one. The latter was supported by scientific rigour, born within the German Bauforschers School, with a *thorough* attention to the compositional and constructional aspects, and the synchronic use of archaeological as well as of architectural methods for the study of details.

When comparing the drawings made by Schazmann, for the Pergamum Gymnasia and the Asklepieion in Kos, with those of Paolini and Finamore for the restoration

FIGURE 1   The second terrace of Asklepieion of Kos. Roman temple on the right. August 2008, looking north-east.
Photo by D. De Mattia

works in Kos, we can see the differences: there was a different purpose to the research, reflected in a different understanding of the nature of preliminary plans. Graphical reconstruction for Schazmann was aimed at spatially reconstructing all the details and the technical-construction solutions of ancient architectures; while Paolini turned his attention mainly to the reconstruction project, to its practical realization, to the use of the original material, to the acquisition of *quantitative* data, and to the planning stage. However, since the 1930s, the planning stage has often not been considered as the step following historical-scientific study of the building, but as a moment exclusively connected to the realization (and not dissemination) stages of an *anastylosis* project. Thus we can infer that the path leading from excavation to conservation can be covered in two diametrically opposed ways: the first focused on the classical *monumentum*, and the second only on the material verification of the works on the ancient building.

We have to deal with the second approach, that is to say with the purely *quantitative* needs of the plan. For sure, scientific rigour applied to the study, and to the different stages of the plan, allow us to achieve a balance: but such balance can never be attained without a thorough knowledge of the building and of the archaeological methods and procedures. At both Pergamum and Kos, the more or less concealed desire to restore the charm and monumentality of the ruins, and enhance them with prestigious new building techniques, is at issue (mostly from a planning point of view) today.

Planning suggestions for the Asklepieion of Kos: project of re-organization of the area

We have seen that the nineteenth-century *Bauforscher* primarily focused on the understanding of the classical architectural plan, both from a compositional and construction point of view. They aimed to use this in planning of the 'new' European capitals, while the early twentieth-century Italian archaeologist-architects wanted archaeological areas to become fully accessible and integrated with bordering spaces and architectures. This principle is particularly evident in the Asklepieion of Kos. Luigi Morricone and Paolini initiated extensive restoration works and planned further reconstructions with the purpose of making the area accessible; a purpose they fully achieved.

But *accessibility* is more complex, as even if the restoration of routes and the consolidation of the crumbling parts have allowed thousands of visitors to crowd the Sanctuary, that does not mean that they can have the correct *view* of the architectural plan of the Sanctuary. Both the Germans and the Italians turned their attention to the ancient architectural plan in its entirety, and that led to strategies different from those arising from the sole intention of understanding the single monument. The most difficult thing is the dissemination of the information acquired on the archaeological area, both to visitors and future researchers. De Angelis D'Ossat[4] used different 'levels' through which architecture finds its 'expressions' in order to identify the areas within which authenticity has to be preserved: he upheld the need to 'preserve authenticity at the territorial, urban and architectural unity level and therefore of form and matter' (D'Ossat, 1979: quoted in Docci, 2008). D'Ossat's levels include that of the formal and material architectural unity. In monumental complexes, such as the

Asklepieion, it is important to preserve also the unity of the overall architectural plan, and that means preserving the legibility of its compositional, morphological, and construction aspects.

When planning works in a complex archaeological area, the relationship of the site with the territory, and therefore the route to reach it, must be taken into account. In the case of the Asklepieion, the best path starts from the city of Kos. The project aimed at restoring a second access to the site, reserved for bike and motorbike riders, while today's entrance area, endowed with a vast (maybe too vast) car park, would be reserved for visitors reaching the site by car or coach.

The site also needed visitor facilities, and at present these are spread along the access path to the *propylaea* of the *stoa* of the third terrace. The project sought to equip the site with a ticketing area, bookshop, bars, and services. We proposed modifying these structures by redesigning the area that runs along the access path, along the orientation of the third terrace, to allow the visitor to have an overall view of the Sanctuary at the beginning of the tour.

Another important issue is the borders of the archaeological area. Such borders should be well defined and guarded, whereas in the case of the Asklepieion the eastern and the western sides of the terrace face the surrounding woods, without clear edges. We propose solving both the boundary and paths by laying out three different paths to climb to the terraces along the east-facing slope of the Sanctuary. These would allow visitors to reach the museum, the refreshment area, the bookshop, and the box office, as well as to climb to the terraces on an acceptable gradient. The archaeological area would then have clear borders and at the same time easy visiting routes, increasing the accessibility to higher terraces and allowing people to reach the museum, which is not used today and all but hidden to visitors.

Having a museum on site is the key to the perfect conservation of the finds at an archaeological site. The museum was envisaged within the ruins of the Roman Baths of the third terrace, and marked on the plans of the Sanctuary by Herzog's first mission. Later, the Italians dismantled this structure in order to continue the study of the baths and erected a new *Antiquarium* further east. It also proposed the restoration of the *Antiquarium* for use as a museum and laboratories for conservation and restoration. The museum should house models of the Sanctuary in the different epochs, and drawings and models of the single monuments.

Other issues include:

- Within each terrace two illustrative panels should be installed: one depicting the terrace in its entirety, in relation with the rest of the Sanctuary, and a more detailed one dedicated to the architecture of the area.
- All-night lighting should be set up in order to control and guard the area. Such a system would not be installed near the ruins, but along the terraces and the retaining walls restored by the Italians, and it would not outline routes, not to misrepresent the original directions to access the Sanctuary, but it would diffusely illuminate the terraces and the remaining monuments according to the orientation of the terraces.
- In order to enhance the understanding of the monumental complex, it is necessary to make the plans of the structures identifiable, which may involve the repositioning the original blocks. The Italians, for instance, lifted parts of

columns of the front of the Ionic temple of the second terrace. Architect Paolini had planned further *anastylosis* operations on two portions of the *stoa* of the third terrace and three *intercolumni* of the *stoa* of the first terrace. We propose verifying the feasibility of such operations and, if possible, carrying them out. First, an accurate work of identification and cataloguing of the blocks should be undertaken.

• In the three-dimensional models of the project we included such reconstructions, because they would allow the visitor to understand the scale of the *stoai* and to compare the order and the serial elements with the monumental architecture (Figures 2 and 3).

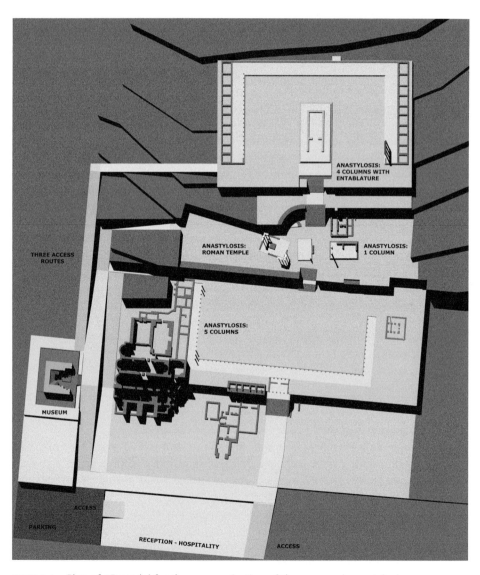

FIGURE 2   Plan of 3D model for the re-organization of the area and *anastylosis*.

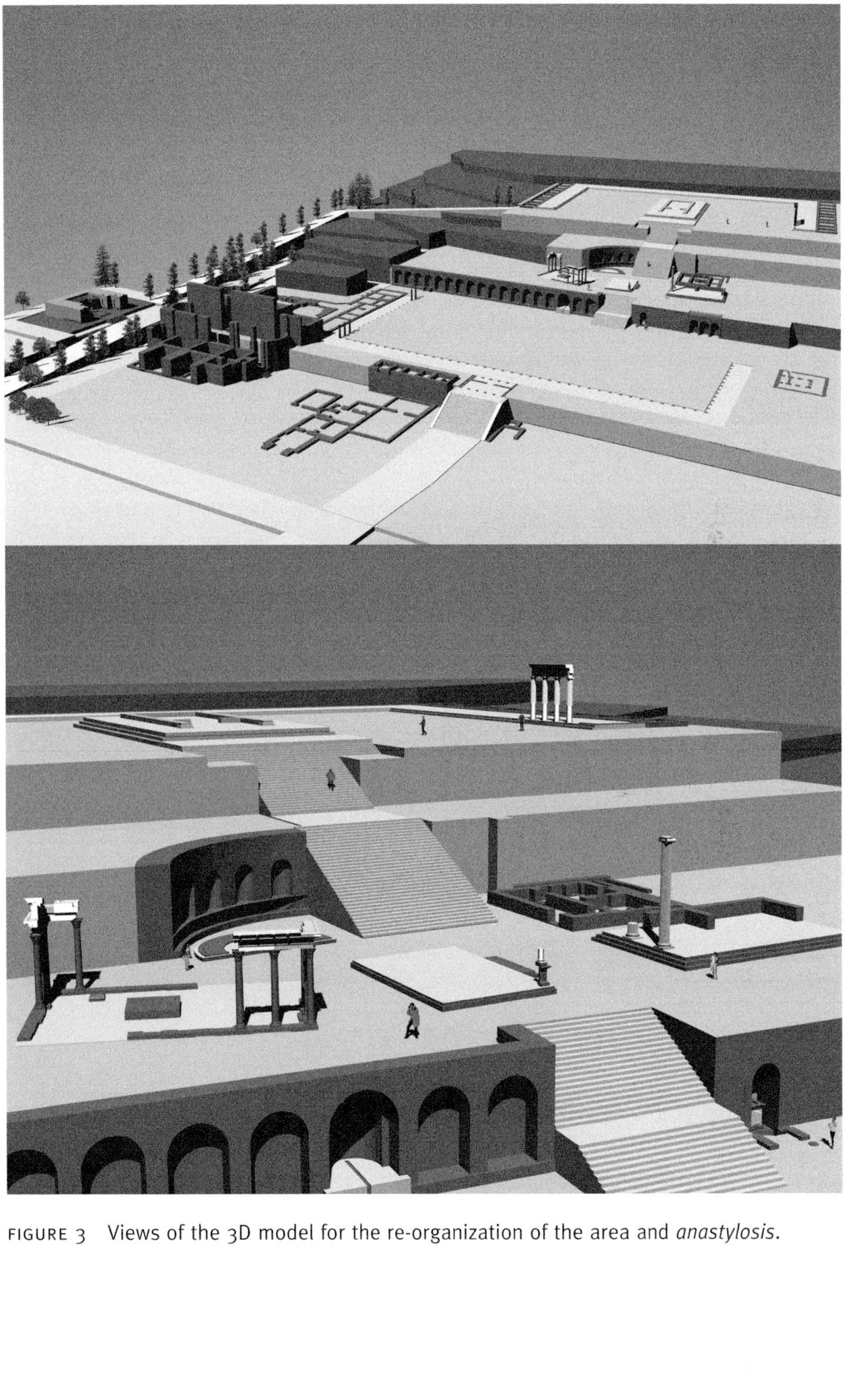

FIGURE 3   Views of the 3D model for the re-organization of the area and *anastylosis*.

Anastylosis project of the Roman temple of the Asklepieion of Kos

The *anastylosis* project of the Roman temple has been elaborated by analysing the surveys carried out in the early 1900s by the German researchers Herzog and Schazmann, and a 1930s project undertaken, but never finalized, by the Paolini.[5] The database and the CAD/CAM model (Figure 4) represent two ways to rigorously store scientific data. The database enables the filing of two- and three-dimensional data, thereby creating a complete catalogue for future researches and supporting the architectural work. The CAD/CAM model provides scale documentation in the reconstruction project, and at the same time creates the possibilities for museum displays of the material model and the archaeological heritage. CAD/CAM models, resulting from accurate studies of the architectural and archaeological aspects of the monuments, represent today's evolution of the traditional models of the twentieth century, preserved in the Glyptotheks of Copenhagen or Munich.

Conclusion

The research demonstrates the importance of the integration of different study tools and the museum display of architecture in an archaeological area. It also shows the possibility to use such tools in a synchronic way, to conserve *in situ* archaeological heritage and to compensate for the absence of the originals in the museum or research laboratory.

FIGURE 4   Views of the CAD/CAM model of the *anastylosis* project of the Roman temple, constructed by single architectural elements. (By D. De Mattia at the laboratory 'CAM and Rapid Prototyping' of the Faculty of Architecture of Bari, Italy.)

The new project at the Sanctuary of Kos proposes some approaches, to:

- Respect, preserve, and enhance the architectural composition of the monumental complex;
- Allow public access through the paths of the original project, with additional pathways for the elderly, children, and people with disabilities;
- Restore the legibility of the relationship between the settlement and architectural elements;
- Complete the *anastylosis* of structures, where a high percentage of the original elements allows their reconstruction;
- Integrate *in situ* conservation with conservation in the museum; the latter providing space for conservators, exhibitions, and educational activities.

The project emphasizes the importance of the authenticity of architectural composition at an archaeological site: an overall project that guided the construction of each architecture. The quality of architectural composition should be preserved and made legible, even through the study of itineraries that retrace the original route of the monumental complex.

The architects who originally designed the Asklepieion of Kos understood the proportion of open space in relation to the elevation and volume of architecture, and the perspectives to the landscape and to the monumental architecture. The rules and quality of architectural design must be part of the intangible heritage studied and protected, because only if we understand and respect composition can really understand the architectural monuments of antiquity. Often we plan itineraries completely disconnected from the original. Too often we isolate the architecture, detaching it from its context.

Permanence is another value that has the power to guide interventions in archaeological sites: the value of what has come down to us today, untouched or transformed, through the historical processes. In the case of the Roman Temple of Asklepieion of Kos, the first reconstruction (never completed) changed the status of the temple: now an intervention historicized. Currently, the conserved elements are in a state of abandonment, exposed to the weather. These factors have led to the development of a new reconstruction project, presented here, which seeks to retrieve what has been achieved, correct inaccuracies, and enable the conservation of the marble architectural elements. The value of permanence will inevitably influence this choice. The number of conserved elements, and the existence of a partial reconstruction, prevent other interventions. The proposed partial reconstruction of the Roman Temple would make the proportional system of the second terrace legible, and restore some dignity to the first reconstruction, which currently leads to erroneous interpretation.

Ancient monuments have undergone several transformations, often dependent upon the permanence of the architecture. Often this approach has led to interventions that alter the sites and give them a new meaning, focusing on single monuments in contrast to the wider context. The value of Palmyra (Syria), for example, is contained in the permanence of the colonnaded street and monuments at its hub; the value of Pergamon (Turkey) is contained in the permanence of the Traianeum and the theatre; the value of the Acropolis of Athens (Greece) is contained in the 'struggle' between the permanence of the Propylaea, Parthenon, and Erechtheion. Permanence is a value that you could not betray. There are no remains that allow us to reconstruct the city block behind the colonnaded street of Palmyra, or the elevations of the buildings of the Hellenistic period in Pergamum, or the architecture described by Pausanias in his visit to the Acropolis of Athens. Designers, trained in archaeology and architecture, should identify the value of ancient architectural design, its readable form, and the relationship between settlement system and architectural structure, in order not to neglect information, or to exceed the limit of reconstruction for a single architecture, losing significance and readability of context.

In conclusion, the integrated project of conservation presented here aims to make the visitor not just a spectator, but an active user of the architectural composition, able to understand the features of the place and the changes that it has undergone during the evolving historical process of which every architecture is a part.

Acknowledgements

I am grateful to the supervisor of my PhD thesis, Prof. Claudio D'Amato Guerrieri. I also thank Profs George Rocco and Monica Livadiotti from the Faculty of Architecture of Bari, directors and coordinators of the Italian archaeological research in Kos, who have made possible my research missions to Asklepieion of Kos. I am also grateful to the Directors dell'Eforia Prehistoric-Classical Rhodes and the Archaeological Institute of Aegean, Dr Melina Philimonos and Dr Aggeliki Iannikourì; the inspectors archaeologists of Kos, Dr Dimitri Bosnakis and Dr Elpida Skerlou; the director of the Archaeological School of Athens, Prof. Emanuele Greco; the director of the photographic library of the German Archaeological Institute in Athens (DAI), Dr Joachim Heiden.

I would also like to remember Prof. Antonino Di Vita (1926–2011), noted archaeologist, former Director of the Italian Archaeological School in Athens, and Member of the Accademia dei Lincei, for his teaching and suggestions regarding my research on the *Bauforschung*. He has been, and will always be, a master of the study of ancient architecture, the teaching of antiquity, and interventions at archaeological sites.

Notes

[1] Treaty of Valletta: Council of Europe 1992. *The European Convention on the Protection of the Archaeological Heritage (Revised)*, usually referred to as the Valletta Treaty or Malta Convention.

[2] *Bauforschung* (architectural research) is a German term referring to the scientific and analytical study of structures and their related graphic documentation and analysis. *Bauforschung* applied during the fieldwork allows for the reconstruction of the historical architecture, of its settlement system, and of its building process, through the integrated analysis, which is both philological (historical sources and typo-morphological comparisons) and scientific (stratigraphic excavation and survey), of the tectonic and formal aspects of architecture.

[3] The *Bauforscher* were the protagonists of 'Great Archaeology', which advanced the discovery of ancient cities, such as Olympia and Pergamon, through stratigraphic excavation. The *Bauforscher* had specific competences in the history of architecture, building sciences, composition rules, and *ex-novo* design, in order to study ancient architecture through systematic survey. Such an architect was educated in the history of ancient architecture, archaeology, history of construction, architectural survey techniques, the representation of ancient architecture, stratigraphic excavation techniques, and topography.

[4] Guglielmo De Angelis D'Ossat (1907–92): Italian engineer, architect, and architectural historian.

[5] Ink and pencil drawings on tracing paper, 1938, planoteca S.A.I.A. Athens, PD 681, PD 682, PD 688.

Bibliography

De Angelis D'Ossat, G. 1979. Preserver l'antiquité, but fondamental de la conservation, I (International Symposium of the Conservation of the Monuments of Architecture and Town-planning). Reproduced in: M. Docci, ed. 2008. *Il restauro architettonico nel pensiero di Guglielmo De Angelis D'Ossat*. Bollettino del Centro Studi per la Storia dell'Architettura, 41. Rome: Gangemi, pp. 81–83.

De Mattia, D. 2009. L'architetto e l'intervento sull'architettura antica. Dalla Bauforschung al progetto di ricostruzione in situ e in museo (The Architect and the Intervention on Ancient Architecture. From *Bauforschung* to the Reconstruction Project Carried Out *In Situ* or in a Museum). Unpublished PhD thesis in Architectural Design, Faculty of Architecture — Politecnico di Bari (Italy).

De Mattia, D. ed. 2010. The Figure of the Architect-Archaeologist. The Bauforschung, The Realization of the Model and the Anastylosis of Ancient Architecture. In: F. Javier Melero, P. Cano, and J. Revelles, eds. *Fusion of Cultures, Abstract of the XXXVIII Annual Conference on Computer Applications and Quantitative Methods in Archaeology, Granada (Spain) 6–9 April 2010*. Granada, pp. 403–06.

De Mattia, D. ed. 2011. Catalogue 'Three Dimensional' 3D-Data. In: *Proceedings of the Fifth Workshop Archeofoss. Open Source, Free Software and Open Format in the Process of Archaeological Research, Foggia (Italy) 6–7 May 2010*. Bari: Edipuglia, pp. 57–64.

Docci, M. ed. 2008. Il restauro architettonico nel pensiero di Guglielmo De Angelis D'Ossat, In: *Bollettino del Centro di Studi per la Storia dell'Architettura. Roma*, 41. Roma: Gangemi.

Herzog, R. and Schazmann, P. 1932. *Asklepieion. Baubeschreibung und Baugeschichte, in Kos. Ergebnisse der Deutschen Ausgrabungen und Forschungen*. Berlin: Heinrich Keller Verlag.

Livadiotti, M. and Rocco, G. eds. 1996. *La presenza italiana nel Dodecaneso tra il 1912 e il 1948*, Catalogo della Mostra. Catania: Edizioni del Prisma.

Radt, W. 1988. *Pergamon. Geschichte und Bauten, Funden und Erforschung einer antiken Metropole*. Köln: DuMont Buchverlag.

Schazmann, P. v. 1923. *Altertümer von Pergamon Band 6, Das Gymnasion der Tempelbezirk der Hera Basileia*. Berlin: De Gruyter.

Notes on contributor

Daniela De Mattia was born in 1981 in Gioia del Colle (Bari, Italy), graduated in Architecture in 2005, with a thesis on the ancient city of Palmyra (Syria). In 2009 she obtained a PhD in Architectural Design, and from 2011 is Post-Doctoral Researcher on the relationship between the discipline of architectural design and *Bauforschung* from the nineteenth to the twentieth century.

Correspondence to: Daniela De Mattia, 29 via Leonardo da Vinci, 70023, Gioia del Colle (Bari), Italy. Email: daniela.demattia@libero.it

CONSERVATION AND MGMT OF ARCH. SITES, Vol. 14 Nos 1–4, 2012, 284–93

A Predictive Map of Compression-Sensitivity of the Dutch Archaeological Soil Archive

G. de Lange
Deltares, The Netherlands

M. Bakr
Deltares, The Netherlands

J. L. Gunnink
TNO-Geological Survey of the Netherlands

D. J. Huisman
Cultural Heritage Agency, The Netherlands

Weak soils like unconsolidated clay and peat may deform and compress considerably by loading, for example, by sand bodies for roads and railways. Archaeological sites within such easily compressible soil layers may therefore be heavily affected by different kinds of construction works. The vulnerability of archaeological sites to compression is largely dependent on soil properties like lithology, grain-size, and previous loading history. This may therefore differ considerably. Predicting the compression sensitivity is of great value for planners, since they can estimate in which areas *in situ* protection of archaeological sites may be feasible and where it would require (costly) technical measures or plan adaptations.

As part of the Cultural Heritage Agency's research programme on construction and archaeology, we prepared predictive maps of the compression sensitivity of the subsurface sediments in the Netherlands for 1 m depth intervals from 0 to 20 m depth.

The maps were constructed using a full 3-D model of the subsurface of the Netherlands.

In combination with the Indicative Map of Archaeological Values (IKAW) that is already available, these maps can be used to better estimate the technical measures needed and costs involved for *in situ* protection of archaeological sites in the planning phase of construction projects.

KEYWORDS vulnerability, civil engineering works, compression, The Netherlands

© Taylor & Francis 2012   DOI 10.1179/1350503312Z.00000000024

Introduction

Civil engineering and construction activities can have a detrimental effect on buried archaeological remains. Apart from the obvious effects of building excavations, the effects of (bio-)chemical changes due to the building over or coverage by fill of a site are described in the literature (Huisman, 2009), as well as the potential damage of foundation construction (Huisman et al., 2011). Weak soils like unconsolidated clay and peat may deform and compress considerably under surcharge loading, for example, by sand bodies for roads, railways, and building developments. This may damage archaeological sites within such easily compressible soil layers. The vulnerability of archaeological sites to loading is thus largely dependent on soil properties like lithology, grain-size, and previous loading history.

Predicting the sensitivity of archaeological sites to loading enables planners to estimate in which areas *in situ* protection of archaeological sites may be feasible, or where it would require (costly) technical measures or plan adaptations.

As part of the Cultural Heritage Agency's programme on construction and archaeology, the need arose to interpret the subsurface information available at the Geological Survey of the Netherlands into predictive maps of the compression sensitivity of the subsurface in the Netherlands. The object was to have a representation of the degree of compression at different levels below the surface.

Compaction due to surcharge loading

When a surcharge is placed on the ground surface, the underlying soils will be compressed. Common examples of surcharges are sand fills on terrains where new residential or industrial areas are constructed, road embankments, dikes, and buildings on shallow foundations or even heavy vehicles. Sometimes these surcharges are temporary. Excess surcharges of sand fill are often left in place for a couple of years to speed up the compaction process of soft layers before construction begins.

How the ground reacts is determined by the physical properties of the respective soils, in particular the deformability of the soils skeleton and the permeability. When the stress imposed by the surcharge compresses the soil skeleton, the pore water pressure increases, causing an excess pore pressure over the hydrostatic pore pressure. The soil will compact at a rate governed by the permeability, which allows the excess pore pressure to dissipate until the soil stresses are again in equilibrium.

Effects on the archaeological archive

The compaction of soil layers affects a number of properties of archaeological sites. Layers are deformed, which could lead to the loss of coherence of delicate remains. Organic and botanical remains could be affected, not only by compression, but also by the dissipation of the pore water. On a detailed scale, the stratigraphy could be compromised. Due to the heterogeneity of the soil and its stratigraphy, the compression under even a relatively evenly distributed sand fill results in differential settlements on a scale that can affect the context of archaeological objects in various ways. Figures 1 and 2 illustrate two common cases (Huisman, 2011). Figure 1 shows that, after compression of a highly compressible layer, foundations and artefacts partly lie in layers where they originally did not occur and may have changed orientation. The

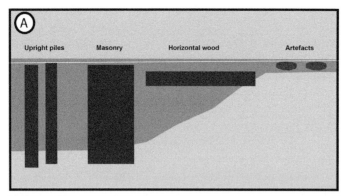

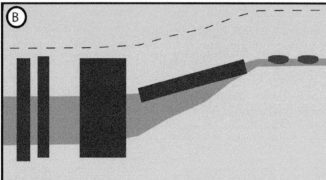

FIGURE 1 Schematic representation of disturbance of artefact-soil relationship by compression of a soil layer. The vertical scale is exaggerated. A: Situation before applying surcharge. B: after 50% compression of the compressible layer.

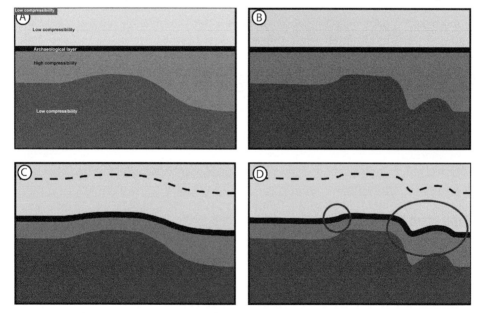

FIGURE 2 Schematic representation of the influence of variability in differential compaction on the deformation of overlying layers. Vertical scale is exaggerated. A: initial situation with low base relief; B: initial situation with high base relief. Height differences are similar, but the undulations are sharper. C and D: as A and B, after 50% compaction of the highly compressible layer.

horizontal wood object has tilted. Figure 2 illustrates the effects of lateral variability of the layers. In this example, the differential settlement of the archaeological layer is solely caused by the variation in layer thickness of the underlying compressible layer.

In practice, variations in layer properties, such as sand or clay content, often play a role as well. The deformation of the archaeological layer varies according to the subsurface relief. Due to the sharper initial undulations in the basal surface in case B the deformation in the highlighted zones in D is more pronounced.

The detail shown in Figures 1 and 2 requires the gathering and analysis of information on a local scale. We have endeavoured to present a map on a national scale that can serve as a first approximation of the sensitivity to surcharge loading of the subsurface.

Method

The method used is illustrated schematically in Figure 3. The calculation utilizes a full 3-D representation of the subsurface in the form of a stack of 3D 'voxels' (= volume pixels). The voxels typically have dimensions of 100 *100 * 0.5 m (l*w*h).

Steps 1 and 2

The model is a geostatistical interpretation of all shallow boreholes in the national database DINO ('Data en Informatie Nederlandse Ondergrond'). Each voxel is characterized by a simplified lithology: either sand, clay, or peat, representing respectively low, medium, and high compressibility. The most likely lithology in each voxel is derived by interpolation between the boreholes by the kriging method, thereby taking into account the spatial distribution of each lithology according to the technique developed by Soares (1992). A depth of 20 m below the surface was chosen as the base of the model, making sure that it contains the complete Holocene profile.

Step 3

In order to come up with a national map showing the sensitivity of the ground to compaction due to a surcharge load we introduced a number of generalizations. We assume that the entire surface of the Netherlands is covered by a 1 m thick blanket of sand fill with a unit weight of 16 kN/m² (kPa). This type of surcharge, left to settle for one or two years, is a relatively common type of ground improvement in preparation of new housing developments in areas with compressible soil in the Netherlands. This uniform load allows us to calculate the compaction with a one-dimensional, vertical consolidation model. This ignores the edge effects that occur along the boundary of the fill. There the stresses, and consequently the strains, are not vertical. Nevertheless, sensitivity to vertical compaction can be considered as representative of sensitivity to any non-vertical deformation also. Because we want to calculate only the vertical effects of a surface surcharge, the topographic relief of the top of the model is levelled.

Step 4

In every column of a 3D voxel model of the subsurface a one-dimensional consolidation calculation is performed according to the consolidation model proposed by

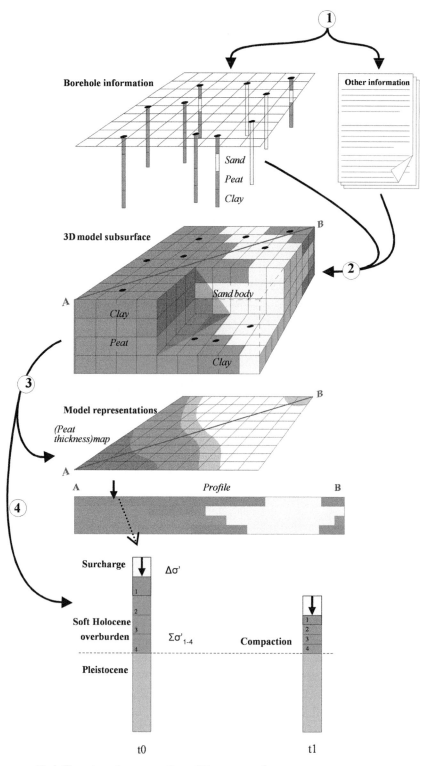

FIGURE 3   Modelling steps in preparation of the compaction map.

Koppejan (1948). This is a modified Terzaghi formula that until recently has been in use in the Netherlands as the standard method to predict settlement:

$$\frac{\Delta h_t}{h} = \left(\frac{U_{(\Delta t)}}{C_p} + \frac{1}{C_s} \log \frac{\Delta t}{\Delta t_d} \right) \ln \left(\frac{\sigma_i' + \Delta \sigma'}{\sigma_i'} \right)$$

in which:

h = layer thickness (m)

Δh_t = compaction (m)

U = degree of consolidation (at time Δt, values between 0 at start of loading and 1 at end of dissipation of excess pore pressure; in this study $U=1$)

$C_{p,s}$ = compression coefficients, p = primary or hydrodynamic, s = secondary or creep)

σ_i = initial effective stress (kPa)

$\Delta \sigma'$ = effective stress increase

Δt = loading time (days)

Δt_d = model reference time of compression coefficients (= 1 day).

We have assigned general compaction coefficients to these lithologies, derived from the Dutch building standard NEN 6740 (Table 1). A distinction is made between Holocene (soft, compressible) and Pleistocene (overconsolidated, stiff) soils. The compaction model distinguishes two domains of compressibility, a stiff, elastic behaviour (high compression coefficients), when surcharge loads are smaller than the load experienced by the soil in the past, the so-called pre-consolidation pressure, and a softer, plastic behaviour (low compression coefficients), when the loads exceed the pre-consolidation pressure. Because the relative increase in stress reduces downwards, the compaction behaviour in the upper, Holocene layers is predominantly in the plastic mode, the compaction behaviour in the Pleistocene layers is in the stiff, elastic mode.

The compaction of each voxel after thirty years of loading is calculated. Thirty years is taken as the theoretical end of consolidation. All excess pore water pressures caused by the surcharge in the relatively poorly permeable clay and peat layers will

TABLE 1

COMPRESSION PARAMETERS USED

	dry vol. weight [kPa]	wet vol. weight [kPa]	Cp elastic	Cs elastic	Cp plastic	Cs plastic	preconsolidation pressure [kPa]
Holocene							
Clay	15	15	60	400	15	100	50
Peat	11	11	20	80	5	20	12,55
Sand	15	19	1600	4000	400	1000	50
Pleistocene							
Clay	19	19	100	1200	25	320	300
Peat	13	13	40	160	10	40	300
Sand	16	21	4000	10000	1000	4000	300

then be dissipated. However, compaction continues at a very slow, logarithmically decaying rate in a process described as creep. For the purpose of illustrating the sensitivity of the ground to surcharge loading, we ignored this relatively small creep component. The compaction values were added up to 1 m intervals and compiled in maps showing the compaction in each consecutive interval of 1 m from the surface to 20 m depth.

The results

Three examples of the maps are reproduced here: in Figures 4, 5, and 6 the compression in the depth intervals 0–1 m, 3–4 m, and 7–8 m depth are illustrated. Because the assumptions used in the model and the calculations are based on generalizations

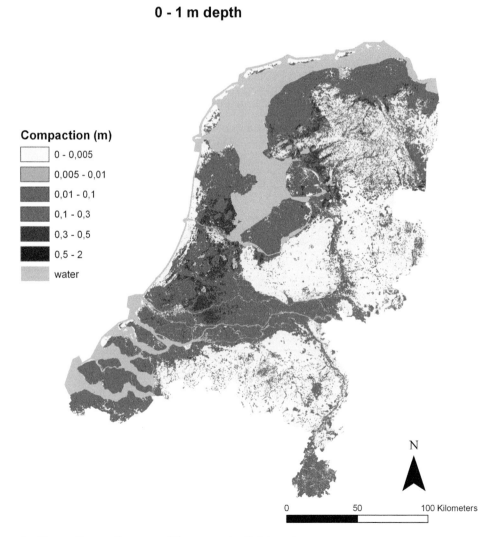

FIGURE 4   Compaction map of the 0–1 m depth interval.

3 - 4 m depth

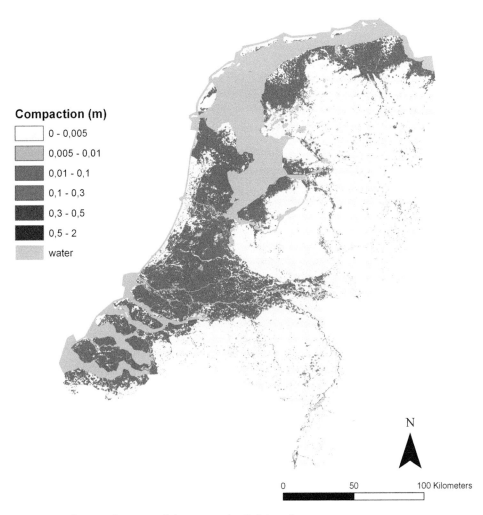

Compaction (m)

☐	0 - 0,005
▨	0,005 - 0,01
▨	0,01 - 0,1
▨	0,1 - 0,3
▨	0,3 - 0,5
▨	0,5 - 2
▨	water

N

0   50   100 Kilometers

FIGURE 5   Compaction map of the 3–4 m depth interval.

for the whole area, the sensitivity to loading given on the maps must be interpreted on a relative scale, as a proper prediction would need local data.

With this in mind the maps in the present form serve as a risk zonation map on which the need for further investigation can be based.

As can be seen from the patterns in the maps, the layers that are sensitive to compaction predominantly occur in the western part of the Netherlands and the river basins. This represents the gradual dip of the Pleistocene base towards the west and north-west. The most highly compressible layers on the maps are the peat layers of the Hollandveen Member of the Nieuwkoop Formation.

The maps are made available through the internet on the website of the Cultural Heritage Agency.[1] In combination with the Indicative Map of Archaeological Values (IKAW) they can be used to better estimate the technical measures needed and

7 - 8 m depth

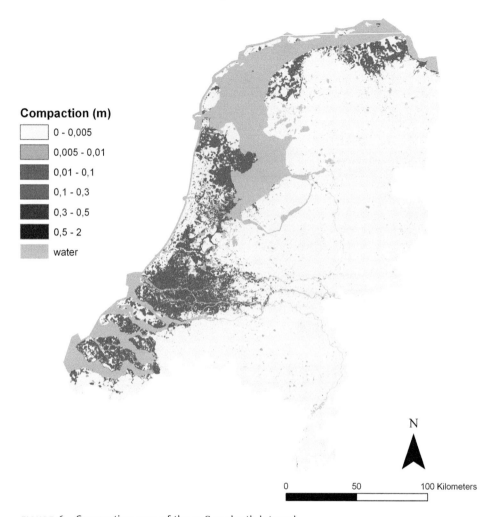

FIGURE 6   Compaction map of the 7–8 m depth interval.

costs involved for *in situ* protection of archaeological sites in the planning phase of construction projects. As such they also play a role in the granting of permits of these projects.

Acknowledgements

The research for and preparation of the maps was commissioned by the Cultural Heritage Agency, Ministry of Education, Culture and Science of the Netherlands.

Note

1   <http://www.cultureelerfgoed.nl/bouwen-en-archeologie>

Bibliography

Huisman, D. J. ed. 2009. *Degradation of Archaeological Remains*. Den Haag: SDU.

Huisman, D. J. ed. 2011. *De invloed van bouwwerkzaamheden op archeologische vindplaatsen*. Amersfoort: Rijksdienst voor het Cultureel Erfgoed [accessed 10 October 2012]. Available at: <http://www.cultureelerfgoed. nl/sites/default/files/u6/De invloed van bouwwerkzaamheden op archeologische vindplaatsen.pdf>.

Huisman, D. J., Muller, A., and van Doesburg, J. 2011. Investigating the Impact of Concrete Driven Piles on the Archaeological Record using Soil Micromorphology: Three Case Studies from the Netherlands. *Conservation and Management of Archaeological Sites*, 13(1): 8–30.

Koppejan, A. W. 1948. A Formula Combining the Terzaghi Load Compression Relationship and the Buisman Secular Time Effect. *Proc. 2nd Int. Conf. Soil Mech. And Found. Eng.*, Rotterdam, 3: 32–38.

NEN 6740. 2006. Geotechnics — TGB 1990 — Basic Requirements and Loads.

Soares, A. 1992. Geostatistical Estimation of Multiphase Structure. *Mathematical Geology*, 24(2): 149–60.

Notes on contributors

Ger de Lange is researcher and advisor on engineering geological aspects of civil engineering works in soft ground. He specializes in land subsidence modelling and mapping of land subsidence due to water management and climate change. For this purpose a time-dependent subsidence model was developed to interact with the TNO subsurface models.

Correspondence to: Ger de Lange, Deltares, Postbus 85467, 3508 AL Utrecht, the Netherlands. Email: ger.delange@deltares.nl

Mahmoud Bakr is researcher and advisor on soil and groundwater systems. He specializes in inverse and forward groundwater flow and mass transport modelling, modelling land subsidence due to groundwater management, and the assessment of worth of data and uncertainty reduction. He is involved in land subsidence projects in the Netherlands, Indonesia, and Vietnam.

Correspondence to: Mahmoud Bakr, Deltares, Postbus 85467, 3508 AL Utrecht, the Netherlands. Email: mahmoud.bakr@deltares.nl

Jan Gunnink develops 3D geological models at TNO — Geological Survey of the Netherlands. He advises users of the geological data and lithological models stored in the national subsurface database DINO on the stochastic characterization of geology in projects such as the modelling of land subsidence due to water management in the Netherlands.

Correspondence to: Jan Gunnink, TNO, Postbus 80015, 3508 TA Utrecht, the Netherlands. Email: jan.gunnink@tno.nl

Hans (D. J.) Huisman is a soil scientist and geochemist. Since 2003, he has worked for the cultural heritage agency as senior researcher soil science and degradation. He has done a series of research projects on degradation of archaeological remains and monitoring of archaeological sites and edited and co-wrote a book on degradation of archaeological remains.

Correspondence to: Hans (D. J.) Huisman, Cultural Heritage Agency, Postbus 1600, 3800 BP Amersfoort, the Netherlands. Email: h.huisman@cultureelerfgoed.nl

CONSERVATION AND MGMT OF ARCH. SITES, Vol. 14 Nos 1–4, 2012, 294–302

Take the Right Decision Everybody

Anke Loska and Ann Christensson

Riksantikvaren (Norwegian Directorate for Cultural Heritage), Norway

The archaeological deposits in medieval towns are among the most important and distinctive heritage monuments in Norway. At the same time they are among the more challenging phenomena confronting heritage management authorities, municipal planners, and property owners/developers alike, especially in relation to building and infrastructure projects. The modern settlement has developed on top of medieval and younger deposits which means that not only are they an irreplaceable depository of historical information, but they also form a significant part of the modern town's physical foundation.

Since 2002 the Directorate for Cultural Heritage in Norway (Riksantikvaren) has been funding systematic monitoring of archaeological deposits of the World Heritage Site Bryggen in Bergen. The monitoring programme consists of several approaches: archaeological assessment of the deposits state of preservation, biochemical investigation of preservation conditions within the deposits, hydrogeological mapping of the water table, water flow, and other given parameters.

Continuous systematic monitoring by using testable, replicable methods and measures, data, and results acquire increased quality and validity. These in turn provide the cultural heritage management with a toolbox for making correct decisions and thereby allow the government's preservation targets to be attained. But, most important, it guarantees the preservation of the 'underground archives' and at the same time allows the urban centres to develop.

This paper presents the knowledge developed through monitoring the Bryggen site as a basis for an official Norwegian standard covering archaeological, biochemical, and hydrogeological deposit investigations.

KEYWORDS cultural heritage, urban landscape, archaeological deposits, state of preservation, environmental monitoring, standardization

Introduction

The archaeological deposits in medieval towns are the largest continuous, automatically protected sites of historical and archaeological significance in Norway. The

DOI 10.1179/1350503312Z.00000000025

modern settlement has developed on top of medieval and younger deposits which means that not only are they an irreplaceable depository of historical information, but they also form a significant part of the modern town's physical foundation. In most of the towns, the medieval town remains coincide with today's city centre and they form the basis for the urban culture that we observe today.

The Norwegian Ministry of the Environment's stated aim is 'to preserve the "underground archives" and at the same time establish conditions for continued use of the pertinent areas and the development of vital inner cities' (Det kongelige Miljøverndepartementet, 2004–05). This is also in line with the national attainment goals that by 2020 the annual losses of archaeological monuments and sites that have automatic statutory protection not exceed 0.5 per cent of the total, and a standard of repair where only normal maintenance is required will be achieved for protected buildings, installations, and vessels, this applying equally to urban archaeological deposits.[1]

Riksantikvaren (the Directorate for Cultural Heritage) is part of the national environmental management, and answers to the Ministry of the Environment. It is responsible for

- the management of all archaeological and architectural monuments and sites andcultural environments in accordance with the relevant legislation
- ensuring that cultural heritage considerations are taken into account in all planning processes.

It is a national objective to ensure that a representative selection of monuments and sites of all periods is preserved for present and future generations. All aspects of cultural heritage have to be treated as finite and non-renewable resources, because, once destroyed, they can never be replaced. Riksantikvaren is dedicated to improving the preservation conditions of the country's cultural heritage. It is therefore mandatory on heritage management to keep pace with modern developments, through active acquisition of knowledge, greater outreach, and a solid comprehension of the principal mechanisms and consequences of the changes taking place.

The medieval town Bergen in Norway, general remarks

The earliest settlement in Bergen dates from the latter half of the eleventh century, and was located towards the north-western end of the Vågen bay's north-eastern shore. This is the same area as today's UNESCO World Heritage Site of Bryggen in Bergen. The typical building patterns of Bryggen are the wooden long, parallel tenements running vertical to the waterfront. This pattern dates back to the town's earliest period, and was well established long before the Hanseatic League in the fourteenth century (Figure 1).

Settlement expanded south-eastwards along the shore and into the area at the head of the harbour, which is today known as Vågsbunnen. If one includes the modern quay front area, we find that settlement at Bryggen has advanced into the former harbour area by up to 140 m — thus generating archaeological deposits which we want to preserve today.

The deposits are mainly organic and derived from both settlement and leather-working activities (Figure 2), as a large part of Vågsbunnen was occupied by German

FIGURE 1   Aerial view of the World Heritage Site Bryggen in Bergen, Norway.

FIGURE 2   Archaeological deposits — the ground beneath the World Heritage Site Bryggen in Bergen, Norway.

shoemakers and tanners from *c.* 1300 to 1600. The deposits in most of the inner part of the Bryggen area were removed after a fire in 1916.

Even at its maximum extent, supposed to be prior to the Black Death, medieval Bergen was probably covered no more than 620,000 m^2. Nonetheless, it is believed that Bergen has been the largest town in Scandinavia during most of the Middle Ages. It is roughly estimated that the total volume of archaeological deposits within Bergen's scheduled area may be well upwards of two million m^3.

The problem in focus

The archaeological deposits in medieval towns are among the most important and distinctive heritage monuments in Norway. The archaeological remains at these sites have a distinguished and significant character, developed more or less continuously from thousand years ago and up to the modern city. The following towns have known medieval deposits preserved beneath them and are designated as scheduled ancient monuments: Oslo, Bergen, Trondheim, Tønsberg, Hamar, Stavanger, Sarpsborg, and Skien.

The modern settlement has developed on top of medieval and younger deposits. While older methods of construction did not normally come into significant conflict with the underlying cultural deposits, these deposits have now become vulnerable to destructive penetration in connection with, for example, road building, technical infrastructure, and building constructions. Penetration into the cultural deposits often results in drainage of any adjacent cultural deposits, and therefore changing the geochemical ground conditions which again change the deposits state of preservation. To put it in other words, penetration into the cultural deposits can provide renewed access for oxygen, which increases the rate of decomposition of organic material. With the organic material gone the soil loses its volume, thus contributing to mechanical settling with possible building damages and loss of historic information as a consequence.

How can monitoring contribute?

The Norwegian government considers archaeological strata a non-renewable resource and direct or indirect damage to them poses a threat to continued *in situ* preservation (Malta Convention, 1992). Development of such sites requires archaeological assessments of the state of preservation and chemical and physical assessments to evaluate the conditions of preservation. Preservation conditions can vary considerably from area to area within each town, as well as from town to town. Organic deposits can even have deteriorated completely, or have been removed en masse. The level of vulnerability to further damage varies within each area, and from city to city.

To keep pace with modern development and ensuring sustainable management of all archaeological and architectural monuments and sites, Riksantikvaren initiated in 2002 a monitoring programme of archaeological deposits of the World Heritage Site Bryggen in Bergen. This activity brought together a research group of archaeologists, hydrologists, physicians, and technicians under the leadership of the cultural heritage management.

The need for standard procedures became more evident with every passing year of monitoring the Bryggen site, as well as the later approaches to gather data on the other medieval sites and mayor cities Trondheim, Oslo, and Tønsberg. Measure results showed clearly that archaeological remains at Bryggen are threatened. The groundwater level at one particular location, namely close to the hotel built in 1980, sank almost 3 m.a.s.l. over a period of twenty-five years. It was estimated that the Bryggen buildings had a settling rate of about 8 mm per year.

What was happening here?[2]

The researchers involved in monitoring Bryggen focused on identifying certain key parameters as early warning indicators, thus developed various requirements concerning monitoring and investigation of the archaeological deposits. As a result, a guidance document, the Monitoring Manual, was developed in 2007.

The long-term monitoring activity at Bryggen provided Riksantikvaren with the knowledge of quantitative and qualitative changes that are occurring beneath the Bryggen buildings. This in turn is essential for making correct decisions about appropriate countermeasures. At the same time this knowledge-based management helps to ensure sustainable management.

The significance of a standard

One of the most important fields to be described in the Monitoring Manual is the preservation category and the use of the state of preservation scale (SOPS; see Table 1), for archaeological layer recording, thereby classifying each documented sample in a preservation category. The state of preservation is determined by the archaeologist by means of a range of criteria such as odour, colour/colour change, the amount of force needed to snap or pull apart organic material, the sponge reaction of soil, and general appearance. The correct preservation category is then found by reference to the state of preservation scale.

By using this scale the degree of preservation will be assessed and can be compared both over time and between locations.

The state of preservation is closely linked to preservation conditions, meaning geochemical conditions in the soil and water, and the hydrological environment. Any changes to the preservation conditions are likely to change the state of preservation.

Process identification and quantification requires chemical analysis of the individual strata. At the same time the preservation conditions can vary considerably from area to area within each town, as well as from town to town. Thus, a standardized

TABLE 1

STATE OF PRESERVATION SCALE (SOPS), DEVELOPED BY RORY DUNLOP, NIKU, IN NORSK STANDARD, 2009

Position in relation to groundwater level	Degree of preservation					
	0 Null value	1 Lousy	2 Poor	3 Medium	4 Good	5 Excellent
Unsaturated zone (A)	A0	A1	A2	A3	A4	A5
Seasonally saturated zone (B)	B0	B1	B2	B3	B4	B5
Saturated zone (C9)	C0	C1	C2	C3	C4	C5
Fill, later than ca 1900 AD (D)	D0	D1	D2	D3	D4	D5

methodology and a set of required measurements of selected parameters are necessary to guarantee genuine comparability of data and results throughout time and between different investigations.

Consequently, to formalize the manual's methods and procedures, the official Norwegian standard was produced in 2009.[3] Its overall aim is to assist both developers and those responsible for sites of archaeological/historical significance in abiding by the relevant legislation and conditions for environmental monitoring when disturbing or building upon deposits of archaeological or cultural significance. It also specifies the responsibilities of the developer in such cases.

According to the standard monitoring is required in the case of building or redevelopment works and also in the case of other types of activity potentially disturbing the archaeological deposits. The monitoring will be carried out before, during, and after the development phase. Different monitoring methods are available, but the selection of an appropriate method will depend on ground conditions.

The use of traceable and reproducible methods and actions will increase the quality and reliability of the data collected. Changes in the cultural deposits will be detected and prompt remedial action can be undertaken. The objective of this is not necessarily a permanent preservation of degradable cultural deposits in medieval towns. What is important is the systematic mapping and checking of the state and conditions of preservation of the deposits and, in that way, the acquisition of valid, high-quality data on their rate of decomposition. Increased knowledge will, through time, provide a better basis for protection strategies and decisions about permitted developments.

Having undertaken numerous measurements over the last ten years in more than thirty dipwells and boreholes at the World Heritage Site Bryggen in Bergen, the large amount of monitoring data needed to be analysed and the results needed to be presented visually to better communicate risks of *in situ* decay. Riksantikvaren needs model outputs as a decision support system for cultural heritage management and to facilitate the communication between different stakeholders. As a World Heritage Site and one of Norway's main tourist attractions, stakeholders vary from cultural heritage authorities at national, regional, and local levels, spatial planners, municipal services, building- and shop-owners, to the general public.

As a result, a framework model of the underground in three dimensions at Bryggen is under development by Hans de Beer from the Geological Survey of Norway (NGU) using proprietary software GSI3D (Geological Surveying and Investigations in 3 Dimensions) (de Beer et al., in press). GSI3D not only produces detailed 3D geological models, but bulk-attributed models with physical, chemical, hydrogeological, or archaeological parameters. Once an attributed model is completed, a large number of customized geoscientific outputs can be generated with little computation (an example of the subsurface model for Bryggen is shown in Figure 3).

Although there are still a lot of challenges to design this framework model to fully perform a spatial risk assessment of *in situ* decay, it already is able to explain the vulnerability of the archaeological deposits in their complex interplay with the natural and anthropogenic environments. Thus, it will contribute to a decision support system for sustainable urban (re)development and regeneration in cities, while preserving cultural heritage.

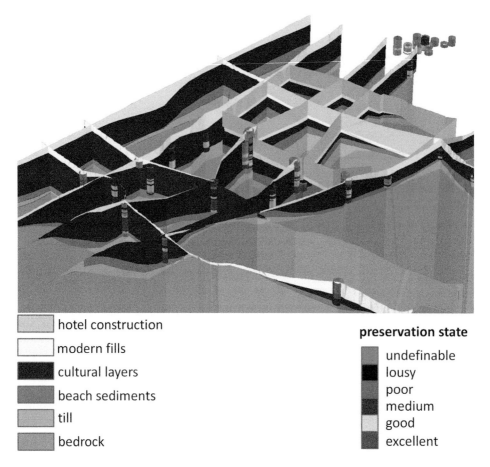

◻	hotel construction
◻	modern fills
◼	cultural layers
◼	beach sediments
◻	till
◻	bedrock

preservation state

	undefinable
	lousy
	poor
	medium
	good
	excellent

FIGURE 3   Example of 3D subsurface model for Bryggen, including borehole sticks with attributes showing state of preservation.
By permission of Hans de Beer, NGU

Outreach

To make certain that we at Riksantikvaren do our job, to work out a consistent management policy for the preservation and safeguarding of the country's automatically protected cultural heritage, we have to be on top concerning knowledge-based management, to communicate the results, the effects, and take correct decisions about appropriate counter-measures.

And we actually are convinced that we are heading in the right direction. In 2011 the Ministry of Environment granted 6 million Euros to the World Heritage Site Bryggen to preserve it from further settling damages. The ground beneath the earlier mentioned hotel site will now be subject to install technical means in order to stabilize the groundwater, thus stopping the leakage of groundwater and thereby decreasing access for oxygen. One alternative, for example, is to install a new drainage system to raise the groundwater level ensuring that the archaeological deposits again will be waterlogged.

The Minister of Environment, Erik Solheim, stated: 'Bryggen is of outstanding cultural value, and it will now be safeguarded from further damage caused by low groundwater levels. We will spend 6 million Euros to reverse the groundwater drainage in a years' time. The task is complex and comprehensive, but we now have the money and the competence to secure Bryggen for the future'.

But of course, although we have come very far on that area of expertise, a standard and 6 million Euros is only the basis. The cultural heritage management still has a long way to go. Together with the researchers from the different disciplines we have to elaborate further on what the monitoring results mean. What does it mean if the water temperature rises 0.5° C?

That is why it is important that everybody who is working with *in situ* preservation come together and meet and exchange knowledge and generate new collaborations. But the most important thing is that researchers and cultural heritage management are willing to work united towards the same objective.

Acknowledgements

All the results, the manual, the standard, and the competency were only made possible by the overwhelming engagement of the researchers involved in the monitoring activity and by the leadership of Ann Christensson. Riksantikvaren wants to thank the following researchers and their institutions: Rory Dunlop (NIKU, Norwegian Institute for Cultural Heritage Research); Henning Matthiesen (National Museum of Denmark); Hans de Beer (Geological Survey of Norway); Jann Atle Jensen (Multiconsult AS); and Bioforsk (Norwegian Institute for Agricultural and Environmental Research).

Notes

[1] <www.environment.no>. Goals and indicators <http://www.environment.no/Goals-and-indicators/>.

[2] For information about the monitoring results for Bryggen in Bergen, please contact the authors for a literature overview.

[3] Norsk Standard, Cultural Property, Requirements on environmental monitoring and investigation of cultural deposits, NS 9451:2009, available in English by winter 2011 on Riksantikvarens website <www.ra.no>.

Bibliography

de Beer, H., Price, S., and Ford, J. In press. 3D Modeling of Geological and Anthropogenic Deposits at the World Heritage Site of Bryggen in Bergen, Norway. *Quarternary International*.

Det kongelige Miljøverndepartementet, 2004–05. *Stortingsmelding nr 16, Leve med kulturminner* [Report no. 16 (2004–05) to the Storting, Living with our Cultural Heritage]. In Norwegian only [accessed 10 October 2012]. Available at: <http://www.regjeringen.no/nb/dep/md/dok/regpubl/stmeld/20042005/stmeld-nr-16-2004-2005-.html?id =406291>.

Malta Convention 1992. European Convention on the Protection of the Archaeological Heritage (Malta Convention or Valletta treaty).

Riksantikvaren and Norsk institutt for kulturminneforskning, 2007. The Monitoring Manual — Procedures and Guidelines for the Monitoring, Recording and Preservation/Management of Urban Archaeological Deposits [accessed 10 October 2012]. Available at: <http://www.riksantikvaren.no/filestore/Veileder_komp.pdf>.

Norsk Standard NS 9451: 2009. Kulturminner, Krav til miljøovervåking og –undersøkelse av kulturlag [accessed 10 October 2012]. English translation available at: <http://brage.bibsys.no/riksant/retrieve/1775/Requirements_eng_versjon_Norwegian_National_Standard_2012.pdf>.

Notes on contributors

Anke Loska, MA, is Senior Adviser at Riksantikvaren, section for Research and Development, responsible for initiation and administration of environmental monitoring programs for cultural heritage sites, monuments, and environments.

Correspondence to: Anke Loska, Riksantikvaren, PO Box 8196, N-0034 Oslo, Norway. Email: anke.loska@ra.no

Ann Christensson is Senior Adviser at Riksantikvaren, section for archaeology, and project leader for the environmental monitoring programme at Bryggen in Bergen.

Correspondence to: Ann Christensson. Email: ac@ra.no

CONSERVATION AND MGMT OF ARCH. SITES, Vol. 14 Nos 1–4, 2012, 303–09

In Situ Preservation of Ancient Floor Mosaics in Turkey

HANDE KÖKTEN

Ankara University, Turkey

As stated in the Burra Charter (1979) 'A building or work should remain in its historical location. The moving of all or part of a building or work is unacceptable unless it is the sole means of ensuring its survival'. This statement has been neglected many times during rescue excavations in Turkey (e.g. Zeugma), whereas the destruction of ancient floor mosaics caused by lifting, especially when carried out by incompetent or inexperienced personnel at systematic archaeological excavations, has steered the authorities desire to preserve them *in situ*. However, due to the lack of conservation professionals and insufficient resources for conservation, it becomes a difficult issue to provide an effective preservation scheme for archaeological excavations. This paper aims to discuss this important issue in terms of the national legislation, preventative and interventive conservation approaches at various sites, exhibition and maintenance of mosaics, as well as the training of conservation technicians in Turkey.

KEYWORDS mosaic floors, archaeological sites, *in situ* preservation, preventive conservation, legislation, site management

Introduction

Floor mosaics form a significant part of Turkey's archaeological heritage and are often discovered during long-term scientific excavations, as well as rescue projects carried out by state museums. However, it is not difficult to predict that many others still wait to be discovered, at many significant ancient sites (e.g. Pergamon, Aphrodisias, Sardis, Sagalassos, Arykanda, Erythrai, Ephesus, Zeugma) where archaeological research still continues.

Due to the large number of *in situ* preserved mosaic floors that survive, preservation issues are unavoidable. Assessing the causes of these problems seems to be the most practical and direct approach.

   DOI 10.1179/1350503312Z.00000000026

Problems related to the current legislation for the protection of the cultural and natural heritage of Turkey

In the National Legislation No. 2863 for the Protection of the Cultural and Natural Heritage,[1] Article 6 defines cultural and natural properties and names 'floor mosaics' as one of the immovable archaeological property that should be preserved *in situ*. In Article 20 of the same legislation, which classifies the lifting and removal of the immovable heritage, it states that 'it is essential to preserve the immovable cultural property and its components in their original locations'. If there is a necessity to remove the immovable cultural property to a different location, or if its properties make this removal unavoidable, such an action can be taken by the Ministry of Culture and Tourism, after the approval of the District Preservation Boards (Article 9)[2] and after necessary security measures are provided. The point that draws ones attention in this article, is the lack of clarification of the reasons that cause 'the necessity for removal'.

As a matter of fact, in practice, the removal of a mosaic floor unearthed during a systematical archaeological excavation depends on the approval of the government representative, who serves at every excavation and survey project in Turkey and who is assigned by the General Directorate of Cultural Property and Museums. Since it is a time consuming process to inform the District Preservation Board, to make an appeal for the removal of a mosaic floor and to wait for the decision of the board, the approval authority seems to be assigned to the government representative to speed up the process. However, the guidelines that the representative takes into account during her approval, are not different than those mentioned in Article 20. In other words, as the legislation does not specify the 'acceptable necessities for the removal of a mosaic floor from its original location' in detail, removal decisions are made with the proposal of the archaeologist/project director and the approval and permission of the government representative.

In this case, the obvious reason for the transfer of a floor mosaic proposed by an archaeologist is likely described as 'the necessity to reach the earlier archaeological layers that are covered by the mosaic floor'. There may be, according to the conservator, other reasons for lifting the mosaic floor, such as detached tesserae, deteriorated preparatory layers, destruction of supportive structures, and risk of destruction due to landslide.

As these causes are not clearly indicated in a code associated with the legislation, and in the absence of an experienced conservator, it may be that this important decision is made by the archaeologist and the representative who may not necessarily be qualified to evaluate the mosaics' condition.

Meanwhile, in the articles of the legislation referring to the immovable cultural property, there is no mention of a code or guidelines that apply to their *in situ* preservation; thus archaeologists and government representatives are lacking the standards to rationalize the methodology and compatibility of the approaches taken by the conservator, especially when the conservation professional is not specialized in mosaics.

All too often, when the floor mosaic is preserved *in situ*, the initiative concerning the post excavation care of the mosaic (e.g. re-burial method and material, monitoring mosaic's condition, maintenance procedure) is left to the field director.

On the other hand, very few archaeological expeditions in Turkey employ a field conservator, and the conservation work mostly focuses on movable cultural remains. This situation reduces the chance of professional consultancy and expertise for the *in situ* conservation of floor mosaics, immediately after their discovery.

Problems related to damage that occurs during the excavation of the mosaic floor

There is no doubt that there is an obligation to plan the conservation work prior to the excavation campaign for the success of the fieldwork, and the following should be determined in advance:

- The scope and content of the conservation work
- The expertise and experience of the conservation team fulfilling the needs of the site
- Budget needed for the proposed conservation project
- Standards that will be applied during all conservation work
- Concerns, responsibilities and priorities of the archaeologist, field conservator and architectural restorer during the decision making process for the preservation of the immovable cultural properties should be clarified.

However, as mentioned above, the availability of professional and experienced field conservators is limited to very few excavations in Turkey and thus planning for on-site conservation is not a common practice (Kökten, 2006). In many cases, this situation results in the damage or even destruction of the floor mosaics. As Sease says, 'too frequently, conservators are brought in only after problems have arisen; after a mosaic has been completely uncovered; and above all after it has sustained some degree of damage' (Sease, 2003: 4).

Even at archaeological sites where floor mosaics have been discovered before, the absence of an experienced field conservator, and a lack of awareness by the archaeologist concerning preventive measures produces severe problems, particularly when the floor mosaic is in a poor state of preservation.

In the case of the discovery of heavily damaged mosaics excavation and first aid treatments should be applied simultaneously with excavation by an experienced mosaic conservator or a conservation technician.

At many archaeological projects in Turkey, the lack of qualified conservators and conservation planning means newly discovered mosaic floors do not receive any level of stabilization or first aid treatment during the excavation (Kökten, 2008). Hence, even the excavation procedure becomes a threat for the mosaic, especially when its physical condition is poor. Under these circumstances, depending on the mosaic's state of preservation, the act of archaeological excavation causes its destruction, rather than preserving the data it provides. In addition, a mosaic floor re-buried with an inadequate fill layer for an extended period of time will exacerbate the series of mistakes.

To avoid severe and sometimes irreversible damage to mosaic floors, it is essential to find solutions to two major problems:

1. In the absence of professional conservators, particularly when the mosaic floor is in poor condition, archaeologists should be aware of their responsibility to protect and stabilize the mosaic, and therefore must approach the mosaic floor

more cautiously. Moreover, there should be guidelines to orient them towards safe and proper stabilization systems, which are easy to figure out and use. These guidelines should contain the basics of preventative conservation techniques and standards of preservation.

2. Standards referring to the material characteristics, layering, depth, and duration of the re-burial fills should be clearly defined, as there are quite a number of floor mosaics that must be covered without receiving of stabilization treatment.

Problems caused by the absence of a qualified and experienced field conservator

1. Aside from the fact that there are very few professionals in Turkey specialized in mosaic conservation, inappropriate conservation interventions undertaken by archaeological conservators and conservation technicians who are not well enough qualified in this particular field are also damaging. This is a common problem both for Turkish and foreign expeditions, when the project director requests the help of an object conservator or the architectural restorer who are also involved in preservation, but in completely different contexts. The use of improper or irreversible materials (i.e. filling the cracks and lacunae with cement mortar), misapplication of complicated treatments (e.g. lifting mosaics), misuse of conservation methods (e.g. lifting and re-laying mosaics unnecessarily) are the most dramatic examples, which results in the destruction of the original floor.

2. These issues clearly indicate that the presence of a conservation professional does not always guarantee the success of the treatments applied to a mosaic floor; as it is the qualification and experience of the conservator that really matters. Thus, there is an urgent need for a reliable and efficient selection procedure of conservation professionals, or an approval system under the authority of the Department of Antiquities. Unfortunately, due to the lack of conservation experts among the staff of the Department of Antiquities to evaluate the qualification of the candidates, conservation professionals are not subject to approval.

3. In other words, the Ministry of Culture holds the field director responsible for all conservation and restoration treatments undertaken during the project, but neither describes the conservation standards expected, nor defines or evaluates the qualifications and experience that a conservator should have. This situation certainly indicates a major deficiency in the legislation, which can be resolved with a 'code of standards and qualifications'.

Problems related to the post-excavation period: lack of monitoring and maintenance

Another important issue related with the preservation of *in situ* floor mosaics in archaeological projects is the post-excavation period. Not only the recently uncovered mosaics, but especially those which have been discovered and reburied long time ago, usually receive no monitoring or maintenance throughout the years. Eventually, this situation affects the condition of the mosaics even if they have been properly treated and stabilized prior to reburial. Such a risk also exists for the *in situ* mosaics displayed under a roof or in a protective structure, as their maintenance is often neglected or ignored by the expedition.

Re-buried mosaic floors

As mosaics floors backfilled for long-term may still be affected, depending on the method and material of backfill, as well as the duration of re-burial period and environmental factors; it is necessary to inspect and monitor their condition on a regular basis, in order to understand whether the chosen method and material is effective (Podany et al., 1994). At the same time, once the mosaic floor is covered with whatever material available, it may also be buried deep in mind and forgotten. For instance, in cases in which the fill layer is not solid, tesellatum will be exposed with the effect of wind and rain, thus weathered throughout the year. In the spring this uncontrolled, undesirable, improper display will even expand further with the efforts of curious visitors. Such conditions are often encountered at ancient sites where archaeological field projects were completed; and obviously these mosaics are at great risk.

Mosaic floors that are displayed under a shelter or in a protective structure

For the mosaics on display in a shelter (e.g. Aizanoi, Roman Baths; Sagalassos, Neon Library; Ephesos, Slope Houses; Pergamon, Building Z), the maintenance and monitoring process seems to function in a different manner. Due to the vast number of tourists visiting archaeological sites, both excavation directors and local museum authorities often feel obliged to keep the mosaics in good shape. At some of these sites there are more than mosaic floors to care for (e.g. Ephesos and Pergamon), as the walls of the ancient buildings are decorated with elaborate frescoes and wall plasters; and regular observation and maintenance procedure of these unique archaeological remains are taken more seriously.

However, uncleaned or broken rain gutters, damp walls, insufficient ventilation, worn and leaking roofs often result in the damage of the mosaic floor. These detrimental processes are often neglected and not considered destructive until a severe damage occurs on the mosaic floor. As the damage develops gradually and the signs of deterioration are ignored for a long period of time, even treated and restored mosaics are affected by these adverse conditions, and unfortunately in most cases they do not receive a second conservation treatment due to the cost of operation.

However, we must admit that the following questions still remain unanswered:

- Who will examine the condition of the roofs and shelters?
- Who will maintain the mosaic floors on a regular basis?
- How often the monitoring will take place?
- What are the intervention levels for mosaics in different states of preservation?
- Who will retreat the damaged mosaics and to what extend the necessary measures be taken?

Once again, this situation brings us back to the statement in the Turkish Legislation[3] (Article 45) that appoints the excavation director as the sole authority who is responsible from the conservation-restoration work of all movable and immovable archaeological remains. However, as the effectiveness of maintenance depends on the excavation director's skill in site management, the current situation proves that without well-defined guidelines there will be inadequate and temporary recipes instead of professional and long-lasting solutions, confusion instead of order, and neglect instead of attention.

Short- and long-term approaches to resolve preservation issues

All these issues mentioned above indicate that *in situ* mosaics unearthed at archaeological sites in Turkey are under severe risk and the major cause of this reality is the absence of an 'archaeological site management code'. Besides, although the focus of this paper is mosaic floors, there is no doubt that all *in situ* preserved archaeological remains (e.g. wall plasters and paintings, marble revetments, inscriptions, tiles, terracotta water pipes, etc.) deserve the same degree of attention and care.

Hence, a three-phased action programme is recommended in order to resolve these issues before the mosaic heritage of Turkey is more severely and irreversibly damaged.

Protection of *in situ* mosaics with preventative conservation methods

1. Informing archaeologists, site managers, and non-specialist conservators about the preventative conservation measures and materials to be applied during the excavation of a mosaic floor. Especially in the absence of a qualified conservation professional, the scope of archaeologist's responsibility shall expand to ensure the safekeeping of the mosaic.
2. Providing information about the characteristics of an ideal backfill, and also an illustrated description of the backfilling process for the archaeologist and non-specialist conservator. Guidelines and illustrations will prevent the use of improper and destructive materials and methods.
3. Improving guidelines for the observation and maintenance programme that will clarify the level and content of this assignment, as well as the qualifications of the keeper. Guidelines will help the site manager and the museum director to follow the condition of mosaics and the sheltering structures systematically and hence to realize problems more rapidly.

Definition of the qualifications and competence of the conservation professionals who will undertake the conservation treatments

Excavation directors and authorities at the Department of Antiquities should be aware of these definitions and criteria to evaluate the suitability of the candidate to the conservation work.

A code of archaeological site management should be prepared by a commission of professionals, including field conservators and restorers. This code must be referred in the related articles of the Legislation for the Protection of the Cultural Property, and should be released to all the professionals working at archaeological sites.

Keeping in mind that every archaeological excavation is a scientific destruction, we need to trust that *in situ* preservation of ancient mosaics in Turkey can still be achieved with the help of concerned archaeologists, experienced conservators, and caring site managers under the shield of standards, codes, and ethics.

Notes

1 Turkish Legislation No. 2863 for the Protection of the Cultural and National Heritage. Available at: <http://teftis.kulturturizm.gov.tr/belge/1-41685/kultur-ve-tabiat-varliklarini-koruma-kanunu.html>.

2 Legislation of the Preservation District Boards. Available at: <http://teftis.kulturturizm.gov.tr/belge/1-41644/kultur-ve-tabiat-varliklarini-koruma-yuksek-kurulu-ile-.html>.

3 Turkish Legislation No. 2863 for the Protection of the Cultural and National Heritage. Available at: <http://teftis.kulturturizm.gov.tr/belge/1-41685/kultur-ve-tabiat-varliklarini-koruma-kanunu.html>.

Bibliography

Kökten, H. 2006. Archaeological Conservation in Turkey. In: *Proceedings of the Conservation Theme of the 5th World Archaeological Congress, of the Past, for the Future: Integrating Archaeology and Conservation.* Los Angeles: Getty Conservation Institute, pp. 224–31.

Kökten, H. 2008. Mosaic Floors Unearthed at Rescue Excavations in Turkey: A Philosophical and Ethical Evaluation of the Decision Making Process. In: *Proceedings of the 9th Conference of the International Committee for the Conservation of Mosaics, Lessons Learned: Reflecting on the Theory and Practice of Mosaic Conservation,* Los Angeles: Getty Publications, pp. 131–35.

Podany, J., Agnew, N., and Demas, M. 1994. Preservation of Excavated Mosaics by Reburial: Evaluation of Some Traditional and Newly Developed Materials and Techniques. In: *Proceedings of the 5th Conference of the ICCM, Conservation Protection Presentation, Conimbriga,* ICCM, pp. 1–19.

Sease, C. 2003. Planning for Conservation of an In Situ Mosaic, Before, During and After Excavation. In: *Proceedings of the 6th International Conference of the International Committee for the Conservation of Mosaics, Mosaics Make a Site: The Conservation in situ of Mosaics on Archaeological Sites, Italy,* pp. 67–83.

Notes on contributor

Hande Kökten has been a professor at the Conservation Program of Baskent Vocational School, Ankara University, since 1991 and is currently the director of this institution. She specialized in conservation training, preventive conservation and preservation of archaeological materials, floor mosaics in particular. She is a member of IIC, ICCM, and ICOM.

Correspondence to: Hande Kökten, Ankara Universitesi, Gumusdere Yerleskesi, Baskent Meslek Yüksekokulu, Fatih Cad. 33A, Kecioren — Ankara, Turkey. Email: hkokten@ankara.edu.tr

CONSERVATION AND MGMT OF ARCH. SITES, Vol. 14 Nos 1–4, 2012, 310–21

The Results of Cultural Management of the Croatian Archaeological Heritage with Special Consideration for Cost Effectiveness: The Case of Roman *Iovia* (Ludbreg)

Tajana Pleše

Croatian Conservation Institute, Croatia

During the four seasons of excavations of the Roman town of *Iovia-Botivo* (present-day Ludbreg, Croatia), a smaller bath and sizeable (presumably public) building were discovered. An optimal plan for presentation was made with all due consideration for the site's specific situation. The plan encompassed scholarly and professional requirements concerning conservation *in situ* combined with the needs of successful cultural management, thus resulting in alignment between the latter two factors as well as cost effectiveness. By applying the aforementioned principles (which served more as guidelines rather than rigid edicts) and facilitating successful, inter-disciplinary cooperation between the national government, the municipal authorities, and researchers, it was possible to provide a sound, legally secure future for this site.

KEYWORDS *Iovia-Botivo* (Ludbreg), Croatia, conservation, presentation, management, archaeological sites

Introduction

Civitas Iovia-Botivo (Ludbreg, Croatia), an early Roman Imperial settlement, was founded in the first century AD along the left bank of the Bednja River. *Iovia* was situated on an important route that ran along the Drava River, connecting Pannonia's major provincial centres, for example, *Poetovio* (Ptuj) and *Mursa* (Osijek). A connection with the southern regions of the province was made possible by a route passing through nearby *Aquae Iasae* (Varaždinske Toplice) which continued down to *Siscia* (Sisak). After several centuries of prosperity, *Iovia* was most likely devastated during

    DOI 10.1179/1350503312Z.00000000027

the invasion of the Goths in the late fourth century AD. The tradition of urban life was not abandoned; instead, this Pannonian town has existed in continuity up until today (Mayer, 1935: 69–82; Mócsy, 1974: 222, 225, 309; Deluka et al., 2003: 733–42; Gračanin, 2010: 20) (Figure 1).

Archaeological excavations of Iovia-Botivo (1968–79 and 2008–10)

The first archaeological excavations were conducted by the Archaeological Museum in Zagreb from 1968 until 1979. These excavations were confined to free, green surfaces, mostly in the backyards of private lots, therefore limited solely to small test trenches. Since Ludbreg is an active small town with the corresponding infrastructure, it was not possible to expand the research area of these certainly intriguing finds. The results of this pioneering work made it possible to presume the general urban layout of Roman *Iovia* (covering estimated area of 6 to 9 ha) and the disposition of the two main thoroughfares — *cardo* and *decumanus* — along which the main public and residential buildings were situated. A suburban area, with residential buildings, businesses, and workshops, was discovered along the northern side of the town, near the Batthyány Castle. All of the discovered architectural structures may be dated from the second to fourth centuries AD (Vikić Belančić, 1984: 119–66).

The most interesting results that came to light in the test trenches were two semicircular bath pools in the Somogy garden, a large private estate in the very heart of the present-day town. Based on the interpretation of the aforementioned pools as baths that were remodelled and converted into a Christian church (as done in nearby

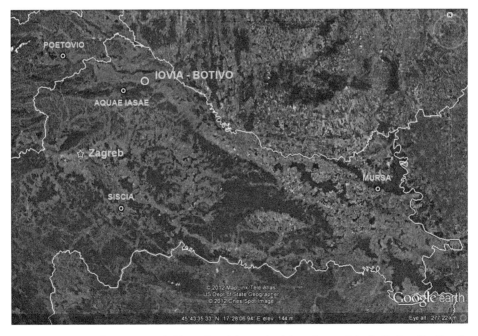

FIGURE 1   Map of Croatia and Slovenia with marked locations of *Iovia-Botivo* (Ludbreg), *Poetovio* (Ptuj), *Aquae Iasae* (Varaždinske Toplice), *Siscia* (Sisak), and *Mursa* (Osijek) marked. © *www.earth.google.com*

Aquae Iasae) and R. Egger's theory, many scholars were eager to accept the hypothesis that Croatian *Iovia* was where Arian Bishop Amantius was exiled after the Council in Aquileia in AD 381 (Egger, 1924: 340–41; Mócsy, 1974: 329–42; Jarak, 1994: 35–36; Migotti, 1994: 51–53; 2002: 51–66; Tomičić, 1997: 34; Gregl and Migotti, 2004: 131–43). A great deal of scholarly importance was attached to the continuation of research in order to discover another piece of the puzzle that would resolve the long-lasting debate on the Iovian diocese (and knowing that the Croatian part of the Roman province of Pannonia has not been sufficiently examined because later settlements were built over their Roman predecessors). Fortunately, even though the present town of Ludbreg entirely covers the general layout of the Roman settlement, it was possible to launch excavations on a larger scale due to the large amount of open space that defined the southern portion of the Somogy garden (total area of 3700 m²).

Although it is entirely clear that these excavations will never be comprehensive because Ludbreg completely overlays the previous Roman settlement, the opportunity created by the earlier, pioneering efforts had to be seized. Prior to the continuation of excavations, it was imperative to resolve the legal aspect of ownership of the Somogy garden. Since reimbursement is guaranteed to the proprietors of properties during archaeological research (as stipulated by the Cultural Heritage Protection and Preservation Act), the best long-term option was to purchase the Somogy garden. This also ensured that there would be no legal obstacles to any future presentation of potential finds. Since the Somogy garden was private property, it took several years to reach a settlement with the estate's heirs. After long negotiations, proprietary issues were finally resolved and the town of Ludbreg became the new owner.

Mindful of their Roman heritage, the municipal authorities were eager to proceed with the excavations, making the legislation regulating archaeological sites very easy to put into practice. In addition to their interest in broadening their knowledge of the past, the authorities also conducted a SWOT analysis and compiled cost-effectiveness studies that showed how this type of tourism product could nicely supplement with the very potent religious tourism based on a pilgrimage site of the Shrine of the Precious Blood of Christ (Klamer and Throsby, 2000: 130–45; European Commission, 2007; Choi et al., 2010: 213–20; Throsby et al., 2010).

Careful coordination of dual funding (research was financed by the Croatian Ministry of Culture and by the Ludbreg municipality) facilitated the achievement of outstanding results in a short period. During the four seasons of excavations, small baths and a sizeable (presumably) public building were discovered. Archaeological excavations (2008–11; the last season of excavations was still ongoing at the time of writing) were conducted by the Croatian Conservation Institute.

As demonstrated during the first archaeological excavations, the centre of modern Ludbreg was continuously inhabited over the past two millennia. Each new generation completely demolished older structures to build the new ones. Hence, there was no stratigraphy and it was only possible to determine a mixture of layers, from the La Tène culture to modern layers (visible mainly as installations and sewers). The Somogy garden was also intersected (and therefore devastated) by many utility installations and modern infrastructure.

During the first three seasons of excavations (2008–10), a small *balnea* situated in the south-eastern part of the Somogy garden was discovered. The Iovian baths

(231 m²) belong to a group of smaller city baths, widespread throughout the Empire. Built as compact, unpartitioned buildings (*Blocktyp*), they fulfilled the rules of economical and structural efficiency. This Iovian example was built as an irregular rectangular building with *apodytierii* (changing rooms), a *tepidarium* (warm bath), *frigidarium* (cold bath), *caldarium* (hot bath), and a small *sudatorium* (steam room). Similar baths were discovered in Baden-Baden, Pforzheim-Hagenschieß, Saint-Rémy de-Provence, and Heilbronn-Wartberg (Smith, 1875: 188; Durm, 1904: 200–17, 700–18; Heinz, 1983: 9–23, 176–85; Yegül, 1992: 48–91). Although these baths did not confirm aforementioned hypothesis of an Early Christian diocese, the results were valuable enough to ensure the continuation of excavations on a larger scale, that is, over the entire area of the Somogy garden (Figure 2).

On the northern side of the baths, a large portion of a (presumably public) building was discovered (assumed total area: *c.* 1500 m²) (Figure 3). The dimensions had to be estimated by extrapolation and mirroring symmetry of all collected data with ILRIS-3D laser scanning because of the Somogy house and its very deep foundations (Figure 4). Its western façade was defined by a colonnaded portico. Through the porch one could enter a wide space divided into five rectangular rooms. This building was remodelled during several construction phases, but it is still not possible to deduce their precise sequential order or how they changed the primary function of the main building. This point is mainly emphasized with two constructional interventions. The first was a large semicircular space that was built alongside the southern façade of the south-eastern room of the main building, while the second one was done along the eastern façade. With a bias of 2° in relation to the southern façade of the

FIGURE 2   Aerial photograph of the small baths after the archaeological excavations in 2009.
Photograph by J. Kliska; by permission of the Croatian Conservation Institute, Zagreb

FIGURE 3   Aerial photograph of the site after archaeological excavations in 2010.
Photograph by J. Kliska; by permission of the Croatian Conservation Institute, Zagreb

structure's main section, a (presumed) rectangular space was built. This space was modelled around a courtyard defined with corridors (only the western and southern corridors were discovered by the end of excavations in 2010). A wing with five smaller rectangular spaces was found alongside the southern corridor. Since the excavations within the Somogy garden have not been completed, it is still not possible to determine the function of the architecture or specify the date of construction and interaction of the researched buildings.

The documentation made by ILRIS-3D scanning (Intelligent Laser Ranging and Imaging System) and GPR (ground-penetrating radar) was incorporated in the land register and compared to aerial photographs. Worthwhile noting here is that a Z+F Imager5006i, the fastest scanner in the small- and medium-range class (500,000 points per second) was used for 3D data gathering. These data, shown as a geo-referenced

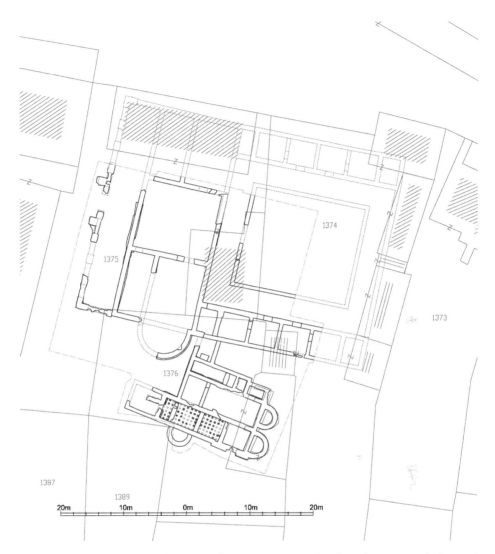

FIGURE 4   Ground plan of the site with ideal reconstruction based on extrapolation and mirroring symmetry of the data collected with ILRIS-3D laser scanning ('Vektra-Geo3D').
By permission of the Croatian Conservation Institute, Zagreb

3D model in a point cloud shape (Polyworks application), were processed by a CAD program, obtaining a polygonal mesh 3D model as the final product. The data may be further used to make 3D animation (Autodesk Maya application) or a CAD wire model (TIN) (Figure 5). By using extrapolation and mirroring symmetry of all collected data (via the above methods), it was possible to assume that a large (presumably) public building with a colonnaded portico was situated on the eastern side of the *cardo*, while the northern façade of the same building followed the southern line of the *decumanus*. The general Roman urban layout of the main communications was utilized throughout the centuries, so that the hypothesis of Holy Trinity Square overlapping the Roman forum is quite possible (Pleše, in press).

FIGURE 5   Aerial photograph of the site after archaeological excavations in 2010 with results of GPR scanning.
Photographed by J. Kliska; GPR scanning by 'Dr Beton'; by permission of the Croatian Conservation Institute, Zagreb

Management plan for the 'Iovia-Ludbreg' archaeological site

The decision to pursue the idea of presenting this Roman site was made on the basis of several factors. First, that was the clear scholarly value, as new data will enhance the rather meagre knowledge of Roman settlements in the Croatian part of Roman province of Pannonia. Equally important was the enhancement of cultural (very few archaeological parks in Croatia), social (awareness of the Roman heritage by the local population), and economic (endorsing small and medium-sized local businesses) value. Furthermore, since the site is easily legible and therefore relatively simple to present, it would be a great loss not to make the most of its educational value. Because of these factors, instead of reburying after excavations, the decision was made to present this site as an archaeological park and open-air museum (Klamer, 1997: 74–87; Klamer, 2003: 10–12; European Commission 2005; 2006).

Strategic planning

Although archaeological excavations are still ongoing, it was very important to ensure written confirmation of release of the Somogy garden from the municipal authorities to ensure that the site is not used for some other function. By obtaining this confirmation, which legally defined the Somogy garden as an archaeological park, it was possible for preparations to continue.

A cost effectiveness study concerning the modes of presentation and final conservation of this archaeological site was compiled. Employing management principles, the project's main vision is to open a self-sustaining, open-air museum within ten years (as of the beginning of excavations). The mission statement was formulated through the scholarly aim of supplementing knowledge on the Croatian part of the Roman province of Pannonia and making this site a mainstay of Outdoor Education Days (required by the *curricula* of elementary and secondary schools). Another mission principle was the strategy rooted in the merger of strong religious tourism (based on pilgrimages to the Shrine of the Precious Blood of Christ) as well as with other open-air museums in the northern parts of the Roman province of Pannonia, for example, *Flavia Solva* (Leibniz, Austria), *Poetovio* (Ptuj, Slovenia), and *Aquae Iasae* (Varaždinske Toplice, Croatia). The value of this site is defined by making it the hub of successful collaboration between the local community and researchers. It is hoped that the open-air museum will effectively meld both scholarly and popular demands, up-to-date techniques of excavation and documentation, proper conservation and restoration methods, and a diverse tourism product. By adhering to these principles, we ensured that this valuable archaeological site would avoid the fate of excavated monuments that were later abandoned and forgotten.

Conservation of the site

All excavated structures were built out of Lithothamnium limestone from local quarries in compliance with standard Roman construction techniques (predominantly *opus mixtum*, as well as *opus caementicium* and *opus spicatum*). All structures were found in a stable, solid condition.

The foundations of the baths excavated in 1969 and 1971 were conserved with cement mortar (Figures 6 and 7). Before its repair, this part was used for experiments on application of different types of stone and binding materials. By using these data, it was possible to gain insight into the best way to permanently preserve the entire

FIGURE 6   View of the south-eastern part of the small baths before conservation-restoration construction works.
Photograph by J. Kliska; by permission of the Croatian Conservation Institute, Zagreb

FIGURE 7   View of the south-eastern part of the small baths after conservation-restoration
construction works.
Photograph by J. Kliska; by permission of the Croatian Conservation Institute, Zagreb

site. Based on observation of the applied materials, the decision was made to proceed
with conservation — restoration works by using limestone from the local quarry
(most closely matching the features of the original stone) bound with a lime mortar
mixture. Testing of the different mixtures is ongoing, and the one that meets all
specifications will be used as the final solution.

   After the completion of the conservation — restoration works on the foundations
and the construction of a drainage system, the original Roman walking surface will
be levelled. Alignment with the higher surrounding level will be accomplished with
several unobtrusive low steps, thus avoiding visually aggressive fences and structures.
All communications will be adapted for disabled persons and strollers.

Presentation plan for the site

The presentation plan was drafted with regard to the site's specific situation. The plan
encompassed the scholarly and professional demands concerning conservation *in situ*,
combined with the needs of successful cultural management, thus resulting in alignment between the latter two factors as well as cost-effectiveness. Since excavations at
the site are drawing to a close, it was possible to launch a conservation study. Given
the fact that mainly building foundations were found (due to the aforementioned
reasons), a decision had to be made as to how to present them. Complete restoration
(in the manner of *Carnuntum*, present-day villages of Petronell and Bad Deutsch-
Altenburg, Austria) was out of the question due to the lack of data. Presentation of
the site at ground level was dismissed because in the long run it is very expensive to
maintain and also hard for visitors to understand. Building a structure over the entire
site would be very complex and rather difficult to justify. Reburial of the site was not
taken into consideration due to all of the reasons cited above. Therefore, conservation
of the foundations and restoration of the walls in a height of approximately 120 cm
was chosen, as this will secure clear visual communication with visitors. Although

this solution is not ideal (and since researchers could only advise and make any final decisions), the municipal authorities were very clear that the chosen method would have to satisfy the needs of their comprehensive socio-economical development plan.

Archaeological park and open-air museum

At each visually expressive point, a 3D reconstruction with a brief, simple explanation will be set up, thus emphasizing the accessibility of information. In the northeastern part of the site, several Roman military tents with Roman games (*latrunculi*, *reges*, *duodecim scripta*, etc.) will be displayed. The whole site, according to the landscaping study, will be defined with 'green walls' that will also define the boundaries with neighbouring properties. A dilapidated two-storey building in the northeastern corner of the estate was torn down, thus improving the visual ambience and making space for the educational corner. The south-eastern part of the Somogy garden will be left unexplored for the next generations and future technology.

The only remaining building on the estate (the Somogy house) will be reused. One part will be remodelled as the head office of the tourism board. Among its primary functions, it will provide exemplary protection of the site and enable monitoring of the entrance. A small museum will be arranged in the other part of the Somogy house. A permanent display, formed as a cross-section of Ludbreg from prehistory to the present, will be based on archaeological finds, that is, a glass La Tène bracelet, Roman coins, and Roman, medieval, and Early Modern pottery. The excavated part of Roman *Iovia* will be explained through 3D interactive models and videos. The Ministry of Tourism will finance maintenance of the tourism board and Varaždin County will finance the museum. The third part of the Somogy house will (probably) be converted into an exclusive wine cellar. The annual lease revenues will be directly used to maintain the site.

The first series of souvenirs with a trademark (Iovia-Ludbreg) were introduced to successfully promote Iovia. These souvenirs were made in cooperation with the municipal authorities and produced exclusively by local small and medium-sized businesses, thus serving as an anti-recessionary measure. The collection is represented by two Roman coins (a nummus of Maximianus and a denarius of Lucilla, both made of zamak, an alloy of zinc, aluminium, magnesium, and copper), *Conditum paradoxum* (made according to the instructions from *De Re Coquinaria* by Apicius), *Mel Ioviae* (acacia honey), *Spiritus mellis Ioviae* (mead), and *Spiritus pruni cerasi Ioviae* (cherry brandy), an homage from Ludbreg's beekeepers and winemakers to their Roman ancestors. Apart from these souvenirs, a collection of environmental tote bags, T-shirts, caps, mugs, and so on, all with the Iovia-Ludbreg trademark, will also be available.

Since all of these activities brought immense changes to the small town of Ludbreg, it was necessary to raise the local population's awareness: therefore, a mesh banner with aerial photographs, a 3D display, and a simple text were set up in the main square (near the main entrance to the site), which were updated at the end of each season of excavations (Figure 8). Any suggestions for improvements to this public project can be made on the town's official website. There is also a strong media campaign (Internet, television, daily press) as well as annual public lectures that inform the wider public of the progress of excavations.

FIGURE 8   Ideal 3D reconstruction of the small baths ('Vektra-Geo3D').
By permission of the Croatian Conservation Institute, Zagreb

Concluding remarks

The *Iovia*-Ludbreg project can be considered a model of successful, interdisciplinary collaboration between the national government, municipal authorities, and researchers, all of them acting for the benefit of the site and its visitors. Cost-effectiveness was achieved through adherence to legal guidelines and fundamental management principles. By applying all of the aforementioned principles, which were set forth more as guidelines than rigid edicts, it was possible to provide a sound, legally secure future for this site.

Bibliography

Choi, A. S., Ritchie, B. W., Papandrea, F., and Bennett, J. 2010. Economic Valuation of Cultural Heritage Sites: A Choice Modelling Approach. *Tourism Management*, 31: 213–20.

Deluka, A., Dragcevic, V., and Rukavina, T. 2003. Roman Roads in Croatia. *Proceedings of the First International Congress on Construction History*, pp. 733–42.

Durm, J. 1905. *Handbuch der Architektur (Zweiter Teil: Die Baustille. Historische und Technische Entwickelung)*. Stuttgart.

Egger, R. 1924. Historisch-topographische Studien in Venezien. *Jahreshefte des Österreichischen Archäologischen Institutes*, 21–22: 327–41.

European Commission 2005. Enhancing the Values of Urban Archaeological Sites. A Practical Guide. Ed. M. Fohn, M. Tinant, and A. Warnotte. Research Report 30/3. Available at: <http://www.in-situ.be/draft_en.pdf>.

European Commission 2006. The APPEAR Method. A Practical Guide for the Management of Enhancement Project on Urban Archaeological Sites. *Research Report* 30/4. Available at: <http://www.in-situ.be/guide_en.pdf>.

European Commission 2007. Managing Archaeological Remains in Towns & Cities from Discovery to Sustainable Display. Available at: <http://139.165.122.87/downloads/Appear.pdf>.

Gračanin, H. 2010. Rimske prometnice i komunikacije u kasnoantičkoj južnoj Panoniji (Summary: Roman Roads and Communications in Late Antique South Pannonia). *Scrinia Slavonica*, 10: 9–69.

Gregl, Z. and Migotti, B. 2004. Civitas Iovia (Botivo). *Situla*, 42: 131–43.

Heinz, W. 1983. *Römische Thermen — Badewesen und Badeluxus im Römischen Reich*. München.

Jarak, M. 1994. Povijest starokršćanskih zajednica na tlu kontinentalne Hrvatske [The History of Early Christian Communities in Continental Croatia]. In: Ž. Demo, ed. *Od nepobjedivog sunca do sunca pravde*. Zagreb, pp. 17–39.

Klamer, A. 1997. The Value of Cultural Heritage. In: M. Hutter and I. E. Rizzo, eds. *Economic Perspectives on Cultural Heritage*. London, pp. 74–87.

Klamer, A. 2003. A Pragmatic View on Values in Economics. *Journal of Economic Methodology*, pp. 10–12. Available at: <http://www.klamer.nl/docs/pragmatic.pdf>

Klamer, A. and Throsby, D. 2000. Paying for the Past: The Economics of Cultural Heritage. In: *World Culture Report*. Paris: UNESCO Publishing, pp. 130–45.

Mayer, A. 1935. Iasi. *Vijesnik hrvatskog arheološkog društva*, 16: 69–82.

Migotti, B. 1994. Arheološka građa iz ranokršćanskog razdoblja u kontinentalnoj Hrvatskoj [The Archaeological Material of the Early Christian Period in Continental Croatia]. In: Ž. Demo, ed. *Od nepobjedivog sunca do sunca pravde*. Zagreb, pp. 41–67.

Migotti, B. 2002. Early Christianity in Aquae Iasae (Varaždinske Toplice) and Iovia (Ludbreg) in Pannonia Savia. *Zalai Múzeum*, 11: 51–66.

Mócsy, A. 1974. *Pannonia and Upper Moesia*. London-Boston.

Pleše, T. In press. Iovia-Botivo (Ludbreg): prilog poznavanju kroz rezultate arheoloških istraživanja 2008–2010 [Contribution to our Knowledge of Iovia-Botivo (Ludbreg) as a Result of Archaeological Excavations in 2008–2010]. *Izdanja Hrvatskog arheološkog društva*.

Smith, W. 1875. *A Dictionary of Greek and Roman Antiquities*. London.

Throsby, D. et al. 2010. Measuring the Economic and Cultural Values of Historic Heritage Places. *Environmental Economics Research Hub — Research Reports from the Economics and Environment Network Symposium*, Canberra. Available at: <http://purl.umn.edu/107584>.

Tomičić, Ž. 1997. Arheološka topografija i toponimija (Iovia — Botivo — Ludbreg). In: K. Horvat Levaj and I. Reberski, eds. *Ludbreg — Ludbreška Podravina*. Zagreb, pp. 21–41.

Vikić Belančić, B. 1984. Sustavna istraživanja u Ludbregu od 1968–1979 [Systematic Excavations at Ludbreg 1968–1979]. *Vijesnik Arheološkog muzeja u Zagrebu*, 16–17: 119–66.

Yegül, F. 1992. *Baths and Bathing in Classical Antiquity*. Cambridge.

Note on contributor

Tajana Pleše (PhD in Archaeology, from the Faculty of Arts and Letters, University of Zagreb, 2010) is a senior conservator-archaeologist in the Croatian Conservation Institute (Division for Archaeological Heritage, Department of Land Archaeology) and head researcher of *Iovia-Botivo* (Ludbreg), the late medieval burgs of Garić and Krčingrad (Plitvice Lakes National Park), and late medieval Pauline monasteries (Lepoglava, Streza, Zlat, Moslavina highlands, and Šenkovec). She has published a number of original scholarly and research papers and participated in several international conferences.

Correspondence to: Tajana Pleše, Department of Land Archaeology, Division of Archaeological Heritage, Croatian Conservation Institute, Kožarska 5, Croatia — 10000 Zagreb. Email: tplese@h-r-z.hr

CONSERVATION AND MGMT OF ARCH. SITES, Vol. 14 Nos 1–4, 2012, 322–32

Advisory Commissions for Archaeology — Sense or Nonsense? The Case of Belgium

Jonas Van Looveren

Faculty of Design Sciences, Artesis University College, Antwerp University Association, Belgium

Belgium has a long tradition of consultative commissions, responsible for the preservation of heritage. In the 1940s and 1950s, Belgian archaeologists expressed a need for such an institute, specifically competent for archaeology and the supervision of excavations. Only in 1965, the first members of a National Commission for Excavations were appointed. They had modest powers, but were able to advocate the value of archaeological heritage and, to a limited extent, supervise fieldwork performed by amateurs. The Commission was also asked to prepare a legal text that would protect archaeological heritage. However, ratified laws were not accomplished and, despite much regret of Belgian archaeologists, the Commission was abolished in 1979.

During the 1980s, Belgium underwent several state reforms which ultimately resulted in the complete regionalization of archaeology (1988–89). Throughout this period, a shift in opinion occurred between Walloon (French-speaking) and Flemish (Dutch-speaking) archaeologists. This resulted in different arrangements of governmental agencies responsible for immovable heritage and archaeology. Nonetheless, as UNESCO had recommended in 1968, all three Belgian regions (including the Brussels-Capital Region) installed advisory commissions that were involved in the preservation *in situ* of archaeological remains. However, these consultative bodies had little influence on politics and policy. Especially in Flanders, the Archaeological Council achieved very little. Probably, the lack of continuity retained the Council from building up a reputation and authority. Nevertheless, advisory commissions for archaeology do make sense in Belgium. They provide a necessary 'forum' to discuss problems and to express undivided opinions; they form a 'channel' to communicate with policy makers; and they present an 'instrument' for advocating the preservation of archaeological heritage.

KEYWORDS Belgium, archaeological heritage management, governmental agencies, legislation, preservation *in situ*

    DOI 10.1179/1350503312Z.00000000028

Introduction

In 1968, UNESCO advised their member states to give responsibility for *in situ* preservation of endangered cultural property, to a representatively composed consultative body. Indeed, several countries had and have advisory institutions for immovable heritage (e.g. the British Council for British Archaeology, the French Commission interrégionale de la recherche archéologique, and the Dutch Monumentencommissies). The Belgian regions (Flanders, Brussels, and Wallonia) all have commissions charged with archaeology and excavations. This is no coincidence, seeing that Belgium has much experience with and a strong tradition of consultative commissions for the preservation of cultural resources. However, as I will show, the Belgian commissions for archaeology nevertheless knew a difficult genesis. Furthermore, for a number of reasons, these commissions struggled to fulfil their quest for the preservation *in situ* of archaeological heritage. This paper will explore why. In addition, I will study the commissions' success and failure. Finally, I will reflect on why consultative bodies for archaeology do make sense within the Belgian context.

The seeds for an archaeological advisory commission

In 1835, shortly after the Belgian independence, a Royal Commission for Monuments (Commission royale des Monuments) was founded. In Europe, it was the first policy body of this nature (Stynen, 1985: 6).[1] However, Belgium was far less progressive with respect to buried archaeology. It was only in 1903 that the Royal Museums for Art and History founded a Service for Excavations. This was the first official institute for archaeology in Belgium (Meylemans et al., 2005: 6). However, the legal framework for protecting archaeological sites and other forms of immovable heritage was nonexistent. In 1909, this situation seemed to change when the Royal Commission published a bill for a *loi sur la conservation des monuments et des sites*. Originally, the proposed bill contained arrangements for archaeological research. However, when the 'Monuments and Landscapes Act' was implemented in 1931, the articles on excavations were left out (Stynen, 1998: 267); at the time, objections about the implied limitations on private property were too strong (Archives of the Belgian Senate, 1929). On the other hand, built heritage and landscapes that were of national interest, for historic, artistic, or scientific reasons, could be designated (legally protected). This way visible, often excavated archaeological sites could gain protection from the Belgian State (Draye and Reap, 2008). Invisible sites, known through field survey, historical research, or other non-destructive methods, could however not gain this form of protection.

After the Second World War, Belgian archaeologists became more and more concerned with this lawlessness. One of Belgium's first professors of 'national' archaeology, Sigfried J. De Laet (1949: 22) stated: 'The situation is thus serious, very serious. Half a million years of our national history are at risk through lack of legislation and proper organization'. He therefore proposed several solutions, one of which was the foundation of a Conseil National des Fouilles Archéologiques (National Council for Archaeological Excavations). According to De Laet, this Council was to be composed of representatives of the Ministry of Culture, the state museums, the universities, the national fund for scientific research, and the provinces. The Council was to have a monopoly over all excavations on Belgian territory (which could be outsourced) and to support the publication of excavation reports. De Laet was evidently inspired by the Dutch State Commission for Archaeological Investigations and by several comparable Belgian institutes that existed for Monuments and Landscapes, History, and Ethnography (Roosens, 1962: 209).

In May 1949, a Comité consultatif des fouilles (Advisory Committee for Excavations) was indeed founded by the Royal Museums for Art and History. Its task was to supervise the Excavation Service and to coordinate communication with other bodies involved in archaeological research. Additionally, its members were to advise the relevant minister about all matters concerning excavations (Belgisch Staatsblad, 1949). However, the responsibilities given to the Consultative Committee were clearly not satisfactory. Art history professor Herman F. Bouchery (1955: 23), for example, stated that a National Council for Archaeology was needed to play an inquisitorial role. According to him, the members were to supervise ownership and preservation of artefacts, monitor the publication of excavation results, and inspect whether excavations met legal and scientific demands. Bouchery thus wanted to offer the Council the authority to suspend excavations. Furthermore, he envisioned the Council would be a coordinating institute that offered grants for excavations. Also Jean Verheyleweghen (1958: 214–19), president of the Royal Society for Anthropology and Prehistory, suggested to create an independent commission that would coordinate archaeological research. As there was 'no global supervision of research, and nobody in Belgium knew where, when and how was being excavated'.

The National Commission for Excavations

In 1958, the efforts of De Laet, Bouchery, and Verheyleweghen achieved result. A royal resolution led to the creation of a National Commission for Excavations and a National Service for Excavations, disconnected and independent from the Royal Museums for Art and History (Belgisch Staatsblad, 1958). However, no commission members were appointed and the Comité consultatif des fouilles had been abolished. According to Heli Roosens (1962: 209), the director of the National Service for Excavations, this was very problematic. He believed the absence of a commission had lead to incoordination of archaeological research and mistrust between amateurs and official archaeologists. Moreover, Belgium was still lacking archaeology legislation and Roosens postulated that this would only be accomplished through a National Commission for Excavations. In 1965, the commission members were finally appointed, including De Laet, Verheyleweghen, and Roosens. Frère, a judge and legal expert, was chosen as chairman (Belgisch Staatsblad, 1965). This clearly illustrated the fact that the Commission was to prepare a legal text regarding archaeological heritage and research. Furthermore, the National Commission was to provide advice and solutions to problems with excavations and the allocation of artefacts (Belgisch Staatsblad, 1958). Mostly, though, the commission members dealt with the assignment of grants to archaeological associations that wanted to conduct fieldwork. The societies that accepted funding were submitted to supervision and inspection from the commission members. This way, the quality of their work could be guaranteed (Archives of G. De Boe).

In October 1973, the National Commission for Excavations finished the requested legal draft (Archives of J. Fleerackers, 1974a). In the prepared bill, the Commission explicitly referred to the UNESCO Recommendation of 1954 and the European Convention of 1969. Amongst the protective provisions, the Commission proposed to temporarily safeguard scheduled archaeological zones. The members claimed that, this way, archaeological reserve zones could be created. However, in reality, their bill would only have resulted in salvage archaeology when construction involving ground disturbance took place within these zones. The possibility of withholding building permits was not foreseen.

For more permanent and long-lasting designation, the text referred to the Belgian Monuments and Landscapes Act of 1931, which was only applicable to fully excavated or visible sites. The 1931 Act was enforced by the Royal Commission for Monuments and Landscapes, which, however, was considered to be careless of archaeological remains. Roosens (1973: 18), for example, sceptically stated: 'Is it not ironic that the benefits, offered by the law, have been so little used?'. Although he also admitted that archaeologists as well could be blamed: 'Whether the reason is the Commission's lack of interest for the remains of our distant past, or negligence by archaeologists themselves, this situation has adverse consequences for the protection of our archaeological heritage'. The members of the National Commission for Excavations therefore probably tried to gain a distinct role in the protection of archaeological remains. Through their proposed legislation, they sought to expand their involvement with the advice on and the nomination of sites suitable for temporary and long-term designation (Archives of D. Coens, n.d.).

Nonetheless, the National Commission did not accomplish a ratified Archaeology Act. At that time, Belgium was undergoing institutional reforms that eventually gave cultural autonomy to the French-speaking, Dutch-speaking, and German-speaking communities. In other words, they formed separate cultural 'parliaments' alongside the national parliament (De Pauw, 2005). Consequently, this led to confusion about which level had authority over archaeology (Archives of J. Fleerackers, 1974b; 1974c). As a result, the drafted legislative documents were never submitted to any parliament. Moreover, when the Commission's second mandate ended in 1977, it was not renewed. A 'National' Commission had become redundant.[2]

Attempts to fill the void

The dissolution of the National Commission for Excavations caused disappointment amongst archaeologists. The bill, drafted by the National Commission, was remembered as a sound and useful document that was supported by all interest groups. This support had been the result of the Commission's balanced composition (Archives of L. Van Impe, n.d.).[3] It is therefore no surprise that several interest groups, active in drafting archaeology legislation during the 1980s, suggested the reinstatement of a representatively composed advisory board.[4] However, French-speaking (Walloon) and Dutch-speaking (Flemish) Belgian archaeologists seemed to have had different opinions on its tasks. In Walloon bills, the Council for Archaeological Excavations was thought to have a central and coordinating position. This even included granting, or rejecting, permissions to excavate. Contrary, in Flemish bills, the Council's role in the protection of *in situ* archaeological heritage was highlighted. The Flemish

Archaeological Council was to nominate suitable zones for designation, and to recommend them to the relevant minister (Archives of F. Vermeulen, 1983; Archives of D. Coens, 1986; Archives of the Flemish Parliament, 1986–87).

However, politically and institutionally, the time was not yet right for the implementation of archaeology legislation. By the end of the 1980s and due to new State Reforms, Belgium transformed from a unitary country to a federal state consisting of three communities, which had power over matters linked to 'people', and three regions, which had power over matters linked to 'territory'. The authority on immovable heritage was completely regionalized and was now the independent jurisdiction of Flanders, Brussels, and Wallonia. This finally made the implementation of archaeology legislation achievable.

Regional archaeological councils

Wallonia

The Walloon government (c. 16,800 km²) voted on their archaeology legislation in 1991 (Belgisch Staatsblad, 1992: 5). The Walloon Region clearly opted for an integral approach of its immovable heritage management. The budgets and francophone personnel of the National Service for Excavations were transferred to the Walloon administration for immovable heritage (Matthys, 1992: 285–87). Additionally, the Walloon division of the Royal Commission for Monuments and Landscapes was supplemented with a section for excavations. This section was given a central position in the organization of archaeological fieldwork. The Commission was to give advice on granting licenses for excavations and the recognition of archaeological sites as 'patrimoine exceptionnel de Wallonie' (only to be excavated by or in cooperation with universities, scientific institutes or the Walloon administration for immovable heritage) and 'for the benefit of the public' (the relevant minister could then suspend construction works, withdraw building permits, and/or expropriate a site if archaeological remains were found by chance). Furthermore, its members were to advise administrations and the relevant minister on all matters linked to archaeology, including the designation of buried and unexcavated archaeological sites. All designations of archaeological sites were to be based on an archaeological atlas, or inventory, which would indicate a hierarchy of importance and which would also be used for spatial planning. In addition, designation as 'monument' or 'site' remained an option.

Until now, designations as 'archaeological site' occurred sporadically in the Walloon Region, resulting in nine designations (DGO4, n.d.). However, in 1999, fourteen archaeological sites (that were designated as monument or landscape) gained the status of 'exceptional heritage' (Belgisch Staatsblad, 1999), in 2006 four (Belgisch Staatsblad, 2006), and in 2009 thirty-one (including 25 tumuli-sites) (Belgisch Staatsblad, 2009). As such, the archaeological subsoil of these monuments and landscapes also gained additional legal protection.

Brussels

The Brussels-Capital Region (c. 161 km²) implemented archaeology legislation in 1993 (Belgisch Staatsblad, 1993a). Regarding the organization of the governmental agencies, Brussels followed the Walloon example. Moreover, emergency excavations became possible on the basis of archaeological atlases. Long-term preservation *in situ* was enabled through designation as archaeological site. The Brussels' Commission was to recommend and advise on monuments, landscapes, and archaeological sites suitable for designation, and on modifications of legally protected goods. The small Brussels-Capital Region has designated six archaeological sites (Ministerie van het Brussels Hoofdstedelijk Gewest — Directie Monumenten en Landschappen).

Flanders

The Flemish Region (*c.* 13,500 km²) voted on their Archaeology Decree in 1993 (Belgisch Staatsblad, 1993b). As expected, the Flemish Region also reinstituted an advisory board: the Flemish Archaeological Council or Vlaamse Archeologische Raad. The composition of this Council had to reflect and represent the diverse archaeological sector. Its members had to provide the minister with advice at his request or on their own initiative (Belgisch Staatsblad, 1994). The eventual mandate of the Council was similar to that of the National Commission for Excavations. Nevertheless, the emphasis of the Council's task was strongly put on actively contributing to the protection and promotion of archaeological heritage. The implementation of the Valetta Convention (1992) was not accomplished through the Flemish Archaeology Decree, as the legislative process had already reached its final stage when the convention was issued. However, this decree did enable the designation of archaeological zones and monuments. Since this designation was more or less permanent (Draye and Reap, 2008: 333), the administration became capable to opt for a site's *in situ* preservation if it was endangered. All other sites were preserved *ex situ* (i.e. excavated), when threatened by ground disturbance from construction commissioned by the federal, regional or local governments (Belgisch Staatsblad, 1993).

The Flemish Archaeological Council held its first meeting in November 1995. From the start, the Council took its advisory role seriously. Throughout its meetings, the members discussed and reasoned opinions on various subjects like for example legislation and implementing integrated archaeological heritage management. Often, the Council's recommendations were fruitless attempts with little impact on policy. This included several themes which, today, still form the subject of discussion for a solution (for instance, the need for archaeological depots, the implementation of the Valetta Convention, and the insertion of archaeological zones in the Flemish spatial structure plan) (Archives of the Flemish Archaeological Council, VIOE and Province of Antwerp).

At every gathering, the Council left room for discussing archaeological sites that were suitable for legal protection. Had the Council prepared documents for enlisting archaeological monuments, they would have been able to advise the minister to take the necessary actions. However, the advisory board never produced such files. Its members attributed their failure to their inexperience with the (young and new) regulations, limited time and understaffing of the Flemish Archaeological Heritage Institute. On the other hand, the Flemish Minister of Immovable Heritage did not take any initiative, ask questions, or demand advice from the Council concerning the designation of specific archaeological sites (Archives of the Flemish Archaeological Council, 1995; 1996a; 1997). The Council was thus not the only one to blame. Furthermore, its members were definitely aware of what the consequences could be.

In 1998, for example, one of them uttered that the longer they waited before legally protecting archaeological heritage, the less credible archaeologists would become (Archives of the Flemish Archaeological Council, 1998). The Council therefore tried to analyse the failing process of enlistment. In 2001, the members compared the preservation of archaeological heritage with the preservation of historic buildings and landscapes. They concluded that, with regard to built and natural heritage, initiatives for legal safeguarding were taken far more seriously by their guardian administrations and based on an inventory.[5] Furthermore, it was decided that the Archaeology Decree was not to be blamed. The Council concluded that an archaeological inventory[6] and a specialised team were needed for the preservation of archaeological heritage (Archives of the Flemish Archaeological Council, 2001).

The abovementioned problems were one of the reasons why the official institutes for immovable heritage were reorganized and rationalized in the Flemish Region. The reformation started in January 2004, when ten 'archaeological heritage managers' were hired by the Administration for Monuments and Landscapes (Van Daele et al., 2004: 45–46). Furthermore, the Flemish Archaeological Council was merged with the Flemish division of the Royal Commission for Monuments and Landscapes (Belgisch Staatsblad, 2004). Flanders thus achieved an administrative organization for immovable heritage, similar to Wallonia and Brussels. This had a positive influence on the failing protection policy. In April 2005, the Minister responsible for Immovable Heritage signed the first resolution that legally protected an archaeological zone: the Chartreuse area in Bruges. Nevertheless, the protection regime remained problematic. Eighteen years after the Flemish Archaeology Decree was ratified, only six archaeological sites gained the definitive status of protected monument or zone (Ruimte and Erfgoed, n.d.).[7]

Advisory commissions for archaeology — sense or nonsense?

In the 1940s and 1950s, Belgian archaeologists expressed a clear need for an institute that would supervise excavations. Clearly, not all fieldwork met up with scientific demands and ethics. Furthermore, problems with the allocation of artefacts (to museums) and grants (to archaeological associations) existed. It is obvious that this was the result of a lack of legislation. One of the solutions, offered by influential people like De Laet, was therefore to create a National Council for Excavations, composed of a balanced representation of the archaeological sector. It is probable that this was necessary to avoid conflicts. In 1949, a first Advisory Committee for Excavations was founded at the Royal Museums for Art and History. Although the committee's powers were very limited, the Committee did have the privilege of advising the relevant minister about excavations, and had induced a pacification between official and amateur archaeologists.

Nevertheless, Belgian archaeologists pursued the installation of an advising and coordinating body with authority and influence on a national scale. If only to know 'where, when and how was being excavated'. In 1965, a National Commission for Excavations was therefore assembled. This Commission had modest powers, but enabled advocating the value of archaeological heritage and, to a limited extent, scientific supervision over fieldwork. Most importantly, the members were to prepare a legal text that would protect archaeological heritage. The Commission's balanced composition did not lead to a progressive legislative proposal, but nevertheless secured the support of the entire archaeological sector. As was recommended by UNESCO, the commission members showed commitment towards the preservation of archaeological heritage and sought control over the designation of archaeological sites. However, institutional reforms prevented archaeology legislation to be voted and the National Commission for Excavations was no longer convened.

Belgium was being transformed into a federalized country. This resulted in regional differences when Flanders, Wallonia, and Brussels implemented archaeology legislation and created their own administrative substructures. Flemings chose to install an advisory board with less power but greater emphasis on preservation than its Walloon counterpart. Surprisingly, this is exactly the subject on which the Flemish Archaeological Council failed. Not only had the Council little influence on politics and policy, its members also seem to have had little belief in the designation of archaeological sites. Additionally, the organization of the administration for immovable heritage and the absence of important instruments like an inventory had a big impact on the stagnating situation.

In conclusion, we can state that the Belgian consultative bodies for archaeology had little impact on the preservation (*in situ*) of archaeological remains. Especially on Flemish side, the lack of continuity retained the consultative bodies from building up a reputation, preventing them from influencing politics. Under the wings of the Royal Commission for Monuments and Sites, an old and respected institute, the committee for archaeology can perhaps now affect decision-making. This is important, since advisory commissions for archaeology do make sense. Foremost, archaeologists need a 'forum' to discuss certain problems and to express undivided opinions; they need an official 'channel' to communicate these opinions to policy makers; and they need an 'instrument' for advocating the value of archaeological heritage, archaeological research and *in situ* preservation. The Belgian commissions unite archaeologists from different subfields and background, often with dissimilar opinions or visions about policy. A divided sector, though, is damaging for archaeological heritage and the reputation of archaeologists. A commission creates the possibility to defend archaeological heritage by speaking with a unified and unambiguous voice.

Notes

[1] The Royal Commission for Monuments was to give the Minister responsible for Heritage, advice on the preservation of valuable historical buildings. In 1912, the Commission was extended with a section for historical landscapes and urban sites and was renamed as 'Royal Commission for Monuments and Landscapes (Stynen, 1985).

[2] Contrary to the National Commission for Excavations, the Royal Commission for Monuments and Landscapes had been divided into two sections in 1968: one for the Dutch-speaking area and one for the French-speaking area. When dealing with the monumental heritage situated in the German-speaking area and in the bilingual (French-Dutch) area of Brussels, both the Dutch-speaking and the French-speaking sections of the Royal Commission for Monuments and Landscapes assembled together (Draye, 1993).

[3] The National Commission for Excavations was composed of researchers of the National Service for Excavations, university professors, museum curators, representatives of associations of amateur archaeologists, city archaeologists …

[4] After the aforementioned state reforms, the proposed archaeology legislations and advisory boards were now (mostly all) community-based.

[5] A thorough inventory of the Flemish archaeological heritage was non-existent. For too long, the focus of Flemish archaeology had been on research and not on preventive archaeological heritage management.

In 1996, the Council reported to the minister that such an instrument was absolutely necessary to implement a selective, yet consistent, preservation policy. The members therefore asked the minister to install an inventory team at the Flemish Archaeological Heritage Institute (Archives of the Flemish Archaeological Council, 1996b).

6 A Central Archaeological Inventory (Centrale Archeologische inventaris) was initiated in 2000 (Meylemans, 2004).

7 In Flanders, the low amount of designated archaeological sites will hopefully multiply in the near future. In 2010 the Flemish Heritage Institute started to develop a new inventory containing information on where sites are possibly preserved. It will show the archaeological potential of a place. This new inventory will hopefully form the basis of a more thorough and sensible designation regime for archaeological monuments (Handleiding voor het afbakenen van archeologische zones, 2010).

Bibliography

Belgisch Staatsblad. 12 August 1949. *Besluit van de Regent van 15 mei 1949 — Organiek reglement der Koninklijke Musea voor Kunst en Geschiedenis*, pp. 7732–34.

Belgisch Staatsblad. 23 April 1958. *Koninklijk Besluit van 29 maart 1958 betreffende de Dienst voor Oudheidkundige Opgravingen*, pp. 3030–31.

Belgisch Staatsblad. 11 August 1965. *Koninklijk Besluit van 19 april 1965 houdende de benoeming van de voorzitter, de ondervoorzitter en de leden van de Nationale Commissie voor Opgravingen*, pp. 9495–97.

Belgisch Staatsblad. 1 January 1992. *Décret du 18 juillet 1991 relatif aux monuments, aux sites et aux fouilles*, p. 5.

Belgisch Staatsblad. 7 April 1993a. *Ordonnantie van 4 Maart 1993 inzake het behoud van het onroerende erfgoed*, p. 7507.

Belgisch Staatsblad. 15 September 1993b. *Decreet van 30 juni 1993 houdende de bescherming van het archeologisch patrimonium*, p. 20414.

Belgisch Staatsblad. 7 April 1994. *Besluit van de Vlaamse regering van 12 januari 1994 betreffende de samenstelling en de werking van de Vlaamse Archeologische Raad*, pp. 9257–58.

Belgisch Staatsblad. 31 August 1999. *Besluit van de Waalse Regering van 3 juni 1999 tot vaststelling van de lijst van het uitzonderlijke onroerende patrimonium van het Waalse Gewest*, pp. 32238–46.

Belgisch Staatsblad. 16 April 2004. *Besluit van de Vlaamse Regering van 5 maart 2004 betreffende de samenstelling, de organisatie, de bevoegdheden en de werking van de Koninklijke Commissie voor Monumenten en Landschappen van het Vlaams Gewest*, pp. 22360–63.

Belgisch Staatsblad. 9 June 2006. *Besluit van de Waalse Regering van 11 mei 2006 tot vaststelling van de lijst van het uitzonderlijke onroerende patrimonium van het Waalse Gewest*, pp. 29774–86.

Belgisch Staatsblad. 17 August 2009. *Besluit van de Waalse Regering van 27 mei 2009 tot bepaling van de lijst van het buitengewoon onroerende erfgoed van het Waalse Gewest*, pp. 54441–62.

Bouchery H. F. 1955. *Noden en toekomst van de Vlaamse Kunstgeschiedenis*, Kortrijk: August Vermeylen-Fonds.

Council of Europe. 1969. *European Convention on the Protection of the Archaeological Heritage (ETS no. 066)*, London [accessed 11 January 2012]. Available at: <http://conventions.coe.int/Treaty/en/Treaties/html/066.htm>.

Council of Europe. 1992. *European Convention on the Protection of the Archaeological Heritage, revised (ETS no. 143)*, La Valetta. [accessed 11 January 2012]. Available at: <http://conventions.coe.int/Treaty/en/Treaties/html/143.htm>.

De Laet, S. J. 1949. Pour une protection efficace des sites, monuments et documents archéologiques, *Alumni. Tijdschrift van de Kring der Alumni van de Universitaire stichting*, pp. 15–28.

De Pauw, W. 2005. *Minister Dixit. Een geschiedenis van het Vlaamse Cultuurbeleid*. Antwerpen/Apeldoorn: Garant.

DGO4 (Direction générale opérationnelle — Aménagement du territoire, Logement, Patrimoine et Energie). N.d. Liste des biens classes [accessed 11 January 2012]. Available at: <http://lampspw.wallonie.be/dgo4/site_thema/index.php>.

Draye, A. M. 1993. *Monumenten en Landschappen in België: Juridische aspecten*. Maklu, Antwerpen and Apeldoorn.

Draye, A. M. and Reap, J. 2008. The protection of archaeological heritage. The United States and Belgium compared. In: B. Demarsin, E. J. H. Schrage, and B. Tilleman, eds. *Art & Law*. Brugge: Die Keure, pp. 322–38.

International Committee on Archaeological Heritage Management (ICAHM). 1990. *ICOMOS Charter for the Protection and Management of the Archaeological Heritage*, Lausanne.

Matthys, André. 1992. Het bestuur van de opgravingen in de Waalse regio. In: G. Bauchhenss, M. Otte, and W. J. H. Willems, eds. *Spurensicherung: archäologische Denkmalpflege in der Euregio Maas-Rhein*, Mainz: Zabern, pp. 284–94.

Meylemans, E. 2004. Drie jaar Centrale Archeologische Inventaris: een overzicht en stand van zaken. In: E. Meylemans, ed. *Centrale Archeologische Inventaris (CAI) I: De opbouw van een archeologisch beleidsinstrument*. IAP-rapporten 14. Brussel: Instituut voor het Archeologisch Patrimonium (IAP), pp. 9–28.

Meylemans E., De Decker, S., and Hofkens, E. 2005. *The Environmental Impact Assessment Procedure and Archaeological Heritage Management in Flanders. Past Present and Future (A Planarch II report)*. Brussels.

Ministerie van het Brussels Hoofdstedelijk Gewest — Directie Monumenten en Landschappen. 2011. Register van het beschermd onroerend erfgoed van het Brussels Hoofdstedelijk gewest [accessed 11 January 2012]. Available at: <http://www.monument.irisnet.be/nl/download/REGISTER/register_lijst_NL.pdf>.

Roosens H. 1962. Voor een Nationale Commissie voor Opgravingen. *Bulletin Koninklijk Instituut voor het Kunstpatrimonium*, 5: 209–11.

Roosens H. 1973. Préservation de sites archéologiques en Belgique. *Archaeologia Belgica*, 149.

Ruimte and Erfgoed. N.d. Databank beschermd erfgoed. [accessed 11 January 2012]. Available at: <www.erfgoed.net/beschermingen>.

Stynen H. 1985. De Koninklijke commissie voor monumenten en landschappen: een terugblik over de periode van 1835 tot de jaren zestig. *M&L — Monumenten, Landschappen & Archeologie*, 4(1): 6–31.

Stynen H. 1998. *De onvoltooid verleden tijd: een geschiedenis van de monumenten- en landschapszorg in België, 1835–1940*. Brussels: Stichting Vlaams Erfgoed.

Van Daele, K., Meylemans, E., and de Meyer M. 2004. De Centrale Archeologische Inventaris: een databank van archeologische vindplaatsen. In: E. Meylemans, ed. *Centrale Archeologische Inventaris (CAI) I: De opbouw van een archeologisch beleidsinstrument*. IAP-rapporten 14. Brussel: Instituut voor het Archeologisch Patrimonium (IAP), pp. 45–46.

Verheyleweghen J. 1958. Examen de la situation de la Recherche scientifique en ce qui concerne les sciences pré- et protohistoriques en Belgique. *Bulletin de la Société d'Anthropologie de Bruxelles*, 69: 214–19.

UNESCO. 1956. *Recommendation on International Principles Applicable to Archaeological Excavations*. New Delhi. Available at: <http://portal.unesco.org/en/ev.php-URL_ID=13062&URL_DO=DO_TOPIC&URL_SECTION=201.html>.

UNESCO. 1968. *Recommendation Concerning the Preservation of Cultural Property Endangered by Public or Private Works*, Paris. Available at: <http://portal.unesco.org/en/ev.php-URL_ID=13085&URL_DO=DO_TOPIC&URL_SECTION=201.html>.

VIOE (Vlaams Instituut voor Onroerend Erfgoed). 2010. Handleiding voor het afbakenen van archeologische zones [accessed 11 January 2012]. Available at: <http://www.vioe.be/images/uploads/content/downloads/Handleiding_voor_het_afbakenen_van_archeologische_zones_versie_101215.pdf>.

Archive material

Archives of the Belgian Senate. 15 January 1929. No. 52, Memorie van toelichting bij het wetsvoorstel op het behoud van monumenten en landschappen.

Archives of D. Coens, KADOC Documentatie- en Onderzoekscentrum voor Religie, Cultuur en Samenleving. N.d. *Werkdocument voor de leden van de Commissie 'voorontwerp van wet tot bescherming van het archeologisch patrimonium'*.

Archives of D. Coens, KADOC Documentatie- en Onderzoekscentrum voor Religie, Cultuur en Samenleving. 1986. *Voorontwerp van wet ter bescherming van het archeologisch Patrimonium*.

Archives of G. De Boe, privately owned. 1972–1977. *Nationale Commissie voor Opgravingen*.

Archives of J. Fleerackers, KADOC Documentatie- en Onderzoekscentrum voor Religie, Cultuur en Samenleving. 18 November 1974a. *Nota betreffende een voorontwerp van wet op het oudheidkundig bodemonderzoek*.

Archives of J. Fleerackers, KADOC Documentatie- en Onderzoekscentrum voor Religie, Cultuur en Samenleving. 25 November 1974b. *Letter from J. Fleerackers to O. Coenen and L.P. Suetens.*

Archives of J. Fleerackers, KADOC Documentatie- en Onderzoekscentrum voor Religie, Cultuur en Samenleving. 4 December 1974c. *Letter from L.P. Suetens to J. Fleerackers.*

Archives of the Flemish Archaeological Council, VIOE Vlaams Instituut voor Onroerend Erfgoed. 1995. *Jaarverslag.*

Archives of the Flemish Archaeological Council, VIOE Vlaams Instituut voor Onroerend Erfgoed. 1996a. *Jaarverslag.*

Archives of the Flemish Archaeological Council, VIOE Vlaams Instituut voor Onroerend Erfgoed. 15 March 1996b. *Letter from Frans Verhaeghe to the Minister of Immovable Heritage Luc Martens.*

Archives of the Flemish Archaeological Council, VIOE Vlaams Instituut voor Onroerend Erfgoed. 1997. *Jaarverslag.*

Archives of the Flemish Archaeological Council, VIOE Vlaams Instituut voor Onroerend Erfgoed. 15 April 1998. *Verslag van de bijeenkomst.*

Archives of the Flemish Archaeological Council, Provincial Government of Antwerp, Department of Culture. 9 February 2001. *Verslag van de vergadering van de werkgroep 'Beschermingen'.*

Archives of the Flemish Parliament. 1986–1987. Stuk 188, No. 1, *Voorstel van decreet houdende bescherming van het archeologisch patrimonium.*

Archives of F. Van Impe, privately owned. N.d. *Werknota over een rozig ideaal en de realiteit van een nationale wetenschappelijke Rijksinstelling.*

Archives of F. Vermeulen, University of Gent. N.d. *Ontwerp van Decreet tot bescherming van het Archeologisch Patrimonium.*

Notes on contributor

Jonas Van Looveren received a Master's degree in Archaeology from the Katholieke Universiteit Leuven and a Master's degree in Conservation of Monuments and Sites from the Artesis University College of Antwerp. Currently, he is a PhD candidate in Conservation of Monuments and Sites at the University of Antwerp. In his research, he focuses on the history of archaeological heritage management and the genesis of archaeology legislation in Belgium. His PhD research is financed by the Artesis University College of Antwerp.

Correspondence to: Jonas Van Looveren. Email: jonas.vanlooveren@artesis.be

CONSERVATION AND MGMT OF ARCH. SITES, Vol. 14 Nos 1–4, 2012, 333–40

A Qualitative Approach for Assessment of the Burial Environment by Interpreting Soil Characteristics; A Necessity for Archaeological Monitoring

BERTIL VAN OS, J. W. DE KORT, and HANS HUISMAN

Dutch Cultural Heritage Agency, Netherlands

Modern-day archaeological monitoring is often hampered by lack of money, lack of time, inadequate measuring equipment, and lack of insight in the conservation potential of a site.

Although in modern archaeological excavations soil characteristics are noted (colour, texture, groundwater level, and sometimes mineralogy), these characteristics are mainly used for the interpretation of a site. However, by looking to these characteristics from a conservational view eventually combined with the conservation status of the archaeological objects, much can be learned about the burial environment. This is essential for optimizing archaeological monitoring.

Degradation processes result from the change of reactive phases in the soil or the site. Reactive phases are soil components such as organic matter, sulfides, iron(hydr)oxides and carbonates (chalk, shells), and, if present, components in the ground or interstitial water such as hydrogen ions and sulphate. The presence of these phases can easily be established by the archaeologist or soil scientist in the field. We propose a simple field-based method for assessing degradation processes essential for in situ preservation and monitoring.

KEYWORDS archaeology, *in situ* preservation, reactive phases, monitoring, burial environment, soil

Introduction

Since the adoption of the treaty of Valetta in 1992, *in situ* preservation of archaeological remains should have become the guiding principle for threatened archaeology in Europe. For this reason, in the Netherlands an Archaeological Monitoring Standard (SAM) was developed in 2005 (Smit et al., 2006). In this standard, degradation

   DOI 10.1179/1350503312Z.00000000029

parameters for several types of archaeological remains were defined. In addition, an outline was given for setting up a monitoring scheme for sites. The emphasis of this work was on the technological part of *in situ* preservation and created a new specialist, the geoconservator. In the SAM the focus was primarily on specialist laboratory research on the degradation of archaeological material, or measuring degradation indicators in the field such as Eh and pH. This has led to the situation that in the process of conservation of a site, the assessment of a site is performed by the archaeologist. After that, the geoconservator decides independently what the risks of degradation are and what kind of monitoring should be applied. In the actual monitoring stage, the archaeologist is not involved.

In addition, most disturbers do not want to pay for 'expensive' monitoring for many years. Moreover, there is no consensus on which measures should be taken if certain decay thresholds are exceeded, and what the minimum time for monitoring for a specific site should be.

A simple method for assessing the burial environment would be very helpful to quickly determine the conservation potential of a site. This assessment should be performed by the field archaeologist and should immediately lead to a decision to excavate or to preserve a site *in situ*. In this paper, we will discuss the parameters that are important for site preservation. In modern-day archaeology these parameters are similar to the parameters that are used for assessment of a site. As an example, for the reconstruction of the past landscape, essential for evaluation of a site, important parameters are lithology, organic matter content, bioturbation, and carbonate content. Such information can also be used for assessing the conservation potential of a site. We present a parameter list that will enable the archaeologist to determine the conservation potential of a site.

Parameters

In most cases a site is an ensemble of soil features, finds, and landscape. Especially in agricultural areas, the survival of a site depends primarily on its depth. In the Netherlands, 90 per cent of the finds with known depth registered in the national archaeological database (ARCHIS) (10,000) have been found within the first metre below the surface (Beukers et al., 2009). This means that serious damage would occur if such sites are levelled or deep ploughed. *In situ* preservation in such cases requires a change in land use, for example from arable land into grassland.

Degradation occurs because archaeological remains are not resistant to the prevailing — or changing — burial conditions (Huisman, 2009). However, the fact that (intact) archaeological finds are present at a site indicates that preservation conditions have been adequate in the past.

The most reactive component in the soil is organic matter. The presence or absence of organic matter determines the impact of oxygen or other oxidizing substances (iron and manganese oxides, sulphate) on degradation processes. Textural characteristics and lithology — that is, the presence of clay, peat, or sand — also have a bearing on the transport of reactive components and water. A clayey soil will keep moisture trapped even if the groundwater level is several metres deep. Another factor of importance is the presence of lime, which will buffer pH values in the soil between 7.5 and 8. In organic rich coastal deposits like peat, the presence of pyrite is important, especially in reclaimed land areas like in the Dutch Polders where the groundwater table is artificially lowered. Oxidation of pyrite will lead to a dramatic lowering of the pH, gypsum formation and degradation of organic matter (Kaczorek and Sommer, 2003). Gypsum formation can then be used as a proxy for unfavourable burying conditions.

Yellow/red/brown colours indicate oxidized sediment or soils as, black, grey, or blue colours indicate the absence of oxygen thus suboxic or anoxic conditions. The latter conditions are in most cases favourable for the preservation of archaeological remains. Together with the conservation conditions of the archaeological finds, this will give a good estimation of the conservation potential and baseline.

An example of the parameters to be observed in the field by the archaeologist to assess the conservation potential of a site can be found in Table 1.

TABLE 1

CONSERVATION POTENTIAL AND BASELINE SURVEY PARAMETERS TO BE OBSERVED IN THE FIELD

Intactness and conservation	Qualification			
	intact	slightly degraded	degraded	disturbed
• Soil type and profile intactness • Geomorphology				
Archaeological remains • Wood • Textile/ leather • Bone • Seeds/organic remains • Charcoal • Soil features • Iron • Non-ferro metal • Ceramics • Glass • Flint				
Reactive components • Iron (hydr)oxides • CaCO3 • Sulfides • Gypsum • Organic matter/black layers				
Features Depth of	0–30	30–60	60–100	>100
• Thickness of agricultural/ tillage layer • Bioturbation • Oxidation/reduction boundary • Groundwater table • Vadose zone • (Groundwater) barriers • Soil moisture • (Clay) illuviation/eluviation				

Examples

From Figure 1 it is clear that oxidation of the soil profile has occurred, which started after the reclamation the land in 1957. The redox boundary coincides with the change in lithology. The marine clay contains organic detritus that has shrunk upon drying causing the clay to crack. The fluviatile clays do contain (diagenetic) pyrite but remain almost impenetrable by groundwater. Oxygen is consumed in the brown layers, enhancing the preservation of the archaeological layer below. In addition, the early Neolithic layer is protected by the black organic rich layer that formed during the inhabitation of the site. The marine deposits contain also shells, not only neutralizing the acid produced by pyrite oxidation but also CO_2 from infiltrating groundwater. All finds (bone, soil features, and botanical remains) are intact or only slightly degraded.

On the basis of this assessment, *in situ* preservation would be the method for conservation of the archaeological remains. Ongoing or future monitoring of the site is not necessary because of the indications that oxidation has stopped and the excellent preservation of the archaeological remains. A part of this site has been excavated to gain academic knowledge about this period.

Figure 2 shows a podzolic soil profile with soil features of a medieval track. Soil formation has stopped after deposition of the drift sand. Carbonate minerals are not

FIGURE 1   Soil profile of an middle Neolithic site (dating from *c.* 4300–4000 cal. BC) in the Flevopolder near Swifterbant (Huisman et al., 2009). From top to bottom: Clay-rich tillage layer (A), marine sand and clay deposit with detritus (B), brown lacustrine clay with cracks (C). Hiatus with peat (C–D) and grey fluvial deposits (D). Black archaeological layers (E) followed by clean fresh water estuarine to fluviatile clay (F). (Photograph by de Kort).

FIGURE 2   Profile of a podzolic soil (A) covered with drift sand (B). In the E-horizon (grey layer, C) a medieval track (thirteenth–fifteenth century) is visible. (D) Road from Hamont to Eindhoven.
Photograph by de Kort

present and pH values therefore are low. The soil is well drained and the groundwater level is significantly deeper than the excavated surface. Bone, metals, and other archaeological remains are therefore not expected to have survived under these oxidized conditions. However, due to the low reactivity of the available (humic) organic matter, the low content of reactive phases (carbonates, iron hydroxides) and stable environment, the features of the medieval track were well preserved for more than five hundred years. Therefore, *in situ* preservation can be applied without further monitoring as changes in the burial conditions are not expected.

Dwelling mounds (*terps*) were originally built in the tidal area of the northern Netherlands. As a result of dike-building, they have not been surrounded by the sea anymore since the Middle Ages. The archaeological layers are well above groundwater but preservation conditions for archaeological remains are often excellent, as can be seen in Figure 3. Organic matter and other reduced components have consumed oxygen. Ultimately, this has led to iron reducing conditions as indicated by the grey colours. The organic rich settlement debris and clayey lithology are therefore responsible for anaerobic conditions that enhance the preservation of bone, metal, seeds, and other organic remains. It is remarkable that humans have often created the perfect preservation conditions for their own remains.

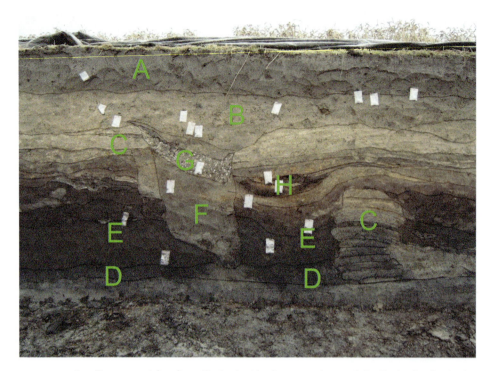

FIGURE 3   Dwelling mound (*terp*) profile in the Northern provinces of the Netherlands. At the top a small tillage layer is visible (A), followed by an anthropogenic filling (B) with plaggen (C) (sods, organic rich topsoil, settlement debris, and clay). At the lower part, a black layer is observed (D), indicating the first habitation of the mound during the Iron Age. Brown layers are rich in organic matter (peat; E). In the middle a trench (F) can be seen, filled afterwards with silty clay and covered with a shell-rich layer (G). The red parts (H) are the remnants of slag and burnt material.
By permission of Rijksuniversiteit Groningen/Groninger Instituut voor Archaeologie

In situ conservation is again a feasible option for this site. Monitoring of the burial environment is not necessary, but — since many *terp* sites are under agriculture — erosion monitoring may be necessary in some cases.

In urban environments, like sites in towns and cities, the conservation of archaeological remains is much more dependent on building activities. Archaeological remains in urban environment (in Europe) are often remnants of medieval buildings. Unless physically disturbed, such remains are mostly stable. Organic remains (wood, textile, leather) in the urban sphere are most often found at places like cesspits, water wells, canal infills, and waste dumps where they are well preserved. Preservation conditions in general in such environments are, in general, excellent. This is because the archaeological interesting objects were deposited together with undefined organic waste. Subsequently, reduced and often semi-impermeable conditions were established quickly, sealing of these remains. The fact that in an urban environment organic remains are found in such settings means that preservation conditions for this type of finds were good. In fact, in the Netherlands, in some cities only one in ten cesspits are dug up when threatened by development because an excavation will only give limited additional information and the conservation of the often numerous finds, associated with such sites, is expensive. Furthermore, as urban sites are often characterized by a lot of building debris (mortar, brick, rock, etc.) pH may be buffered by lime often associated with such debris. So if the archaeologist is able to determine black layers, pieces of mortar, impermeable horizons (or the absence of those), and also material like bone, leather, metal (was it buried under anaerobic conditions or not, observing the type of corrosion), he or she will be able to predict the conservation potential of a site.

Conclusions

By looking at soil features, intactness of archaeological remains and reactive phases, much can be learned about the burial environment. Such assessment can be carried out without any technical measurements in the field or in the laboratory. The trained archaeologist can easily carry out such an assessment together with the archaeological evaluation of a site. On the basis of this assessment, the effects of environmental changes can be predicted. This will help the decision for *in situ* or *ex situ* preservation and avoid complex and costly long-term monitoring.

Acknowledgements

The organization of the Paris 4 conference is thanked for the opportunity to present our paper. Two anonymous reviewers are thanked for their critical comments that, we think, have improved the manuscript considerably.

Bibliography

Beukers, E. 2009. *Erfgoedbalans 2009: archeologie, monumenten en cultuurlandschap in Nederland*. Amersfoort: Cultural Heritage Agency of the Netherlands.

Huisman, D. J. 2009. *Degradation of Archaeological Remains*. Den Haag: SDU.

Huisman, D. J., Jongmans, A. G., and Raemaekers, D. C. M. 2009. Investigating Neolithic Land Use in Swifterbant (NL) using Micromorphological Techniques. *Catena*, 78(3): 185–97.

Kaczorek, D. and Sommer, M. 2003. Micromorphology, Chemistry, and Mineralogy of Bog Iron Ores from Poland. *Catena*, 54(3): 393–402.

Smit, A., van Heeringen, R. M., and Theunissen, E. M. 2006. *Archaeological Monitoring Standard*. Amersfoort: National Service for Archaeology, Cultural Landscape and Built Heritage.

Notes on contributors

Bertil van Os was educated as a marine geochemist at Utrecht University. Since 2007 he has been employed by the Cultural Heritage agency as senior scientist. He works mainly on projects concerning the conservation of archaeological remains *in situ* and inorganic materials. His latest projects are the evaluation of the implementation of the Malta agreement in Dutch regulation, the influence of climatic change on the spreading of ship worm in the Baltic (Wreckprotect), lead corrosion in organ pipes, and the application of mitigating measures and the study of their effect on important threatened archaeological monuments.

Correspondence to: Bertil van Os, Dutch Cultural Heritage Agency, Smallepad 5, 3811MG Amersfoort, Netherlands. Email: B.van.os@cultureelerfgoed.nl

Jan Willem de Kort trained as archaeologist at Leiden University (Archaeology of North Western Europe) and specialized in prehistoric archaeobotany and archaeology. He now works as a senior archaeologist and is responsible for all archaeological field activities from the Cultural Heritage Agency in the Pleistocenic part of the Netherlands.

Hans (D. J.) Huisman is a soil scientist and geochemist. Since 2003, he has worked for the Cultural Heritage Agency as senior researcher soil science and degradation. He has undertaken a series of research projects on degradation of archaeological remains and monitoring of archaeological sites, and edited and co-wrote a book on degradation of archaeological remains.

CONSERVATION AND MGMT OF ARCH. SITES, Vol. 14 Nos 1–4, 2012, 341–49

Founding of a Monumentenwacht for Archaeological Heritage in Flanders (Belgium)

Nele Goeminne

Monumentenwacht Vlaanderen vzw, Belgium

In August 2009, Monumentenwacht Vlaanderen set out to develop a new service and monitoring system for archaeological heritage in Flanders. Such an initiative takes time, for it needs to be done thoroughly, and there are many questions that need to be addressed. The answers can be found partly in examples in other countries, but must also be evolved in practice within the Flemish context, where a policy on *in situ* preservation of archaeological heritage is still in its infancy. This paper explains how this new service has been set up.

KEYWORDS Belgium, monitoring, *in situ* preservation

Organizational framework

Monumentenwacht[1] has been well established on the Flemish heritage scene for nearly twenty years now as a group of six non-profit associations. The umbrella organization, Monumentenwacht Vlaanderen, was founded in 1991. In the course of 1992, the five provincial Monumentenwacht organizations were set up.[2] The initiative was inspired by the Netherlands, where a national federation of provincial Monumentenwacht organizations had already been in existence since 1973.

Monumentenwacht seeks to contribute to the long-term conservation of cultural heritage in Flanders, more particularly by supporting, informing and raising awareness among its members about sustainable conservation and management of their heritage site. The emphasis is on a preventive approach, aimed at stimulating regular maintenance. Such regular maintenance can help postpone and even avoid major and costly restoration works.

The preventive approach is reflected in regular site inspection visits during which the condition of the heritage is assessed and recorded by a team of specialists (condition/risk surveys and assessments). The results are presented in a well-documented and clearly formulated status report, in which concrete, practical, and prioritized recommendations on maintenance, repair, preventive conservation, daily care,

    DOI 10.1179/1350503312Z.00000000030

housekeeping, and management are given. Additional services to members include on-site advice, publications, helpdesk assistance, workshops, and demonstrations. Monumentenwacht offers its services as an independent and objective advisory body.

Owners, managers, or caretakers of heritage sites (private individuals, associations, companies, or public authorities) become members of Monumentenwacht on a voluntarily basis (bottom-up approach). The voluntary nature of membership is of the utmost importance, starting from the personal engagement of the owner and thus guaranteeing a commitment to regular and adequate maintenance of the site in question. Thanks to substantial financial support of the five Flemish provinces and of the Flemish government, the cost for owners-administrators can be kept very low. Furthermore, the site inspection reports can serve as a basis to apply for a maintenance grant for listed monuments.

What initially began as one umbrella organization and five provincial organizations, each employing a team of two architectural assessors, has since developed into an organization with 3109 members and a permanent staff of sixty-nine. In the early years the focus was on architectural heritage; it was extended in 1997 to historic interiors and in 2008 to naval heritage. Since its foundation, 5955 buildings and seventy-three vessels have been described, and tens of thousands of condition surveys have been carried out.

Following a feasibility study in May/June 2008, it was decided in August 2009 to develop also a new service for owners of archaeological heritage ('Archaeological Monumentenwacht'). After a pilot and development phase (August 2009–December 2010), this service was officially offered as of January 2011 to prospective members.

Archaeological Monumentenwacht: what and why?

The development of a service centring on archaeological heritage was initiated and supported by the Flemish government in 2008.[3] With the official ratification by Belgium of the Malta Convention on 8 October 2010 (European Convention on the Protection of the Archaeological Heritage, Valetta, 16 January 1992) and its planned implementation in the new Decree on the Immovable Heritage in Flanders, emphasis in future heritage conservation will increasingly shift to *in situ* preservation of archaeological heritage.[4]

By broadening its range of services, Monumentenwacht wants to support, inform, and advise owners in the *in situ* preservation and management of their site(s). Like architectural and naval heritage, archaeological heritage does not automatically remain in a good condition, but is subject to a whole number of deterioration processes.

In situ preservation of archaeological heritage therefore calls for an appropriate and active conservation (management and maintenance) policy. The idea is that our archaeological heritage, which is often the only — vulnerable — archive still remaining of our past, should be preserved in the long term as a source of knowledge and experience. Monumentenwacht wants to support and advise its members in this process by developing and offering initiatives of a preventive nature. This is mainly done by carrying out periodic and systematic condition and risk assessments, resulting in the production of status reports with recommendations for preservation and management.

This broadening by Monumentenwacht of its range of services also opens up new possibilities for integrated heritage inspections, for example, in castle and monastery grounds where upstanding architectural heritage and (subsurface) archaeological heritage has been preserved.

Inspiration abroad

When developing this new service for archaeological sites, inspiration was sought in existing initiatives in other countries, particularly in the Netherlands where a similar service is already offered by the Stichting Archeologische Monumentenwacht Nederland, and in England, in the work of English Heritage.

The Archeologische Monumentenwacht Nederland (AMW) is a private foundation, set up in 1991 with the support of the Prince Bernhard Cultural Foundation and working all over the Netherlands. The main objective of the AMW is to prevent the deterioration of archaeological monuments by advising landowners about mitigating measures that should be taken and what kind of maintenance should be executed to prevent decay of the archaeological remains. To this end AMW carries out archaeological baseline surveys and periodical monitoring of the condition of archaeological monuments. In the archaeological baseline survey the features of the monument and its direct surroundings and its (possible) threats are recorded. The monitoring reports contain specific recommendations on the maintenance and the archaeological management of the monument. Initially the monitoring method was based on visual observations, but recently the services were broadened with monitoring techniques to study also the burial environment. Landowners and managers, but also local authorities, can subscribe to the (paying) services of AMW.[5]

English Heritage is a quasi-independent public body holding wide-ranging powers to manage the historic environment of England. It gets approximately three-quarters of its funding from the Department of Culture, Media and Sport. Since the late 1970s, a group of advisors (currently called Historic Environment Field Advisers — HEFAs) have been responsible for periodically monitoring the condition, threats, and management of designated archaeological monuments in their geographical area. This monitoring is based on visual observation and periodical site visits. The findings are recorded in a form that is entered in an internal database system. The HEFAs constitute the front line of English Heritage and report to the Inspectors of Ancient Monuments. They play an essential advisory and supporting role for the owners of monuments. For example, they help to draw up and oversee management plan, offer advice on suitable options for funding, and provide preliminary advice on applications for permission to carry out works.

Both organizations played an important supporting role in the start-up of the new service. The adviser on Archaeological Heritage of Monumentenwacht Vlaanderen took part in a training course for the HEFAs and completed an internship with AMW. The Flemish organization also worked closely together with the latter organization during the pilot inspections that were carried out during the period March–May 2010.

Archaeological Monumentenwacht: for whom?

Owners and administrators of archaeological heritage sites in Flanders can call upon the services of the 'Archaeological Monumentenwacht' and become members on a voluntary basis. For the pilot inspections, cooperation was mainly with land management agencies (such as Agentschap Natuur en Bos — Nature and Forest Agency) and public authorities.

The Archaeology Decree (Decree of 30 June 1993 on the Protection of the Archaeological Heritage) defines archaeological heritage as 'archaeological monuments and zones in all their forms' (Art. 3 § 1). Archaeological monuments are defined as 'all remains and objects and any other traces of mankind that bear witness to epochs and civilizations for which excavations or finds constitute a significant source of information' (Art. 3 § 2). Archaeological zones are defined as 'all grounds that are of scientific and cultural-historical value because of the potential presence of archaeological monuments, including a buffer zone' (Art. 3 § 3).

Monumentenwacht uses a more practice-based definition, in which archaeological heritage may encompass buried sites as well as visible cultural-historical relics (such as burial mounds, moated sites as, for example, Figure 1) and excavated building remains (Figure 2).

In order to be accepted as a member of Monumentenwacht the archaeological heritage site must be 'valuable' (which means worth to preserve *in situ*). It may be listed, though this is not necessary. For architectural and naval heritage, there are elaborate Monument Registers and Inventories that can be consulted quite easily

FIGURE 1   A moated site in Kortemark.

FIGURE 2 Excavated building remains of a former water mill in Zwalm.

for this matter. These instruments are not yet fully developed for archaeological heritage.

The register of listed archaeological assets currently (10 October 2012) contains only fourteen listed archaeological zones. This type of protection (in accordance with the Archaeology Decree) only came into effect in 2004, when the structural management and protection of the archaeological heritage in Flanders was entrusted to the former Department of Monuments and Landscapes (now the Immovable Heritage Agency). This, of course, does not mean that Flanders has only fourteen valuable archaeological sites; it simply means that the protection and valuation process is still under way. Before 2004, archaeological heritage was protected under the Monument Decree (enacted for architectural monuments) or the Landscape Decree. The archaeological remains listed according to those decrees essentially covered visible archaeological heritage. The listing did not involve an extensive archaeological valuation. In addition, there is no separate register for archaeological assets that were listed under one of those decrees. Our own — far from complete — search in the listed heritage database, however, produced at least some 160 archaeological sites listed under the Monument or Landscape Decree.

Furthermore, as far as an inventory is concerned, the Immovable Heritage Agency has only recently (2009/10) started a valuation project, that will produce and partly publish an inventory of 'demarcated archaeological zones' in Flanders. These are zones in which most probably archaeological remains are *in situ* preserved. This means that, for the time being, it is difficult to judge the size and demand of our target group.

Given that a sustainable policy on *in situ* preservation and management of archaeological heritage in Flanders is still in an early stage of development, there is a need for capacity-building among heritage professionals and researchers as well as among owners. Awareness raising should therefore be seen as one of the main tasks of the 'Archaeological Monumentenwacht'.

Archaeological Monumentenwacht: services?

Site inspections

In return for membership, the archaeological site is periodically inspected (Figure 3). During those site inspections, the current condition of the archaeological heritage is recorded and assessed. For this purpose, old and new damage and (unwanted) growth is recorded in detail. A survey is also made of (potential) threats, such as planned management works. The findings are based on visual observations and also extend to a peripheral (buffer) zone around the archaeological relic. The first site inspection constitutes the archaeological baseline measurement against which the periodical follow-up inspections are carried out (monitoring). By regularly and systematically monitoring and assessing the state of preservation, new damage and threats can be detected in time, and changes can be made to the management of the site if necessary.

FIGURE 3   The (pilot) inspection of an erosion channel in a burial mound in Tongeren.

The preventive and awareness-raising effect of the inspections is very important, since (further) decay must be prevented. Close consultation with the owner or administrator of the site forms therefore an essential part of the inspection procedure (Figure 4).

The inspection methodology used, based on visual observations, is inspired by that operated by the Archeologische Monumentenwacht Nederland (AMW) and the Historic Environment Field Advisers (HEFAs) of English Heritage. Nevertheless, the inspection and reporting methodology is still in development. It has been tested and assessed in pilot inspections carried out under the supervision of AMW during the period March–May 2010 at various sites across Flanders. A total of sixteen burial mounds (Figure 5), one site with surface finds and two sites with buried remains, were inspected. In the future we will investigate whether this methodology could be extended to subsurface monitoring of the burial environment.

Status reports

The results from the site inspections are recorded in a status report with recommendations for conservation and management. These results are illustrated with photos, maps, and illustrations. The recommendations are primarily concerned with preservation and maintenance. Advice on consolidation and opening up to the public is given as part of a separate, specialized service. Depending on the demand for and the current supply of these services, we will decide whether Monumentenwacht should specialize further in this area. The (maintenance) works to be carried out are described as specifically as possible and an indication is given as to urgency. If

FIGURE 4   Dialogue with the administrator during the pilot inspection of a below-ground parish church in Halen.

FIGURE 5   The (pilot) inspection of a burial mound ('Avernassetom') in Gingelom.

necessary, owners and administrators are referred to competent authorities, specialists, and contractors. Monumentenwacht also refers them as precisely as possible to the relevant agencies for information about grants and permits. The status report also contains background information which may be useful for the purpose of displaying the archaeological site to the public.

The owner can act on the recommendations contained in the report, or use the report as a basis to apply for government grants for works to be carried out on listed heritage. The reports may also be used as reference material in the elaboration and evaluation of all sorts of management plans, such as forestry conservation plans, and management contracts.

Outlook

In a context where a sustainable policy on *in situ* preservation and management of archaeological heritage is still in an early stage of development, the new service of 'Monumentenwacht Archaeology' is breaking fresh ground. It is an important initiative, but no easy task. The new Decree on the Immovable Heritage, in which the principles of the Malta Convention will be implemented, is awaited with baited breath. We hope that the decree will encourage periodic monitoring and active management as important strategies for *in situ* preservation of archaeological heritage. We look also forward to the further elaboration of the register of listed archaeological zones and of the inventory of 'demarcated archaeological zones' in Flanders.

At this moment however, support for *in situ* preservation and management of archaeological sites, and awareness that this calls for an active preservation policy, based on archaeological baseline measurement and monitoring, is still tentative; likewise there is a considerable need for awareness raising. In this light, the implementation and further development of the new service will take time and success will be closely linked to the developments that occur in the archaeological heritage sector.

Notes

[1] For further information, see <www.monumenten wacht.be>.

[2] The political structure of Belgium is rather complex after four phases of state reform between 1970 and 1993. Today, Belgium is a federal state where the decision-making power is no longer exclusively in the hands of the federal level. The management of the country falls to several partners, which exercise their competences independently in different fields. The Kingdom is subdivided in three regions (Flemish, Brussels Capital, and Walloon) and three communities (Dutch, French, and German). The competences on the regional level are divided between those regions and communities. The regions are responsible for all territorially linked matters such as transport, town and country planning, environment, cultural heritage, and employment; the communities' competences are, amongst others, education, culture, and welfare. This political structure explains why Monumentenwacht can only operate in the Flemish region. The Flemish region is in itself divided in five provinces. This has determined the structure of the organization.

[3] See also the paper by Jonas Van Looveren in this issue.

[4] The Flemish government is currently working on a new Decree on the Immovable Heritage. This umbrella decree is meant to replace all previous decrees (i.e. Monument Decree of 1976, Archaeology Decree of 1993, and Landscape Decree of 1996). Since the current laws, decrees and regulations on immovable heritage have tended to come about organically, the different inventories, protection statuses, procedures, and enforcement rules are not always ideally attuned to each other. Furthermore, as a result of consecutive amendments, this body of regulations had in recent decades become very incoherent. The new decree will be in keeping with an integrated and holistic approach to the immovable heritage concept and is designed to ensure the management and conservation of the value of our landscapes, monuments and archaeological sites. This decree will also effectively implement the principles of the Malta Convention. A first draft proposal of this decree was presented on 23 July 2010.

[5] <http://www.archeomw.nl/en.home> [accessed 20 February 2012].

Notes on contributor

Nele Goeminne is an advisor on archaeological heritage at Monumentenwacht Vlaanderen vzw. She has an MA in Archaeology (2005) and a postgraduate degree in Conservation of Monuments and Sites (2008). She has worked previously in the conservation of built heritage, at the Immovable Heritage Agency in Flanders.

Correspondence to: Nele Goeminne, Archaeology Adviser, Monumentenwacht Vlaanderen vzw, Erfgoedhuis den Wolsack, Oude Beurs 27, 2000 Antwerp, Belgium. Email: nele.goeminne@monumentenwacht.be

CONSERVATION AND MGMT OF ARCH. SITES, Vol. 14 Nos 1–4, 2012, 350–59

Long-Term Preservation of Dendroarchaeological Specimens and *In Situ* Preservation: Problems and Practical Solutions

PEARCE PAUL CREASMAN

Laboratory of Tree-Ring Research, University of Arizona, USA

Dendrochronology offers a unique opportunity to address archaeological questions with minimal invasiveness. Often, archaeological tree-ring sampling, and occasionally analysis itself, can be performed while the larger structure or object remains *in situ*. In comparison to the costs and benefits of excavation (complete or partial) and a growing international call for *in situ* preservation, dendrochronology provides an effective compromise for the interpretation of wooden material culture.

The current number of archaeological tree-ring specimens worldwide probably exceeds 2,000,000. These specimens have been obtained from thousands of historic buildings, shipwrecks, and other sites and artefacts. These specimens are housed by a variety of public and private entities: museums, universities, governments, private corporations, and individuals. Despite their importance as vouchers for archaeological dates and great potential for future use and new applications, generally little attention has been paid to the long-term curation of tree-ring specimens. This paper identifies some pressing curation problems and suggests that the value and nature of dendroarchaeological research is compatible with international calls for *in situ* preservation. Some practical suggestions, provided here, could drastically improve the long-term curation of dendroarchaeological specimens, further demonstrating the methodology as a viable and valuable partner to *in situ* preservation.

KEYWORDS dendrochronology, dendroarchaeology, conservation, preservation, specimens, archives

Introduction

Dendrochronologists study the annular rings and other growth features of trees as natural chronometers and as recorders of change in the environment with which all

DOI 10.1179/1350503312Z.00000000031

biological life and human cultures are inescapably linked. Tree rings provide access to a pre-industrial perspective on cultures and environment that is otherwise unattainable and is of great importance to the public and academics alike.

The value of dendrochronology to archaeology is difficult to overstate: over the past eighty years, it has become the gold standard for referencing chronological, behavioural, and environmental events when wood is found on archaeological sites (Dean, 1996; 2009). With its origins rooted in the south-western region of the United States, dendroarchaeology has spread to much of the rest of the world and has been a mainstay of European archaeology for at least four decades (Kuniholm, 2001; Baillie, 2002; Čufar, 2007; Dean, 2009; Eckstein and Cherubini, 2012).

Archaeological tree-ring studies are especially valuable for yielding absolute, single-year dates for past events and processes. Cultural and natural history insights from this kind of work have arisen worldwide. To cite an early example, A. E. Douglass (1929), founder of the discipline in the United States, used architectural timbers and archaeological charcoal to date the rise and fall of pre-European populations of the US South-west (Robinson, 1979). They also have shed light, for example, on the historic and pre-historic record of Europe (e.g. Billamboz, 2004; in which waterlogged timbers from Neolithic and Bronze Age settlements in the northern Alps were used to understand bog and lake-shore occupation over time). Knowledge gained from tree rings in archaeological contexts has been central to revealing and understanding cultural and environmental change over time, with valuable lessons for the present and future. Such studies continue today and have expanded to include virtually all periods of history, cultures, and a variety of wood-use behaviours worldwide (e.g. see Nash, 2002 for a review of archaeological tree-ring dating methods and applications; see Creasman, 2010a for applications of dendrochronology to better understand human/environment interactions based on ship and boat timbers).

Dendrochronology is often compared to the assembly of a jigsaw puzzle. The pieces, gathered from a wide variety of independent sources, are assembled over a period of years. Long-term preservation and continued access to specimens are thus crucial to this field, as an individual sample may prove to be significant only decades after its collection, when sufficient others have been obtained for comparison, allowing completion of the 'puzzle'. Despite this necessarily far-sighted scope, practitioners and stakeholders alike have largely neglected development of a comprehensive solution for the long-term needs of expanding collections.

In most cases, analysis in archaeological dendrochronology involves only a small portion of the parent timber, which can remain *in situ* (Figure 1). Although analysis and future reference might require removal of a portion of the specimen (a 'core'; Figure 2) (Bannister, 1963; Stokes and Smiley, 1968; Ferguson, 1970; Towner, 2001), this is not always the case. Various studies of art historical objects and structures demonstrate that there are effective techniques for the analysis of wooden archaeological remains *in situ* and/or without sampling: narrowing the origin and earliest possible dates of wood-panel paintings by several Dutch masters (Eckstein et al., 1986; Wazny, 1992; 2005; Haneca et al., 2005); identifying whether certain reputed Antonio Stradivari stringed instruments could have been crafted during his lifetime (Bernabei et al., 2009; Čufar et al., 2010; Grissino-Mayer et al., 2010); using digital methodologies to acquire tree-ring data and measurements from Buddha statues and other wooden artefacts that cannot be cored or sampled (NARA, 2004); and

FIGURE 1   A University of Arizona student taking a dendroarchaeological sample.
Photograph by R. H. Towner

correlating photographs and terahertz reflection imaging to measure inaccessible tree rings (Jackson et al., 2009), to name but a few.

Given the inherently destructive nature of archaeological excavation, dendro-chronological specimens collected from a site should be held to the same standards of care and preservation as any other component of material culture. Collecting and processing of specimens can be costly in time and funds, but, too few researchers possess the sense of urgency that leads to the development or execution of procedures that can support future use of the specimens and thus the maximization of resources (Creasman, 2011: 103). Lacking such resources or vision, development and implementation of non-invasive dendrochronological methods should be encouraged, as more *in situ* analysis may both mitigate growth of collections and help to better preserve archaeological sites and artefacts (Figure 3).

While anecdotes of the loss or destruction of valuable dendrochronological material are prevalent, few potent accounts can be confirmed (see Creasman, 2011). It seems the primary curation problems have been the result of a shortage of storage capacity, limited personnel resources, inadequate preservation technology, or lack of vision regarding potential future uses (see Baillie, 2002; Dean, 2006). Yet, the confirmed examples do not necessarily portend a dim future for dendrochronological collections, as most seem to have received adequate care. With greater education on the part of customers and researchers involved in dendroarchaeological analysis, curation problems should be a thing of the past.

FIGURE 2   Representative dendroarchaeological samples.

FIGURE 3   An historic American wooden farm structure, *in situ* after dendroarchaeological sampling: identical condition as prior to sampling.
Photograph by R. H. Towner; Towner and Creasman, 2010

Dendrochronological collections

The nature of dendrochronology, especially for chronology-building, often calls for the collection of a large volume or quantity of specimens and their long-term curation (Figure 4; Stokes and Smiley, 1968; Baillie, 1982; Creasman, 2011).[1] Because absolute dating is the 'backbone of all [archaeological] tree-ring research' (Kuniholm, 2001: 38) and an 'ample supply' of wood is one of Bannister's prerequisites for successful dendrochronology (1963: 164), it is not a coincidence that many large and diverse collections have been built during the past century (e.g. the University of Arizona's combined cultural and natural history dendrochronology collection includes approximately 2,000,000 specimens, of which approximately 700,000 are archaeological; Figure 5).

There are broad disparities in the significance placed on archaeological dendrochronology by national research agencies and agendas. For example, the Dutch

FIGURE 4   A small portion of the general dendrochronology collection of the University of Arizona.
Photograph by G. Mackender

FIGURE 5   Approximately 50 per cent of the boxed dendroarchaeology collection of the University of Arizona.
Photograph by G. Mackender

National Research Agenda for Archaeology has included dendrochronology in its scope (Jansma, 2006). While English Heritage outlined techniques for collection, preparation, and analysis of dendrochronological specimens (Laxton et al., 2001; Jones, 2010), it has not defined standards for storage and safekeeping, which is left to individual laboratories (Hillam, 1998). Consistency is also lacking in the United States: in the guide to responsible conduct in scientific research authored by the National Academy of Sciences et al. (2009), collections of all kinds are critically overlooked. However, the National Science and Technology Council (2009) have specifically addressed scientific collections.[2] As there is no national agenda or agency for archaeology in the United States, the protection of archaeological heritage is left to state and local governments.

This paper is not and should not be construed as an indictment of past practices within the fields, but as a call to arms. In all subfields, stakeholders need to deepen their commitment to collections, especially archaeological materials, and/or identify alternative practices for analysis that decrease collections growth, such as *in situ* analysis.

Challenges

The potential exists for much greater use of the existing dendrochronological collections worldwide (e.g. Santiago-Blay et al., 2011), but this expansion depends upon their proper housing and management and upon improved knowledge of and access to them. Organized and readily accessible collections will encourage greater use of the materials by scholars, as well as for public outreach (e.g. primary school demonstrations and museum displays). Further, ongoing loss of tree-ring resources due to environmental and social changes means that existing collections will be increasingly valuable in coming decades and centuries for study by archaeologists, biologists, chemists, and a variety of earth scientists, among others.

With the increasing recognition of and demand for archaeological applications of dendro-analysis (e.g. Creasman, 2010b), collections are continually growing, thus compounding the challenges. For example, it is likely that thousands of unique wet palaeoecological and archaeological specimens spanning from 8000 BC to present have been amassed in the past few decades and are sitting on shelves throughout Europe without proper attention being paid to the specific conservation needs of waterlogged wood or their future utility (see Creasman, 2011).

Collecting and preparing a usable tree-ring specimen require a considerable initial investment of time and funds. Even thereafter, the physical specimens often remain largely inaccessible to those beyond the host institution/repository; in some cases, they are totally unavailable. Indeed, some tree-ring collections have been destroyed, in part or in full, following their initial use (for specific examples, see Creasman, 2011). As archaeological resources generally cannot be re-collected, any loss is significant.

Suggested solutions

The various methods offered by dendrochronology provide opportunities to balance the desire to preserve sites *in situ* with the desire to derive information. Often, archaeological tree-ring sampling, and occasionally analysis itself, can be performed while the larger structure or object remains *in situ*. Given that standard sampling and analysis for dendrochronology is minimally invasive, especially relative to excavation, dendrochronology should be embraced by all those who wish to preserve our archaeological heritage for the future without sacrificing the ability to derive data about our collective past. However, as with any technique in archaeology that calls for *in situ* preservation, certain curation challenges are present and should be resolved before accelerating study.

While the suggestions provided here would, *ideally*, be applied indiscriminately across all sectors of the field, it must be acknowledged that a division exists between academic or public sector and commercial or private sector work. The fundamental differences between these two branches and their business models often result in drastically different standards of care. This division and its implications are outside of the scope of this manuscript and will be explored by the author in a future work.

Those seeking dendrochronological analysis for their site/artefacts, the organizations that fund the research and venues that publish such work should collectively and actively require confirmation of viable long-term management plans for the specimens in question. Perpetual institutional commitments are and will be critical to the future of dendrochronological specimens. Yet, after the primary researchers are gone or a discipline falls out of favour, institutions can unilaterally revise such agreements. If specimens remain *in situ* they can escape the pitfalls of such possibilities, but are, inevitably, exposed to other hazards. Perhaps the safest way to ensure preservation of specimens would be to build endowments exclusively for this purpose. It has been suggested that such resources could be secured through estate planning by those involved in the research (P. I. Kuniholm, International Tree-Ring Data Bank Forum, 6 May 2010), but how many people are dedicated enough to their work to support it in this way?

The practice of sampling should be predicated on a demonstrated ability to care for any material culture collected from archaeological contexts. If dendroarchaeological specimens are analysed with greater frequency *in situ*, there is far less likelihood of losing all or part of the critical associated data or other common collection problems. Whenever practical, *in situ* analysis of dendroarchaeological specimens should be practised, which will, in turn, help to reduce the stress on dendrochronological collections. The issue at hand is how to progress. It is hoped that this manuscript can be used to further advance the case for curation of dendrochronological specimens and greater application of the method even when the decision is made to preserve a wooden structure *in situ*.

Acknowledgements

The presentation of this material was supported by the University of Arizona's Appointed Professional Advisory Council professional development scholarship. This manuscript is derived in part from a more detailed article by the author (Creasman, 2011). The author wishes to acknowledge the following people for their contributions to this work or reflections on the status of dendrochronological collections: Rex

Adams, Joan Bacharach, Chris Baisan, Bryant Bannister, Gretel Boswijk, Peter Brown, Jeff Dean, Noreen Doyle, Catherine Hawks, Malcolm Hughes, Esther Jansma, Steve Leavitt, Greg McDonald, Daniel Nievergelt, Jim Speer, Elaine Sutherland, Tom Swetnam, Jacques Tardif, Willy Tegel, and Valérie Trouet. Of course, errors and opinions are solely the responsibility of the author and do not necessarily reflect the thoughts or policies of any institution with which the author is affiliated.

Notes

[1] Chronology-building is necessary for most dendroarchaeological analysis. 'Master chronologies' are the backbone upon which archaeological dating and other interpretations are based. However, chronology-building is not necessarily reliant only on archaeological material. It often incorporates a substantial component of living-tree or other non-archaeological material.

[2] It is important to note that in the United States archaeology is most often considered part of the humanities or a social or behavioural science and is less often included in discussions of the 'hard sciences'. For example, Hodder has posed and addressed the question: 'Is archaeology a soft science or an expensive humanity?' (1984; 2005).

Bibliography

Baillie, M. G. L. 1982. *Tree-Ring Dating and Archaeology*. Chicago: University of Chicago Press.

Baillie, M. G. L., 2002. Future of Dendrochronology with Respect to Archaeology. *Dendrochronologia*, 20(1/2): 69–85.

Bannister, B. 1963. Dendrochronology. In: D. Brothwell and E. Higgs, eds. *Science in Archaeology*. New York: Thames and Hudson, pp. 161–76.

Bernabei, M., Bontadi, J., and Rognoni, G. R. 2009. Dendrochronological Dating of the Cherubini Stringed Instruments Collection, Florence. *Journée d'étude Dater l'instrument de musique*, June: 96–106.

Billamboz, A. 2004. Dendrochronology in lake-Dwelling Research. In: F. Menotti, ed. *Living on the Lake in Prehistoric Europe: 150 Years of Lake-Dwelling Research*. New York: Routledge, pp. 117–31.

Creasman, P. P. 2011. Basic Principles and Methods of Dendrochronological Specimen Curation. *Tree-Ring Research*, 67(2): 103–15.

Creasman, P. P. 2010a. Extracting Cultural Information from Ship Timber. Unpublished PhD dissertation, Texas A&M University.

Creasman, P. P. 2010b. An Evaluation of Dendrochronology as a Tool for the Interpretation of Historical Shipwrecks. In: C. E. Horrell and M. Damour, eds. *ACUA Underwater Archaeology Proceedings from the Society for Historical Archaeology's Annual Meeting 2010*. Advisory Council on Underwater Archaeology, pp. 250–54.

Čufar, K. 2007. Dendrochronology and Past Human Activity — A Review of Advances since 2000. *Tree-Ring Research*, 63(1): 47–60.

Čufar, K., Beutring, M., and Grabner, M. 2010. Dendrochronological Dating of Two Violins from Private Collections in Slovenia. *Zbornik gozdarstva in lesarstva*, 91: 3–10.

Dean, J. S. 2009. One Hundred Years of Dendroarchaeology: Dating, Human Behavior, and Past Climate. In: S. Manning and M. J. Bruce, eds. *Tree-rings, Kings, and Old World Archaeology and Environment: Papers Presented in Honor of Peter Ian Kuniholm*. Oxford: Oxbow Books, pp. 25–32.

Dean, J. S. 2006. In Memoriam: Robert E. Bell 1914–2006. *Tree-Ring Research*, 62(1): 33–34.

Dean, J. S. 1996. Dendrochronology and the Study of Human Behavior. In: J. S. Dean, D. Meko, and T. W. Swetnam, eds. *Tree Rings, Environment and Humanity: Proceedings of the International Conference, Tucson, Arizona 17–21 May 1994*. Ann Arbor: Cushing-Malloy, Inc., pp. 461–69.

Douglass, A. E. 1929. The Secret of the Southwest Solved by Talkative Tree Rings. *National Geographic Magazine*, 56(6): 736–70.

Eckstein, D. and Cherubini, P. 2012. The 'Dendrochronological Community' at Rovaniemi, Finland, 2010: Lessons Learned from the Past and Perspectives for the Future. *Dendrochronologia*, 30(2): 195–97; doi:10.1016/j.dendro.2011.02.001.

Eckstein, D., Wazny, T., Bauch, J., and Klein, P. 1986. New Evidence for the Dendrochronological Dating of Netherlandish Paintings. *Nature*, 24(625): 25–30.

Ferguson, C. W. 1970. Concepts and Techniques of Dendrochronology. In: R. Berger, ed. *Scientific Methods in Medieval Archaeology*. Berkeley: University of California Press, pp. 183–200.

Grissino-Mayer, H., Sheppard, P. R., Cleaveland, M. K., Cherubini, P., Ratcliff, P., and Topham, J. 2010. Adverse Implications of Misdating in Dendrochronology: Addressing the Re-dating of the 'Messiah' Violin. *Dendrochronologia*, 28: 149–59.

Haneca, K., Wazny, T., Van Acker, J., and Beeckman, H. 2005. Provenancing Baltic Timber from Art Historical Objects: Success and Limitations. *Journal of Archaeological Science*, 32: 261–71.

Hillam, J. 1998. *Dendrochronology: Guidelines on Producing and Interpreting Dendrochronological Dates*. London: English Heritage.

Hodder, I. 2005. *Theory and Practice in Archaeology*. 3rd edn. New York: Routledge.

Hodder, I. 1984. Archaeology in 1984. *Antiquity*, 52: 25–32.

Jackson, J. B., Mourou, M., Labaune, J., Whitaker, J. F., Duling III, I. N., Williamson, S. L., Lavier, C., Menu, M., and Mourou, G. A. 2009. Terahertz Pulse Imaging for Tree-Ring Analysis: A Preliminary Study for Dendrochronology Applications. *Measurement and Sciences Technology*, 20(075502): 1–10.

Jansma, E. 2006. NOaA 3 Dendrochronologie. *Dutch National Research Agenda for Archaeology* [accessed 1 April 2011]. Available at: <http://noaa.nl/toc/balk1-4-3.htm>.

Jones, D. M., ed. 2010. *Waterlogged Wood: Guidelines on the Recording, Sampling, Conservation and Curation of Waterlogged Wood*. Belgium: English Heritage Publishing.

Kuniholm, P. I. 2001. Dendrochronology and Other Applications of Tree-Ring Studies in Archaeology. In: D. R. Brothwell and A. M. Pollard, eds. *Handbook of Archaeological Sciences*. London: John Wiley & Sons Ltd, pp. 36–46.

Laxton, R. R., Litton C. D., and Howard, R. E. 2001. *Timber: Dendrochronology of Roof Timbers at Lincoln Cathedral*. London: James and James Ltd.

NARA. 2004. Dendrochronology and the Latest Imaging Equipments: Applications to Ancient Architecture, Carved Wooden Buddha Statues, and Wooden Artifacts. *Japan: Buried Cultural Properties News*, 116.

Nash. S. E. 2002. Archaeological Tree-Ring Dating at the Millennium. *Journal of Archaeological Research*, 10(3): 243–75.

National Academy of Sciences, National Academy of Engineering, and the Institute of Medicine (USA). 2009. *On Being a Scientist: A Guide to Responsible Conduct in Research (Third Edition)*. Washington DC: The National Academies Press.

National Science and Technology Council, Committee on Science, Interagency Working Group on Scientific Collections (USA). 2009. *Scientific Collections: Mission-Critical Infrastructure of Federal Science Agencies*. Washington DC: US Office of Science and Technology Policy.

Robinson, W. J. 1979. Tree-ring Dating and Archaeology in the American Southwest. *Tree-Ring Bulletin*, 36: 9–20.

Robinson, W. J., Cook., E., Pilcher, J. R., Eckstein, D., Kairiukstis, L., Shiyatov, S., and Norton, D. A. 1992. Some Historical Background in Dendrochronology. In: E. Cook and L. A. Kairiukstis, eds. *Methods of Dendrochronology: Applications in the Environmental Sciences*. Dordrecht: Kluwer Academic Publishers, pp. 1–22.

Santiago-Blay, J. A., Lambert, J. B., and Creasman P. P. 2011. Expanded Applications of Dendrochronology Collections: Collect and Save Exudates. *Tree-Ring Research*, 67(1): 67–68.

Stokes, M. A. and Smiley, T. L. 1968. *An Introduction to Tree-Ring Dating*. Tucson: University of Arizona Press (reprinted 1996).

Towner, R. H. 2001. Dendroarchaeology. In: S. A. Elias, ed. *Encyclopedia of Quaternary Science*, II. Amsterdam: Elsevier, pp. 2307–15.

Towner, R. H. and Creasman, P. P. 2010. Historical Dendroarchaeology in the El Malpais Area: Lessons from the Savage Homestead. *Historical Archaeology*, 44(4): 8–27.

Wazny, T. 2005. The Origin, Assortments and Transport of Baltic Timber. In: C. van de Velde, J. van Acker, H. Beeckman, and F. Verhaeghe, eds. *Constructing Wooden Images: Proceedings of a Symposium on the Organization of Labour and Working Practices of Late Gothic Carved Altarpieces in the Low Countries, Brussels 25–26 October 2002*. Brussels: VUB Press, pp. 115–26.

Wazny, T. 1992. Historical Timber Trade and its Implications on Dendrochronological Dating. *Lundqua Report* (*Proceedings International Symposium Tree-Rings and Environment 1990, Ystad*), 34: 331–33.

Notes on contributor

Pearce Paul Creasman is Curator of Collections and Assistant Research Professor in the Laboratory of Tree-Ring Research at University of Arizona (USA), and is Director of the University's Egyptian Expedition. His research interests include the use of ship timber to understand human/environment interactions, maritime archaeology, dendrochronology, and Egyptian archaeology.

Correspondence to: Pearce Paul Creasman, Laboratory of Tree-Ring Research, University of Arizona, 105 W Stadium Drive, Tucson AZ 85721, USA. Email: pcreasman@ltrr.arizona.edu

CONSERVATION AND MGMT OF ARCH. SITES, Vol. 14 Nos 1–4, 2012, 360–71

The RAAR Project — Heritage Management Aspects on Reburial After Ten Years of Work

Inger Nyström Godfrey,[1] Thomas Bergstrand,[2] Håkan Petersson,[3] Carola Bohm,[4] Eva Christensson,[5] Charlotte Gjelstrup Björdal,[6] David Gregory,[7] Ian MacLeod,[8] Elizabeth E. Peacock,[9] and Vicki Richards[10]

[1] Studio Västsvensk Konservering, Västarvet, Göteborg, Sweden
[2] Bohusläns Museum, Västarvet, Uddevalla, Sweden
[3] Bohusläns Museum, Västarvet, Uddevalla, Sweden
[4] National Heritage Board, Stockholm, Sweden
[5] National Heritage Board, Stockholm, Sweden
[6] Swedish University of Agricultural Science, Uppsala, Sweden
[7] National Museum of Denmark, Brede, Denmark
[8] Fremantle Museums and Maritime Heritage, Western Australian Museum, Fremantle, Australia
[9] Norwegian University of Science and Technology, Trondheim, Norway
[10] Department of Materials Conservation, Western Australian Museum, Fremantle, Australia

The general purpose of the international reburial project, Reburial and Analyses of Archaeological Remains (RAAR), is to evaluate reburial as a method for the long-term storage and preservation of waterlogged archaeological remains. Since 2001 material samples have been buried, retrieved, analysed systematically, and the results reported.

RAAR has mainly focused on the degradation of materials commonly encountered on archaeological sites, and on environmental monitoring techniques in order to determine what type of material can be reburied and for how long. The project has concluded that a heritage institution could provide short- or long-term curation for its archaeological archive by using reburial depots provided they are set up according to guidelines and restrictions stipulated by the RAAR project.

However, there are management and legal aspects that need to be discussed and resolved before each reburial project. Actual reburials that have been carried out so far are often a solution to emergency situations and lack

DOI 10.1179/1350503312Z.00000000032

collection and management policies. The questions 'what', 'why', and 'for how long' have been forgotten and need to be addressed. The legal protection of a reburial site is also important. This paper discusses these aspects and their consequences and highlights possible differences in approaches between the countries involved in the RAAR project.

KEYWORDS reburial, heritage management, underwater archaeological heritage

Introduction

In situ preservation of shipwrecks and other archaeological underwater sites represents a new field of interest. Over the past few years it has received increased attention by both policy makers, as well as heritage management institutions, such as museums.

Non-destructive and non-intrusive conservation strategies, such as *in situ* preservation, are emphasized in the UNESCO Convention of 2001 (UNESCO, 2001). Furthermore, they are highlighted in the ICOMOS Charter for the Protection and Management of the Underwater Cultural Heritage from 1996 (ICOMOS, 1996) to protect fragile and non-renewable archaeological heritage.

Reburial can be seen as the other side of the coin in that it seeks to emulate a pre-excavation (*in situ*) environment that has been conducive to the preservation of archaeological remains. The approach also offers the potential to create alternative storage repositories for the preservation of underwater archaeological heritage.

Perhaps because *in situ* preservation is a fairly new field, the terminology is still not strictly defined. In particular, this seems to be true for 'reburial'. During the work with the RAAR project, it has become increasingly clear that we need, for legal reasons if for nothing else, to differentiate between artefacts that are recovered, recorded, and reburied on the site from which they were discovered (*in situ*) and artefacts that are reburied elsewhere (*ex situ*). The term *in situ* storage has been used for artefacts reburied in a new, specially created site (Ortmann et al., 2010: 28). In our view, this is neither a correct nor adequate term to use. It is likely that more adjustments to *in situ* preservation terminology will be necessary as we fine-tune the methods, but until general agreement dictates differently, the RAAR project will use the following definitions regarding reburial:

- Reburial *in situ*: artefacts that are recovered, recorded, and reburied on the same site from which they originated.
- Reburial *ex situ*: artefacts that are recovered, recorded, and reburied on a specially created site outside the original site; that is, artificially created reburial depots.

The aim and structure of the project

In 2011, ten years have passed since the RAAR project was initiated. Extensive archaeological investigations that took place in Marstrand harbour from 1998 to 1999 and the subsequent reburial *ex situ* of recovered artefacts was the catalyst for RAAR.

FIGURE 1   The reburial site at Marstrand (foreground).

The principle goal of RAAR is to evaluate reburial as a method for long-term storage and preservation of waterlogged archaeological remains. The scope of the study is to provide, where possible, guidelines for the material types that can safely be reburied in environments similar to the one at Marstrand (Figure 1) and to identify those that should not be reburied.

RAAR is coordinated by the Bohusläns Museum and Studio Västsvensk Konservering in Sweden and consists of six sub-projects co-ordinated by museums and universities in Sweden, Denmark, Norway, and Australia (Table 1). The study aims to

TABLE 1

THE SIX SUBPROJECTS AND THEIR COORDINATORS

Sub-project	Coordinator	Institute/University
Silicates	Carola Bohm and Eva Christensson	National Heritage Board, Sweden, (RAÄ)
Metals	Vicki Richards and Ian MacLeod	Western Australian Museum, Fremantle, Australia, (WAM)
Wood	Charlotte Björdal and Thomas Nilsson	Swedish University of Agricultural Science, Uppsala, Sweden, (SLU)
Organic non-wood materials	Elizabeth E. Peacock	Norwegian University of Science and Technology, Trondheim, Norway, (NTNU)
Packing and labelling materials	Inger Nyström Godfrey	Studio Västsvensk Konservering, Göteborg, Sweden, (SVK)
Environmental monitoring	David Gregory	National Museum of Denmark, Brede, Denmark, (NM)

TABLE 2

RETRIEVAL PROGRAMME FOR THE PROJECT

Phase	Proposed retrieval year	Proposed reburial interval (yr)	Retrieval year	Reburial interval (yr)	Comments
1	2003	1	2003	1	Final report published in 2007
	2004	2	2004	2 (1)[1]	
	2005	3	2005	3 (2)	
2	2008	6	2009	7 (6)	Final report published in 2011
2	2014	12			Subject to funding
3	2026	24			Subject to funding
3	2050	48			Subject to funding

[1] Number in brackets denotes the reburial interval for the metal samples, which were reburied in 2003 one year after the other sample units.

determine the stability of the most commonly encountered materials on archaeological excavations, as well as that of packing and labelling materials. The project concurrently monitors the burial environment in Marstrand to complement the studies on materials degradation and to determine the physico-chemical criteria necessary for a successful reburial programme. In order to determine the long-term effects of reburial on the different material types, sufficient samples were buried to allow sampling to continue for up to fifty years (Table 2).

The results of the project to date have been extensively reported and published (e.g. Bergstrand and Nyström Godfrey, 2007; Nyström Godfrey et al., 2009; 2011; in press; RAAR website, 2002). This paper will focus on legal and management aspects that are connected with the reburial preservation method.

Consequences for heritage management

Legal aspects of reburial

There are differences between countries with regards to the legal protection of maritime archaeological heritage. However, if we look at Swedish law, there are important differences between the protection of *in situ* and *ex situ* reburial sites, and it is likely that there are similar differences in other countries.

In Sweden, a reburial *in situ* will be protected by the Swedish Heritage Act (1988), which is the same Act that protects the site itself. The finds will belong to and be the responsibility of the Swedish state. It will be marked on maps and charts and registered in the Heritage Site Register available for national planning.

A reburial *ex situ*, on the other hand, is not a heritage site; therefore, it is not protected by the Heritage Act. The artefacts would be managed by the state or a regional museum and protected by civil laws. Whether or not a museum is responsible for archaeological artefacts depends upon whether it seeks and is given permission by the state to curate the finds. However, this legal process has not been fully investigated (Bergstrand and Nyström, 2001; Statens Maritima Museer, 2005:14–16; Riksantikvarieämbetet, 2008: 17–18).

The procurement of land for the reburial depot is an important consideration. Depending on where the *ex situ* depot is located, the land might need to be purchased, leased, or encumbered with an easement. An easement should contain all details on timeframes, management, and closure and marked on maps and charts. Most construction developments in water are regulated by the water rights court. It is possible that an underwater *ex situ* reburial depot would need to be granted permission by such a court.

Collection strategies for reburial?

Today many museums are updating their collection strategies regarding, not only what to collect and keep, but also what to de-access from their collection. With a constant increase in the number of finds comes the need for larger storage areas. Already, many museum storage areas are almost full and, with often limited funds, it is valid to question what should be preserved and at what cost.

In the same way that traditional conservation and storage preserves an object for future study and exhibition purposes, so too is reburial designed for preservation so that artefacts can be accessed and researched in the future. Reburial of artefacts *in situ* is no doubt the better and less complicated option, since the artefacts are returned to their original context and protected by the same heritage legislation as the site itself. However, in many cases underwater archaeology occurs when a heritage site is threatened because of planned construction work. After the archaeological excavation, the heritage site will no longer exist, so any reburial would have to be *ex situ*.

A reburial *ex situ* is a museum storage area that requires management and the application of collection strategies. It is easy to use reburial depots as 'archaeological artefact dumps' when the decision to discard is difficult or controversial. However, it is important to make a clear distinction between reburial and disposal. Reburial is preservation. If there are no thoughts about future use of an artefact or a collection, there is little point preserving it at all. Reburied artefacts are not meant to be forgotten in the sediments. Reburial *ex situ* should not be chosen instead of conscious disposal if the artefacts have been evaluated as of no or little use based on, for example, scientific, technological, educational or aesthetic grounds. In reality, even if there are three ways of dealing with the physical finds from an excavation: conservation, reburial (*in situ* or *ex situ*) and disposal, the decisions the practitioners face are between preservation and disposal.

The Swedish Heritage Act (1988) demands that every archaeological excavation has a find strategy. This strategy contains an assessment of the expected number and types of finds, how these are to be collected and managed during the excavation, and, furthermore, the motives for the collection and selection of finds to be conserved. These motives should be guided by the scientific aim of the individual excavation. A similar attitude and strategy is appropriate for artefacts that are to be reburied *ex situ*.

Collection dilemmas

Preservation strategies should be based on scientific reasoning — first of all site-specific questions, but sometimes taking into account regional and national aspects. While most practitioners would agree, in reality, it is not always that easy. An examination of existing archaeological stores would confirm the presence of an endless number of small flint artefacts (inexpensive to preserve and store) but fewer large conservation/storage-costly artefacts. A preservation strategy based on what is affordable, while realistic, is not acceptable as it leads to an unrepresentative picture of a particular archaeological site or region.

Consequently, collection and preservation strategies are necessary. These will vary from one country to another and over time. The Marstrand project used a set of general criteria to help decide what to conserve and what to rebury (Nyström, 2002). However useful, such general criteria tend to be just that, and each excavation needs its own, more detailed guidelines based on the particular situation at hand.

Limited time for the assessment process is a situation that is common to most excavations. The discussions of what to preserve or discard often begin too late. The assessment of sites and artefacts are not easy, but it would become less difficult if the process started early and was coherent and consistent with regional and/or national collection policies. With such policies in place and collaboration between the site manager, conservator, and other specialists, the process has a chance of being as successful as possible. However, only the future can tell if coming generations will praise or curse us for what we choose to preserve or discard.

Reburial time frames

If we accept that artefacts reburied *ex situ* should be used in the future, we need to discuss time frames and strategies for closure. The RAAR project recommends that stipulated time frames be part of any reburial strategy. The project has previously used the terms short- and long-term reburial as a way of categorizing the reburial potential of different materials, but it was only recently we asked ourselves what we actually meant by these terms. How long is long term, and does the short term get longer with coming retrievals, if the material survives? Long term certainly does not mean eternity, since reburial depots (*ex situ*) are not meant to last forever.

Retrievability has been discussed by RAAR as a way of defining long-term reburial, relating it to the working life of a person, for example, approximately twenty-five years. This definition argues that information gets lost, and foci and agendas change when a person retires. Against this, one could argue that a reburial depot is the responsibility of a museum or similar institution and is, thus, secure. Unfortunately, in reality it is often not the case. Eventually, it was decided that, for the RAAR project, long-term reburial is twenty-five to fifty years, since fifty years is the planned life of the project. The project defined short-term reburial as lasting between nought to five years. A third term was introduced, medium-term reburial. Below is a first draft of the suggested time frame categories:

- *Short term: 0–5 years.* Storage solution while preparing for documentation, conservation, traditional storage, and/or analyses.
- *Medium term: 5–25 years.* Artefacts or collections awaiting analysis to answer future research questions, improved analytical techniques, and/or the development of more suitable conservation treatments.
- *Long term, 25–50 years.* Exceptional conditions. Finds with a very high archaeological potential, but where documentation and conservation is not possible due to a structural lack of resources and/or competence.

To these time frames, collection strategies and programmes should be added: documents that describe the intentions with the reburied finds, time schedules, and funding proposals. Failure in this system must also be considered. Even if a reburial programme is designed with strategies for future retrieval and funding, there is always the potential risk that this will not occur. How do we prepare for that? Do we physically dispose of the artefacts in such circumstances or can we 'only' rid ourselves of the problem legally and administratively? An easement can and should be very precise, but could an *ex-situ* reburial easement state that the depot is no longer a depot after a certain number of years? Would that be a way to part with ownership and responsibility? Would that be ethical?

Reburial — comparing the situation in the RAAR countries — Australia, Denmark, Norway, and Sweden

A minor questionnaire was sent to the RAAR participants in order to get an update on what is happening in the respective countries with regards to reburial and heritage management issues. The questions addressed general perceptions, as well as legal and management issues. The summary below is based on the answers received, which may not necessarily be the complete picture of the reburial situation in each respective country.

- Has your perception (opinion) on reburial changed during the last ten years?
- If so, in what sense?

The RAAR participants' view on reburial has changed over the past ten years, and become more nuanced. Initially, some had more positive and others more negative opinions of the method as a way of preserving archaeological artefacts. We now believe that the method is scientifically valid for certain materials. However, there is a danger that heritage managers and government officials will apply these methods as the cheaper alternative to full or even partial excavation and conservation of recovered materials. Recent research results highlight the fact that these techniques cannot be simply used as a blanket model for all sites and each site must be analysed and considered separately.

If there is consensus between the RAAR participants on the technical side of reburial, there is less so when we discuss why and when we should rebury artefacts — this is particularly true for reburial *ex situ*. For some of us, reburial *ex situ* should be the very last option after traditional conservation or disposal. It should be temporary storage with time limits and programmes of intent. Decisions regarding what to preserve must be made at the time of excavation. Others believe that when faced with the loss of cultural heritage, reburial is a good method and a better option than 'preservation by record'. These differences in opinion within the RAAR project probably reflect a more general opinion on the subject among museum/heritage practitioners.

- Under what legal act would a reburial depot be protected, if the depot is not on the archaeological site?
- Who is the owner of the artefacts in a reburial depot in your country?
- Are the legal aspects of a reburial depot discussed in your country?

There has been no reburial depots (*ex situ*) established in Australia; therefore, the legislation has not been tested and the legal aspects are rarely discussed. In Australia, the Commonwealth would be the legal owners of artefacts in a reburial depot and there are possibly two ways in which a reburial depot might be protected under the legislation.

1. The legislation has the capacity to protect shipwreck artefacts even if they are not physically located on an actual shipwreck site.
2. The reburial depot is placed in close proximity to the actual shipwreck site, and a protected zone is established (large enough to incorporate the wreck site and the reburial depot together) through Commonwealth legislation.

In Sweden, Denmark, and Norway the legal aspects have been discussed, but are not a prioritized topic. Actual depots have most often been *ad hoc* solutions. In Sweden, the archaeological finds would be owned and managed by the state or a regional museum and protected by civil laws, not by the Heritage Act. In Denmark the *ex situ* finds would be protected by the Museum law, which is the same law that protects the archaeological site and management would be performed by the state or delegated to the regional museum. The current Norwegian law does not address the concept of artefact reburial. Several instances of the reburial of marine finds (both on land and in the marine environment) have now led to discussion of the legal aspects.

The long-term aspects of reburial are rarely considered. Even though there has been a step in the right direction in terms of international legislation (e.g. UNESCO, 2001; European Convention, 1992), the implications cannot be seen on the national level in terms of heritage agency or local museum policies.

- Are reburial depots managed locally, regionally, nationally, or a combination of all?
- Are reburial management issues discussed in your country?
- Are you aware of any reburial cases where reburial programmes have been put in place to outline why, what, and when the artefacts should/could be used or cases where time frames have been set?

General *in situ* preservation management issues are discussed in Australia, but the idea of reburial depots are not. If reburial depots were established in Australia, the delegated authority for the Commonwealth in each State would be the managers. For example, in Western Australia, the Commonwealth's delegated authority is the Western Australian Museum and they would be the managers of the depot.

In Demark and Sweden there are discussions both on general *in situ* management issues, but also on reburial depots. Money has been invested in research in Denmark and Sweden, but the problem is obtaining continued funding for monitoring of sites and a general acceptance of the strategy. In Denmark there has been no obvious general strategy — reburial depots are managed locally, regionally, and nationally. In Sweden, to date, depots have only been managed locally. In Norway, there is no general strategy. Marine reburial depots are managed regionally, if at all. However, several instances of reburial in the marine environment have initiated a review of the legal aspects.

In terms of the practicalities of *in situ* preservation both on land and underwater, questions of accessioning and so on underpin the problems. When the decision is made, procurement of suitable pieces of land or areas of seabed has not usually been considered. No one is really prepared to pay for any subsequent monitoring.

No participant was aware of any reburial cases where reburial programmes have been put in place to outline why, what and when the artefacts should/could be recovered and used or cases where time frames had been set.

Final remarks

It seems apparent that the reburial method has been studied mainly from a degradation point of view. Different reburial studies have focused on the long-term physical stability of the different materials and much less on the long-term consequences of administration and management of the reburial site. Looking at actual reburials (both *ex situ* and *in situ*), they seem to have come about *ad hoc*. They are often responses to emergency situations and heterogeneous in their character. To make reburial a useful and comprehensive tool for heritage management we need to:

- Understand the pros and cons of reburial.
- Preferably use *in situ* reburial (depending on the laws of the country).
- Only use *ex situ* reburial depots that are fully managed and legally protected.
- Improve reburial programmes.
- Collaborate and actively discuss collection policies (what to preserve) on a local, regional, and national level.
- Stress the need for improved national legislation that incorporate *in situ* preservation and reburial strategies.

Bibliography

Bergstrand, T. and Nyström, I. 2001. *Återdeponering av arkeologiskt fyndmaterial — en metod?* Bohusläns Museum rapport 2001:32, ISSN 1650-3368.

Bergstrand, T. and Nyström Godfrey, I. eds. 2007. *Reburial and Analyses of Archaeological Remains. Studies on the Effect of Reburial on Archaeological Materials Performed in Marstrand, Sweden 2002–2005*, Kulturhistoriska dokumentationer nr 20, Uddevalla: Bohusläns Museum, ISSN 1102-528X.

The European Convention on the Protection of the Archaeological Heritage. 1992. Council of Europe. Valetta, Malta, 16 January 1992. Available at: <http://conventions.coe.int/treaty/en/treaties/html/143.htm>.

ICOMOS, 1996. *Charter for the Protection and Management of the Underwater Cultural Heritage.* Ratified by the 11th ICOMOS General Assembly, held in Sofia, Bulgaria, from 5–9 October 1996. Available at: <http://www.international.icomos.org/under_e.htm>.

Nyström, I. 2002. Preventive Conservation and Re-burial of Archaeological Objects. In: P. Hoffmann, J. A. Spriggs, T. Grant, C. Cook, and A. Recht, eds. *Proceedings of the 8th ICOM Group on Wet Organic Archaeological Materials Conference, Stockholm 11–15 June 2001.* Bremerhaven: International Council of Museums (ICOM), Committee for Conservation Working Group on Wet Organic Archaeological Materials, pp. 167–74.

Nyström Godfrey, I., Bergstrand, T., Bohm, C., Christensson, E., Gjelstrup Björdal, C., Gregory, D., MacLeod, I., Nilsson, T., Peacock, E. E., and Richards, V. 2009. Reburial and Analyses of Archaeological Remains. The RAAR Project. Project Status and Cultural Heritage Management Implications based on the First Preliminary Results. In: K. Strætkvern and D. J. Huisman, eds. *Proceedings of the 10th ICOM Group on Wet Organic Archaeological Materials Conference, Amsterdam, 10–15 September 2007.* Amersfoort: Rijksdienst voor Archeologie, Cultuurlandschap en Monumenten (RACM), pp. 169–96.

Nyström Godfrey, I., Bergstrand, T., Bohm, C., Christensson, E., Gjelstrup Björdal, C., Gregory, D., MacLeod, I., Peacock, E. E., and Richards, V. in press. Reburial and Analyses of Archaeological Remains. The RAAR

Project. Phase II — Project Status and New Findings. In *Proceedings of the 11th ICOM Group on Wet Organic Archaeological Materials Conference, Greenville, 24–28 May 2010*.

Nyström Godfrey, I., Bergstrand, T., and Petersson, H. eds. 2011. *Reburial and Analyses of Archaeological Remains. Phase II — Results from the 4th Retrieval in 2009 from Marstrand, Sweden*. Kulturhistoriska dokumentationer nr 28, Uddevalla: Bohusläns Museum and Studio Västsvensk Konservering.

Ortmann, J., McKinnon, J. F., and Richards, V. 2010. In-Situ Preservation and Storage: Practitioners Attitudes and Behaviours. *Bulletin of the Australasian Institute for Maritime Archaeology*, 34: 27–44.

The RAAR website, 2002. Available at: <http://www9.vgregion.se/vastarvet/svk/reburial/index.htm>.

Riksantikvarieämbetet 2008. *Kulturmiljövård under vatten. En rapport till vägledning för arkeologer och handläggare verksamma inom kulturmiljöområdet*. Ed. Cecilia Borssén. Riksantikvarieämbetet Rapport 2008:5, ISSN 1651-1298, ISBN 978-91-7209-525-0.

Statens Maritima Museer, 2005. Återdeponering av arkeologiskt fyndmaterial. Unpublished report from Statens Maritima Museer, dnr 1320/05-51.

The Swedish Heritage Act, 1988. *Lag om kulturminnen m.m.* Svensk författningssamling SFS nr 1988:950. Available at: <http://www.riksdagen.se/Webbnav/index.aspx?nid=3911&bet=1988:950>.

UNESCO, 2001. *Convention on the Protection of the Underwater Cultural Heritage 2001*. The General Conference of the United Nations Educational, Scientific and Cultural Organisation, 31st Session, Paris, 15 October to 3 November 2001. Available at: <http://portal.unesco.org/en/ev.php-URL_ID=13520&URL_DO=DO_TOPIC&URL_SECTION=201.html>.

Notes on contributors

Inger Nyström Godfrey has a BSc in Conservation and a BA in Classical Archaeology from the University of Göteborg. She is a senior archaeological conservator and has worked in the field of conservation since 1989. She has been involved in reburials and *in situ* preservation of marine archaeological sites since 1998 and is one of the coordinator the RAAR project.

Correspondence to: Inger Nyström Godfrey. Email: inger.nystrom@vgregion.se

Thomas Bergstrand has an MA in Archaeology from the University of Gothenburg. He has been employed since 1997 at Bohusläns Museum, Uddevalla, Sweden, in the field of marine archaeology. His main focus is marine contract archaeology and heritage management; including issues concerning *in situ* preservation, reburial and similar questions. He is one of the coordinators of the RAAR project.

Correspondence to: Thomas Bergstrand. Email: thomas.bergstrand@vgregion.se

Håkan Petersson has a doctor's degree in Archaeology from the University of Gothenburg and is since 2004 employed as research co-ordinator at Bohusläns museum, Uddevalla. One of his main scientific areas of interest is methodological studies connected to Archaeological development.

Correspondence to: Håkan Petersson. Email: hakan.petersson@vgregion.se

Carola Bohm has a BA in Archaeology (Uppsala University) and a BSc in Archaeological Conservation and Materials Science (Institute of Archaeology, University of London). She worked in the Conservation Department at the Swedish National Heritage Board for twenty-seven years, specializing in ceramics and glass and with particular interest in glass deterioration — atmospheric as well as terrestrial and marine. Since 2008 she is engaged in private practice in Stockholm.

Correspondence to: Carola Bohm, Acta Konserveringscentrum AB, Riddargatan 13D, 114 51 Stockholm, Sweden. Email: carola.bohm@actakonservering.se

Eva Christensson has a BA in Archaeology, Ethnology, and Art History (1972), and further studies in Classical Archaeology (1989) from the University of Lund, Sweden. She has a BSc (1991) from the University of Wales, College of Cardiff in Archaeological Conservation. Since 1994 she has been working as a conservator at the Swedish National Heritage Board mainly with ceramics, bone, ivory, and amber in close cooperation with, especially, the Mediterranean Museum and the National Historical Museum in Stockholm.

Correspondence to: Eva Christensson, National Heritage Board, Artillerigatan 33A, 621 38 Visby. Email: eva.christensson@raa.se

Charlotte Gjelstrup Björdal gained her BSc in conservation from the Royal Academy of Arts, Copenhagen, 1986, and specialized in conservation of waterlogged archaeological wood. In 2000, she defended her doctoral thesis 'Waterlogged Archaeological Wood – Biodegradation and its Implication for Conservation', at the Dept of Wood Science, Swedish University of Agricultural Sciences. During the last fifteen years, her research has focused on microbial degradation processes in archaeological wood from marine and terrestrial environments, and their implications and consequences for long-term preservation of cultural heritage. Charlotte Gjelstrup Björdal is associate professor and Director of the Conservation Program at the Department of Conservation, University of Gothenburg, Sweden.

Correspondence to: Charlotte Gjelstrup Björdal, Conservation Program at the Department of Conservation, University of Gothenburg, Sweden. Email: charlotte.bjordal@conservation.gu.se

David Gregory worked for several years in the pharmaceutical industry as an analytical chemist. After that he obtained a BSc in archaeology (University of Leicester), MPhil in Maritime studies (St Andrews University), and PhD ('Formation processes in underwater archaeology: a study of the deterioration of archaeological materials in the marine environment', 1996 (University of Leicester). He is currently employed as a senior scientist at the National Museum of Denmark investigating methods of *in situ* preservation in waterlogged and underwater environments.

Correspondence to: David Gregory. Email: david.john.gregory@natmus.dk

Ian MacLeod has a PhD and a Doctor of Philosophy from Melbourne University. He has been solving deterioration problems with shipwreck artefacts since 1978. He is passionately interested in the decay of glass, ceramics, wood, and metals. He was granted a Senior Fulbright Fellowship in 1993 and a Getty Conservation Institute fellowship in 2010 that allowed him to develop his research.

Correspondence to: Ian MacLeod, Western Australian Maritime Museum, Peter Hughes Drive, Victoria Quay, Fremantle, WA 6160, Australia. Email: ian.macleod@museum.wa.gov.au

Elizabeth E. Peacock is a Professor of Conservation at the Norwegian University of Science & Technology and University of Gothenburg, focusing on conservation research and education following extensive experience in practical conservation. She has researched in pedagogy and organic archaeological materials addressing biodeterioration, *in situ* preservation, reburial, and environmental monitoring, as well as remedial conservation.

Correspondence to: Elizabeth E. Peacock, NTNU Museum, Norwegian University of Science and Technology, Trondheim, Norway, & Department of Conservation, University of Gothenburg, Sweden. Email: elizabeth.peacock@ntnu.no

Vicki Richards has a B.App.Sci. (Hons) (Curtin University) and an MPhil in chemistry (Murdoch University). Vicki Richards has been a Conservation Scientist in the Materials Conservation Department of the Western Australian Museum for the past twenty-four years. One of her primary research areas is investigating deterioration mechanisms of metals and organic materials on shipwreck sites and devising and implementing appropriate on-site management plans for the long-term *in situ* preservation of these sites.

Correspondence to: Vicki Richards, Department of Materials Conservation, Western Australian Museum, Shipwreck Galleries, 45–47 Cliff St, Fremantle, WA 6160, Australia. Email: vicki.richards@museum.wa.gov.au

CONSERVATION AND MGMT OF ARCH. SITES, Vol. 14 Nos 1–4, 2012, 372–83

PARIS London: One Hundred and Fifty Years of Site Preservation

Jane Sidell

English Heritage, UK

This paper outlines the history of preservation *in situ* as practised in London over the last hundred and fifty years. It touches upon the early development of the City of London and the destruction of significant remains, which gradually lead to a heightening of sensitivities and public concern for preservation, particularly of built fabric such as the Roman defences. The role of cases such as the Walbrook Mithraeum and Rose Theatre are discussed, both influential in changing the relationship between development and archaeology. The paper concludes by noting how much we have learnt from past mistakes, but notes that more can be done to make these sites more accessible.

KEYWORDS London, archaeology, Roman, Rose Theatre, urban preservation *in situ*

Introduction

The archaeology of London is often exceptionally well preserved owing to the River Thames and its tributaries, and extensive waterlogging. Additionally, the focus of occupation has shifted within the city, leading to periods of stasis for monumental remains. Furthermore, there is a clear history of interest in the past. Even before the Age of Enlightenment, evidence exists of recording and preservation of monuments by early antiquarians such as John Aubrey (1626–97) and William Stukeley (1687–1765), whilst John Stow in his famous *Survey of London* (1598) records a Roman cemetery at Bishopsgate, and William Dugdale similarly noted Roman finds in Southwark in 1662.

With the rapid expansion of London in the eighteenth century, more archaeological remains came to light, and antiquarians sought to understand artefacts and structures in context (Cotton, 1999). A more focused appreciation of archaeological deposits in London can be seen through the works of Flaxman Spurrell (Scott and Shaw, 2009), and particularly Charles Roach-Smith (Sheppard, 1991). The mid-nineteenth century also saw the formation of a new generation of societies — rather than the formal grandeur of institutions like the Society of Antiquaries, more modest organizations

DOI 10.1179/1350503312Z.00000000033

developed, including the British Archaeological Association (1843), the London and Middlesex Archaeological Society (1851), the Surrey Archaeological Society (1854), and the Kent Archaeological Society (1857). These societies were concerned with studying and recording remains, but also preservation. The London and Middlesex Archaeological Society constitution reads: 'To promote the preservation and recording of historic buildings, ancient monuments, documents and other remains'.

Early sites

Possibly the earliest known example of a deliberate attempt at preservation *in situ* can be traced back to Christopher Wren. William Stukeley noted in 1748, whilst lamenting the damage done through construction at Mansion House, that Wren 'had taken great care to preserve by casing it', the London Stone (Celoria and Spence, 1968: n. 43). This rather legendary stone is considered, amongst other wilder ideas, to be the marker stone from whence all distance in the Roman province of Britannia was measured (Clark, 2010). It now sits, sadly, on one side of Cannon Street, having been moved from the centre of the road in 1742 (Figure 1). Wren took rather less care elsewhere, however, for whilst he discovered significant Roman remains during the rebuilding of St Paul's Cathedral, he did not preserve them. Fortunately some records were made by John Conyers, considered to be London's first archaeologist (Schofield, 2011).

It is not until significantly more recently that deliberate decisions were made to protect archaeological sites *in situ*. Records of discoveries exist from the eighteenth century (Sloane, 2008), including mosaics (Woodward, 1707) and the City Wall (Price, 1880), but there is no evidence of attempts to preserve *in situ*. Perhaps the earliest well-publicized example is the Anglo-Saxon barrow cemetery in Greenwich Park. The first known mention of the cemetery is in Harris' History of Kent (1719), and in 1784 extensive excavation of the barrows occurred. Records are almost non-existent — only eight are described, noting primary burials, some in wooden coffins (Douglas, 1793). It was a subsequent intrusion that caused a public outcry.

22 June 1844 — *Illustrated London News*:

> We are sorry to see it stated that there is pending an invasion of the sylvan shades of Greenwich, that most favourite resort of smoke-dried Londoners. An immense tank, to supply the hospital with water is to occupy with its unslightlyness one of the prettiest spots in the park, sweeping away the ancient barrows which have hitherto been carefully preserved as objects of antiquarian interest.

29 June 1844 — *Illustrated London News*

> Ten days ago while a public meeting [...] was being held for the purpose of taking the sense of the public on the threatened trespass and desecration, a set of worlds-end wretches were let loose on the barrows and in a few short hours, three-fourths of them were actually and IN SPITE cleanly and smoothly shaven from the face of the ancient sward. This was to add insult to oppression. The historic affections of the people were not only wounded, but their rights as Englishmen-ay and as the park-owners were defied. The thing was not to be borne. Meeting after meeting was led; remonstrances were urged, consequences threatened and at length the Admiralty navigators have been withdrawn from the Park.

LONDON STONE WHICH HAS LONG PUZZLED THE ANTIQUARIES   McLeish

Set in a stone casing in the wall of St. Swithin's, Cannon Street, is this block of oolite, guarded by a grille. It was placed there in 1798, having been transferred from the other side of the road. Camden, the historian, 1551–1623, held that it was the milliarium, or milestone, from which distances were calculated on the main roads in days when London was Londinium Augusta. There was a similar stone in the Forum at Rome. If Camden is right, Roman lictors may have stood, like this policeman, in front of the stone 1,600 years ago.

14

FIGURE 1   London Stone.

The strength of feeling meant the reservoir was moved to the south, and the barrows have remained preserved ever since. It was a central principle with Greenwich that the barrows be preserved within their landscape, following a tradition of incorporating the barrows within new schemes in the Park, including in the fifteenth and seventeenth centuries. Quite how much of this was deliberate and how much chance is uncertain, but the significance of context is clear.

Unfortunately most areas of London cannot claim the same longevity of undisturbed tranquillity. This is superlatively true of the City of London, which incorporates the Roman city and much of the medieval city; it is practically an obscured tell, with over nine metres of archaeological stratigraphy surviving at its heart (Rowsome, 2000). By the early medieval period, it is clear that earlier structures were used as new foundations, but doubtless for ease of construction and building material rather than to preserve these earlier structures for their intrinsic importance.

Even before the outcry in Greenwich, an understanding of the antiquities being destroyed in the City of London is documented, along with attempts to reduce the destruction and preserve remains *ex situ* if *in situ* could not be managed. The new sewer network required vast trenching operations and generated a significant number of finds. Roach Smith noted half a dozen Roman mosaics destroyed in 1836–37 (Sheppard, 1991), as well as some sections of the Roman Wall (see RCHM(E) 1928). The Commissioners of Sewers donated many finds and, whilst this scheme did not lead to preservation *in situ*, it heightened awareness of the wholesale destruction inherent in infrastructure schemes, noted in a letter of 1847 from the Guildhall library to the Commissioners indicating the disastrous effect upon the Roman City (Sheppard, 1991).

It seems likely this contributed to the earliest deliberate case of preservation *in situ* in the City the following year, when the Billingsgate bathhouse was discovered (Figure 2). The *tepidarium* was uncovered during the construction of the Coal Exchange, and preserved, by order of the City Architect, J. B. Brunning (Marsden, 1968), who by this act becomes an important figure in the history of London's archaeology. This was underscored a decade later, when the site next door was developed and more of the bathhouse was uncovered, and the precedent of retaining the fabric was continued. A century passed and in 1968 the Coal Exchange and warehouses were demolished and yet more of the complex was preserved.

It appears that successes depended on serendipity. Were the right people involved? What was the scheme? And also what was the aesthetic quality of the remains. In 1805, for instance, the Bank of England mosaic, discovered during construction, was lifted and given to the British Museum. Yet, in the 1830s, many more were destroyed by the sewers. In 1848 and 1859 parts of the Billingsgate Bathhouse were saved, yet in 1864, during the construction of Cannon Street Railway Station, 'the Roman masonry was so hard that some stretches had to be blown up with dynamite to remove them' (Sheppard, 1991: 20). Yet, the Bucklersbury Pavement, found in 1869, was on show for three days in which an estimated 33,000 people visited and then the mosaic was then carefully removed to the Guildhall Museum (Price, 1870).

The Roman city wall

The history of the Roman city wall, thought to have been approximately 3 km in length (RCHM(E), 1928; Maloney, 1983), is a curious mixture of casual destruction

FIGURE 2   The Billingsgate bathhouse, from the *Illustrated London News* (1848).

and careful preservation, with no learning from the mistakes of the past to preserve what remained for the future. It is a microcosm of preservation *in situ* across London; sporadic successes when particular circumstances combine, but also tragic and preventable losses.

Nineteenth century

Destruction of the wall was extensive, during construction of new buildings, but particularly the Southend Railway and the Circle Underground Line. This included the wall, several bastions, also some culverts at Moorgate thought to be for the passage of the Walbrook Stream. Small sections survived, some deliberately, such as the large stretch at Tower Hill (Figure 3) but usually only by chance, when the wall could be reused, or quirkily, as in the basement of the electricity substation to power the Circle Line. Sections of what is thought to be the riverside wall were observed, and probably survived as it was more extensively eroded and robbed than the landward wall and so did not form such a significant obstacle to development, only surviving below ground level.

Early twentieth century

Extensive development occurred in the early years, particularly 1905, and a number of sections were lost, however, more efforts were made to preserve elements, such as in the current Roman Wall House, All Hallows on the Wall, the Tower of London, and the angle bastion found at Christ's Hospital (Norman and Reader, 1912).

FIGURE 3   London Wall at Tower Hill.

Post-war

There were extensive finds made by Grimes in this period, and very little development in the immediate post-war years. This lead to extensive preservation of stretches, particularly in the area of the Cripplegate Fort, much of which was revealed through bombing and subsequent clearance of the more modern fabric (Grimes, 1968). However, with increased development, even whilst it would be hoped that by this date the significance and rarity of the wall was well established, there have still been losses.

This includes an internal turret removed in 1966, more at Baynard's Castle riverside wall (Maloney, 1983). And yet, new stretches of the wall are still appearing: in 2009 a section joining the Coopers Row stretch was uncovered following demolition, and awaits incorporation into a new hotel scheme.

Post-war archaeology

Following the Blitz, it was clear that rebuilding was going to be the work of decades and it was noted, in typical style by Mortimer Wheeler, that this could significantly threaten the remaining surviving fabric:

> In rebuilding itself, on this occasion, London will destroy more of her history than has any single one of the many great fires. At stake is nearly 2000 years of accumulated material bearing upon the history and everyday life of the greatest city in the world, potential knowledge which can now be acquired for relatively modest cost but can never again be bought. (Wheeler, 1944)

This coincided with the birth of professional archaeology, with qualified staff (albeit very few) undertaking fieldwork under the aegis of the Roman and Medieval London Excavation Council (Grimes, 1968). Preservation was not seen as a priority at this period — it was very much an opportunistic time to gain knowledge of the Roman and medieval cities.

A turning point came in 1954, with what became known as 'the famous Mithras incident' (Shepherd, 1998). Grimes was excavating a Roman temple, and following normal practice the site was being recorded, and then it would have eventually have been dismantled. A sculpted head of Mithras was discovered on 18 September, word of the discovery of the Temple got out, and the public broke into the site on Sunday the 19th. The case was reported in *The Times*, 20 September 1954, and included the statement:

> There is something grievously wrong with our planning if an important antiquity of this sort can be destroyed almost before it has been seen. What other civilised nations may think of the matter is a point upon which once can only speculate apprehensively. It is no wonder that many of those who visited the site yesterday (some of whom came to The Times office to lodge their protests) were asking why no arrangements could be made either to arch over the remains in a sort of crypt, or to remove them stone by stone for re-erection elsewhere.

The paragraph is significant for two reasons — consideration of the impact made outside Britain on how cultural remains were treated, and for the public expressing a desire to protect remains *in situ*. The Minister of Works, Sir David Eccles, visited the site with Grimes and scheduling was discussed which would have led to preservation *in situ*. The cost of compensation to the developer, and delays to crucial post-war redevelopment meant, unsurprisingly, that scheduling was discounted.

And yet approximately 30,000 visitors queued over nine days; strikingly reminiscent of the Bucklersbury pavement nearly a hundred years before and a hundred yards away. A rather uneasy compromise was achieved — the remains were largely dismantled for re-assembly a few hundred yards from the original location. There are some woeful errors in the reconstruction, nevertheless, it is a popular site; and has been listed at Grade II as an important part of the social history of the City.

Subsequently, redevelopment of the City progressed more rapidly, with extensive excavations. Very few professional archaeologists were employed; Ivor Noel Hume, Peter Marsden, Francis Celoria, Roy Canham, Brian Hobley, and Harvey Sheldon bore the brunt, supported by an army of amateur archaeologists. A growing unease developed about the loss of many important sites, such as Baynard's Castle; a substantial site on the City waterfront with monumental remains but too little time to record them before the site was cleared for development in 1972. This Corporation of London was both developer and planning authority, and received stern criticism over the way the site was treated (Sheldon and Haynes, 2000), underscoring the need for a stronger link between archaeology and planning.

Fear for the future was also growing, with a consciousness that archaeological remains were finite and it would be possible to run out of archaeology. This led to the survey known as the *Future of London's Past* (Biddle et al., 1973) and the profession moved from one which simply rescued archaeology to understanding, and managing it as a resource. This is really when preservation *in situ* as we understand it evolved; unfortunately this coincided with a boom in development which has never really gone away. Using site codes is simplistic but an indicative way of establishing fieldwork quantities. In the 1970s 538 site codes were issued, in the 1980s 871 and 2800 in the 1990s.

Planning Policy Guidance note 16

Things came to a head in the late 1980s with the Huggin Hill bathhouse and the Rose Theatre. The story of the Rose is well known (Bowsher, 1996), the bathhouse, less so (Orton, 1989). They were both of clear national if not international importance. It was almost as if both the professionals and the public decided a line had to be drawn, and both sites received extensive media coverage, and questions in Parliament. The coverage of the Rose was on an international scale, including uniquely (it can only be hoped), the release of a campaigning soft-rock ballad.

If our complacency had been jolted with the Temple of Mithras, history was changed by the Rose and Huggin Hill. The public outcry brought the growing unease of the previous decades into sharp relief, bringing forward documentation to firmly incorporate the protection of archaeology within the planning process and enshrine the principle of preservation *in situ*:

> Where nationally important archaeological remains, whether scheduled or not, and their settings, are affected by proposed development there should be a presumption in favour of their physical preservation. (PPG16 para 8, Department of the Environment 1990)

Yet it has not all been a perfect dream of preservation since then. It has taken time to explore mechanisms of preservation. Sometimes, whole zones of a development site have been preserved in their entirety, whilst elsewhere some deposits are excavated away, leaving the remainder *in situ*. Masonry tends to be preserved whilst soft archaeology is excavated away. This is philosophically problematical; separating masonry from its context can really only be seen as partial preservation; however, it is acknowledged that masonry is the most 'readable' form of archaeology as well as the most robust, usually able to survive changes in ground conditions. A good example of where masonry has been preserved and soft archaeology removed is the

FIGURE 4   Roman bathhouse at Shadwell.

Shadwell bathhouse (Figure 4; Douglas et al., 2011), where the decision to preserve the site was taken part way through the scheme, and the costs offset by the granting of permission to increase the height of the development. The most spectacular example remains the Guildhall Amphitheatre (Bateman, 2000), presented within a bespoke viewing chamber (Figure 5).

A particularly contentious area is organic remains. It is recognized that soil hydrology is still poorly understood, and thousands of Roman and medieval timbers have been removed over time. The main reason such structures and sites are excavated and not preserved stems from doubt over whether the material would preserve long term, given unavoidable irregularities in water quality and level. The other main reason for the removal of timber structures include the need to carefully unpick the layers of timber buildings, drains, wells, water pipes, trackways, and so on to fully understand the complexity of urban deposits. A balance needs to be struck between what we preserve and what we excavate to develop our knowledge of the City.

Legacy

Interestingly, now that some sites have been preserved for so long, legacy issues are arising. The Rose Theatre has been monitored for over twenty years; at what point does the exercise simply become one of data gathering for its own sake, rather than to examine chemical and hydrological trends and plan management of the site? (See

FIGURE 5   The Guildhall Amphitheatre.
By permission of the Museum of London

Corfield, this volume, for extended discussion of this site.) The original site of the Temple of Mithras is being redeveloped and the listed reconstruction has been carefully dismantled prior to re-reconstruction close to the original location, where more foundations have recently been uncovered. Suggestions have been made to move the London Stone again, to improve its visibility, but have been met with vehement opposition. Other sites such as Billingsgate now require extensive conservation owing to gradual degradation. Even the Guildhall amphitheatre, the best maintained example in London, requires conservation from time to time owing to the impact of visitors. Furthermore, preservation has to be balanced with interpretation. Our understanding of the structures changes with new discoveries, as does the way the public like to be informed. The existing panels on the City Wall are practically artefacts themselves, whilst a new smartphone application has just been created for Roman Londinium.

Conclusion

It makes uncomfortable reading, but it appears that whilst the spirit of PPG16 and its new replacement Planning Policy Statement 5 are broadly followed, formal examples of preservation *in situ* are relatively rare, and the main cases tend to be associated with scheduled monuments where the legal controls are much stronger. Even rarer are those examples where is it possible to preserve and present the fabric to the public. When this occurs it appears to be less a result of enforcing policy but where serendipitous circumstances coalesce to make it desirable, possible and economical to do so. The history recounted above shows this paradigm dates back almost 200 years.

Nevertheless, considering the continual occupation of central London for two millennia, the wars, the greed, self-aggrandisement, and expansionism, we still have a remarkable range of heritage on show. Some of it may be in nightclubs, car parks, pub cellars, cupboards, down manholes, and behind lavatory panels, but there remains a body of archaeologists willing to do battle to protect as much as possible, and the fabric of modern London is all the better for it.

Acknowledgements

This paper has drawn upon the work of many who have preserved and written about archaeology. In addition to those named in the text and references, thanks go to Sally Brooks, Cath Maloney, Roy Stephenson, John Stewart, Kathryn Stubbs, and Krysia Truscoe.

Bibliography

Bateman, N. 2000. *Gladiators at the Guildhall. The Story of London's Roman Amphitheatre and Medieval Guildhall*. London: Museum of London Archaeology Service.

Biddle, M. and Hudson, D., with Heighway, C. 1973. *The Future of London's Past*. Rescue publication 4.

Bowsher, J. 1996. *The Rose Theatre. An Archaeological Discovery*. London: Museum of London.

Celoria, F. and Spence, B. W. 1968. Eighteenth Century Fieldwork in London and Middlesex: Some Unpublished Drawings by William Stukeley. *Transactions of the London and Middlesex Archaeological Society*, 22: 23–31.

Clark, J. 2010. London Stone: Stone of Brutus or Fetish Stone — Making the Myth. *Folklore*, 121(1): 38–60.

Cotton, J. 1999. Ballast-heavers and Battle-axes: The 'Golden Age' of Thames Finds. In: A. Coles and M. Dion, eds. *Mark Dion: Archaeology*. London: Black Dog Press, pp. 58–71.

Department of the Environment, 1990. *PPG 16; November 1990, Planning Policy Guidance: Archaeology and Planning*. London: HMSO.

Douglas, A., Gerrard, J., and Sudds, B. 2011. *A Roman Settlement and Bath House at Shadwell. Excavations at Tobacco Dock and Babe Ruth Restaurant, The Highway, London*. London: Pre-Construct Archaeology Ltd.

Douglas, J. 1793. *Nenia Britannica, or a Sepulchral History of Great Britain, from the Earliest Period to its General Conversion to Christianity*. London.

Dugdale, Sir W. 1662. *History of Imbanking and Drayning*.

Grimes, W. F. 1968. *The Excavation of Roman and MEDIEVAL London*. London: HMSO.

Harris, J. 1719. *History of Kent*.

Maloney, J. 1983. Recent Work on London's Defences. In: J. Maloney and B. Hobley, eds. *Roman Urban Defences in the West*. CBA Research Report 51, pp. 96–117.

Marsden, P. 1968. Roman House and Bath at Billingsgate. *The London Archaeologist*, 1(1): 3–5.

Norman, P. and Reader, F. W. 1912. Further Discoveries Relating to Roman London, 1906–12. *Archaeologia*, LXIII: 257–344.

Orton, C. R. 1989. A Tale of Two Sites. *The London Archaeologist*, 6(3): 59–65.

Price, J. E. 1870. *Description of the Roman Tessellated Pavement found in Bucklersbury*. London.

Price, J. E. 1880. *On a Bastion of London Wall*. London.

Rowsome, P. 2000. *Heart of the City: Roman, Medieval and Modern London Revealed by Archaeology at 1 Poultry*. London: Museum of London Archaeology.

Royal Commission on Historic Monuments (England), 1928. *Royal Commission on Historical Monuments (England), An Inventory of the Historical Monuments in London 3. Roman London*. London: HMSO.

Schofield, J. 2011. *St Paul's Cathedral before Wren*. London: English Heritage.

Scott, B. and Shaw, A. 2009. The Quiet Man of Kent: The Contribution of F.J.C. Spurrell to the Early Years of Palaeolithic Archaeology. In: R. Hosfield, F. Wenban-Smith, and M. Pope, eds. *Great Prehistorians: 150 Years of Palaeolithic Research 1859–2009* (Special volume 30 of *Lithics: The Journal of the Lithic Studies Society*), pp. 53–64.

Sheldon, H. and Haynes, I. 2000. Introduction, Twenty-Five Years of London Archaeology. In: I. Haynes, H. Sheldon, and L. Hannigan. eds. *London Under Ground, the Archaeology of a City*. Oxford: Oxbow, pp. 1–8.

Shepherd, J. 1998. *The Temple of Mithras in London. Excavations by W F Grimes and A Williams at the Walbrook*. London: English Heritage.

Sheppard, F. 1991. *The Treasury of London's Past: An Historical Account of the Museum of London and its Predecessors, the Guildhall Museum and the London Museum*. London: HMSO.

Sloane, B. 2008. Images of Empire: Illustrating the Fabric of Roman London. In: J. Clark, J. Cotton, J. Hall, R. Sherris, and H. Swain, eds. *Londinium and Beyond. Essays on Roman London and its Hinterland for Harvey Sheldon*. York: Council for British Archaeology Research Report 156, pp. 11–24.

Stow, J. 1598. *Survey of London*.

Wheeler, R. E. M. 1944. The Rebuilding of London. *Antiquity*, 18(71): 151–53.

Notes on contributor

Jane Sidell is an archaeologist who has worked in London for over twenty years, following degrees undertaken at University College London and the University of Durham. The first half of this time was spent working for the Museum of London as an environmental archaeologist and the latest decade for English Heritage as archaeological science advisor and currently Inspector of Ancient Monuments for London. She has a keen interest in archaeological science, and the interface of science with archaeology undertaken in the commercial sphere. The interest in the history of preservation *in situ* arose from firstly learning how to preserve sites, and then uncovering methods and reasons for past cases of preservation.

Correspondence to: Jane Sidell, English Heritage, 1 Waterhouse Square, 138–42 Holborn, London EC1N 2ST, UK. Email: jane.sidell@english-heritage.org.uk

CONSERVATION AND MGMT OF ARCH. SITES, Vol. 14 Nos 1–4, 2012, 384–96

The Rose Theatre: Twenty Years of Continuous Monitoring, Lessons, and Legacy

MIKE CORFIELD

Hon. Research Fellow University of Cardiff & Trustee of the Rose Theatre, UK

The discovery of the Rose Theatre in 1989 led to the implementation of new planning guidance focused on the presumption that the preferred response to development impacting on archaeological sites would be mitigation and preservation *in situ*. There was little understanding of what the impact of mitigation would be on the quality of the buried evidence and the Rose Theatre site was the first to be scientifically monitored. As a direct result research was implemented and the PARIS series of conferences were initiated.

KEYWORDS Elizabethan theatre, *in situ* preservation, monitoring, reburial

Introduction

The discovery of the site of the Rose Theatre in 1989 and the campaign to have it preserved have been fully documented by Wainwright, Biddle, Chippendale, Orrel and Gurr, and Tilly (Antiquity articles, 1989). The report of the excavation of the site and of a small part of the nearby Globe Theatre has been published by Museum of London Archaeology (Bowsher and Miller, 2011), and the methodology for the reburial of the site has been described (Ashurst et al., 1989). The reburial system was designed to maintain the waterlogged and anaerobic conditions that had preserved the site's organic remains for four hundred years, as well as providing physical protection for the site from accidentally falling debris during the construction of the building over the site. The Government had provided some £5 million to enable the site developer to redesign the building in such a manner that the theatre remains would be preserved and remain accessible for the study of the evolution of Elizabethan Theatres and for future development as a tourist venue. As a condition of this, English Heritage were required to monitor the site to ensure that there was no deterioration of the reburied remains and the yet unexcavated third of the site. The physico-chemical monitoring of the site has continued at monthly intervals and has

DOI 10.1179/1350503312Z.00000000034

been reported (Corfield, 1993; 1996; 2004). For much of the time the monitoring has shown that the conditions for the preservation of the site were being maintained, despite the planned lifetime of the covering system being just two years, this being the time scale for the construction of the new building, after which it was anticipated plans and finance for a more permanent solution would have been developed. However, in recent years there have been indications of possible loss of effectiveness and this been sufficient for English Heritage to place the site on its list of Heritage at Risk.

Since 1989 there has been a considerable improvement of the South Bank of the Thames and the area has become a place of great cultural interest with the replica of the Globe Theatre, the design of which was guided by the evidence revealed by the excavation of the Rose Theatre site; the Tate Modern Art Gallery is in the former Bankside Power Station, and there is a new footbridge linking the area to the City of London. This culturally led regeneration has resulted in the development of cafes and restaurants as well as the offices of major companies. The Rose Theatre site has been a part of this: the Rose Theatre Trust has developed an exhibition space and the outline of the theatre has been marked out by strips of coloured lights, partly submerged beneath a pond of water that is needed to ensure that the higher outer part of the theatre is kept fully saturated. Audiovisual presentations have been produced with contributions by leading actors, and more recently the Trust has developed an

FIGURE 1   Cutaway reconstruction drawing of the Rose Theatre.
With kind permission of Bill Dudley © Rose Theatre Trust

ambitious programme of theatrical productions that have proved very popular even though the audience is restricted to only forty.

It has always been the Trust's ambition to make the site more accessible to visitors, and particularly to be able to show the actual remains of the theatre. Soon after the discovery of the site a meeting of international experts was convened by English Heritage to explore ways whereby the remains could be left exposed. However, it was impossible to overcome the fundamental problem that the site has to be kept fully saturated to prevent shrinkage of the clay silts on which the theatre was built. The effect of drying the silts was clearly seen during the course of the excavation when deep fissures opened up, threatening the integrity of the site. Further damage was limited by the installation of a water-spraying system that remained in place until the excavation was completed and the site reburied. Subsequent geotechnical tests showed that the clay had a water content of 56–83% and that a reduction of the water content from 50% to 40% would result in 13% volumetric shrinkage, while drying to 20% would lead to shrinkage of a third volumetric. A further concern was the risk that the cracking of the ground surface could extend to the intercalated peat beds where the water content is 226%. Drying of these beds would be catastrophic because the vertical cracking would be coupled to horizontal shrinkage of the peat beds leading to subsidence of the ground surface (Huntings Land and Environment, 1994).

Reluctantly, those who were anxious for the public to be able to see the actual remains of the theatre have come to accept that they have to remain buried. However, the significance of the theatre is so great that improvements to its preservation and presentation have become an urgent necessity.

The theatre is significant for a number of reasons:

1. Architectural context: it is one of only five Elizabethan theatres to have been excavated in London and first on the South Bank where several other theatres were subsequently built outside the restrictive regime of the City of London. It is also the most developed and one of only a few Elizabethan theatres where the entire ground plan survives and is accessible.

2. Survival: it is the most complete and best preserved of the Elizabethan theatres; although other theatres have been found in Hackney on the north bank of the Thames, these are smaller and less well preserved than the Rose.

3. Documentation: there is a comprehensive archive of its owner Philip Henslowe from 1592, including his diaries that were preserved by his son-in-law and partner Edward Alleyn who donated them to Dulwich College which he founded. Henslow's diaries give details of the productions at the theatre, the companies of actors presenting them, the profits of the theatre, and the alterations and repairs carried out and their costs.

4. Changing planning guidance: the circumstances of the discovery of the theatre and the subsequent furore that led to its protection resulted in the Government bringing forward new Planning Policy Guidance for the development of sites of high archaeological potential putting emphasis on impact assessments, mitigation, and funding by the developer under the polluter pays principle.

5. A test bed for reburial and scientific monitoring: the site was the first to be reburied in a manner designed to give positive protection to the archaeological evidence, and to be scientifically monitored. The twenty-year record of the

monitoring is the longest continuous record from any site and led to further studies and practical applications of ground environments and the impacts of change on the archaeological record.

6. Regeneration of the South Bank: when the site was discovered the South Bank was very neglected and run down, the presence of the site was one of several factors that contributed to the revitalization of the South Bank.

By 2010 it was recognized that the theatre remains could not be held in limbo indefinitely, English Heritage had expressed its concern that the site might be deteriorating and the site was becoming an ever more popular venue for visitors and for performance. The preparation of a bid for financial support from the Heritage Lottery Fund for the development of the site brought into focus the need to devise a means of covering the remains that would meet specific criteria:

- the waterlogging of the soils must be maintained by the natural groundwater regime of the site and its environs
- the depth of the covering system must be reduced to achieve maximum head-room for the development of visitor facilities
- the covering should be as near as possible a faithful representation of the real ground surface
- there should be space to locate any of the original structural foundation material in its original position on the replicated surface
- as much as possible of the replicated theatre ground surface should be visible to the public
- maintenance should be low cost.

The method that has been proposed by the author is dependent on the outcome of a review of all the monitoring data. This will be complicated because there have been unquantified inputs of additional water through a network of 'leaky pipes' to maintain the required depth of water to ensure complete saturation of the highest parts of the theatre. A study of the natural hydrological inputs to the site and particularly the inputs from the river to the north and the land to the south will be conducted to ensure that the piezometric pressure is sufficient to ensure that the highest parts at the outer periphery of the theatre will be fully wetted after the site is sealed and there are no more external inputs of water. The review will also determine the best position and methodology for continued monitoring that will focus on the soil moisture content and which should be recorded remotely.

The present covering of the site was designed to ensure the maintenance of saturated soil conditions and to protect the site from physical damage during the construction of the building above the site. A key concern was to prevent physical damage to the site from falling debris and it is for this reason that a 1 m depth of sand was interposed between the geotextile placed immediately over the site and the polyethylene sheet that seals the site. A final capping of the site with 100 mm thickness of concrete was to protect the covering materials and to allow access over the site by foot.

In the new design for the site the covering can be much thinner because the risk of physical damage is now removed. If in the future the site is redeveloped, it will be for the developer to ensure the protection of the site and the infrastructure provided for

FIGURE 2   View
of the Rose
Theatre as
excavated.
*Photographer
Andrew Fulgoni
© Fulgoni
Copyrights Ltd
1989–2009*

public access and interpretation. There will be the need for access onto the covering to enable the theatre remains to be positioned and to allow cleaning and maintenance to be carried out. Significantly for the architect, the sand layer will no longer be needed, giving him an additional metre of airspace that will be essential for the realization of his design. The new covering will still retain the geotextile that acts as a protective barrier between the site surface and the covering materials avoiding contamination of the former by the latter. Over the geotextile a load spreading layer will provide physical protection against the light access permitted to the reconstructed theatre surface; a cellular material Erocell™ 100 mm deep will be used with the cells being packed with iron-free sand (actually reusing some of the present sand layer). An impervious sealing layer will be the final layer which will be sculpted to replicate the actual theatre surface.

Above this a steel framework will be installed, glass panels will be fitted into the framework initially at strategic points so that visitors are able to view the remains, but eventually it is hoped that there will be a complete glass floor. The object is to

FIGURE 3   The Theatre is delineated by the coloured lights, saturation of the buried remains is maintained by the pool of water.
© *Rose Theatre Trust*

enable the visitors to get as close to the actual theatre and the stage where the great works of the Elizabethan playwrights were performed, while at the same time maintaining the integrity of the actual site.

Lessons

It has to be said that there must be very few sites where the sort of long-term monitoring undertaken at the Rose could be justified. In this case it was made necessary by the requirement imposed by the then Government that the survival of the site had to be guaranteed until such time as those wishing to be able to present the site to the public had raised the necessary money to do this. The sensitivity of the Government was demonstrated to the author following a comment in a presentation to a conference in the USA that there were signs of decay to the cement piles that supported the former building on the site. This was reported in *The Times* and resulted in questions being asked in the House of Commons.

The twenty years of records are a significant research resource in their own right, even though they only relate to a single and somewhat unrepresentative site. As part of the reburial, the hydrology consultants have been asked to review the accumulated data and to put it into the context of the wider hydrology of the surroundings of the site and it is hoped that this will provide the basis for a further paper.

The reburial method used for the Rose has become the benchmark for site reburial elsewhere, though it has been recognized that the Buckland Sand used in this reburial because it is entirely free of iron and other impurities is not strictly necessary. It is a scarce and expensive material more commonly used in metal casting, and research has shown that sand with firmly bonded iron in it does not result in the sand leaching into the archaeological deposits (Canti and Davis, 1999). It is also the case that depth of sand used was for the specific purpose of protection of the site during demolition of the old building and building the replacement. It will not be necessary for other than the specific circumstances of the time and indeed, because the natural hydraulic pressure was altered by it being there the external irrigation system was needed to ensure that the site was fully saturated. Ideally the aim of reburial should be to reinstate the ground conditions that existed before excavation so that the pre-existing hydrology can be re-established. Had it been known that the 'temporary' reburial would still be in place twenty years later, it is doubtful if such a burial scheme would have been put in place.

The legacy of the Rose Theatre

It is an opportune moment to reflect on the impact that the Rose Theatre has had on mitigation, *in situ* preservation in particular, and on increasing understanding of the ground environment. There is nothing new about seeking to preserve archaeological sites. Very many sites have been partially excavated and then backfilled in the expectation that it would be possible to carry out further investigation at a later date. In the United States the Corps of Engineers has a long tradition of developing methods to give physical protection to archaeological sites affected by a range of threats and has published numerous guidance reports that are available on the web, see for example Nickens, 1991. Site preservation and protection has been an important component of US university archaeological programmes since at least the 1980s and more recently the National Parks Service has implemented programmes for the reburial of numerous Native American sites in the south-west states. To validate this reburial policy a colloquium was held in Santa Fe to share experiences of reburial and monitoring (Burch, 2004). Apart from the last-mentioned initiative, most attention given to the physical attrition of sites (e.g. Darville and Fulton, 1995) rather than to changes to the burial environment.

As noted above, the extraordinary demonstrations during the excavation of the Rose demanding it to be preserved and made accessible led to large sums of government money being made available for the redesign of the proposed building on the site. This quickly led to the issue of Planning Policy Guideline 16, Archaeology and Development, which formalized the requirement for developers to pay for development sites to be evaluated before planning permission was given. If significant archaeological evidence was found to be present, then the developer had either to minimize the impact of the development on the archaeology, or pay the full costs of the excavation of the site if mitigation were not possible. Subsequently, following a study of archaeology in York, a figure of 5 per cent loss of the archaeological resource to unavoidable engineering requirements of development was deemed to be acceptable (Ove Arup, 1991). This was the first time that there had been any formal constraint on development because of the presence of archaeology. Planning Policy

FIGURE 4   Public exhibition space.
© *Rose Theatre Trust*

Guideline 15 has now been replaced by Planning Policy Statement 5: Planning and the Historic Environment, which brought into the same framework all aspects of the historic environment.

The author, recognizing the absence of any study of the hydrology of archaeological sites commissioned a number of projects directly funded by English Heritage, particularly in wetlands and former wetlands where archaeological evidence survived below the depleted water table and to some extent in the capillary zone above it (Corfield, 1993). Postgraduate studentships were also supported to examine the impacts of human activities such as sewage disposal on biological activity (e.g. Powell, 2000). A bid for a broader European-funded programme was unsuccessful, as was a bid for a UK Research Council-funded project, but research activity increased, although still predominately focused on north-west Europe.

In 1992 the Council of Europe enacted the European Convention on the Protection of the Archaeological Heritage, otherwise known as the Valetta Treaty. This brought the same standards of archaeological impact assessments as had been developed in the United Kingdom to the countries of the Europe that ratified the Convention.

Remarkably, these instruments were implemented as if all that was necessary to protect archaeological evidence was to prevent the ground which contained the evidence being disturbed by development. Little attention was paid to the potential reduction in the quality of the evidence, or indeed of its total loss because of collateral impacts, for example changes to the local hydrology as a consequence of ground compression or the introduction of oxygen into ground depleted in it. A few archae-ologists had recognized the impacts of development: Biddle (1994) recorded the dis-tortion of stratigraphy caused by piling, and French and Taylor (1985) reported the sudden and dramatic dewatering of archaeological deposits following the opening of a quarry at some distance from the site. In order to address the knowledge deficit, a number of projects were initiated aimed at increasing understanding of hydrology and the impacts of human activities on it, and the implications for archaeological evidence. In England, much of the research was focused on a major programme of investigation of the management of the archaeology of the Somerset Levels, the Fens of East Anglia, the wetlands of the River Humber and its tributaries, and the wetlands of the north-west. In Europe, mainly Scandinavia and the Netherlands, strong research programmes were also developed. The first PARIS conference was held in 1996 with the specific aim of bringing together archaeologists and scientists from interrelated disciplines to share experiences and stimulate collaborative research. By the time of the second PARIS conference in 2001, English Heritage had appointed a team of Regional Science Advisers whose primary role was to assist the archaeologists dealing with development proposals with the preservation issues. The papers showed that there was a closer focus on the viability of preservation *in situ* policies with a wider range of research being reported and a broader range of environments being studied. The bias continued to be towards wetland sites, but the scope broadened to include sites on non-saturated soils and made ground (ground created as a conse-quence of successive generations building on the detritus of previous ones). The impacts of climate change became increasingly important from the second conference onwards with coastal changes being a particular concern, and more recently changes in salinity of the Baltic (these proceedings).

From the third conference there was an increasing awareness that it was not enough just to monitor the site itself, there had to be a broader understanding of the broader hydrological context that maintained the preservation conditions of sites. Studies in the Netherlands of the World Heritage Site of Schockland (Van Heeringen et al., 2004) and of the desiccated landscape of Voorne-Putten (Van Heeringen and Theunis-sen, 2002) were published showing how the demand for agricultural land and land for new housing and industry was impacting on the preservation of archaeological evidence. In Norway extensive studies of the hydrological inputs to the medieval harbour of Bryggen in Bergen demonstrated the relationship between inputs of sea water and run-off water from the land and the impact on this of a new hotel constructed alongside the medieval buildings built on wooden piles (see de Beer et al. in this issue).

Studies have also been made of the physical impacts of development on archaeo-logical sites. Hughes et al. (2004) reported a number of projects in London and English Heritage published a study of the mitigation of construction impacts (Davis et al., 2004) that included a summary of the construction impacts and how they may affect the quality of archaeological evidence as well as a database of sites where mitigation had been adopted. Recognizing that the one impact that was unavoidable on major constructions was piling guidelines have been published to enable archae-ologists to understand the effects of the various methods used and to decide which will have the least impact on their site (Williams et al., 2007).

FIGURE 5   Erocell load spreading geosynthetic material.
© *Terram*

Finally, there is the need to establish standards for documenting the preservation status of archaeological sites. Needless to say there are a wide range of soils and climatic conditions that enable more or less evidence to survive that would be difficult to encapsulate in a single reference work or guideline. Furthermore, *in situ* preservation is a young discipline with few dedicated practitioners. The Netherlands has led the way by setting out standards for monitoring that explain the terminology, give an overview of the parameters and the procedures for documenting them (Smit et al., 2006) while the application of monitoring results to the preservation of urban archaeology has been provided by the Norwegian Monitoring Manual (Riksantikvaren og Norsk Institutt for Kulturminneforskning, nd). A useful summary of the degradation of the broad categories of archaeological evidence and including a chapter on monitoring has been published by the Cultural Heritage Agency of the Netherlands, and this unlike many other publications also includes a valuable chapter on soils and their evidence value (Huismann, 2009). Both these publications are focused on the sort of burial environments to be found in the Netherlands and naturally waterlogged sites predominate. Similar publications to address preservation in unsaturated soils and in climatic conditions other than that of north-west Europe would be welcome.

Wither PARIS

In the twenty-three years since the discovery of the Rose Theatre, therefore, there has been an explosive increase in the understanding of the scientific issues affecting the

FIGURE 6   Model of the proposed visitor centre.
© Helm Architecture

preservation of archaeological evidence in the ground, and there have been notable efforts to manage the burial environment in order to mitigate the impact of changed land use. As pressures increase on the need to use land for housing, industry, transportation, and for food production, there will be continued risks that the value of the evidence contained in archaeological sites will be degraded or lost. Archaeologists and scientists should be setting out protocols to identify areas of archaeological interest, to categorize them according to broad preservation parameters, and to assess how threats to their integrity can be assessed and managed. In doing this it will be necessary to assess the impact on ground conditions of developments that may be at a considerable distance from the site — altering local hydrology by construction of deep cuttings or underground car parks for example may result in dehydration if the supply is cut off or flooding if the drainage routes are cut.

PARIS, as has been already stated, is a predominantly northern European discipline. It has been a great pleasure to see the scope being extended both geographically and in terms of the types of sites and burial environments covered. Hopefully, this will continue to develop so that at the next PARIS Conference we can see the results of research on an even wider range of site types and climatic conditions. Fundamentally, though, the emphasis should be on scientific understanding to underpin decisions to preserve sites for future generations.

Bibliography

Ashurst, J., Balaam, N., and Foley, K. 1989. The Rose Theatre. *Conservation Bulletin*, 9: 9–10.

Biddle, M. 1989. The Rose Reviewed: A Comedy (?) of Errors. *Antiquity*, 63: 753–60.

Biddle, M. 1994. What Future for British Archaeology. In: *Eighth Annual Conference of the Institute for Field Archaeologists, Bradford, 13–15 April 1994, Archaeology In Britain Conference, Oxford*. Oxford: Oxbow Books, pp. 4–6.

Bowsher, J. and Miller, P. 2009. *The Rose and the Globe Playhouses of Shakespeare's Bankside, Southwark, excavations 1988–1990*. MOLA Monograph 48. London: Museum of London Archaeology.

Burch, R. ed. 2004. Selected Papers from the Colloquium 'Reburial of Archaeological Sites'. *Conservation and Management of Archaeological Sites*, 6 (3&4): 133–399.

Canti, M. and Davis, M. 1999. Tests and Guidelines for the Suitability of Sands to be Used in Archaeological Site Reburial. *Journal of Archaeological Science*, 26: 775–81.

Chippendale, C. 1989. Editorial. *Antiquity*, 63: 411–13.

Corfield, M. C. 1993. Monitoring the Condition of Wet Archaeological Sites. In: P. Hoffmann, ed. *Proceedings of the 5th ICOM Group on Wet Organic Archaeological Materials Conference*. Bremerhaven: Portland Maine, pp. 423–36.

Corfield, M. 1996. Preventive Conservation for Archaeological Sites. Preprints of the contributions to the *Copenhagen Congress, 26–30 August 1996: Archaeological Conservation and its Consequences*, pp. 32–37.

Corfield, M. 2004. Saving the Rose Theatre: England's First Managed and Monitored Site. *Conservation and Management of Archaeological Sites*, 6 (3&4): 305–14.

Council of Europe, 1992. European Convention on the Protection of the Archaeological Heritage (Revised), Valetta.

Darvill, T. and Fulton, A. 1995. *The Monuments at Risk Survey of England*. London: English Heritage.

Davis, M., Gdaniac, K., Brice, M., and White, L. 2004. *Mitigation of Construction Impact on Archaeological Remains*. London: Museum of London Archaeological Service.

French, C. and Taylor, M. 1985. Desiccation and Destruction. *Oxford Journal of Archaeology*, 4 (2): 139–56.

Hughes, R., Coles, B., Henley, R., Seaman, J., Butler, J., Lawrence, A., Patel, D., Dillon, J., McKinley, J., and Sheilds, H. 2004. Design and Decision on Five Development Sites in London: Governor's House, Millenium Footbridge, Alder Castle, Plantation Place and Park Lane, Croydon. In: *Preserving Archaeological Remains in Situ Proceedings of the Second Conference, 12–14 September 2001*. London: Museum of London Archaeological Service, pp. 98–136.

Huismann, D. J. 2009. *Degradation of Archaeological Remains*. Den Haag: Sdu Uitgevers b.v.

Huntings Land and Environment, 1994. Investigation of site conditions and repair and replacement of monitoring points. Huntings Report R898: HER-07 to English Heritage.

Nickens, P. R. ed. 1991. *Perspectives on Archeological Site Protection and Preservation*. Technical Report EL-91–6, Waterways Experiment Station. Vicksburg, Mississippi: US Army Corps of Engineers.

Orrell, J. and Gurr, A. 1989. What the Rose Can Tell Us. *Antiquity*, 63: 421–29.

Ove Arup & Partners and the Department of Archaeology, University of York, in association with B. Thorpe, 1991. *York Development and Archaeology*, Manchester.

Powell, K. L., Pedley, S., and Corfield, M. 2000. The Effect of Water Quality upon the Integrity of Buried Archaeological Wood. In: *Proceedings of the Archaeological Sciences Conference, Durham, UK*.

Riksantikvaren og Norsk Institutt for Kulturminneforskning, n.d. The Monitoring Manual, Procedures & Guidelines for the Monitoring, Recording and Preservation/Management of Urban Archaeological Deposits. Riksantikvaren and Norsk Institutt for Kulturminneforskning.

Smit, S., van Heeringen, R. M., and Theunissen, E. M. 2006. Archaeological Monitoring, Standard Guidelines for the Non Destructive Recording and Monitoring of the Physical Quality of Archaeological Sites and Monuments. Nederlandse Archeologische Rapporten (NAR) 33. Amersfoort: National Service for Archaeology, Cultural Landscape and Built Heritage.

Tilly, C. 1989. Excavation as Theatre. *Antiquity*, 63: 275–80.

van Heeringen, R. M., Mauro, G. V., and Smit, A. eds. 2004. *A Pilot Study on the Monitoring of the Physical Quality of Three Archaeological Sites at the UNESCO World Heritage Site at Schokland, Province of Flevoland, The Netherlands*. Amersfoort: Nederlandse Archeologische Rapporten 26, ROB.

van Heeringen, R. M., and Theusnissen, E. M. 2002. *Desiccation of the Archaeological Landscape at Voorne-Putten*. Amersfoort: Nederlandse Archaeologische Rapporten 25, ROB.

Wainwright, G. 1989. Saving the Rose. *Antiquity*, 63: 430–35.

Williams, J., Sidell, J., and Panter, I. 2007. *Piling and Archaeology, An English Heritage Guidance Note*. English Heritage.

Notes on contributor

Mike Corfield joined English Heritage in 1991 following nearly twenty years as Head of Conservation in Wiltshire and at the National Museum of Wales. As Head of Conservation (and later Head of the Ancient Monuments Laboratory and Chief Scientist) he assumed responsibility for the monitoring programme and the site preservation of the Rose Theatre. He promoted a number of research projects to investigate the ground environment and hydrology and to study the quality of preservation of archaeological evidence, and supported the first and second PARIS conferences. Since his retirement he has retained his interests presenting and publishing papers and giving advice on site preservation. He is a Trustee of the Rose Theatre Trust and of the Alderney Maritime Trust.

Correspondence to: Mike Corfield. Email: mike1corfield@btinternet.com

CONSERVATION AND MGMT OF ARCH. SITES, Vol. 14 Nos 1–4, 2012, 397–405

Partial Solutions to Partially Understood Problems — The Experience of *In Situ* Monitoring and Preservation in Somerset's Peatlands

RICHARD BRUNNING

Somerset County Council, UK

The peat moors of lowland Somerset contain a wealth of waterlogged archaeological sites, including some of the most significant prehistoric monuments in the country. There has been a long history of attempts to preserve archaeological sites *in situ* and monitoring of the burial environment began in 1982. The monitoring has become more complex over time, but the results suggest the same continuing problem of a drop in the water table over the summer months across the whole landscape. With the sole exception of the portion of the Neolithic Sweet Track that benefits from an irrigation system, all the other known sites remain at risk of gradual destruction. The solutions must be found on a landscape scale using agri-environment payments to secure sustainable management of the peat resource. Unfortunately, short-term changes to these payments and long-term changes to the climate are likely to worsen the situation and eventually to require a more drastic solution to the problem. Evidence has been generated to support an ecosystems approach to sustainable peatland management.

KEYWORDS peat, Somerset, wood, preservation, monitoring, prehistoric, waterlogged

Introduction

At the heart of Somerset is an extensive floodplain containing deep Holocene deposits. The area can be broadly divided between the clay dominated 'levels', found mainly along the coast, and the peat-dominated 'moors' further inland. Only the peat areas are considered in this paper because they contain a particular wealth of waterlogged archaeology and are vulnerable to particular agencies of destruction.

The Somerset lowland peat moors cover an extensive area north and south of the Polden ridge. The depth of the peat varies from under 1 m to over 8.5 m (Cope and

DOI 10.1179/1350503312Z.00000000035

Colborne, 1981). In some areas the peat is covered by alluvial deposits many metres thick and interdigitates with layers of alluvium.

The peatlands of Somerset have produced some of the most important archaeological discoveries of the prehistoric period in the UK. The best-preserved prehistoric settlement ever discovered in the country was the Iron Age 'Glastonbury lake village', excavated by Arthur Bulleid and Harold St George Gray between 1898 and 1911 (Bulleid and Gray, 1911; 1917). Their subsequent work at 'Meare lake village' was also influential in improving understanding of Iron Age material culture and society (Bulleid and Gray, 1948; 1953; Gray, 1966).

The peatlands are also noted for the numerous prehistoric wooden trackways that crossed the wetlands and linked together the islands of hard geology. The earliest and most significant of these was the Neolithic Sweet Track, built in 3807/6 BC through 2 km of reedbed. As well as being the oldest surviving wooden structure from the UK, the votive offerings found beside it suggest that it is also probably the earliest religious structure in the country.

The rescue archaeology conducted in advance of peat extraction on the 1920s and 1980s by the Somerset Levels Project highlighted the great potential of the area, but also demonstrated its vulnerability to various forces of destruction (Coles and Coles, 1986). At least fifty-three waterlogged prehistoric sites are known to exist in the Somerset lowland peat moors. Many of these are protected as Scheduled Monuments and the area contains more of such designated waterlogged prehistoric sites than all of the rest of England combined. The deep Holocene deposits undoubtedly contain a host of undiscovered sites whose numbers and significance would probably equal or surpass that part of the record that has been investigated to date.

Although the majority of sites have been investigated in the central Brue valley, where peat extraction took place, there is ample evidence to demonstrate that all the other moors have a similarly high potential. The analysis of peat deposits by Sir Harry Godwin, the Somerset Levels Project, and later researchers has also demonstrated that the peat itself holds a unique record of Holocene climate and landscape change that is central to understanding human activity in the wetlands and the surrounding region (Godwin, 1948; 1955; Caseldine, 1984; 1988).

The problems

The most significant threats to the waterlogged archaeological remains on the Somerset moors can be divided into three categories:

- Peat extraction
- Other development
- Desiccation.

The scale of peat extraction in the county has significantly diminished over the last two decades and archaeological mitigation can be enforced through the planning system. The UK government has issued a target for the voluntary ending of peat compost (67% of the current market) by 2020 and all peat use by 2030. If these targets are met it will mean that this threat will be eliminated and is very unlikely to reoccur. Other development, such as house building, power-line construction, or road creation affects only a very small area and can be governed and mitigated through the planning system.

The widest and most significant threat comes from the desiccation of the peat itself and its eventual loss through peat wastage. This threat is present on a landscape scale and is likely to increase over coming decades for reasons outlined below. Only this threat is therefore considered in the remainder of this paper. The speed of peat wastage varies considerably from one area to another because of differing land use, water table management, and the character of the deposits themselves. The most rapid destruction takes place in arable areas, but no area is immune from the problem. For this reason all the waterlogged Scheduled Monuments in the Somerset moors are classified as at high risk of destruction. The subsequent sections will show how this threat has been monitored and what solutions may be possible.

Monitoring preservation

The monitoring of the condition of the waterlogged archaeology of the peat moors can take simple or intensive forms. Some of the most obvious forms of destruction, such as arable ploughing on peat soils, are immediately visible. The speed of peat wastage in these instances means that changes are identifiable over a few years, especially where islands of hard geology are progressively revealed. The installation of under drainage can also show immediate destruction, as was the case of a Bronze Age oak and alder forest that was ripped out of the peat near Athelney during one such operation.

Peat wastage in pasture fields can also be seen to have taken place when ground shrinkage reveals archaeological remains (Figure 1). This was evident at Harter's Hill on Queen's Sedgemoor, where a late Bronze Age ritual site was discovered when oak piles began to protrude from the ground (Brunning, 1998). It is also apparent where the Sweet Track crosses the sand island of Shapwick Burtle. In that location, prehistoric bog oaks are beginning to 'pop up', with worrying implications for the continued preservation of the trackway.

Monitoring of individual sites has occurred on only eleven of the waterlogged fifty-three sites thought to exist *in situ*. While this may seem a small proportion, it compares favourably to the situation in the rest of the UK.[1] One site, the Neolithic Sweet Track, has one of the longest histories of monitoring in Europe. That site is considered below along with nine other sites that were monitored as part of a single project. The remaining site was a late Bronze Age ritual deposition area that was monitored as part of an MSc dissertation (Cheetham, 1998).

The Sweet Track

The Sweet Track was discovered in 1970 by a peat cutter, Ray Sweet, after whom it was named. It was a raised wooden walkway built in 3807/6 BC to connect Westhay island to the high ground to the south (Figure 2) across 2 km of reedswamp (Coles and Coles, 1986; Coles and Brunning, 2009). Between 1970 and 1982 370 m of the original length of 1980 m was excavated by the Somerset Levels Project, in advance of destruction by peat extraction or river widening (Coles et al., 1973; Coles and Orme, 1976; 1979). Between 1980 and 1982 small excavations were carried out along the length of the trackway to confirm its route, assess survival, and excavate the most

FIGURE 1   Peat wastage led to the discovery of this Late Bronze Age ritual pile alignment, at Harter's Hill, Somerset, when the tops of the piles started protruding from the ground surface.

endangered sections (Coles and Orme, 1984). This information was used to support a scheme for the creation of a National Nature Reserve to help protect part of track in an area that had been partly cut for peat (Coles and Orme, 1984).

In 1982 the land was successfully purchased and a water management system was created to supply water to a ditch system running parallel to the trackway over a distance of 500 m. Weekly (later monthly) monitoring of the water table in the new Shapwick Heath National Nature Reserve (NNR) was carried out from 1982 to 1995, firstly by the Somerset Levels Project and subsequently by Somerset County Council. In 1982 the summer water table was below the top of the track, largely because of the draw-down effect from the neighbouring peat-cut fields where water was pumped out in the summer. The irrigation ditch helped to ameliorate this situation, but in several places summer water levels remained a problem until 1994 when the adjoining areas changed from exhausted peat cuttings to reedbeds and became part of the reserve.

In 1995 a more intensive monitoring programme was carried out to determine if the irrigation system in the reserve was achieving sustainable *in situ* preservation of the trackway. In addition to water levels, the project examined pH, redox, hydraulic conductivity, and water chemistry (Brunning et al., 2000). This largely confirmed the positive impression of the water-table monitoring. Information on the baseline condition of the monument was also gathered by analysis of the wooden remains using moisture content, density, loss on ignition, SEM sections, and FT-IR spectrometry. As the palaeoenvironmental information was also considered to be a key part of the site record, pollen, plant macrofossil, and beetle preservation was also studied.

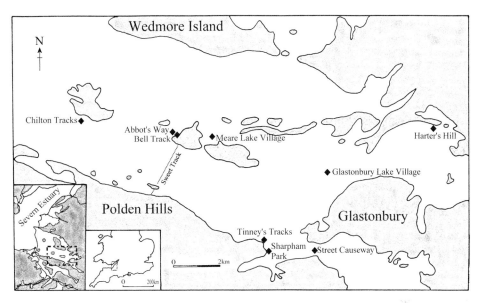

FIGURE 2   Location map of the Sweet Track and MARISP sites.

The MARISP Project

As it was recognized that many other sites were also threatened with desiccation the Monuments at risk in Somerset's peatlands (MARISP) project was begun in 2003 to examine the condition and burial environment of nine prioritized monuments (Brunning, 2007). The methodology largely followed that taken during the 1995 work on the Sweet Track, although an improved methodology of determining the condition of pollen and plant macrofossil remains was developed (Jones et al., 2007).

The results varied significantly from site to site, but centred on the lingering problem of the summer water table. A simpler programme of water table monitoring alone would have reached virtually the same conclusions, but the MARISP methodology allowed greater academic reliance on the results. Quantifiable and replicatable analysis of the monument components also produced reliable baseline condition information against which future investigations can be compared.

Although the majority of the MARISP sites were simple in both their stratigraphy and structure, Glastonbury Lake Village was identified as being more complex and deserving of more intensive monitoring. The section of the Sweet Track that bordered the sand island at Shapwick Burtle was also identified as endangered, so these two sites were recommended for further work, currently being carried out by Reading University in partnership with English Heritage and Somerset County Council.[2]

The solutions

The monitoring that has been undertaken to date has identified preservation *in situ* problems on individual sites. In some instances localized actions can provide a solution. For the Sweet Track in the Shapwick Heath NNR, de-silting of the irrigation ditch is required as well as felling of the trees and scrub along the line of the trackway to prevent root damage and to keep down rates of evapo-transpiration. Improved sub-surface irrigation is needed in one field and the Reading study[2] has shown that enhanced conditions are also required in the Burtle field.

For the other sites, the shared character of the water management system means that only a broader approach is likely to achieve success. The broad conditions required to achieve sustainable management of peat soils in Somerset have long been known (e.g. Spoor et al., 1999). They are a summer water table a maximum of 400 mm below the field surface maintained by ditch or sub-surface irrigation at 40 m spacing. Such regimes would not interfere with the traditional pasture farming and might even increase yields. The main problems are a lack of capital money to install the irrigation and insufficient summer water to feed such a system.

To overcome these obstacles a very robust evidence base is required to convince those parts of the government that might be able to fund a solution. As the archaeological goal is of sustainable peat management, the objective is shared by many other 'ecosystem service' interests such as nature conservation, sustainable flood management, and carbon storage. This is the approach that has been fostered by the 'Wetland Vision' for England and by local wetland visions presently being generated for the peatland of the Brue valley in Somerset.

The need to pursue a landscape approach is reinforced by the ending of the current Environmentally Sensitive Area payments to farmers on the Somerset lowland moors over 2011–13. The Environmental Stewardship scheme that replaces it will only be able to cover a much smaller proportion of the peatland area. This entails a risk that a large-scale conversion to arable may occur, resulting in rapid degradation of the peat resource and the archaeology it contains.

A series of studies have been undertaken by Somerset County Council to provide the information base upon which to argue the case for increased targeting of financial resources towards a sustainable future for Somerset's peatlands. They constitute the following:

- 2001 Peat wastage desktop study
- 2003 Peat wastage field study
- 2009 Peatland carbon storage report
- 2011 Peat risk mapping exercise
- 2011–12 LIDAR and water-table analysis.

The initial desktop study (Brunning, 2001) identified the areas of lowland peat and their character and assessed the known archaeology within them. The rates of peat wastage were taken from existing UK and European studies and from ground anchor measurements from Somerset. This suggested wastage in arable areas at a rate of 10–40 mm per year and 10–20 mm in pasture regimes. The ground anchor data from wet permanent pasture suggested annual wastage rates of 0.44–0.79 mm.

The 2003 study (Brown et al., 2003) was designed to provide dating information for the peat sequence, especially where the date of the top of the surviving peat was not known. The report also assessed peat wastage using humification classification, bulk density analysis, Eh, loss on ignition, UV reflectance, and multiple radiocarbon determinations to provide age-depth profiles. The latter was used to estimate historic peat wastage rates of between 0.20 mm and 0.57 mm per year.

The 2009 study (Brown, 2009) was initiated to help inform decision-making about the peat extraction component of a new mineral plan for Somerset. It estimated the volume of the lowland peat in Somerset at 663.61M m^{-3} and that there was 3.33M metric tons of organic carbon in the top 1 m of peat that was most at risk from wastage. The annual carbon loss due to peat wastage was estimated at 200,000 tons. This study helps to make the climate change case for protecting the peatland resource.

The 2011 study is designed to help target the limited financial resources available in the Environmental Stewardship scheme towards those areas most at risk from peat wastage. The maps produced use the varying depth of alluvium over peat to identify areas most at risk of wastage. The highest risk areas will be subjected to more research in 2011–12 comparing ground heights from existing Environment Agency LIDAR data to summer water penning levels in the ditch systems managed by the Internal Drainage Boards. This will help to identify where the greatest problems exist in the high-risk areas. The spacing of ditches and sub-surface irrigation will also be incorporated into a GIS risk model and it is intended that the hydraulic conductivity of peat in different moors will also be considered.

These studies should allow proposals for sustainable peatland management to be generated but over the longer term the predictions for climate change suggest that a significant problem of summer water supply will occur. By 2080 the rather optimistic medium emissions scenario suggests that SW England will enjoy 30–40 per cent less summer rainfall than present levels and will suffer summer temperatures 3–4 degrees centigrade higher (UKCIP09). This suggests that more winter rainfall will have to be retained on the floodplain in some form to provide summer irrigation.

Conclusion

The internationally important wetland archaeological resource in Somerset's lowland peatland is at significant risk from desiccation and degradation. This process of destruction is now well understood at both a site and landscape level. The priorities for the coming years are fourfold:

- To convince farmers in the area that arable farming is not in their medium- or long-term interest
- To convince the UK government that the ecosystem services provided by the lowland peat moors in Somerset are worth the investment to secure their sustainable management
- To prepare a long-term strategy to cope with the challenges posed by predicted climate change over the next 60–70 years
- To assess and research the wetland monuments that have not yet been properly investigated.

The first four actions must be carried out in cooperation with numerous partner organizations such as Defra, English Heritage, English Nature, the Internal Drainage Boards, the Environment Agency, nature conservation organizations, and the farming community. The last action is up to the heritage community. Baseline condition information on the most important monuments should be obtained where this has not already been done, and wherever possible research questions about the sites should be answered at the same time.

The wetland archaeological resource in Somerset faces an uncertain future. A sustainable future for the peatlands is possible but may not happen, and most of the known sites are in the areas of highest risk. Research questions about the known sites should be answered through minimally intrusive investigations while the resource still exists. Longer-term preservation must focus on the peat resource itself and the waterlogged sites yet to be discovered.

Acknowledgements

The MARISP project and the 1999–2000 work on the Sweet Track was co-funded by English Heritage and Somerset County Council. Somerset County Council, the Environment Agency, and Natural England funded the various peat studies. The author would like to thank Gareth Watkins, the English Heritage project monitor, for his continued advice and support and all the numerous specialists who have been involved in the different projects.

Notes

[1] See Williams in this volume.   [2] See Jones in this volume.

Bibliography

Brown, A. G. 2009. Carbon Storage and Sequestration in the Somerset Levels, UK. Unpublished report prepared for Somerset County Council.

Brown, A. G., Dinnin, M., and Toogood, T. 2003. Peat Wastage in the Somerset Levels. A Study Based on Field Evidence. Exeter: Exeter University.

Brunning, R. 1998. Two Bronze Age Wooden Structures in the Somerset Moors. Archaeology in the Severn Estuary, 9: 5–8.

Brunning, R. 2001. Archaeology and Peat Wastage on the Somerset Moors. Taunton: Somerset County Council.

Brunning, R. 2007. Monuments at Risk in Somerset's Peatlands. In: J. Barber, C. Clark, M. Cressey, A. Crone, A. Hale, J. Henderson, R. Housley, R. Sands, and A. Sheridan, eds. Archaeology from the Wetlands: Recent Perspectives, Proceedings of the 11th WARP Conference, Edinburgh 2005. WARP Occasional Paper 18. Edinburgh: Society of Antiquaries of Scotland, pp. 191–98.

Brunning, R., Hogan, D., Jones, J., Jones, M., Maltby, E., Robinson, M., and Straker, V. 2000. Saving the Sweet Track. The In Situ Preservation of a Neolithic Wooden Trackway, Somerset, UK. Conservation and Management of Archaeological Sites, 4: 3–20.

Bulleid, A. and Gray, H. St G. 1911. The Glastonbury Lake Village Volume 1. Glastonbury.

Bulleid, A. and Gray, H. St G. 1917. The Glastonbury Lake Village Volume 2. Glastonbury.

Bulleid, A. and Gray, H. St G. 1948. The Meare Lake Village Volume 1. Glastonbury.

Caseldine, A. E. 1984. The Somerset Levels. In: H. C. M. Keeley, ed. Environmental Archaeology: A Regional Review. Department of the Environment. DAMHB Occasional Paper No. 6, pp. 66–77.

Caseldine, A. 1988. A Wetland Resource: The Evidence for Environmental Exploitation in the Somerset Levels during the Prehistoric Period. In: P. Murphy and C. French, eds. The Exploitation of Wetlands. BAR Series 186, pp. 239–65.

Cheetham, J. L. 1998. Characterisation of Burial Environments Exhibiting Well Preserved Wet Archaeological Wood: An Investigation at Greylake, Somerset. Unpublished MSc dissertation, University of Hull, Hull.

Coles, B. and Brunning, R. 2009. Following the Sweet Track. In: G. Cooney, K. Becker, J. Coles, M. Ryan, and S. Sievers, eds. Relics of Old Decency: Archaeological Studies in Later Prehistory. Dublin: Wordwell, pp. 25–37.

Coles, J. M., Hibbert, F. A. and Orme, B. J. 1973. Prehistoric Roads and Tracks in Somerset, England 3. The Sweet Track. *Proc. Prehistoric. Soc.*, 39: 256–93.

Coles, B. J. and Coles, J. M. 1986. *Sweet Track to Glastonbury: The Somerset Levels in Prehistory*. London: Thames and Hudson.

Coles, J. M. and Orme, B. J. 1976. The Sweet Track, Railway Site. *Somerset Levels Papers*, 2: 34–65.

Coles, J. M. and Orme, B. J. 1979. The Sweet Track, Drove Site. *Somerset Levels Papers*, 5: 43–64.

Coles, J. M. and Orme, B. J. 1984. Ten Excavations along the Sweet Track (3200 bc). *Somerset Levels Papers*, 10: 5–45.

Cope, D. W. and Colborne, G. J. N. 1981. *Thickness of Peat in the Somerset Moors*. Map at 1:50,000. Harpenden: Soil Survey of England and Wales.

Godwin, H. 1948. Studies of the Post-Glacial History of British Vegetation. X. Correlation between Climate, Forest-Composition, Prehistoric Agriculture and Peat Stratigraphy in Sub-boreal and Sub-Atlantic Peats of the Somerset Levels. *Phil. Trans. Royal Society*, B233: 275–86.

Godwin, H. 1955. Studies of the Post-Glacial History of British Vegetation XIII. The Meare Pool Region of the Somerset Levels. *Phil. Trans. of the Royal Society*, B239: 161–90.

Godwin, H. 1960. Prehistoric Wooden Trackways of the Somerset Levels: Their Construction, Age and Relation to Climate Change. *Proc. Prehistoric Soc.*, 26: 1–36.

Gray, H. St G. and Bulleid, A. 1953. *The Meare Lake Village Volume 2*. Glastonbury.

Gray, H. St G. 1966. *The Meare Lake Village Volume 3*. Glastonbury.

Jones, J., Tinsley, H. M., and Brunning, R. 2007. Methodologies for Assessment of the State of Preservation of Pollen and Plant Macrofossil Remains in Waterlogged Deposits. *Environmental Archaeology*, 12(1): 71–86.

Spoor, G., Gilbert, J., and Gowing, D. 1999. *Conservation of Peat Soils on the Somerset Levels and Moors, Part 4: Safeguarding Peat Soils*. Silsoe College, Cranfield University.

Notes on contributor

Richard Brunning has specialized on the excavation and analysis of prehistoric waterlogged wood in the UK and has compiled the English Heritage guidelines on waterlogged wood. For nineteen years he has been the Somerset Levels and Moors Archaeologist for Somerset County Council with responsibility for all aspects of the heritage of that area.

Correspondence to: Richard Brunning, Somerset Heritage Centre, Brunel Way, Norton Fitzwarren, Taunton TA2 6SF, UK. Email: rbrunning@somerset.gov.uk

CONSERVATION AND MGMT OF ARCH. SITES, Vol. 14 Nos 1–4, 2012, 406–28

The Never-Ending Story? The Lessons of Fifteen Years of Archaeological Monitoring at the Former Island of Schokland

D. J. Huisman

Cultural Heritage Agency, Netherlands and Leiden University, Faculty of Archaeology, Netherlands

G. Mauro

Leiden University, Faculty of Archaeology, Netherlands

The former island of Schokland became part of the mainland of the Netherlands when the Noord-Oost polder was drained in the 1940s. Mesolithic camp sites, Neolithic and Bronze age settlements, and medieval dwelling mounds (*terps*) on Schokland and in its immediate surroundings now form a UNESCO World Heritage site.

The main threat to the former island and the archaeology is drying out of the soil profiles, causing degradation of organic remains. Because of this, on the island and in its immediate surroundings the groundwater table is kept high in a specially created hydrological zone.

Schokland was one of the first sites in the Netherlands to be monitored in order to assess threats to the archaeological record and ongoing degradation processes. Monitoring started in 1999, and subsequent measurements were taken in 2001, 2006, and 2009/10. This included measurements of groundwater tables, water composition, redox, soil moisture and soil chemistry, micromorphology, and the degradation of botanical remains and bone. This time series of measurements makes it possible — first and foremost — to study long-term effects and changes in the Schokland burial environment, and their effects on the archaeology. In addition, the development of monitoring techniques around Schokland illustrates how the field of archaeological monitoring has evolved over the years.

Since the first monitoring round in 1999, developments in monitoring have included (1) technological developments enabling monitoring of high-frequency variations in groundwater, redox, and moisture contents, for

     DOI 10.1179/1350503312Z.00000000036

example; (2) growing knowledge of degradation processes and the relevant characteristics of the burial environment; and (3) an increase in easily accessible datasets from third parties. Worries have arisen about the long-term storage and availability of monitoring data.

For future monitoring rounds, the value of the various monitoring techniques need to be critically evaluated, and the purpose of monitoring specific sites need to be reconsidered.

KEYWORDS monitoring, groundwater, redox, soil moisture, bone, botanical remains

Introduction

The former island of Schokland was one of the first sites in the Netherlands to be monitored to assess threats to the archaeological record and ongoing degradation processes. In addition, the measurements and tests performed at the site also form part of a larger effort to increase our knowledge of degradation processes and develop monitoring techniques. Monitoring started in 1999, and subsequent measurements were taken in 2001, 2006, and 2009/10. They included measurements of groundwater tables, water composition, redox, soil moisture and soil chemistry, micromorphology, and degradation of botanical remains and bone. This time series of measurements makes it possible — first and foremost — to study long-term effects and changes in the Schokland burial environment, and their effects on the archaeology. In addition, the development of monitoring techniques around Schokland illustrates how the field of archaeological monitoring has evolved over the years.

In this paper, we intend to show how techniques for monitoring have evolved over the years and how new knowledge of degradation processes has affected the techniques and the interpretations. But we also want to critically evaluate which techniques give the information needed for monitoring a site successfully and make recommendations for the future of the monitoring set-up at Schokland.

The world heritage site and its protection

Schokland

For several centuries, Schokland was an island in the Zuyder Zee. It was inhabited from the Middle Ages. However, towards the mid-nineteenth century the island had eroded so much that only a narrow strip of land remained. The residents had withdrawn to four *terps* constructed on the eastern side of the island. Given the poverty there and the threat to the residents' safety, the entire island was evacuated between 1855 and 1859.

After the Zuyder Zee had been cut off from the North Sea and the Noord-Oost polder had been created, Schokland became an 'island on dry land' (Figure 1). In 1995 UNESCO designated the former island and its immediate surroundings a World Heritage Site. Schokland is regarded as the symbol of the Netherlands' centuries-old battle against the encroaching water. The historic occupation of the island and the

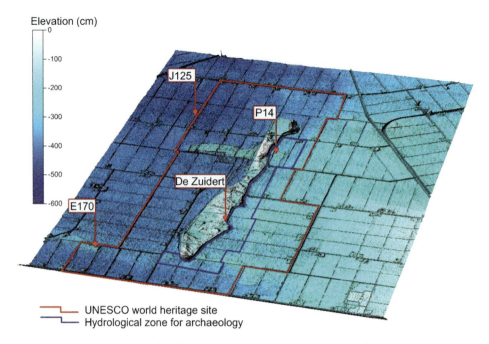

Elevation (cm)

UNESCO world heritage site
Hydrological zone for archaeology

FIGURE 1   Modern-day Schokland is an island on dry land. The AHN (Lidar) semi-3D image with exaggerated relief clearly shows how the former island is elevated above the surrounding former seafloor. Relief on the former seafloor represents a relic glacial feature consisting of boulder clay (across the former island between P14 and J125) and Late Glacial river dunes (e.g. at Schokkerhaven-E170). The boundaries of the UNESCO World Heritage Site and the hydrological zone are indicated. Archaeological sites that were monitored are also indicated.

reclamation of the land, with its characteristic parcelling, are seen as part of this battle. The contours of the island and the remains of the *terps* and historic buildings are tangible mementoes.

However, the exposed former sea floor surrounding the island also includes remains from a time when the sea was still far away. Finds from the Late Palaeolithic and the Mesolithic (remains of hunting camps) have been found, though little else is known about this period. Several Neolithic and Bronze Age sites have however taught us a little about how people lived there in the period 4900–1500 BC. These remains were also a factor in the UNESCO listing. They reveal a past in which people were able to live in a dynamic landscape with, and partly thanks to, the water in two old rivers (the IJssel and Vecht) (Figure 2). Natural levees and river dunes ran alongside both rivers. A boulder clay outcrop partially covered by driftsand is also situated beside the river Vecht. These raised features in the landscape were attractive places to live.

History of protection

In 1996 Flevoland provincial authority launched the Schokland area project, designed to improve protection of the cultural heritage, landscape, and natural values at the World Heritage site. The idea was also to boost the local economy.

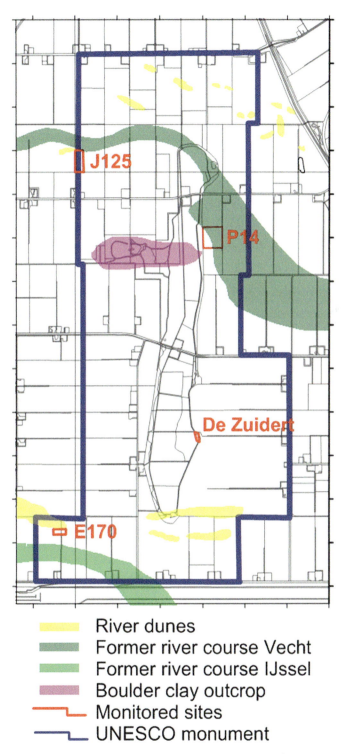

FIGURE 2   The Schokland area during the Neolithic and Bronze Age (based on Van Doesburg and Mauro, 2007: fig. 4).

This resulted, two years later, in the 'New Schokland 1998' strategy. The Cultural Heritage Agency of the Netherlands (RCE; formerly Rijksdienst voor het Oudheidkundig Bodemonderzoek; ROB) (then the ROB) was a stakeholder in the project. Besides the provincial authority and the RCE, other parties were actively involved, including the Zuiderzeeland water board, the Noord-Oost polder local authority, nature conservancy *Stichting Flevolandschap*, the northern branch of the agricultural and horticultural association and the central government property management agency, then known as *Domeinen Onroerende Zaken*, now RVOB. The World Heritage status of the area was an important factor in the development of the plan.

In 1996 the plots around Schokland were being used for intensive agriculture and grazing. The boulder clay outcrop and the former island themselves were being used for forestry and extensive agricultural purposes respectively.

Intensive agriculture is not compatible with the preservation of subsurface archaeology. Soil working operations like ploughing adversely affect the uppermost layers of a site, generally to depths of some 30–50 cm. Locally, where the archaeological remains are near the surface, the old soil profile and archaeological remains have been incorporated into the topsoil. Only the deeper parts of soil features are still present at those spots. Secondly, groundwater management for agricultural purposes causes desiccation and the degradation of organic remains.

The initial phase of the project not only identified archaeological issues, it also found that improvements were required for the benefit of agriculture and the natural environment. For example, the hydrology was less than optimum both from an agricultural perspective, and for wildlife. The land surface had fallen considerably since the polder was created in 1942 (by at least 1 to 1.5 m), as a result of settling and peat degradation. The former island is still clearly visible as a raised feature in the landscape. Without measures to prevent further subsidence, however, Schokland would probably lose its characteristic image as an island on dry land (Plan van Aanpak Nieuw Schokland, 1998; Van Doesburg and Mauro, 2007).

One of the measures included in the project was the creation of a 'hydrological zone' in 2004 (see Figure 1 for extent of hydrological zone). To the east and south of Schokland plots totalling more than 135 ha were voluntarily taken out of agricultural production. The farmers affected were compensated in the form of replacement agricultural land or cash payments. The water level was raised in the hydrological zone by blocking waterways and adapting the pumping regime (the area constantly receives groundwater from upward seepage) and the area was turned into natural habitat under wet grassland management. This was designed to achieve two key cultural heritage objectives. First, the raised groundwater level should put a stop to the subsidence, thus preserving the unique character of Schokland as an island on dry land. Furthermore, the degradation of archaeological remains in the zone should be halted by putting an end to agricultural activities and raising the water level. The hydrological zone was divided into several sections where the water level is determined by the top of the archaeological remains.

Around 2007 the plots to the west, bordering the former island, were taken out of agricultural production, too, and converted to wetland habitat. This as it were created a shell around Schokland in which the water level is higher than normal. The area to the west of the island was initially made wetter with the aim of enhancing natural values, however. Of course, the archaeological remains in this area would also benefit from the measure. However, in this publication, the 'hydrological zone' refers to the wetland area created for the benefit of landscape and archaeological values.

In the years following the completion of the hydrological zone, the water level was slowly raised. This was done gradually to allow a covering of grass to develop and prevent the growth of reeds. The grass was mown for the same reason. Reeds are not good for archaeological remains. Not only do their long roots grow through most archaeological materials, the rhizomes also allow oxygen into the soil.

The hydrological zone is owned and managed by nature conservancy *Stichting Flevolandschap*, a civil-society organization. The Zuiderzeeland water board is responsible for managing the water level.

Monitoring is needed to establish whether the measures have actually been effective. Rounds of monitoring were conducted in 1999–2001, 2003–04, and 2009–11. Data from fieldwork conducted in 2006 have also been used in the last round. From the start, a further aim of the monitoring programme has been the acquisition of knowledge of archaeological monitoring in general, given the fact that it was in its infancy at the outset.

Monitored sites

Two prehistoric sites (P13/P14 and Schokkerhaven-E170) and a medieval *terp* (De Zuidert) were initially included in the monitoring programme. In 2003 the programme was extended to include site J125 on a small river dune, where prehistoric remains have also been found.

Site P13/P14

Site P13/P14 is on the easternmost part of the boulder clay outcrop, which is covered by drift sand. During the Neolithic and Bronze Age it acted as a riparian buffer of the Overijsselse Vecht (see Figure 2). Remains from the period 4900–1500 BC have been found there, including house plans, a number of graves, and a field. The occupation was not, however, continuous (Hogesteijn, 1991; Gehasse, 1995; Ten Anscher, 2012). The highest sandy parts of the site are immediately beneath the ploughsoil, and have been eroded. The flanks are protected by layers of clay, peat, and detritus.

The site is in the hydrological zone, has been taken out of agricultural production and is currently natural habitat. It has been listed as a national archaeological monument.

Schokkerhaven-E170 site

This site is situated on river dunes immediately to the north of an old section of the river IJssel to the south-west of Schokland. A layer of waste from the Middle Neolithic has been found on the southern flank of the dune, which includes flint artefacts, potsherds, and bone fragments. A number of oak posts and beams have been found which may have formed part of a palisade. C14 dating of hazelnut shells from the bottom of the waste layer suggests that it began to accumulate in *c*. 3900–3800 BC. Dendrochronological analysis has dated the wooden structure to between 3350–3300 BC (Hogesteijn, 1991; Gehasse, 1995). Here, too, the top of the dune is eroded and the flanks are covered with layers of clayey-peat and detritus. The site is used for agricultural purposes, and is currently mainly used for growing crops.

Site J125

Site J125 is on an isolated river dune to the west of the former island. Several flint artefacts and potsherds have been found there, along with a number of hearth pits. A C14 dating of the pottery has dated the site to the Late Mesolithic and Early Neolithic. The site continues into the neighbouring plot J126, but is highly degraded there due to agricultural activities. The site has been much better preserved in plot J125. Uneroded soils can still be found in the higher parts of the dune. The flanks are covered with reed and brook peat and clay. The site is on agricultural land, and is partly situated under a path between plots.

De Zuidert terp

De Zuidert is the smallest dwelling mound on Schokland, and forms part of the hamlet of Ens. It was raised several times, the most recent layer having been added in the fifteenth century. The *terp* remained occupied until the evacuation of 1855, when sixteen small homes were still scattered there. After the evacuation, the buildings were demolished, the sea defences were lowered, and parts of the *terp* immediately behind the sea defences were dug out to raise other *terps* on Schokland.

Several raised layers can be identified in the soil, in which materials like clay, reeds, sea grass and dung can be recognized (Van der Heide, 1950; Van Doesburg and Mauro, 2007).

The *terp* is currently covered with grass. A shelter stands on top of the mound, and a restored well can be seen. The *terp* enjoys statutory protection as a national archaeological monument.

Monitoring Schokland

In each phase of the monitoring of Schokland, a series of measurements were taken in the field, or from samples taken to the lab. The methods used can be divided into measurements to characterize the burial environment, to determine the quality and degree of degradation of archaeological remains or to identify active (and past) processes. An overview of the methods is presented in Table 1. A brief history is given below.

Phase 1: first assessment and baseline survey (1999–2001)

A first round of measurements — a combined first assessment and baseline survey *sensu* Huisman et al. (2009) — was initiated at three sites at the Schokland monument in 1999. The monitoring set-up and results were reported in Van Heeringen et al. (2004). Monitoring was performed at three selected sites: De Zuidert, P14, and Schokkerhaven-E170. All three sites contain well-preserved organic remains; the *terp* may also contain metals.

To characterize the burial environment, groundwater levels, groundwater composition, temperature, and chemical parameters (Electrical Conductivity, oxygen content, redox, pH) were measured directly in dipwells. Water levels were monitored on a monthly basis in these dipwells until 2002. Botanical macroremains and bone fragments from samples taken in 1999 and 2001 were studied to determine the quality and degradation of archaeological material. The bone remains were studied histologically, and using FTIR, XRD, and collagen extractions. The processes were studied using

TABLE 1

METHODS USED IN THE VARIOUS MONITORING ROUNDS AT THE SCHOKLAND UNESCO WORLD HERITAGE SITE

Year	Sites				Monitoring techniques						Archaeological remains	
	De Zuidert	P14	E170	J125	Burial environment					Processes	Botany	Bone
					Groundwater levels	Moisture content	Redox: oxygen	pH	Chemical analyses	Micromorphology		
1999-2001	x	x	x		Monthly (hand) measurements		Electrodes in dipwells for Eh and oxygen contents. **	pH H2O (laboratory)	Groundwater composition, pH and EC	Small thin sections	Macroremains	Histological analysis, collagen extraction and FTIR
2003-2004	x	x	x	x	Loggers	Logger*	Monthly hand measurements	pH CaCl2	Soil pH			
2006/2007 and 2009-2010	x	x	x	x	Logger	Logger****	Logger****	pH H2O (laboratory)	Soil pH. Chemical analyses of soil samples (organic matter, sulfur, XRF)	Kubiena-size thin sections (80 x 80 mm)	Pollen and macroremains	Planned, but not executed due to limited amount of bone fragments found

*: measurements failed.
**: data discarded because of reliability issues.
***: data probably onreliable.
****: Only P14 and De Zuidert.

soil micromorphology on 2.5 cm wide samples from 1999 and 2001. If 1999 was the first assessment and the baseline survey, the 2001 measurements can be seen as the first monitoring round, but the time between 1999 and 2001 is too short to expect major differences.

During this phase, it became clear that the redox and oxygen measurements from dipwells were not reliable, because atmospheric oxygen diffusion into the groundwater during the measurement interfered with the results. In the end, therefore, they were not reported in Van Heeringen et al. (2004). The groundwater composition data were reported but not used, because 'no peculiarities were observed' (Van Heeringen et al., 2004).

Step 2: second round (2003/4)

The second round of monitoring came directly after the establishment of the hydrological protection zone. J125 was added as a fourth monitoring site just outside the UNESCO World Heritage Site. In this round, the burial environment was characterized by taking monthly measurements of redox conditions with a redox probe (thus preventing atmospheric oxygen from interfering with the measurements), by measuring the pH of soil samples, and by monitoring groundwater levels four times a day using an automated pressure gauge. The results of this round were reported in Smit et al. (2005). Around this time, the water board installed an extensive set of dipwells with automatic recorders to monitor groundwater levels around the former island. Some of these data were also presented in Smit et al. (2005).

Step 3: third round (2006 and 2009/10)

In 2006, an archaeological survey was carried out at the Schokkerhaven-E170 and J125 sites to better characterize and delineate the archaeological deposits and their state of degradation. This entailed an augering survey and digging small test-pits, coupled with micromorphological research, characterization of the inorganic soil composition and analysis of botanical remains and pollen. These results were reported in Huisman et al. (2008b). They were also used as part of the third monitoring round. The rest of this round was carried out in 2009–10 and consisted of monitoring groundwater levels, redox, and soil moisture using automated data-loggers at all four sites. Cores from De Zuidert and P14 were analysed for chemical composition and micromorphology — this time using 8 x 8 cm slides. Botanical analyses were also performed. Histological bone analysis was planned but the quantity of bone fragments recovered during augering was too low. The results of this monitoring round are scheduled for publication in late 2011/early 2012.

Developments in the monitoring of Schokland

Introduction

In proper monitoring programmes, it is customary to measure the same parameters repeatedly over time. However, in the Schokland project there have been considerable changes in the set-up and monitoring methods used. This is understandable if we consider the fact that, at the time of the first monitoring round, knowledge of degradation processes was scarce, and the monitoring techniques were still in their infancy.

At the same time, however, the Schokland sites are among the most intensely monitored archaeological monuments in the world.

A summary of developments in monitoring and their impact on the Schokland monitoring programme is given below. A critical evaluation of the applicability of the applied methods leads to recommendations as to how to proceed with monitoring this area in the future.

The burial environment: developments in techniques and interpretation of groundwater levels, redox and moisture contents

Phase 1: From the start of the monitoring of wetland archaeological sites, it was clear that groundwater levels are key for the preservation of organic remains. Low concentrations of oxygen and negative redox values were also considered important. It is therefore logical that these parameters were a major focus of monitoring. In the first phase, groundwater measurements were taken by hand in dipwells. The dipwells were also used for redox and oxygen measurements. It soon became clear, however, that dipwells are not suitable for redox and oxygen measurements because of interference from atmospheric oxygen. These data were not therefore reported. During this phase, measurements were commonly taken by hand on a monthly basis (Van Heeringen et al., 2004).

Phase 2: Technical developments made it possible to intensify the monitoring of groundwater levels, as automated pressure recorders (Divers) with data-loggers were employed. This made it possible to obtain a much higher data density over time (e.g. four measurements/day), and made fieldwork much more efficient. Redox measurements were taken with a specially designed probe inserted into the soil for each measurement. Oxygen measurements were no longer used due to the technical difficulties of measuring oxygen levels in soil without introducing atmospheric oxygen (Smit et al., 2005). Apart from the monitoring activities at the archaeological sites, around this time the water board installed a large number of dipwells with automated pressure recorders to monitor groundwater levels around the entire former island. They have been taking four measurements a day ever since.

Phase 3: Between the second and third phase, new research results showed that groundwater levels in themselves are not a direct indicator of the preservation potential of the burial environment. Whether organic remains degrade is determined by moisture content in the soil rather than by the groundwater level: above the water table can be well preserved if the moisture content is high enough — below the water table it is by definition wet enough (Theunissen et al., 2006; Huisman and Theunissen, 2008; Huisman et al., 2008a; Huisman and Klaassen, 2009). This may explain the relatively good preservation of the J125 site, which is above the water table. Degradation of metals is determined by a combination of oxygen and sulphate concentrations, salinity, and pH (Huisman, 2009a; Huisman and Joosten, 2009). This is only relevant for the De Zuidert site, since that is the only site where metal artefacts can be expected. For both types of material — organic remains and metal — groundwater levels are in general not the determining factor in degradation processes. They are still relevant, however, since they are the driving force behind changes in the burial environment like moisture contents and oxygen availability.

In the third round, therefore, groundwater and redox measurements were combined with soil moisture measurements. Dipwells with automated pressure recorders and data-loggers were again used for groundwater level recordings. Redox was measured again using redox probes, but now they were permanently installed and equipped with data-loggers, thus considerably increasing the amount of redox data and the temporal resolution.

In this period, doubt also arose as to the reliability of the methods used for redox measurements during the second round (A. Smit, Paleo Terra, pers. comm.). Tests by Rabenhorst et al. (2009) have shown that redox measurements using voltmeters with relatively low input resistance — like the one used in the second monitoring round — alter the soil environment around the probe, and thus do not give a reliable measurement. The equipment used in the third monitoring round does not have this problem.

One cause for concern was the difficulties encountered when trying to retrieve the original data files from monitoring phases 1 and 2. The only copies of these data left were back-up files that happened to be located by A. Smit (who performed the measurements in Phase 1 and 2) on an old computer disk. Thanks to his efforts, the data could be recovered.

Massive datasets

During **phase 1 and 2**, relatively few hydrological data were available from the archaeological sites and the surrounding landscape. The large-scale intensive monitoring by the water board had only just started during phase 2. During **phase 3**, however, for the first time hydrological data were available with high frequencies (mostly four measurements /day), spanning close to ten years, from some 50 locations. This totalled approx. 500,000 measurements that gave a good overview of the hydrological behaviour throughout the seasons in various areas of the monument. An overview of dipwells with available groundwater data is given in Figure 3. A comparison of water levels in adjacent wells inside and outside the hydrological zone, for example, demonstrates to what extent the establishment of this zone has raised water levels (Figure 4).

Because of the availability of this dataset, for the first time the measurements on the archaeological sites could be evaluated within the framework of known hydrological variation. It became clear, for example, that the first monitoring round of 1999–2001 was during a period when groundwater levels in the southern part of the monument were still falling after a temporary high in 1998. This high was correlated with the construction of the IJsseloog sludge depot in Ketelmeer lake, in close proximity to the polder dike (see Figure 5). This resulted in a temporary increase in groundwater pressure in the region.

Active and past degradation processes: development of micromorphological interpretations

During **phase 1**, soil micromorphology was used to identify active degradation processes and their progress. Samples were taken in 1999 and 2001. The report focuses on the state of the organic material, classifying samples according to the fraction of non-degraded tissue in the total organic content. Samples with low fractions of

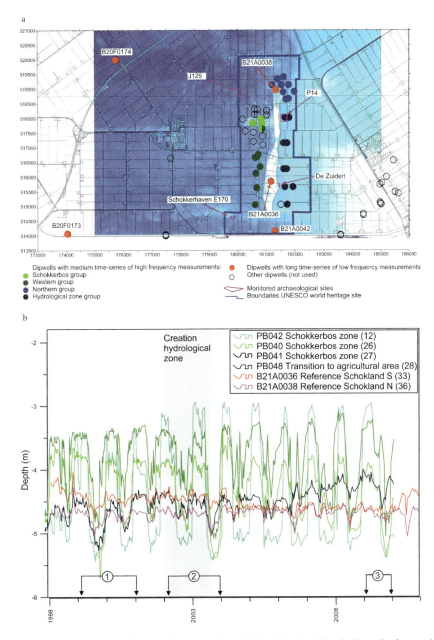

FIGURE 3   Available groundwater data. A: Map of Schokland with all dipwells from which groundwater data are available. Wells are classified according to timespan and frequency of data, and grouped according to hydrological behaviour. Dipwell ID codes are given for those with long times series. Unused dipwell data are from wells where the time series is too short or with data irrelevant for the UNESCO site. Groundwater level data over time in four zones with different hydrological behaviour (Schokkerbos group, Western group, Northern group, Hydrological zone group). Note that the time series differ in length. Groundwater levels in two dipwells on the former island are given for comparison. Background colour according to scale in Figure 1.

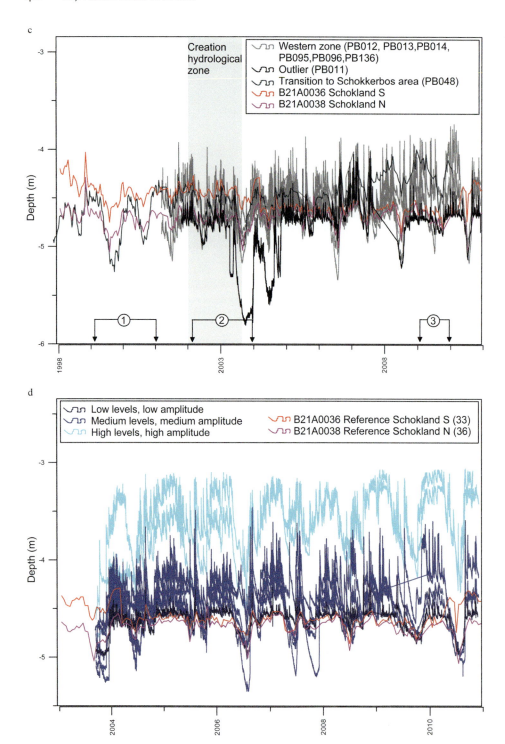

FIGURE 3   Continued.

e

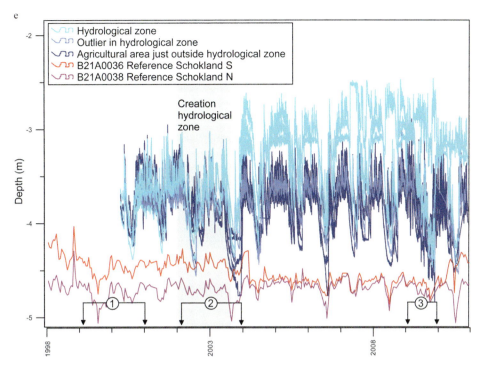

FIGURE 3   Continued.

non-degraded tissue were deemed to be less valuable as an archaeological information source, as the archaeobotanical content would be more degraded. As was expected, because of the short time between sampling, no change in the condition of the site was observed between the 1999 and the 2001 sampling rounds.

During **phase 3**, soil micromorphology was again used. Larger samples were taken, some three times wider than before, in order to better capture the morphological variation within the samples. Also, in the meantime, new insights into the use and applicability of this technique led to a change in the approach and the interpretation of micromorphological slides. It had become apparent that the degraded fraction of organic matter was not well correlated with the archaeobotanical value. Some types of peat may contain low fractions of well-preserved organic tissue due to their mode of genesis, and still be considered well preserved. In those peats, the bulk of the soil mass consists of organic plasma formed by degradation of above-ground plant material before it was submerged in a waterlogged environment. Such peats, as well as peats that consist entirely of well-preserved organic tissue, represent past environments in which botanical remains that are related to human activities and landscape could be well preserved. The biggest issue with preservation and monitoring, however, concerns recent processes that may affect such materials. When using micromorphological samples, the focus should not therefore be on the overall state of degradation of the organic materials so much as on (1) identifying active decay and transformation processes, (2) identifying indicators for changes in the burial environment in the past and (3) establishing the state of preservation of archaeological remains (Huisman, 2009b; Huisman et al., 2009).

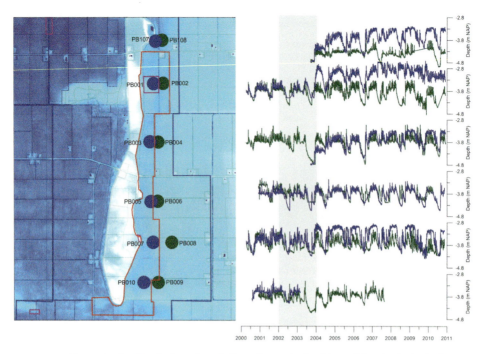

FIGURE 4   Groundwater levels in pairs of dipwells on both sides of the hydrological zone boundary (hydrological zone and buffer zone in red). The two dipwell pairs in the north (including PB001/PB002 on P14) show a permanently elevated water table. PB003/PB004 and PB007/PB008 show longer periods of high water tables in the zone, but not higher than the area outside the zone, and still show dry spells as before. Pair PB005/PB006 shows little change after the hydrological zone was created.

This new approach was used in phase 3. During this round, ample evidence was found for the presence of pyrite at all sites and evidence of oxidation processes in most (all except P14). Pyrite oxidation can have two major negative effects on archaeological sites: (1) strong acidification — if no lime is present as a buffer — due to the formation of sulphuric acid as an oxidation product and (2) damage to artefacts, botanical and zoological remains due to the formation of new minerals — especially gypsum in the presence of carbonates. Schokkerhaven-E170 and De Zuidert showed serious damage to archaeological and botanical materials due to pyrite oxidation and mineral formation. At J125, only minor damage could be seen (Figure 6). The damage at Schokkerhaven-E170 and De Zuidert is the result of downward infiltration of oxygen-rich water, or maybe (partial) drying out of the soil and infiltration of atmospheric oxygen. The reason why J125 shows less damage may be because of generally higher water tables and possibly less permeable layers compared to Schokkerhaven-E170 or De Zuidert.

A comparison between the thin sections from phase 1 and phase 3 would have been a great opportunity to assess whether there were significant changes in the state of the sites over the last decade. However, the thin sections from phase 1 were missing and attempts to locate them were unsuccessful.

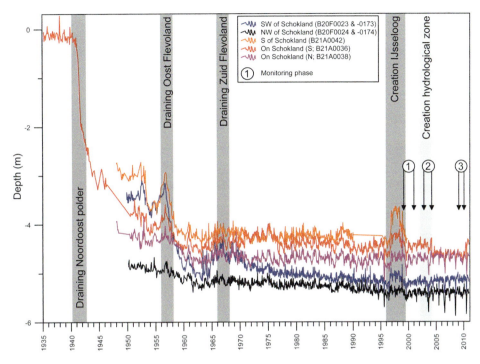

FIGURE 5 Long-term trend in groundwater levels from dipwells, demonstrating the effects of various large-scale hydroengineering works in the region. See Figure 3A for position of the wells.

The burial environment: measuring and interpreting soil and water chemical data

During **phase 1**, the chemical composition of the *groundwater* was measured repeatedly at all three sites monitored in this phase. The results were reported (Van Heeringen et al., 2004), but with the remark that no meaningful conclusions could be drawn from this data. There was no repeat of these measurements in the Schokland monitoring, with the exception of pH (which was measured again in **phase 3**). A reappraisal of these data was made while reporting on phase 3. Piper-plots of the data (Figure 7a) show that Schokkerhaven-E170 has groundwater that is dominated by dissolved species that are typical of saline or brackish conditions (see Appelo and Postma, 1999 for the use of piper plots in general; and Huisman et al., 2009 for their relevance in archaeological monitoring). De Zuidert and P14 have groundwater compositions more in line with fresh water. Most remarkable, however, is the fact that the groundwater composition seems to be heavily influenced by gypsum dissolution, the gypsum being a by-product pf pyrite oxidation in a calcareous environment. The concentrations of calcium and sulphate are correlated, and have a ratio close to the stoichiometry of gypsum (Figure 7b). This supports the micromorphological observations and soil chemical analyses made during phase 3.

During **phase 3**, the chemical composition of the soil was analysed. At Schokkerhaven-E170 and J125, hand-held XRF was used in combination with measurements of the sulphur contents and speciation. The sulphur contents and the occurrence of both

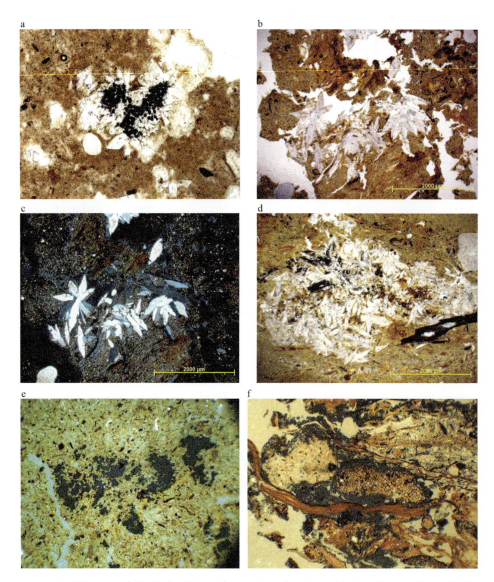

FIGURE 6   Micromorphological evidence for pyrite and pyrite oxidation. Plane polarized light (PPL) unless indicated otherwise. A: Pyrite (black), surrounded by gypsum (white) in peat (J125). B: Clusters of gypsum (white) and iron oxides (reddish) in clayey groundmass (De Zuidert). C: Idem, with crossed polarizers (XPL). Gypsum is grey to brilliant white; iron oxides are reddish. D: Gypsum minerals and iron oxides, associated with charcoal fragments (black). The formation of the gypsum has resulted in the fragmentation of the charcoal (De Zuidert). E: Cluster of unaffected pyrite in deeper, reducing layers (De Zuidert); Oblique incident light (OIL). F: Pyrite precipitated on organic tissue fragments. From the deeper, reducing layers unaffected by oxidation (De Zuidert; OIL).

(a)

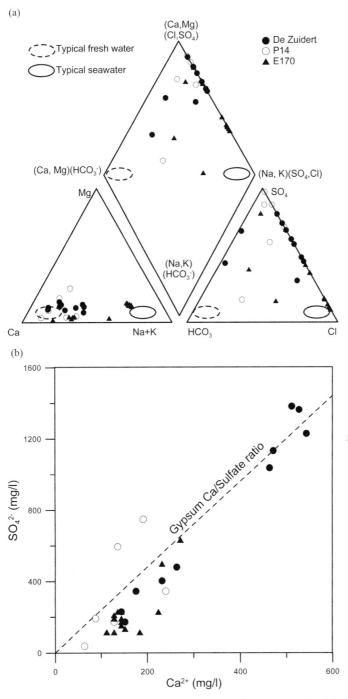

FIGURE 7a   Piper-plots of groundwater composition measurements made during the 1999–2001 monitoring round (Van Heeringen et al., 2004). The lower left (cation) triangle shows that P14 and De Zuidert have a largely freshwater signature, mostly due to high calcium contents, whereas Schokkerhaven-E170 shows some samples that are more saline. The lower right (anion) triangle shows that sulphate dominates at all three sites. This is confirmed in the upper diamond, where the samples are all above the saline and fresh water compositions, and tend strongly to the upper calcium and sulphate contents.

Scatterplot 7b shows that the concentrations of calcium and sulphate correlate well, and are in line with the composition of gypsum. These plots demonstrate the importance of pyrite oxidation and gypsum dissolution and reprecipitation at these three sites. It also shows that saline or brackish water is still present at Schokkerhaven-E170.

sulphide and sulphate species confirmed the micromorphological observations of pyrite oxidation (Figure 8). Moreover, it was possible to estimate the speed and progress of pyrite oxidation (Huisman et al., 2008b), which indicated that degradation due to pyrite oxidation (equivalent to the production of 0.1 g/kg H^+) was worrying, especially at Schokkerhaven-E170. It was estimated that about 30% of the pyrite had been oxidized since 1940, and that acid production would continue for about a century.

Monitoring archaeological materials

In **phase 1**, the degree of preservation of botanical macroremains was analyzed. Bone fragments were analyzed by classifying histological characteristics of decay processes (Jans et al., 2002; 2004) and by chemical characterization (XRD, FTIR, and collagen extraction).

In **phase 3**, analyses of botanical macroremains and histological research of bone fragments was again planned. However, too few fragments of bone were available for a meaningful histological assessment. At one of the sites (Schokkerhaven-E170), a test was performed using quality of pollen as a measure of the preservation of the site.

No clear trend becomes apparent when the quality of botanical remains is compared. Problem is that for many common species and types of botanical remains, a whole range of preservation states are encountered. This may be because the degree of preservation of botanical remains is not determined by recent decay processes alone, but also by decay in the past (especially during site formation) and by resistance to decay processes. Resistance to decay can vary considerably between species and types of fragment (Brinkkemper, 2006). Accumulated (past and recent) decay can also differ from object to object. No meaningful conclusions could be drawn from the monitoring of this type of material.

Bone remains suffer from the same problem of accumulated decay processes. Moreover, they are also commonly present in only minor amounts at archaeological sites, which make them less useful as a material for monitoring.

General developments in monitoring

The Schokland monitoring project demonstrates several general developments:

Trend 1: technological developments

The last decade has seen an increase in options for automatic and high-frequency monitoring of relevant parameters. Especially groundwater levels, moisture contents and redox, in particular, are increasingly being measured automatically. This reduces the need for frequent field visits, and makes monitoring more efficient (although it poses equipment security issues). However, processing and interpreting the massive amounts of data that are generated takes considerable amounts of time and energy.

Trend 2: growing knowledge of degradation processes

At the start of monitoring projects in the 1990s there was no basic overview of the available knowledge of degradation processes and their relationship to soil conditions. Since then, a series of publications have provided a solid base of information

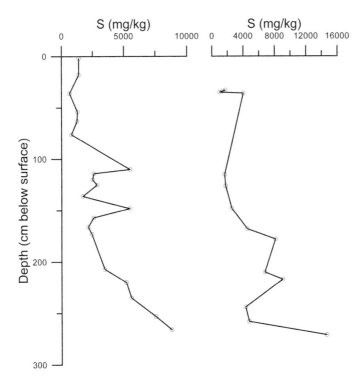

FIGURE 8   Profile of sulphur contents at De Zuidert (data from two boreholes). Sulphur contents reach values of 1–1.5%. Increasing values with depth may indicate that sulphate – from pyrite oxida-tion – leaches to deeper soil layers, where it promotes the formation of new pyrite minerals like those seen in Figure 6E and F.

(Kars and Smit, 2003; Smit et al., 2006; Huisman, 2009c). Some of these (e.g. Smit et al., 2006) are based at least in part on the experiences of the first monitoring rounds in Schokland. Moreover, several research projects and publications have extended the knowledge base. In the Schokland project, this has led to (1) the introduction of soil moisture measurements, (2) a change in the way data from soil thin sections are evaluated and (3) recognition of pyrite oxidation and awareness of its importance for the preservation of the Schokland sites.

Trend 3: increasing availability of external data
Developments in internet-accessible databases makes it easier to access various kinds of data. Weather data can easily be found on and downloaded from the website of the Royal Netherlands Meteorological Institute[1] and collated groundwater data can be obtained from the TNO DINO Loket geoscience database or from Zuiderzeeland water board.

Trend 4: importance of archiving data and materials
It is of key importance in monitoring projects that results from different moments in time can be compared. Therefore, care must be taken to ascertain that it is possible to access data and study materials from each measuring round. In the Schokland case, this has failed to some extent. The monitoring data were recovered by chance, and with the help of A. Smit (Paleo Terra), who found the files on an old computer. The soil thin sections for micromorphological analysis from the first phases of monitoring have been lost.

This problem prompted an initiative to encourage the archiving of digital monitoring data and of thin sections from archaeological sites in the Netherlands. This will hopefully prevent such problems from occurring in the future.

Refocusing for the next rounds

The report on the 2011 monitoring round is scheduled for publication in late 2011/ early 2012. The main question to be answered is whether the costly measures to protect the monument have paid off. This question cannot be answered at this juncture, since not all data from the last monitoring round are available. The following tentative conclusions can however be drawn:

- The dominant threat at all four sites is the oxidation of pyrite, resulting in acidification or damage due to the formation of gypsum crystals.
- Parts of the hydrological zone are experiencing wetter conditions than before, while other parts show little change.
- Conditions at P14 have improved, and the burial environment there seems to be ideal for preservation of the archaeological remains.
- Conditions at De Zuidert have not been influenced by the creation of the hydrological zone. Pyrite oxidation and gypsum formation in the upper layers of the mound constitute the greatest threat.
- Of the two sites that lie far from the hydrological zone, Schokkerhaven-E170 suffers seriously from pyrite oxidation, and is degrading at a fast rate. At J125, pyrite is also oxidizing, but less actively. Damage here seems to be limited.

The report on the third monitoring round will also be a moment to take a critical look at the monitoring programme and to advise on the next steps. Important points to discuss will be:

- What methods provide information on the state of the monument that are precise, reliable and relevant enough that they contribute significantly to the monitoring programme? And which methods are too imprecise, unreliable or irrelevant and should no longer be included?
- At which sites does monitoring contribute to preservation and protection? Is it logical to continue monitoring sites where the burial conditions cannot or will not be changed? For example, archaeological values at Schokkerhaven-E170 are degrading at a worrying rate. If no other action is taken, does it make sense to continue monitoring? At De Zuidert, we see several active degradation processes in the upper layers that are related to the soil moisture regime and oxygen. Deeper layers are in a very good state. The processes active at the site can be seen as normal for *terp* sites, and seem not to have been influenced by the draining of the polder and later human actions. No reasonable measures can be taken to ameliorate the burial environment. This raises the question of what purpose monitoring now serves.

These questions have yet to be answered in relation to the monitored sites at the UNESCO Schokland monument.

Acknowledgements

We would like to thank the waterboard Zuiderzeeland for providing the groundwater-level data. Sue McDonnel checked the English language. Two anonymous reviewers are thanked for their helpful comments. Sander Smit is thanked for providing datasets from earlier monitoring rounds and for discussions on the reliability of redox probe measurements.

Note

1 KNMI; <www.knmi.nl>.

Bibliography

Appelo, C. A. J. and Postma, D. 1999. *Groundwater, Chemistry and Pollution*. Rotterdam: Balkema.

Brinkkemper, O. 2006. Study of the Preservation Quality of Archaeological Sites Using Botanical Macroremains. *Berichten van de Rijksdienst voor het Oudheidkundig Bodemonderzoek*, 46: 303–14.

Hogestijn, J. W. H. 1991. *Archeologische kroniek van Flevoland (Cultureel Historisch Jaarboek voor Flevoland 1)*. Lelystad.

Gehasse, E. F. 1995. Ecologisch-archeologisch onderzoek van het Neolithicum en de Vroege Bronstijd in de Noordoostpolder met de nadruk op vindplaats P14, PhD thesis, Amsterdam University, Amsterdam.

Huisman, D. J. 2009a. Iron. In: D. J. Huisman, ed. *Degradation of Archaeological Remains*. Den Haag: SdU Uitgevers b.v., pp. 91–109.

Huisman, D. J. 2009b. Using Soil Micromorphology to Evaluate the Suitability of the Burial Environment for In Situ Protection. In: K. Straetkvern and D. J. Huisman, eds. *Proceedings of the 10th ICOM Group on Wet Organic Archaeological Materials Conference, Amsterdam 2007*, Nederlandse Archeologische Rapporten (NAR) 37, Amersfoort: RACM, pp. 101–11.

Huisman, D. J. ed. 2009c. *Degradation of Archaeological Remains*. Den Haag: SdU Uitgevers b.v.

Huisman, D. J. and Theunissen, E. M. 2008. Too Good to Be True? The Unexpectedly Good Preservation of the Nieuw Dordrecht Neolithic Peat Trackway and its Consequences. In: H. Kars and R. M. van Heeringen, eds. *Preserving Archaeological Remains In Situ. Proceedings of the 3rd Conference 7–9 December 2006, Amsterdam*, Geoarchaeological and Bioarchaeological Studies Vol. 10, IGBA, VU University, Amsterdam, pp. 15–28.

Huisman, D. J. and Klaassen, R. K. W. M. 2009. Wood. In: D. J. Huisman, ed. *Degradation of Archaeological Remains*. Den Haag: SdU Uitgevers b.v., pp. 13–32.

Huisman, D. J. and Joosten, I. 2009. Copper and Copper Alloys. In: D. J. Huisman. ed. *Degradation of Archaeological Remains*. Den Haag: SdU Uitgevers b.v., pp. 111–24.

Huisman, D. J., Manders, M. R., Kretschmar, E., Klaassen, R. K. W. M., and Lamersdorf, N. 2008a. Burial Conditions and Wood Degradation on Archaeological Sites in the Netherlands. *International Biodedeterioration & Biodegradation*, 61: 33–44.

Huisman, D. J., Müller, A., van Os, B., and Peeters, H. 2008b. Een kleinschalig onderzoek naar de fysieke gaafheid en conserveringstoestand van de vindplaatsen Schokkerhaven-E170 en Schokland-J125 (prov. Flevoland) in het kader van het beheersplan Schokland (UNESCO World Heritage Site). Beknopte Rapportage Archeologische Monumentenzorg (BRAM) 11, Amersfoort: Rijksdienst voor Archeologie, Cultuurlandschap en Monumenten.

Huisman, D. J., Vorenhout, M., Smit, A., van Os, B., and Manders, M. 2009. Preservation and Monitoring of Archaeological Sites. In: D. J. Huisman, ed. *Degradation of Archaeological Remains*. Den Haag: SdU Uitgevers b.v., pp. 177–210.

Jans, M. M. E., Kars, H., Nielsen-Marsch, C. M., Smith, C. I., Nord, A. G., Arthur, P., and Earl, N. 2002. In Situ Preservation of Archaeological Bone. A Histological Study Within a Multidisciplinary Approach. *Archaeometry*, 44: 343–52.

Jans, M. M. E., Nielsen-Marsch, C. M., Smith, C. I., Collins, M. J., and Kars, H. 2004. Characterization of Microbial Attack on Archaeological Bone. *Journal of Archaeological Science*, 31: 87–95.

Plan van Aanpak Nieuw Schokland, 1998.

Rabenhorst, M. C., Hively, W. D., and James, B. R. 2009. Measurements of Soil Redox Potential. *Soil Science Society of America Journal*, 73(2): 668–71

Smit, A., Mol, G., and van Heeringen, R. M. 2005. *Natte voeten voor Schokland. Inrichting hydrologische zone. Archeologische monitoring 2003–2004. Een evaluatie van de waterhuishoudkundige maatregelen.* Rapportage Archeologische Monumentenzorg 124. Amersfoort: Rijksdienst voor het Oudheidkundig Bodemonderzoek.

Smit, A., van Heeringen, R. M., and Theunissen, E. M. 2006. *Archaeological Monitoring Standard, Guidelines for the Non-Destructive Recording and Monitoring of the Physical Quality of Archaeological Sites and Monuments.* Nederlandse Archeologische Rapporten (NAR) 33. Amersfoort: Rijksdienst voor Archaeologie, Cultuurlandschap en Monumenten (RACM).

Ten Anscher, T. J. 2012. Leven met de Vecht: Schokland-P14 en de Noordoostpolder in het neolithicum en de bronstijd. Unpublished PhD thesis. Universiteit van Amsterdam.

Theunissen, E. M., Huisman, D. J., Smit, A., and van der Heijden, F. 2006. *Kijkoperatie in het veen. Kwaliteits-bepalend onderzoek naar de veenweg van Nieuw-Dordrecht (gemeente Emmen).* Rapportage Archeologische Monumentenzorg (RAM) 130.

Van der Heide, G. D. 1950. *Voorlopig opgravingsrapport: Proefopgraving terp Zuidert, Schokland* (ROB report 16C). Amersfoort: Rijksdienst voor het Oudheidkundig Bodemonderzoek.

Van Doesburg, J. and Mauro, G. V. 2007. *Onderzoek en archeologische begeleiding op en rondom Schokland; een kleinschalig onderzoek aan het Enserkerkje en archeologische begeleiding van de herstelwerkzaamheden aan de kerkresten, de waterput op de Zuidert en de aanleg van de hydrologische zone.* Rapportage Archeologische Monumentenzorg (RAM) 142. Amersfoort: RACM.

van Heeringen, R. M., Mauro, G. V., and Smit, A. 2004. *A Pilot Study on the Monitoring of the Physical Quality of Three Archaeological Sites at the UNESCO World Heritage Site at Schokland, Province of Flevoland, the Netherlands.* Nederlandse Archeologische Rapporten 26. Amersfoort: Rijksdienst voor het Oudheidkundig Bodemonderzoek.

Notes on contributors

Hans (D. J.) Huisman is a soil scientist and geochemist. Since 2003 he has worked for the cultural heritage agency as senior researcher soil science and degradation. He has done a series of research projects on degradation of archaeological remains and monitoring of archaeological sites and edited and co-wrote a book on degradation of archaeological remains.

Correspondence to: Hans (D. J.) Huisman. Email: h.huisman@cultureelerfgoed.nl

Guido V. Mauro is an archaeologist. Since 1997 he has worked for the cultural heritage agency as consulate archaeology and cultural landscape. His working area includes Noord- and Zuid-Holland as well as Flevoland. He has done several projects on *in situ* preservation and was involved of the creation of the 'hydrological zone' Schokand.

Correspondence to: Guido V. Mauro. Email: g.mauro@cultureelerfgoed.nl

CONSERVATION AND MGMT OF ARCH. SITES, Vol. 14 Nos 1–4, 2012, 429–41

Is Preservation *In Situ* an Unacceptable Option for Development Control? Can Monitoring Prove the Continued Preservation of Waterlogged Deposits?

Tim Malim

SLR Consulting, UK

Ian Panter

York Archaeological Trust, UK

This paper will outline the approach taken for monitoring of two waterlogged areas in England: the multi-period deposits beneath the historic town of Nantwich, Cheshire, and the Bronze Age timber platform at Whittlesey, Cambridgeshire. These two examples allow contrast and comparison between urban and rural contexts, and between multiple ownerships and single development. The projects also illustrate how English planning guidance can be variously interpreted dependent on conflicting aims and objectives. The paper will describe the characteristics of the sites, their past history and present threats, and the suggested management strategies for each. The duration, spatial interval, and methods of monitoring (including use of *in situ* redox probes, Time Domain Reflectometry, sediment geochemistry, and water-level measurement) will be discussed, and how short-term data-gathering is actually what influences decision-making.

KEYWORDS archaeological site monitoring, UK planning legislation, waterlogged sites, UK

Introduction

The title of this paper seems incongruous to present at the fourth conference designed to discuss how we can endeavour to preserve rather than excavate archaeological remains. However, in the light of recent change to English planning guidance the phrase 'preservation *in situ*' has been made redundant. With the introduction of new planning guidance for archaeology and development (Planning Policy Statement 5,

          DOI 10.1179/1350503312Z.00000000037

usually referred to as PPS5) in March 2010 the terminology is now 'conservation of heritage assets', and, although this may seem a question of semantics, it actually raises some fundamental truths exposed starkly by the experience of the examples outlined here at Nantwich and Must Farm.

The first site comprises the historic core of Nantwich town centre, a medieval salt-producing town with organic remains dating as far back as the Iron Age, over 3 m of waterlogged deposit, and an existing conservation area with attractive timber-frame buildings. Cheshire East Council has taken a proactive approach towards seeking a solution for continued preservation and was supported by English Heritage who funded a pilot study to establish the conditions of preservation and origins for the waterlogged remains, and a three-year monitoring programme to help understand the processes involved in survival and decay of these remains.

The second site is Must Farm, a Bronze Age timber platform constructed on the edge of a palaeochannel in the Cambridgeshire fens on the edge of Peterborough. A management plan (SLR 2007) to preserve the remains in situ in accordance with national planning guidance has been funded by Hanson Building Products (part of Hanson Heidleberg Cement) with a long-term monitoring programme initiated in 2007 and planned to last throughout the lifetime of the quarry. In contrast to Cheshire, however, the local planning authority believes the remains are too valuable to risk and therefore they should be excavated rather than wait to see whether measures implemented will be successful in conserving the site over the twenty-five-year duration of the planning consent and also in the longer term.

Under previous planning guidance (Planning Policy Guidance 16, usually referred to as PPG16) preservation *in situ* allowed maintaining the status quo, but under PPS5 a more pro-active approach is expected. In effect, the question as to whether preservation *in situ* is a pragmatic option will be evaluated by what criteria one wants to apply:

- If indicators of decay are detected does this really imply rapid deterioration of the buried remains, which might have survived for thousands of years with a very slow rate of decay over that period? Although a number of proxy indicators can be used to monitor a site, the implication of the data are complex and interpretation can vary from site to site; and
- If the test is to demonstrate the remains are indeed being preserved, then how do proxy indicators prove this? They need to be verified by intrusive investigation, a method that would introduce the very agents of decay that we seek to exclude.

Nantwich project Phase 1: characterizing the waterlogged deposits

In 2007 English Heritage and Cheshire East Council commissioned SLR Consulting with York Archaeological Trust to review and map existing information on the distribution of waterlogged remains within Nantwich using data from archaeological investigations and boreholes. Subsequently we cored thirty locations in two phases of drilling in order to establish the extent of the waterlogged deposits, and to characterize them. From this dual approach it was possible to suggest why waterlogged deposits occurred, and what threatened their continued survival. The reasons for the waterlogging and thus preservation of organic remains seem to derive from the natural geology of the town which comprises sand overlying Gault clay. In spite of the fact that parts of the town are built several metres above the river Weaver, a series of natural aquifers originally ran through the area, saturating the sands above the impermeable clay, and thus created perched water tables and conditions for domestic and stable refuse to accumulate without substantial decay, a process accelerated in the lower-lying parts of the town by the industrial waste from salt production. Organic remains have been dated to Iron Age and Roman times, but the main period of blanket waterlogging appears to span the late Anglo-Saxon/medieval period (eleventh century through into the thirteenth century). However, these deposits are now liable to desiccation and many of the cores failed to retrieve evidence for organic remains, even within areas of known waterlogged deposits revealed from previous archaeological fieldwork. Our interpretation is that desiccation is probably due to the lack of rainwater recharge caused by drainage and hard surfacing installed after the cholera epidemic in the 1850s, and that the disparate evidence between coring and archaeological excavation reflects the highly localized and variable nature of preservation that can occur within widespread deposits.

As a result of these studies we have written a supplementary planning guidance to advise developers and planners on the sensitivity of the Area of Special Archaeological Potential in Nantwich, and to urge the introduction of a holistic planning strategy for sustainable economic development with joined up thinking between urban planners, water and highways engineers, statutory undertakers, and private developers. In addition, English Heritage and Cheshire East Council have funded a three-year monitoring programme 2011–14, Phase 2 of the Nantwich Waterlogged Deposits project.

Must Farm: characterizing the waterlogged deposits

The baseline conditions at Must Farm were established from samples taken during trial trenching in 2006–07. Two monoliths 10 m apart were assessed for geochemical signatures which showed both weakly reducing and weakly oxidizing sediments. Groundwater was not detected during insertion of all dipwells, and the physical nature of the sediments (roddon silts sandwiching coarser material as part of a cultural horizon) suggested that the small pore spaces were instrumental in retaining moisture and coarser material would be more prone to oxidation. The trench showed that the cultural horizon sloped down the side of the roddon (ancient watercourse) into the palaeochannel, with over 2 m of silt and clay between the cultural horizon and the sand and gravel aquifer. The cultural horizon is sealed beneath at least 1 m of silt and alluvium, with soil and brick debris above. The preservation of organic remains at an elevated level above the aquifer was initially interpreted as due to a perched water table, but subsequent studies has demonstrated that they lie within a tension saturated zone caused by capillary action.

What should we monitor?

The monitoring strategies developed for both Must Farm and Nantwich (Figure 1) were designed to characterize the physical and chemical conditions that have preserved organic and inorganic remains. Methodologies have been devised with reference to

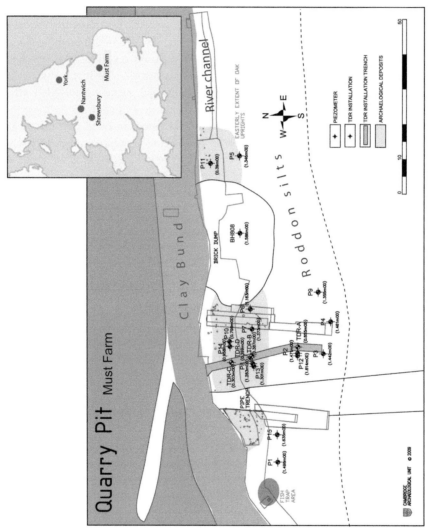

FIGURE 1   Map of the UK showing the location of the two case studies, Must Farm, Cambridgeshire and Nantwich, Cheshire; and detailed plan of Must Farm showing monitoring points relating to cultural deposits.

previous *in situ* schemes and international guidance published by the Norwegian and Dutch government agencies. The development of the monitoring strategies has been an iterative process, adopting new techniques where necessary.

Must Farm

For example, the initial proposals for Must Farm focused on the insertion of thirty-three piezometers and ninety-nine redox probes at eleven monitoring points — monitoring three depths at each location (Figure 1). Rainfall data was provided by MORECS (Meteorology Office Rainfall and Evaporation Calculation System) from the weather station at Wittering, some 10 km away from the site. Interpretation of the water-level data (collected at fortnightly intervals using a simple audible dipmeter since February 2008) revealed that the archaeological deposits were situated within both the water table and its capillary fringe (or tension saturated zone) and recharged primarily through rainfall.

Enhancement to this monitoring regime included the installation of a further four deep dipwells so as to correlate groundwater levels with moisture contents within the capillary fringe (and provide a North–South profile across the site towards the quarry edge) as well as four 'dry' access tubes for Time Domain Reflectometry (TDR) adjacent to them. TDR is now a standard technique for measuring moisture content of sediments within the capillary fringe (piezometers are ineffective in these conditions).

Monitoring of the deep boreholes indicates that groundwater levels are beginning to stabilize following construction of a bund to prevent potential dewatering into the deep quarry adjacent to the site, and that recharge of the site occurs primarily during the winter months when effective precipitation is at its greatest. Groundwater levels are increasing at a rate of approximately 0.2 m per year since 2007. Both TDR and piezometer data suggest that more of the upper deposits of the 'cultural horizon' become saturated during the winter months as the water table rises and the capillary fringe increases.

Direct measurement of redox potentials at Must Farm is achieved using *in situ* platinum tipped probes. Initial problems of installation due to the presence of between 0.5 m and 1.0 m thickness of brick rubble was overcome through the mechanical removal of this brick rubble followed by hand-augering access holes for each probe cluster. These clusters were sleeved and sealed in narrow bore tubing to facilitate insertion. However, exposure to the elements over the last four years has led to the breakdown of the silicone seals and the redox measurements are now likely to be erroneous; similar failures with redox monitoring equipment were encountered at Nydam (Mathiesen et al., 2004). *In situ* redox measurements have been supplemented with geochemical assay of the sediments. Baseline conditions were established during the excavation by Boreham (2007) and subsequent assays of the presence and concentrations of the principal redox sensitive species (e.g. sulphide, sulphate, ferrous and ferric ions, nitrates and nitrites) indicate that reducing conditions prevail within the deeper deposits but that variable conditions exist within the shallow sediments of the 'cultural horizon'.

Such variability within these superficial sediments can be attributed to their physical properties including grainsize, anisotropic permeability, as well as the seasonality of the recharge to the system and differences in vertical and lateral water movement times in the clays, silts, and anthropogenic sediments.

Nantwich

Must Farm is a good example of a complex rural wetland, whilst our second case study, Nantwich, highlights the issues around monitoring and characterization in urban deposits (Figure 2). Being research driven meant that a staged approach could be adopted for the Nantwich Deposit Model study. Baseline conditions were established in 2007 when a programme of geochemical and palaeoenvironmental sampling was conducted in the town using cores extracted by a windowless percussive rig. Each core (1 m long sections and 100 mm diameter) was recovered in a Perspex sleeve which was sealed rapidly and stored in cool and light-free conditions before processing. The lithology of each core was described before sub-sampling to identify the degree of preservation of plant macrofossils, pollen, diatoms, insect remains and wood. As with Must Farm, sediment samples were analysed to identify the predominant redox sensitive species which was used to chemically characterize the deposits in Nantwich. Sub-samples were stored either in grip-lock bags or airtight plastic containers and stored at 5° C before processing. All tests were carried out in an accredited (ISO 17025 compliant) laboratory working to recognized standard testing methodologies (for example, British Standard 1377) using the approach adopted by Matthiesen at Bryggen (Matthiesen, 2008).

After collating the results two clear preservation zones were identified (Figure 2):

- Preservation Zone 1 consists of those deposits in the River Weaver floodplain/valley where preservation is very good/excellent and geochemical data indicates reducing or highly reducing deposits.
- Preservation Zone 2, broadly east of the Weaver including archaeological deposits located above the floodplain and within the core of the medieval town. Preservation here can be described as 'variable', ranging between excellent to actively decaying.

In geochemical terms, both zones were characterized by having relatively low concentrations of sulphates, and higher levels of sulphide and sulphur. However, pockets within Zone 2 were found to have an abundance of sulphate as opposed to sulphides and active decay was observed in the palaeoenvironmental remains (please refer to Malim et al., 2009 for further information about the indicators of state of preservation for bioarchaeologcial materials). Excesses of sulphate are taken to indicate oxidizing conditions where bacteria such as *Thiobacillus ferrooxidans* obtain their energy through the oxidation of inorganic sulphides and ferrous compounds. Where sulphides predominate, bacteria such as *Desulfovibrio desulfuricans* obtain their energy through the reduction of sulphates and are typically found in waterlogged soils. Best preservation of organic materials is assumed to be found in deposits where an excess of sulphides are present.

Based on preliminary results whilst working in the field, eleven dipwells were installed in 2007 to provide a grid for monitoring groundwater levels. Each dipwell comprised a 50 mm slotted PVC tube, bedded into inert sand and sealed with bentonite to prevent water ingress from surface run-off. The tubes were fitted with a gas tap to enable gas samples to be collected and measured. Stage 2 saw an enhance-ment to this initial grid with the installation of six additional dipwells — three in Zone 1 and three in Zone 2 (Figure 3). Those in Zone 1 were at new locations to provide one transect from the upland edge of the known waterlogged deposits to the river's edge. Those in Zone 2 were installed adjacent to three locations where the assessment in 2007 had identified well preserved but potentially decaying organic remains, and hence requiring data capture from varying depths determined by the archaeological stratigraphy.

Water levels are recorded automatically using a pressure transducer (the SOLINST Levellogger system) which is inserted into the dipwell and data capture has been set to twice daily intervals). Stored data is downloaded at monthly intervals and corrected for local atmospheric pressure using a dedicated barometric transducer installed in Nantwich for the project. An audible dipmeter is used to record water levels in the remaining dipwells. Whilst it is too early to detect significant trends the correlation between rainfall and water levels in each of the dipwells is clear (Figure 4, water level data from Nantwich from 26 January 2011 to 11 May 2011). Dipwells AB, AE, and AF are located in the Weaver floodplain (i.e. Zone 1) whereas F1, P, and N1 are located in Zone 2, that is, in the core of the medieval settlement.

A groundwater-monitoring regime, using a Water Quality Meter to measure a wide range of parameters including pH, temperature, conductivity, redox, and dissolved gases (methane, hydrogen sulphide, carbon dioxide, and oxygen) has been imple-mented on a quarterly basis. Additional water samples will be submitted annually for laboratory analyses for the same parameters. Each tube is purged of stagnant water (following procedures described in BS 5930, Annex F) and allowed to recharge before measurements are collected.

Already the authors can begin to see the correlation between certain chemicals and other in situ tests. For example, Figure 5 shows the direct correlation between negative redox values (i.e. reducing conditions), low ratios for sulphate/sulphide, and high levels of methane gas. Whilst methane gas may be derived from a leaking gas pipe (natural gas being a source of methane), the likelihood here is as a result of the slow decay of organic remains under anoxic conditions, and the potential for using methane as a proxy indicator for the character of the burial environment will be explored further during the Nantwich study.

Over the course of the next two and half years further trends will be investigated to ascertain what influence the influx of rainfall has on sediment geochemistry and hence potential impacts upon continued preservation of the archaeological resource.

Lessons learnt?

Our work has confirmed that an holistic approach has to be adopted and as much data gathered at the earliest opportunity as is possible. Monitoring techniques are now well established although concerns are still voiced as to the duration of the monitoring programme and interval between data capture. Our work at Must Farm has demonstrated that fortnightly water level/moisture content and redox measure-ment are adequate, especially where additional information including readings from adjacent deep boreholes are taken into consideration. Although a year of data is the

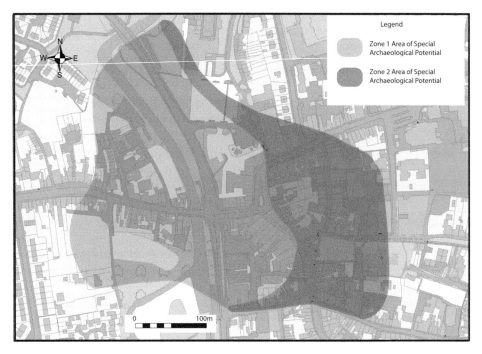

FIGURE 2   Preservation zones in Nantwich, identified as a result of the Nantwich Deposit Model, Phase 1b.

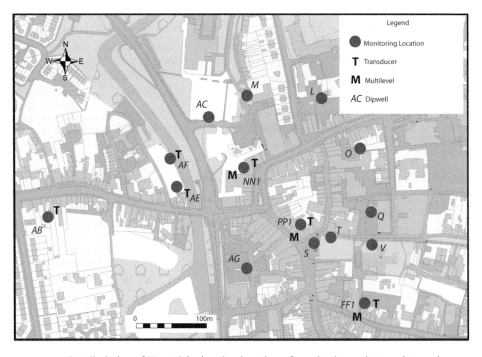

FIGURE 3   Detailed plan of Nantwich showing location of monitoring points and transducers.

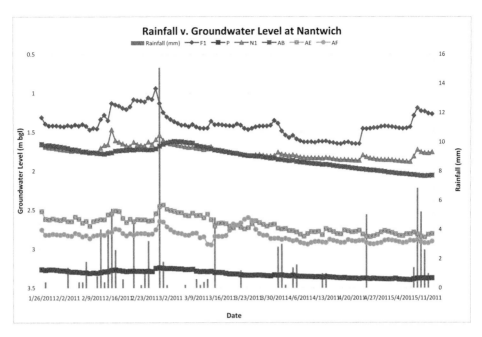

FIGURE 4   Water levels from transducer data from six dipwells in Nantwich, showing relationship between rainfall and groundwater levels.

bare minimum that will be required before trends begin to become clear, our experience at Must Farm (in which waterlogging occurs due to a tension saturated zone rather than a measurable water level) has shown how even three years are insufficient; each review meeting produces further queries requiring more detailed and specific data to answer those questions. Ideally, an initial twelve months of data should be captured before the project commences; however, it is unlikely that such a requirement would ever be enforceable within the current English planning system. It could be argued that without such data there is no point in pursuing *in situ* preservation because there is insufficient information required to reach a decision. Surely, 'informed conservation', as practised by all UK heritage agencies, is the key to successful preservation?

Three years of monitoring the Must Farm deposits have demonstrated the complexity of even 'rural' locations especially where much of the 'cultural horizon' is located above the water table. These complexities are the norm in urban centres which was highlighted in the York study (Holden et al., 2009). Our characterization of the Nantwich deposits, including a baseline assessment of the degree of preservation of the organic remains illustrate just how complex and dynamic the urban environment can be.

As stated previously, we have identified two distinct preservation zones in Nantwich where we can make certain inferences about the state of preservation of the archaeological resource based on the monitoring data. However, these can only remain as assumptions based on the premise that optimum preservation is achieved under highly reducing conditions. *In situ* preservation is about controlling the factors

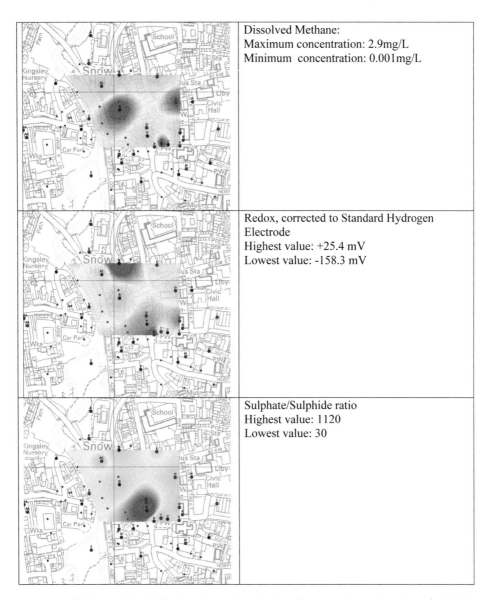

	Dissolved Methane: Maximum concentration: 2.9mg/L Minimum concentration: 0.001mg/L
	Redox, corrected to Standard Hydrogen Electrode Highest value: +25.4 mV Lowest value: -158.3 mV
	Sulphate/Sulphide ratio Highest value: 1120 Lowest value: 30

FIGURE 5   Water quality distribution plots: dissolved methane, redox, and sulphate/sulphide ratios. Red zones: highest values, green zones: lowest values.

that determine the rate at which this decay happens and that this rate can be slowed to an almost imperceptible level in 'reducing' environments because of the type of bacteria able to flourish under such conditions. When we do discover active decay, as we believe we did in Nantwich, we still have to ask ourselves whether we are really looking at recent decay or is it evidence of ancient decay that occurred prior to the onset of conditions conducive to preservation. Our interpretation, based on the geochemical and palaeoenvironmental studies, led us to believe that the decay was recent, but we will not have definite proof until we have collected sufficient information about surface and groundwater levels and movement, that is, after we have a minimum of twelve months' readings.

This highlights the existing gap in our knowledge base — we still lack sufficient information about how materials degrade, so it is often impossible to identify where the remains lie on their individual decay trajectories.

Within the United Kingdom there has been no long-term monitoring study to demonstrate the efficacy of preservation in situ for waterlogged remains. A number of sites have experimented with various data-collection strategies to try to characterize and monitor the diverse nature of burial conditions in which organic remains have survived, including Shinewater Park (Sussex) (Hogan, 1998; 2001), Sutton Common (South Yorkshire) (Cheetham, 2007), Fiskerton (Lincolnshire) (Williams et al., 2008a), and Shardlow Quarry (Derbyshire) (Williams et al., 2008b). There is no definitive 'one size fits all' approach that can be adopted, especially as the deposits in which organic remains are found can vary from clays to peats and even saturated sands, and valid comparative data is lacking; even laboratory analyses for the same proxy indicators from the same samples can provide very different results depending on the methods and interpretation of results employed by each laboratory. Each site is unique and therefore requires a bespoke and iterative management plan, which can be flexible and subject to ground-truthing, rather than relying on proxy indicators. The studies at Nantwich and Must Farm are thus of immense significance in establishing whether national policy can actually be applied to the realities of archaeological resource management, and that the design of effective monitoring programmes, data-gathering, and interpretation of results are not easily compatible with processes requiring short-term decision-making.

Acknowledgements

The work presented in this paper would not have been possible without the input from the following individuals: Mark Swain (SLR Senior Geotechnical Engineer), David Morgan (SLR Technical Director), Claire Parsons (SLR GIS and data management), Caroline Malim (SLR Senior Illustrator), John Carrott (Palaeoecological Research Services who assessed the level of preservation of the bioarchaeological remains), Mags Felter (YAT), Steve Boreham (University of Cambridge), David Gibson and Mark Knight and their team from the Cambridge Archaeology Unit who excavated the site at Must farm. In addition the Nantwich project has been made possible through the vision and invaluable input of the steering group: Jill Collens and Mark Leah (Cheshire East Council), Sue Stallibrass (English Heritage Regional Science Advisor), and Jennie Stopford (English Heritage, Inspector of Ancient Monuments).

Bibliography

Boreham, S. 2007. Stratigraphy, Physical and Chemical Analyses from Bronze Age sediments at Must Farm, Whittlesey, Peterborough. Unpublished assessment report for Cambridge Archaeological Unit and Hanson Building Products.

British Standards Institute, 1990. BS1377. *Methods of Test for Soils for Engineering Purposes. Part 3. Chemical and Electro-Chemical Tests.* BSI London.

British Standards Institute, 1999. BS5930. *The Code of Practice for Site Investigations. Annex F*. BSI. London.

Cheetham, J. 2007. An Assessment of the Potential for In-Situ Preservation of buried Organic Archaeological Remains at Sutton Common, South Yorkshire: PhD thesis, University of Hull. (2004) [online] [accessed 3 February 2012]. Available at: <doi: 10.5284/1000272>.

Department for Communities and Local Government, 2010. *Planning Policy Statement 5 Planning and the Historic Environment* [accessed 3 February 2012]. Available at: <http://www.communities.gov.uk/publications/planningandbuilding/pps5>.

Department of the Environment, 1990. *Planning Policy Guidance 16: Archaeology and Planning* [accessed 3 February 2012]. Available at: <http://www.communities.gov.uk/documents/planningandbuilding/pdf/156777.pdf>.

Hogan, D. V. 1998. *Environmental Investigations at Shinewater Park, East Sussex*. Wetland Ecosystem Research Group Report No. 22.

Hogan, D. V. 2001 *Environmental Investigations at Shinewater Park, East Sussex 1999–2000*. Wetland Ecosystem Research Group Report.

Holden, J., Howard, A. J., West, L. J., Maxfield, E., Panter, I., and Oxley, J. 2009. A Critical Review of Hydrological Data Collection Schemes for Assessing Preservation Risk for Urban Waterlogged Archaeology: A Case Study from the City of York, UK. *Journal of Environmental Management*.

Matthiesen, H., Gregory, D., Jensen, P., and Sorensen, B. 2004. Environmental Monitoring at Nydam, a Waterlogged Site with Weapon Sacrifices from the Danish Iron Age. A Comparison of Methods Used and Results from Undisturbed Deposits. *Journal of Wetland Archaeology*, 4: 55–74.

Matthiesen, H. 2008. Detailed Chemical Analyses of Groundwater as a Tool for Monitoring Urban Archaeological Deposits: Results from Bryggen in Bergen. *Journal of Archaeological Science*, 35: 1378–88.

SLR, 2007. Must Farm Timber Platform Baseline Testing and Monitoring Regime Method Statement. Unpublished report for Hanson Heidleberg Cement.

Smit, A., van Heeringen, R. M., and Theunissen, E. M. 2006. *Archaeological Monitoring Standard. Guidelines for the Non-Destructive Recording and Monitoring of the Physical Quality of Archaeological Sites and Monuments*. Nederlandse Archaeologische Rapporten 33.

Riksantikvaren and NIKU, n.d. *The Monitoring Manual. Procedures & Guidelines for the Monitoring, Recording and Preservation/Management of Urban Archaeological Deposit* [online] [accessed 3 February 2012]. Available at: <www.riksantikvaren.no/filestore/Veileder_komp.pdf>.

Malim, T., Panter, I., and Carrott, J. 2009. Nantwich Waterlogged Deposits. Report No. 2. The Character and Extent of Archaeological Preservation. Unpublished report for Cheshire County Council and English Heritage (Project Number 3839 MAIN).

SLR, 2010. Nantwich Waterlogged Deposits. Report No. 3. Management Strategy: Supplementary Planning Documents for the Historic Environment and Archaeological Deposits. Unpublished report for Cheshire County Council and English Heritage.

Williams, J., Fell, V., Graham, K., Simpson, P., Collins, M., Koon, H., and Griffen, R. 2008a. Re-watering of the Iron Age Causeway at Fiskerton, England. In: H. Kars and R. M. van Heeringen, eds. *Preserving Archaeological Remains In Situ. Proceedings of the 3rd Conference 7–9 December 2006, Amsterdam*. Geoarchaeological and Bioarchaological Studies 10 Vrije Universiteit Amsterdam.

Williams, J., Martin-Bacon, H., Onions, B., Barrett, D., Richmond, A., and Page, M. 2008b. The Second Shardlow Boat — Economic Drivers or Heritage Policy? In: H. Kars and R. M. van Heeringen, eds. *Preserving Archaeological Remains In Situ. Proceedings of the 3rd Conference 7–9 December 2006, Amsterdam*. Geoarchaeological and Bioarchaological Studies 10 Vrije Universiteit Amsterdam.

Notes on contributors

Tim Malim is the Technical Discipline Manager for Archaeology and Heritage at SLR Consulting Ltd. He has been involved in wetland archaeology and monument conservation since being part of English Heritage's Fenland Survey team in the 1980s, and designed archaeological investigation, reinstatement, and monitoring at the Iron Age fort of Stonea Camp whilst head of Cambridgeshire County Council's Archaeological Field Unit in the 1990s.

Correspondence to: Tim Malim, SLR Consulting Ltd, Mytton Mill, Forton Heath, Montford Bridge, Shrewsbury SY4 1HA, UK. Email: tmalim@slrconsulting.com

Ian Panter is Principal Conservator for the York Archaeological Trust and specializes in the assessment of organic archaeological remains, geochemical investigations, and deposit monitoring. Ian is currently working on the Nantwich study and Must Farm *in situ* preservation schemes as well as aspects of the marine environmental characterization of the designated wreck, the *Royal Anne* Galley.

Correspondence to: Ian Panter, York Archaeological Trust, 47 Aldwark, York YO1 7BX, UK. Email: ipanter@yorkat.co.uk

CONSERVATION AND MGMT OF ARCH. SITES, Vol. 14 Nos 1–4, 2012, 442–57

Thirty Years of Monitoring in England — What Have We Learnt?

JIM WILLIAMS

English Heritage, UK

Over the last thirty years, over sixty separate episodes of monitoring water-logged archaeological sites have been carried out in England. This paper lists these projects, summarizes basic information about them, and reviews what we have learnt over these last thirty years. Recommendations are given to help improve future monitoring projects. In particular, it is suggested that more work is needed on assessing the state of preservation of a site before monitoring is considered; that a proper project design needs to be developed at the outset of the work; and that more thought should go into deciding why monitoring is needed for a given site, including identifying mitigation options that can be initiated if monitoring data suggest optimum conditions for survival are no longer being maintained.

KEYWORDS monitoring, waterlogged deposits, site preservation, mitigation

Introduction

The need for monitoring data to influence decision-making for wetland and water-logged archaeological sites has been recognized in England for about thirty years, with early work undertaken in the East Anglian Fens (French and Taylor, 1985) and the Somerset Levels (Coles, 1995; Brunning et al., 2000). Since then, numerous monitoring exercises have been carried out; many have been published, some have not. As such, one of the main aims of this study was to draw together for the first time a definitive list of all monitoring projects carried out on English waterlogged archaeological sites.

This paper is divided into three sections. The first part includes the list of monitoring projects, considers why they were carried out and examines the techniques used. The second section looks at what we have learnt about the monitoring parameters and how our understanding has evolved over time. The final section offers recommendations for those embarking on future programmes of monitoring.

Review of past and existing monitoring projects

Information was gathered for this paper using questionnaires sent to those involved in past or current monitoring projects; the list of sites (for questionnaire survey) was

DOI 10.1179/1350503312Z.00000000038

compiled through peer discussion and from published sources and past reviews (e.g. Lillie and Smith, 2009). Where there was no response or where no one involved was available, the information was gained from published sources. The following questions were asked in the questionnaire to provide comparable information about each site.

- Site name and location
- Lead and contact details
- Reasons for monitoring (aims and objectives)
- What is being monitored (nature of archaeology, date range, survival)
- Duration of project (start date, end or projected end date)
- Development / land use change and natural threats
- Parameters monitored (water level, pH, etc.)
- Constraints / problems / additional notes
- Publications / reports

Sites monitored and duration of monitoring

Since 1982, thirty-six sites have had monitoring projects carried out (see Table 1). Three additional projects were carried out where monitoring was undertaken on multiple sites (work by Caple and Dungworth, 1998; the Monuments at Risk in Somerset's Peatlands (MARISP) project (Brunning, 2008) and monitoring on Exmoor mire sites by Heather Davies). This brings the total number of projects to forty and the total number of sites to fifty-four.

Some sites have been subject to more than one period of monitoring; in fact, if every discrete monitoring project is taken into account, over sixty separate schemes have been initiated in the last thirty years. At Flag Fen,[1] five different monitoring projects have been undertaken. There are also projects that came to light during the writing of this paper that are not included in the data analysis or lists because they were not monitoring projects based on archaeological sites (such as work in the Forestry Commission's Alice Holt woodland, reported at the last PARIS conference by Graham et al., 2008), or where planned monitoring projects were never initiated. For convenience, the following site comparisons are based on the list of thirty-nine projects/sites given in Table 1.

The first project carried out was at Etton in Northamptonshire in 1982. Water-level monitoring also began at the Sweet Track the same year and continued for thirteen years. The longest running monitoring project is the Rose Theatre, which started in 1989 and is still being monitored. The average duration of projects is around 3½ years, and fifteen of the thirty-nine projects are still ongoing today. The types of sites monitored and the nature of remains captured in this survey are highly variable. They range from Mesolithic artefacts and deposits at Star Carr and New Denham, through to the remains of the Globe and Rose Elizabethan playhouses. Almost half of the forty sites contain prehistoric remains, more than quarter contain Roman or Anglo-Saxon material, and at least that many include medieval deposits. Twenty-three sites are in rural locations, and sixteen in urban contexts.

Reasons for monitoring

Monitoring of wetland archaeological sites is often a vital part of their management. Monitoring data demonstrate whether sites are waterlogged and anoxic, and this

TABLE 1

LIST OF SITES IN ENGLAND WHERE MONITORING HAS BEEN UNDERTAKEN. TABLE ALSO SHOWS START YEAR (WHERE KNOWN) AND THE REASONS WHY MONITORING WAS INITIATED. WHERE MORE THAN ONE EPISODE OF MONITORING WAS CARRIED OUT, ALL REASONS ARE SHOWN. REFERENCES FOR THE MAIN OR MOST RECENT PUBLICATIONS ARE ALSO SHOWN. WHERE NO PUBLICATION DETAILS ARE GIVEN, INFORMATION IN THE TABLE AND PAPER WAS SUMMARIZED FROM QUESTIONNAIRE RESPONSES AND MARKED WITH (-)

Site	Locality	Start year	Reason	Publication
Etton	Northamptonshire	1982	Extraction	French & Taylor, 1985
Sweet Track	Somerset	1983	Site management	Brunning et al., 2000; Coles, 1995; Jones, 2010;
Globe Theatre	London	1989	Development	Barber, 2002
Rose Theatre	London	1989	Development	Corfield, 1994; Corfield, 2004
Market Deeping	Lincolnshire	1993	Research	Corfield, 1994; Corfield, 1996
Caple & Dungworth sites	N/A	1994	Research	Caple, 1996; Caple & Dungworth, 1998
Over / Willingham	Cambridgeshire	1994	Extraction	French et al., 1999; French, 2004; 2009
44-45 Parliament street	York	1995	Development	Davis et al., 2002
Flag Fen	Cambridgeshire	1995	Site management / development	Powell et al., 2000; Lillie, 2007; Burks Green RPS, 2009
Shinewater	East Sussex	1995	Site management	-
Tower of London Moat	London	1997	Site management	Keevill, 2004
Sutton Common	South Yorkshire	1998	Research / site management	Chapman & Cheetham, 2002; Douterelo et al., 2011
82-90 Park Street, Croydon	London	2000	Development	Hughes et al., 2004
Knights Hospitallers Preceptory, Beverley	East Yorkshire	2001	Development	Lillie, 2007
Oxford Castle	Oxford	2002	Development	-
A1 soil stack	Yorkshire	2003	Development	Higuchi, 2005
Fiskerton	Lincolnshire	2003	Agricultural land use change	Williams et al., 2008a
Hatfield	South Yorkshire	2003	Research / site management	Douterelo et al., 2011
MARISP Sites	Somerset	2003	Site management	Brunning, 2007; 2008; Brunning et al., 2008

TABLE 1

CONTINUED

Site	Locality	Start year	Reason	Publication
Vindolanda	Northumberland	2003	Site management	-
Dixon's Yard, Walmgate	York	2004	Development	W.A. Fairhurst & Partners, 2004
St Mildred's	Canterbury	2004	Development	Hogan, 2011
The Saltway, Droitwich	Worcestershire	2004	Development	Moffett & Panter, 2005
Newington	Nottinghamshire	2005	Research	Lillie & Smith, 2007; 2008
Shardlow	Derbyshire	2005	Extraction	Williams et al., 2008b
Brooksby	Leicestershire	2006	Extraction	Capita Symonds, 2011
St George's Square, Droitwich	Worcestershire	2006	Development	Woodiwiss, 2007
Alchester	Oxfordshire	2007	Site management	-
Must Farm	Cambridgeshire	2007	Extraction	Panter & Malim in this volume
Brooklyn Garage, Alcester	Warwickshire	2008	Development	Elgy, 2008
Cleeve Abbey	Somerset	2008	Site management	-
Exmoor Mire Sites	Somerset	2008	Research	-
Glastonbury Lake Village	Somerset	2008	Research	Jones in this volume
New Denham	Buckinghamshire	2008	Extraction	Batchelor & Black, 2010
Beccles	Suffolk	2009	Site management	-
Star Carr	North Yorkshire	2009	Site management	Boreham et al., 2011; Brown et al., 2009
Nantwich	Cheshire	2010	Research / site management	Panter & Malim in this volume
Caroon House, Fleet Valley	London	-	Development	-
Hungate	York	-	Development	-

shows the likelihood of long-term preservation. However, the reason for initiating these projects can vary (see Figure 1 and Table 1). Monitoring was set up at fifteen of the thirty-nine sites as a result of, or in response to, development activity. Six of the monitoring projects have been set up to counter dewatering risks from extraction/quarry sites. Combined, these projects represent around 50 per cent of all monitoring projects which have been initiated because of some form of development risk.

Another key reason for monitoring is for site management, often because of a known or perceived threat from agricultural or other drainage works, although other more localized impacts, such as archaeological excavations have also been the driver for monitoring projects. Overall, thirteen projects have site management as the main or ancillary reason for monitoring. The other major reason for undertaking monitoring projects is research, to improve monitoring techniques and understand better the dynamics of water and below ground conditions on wetland archaeological sites.

Monitoring tools and techniques

Table 2 shows the techniques used on the sites covered in this paper. Almost all projects recorded water level, and 90 per cent recorded pH and redox. Conductivity was measured on 50 per cent of sites, and temperature on 25 per cent. A quarter of all projects also collected data on soil or water chemistry, the common parameters monitored include nitrate (NO_3^-), ammonium (NH_4^+), phosphate (PO_4^-), sodium (Na^+), potassium (K^+), calcium (Ca^{2+}), magnesium (Mg^+), chloride (Cl^-), and sulphate (SO_4^{2-}). Soil moisture (recorded using soil moisture cells, neutron probes or Time Domain Reflectometry — TDR) was measured frequently on projects in the 1990s but has been used less frequently in the last ten years.

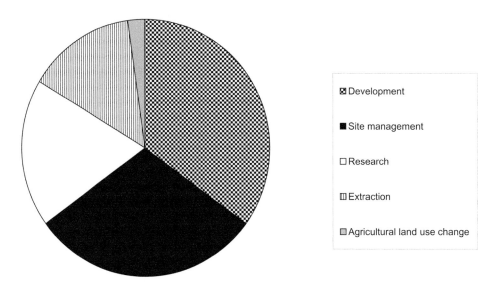

FIGURE 1   Chart showing reasons given for carrying out monitoring projects in England (based on data in Table 1).

TABLE 2

PARAMETERS RECORDED AT THE 39 MONITORING SITES/PROJECTS. WHERE MULTIPLE PROJECTS HAVE TAKEN PLACE, ALL TECHNIQUES USED HAVE BEEN HIGHLIGHTED IN THE TABLE

Site	Water level	pH	Redox	Conductivity	Temperature	Water chemistry	Moisture
Etton	■						
Sweet track							
Globe Theatre		■	■	■		■	■
Rose Theatre		■	■	■			■
Market Deeping		■	■				
Caple and Dungworth sites				■	■		
Over / Willingham		■					■
44-45 Parliament street		■		■	■		■
Flag Fen		■	■				
Shinewater							
Tower of London Moat		■	■	■			■
Sutton Common							
82-90 Park Street, Croydon		■					■
Knights Hospitallers Preceptory, Beverley			■				
Oxford Castle							
A1 soil stack		■		■	■		
Fiskerton						■	
Hatfield					■		
MARISP sites						■	

TABLE 2
CONTINUED

Site	Water level	pH	Redox	Conductivity	Temperature	Water chemistry	Moisture
Vindolanda		▓			▓		
Dixon's Yard, Walmgate	▓	▓	▓		▓	▓	
St Mildred's	▓	▓	▓	▓			
The Saltway, Droitwich	▓	▓	▓		▓		
Newington	▓	▓	▓		▓		
Shardlow	▓		▓				
Brooksby	▓	▓	▓				
St George's Square, Droitwich	▓	▓	▓	▓		▓	
Alchester	▓	▓					
Must Farm		▓	▓			▓	▓
Brooklyn Garage, Alcester		▓	▓	▓			
Cleeve Abbey			▓				
Exmoor mire sites		▓	▓				
Glastonbury lake village		▓	▓	▓			▓
New Denham		▓	▓	▓			
Beccles	▓						
Star Carr	▓			▓		▓	
Nantwich		▓	▓				
Caroon House, Fleet Valley							
Hungate							

What have we learnt from nearly thirty years of monitoring?

During the last thirty years there has been no significant evolution of our tools, for example a shift towards increasingly complex and advanced monitoring equipment; in fact we are still using many of the same tools we were thirty years ago. If anything, the changes during this time have revolved around improving our understanding of what the results mean.

Water level

The evidence from numerous monitoring projects carried out during this time in England and elsewhere has demonstrated beyond doubt that one of the most critical variables in understanding waterlogged sites is water level. Where water levels are consistently above the archaeological deposits being monitored, below-ground conditions are likely to be favourable for long-term preservation. Conversely, where the water level is below the 'preserved' remains, or fluctuates seasonally, the likelihood of preservation is less assured.

Therefore, for fairly simple, perhaps mainly rural sites, just measuring water level is a quick, cheap, and effective method of checking on the likely state of condition of a site (assuming the site's state of preservation has first been characterized). For sites which are well preserved (macro- and microscopically) and where no changes to the current regime are proposed, such a seemingly limited response may well be adequate given our accumulated experience.

Redox potential

Most monitoring projects have measured redox and pH and in the last ten years, these have been the main variables used for monitoring (see papers in Nixon, 2004; Kars and van Heeringen, 2008). Most projects use the presence of non-fluctuating, near neutral pH and redox values between +100mV and -400mV as indicators of good preservation conditions (Patrick and Mahapatra, 1968; Keevill et al., 2004). The majority of projects have run for more than one year, as gathering long-term series data (rather than collecting one-off snap-shots) allows changes over time, often seasonally influenced, to be properly understood. This is particularly important given the acknowledged complexity of redox measurement in the field.

One difference not recorded in the questionnaires (as a result of poor survey design rather than responder failure) is the variation in methods of recording redox (and to an extent pH), either using *in situ* electrodes, or through the use of probes inserted into boreholes or samples bailed from these. A number of projects (in England and Europe) have concluded that *in situ* probes provide a 'more accurate' assessment of redox potential (e.g. Caple and Dungworth, 1998; Smit, 2002: 111), but water samples from boreholes continue to be used for redox analysis. This is because it is a cheaper method (at least in terms of initial material outlay), and, although the data are not as precise as *in situ* measurements, good and useful results can be acquired (see, for example, Williams et al., 2008a).

The use of flow-through cells, where water is pumped from a borehole into separate sealed containers, each housing a single monitoring probe which contact between the sample and the air, provides more accurate results, see Figure 2.

FIGURE 2   Collecting groundwater using a flow-through cell at Brooksby, Leicestershire. Water is pumped from the borehole and into the flow-through cell which contains the redox or pH probe. The data from the meter are noted (left, on the bucket) once the readings have stabilized.

Conductivity and water chemistry

Although conductivity was measured on 50 per cent of the projects, results have not been reported as regularly as for redox or pH data. Conductivity is measured to assess the presence of dissolved ions, which can be used to identify the extent of pollution, for example from agri-chemicals (Caple and Dungworth, 1998). It is also used as a proxy measure, alongside rainfall data, to look at the different contribution of rainwater and groundwater to site hydrology (Caple, 1996). Given that its use has not been ubiquitous, nor its reporting very consistent, more guidance is needed to demonstrate fully its benefits, methods, and application.

The same is, to a great extent, true of the measurement of soil moisture, and recording of other chemical data (anion and cation concentration) from water samples. These parameters are very useful for characterizing a site and measuring changes over time, but they are rarely used to their full potential. In part this reflects a lack understanding about the data we collect. If moisture levels drop from 60 per cent to 45 per cent, if sulphate levels rise by 100 mg/l, or if the deposits become mildly reducing for a few months, do we really know what effect this has on buried archaeological material? This is because we do not have the fundamental knowledge of how such subtle changes in the burial environment effect degradation or understand fully what influences the rates at which any changes occur (Williams, 2009: 27, 46). Undoubtedly, this is an area for further research.

Monitoring challenges and recommendations

From collecting and collating information on sites monitored in the last thirty years, I conclude that many of the sites which have been or are being monitored are insufficiently characterized prior to monitoring. The management of projects and their data needs to be organized better in many cases. Finally, the reasons for carrying out monitoring and the mitigations options available if conditions deteriorate, are not always fully justified and considered. I therefore offer the following recommendations for those contemplating monitoring projects in the future.

Assessment of the state of preservation

Before beginning a programme of monitoring it is essential that the state of preservation of the site is adequately investigated, so that changes seen in the monitoring data can be linked directly to likely impacts on the site. Currently, too many sites have no characterization, or are only investigated during the installation of the monitoring equipment.

I would suggest that thorough assessments of the state of preservation of sites need to be carried out before monitoring is even considered. Such an assessment should look at the state of preservation of artefacts and deposits and study the deposit chemistry. Currently, there are no guidelines on preservation assessments in England, but standards from the Netherlands (Smit et al., 2006) and Norway (Riksantikvaren, n.d.) and recent work in England (Brunning, 2008) demonstrate the range of methods that could be applied. Additionally, efforts should be made to understand how the site functions in its local and wider hydrological environment before commencing long-term and detailed monitoring studies. If archaeological remains are in an active state of degradation, or are buried in oxidized, degraded, or humified deposits that are unlikely to be suitable for long-term preservation, or if there will never be sufficient water available, then I would question what the value of monitoring such a site would be. Resources could be directed better to excavation and further understanding the site.

When I was involved with setting up a monitoring project at Fiskerton, we took the view that, as the site was significant, a 'conservation-led approach' which began with monitoring rather than evaluation was the most sensitive way to proceed. With hindsight, such minimal intervention meant that we never really understood what level the archaeology was situated at in relation to the recorded water level, and could not effectively relate the impacts of changes in monitoring data to site management. When we did subsequently evaluate the site, we found little of the horizontal stratigraphy survived, and the state of preservation of much of the archaeological and palaeoenvironmental material was poor. If we had adequately evaluated the site and artefacts at the beginning of the project we would not have embarked on a programme of monitoring at all.

Better project designs and project management structures

If a monitoring project is initiated, then it needs to be properly planned, resourced, and managed. The starting point for any monitoring project should be the production of a full and comprehensive project design (see, for example, English Heritage, 2006).

Writing a project design forces you to think in more detail about why you want to monitor, what parameters you need to collect, and what you are going to do with the information you have recorded.

Unfortunately, many monitoring projects are rather ad hoc arrangements, hurriedly put together to counter a development risk or to investigate a rapidly degrading site. As such they run the risk of collecting the wrong data, or asking the wrong questions, or, in the worst case, monitoring when this is not the appropriate site-management response.

Any project design should include, as a minimum, information on the nature and condition of the archaeological remains, the purpose of the monitoring, the type of monitoring equipment, the frequency of monitoring, and curation of monitoring data. It is also essential that the project design sets out clearly what the proposed site management (e.g. mitigation) options will be once the data have been collected and analysed.

Perhaps most importantly, though, the project design should be clear about the roles and responsibilities of the project team. Mechanisms should be put in place to ensure that the whole project team, rather than any one individual, is responsible for reviewing and quality-assuring the data. Regular (physical or teleconference) meetings should be arranged to discuss the results and safeguards initiated to ensure that data collection or reporting procedures are unaffected by any staffing changes. Quite a few projects covered in this review just ceased or have interrupted data because either the person responsible for the monitoring, or the person responsible for setting up and managing the project left or changed jobs.

Why is monitoring needed and what mitigation options are available?

There are three main reasons, I believe, why sites are monitored. Firstly, for research, to improve existing and test new monitoring techniques. Secondly, monitoring is carried out to check and record that stable conditions exist and continue at known wetland and waterlogged archaeological sites. Finally, sites are monitored to record the impact of land-use changes, whether those changes are natural, agricultural, development, or abstraction-led in origin.

Research monitoring

To be worthwhile, research-led monitoring should address the big unanswered questions, which include understanding rates of change and the impacts these changes have on archaeological material, given different magnitudes and speeds of change (see Williams, 2009: 27, 46). Research topics to improve current monitoring techniques could include further work on soil moisture (i.e. an increased understanding of TDR) and also a comparison between data from *in situ* redox probes with data from water-based analysis using flow-through cells.

Monitoring stable sites and measuring water table fluctuations

The monitoring of known wetland sites where stable conditions exist can be a fairly simple procedure. It could include a visual assessment of water levels on site, for example in adjacent ditches, as is undertaken at the Sweet Track (Brunning, pers. comm.) or measurement of water levels to check that they do not fall below archaeological levels, as is currently the case for monitoring at the site of Beccles, an alignment of Iron Age timbers. Where monitoring data suggest stable conditions do not exist, then mitigation options (discussed below) should be considered.

Monitoring can also be used as part of the characterization of a site, to look at the range of water level movements or chart redox potential at given depths throughout the year. However, much of this information can be inferred more quickly, and for potentially less cost from a thorough assessment of soil chemistry and by studying the state of preservation of archaeological artefacts and deposits.

Monitoring land-use change

On sites where land-use changes are occurring, monitoring projects should only be initiated if there are clear mitigation options that can be put in place if the data suggest conditions below-ground are deteriorating. At Vindolanda, monitoring was undertaken to investigate the impact of archaeological excavations on adjacent buried material. If the monitoring data had suggested that these excavations were damaging the adjacent material (which they were not), then the obvious mitigation response would have been to cease further excavations. Likewise, a monitoring project was set up in a quarry at Shardlow to ensure that quarrying activities did not impact on a Bronze Age log boat, discovered, then preserved *in situ* in the quarry. Current conditions are good, but if water levels do drop there remains the option to encourage the quarry to raise the water levels, and, if that fails, excavate the boat and remove it for further analysis and conservation.

Where archaeological sites are impacted by the construction of large developments (particularly in urban locations) the removal of a building or buildings because monitoring shows below-ground conditions are deteriorating is thoroughly impractical. There seems to me to be little point in collecting years of data that indicate the site is actively degrading if nothing can be done to alter the below-ground conditions or access the site to carry out an excavation to retrieve what information remains. In these situations, it is questionable as to what the purpose of monitoring actually is, and monitoring should, on the whole, therefore be discouraged.

Monitoring on or near development sites can, however, provide useful data that could improve future planning and management decisions on adjacent sites. In that context, a developer might be encouraged to support the cost of monitoring as a planning gain (a trade-off for not have to pay for a costly excavation). However, for this to be of value, the monitoring needs to be well planned and ideally carried out as part of a systematic programme to understand the waterlogged deposits of a given city or town. Without that, there is a high chance that the data gathered will be *ad hoc* and make little contribution to improving our existing understanding.

On a few sites (containing well-preserved archaeological remains of national or international significance) where preservation *in situ* is proposed, design solutions could be found to build removable basement flooring to allow access to sample or excavate deposits where monitoring indicated rapid deterioration was occurring. Although designed as a temporary solution (which has now lasted over twenty years), this configuration is similar to that built for the Rose Theatre. This construction technique was recommended as a mitigation option in the Ove Arup 'York Development & Archaeology Study' (1991).

Planning-led monitoring decision making

Finally, it should be emphasized that decisions about monitoring on development sites take place in a clearly defined resource management context. Preservation of significant sites *in situ* is the underlying principle in past and present English planning guidance relating to the historic environment (DoE, 1990; DCLG, 2010) and in the Council of Europe's Valetta Convention (1992). In the past twenty years, this has precipitated a 'policy-led' approach when deciding which sites should be preserved *in situ* and therefore monitored, rather than one based on the potential of the site to be preserved *in situ*. Too often, decisions are taken to preserve waterlogged archaeological sites *in situ* during development schemes without assessing their current state of preservation or considering if current or future ground conditions are appropriate for long-term preservation.

Where a 'planning-led' decision is made to preserve organic-rich waterlogged archaeological remains *in situ* during development, monitoring can sometimes seem like an appropriate response. But perhaps this is only because we have no other responses and we opt for monitoring because it makes us feel like we are doing something positive for a site that we will be unable to save if conditions deteriorate. Rather than monitoring such sites, money would be much better spent on adequately characterizing the condition of the remains before the initial development starts so that the potential impacts of the proposed buildings can be properly assessed. Similar assessment could then take place if the site was to be redeveloped in the future. These would assess the impacts of the previous scheme of *in situ* preservation, and to consider whether further preservation was likely to be achievable or if the remaining information from the site should be realized through excavation. Hopefully, in the future such prior assessment would finally be the norm.

Note

[1] References for sites reviewed in this paper are given in Table 1. Where no reference is given in the Table, material discussed in the paper is drawn from questionnaire responses and follow up discussions with those involved.

Bibliography

Barber, B. 2002. Saving the Globe?: Part 2, the Preservation of the Monument. *London Archaeologist*, 9(12): 323–29.

Batchelor, C. R. and Black, S. 2010. Preferred Area 4, Denham, Buckinghamshire: Groundwater Monitoring Report February 2010. Report No. 2. Unpublished Quaternary Scientific (QUEST) Report Project Number 020/09.

Boreham, S., Conneller, C., Milner, N., Taylor, B., Needham, A., Boreham, J., and Rolfe, C. J. In press. Geochemical Indicators of Preservation Status and Site Deterioration at Star Carr. *Journal of Archaeological Science* [accessed 14 July 2010]. Available at: <doi:10.1016/j.jas2011.01.016>.

Brown, A. G., Bradley, C., Boomer, I., and Grapes, T. 2009. Hydrological Assessment of Star Carr Catchment, Yorkshire (5922). Unpublished report prepared for English Heritage.

Brunning, R. 2007. Monuments at Risk in Somerset's Peatlands. In: J. Barber, C. Clark, M. Cressey, A. Crone, A. Hale, J. Henderson, R. Housley, R. Sands, and A. Sheridan, eds. *Archaeology from the Wetlands: Recent Perspectives, Proceedings of the 11th WARP Conference, Edinburgh 2005*. WARP Occasional Paper 18. Edinburgh: Society of Antiquaries of Scotland, pp. 191–98.

Brunning, R. 2008. How Does Monitoring Fit into a Wider Strategy? A Multi-Site Example from a Rural Wetland in the UK. In: H. Kars and R. M. van Heeringen, eds. *Preserving Archaeological Remains In Situ, Proceedings of the Third International Conference* (Geoarchaeological and Bioarchaeological Studies 10). Amsterdam: Vrije Universiteit Amsterdam, pp. 217–25.

Brunning, R., Hogan, D., Jones, J., Jones, M., Maltby, E., Robinson, M., and Straker, V. 2000. Saving the Sweet Track. The *In Situ* Preservation of a Neolithic Wooden Trackway, Somerset, UK. *Conservation and Management of Archaeological Sites*, 4: 3–20.

Brunning, R., Bronk Ramsey, C., Cameron, N., Cook, G., Davies, P., Gale, R., Groves, G., Hamilton, W.D., Hogan, D., Jones, J., Jones, M., Kenward, H., Kreiser, A., Locatelli, C., Marshall, P., Tinsley, H., and Tyres I. 2008. The Monuments at Risk in Somerset's Peatlands Project. Unpublished draft MSS, Somerset County Council.

Burks Green R.P.S. 2009. Site investigation report: Storey's Bar Road, Peterbrough, Cambs. Unpublished Burks Green R.P.S. report C11627 for Peterborough Renewable Energy Ltd.

Capita Symonds. 2011. Brooksby Quarry: Ground Water Monitoring for In Situ Protection of Archaeological Features. 2011 Annual Report for Lafarge Aggregates Ltd. Unpublished report.

Caple, C. 1996. Parameters for Monitoring Anoxic Environments. In: M. Corfield, P. Hinton, T. Nixon, and M. Pollard, eds. *Preserving Archaeological Remains In Situ. Proceedings of the Conference of 1st–3rd April 1996*. Bradford: Museum of London Archaeology Service/University of Bradford, pp. 113–22.

Caple, C. and Dungworth, D. 1998. Waterlogged Anoxic Archaeological Burial Environments. Unpublished Ancient Monuments Laboratory Report 22/98. Historic Buildings and Monuments Commission, London.

Chapman, H. P. and Cheetham, J. L. 2002. Monitoring and Modelling Saturation as a Proxy Indicator for *In Situ* Preservation in Wetlands — a GIS-based Approach. *Journal of Archaeological Science*, 29: 277–89.

Coles, B. 1995. *Wetland Management: A Survey for English Heritage*. Exeter: WARP Occasional Paper 9.

Corfield, M. 1994. Monitoring the Condition of Waterlogged Archaeological Sites. In: P. Hoffmann, ed. *Proceedings of the 5th ICOM Group on Wet Organic Archaeological Materials Conference, Portland, Maine 1993*. Bremerhaven: Ditzen Druck and Verlags-GmbH, Deutsches Schiffahrtsmuseu, pp. 423–37.

Corfield, 1996. Preventive Conservation for Archaeological Sites. In: A. Roy and P. Smith, eds. *Archaeological Conservation and its Consequences*. London: IIC, pp. 32–37.

Corfield, M. 2004. Saving the Rose Theatre: England's First Managed and Monitored Reburial. *Conservation and Management of Archaeological Sites*, 4: 305–14.

Council of Europe, 1992. *European Convention on the Protection of the Archaeological Heritage (revised) (Valletta 1992)*. Council of Europe Treaty Series no. 143.

Davis, M., Hall, A., Kenward, H., and Oxley, J. 2002. Preservation of Urban Archaeological Deposits: Monitoring and Characterisation of Archaeological Deposits at Marks & Spencer, 44–45 Parliament Street, York. *Internet Archaeology*, 11 [accessed 14 July 2011]. Available at: <http://intarch.ac.uk/journal/issue11/oxley_toc.html>.

Department of the Environment, 1990. *Planning Policy Guidance 16: Archaeology and Planning*. London: HMSO.

Department of Communities and Local Government, 2010. *Planning Policy Statement 5: Planning for the Historic Environment*. London: TSO.

Douterelo, I., Goulder, R., and Lillie, M. 2011. *International Biodeterioration and Biodegradation*, 65: 435–43.

Elgy, C, 2008. Assessment of the Burial Environment at Booklyn Garage, Alcester, Warwickshire: A Review of the Data Collected Between March and May 2008. Unpublished report, Historic Environment and Archaeology Service, Worcestershire County Council, report 1628.

English Heritage. 2006. *Management of Research Projects in the Historic Environment The MoRPHE Project Managers' Guide*. Swindon: English Heritage.

French, C. 2004. Hydrological Monitoring of an Alluviated Landscape in the Lower Great Ouse Valley at Over, Cambridgeshire: Results of the Gravel Extraction Phase. *Environmental Archaeology*, 9(1): 1–13.

French, C. 2009. Hydrological Monitoring of an Alluviated Landscape in the Lower Great Ouse Valley at Over, Cambridgeshire: The Quarry Restoration Phase. *Environmental Archaeology*, 14(1): 63–76.

French, C., Davis, M., and Heathcote, J. 1999. Hydrological Monitoring of Alluviated Landscapes in the Lower Great Ouse Valley, Cambridgeshire: Interim Results of the First Three Years. *Environmental Archaeology*, 4: 41–56.

French, C. and Taylor, M. 1985. Desiccation and Destruction: The Immediate Effects of De-watering at Etton, Cambridgeshire. *Oxford Journal of Archaeology*, 4(2): 139–55.

Graham, K., Crow, P., Fell, V., Simpson, P., Wyeth, P., Baker, R., and Griffin, V. 2008. A Woodland Burial Study: Developing Methods to Monitor the Burial Environment. In: H. Kars and R. M. van Heeringen, eds. *Preserving Archaeological Remains In Situ, Proceedings of the Third International Conference* (Geoarchaeological and Bioarchaeological Studies 10). Amsterdam: Vrije Universiteit Amsterdam, pp. 131–38.

Higuchi, T. 2005. Castle Hills (A1) Roman Remains Monitoring. Unpublished report.

Hogan, D. 2011. Environmental Investigations at St Mildred's Tannery, Canterbury Report 4. Unpublished report.

Hughes, R., Dillon, J., McKinley, J., Patel, D., and Shields, H. 2004. The Geotechnical Instrumentation of Park Lane, Croydon, an Early Anglo Saxon Cemetery. In: T. Nixon, ed. *Preserving Archaeological Remains In Situ? Proceedings of the 2nd Conference 12–14 September 2001*. London: Museum of London Archaeology Service, pp. 128–36.

Keevill, G. D., Hogan, D. V., Davis, M., and Howell, D. 2004. Waterlogged Archaeological Remains, Environmental Conditions and Preservation *In Situ*: A Case Study from the Tower of London. In: T. Nixon, ed. *Preserving Archaeological Remains In Situ? Proceedings of the 2nd Conference 12–14 September 2001*. London: Museum of London Archaeology Service, pp. 137–42.

Jones, L. 2010. *In situ* Preservation, Research and Monitoring in the Somerset Levels: An Interim Report. In: J. R. L. Allen and A. Brown, eds. *Archaeology in the Severn Estuary*, 20: 65–79.

Jones, L. and Bell, M. *In Situ* Preservation of Wetland Heritage: Hydrological and Chemical Change in the Burial Environment of the Somerset Levels, UK. In: D. Gregory and H. Matthiesen, eds. *Conservation and Management of Archaeological Sites*, 14(1–4): 114–24.

Kars, H. and van Heeringen, R. M., eds. 2008. *Preserving Archaeological Remains In Situ, Proceedings of the Third International Conference* (Geoarchaeological and Bioarchaeological Studies 10). Amsterdam: Vrije Universiteit Amsterdam.

Lillie, M. C. 2007. *In situ* Preservation: Geo-Archaeological Perspectives on an Archaeological Nirvana. In: M. C. Lillie and S. Ellis, eds. *Wetland Archaeology and Environments: Regional Issues, Global Perspectives*. Oxford: Oxbow Books, pp. 156–72.

Lillie, M. C. and Smith, R. J. 2007. Understanding Water Table Dynamics and their Influence on the Buried Archaeological Resource in Relation to Aggregate Extraction Sites. Unpublished report (March 2007 [2 volumes]), Wetland Archaeology and Environments Research Centre, University of Hull, Hull.

Lillie, M. C. and Smith, R. J. 2008. Understanding Waterlogged Burial Environments: The Impacts of Aggregates Extraction and De-Watering on the Buried Archaeological Resource. Unpublished report (February 2008), Wetland Archaeology and Environments Research Centre, University of Hull, Hull.

Lillie, M. C. and Smith, R. J. 2009. International Literature Review: In Situ Preservation of Organic Archaeological Remains. Unpublished report for English Heritage. Wetland Archaeology and Environments Research Centre, University of Hull, Hull.

Malim, T. and Panter, I. 2012. Is Preservation *In Situ* an Unacceptable Option for Development Control? Can Monitoring Prove the Continued Preservation of Waterlogged Deposits? In: D. Gregory and H. Matthiesen, eds. *Conservation and Management of Archaeological Sites*, 14(1–4): 428–40.

Moffett, L. and Panter, I. 2005. Ground Monitoring at the Waitrose Supermarket Site, The Saltway, Droitwich. Unpublished report.

Nixon, T. ed. 2004. *Preserving Archaeological Remains In Situ? Proceedings of the 2nd Conference 12–14 September 2001*. London: Museum of London Archaeology Service.

Ove Arup & Partners and York University in association with Bernard Thorpe, 1991. *York Development & Archaeology Study*. York: English Heritage and York City Council.

Patrick, W. H. and Mahapatra, I. C. 1968. Transformation and Availability to Rice of Nitrogen and Phosphorus in Waterlogged Soils. *Advances in Agronomy*, 20: 323–59.

Powell, K. L., Pedley, S., and Corfield, M. 2000. The Effect of Water Quality upon the Integrity of Buried Archaeological Wood. In: A. Millard, ed. *Archaeological Sciences 1997. Proceedings of the Conference held at the University of Durham, 2nd–4th September 1997*. Oxford: Archaeopress.

Riksantikvarnen. N.d. The Monitoring Manual. Procedures & Guidelines for the Monitoring, Recording and Preservation/Management of Urban Archaeological Deposits [accessed 14 July 2011]. Available at: <http://www.riksantikvaren.no/filestore/Veileder_komp.pdf>.

Smit, A. 2002. The Preservation Potential of the Burial Environment. In: R. M. van Heeringen and E. M. Theunissen, eds. *Desiccation of the Archaeological Landscape at Voorne-Putten*. Nederlandse Archaeologische Rapporten 25. Amersfoort: Rijksdienst voor het Oudeidkundig Bodemonderzoek, pp. 91–114.

Smit, A., Van Heeringen, R. M., and Theunissen, E. M. 2006. *Archaeological Monitoring Standard. Guidelines for the Non-Destructive Recording and Monitoring of the Physical Quality of Archaeological Sites and Monuments*. Amersfoort: rijksdienst voor archeologie, cultuurlandschap en monumenten.

W. A. Fairhurst and Partners. 2004. Dixon's Yard, York Archaeological Gas and Water Monitoring Strategy and Results. Unpublished documents.

Williams, J. 2009. *The Role of Science in the Management of the UK's Heritage. NHSS Report 1* [accessed 14 July 2011]. Available at: <www.heritagesciencestrategy.org.uk>.

Williams, J., Fell, V., Graham, K., Simpson, P., Collins, M., Koon, H., and Griffin, R. 2008a. Re-watering of the Iron Age Causeway at Fiskerton, England. In: H. Kars and R. M. van Heeringen, eds. *Preserving Archaeological Remains In Situ, Proceedings of the Third International Conference* (Geoarchaeological and Bioarchaeological Studies 10). Amsterdam: Vrije Universiteit Amsterdam, pp. 181–97.

Williams, J., Martin Bacon, H., Onions, B., Barrett, D., Richmond, A., and Page, M. 2008b. The Second Shardlow Boat — Economic Drivers or Heritage Policy? In: H. Kars and R. M. van Heeringen, eds. *Preserving Archaeological Remains In Situ, Proceedings of the Third International Conference* (Geoarchaeological and Bioarchaeological Studies 10). Amsterdam: Vrije Universiteit Amsterdam, pp. 317–25.

Woodiwiss, S. 2007. Evaluation at St George's Square, Droitwich, Worcestershire. Unpublished report, Historic Environment and Archaeology Service, Worcestershire County Council, report 1570.

Notes on contributor

Jim Williams is the English Heritage science advisor for the East Midlands. He is interested in most aspects of preservation *in situ* research and policy, particularly preservation assessment, groundwater monitoring, and construction impacts on archaeological sites, in particular piling.

Correspondence to: Jim Williams, English Heritage, 44 Derngate, Northampton NN1 1UH, UK. Email: jim.williams@english-heritage.org.uk

CONSERVATION AND MGMT OF ARCH. SITES, Vol. 14 Nos 1–4, 2012, 458–68

'I Felt Connected to a Past World': A Survey of Visitors to Colonial Archaeological Sites Conserved *In Situ* in Australia and New Zealand

Tracy Ireland

University of Canberra, Australia

While there is extensive international literature on the technology and techniques of archaeological conservation and preservation *in situ*, there has been only limited discussion of the meanings of the places created and the responses they evoke in visitors. Experience in Australia and New Zealand over the past decade suggests that the conservation of colonial archaeological remains is today seen as a far more desirable option, whereas previously many would have suggested that this kind of conservation was only appropriate in 'old world' places like Greece and Italy; and that the archaeology of the colonial period was not old enough to be of value. This paper discusses a recent survey of visitors to colonial archaeological sites which reveals some of the ways in which these archaeological remains are experienced, valued, and understood, and gives some clues as to why conservation *in situ* is an expanding genre of heritage in this region. The visitors surveyed value colonial archaeological sites conserved *in situ* for the link they provide to place, locality, and memory; for the feeling of connection with the past they evoke; and for the experience they provide of intimacy with material relics from the past. This emphasis on the affective qualities of archaeological remains raises some issues in the post-colonial context, as it tends to reinforce received narratives of identity and history, and relies on the 'European' antiquarian appreciation of ruins — making the urban environment more like Europe by creating evidence of similar historical layering.

KEYWORDS *in situ* conservation, colonial heritage, settler heritage, authenticity

    DOI 10.1179/1350503312Z.00000000039

Introduction

Interest in the archaeology of the colonial period began in Australia and New Zealand in the late 1960s and 1970s. From the outset, this interest encompassed ruined and abandoned sites and building archaeology, as well as maritime and land archaeological sites. Discovery of early Dutch and British shipwrecks was a key impetus for the development of education and research in materials conservation, while recognition of the growing value attributed by communities to historic and Indigenous cultural sites led to the development of government enquiries, followed by protective legislation and specialist heritage management infrastructure in the 1970s (Ireland, 2002).

The *in situ* conservation of colonial archaeological remains, particularly sites of high research or symbolic potential, has been an aim of archaeological heritage management in Australia since the 1970s, largely following trends in historic sites conservation in the United States (Temple, 1986; 1988). However, successful examples of conservation *in situ* have been, until recently, rare and often controversial, not only because conservation *in situ* prevented maximized commercial development, but also because of a lack of consensus in the community about the value, significance, and meaning of the physical remains. In the last decade, however, the number of conservation *in situ* projects in Australia and New Zealand has grown significantly. This process appears to have a number of drivers: consent conditions imposed by regulatory authorities requiring conservation; community lobbying and pressure for conservation; and, perhaps most interestingly, the conservation of archaeological remains by developers and designers, not only to satisfy consent conditions, but also as a means of differentiating and providing a unique identity for their urban design projects.

The material memories project

The research upon which this paper is based focuses on colonial period archaeological remains which have been excavated and then conserved *in situ* (Ireland, 2012). It looks particularly at those sites retained in urban contexts, often at the expense of the full development potential and therefore the full financial return on the land. About twenty-one examples fitting this definition have been identified in Australia and New Zealand, although many further examples of archaeological remains conserved within historic sites and buildings, national parks, and rural areas would expand this number significantly. While any definition of site types is difficult, a focus of this project has been on the urban design context. The research has not included maritime archaeological sites, as their conservation involves a different set of social and economic issues. The aims of the research include increasing understanding of why the conservation *in situ* of colonial archaeological remains has emerged as a significant new genre of urban heritage conservation in the last decade in this region. While there is extensive international literature on techniques and best practice for archaeological conservation and preservation *in situ*, there is a more limited discussion of the meanings of the places created and how they are experienced and understood by visitors. Thus, crucial questions for our region are how should we decide what to conserve and what not to conserve, what version of heritage are we conserving and what community benefits accrue from this process? This paper briefly reviews the background to these questions and presents results from an online survey of visitors to these conserved archaeological sites.

A change in attitude to 'place memory' in Australia and New Zealand

Andreas Huyssen argues that the invasion of urban space by manifestations of memory and temporality is one of the most intriguing cultural phenomena of our times and that historical memory is increasingly being given material form (Huyssen, 2003). The desire for experiences of the past in the present, and for the use of conserved archaeological remains in urban environments as triggers for social memory appears to have intensified and become more broadly shared in communities in many parts of the globe (Matero, 2000). This is generally seen as evidence for a maturing heritage conservation system, linked to the growth of cultural tourism and the building influence of international heritage doctrine, such as the ICOMOS Charter for the Protection and Management of the Archaeological Heritage, the European Convention on the Protection of the Archaeological Heritage, and the Australia ICOMOS Burra Charter (Willems, 2008). While these places are certainly 'conservation successes' and while the effects of conservation doctrine have been significant, these factors do not adequately explain the growth in popularity of archaeological conservation *in situ* in Australia and New Zealand. Of the twenty-one archaeological sites in the study group, five of the *in situ* displays were constructed between 1984 and 1999 and sixteen were constructed between 1999 and 2010. This suggests that over the last decade the conservation and display of colonial archaeological remains was seen as a far more popular and acceptable option by the public than at any other time since the emergence of the contemporary heritage movement in the 1970s.

The growing use of conserved archaeological remains in urban locations therefore needs to be recognized as not only successful conservation, but a distinctive new form of urban design practice which is built on the aesthetic qualities of archaeological authenticity and memory, what Huyssen terms the 'imagined palimpsest' (Huyssen, 2003). This change of attitude has been driven by the expanding category of national heritage and the success of the conservation movement, but also by broader public interest in the past and by the designers and architects who create a vision for how past and present co-exist in the urban landscape. It is not suggested that this phenomenon is unique to this region — in fact, the key point here is that it is not. This genre of conservation appropriates and mimics European forms and this has a range of implications in the post-colonial context.

Appropriating a 'European' form of place making?

It is clear that the phenomenon of urban archaeological places conserved *in situ* is influenced by global architectural examples, but how are local practitioners incorporating local meanings into this idiom? For instance, Australian Indigenous archaeological remains are not being conserved and displayed in similar urban contexts, largely because they lack the formal architectural qualities from which these displays tend to derive the main aesthetic appeal of their presentation. Australian Indigenous sites are of course being conserved, and in some cases displayed, in different, usually non-urban contexts, while in New Zealand the architectural remains of Te Aro Pa, a colonial period Maori village site in Wellington, have been conserved and displayed *in situ* in the ground floor of an apartment building (Kerr, 2008). In Australia however, to conserve a shell midden, hearth site, or other forms of archaeological remains commonly found around Sydney, for instance, would require a significantly different presentation approach. It would require the development of a new conservation and design idiom, and this in turn would require involvement and collaboration with Indigenous communities. Rather than developing such a new idiom in response to the unique nature of the archaeological heritage of the region, the urban conservation of colonial archaeological sites appears to be based on the perhaps uncritical export of the 'in situ conservation concept' from Europe, as Willems has suggested (2009: 656). The 'aesthetic' of archaeological remains from the recent colonial past conserved *in situ* is a device that mimics the historic depth of ancient European cities and the antiquarian appreciation of ruins — making the urban environment more like Europe by creating evidence of similar historical layering (Woodward, 2002). The places created therefore contribute to perceptions of the legitimacy and tradition of the settler nation, ironically highlighting modernity, economic success, and progress from humble beginnings to fully modern nation (Hamilakis, 2001).

Visitor understanding and experience of colonial archaeological places: the survey results

The issues discussed above lead to a need to understand more about how visitors and publics in Australia and New Zealand value, experience, and understand this new genre of colonial archaeological places integrated into urban environments. As many of these places are not staffed or managed in traditional ways, accessing visitors is challenging. It was therefore decided, as a first step in the research process, to target groups known to have an interest in such places and who would be motivated enough to go on line and assist with the survey. In March 2011, a twenty-one-question visitor survey, designed using the Survey Monkey online survey tool, was distributed via various networks, including heritage associations and interest groups, workplaces, and universities. One hundred and ninety responses were received within the month and these are the basis for the results reported here. All responses were anonymous. The geographic spread of the responses was good — as expected the majority (34%) were people living in NSW, Australia, where most of this urban archaeological conservation has occurred, however responses were received in smaller numbers from all states and territories in Australia and from both the north and south islands in New Zealand. In general terms, the findings from this group express an extremely high degree of support and approval for this type of conservation *in situ* of archaeological remains. Very few respondents were critical of any aspect of the places they discussed, even though one might have expected critique from this group on aspects such as interpretation content. It appears most respondents viewed participation in the survey as a way of expressing their support for heritage conservation in general. Most interesting perhaps have been the findings relating to how respondents describe their experience of the places and how they understand 'in situ archaeological sites' as a category of heritage place.

Who responded to the survey?

The respondents to the survey (n = 190) were:

- highly educated (35% had bachelor degrees, while 34% had masters or PhD);
- mostly aged over 40 (50% over 45); and
- mostly (62%) working in a heritage-related area.

Fifty-four per cent of respondents visited heritage places frequently and 47% visited museums occasionally. The group was also well travelled: 82% had visited archaeological sites when travelling overseas. This group therefore reflects the opinions of those already very interested in cultural heritage and with broad experience of visiting cultural heritage sites.

What other sites like these have you visited?

The survey presented the respondent with a list of 19 colonial, urban archaeological sites in Australia and New Zealand, which had been excavated, then conserved and displayed *in situ*. When asked 'what other sites like these have you visited', 70 out of 190 respondents chose to list other places in a free text section. Thirty-four of these 70 respondents listed a number of colonial sites which had been archaeologically excavated, while 36 listed a wide range of colonial and pre-colonial Indigenous heritage places that had not been revealed through archaeological excavation. When offered the option to discuss one of the 19 sites identified in the survey or another place of their own choice, 33 respondents chose to discuss their own example. Of these 33 choices, 15 were ruined places which had not been excavated, three were museum exhibitions about archaeological places, and two were ancient Indigenous archaeological places.

While this question was designed to deliver information about the range of places known to people, it also revealed interesting information about people's understanding of the archaeological conservation *in situ* process — more than half of the group choosing their own place did not distinguish between some of the key categories that are commonly used in heritage management, for example between ruined buildings and excavated archaeological sites, Indigenous pre-contact sites and colonial period archaeological sites, *in situ* remains and *ex situ* museum displays of artefacts.

Interpretation of the archaeological sites

As many of the sites included in the survey have very limited on site interpretation, the results here surprised me in that respondents were overwhelmingly positive about the interpretation of the sites. As shown in Figure 1, respondents agreed that interpretation was:

- informative and educational;
- explained what the things they were looking at were;
- told them most of what they wanted to know about the place; and
- was creative and interesting.

Importance of authenticity and originality

Respondents overwhelmingly found all the sites they visited to be 'original and authentic' and not a reconstruction (Figure 2). When these results were filtered to

INTERPRETATION OF ARCHAEOLOGICAL REMAINS

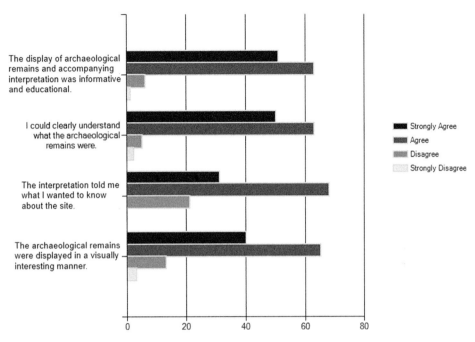

FIGURE 1   Interpretation of conserved sites.

show answers specific to two sites that included some reconstruction, none of the eleven respondents who visited these two sites agreed that they were a reconstruction. This suggests that because the sites included at least a proportion of 'original' archaeological remains, this was sufficient for the perception of the site as original and authentic. Alternatively, the level of reconstruction involved in the conservation *in situ* process may not be clear even to these well informed observers. One of the only slightly critical findings in the survey was that approximately 17 per cent disagreed that the remains were in good condition (Figure 2).

The use of artefacts in displays associated with conserved in situ sites

Respondents also commented on the use of associated displays of artefacts, which is a common feature of the sites in the study group. The findings here correlate with the findings on interpretation discussed above (Figure 1), as the statements posed related to:

- the information conveyed by the artefacts;
- that the display was interesting/intriguing;
- that the artefacts were well explained; and,
- the clarity/purpose of the displays.

Most respondents agreed or strongly agreed that the artefact displays were well interpreted and interesting (Figure 3).

A free text section provided the opportunity for expansion on these answers about artefact displays. Respondents from the minority who were critical of the success of

AUTHENTICITY AND CONDITION OF ARCHAEOLOGICAL REMAINS

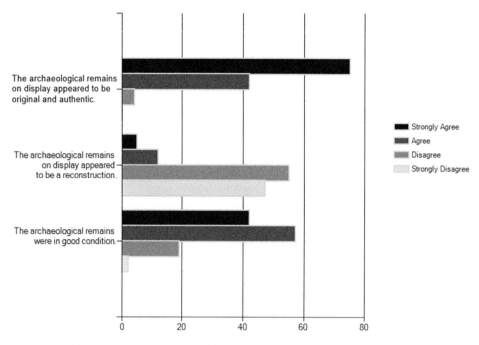

FIGURE 2   Authenticity and condition of the conserved sites.

associated artefact displays took the opportunity to expand here, as did some of the majority of those more appreciative of the displays (direct quotes from survey):

- 'provide a more personal attachment to the history of the place'
- 'artefacts interesting but confusing'
- 'artefacts are beautiful and intriguing but often lacking in context and inter-pretation'
- 'made the architectural remains more relatable'
- 'showed interesting windows into the past in a clear and understandable manner that didn't require 1300 hours in a library to understand'
- 'not clearly explained — displayed as if they spoke for themselves rather than needing interpretation. The objects were fascinating and I wanted to know more about them'
- 'old objects give snap shot views of the past'
- 'they are just objects in a case that reveal nothing about the site'.

Themes emerging from these free text comments include the way in which archaeo-logical objects are perceived by some visitors as providing more intimate or 'personal' links with the past and also how it can be difficult for visitors to interpret the message of artefacts, other than as intriguing or beautiful objects. This perhaps contrasts between those who experience a more emotional response to a place and those who seek more empirical information about a heritage site.

DISPLAY OF ARTEFACTS AND OBJECTS

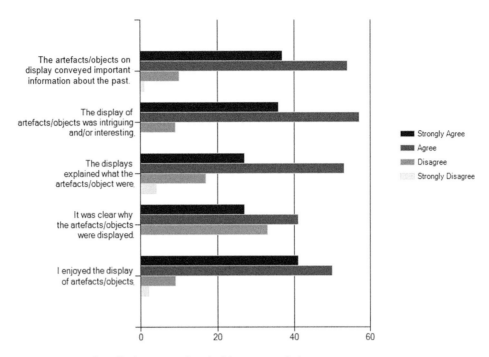

FIGURE 3   Artefact displays associated with conserved sites.

Is it like visiting a museum?

The survey asked for a yes/no response to the question 'was visiting this site just like visiting a museum?'. Sixty-seven per cent of respondents felt that visiting conserved *in situ* archaeological remains was not like visiting a museum. As one of the archaeological sites in the study group (the remains of Sydney's first government house) is located within the Museum of Sydney, some who answered yes to this question had in fact visited that site. When given the opportunity, 109 respondents expanded on this answer in a free text section. Free text responses included comments such as (direct quotes from the survey):

- 'open air, no glass cases'
- 'the site provided a more realistic connection to the past than visiting a museum'
- 'there were no glass walls between me and the place'
- 'it's a more personal experience and gives a better spatial sense of the past'
- 'the experience was more visceral than a boring museum'
- 'no post-modern crap, no museum nazis'
- 'being at the actual site of the past activity gave it a level of immediacy'
- 'provides direct link to the history of the area where it is located'
- 'I felt connected to a past world'
- 'Being outdoors, there was a freedom to understand the place as I wished without being compelled to 'respect' the objects in a semi-religious way, as is

the case in a museum. Because the site was very much a part of the living city [. . .] it appeared to have greater relevance for everyday life'.

Key themes emerging from these comments include:

- The significance of locality — clearly the experience of these archaeological places is deeply embedded in a sense of locality. The remains are acting as an evocative 'place memory'.
- The importance of access and openness — many (although not all) of the archaeological sites in the study group are not contained within a 'glass case' in order to conserve them. The resulting accessibility, openness, and 'closeness' (one respondent used the term 'intimate') available to a visitor appears to be deeply 'affective', in the sense that it provokes an emotional response in the visitor.
- Descriptions of 'affect' (used here in the sociological sense of an emotional response) — terms such as 'personal experience', 'direct link', 'visceral', and 'connection' all describe the emotional response to the perception of age and authenticity of archaeological remains, combined with the link they provide with place or locality (as described above), and also with people from the past.
- Control/freedom of meaning — these responses suggest that meaning at these archaeological sites may be experienced more through 'affect' than through didactic interpretation, such as some people expect to be subjected to in museums. This appears to have made some respondents feel that there was a freedom from ideologically driven interpretation (e.g. the comments about 'post-modern crap' and religion).

Overall impression

When asked to choose phrases that best described the overall impression derived from their visit, 82% of choices were for the phrase 'provides a connection with the past'. The next most popular choices were at 70% for 'interesting', and at 67% for 'provides insight into people and life in the past' (Figure 4). These overall impressions reinforce the findings discussed above, relating to the importance of the emotional response that the archaeological site provides of feeling 'connected to' and 'in touch with' the past.

Conclusions

The findings presented here suggest that this group of visitors highly values colonial archaeological sites conserved *in situ* for the link they provide to place, locality, and memory; for the feeling of connection with the past they evoke; and for the experience they provide of intimacy with material relics from the past. In terms of conservation and display, it is clear that the experience of affective authenticity is enhanced when the remains are not behind glass, and when the visitor can physically appreciate an embodied sense of place and locality through close proximity to the archaeological remains.

It is not clear if it is important to this visitor group that these places have been revealed and displayed through a process of archaeological excavation and then

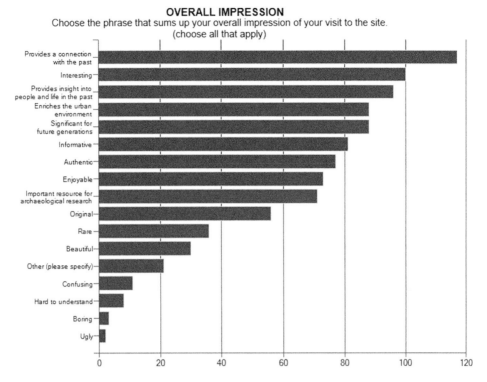

FIGURE 4   Overall impression of the site visit.

conservation *in situ*. Many respondents clearly did not distinguish between different kinds of heritage places, such as ruins or abandoned places, indigenous archaeological sites, and non-indigenous colonial archaeological remains. This suggests that to some visitors all these places are simply 'heritage' and valued highly for that status.

Most of these visitors did not seem to expect or require elaborate interpretation of the conserved remains and they appreciated artefact displays more for the feeling of connection with people in the past that they provided, than for the historical informa-tion they might convey. What emerged most strongly in responses from this educated and expert group of respondents was the emphasis placed on the embodied expe-rience of the past that these historic remains provided, how this experience added to their sense of place, and how they felt that they were free to encounter and construct meanings on their own terms, not as dictated by an institution such as a museum.

This suggests that the recent success and expansion of this category of conservation in Australia and New Zealand is due at least in part to the alternative kind of experience of the past that these sites provide, in contrast to other types of heritage places or cultural institutions. However, the reliance on 'affective authenticity' and related emotional responses for the success of this kind of archaeological conservation has also limited creative local responses to heritage conservation, as it requires links with well-established aesthetics and narratives of history and identity, and tends not to challenge or disrupt received versions of the past with less comfortable ideas. This conservation has tended to be defined through a 'European' antiquarian appreciation of the architectural ruin, rather than a response to the complex material reality of cultural heritage in postcolonial, or de-colonising settler societies. A challenge for the future is for conservation to enable new forms of place memory, providing the bridge which communities seek to build between place, memory, and identity.

Acknowledgements

I gratefully acknowledge the funding for this research provided by the University of Canberra and the contributions of Sarah Webeck, for research assistance, and Beaux Guarini for the poster design for the PARIS IV conference in Copenhagen. I also thank two anonymous referees who provided valuable advice which improved the paper substantially.

Bibliography

Hamilakis, Y. 2001. Antiquities Underground. *Antiquity*, 75(287): 35–36.

Huyssen, A. 2003. *Present Pasts: Urban Palimpsests and the Politics of Memory*. Stanford, California: Stanford University Press.

Ireland, T. 2002. Giving Value to the Australian Historic Past: Archaeology, Heritage and Nationalism. *Australasian Historical Archaeology*, 20: 15–25.

Ireland, T. 2012. Excavating Globalisation from the Ruins of Colonialism: Archaeological Heritage Management Responses to Cultural Change. In: E. Negussie, ed. *Proceedings of the ICOMOS Scientific Symposium. Changing World, Changing Views of Heritage: The Impact of Global Change on Cultural Heritage*. Paris: ICOMOS, pp. 18–28.

Kerr, P. 2008. Downtown Discovery. *Heritage New Zealand Magazine*. Autumn Edition. New Zealand Historic Places Trust/Pouhere Taonga [accessed 30 May 2010]. Available at: <http://www.historic.org.nz/en/Publications/HeritageNZMagazine/HeritageNz2008/HNZ08-DowntownDiscovery.aspx>.

Matero, F. 2000. The Conservation of an Excavated Past. In: I. Hodder, ed. *Towards Reflexive Method in Archaeology: The Example of Catalhöyük*. British Institute of Archaeology at Ankara: BIAA Monograph No. 28, pp. 71–88.

Temple, H. 1986. Marketing, Conservation and Interpretation of Historic Sites in the United States of America and the United Kingdom. *Australian Historical Archaeology*, 4: 3–8.

Temple, H. 1988. Historical Archaeology and its Role in the Community. Unpublished MA (Hons) thesis, University of Sydney.

Willems, W. J. H. 2008. Archaeological Resource Management and Preservation. *Geoarchaeological and Bioarchaeological Studies*, 10: 283–89.

Willems, W. J. H. 2009. European and World Archaeologies. *World Archaeology*, 41(4): 649–58.

Woodward, C. 2002. *In Ruins*. London: Vintage.

Notes on contributor

Tracy Ireland is Director of the Donald Horne Institute for Cultural Heritage at the University of Canberra. Her PhD centred on the relationships between archaeology, heritage conservation, and nationalism, and she has published on archaeological heritage management, landscapes, social significance, and indigenous historic sites in Australia. She is currently working on a series on Ethics and Archaeology for Springer.

Correspondence to: Tracy Ireland. Email: tracy.ireland@canberra.edu.au

CONSERVATION AND MGMT OF ARCH. SITES, Vol. 14 Nos 1–4, 2012, 469–78

Complications and Effectiveness of *In Situ* Preservation Methods for Underwater Cultural Heritage Sites

SORNA KHAKZAD and KONRAAD VAN BALEN

Raymond Lemaire International Centre for Conservation, University of Leuven (KU Leuven), Belgium

Underwater Cultural Heritage (UCH) as an outstanding division of the cultural heritage of humanity appears to be crucial and complicated when more general issues regarding preservation and conservation are raised. The essence of *in situ* preservation should be equally discussable for any kind of archaeological remains; on land or underwater.

There is a long history of different methods and concepts of intervention in a variety of sub-aquatic archaeological sites; from shipwrecks to sub-merged settlements. This paper will present an introduction to different techniques and theories of preservation and conservation of underwater cultural and archaeological sites since this kind of heritage has scientifically been explored and studied. A range of different preservation methodologies, from total or partial transference inland, to preservation underwater, will be compared; the advantages and disadvantages of each option will be highlighted. Different examples of international best practices will be illustrated. Different types of *in situ* conservation/protection will be explained and categorized. Furthermore, there will be a focus on the UNESCO Convention of 2001 on Conservation and Preservation of UCH, where the *in situ* conservation option has been recommended.

Moreover, the technical issue for preservation of UCH sites, either *in situ* or after displacement, will be explained. The implication of relocation for different sorts of sites and materials will be argued; for example, cases where some sites, such as shipwrecks, would more easily be displaced compared with submerged settlements, villages, or ports.

Finally, by stressing that the state of 'being underwater' makes many sites qualified to be regarded as UCH, the *in situ* preservation approach will prevail that this state is maintained.

KEYWORDS underwater cultural heritage, *in situ* conservation, evaluation systems

© Taylor & Francis 2012
DOI 10.1179/1350503312Z.00000000040

Conservation and treatment methods: why and what?

The UNESCO Convention on the Protection of Underwater Cultural Heritage (2001) recommends *in situ* conservation as the best means of protecting cultural heritage underwater. Missing, however, is recognition of different types of cultural heritage underwater, each of which may require different kinds of treatment, and there is no common set of criteria governing the assessment of all materials. This paper has two goals: to highlight the differences between the variety of conservation and protection methods in order to demonstrate that each site has particular characteristics; and to offer a preliminary outline of a common assessment process within which these particular characteristics and needs may be best determined. Ideally, this process may be integrated into the gradually progressing body of international legislation regulating the protection and preservation of cultural heritage underwater.

It worth mentioning that protection, according to Charter for the Protection and Management of the Archaeological Heritage (1990) as well as UNESCO Convention for the Protection of the World Cultural and Natural Heritage (1972), falls under the legislations and policies of each nation regarding the protecting their cultural assets by enforcing laws. Conservation includes actions and management on a site in order to stop or reduce the erosion process and to stabilize the site condition.

Following is a brief introduction to different methods of intervention in underwater cultural sites. Some project examples are presented, to show different scenarios in order to highlight the criteria which should be considered crucial while treating different types of underwater sites.

Displacement, moving onto land

This classical method of excavation is usually followed by the study and conservation of objects and display in museums. This process is similar to the classical archaeology of materials found on land. There are examples of sites which had to be moved onto the land due to the danger of being submerged. Abu Simbel Nubiam Monument in Egypt is a good example of this type of project. Through relocation of the site, the risk of its submergence was eliminated. There are examples in which the submergence occurred a long time ago, such as shipwrecks: the most popular ones are *Vasa* and the *Mary Rose*, amongst others. In these cases the sites were excavated and the objects and all parts of the wreck remains were moved on land. Again the approach was a classical method of excavation of an archaeological site underwater. These cases show different situations in which the best decision was made according to current available technology, current identified priorities of protection and conservation due to natural and human impacts, and expected benefits, for example for educational purposes, and for safeguarding the values of the heritage.

In situ methods for conservation, protection, and presentation of underwater sites

With the advent of new techniques and theories, new methods of excavation, protection and conservation of archaeological sites, either on land or underwater, have been developed. The idea of *in situ* archaeological parks and museums is not a very new topic for terrestrial cultural sites. Nevertheless, for underwater cultural heritage, this method brings more complications due to the special environment, although at the same time it is strongly recommended by the UNESCO Convention 2001. According to the first rule of the annex of the UNESCO Convention on Protection of Underwater Cultural heritage, 'The protection of underwater cultural heritage through *in situ* preservation shall be considered as the first option'. *In situ* conservation/protection can be considered as one of the most convenient methods of safeguarding the significance and location of UCH. Being underwater is a quality which makes the sites underwater eligible to be regarded as underwater cultural heritage. Simply stated, objects or site out of water have not this 'quality' anymore. As mentioned in the UNESCO Convention 2001: 'once out of the water and exhibited on land, objects from submerged archaeological sites are deprived of their context and lose part of their significance'. However, if the intervention significantly contributes to the protection, enhancement of knowledge, or condition of the UCH, the action may be authorized. Additionally, *in situ* conservation may protect the original condition of the site after sinking, and reserves the possibility of using more advanced techniques in the future. Underwater cultural heritage are like a 'time capsule' (Muckelroy, 1978: 55) and as long as they are protected underwater they hold valuable historical, archaeological, and natural data. By moving them out of water this information will be scratched or might be lost. Submerged and buried maritime heritage often exists in an environment that, without disturbance, is conducive to the long-term preservation of a variety of archaeological materials (Corfield, 1996: 32). *In situ* preservation is based on the concept that certain environments are capable of slowing deterioration. As (Holden et al., 2006: 59) indicate, it is this very process that allows archaeologists to uncover the past through excavation. Once these sites are disturbed, chemical, biological, and physical forces begin to destroy the fragile stability of the sites.

In situ conservation is a general term for protecting and conserving underwater sites using different methods. However, looking at different international projects and going through literature, a variety of methods and implementations of *in situ* conservation are identified (Delgado, 1997). Therefore, it is important to be clear about the specific methods of *in situ* conservation/protection used when discussing this in a scientific context. This paper suggests categorizing different *in situ* conservation methods according to the similarity in their approaches as follows:

In situ protection

In some cases any large-scale scientific intervention of underwater sites is impossible due to the high economical cost or due to technical difficulties; however, the sites might be under threat from natural erosion or human intervention (such as fisheries or anchorage). In these cases, rather simple *in situ* protection methods can be used such as covering a site or restricting access can guarantee protection of the sites (Figure 1). The examples of this method can be seen in some countries such as Turkey where the government has limited access, diving and even snorkelling on some underwater sites. Considering the fact that Turkey has a large number of underwater sites (from shipwrecks to submerged cities) *in situ* protection on all sites is not possible, therefore the damage to sites has been reduced through government regulation (Strati, 1995).

FIGURE 1   *In situ* protection, trapezoid protective cage, Cape North of Rab Island, Croatia. © *UNESCO*

In situ conservation

In situ conservation covers a wide range of techniques and forms. This method involves intervention in the sites and sometimes can be combined with reburial. There are remarkable examples of different kinds of *in situ* conservation techniques that still allow access for visitors, such as in Croatia (Figure 1). In the case of the underwater Roman villas in Baiae, Italy hydraulic mortar has been injected between the brick to conserve the walls from collapsing (Davidde, 2002) (Figure 2).[1] There are variety of *in situ* conservation techniques, such as cathodic protection using sacrificial anodes, which are suitable for iron and metal artefacts. The use of sacrificial anodes for iron artefacts by MacLeod on the *Sirius* site (MacLeod, 1996a; 1996b), while promising in terms of *in situ* developments, was originally intended to provide increased stability of the object in conjunction with conventional forms of retrieval and treatment. In many cases, the use of cathodic protection stabilizes the artefacts *in situ* but the site is still accessible to visitors underwater (MacLeod, 1998).

Reburial

In terms of archaeological use of *in situ* preservation, reburial is the first method to be used regularly by attempting to create a more stable reburial environment, slowing chemical, biological, and physical deterioration. This can be accomplished in different ways, such as backfilling of excavated sediment, installing various forms of barriers and encouraging sediment deposition on site (Oxley, 1998a: 97–100, 104; Oxley, 1998b: 159). Both the natural conditions and the material which is used for reburial have a big impact on the effectiveness of this method. Continuous monitoring is required in order to ensure preservation in the long term.

FIGURE 2   Underwater ruins of a Roman villa and the replica of a statue, Baia, Italy.
© *http://underwaterarchaeologicalparkbaia.blogspot.com*

The idea of using a physical barrier to protect sites is based on the notion that the original burial site created conditions conducive to preserving archaeological materials (Harvey, 1996). Recreating or imitating the original conditions should, in theory, provide similar protection (Oxley, 1998a: 91). Barriers can include sandbags and geotextiles while sediment deposition can be encouraged with mats of artificial sea grass, debris netting, or geotextiles (Oxley, 1998a: 100–04; Oxley, 1998b: 159, 165). Each of these techniques has its own inherent advantages and disadvantages. For instance, finer sediment such as sand is often carried away by currents before it has a chance to settle on site (Oxley, 1998b: 168). Heavier sediments, such as gravel, are more successful, though questions remain about whether or not this can damage the site (Oxley, 1998b: 168). While this form of reburial may be cost effective, Oxley (1998b: 168) notes that planning in terms of site environment, type of sediment used, and how the drop is to be completed are key elements in ensuring the success of this technique. Another method of encouraging sediment deposition that has been successful in some situations has been artificial seagrass. Seagrass occurs naturally on many sites, but, once disturbed, is unlikely to re-establish itself (Godfrey et al., 2005: 15, 51). However, the presence of bacteria which can gradually penetrate into the different kinds of protective layers and in any depth (Fazzani et al., 1975), keeps reburial still to be a debatable technique for long-term protection. From a preventive conservation approach it is advised to install monitoring tools when reburying to be able to follow the state of preservation while the objects and the site will remain invisible.

In situ preservation and presentation

Some projects present novel approaches to conservation, protection, and display of UCH such as: underwater parks, aquariums, submerged museums, remote sensing, and so on. The implementation of those cases very much depends on the natural environmental conditions, as well as the available technologies and the economic circumstances of each project. Some of these examples use a combination of different methods, such as *in situ* conservation, reburial as well as relocation of the artefacts together with major interventions in the site by inserting new buildings or access path, which are often innovative and are unique in their design and approach. Examples include the Baiheliang Underwater Museum in China (Figure 3), the underwater museum of Alexandria in Egypt, and the underwater wreck park in Florida. In the first two examples, new techniques and technology were applied to construct infrastructure underwater, in order to prepare a suitable space for underwater sites and artefacts for which no diving was required to visit them. However, in the underwater shipwreck parks (Florida's museum in the sea, 2007), the wrecks are conserved *in situ* (or in similar situ where some sites or object are moved to another location in water where a similar condition of water and nature would be maintained) and visitors with diving equipment can follow the trails and gain information from the text boards which are installed underwater. In these cases a combination of different conservation methods, such as continuous *in situ* conservation, reburial, and protective measures

FIGURE 3   The construction of the Baiheliang Underwater Museum, China.
© UNESCO

have been applied. Since these methods are very diverse and mostly quite recent, the impact of the applied *in situ* conservation techniques are not yet clear and should be monitored and reported in the long term (Manders, 2004).

Considerations

The application of *in situ* conservation techniques not only can preserve an underwater cultural heritage site in its original location but can also preserve the site for future research with the advent of new technologies and innovations. The relocation if needed of shipwrecks and objects is considered feasible. In case of submerged sites that once were above water and are endemic (as immerged harbours or cities, prehistoric landscapes . . .) relocation is mostly not an option.

In the consideration of any kind of cultural heritage site it is important to define the aims of any activity to be undertaken. After proper evaluation of the heritage values of a site, the best conservation and/or excavation methods can be chosen. One example of a project without consideration of the possibilities and consequences of the intervention is the relocation of a metal shipwreck in Iran with the significance being the first steam engine ship used in this country (Figure 4).

Awareness raising and presentation of UCH to the public are as important as research and study of the sites themselves. Therefore, in choosing a methodology for excavation, conservation, and protection, all the aforementioned issues should be regarded as imperative. In addition, monitoring after any kind of intervention is an inevitable task in any long-term management plan.

FIGURE 4   Relocating a metal shipwreck on land, without planning for its proper treatment. Persepolis shipwreck, Maritime Museum of Bushehr, Iran.

As shown in Table 1, a simple matrix is suggested to assess different kinds of intervention according to the significance of the submerged sites. This matrix is a simplified version of some evaluation matrixes; each component of this matrix has more issues to consider. In order to evaluate which method might be the most appropriate, several matrixes have been developed in the author's Master thesis (Khakzad, 2008) and offer an evaluation tool based on international convention, best practices, and the author's experiences in the field. There are several tools to define the significance of land sites, such as the criteria for World Heritage Listing, the Nara document on Authenticity (Nara Document on Authenticity, 1994), and so on. These documents provide a harmonized tool to assess the significance of different kinds of sites in the world. Each factor is evaluated for each method, however, the degree and possibility for each method is relative. For instance, protection for the sites and objects which are moved inland is highly depends on the treatment after recovery, the techniques available for the project in different areas, and budget. If all the variation comes along, then the protection is considered 'High'. Therefore, this matrix is useful, when all the aspects for management of a site has been well foreseen in advance. So in line with the UNESCO Convention on the Protection of UCH (UNESCO Convention, 2001) in order to have a more comprehensive and practical framework, it is important to bring the outcomes of different international projects and documents together in order to use these results and experiences to create an inclusive evaluation tool.

TABLE 1

A SIMPLE MATRIX TO COMPARE AND EVALUATE DIFFERENT TREATMENT METHODS WITHIN THEIR PRACTICAL ADVANTAGES AND DISADVANTAGES

Facts Method	Protection	Conservation	Visit	Location significant	Monitoring
Move in land	**High** If the site treated well inland	**Mid to high** too problematic	**Possible** Usually	**Lost** Underwater significance	**Easier & economical**
In-situ	**Mid to high** Depends on State party or country's regulation	**Varies** due to monitoring, method, context & material	**Possible/impossible** (dependent on the method/s used)	**Preserved** original location & material	**Not easy & expensive** (Compare with land methods)
Reburial	**Mid to high** Depends on State party or country's regulation	**Varies** due to monitoring, method, context & material	**Not possible** Only virtually, providing replica or virtual reconstruction	**Varies** could be done in a different location	**Not easy & expensive** (Relative to where and what is applied)
Other	**High** In most cases	**Varies** due to techniques **Mid to high**	**Possible** diving, remote, Underwater museum, aquarium, etc	**Varies** in-situ or in-similar-situ (displacement of the site to another underwater location where the original water condition is maintained.)	Dependent on the method

Conclusion

The necessity of a standardized evaluation tool in order to have a base, nationally and internationally, to define the values of a site and justify the application of certain actions on different sites has been highlighted. This tool is being further developed in the author's PhD dissertation. This evaluation tool offers a common language and terminology in order to measure the level of significance and condition of different sites. The very simple version of this system (Table 1) can work as a checklist which can be filled in by experts. This tool will help to define *in situ* conservation/protection methodology as well as assessing the success of a project and the effectiveness of the applied technique/s in a standardized way.

The importance of *in situ* conservation in preserving the significance of sites and reserving the right for future techniques and innovation for further studies, visiting and accessibility possibilities has been highlighted.

Some of the more recent *in situ* preservation techniques such as underwater museums, displacement to another underwater location and aquarium are so diverse in nature and design that it is difficult to judge their long-term impacts on the underwater cultural heritage. There are factors which might cause changes in the present condition of the sites; to mention a few, the impacts of climate change on water parameters and natural environment, or urban and industrial development and their impact on geological and biological features of the underwater environment. Therefore, for these kinds of projects a high quality monitoring system should be implemented and the successful examples considered as models for similar cases.

Note

[1] <http://underwaterarchaeologicalparkbaia.blogspot.com/>.

Bibliography

Blake, J. 1994. The Protection of Turkey's Underwater Archaeological Heritage — Legislative Measures and Other Approaches. *International Journal of Cultural Property*, 3: 273–94.

Charter for the Protection and Management of the Archaeological Heritage (1990) [accessed January 2012]. Available at: <www.international.icomos.org/charters/arch_e.htm>.

Corfield, C. 1996. Preventive Conservation for Archaeological Sites. *Conference Paper: Archaeological Conservation and its Consequences: Preprints of the Contributions to the Copenhagen Congress, 26–30 August 1996*. London: International Institute for Conservation of Historic and Artistic Works, pp. 32–37.

Davidde, B. 2002. Underwater Archaeological Parks: A New Perspective and a Challenge for Conservation — the Italian Panorama. *International Journal of Nautical Archaeology*, 31(1): 83–88.

Delgado, J. ed. 1997. *Encyclopedia of Underwater and Maritime Archaeology*. London: British Museum Press.

Division of Historical Resources, Bureau of Archaeological Research, 2007. Florida's Museums in the Sea: Florida's Underwater Archaeological Preserves [accessed May 2011]. Available at: <http://www.museumsinthesea.com/>.

Fazzani, K., Furtudo, S. E. J., Eaton, R. A., and Jones, E. B. G. 1975. Biodeterioration of Timber in Aquatic Environments. *Society for Applied Bacteriology, Technical Series*, 9: 39–58.

Godfrey, I., Reed, E., Richards, V., West, N., and Winton, T. 2005. The James Matthews Shipwreck — Conservation Survey and In-Situ Stabilization. In: P. Hoffmann, K. Strætkvern, J. A. Spriggs, and D. Gregory, eds. *Proceedings of the 9th ICOM Group on Wet Organic Archaeological Materials Conference*. ICOM Committee for Conservation Working Group on Wet Organic Archaeological Materials, Bremerhaven, pp. 40–76.

Harvey, P. 1996. A Review of Stabilization Work on the Wreck of the William Salthouse in Port Phillip Bay. *Bulletin of the Australian Institute for Maritime Archaeology*, 20(2): 1–8.

Holden, J., West, L. J., Howard, A. J., Maxfield, E., and Oxley, J. 2006. Hydrological Controls of In Situ Preservation of Waterlogged Archaeological Deposits. *Earth-Science Reviews*, 78(1–2): 59–83.

International Council of Monuments and Sites, 1994. *Nara Document on Authenticity*.

Khakzad, S. 2008. Underwater Cultural Conservation and Presentation to the Public, Case Study the Current Projects in Belgium. Master thesis, University of Leuven, Belgium.

MacLeod, I. D. 1996a. In Situ Conservation of Cannon and Anchors on Shipwrecks Sites. In: *Archaeological Conservation and its Consequences: Preprints of the Contributions to the Copenhagen Congress, 26–30 August 1996*. London: International Institute for Conservation of Historic and Artistic Workspp. 111–15.

MacLeod, I. D. 1996b. An In-Situ Study of the Corroded Hull of HMVA Cerberus (1926). In: *Proceedings of the 13th International Corrosion Congress*. Melbourne, Australia, pp. 1–10.

MacLeod, I. D. 1998. In-Situ Corrosion Studies on Iron and Composite Wrecks in South Australian Waters: Implications for Site Managers and Cultural Tourism. *Bulletin of the Australian Institute for Maritime Archaeology*, 22: 81–90.

Manders, M. R. and Luth, R. 2004. Safeguarding. In: C. O. Cederlund. ed. *Monitoring, Safeguarding and Visualizing North-European Shipwreck Sites — Challenges for Cultural Resource Management: Final Report*. Helsinki: The National Board of Antiquities, pp. 63–73.

Muckelroy, K. 1978. Introducing Maritime Archaeology. In: L. E. Babits and H. Van Tilburg, eds. *Maritime Archaeology: A Reader of Substantive and Theoretical Contributions*. New York: Plenum Press, p. 55.

Oxley, I. 1998a. The Environment of Historic Shipwreck Sites: A Review of the Preservation of materials, Site Formation and site environmental assessment. Master of Science, Geography and Geosciences, University of St Andrews.

Oxley, I. 1998b. The In-Situ Preservation of Underwater Sites. In: M. Corfield, P. Hinton, T. Nixon, and M. Pollard, eds. *Preserving Archaeological Remains In Situ*. London: Museum of London Archaeological Service and University of Bradford, pp. 159–73.

Strati, A. 1995. *The Protection of the Underwater Cultural Heritage: An Emerging Objective of the Contemporary Law of the Sea*. The Netherlands: Kluwer Law International.

UNESCO Convention for the Protection of the World Cultural and Natural Heritage, 1972 [accessed January 2012]. Available at: <http://whc.unesco.org/en/conventiontext/>.

Notes on contributors

Sorna Khakzad is a PhD Researcher at the University of Leuven (KU Leuven), Belgium. Architect MSc (Azad University of Tehran, 2004), advanced study in Conservation of Monuments and Historic Sites (KU Leuven, 2008). Her PhD deals with management of UCH. She worked as architect-cultural heritage specialist in national and international projects, a member of SPLASHCOST, received awards from UNESCO-Vocations Patrimoine and World Learning Center (USA).

Correspondence to: Sorna Khakzad, 01 Arenberg Castle, RLICC Office, Heverlee, 3001, Belgium. Email: sorna_serena@yahoo.com

Koenraad van Balen, PhD engineer-architect, is a Professor at the University of Leuven and Director of the Raymond Lemaire International Centre for Conservation; he is involved in various international research projects dealing with heritage preservation and on construction materials.

Correspondence to: Koenraad van Balen, Kasteelpark Arenberg 40, B-3001 Leuven (Heverlee), Belgium. Email: koenraad.vanbalen@bwk.kuleuven.be

CONSERVATION AND MGMT OF ARCH. SITES, Vol. 14 Nos 1–4, 2012, 479–86

Nydam Mose: *In Situ* Preservation at Work

DAVID GREGORY and HENNING MATTHIESEN

National Museum of Denmark, Denmark

The site of Nydam Mose saw the beginning of systematic research into *in situ* preservation of waterlogged archaeological sites on land at the National Museum of Denmark. In the past fifteen years a generic approach to *in situ* preservation of archaeological sites has been developed based on this research. This article is primarily a review of this generic approach, summarizing the methods and results with particular reference to the published results from the investigations in Nydam Mose.

KEYWORDS Nydam Mose, *in situ* preservation, deterioration, mitigation, monitoring

Introduction

During the Iron Age, Nydam Mose was a small lake into which several thousand artefacts were deposited on several occasions between approximately ad 200 and 500 (Rau, 2012). The present-day site is a waterlogged water meadow and since 1859 several archaeological campaigns have taken place. The last of these was conducted in 1997 when, because of the volume of finds (over 16,000 artefacts excavated between 1989–97; Figure 1) and the resources required for their conservation, it was decided to stop further excavations and investigate the feasibility of preserving the site *in situ*. Over the following fifteen years a generic approach to *in situ* preservation has been developed which we believe can be applied when considering the *in situ* preservation of other archaeological sites.

Approach to *in situ* preservation

The authors use the term *in situ* preservation to mean a form of preventive conservation whereby preservation of artefacts and cultural deposits is assured by a sequence of artefact analysis, initiation of stabilization strategies and environmental monitoring (Gregory and Matthiesen, 2007). In order to achieve this there are five fundamental points related to the successful *in situ* preservation of archaeological sites, these are:

      DOI 10.1179/1350503312Z.00000000041

FIGURE 1   The archaeological richness of Nydam. To left, metal artefacts, including swords and shield bosses. To right, wooden artefacts, including shield fragments, spear, and arrow shafts.

The extent of the site

The ability to delimit the size or area of an archaeological site is of paramount importance in designing an effective *in situ* preservation strategy. With the increasing development in land survey techniques, remote sensing, and geophysical methods, it is essential to embrace this technology in combination with more traditional archaeological methods of site prospection such as soil sampling through coring and trial excavations. Currently, only a few per cent of the Iron Age lake at Nydam have been excavated. However, several geophysical surveys and ground truthing of the results has been carried out in recent years, including metal detector, flux gradiometer, and ground penetrating radar (Dobson et al., 2008). These have shown the site extends over a greater area than where archaeological excavations have been carried out (Figure 2) and this information has been taken into consideration when prioritizing which areas of the site to protect.

The types of archaeological materials present on the site and state of preservation

Either through test excavation or previous knowledge gained from archaeological excavations on the site, the types of material likely to be encountered on a site needs to be known. Having identified what materials are present they need to be analysed in the laboratory so as to get an indication of the typical state of preservation of the material and begin to identify the processes of deterioration that have taken place previously, and the factors controlling future preservation. In Nydam concern originally arose about the state of preservation of both iron and wooden artefacts, which were the predominant materials. However, it was shown that much of the poor 'visible' state of preservation was the result of depositional formation processes. Many artefacts were thrown out into the Iron Age lake; wooden artefacts had floated around and been attacked by wood-boring insects, giving them a gnarled/roughened surface, prior to incorporation in the bog (Gregory and Jensen, 2006; Gregory et al., 2002). Similarly, metal artefacts had been exposed to the waters of the lake, where

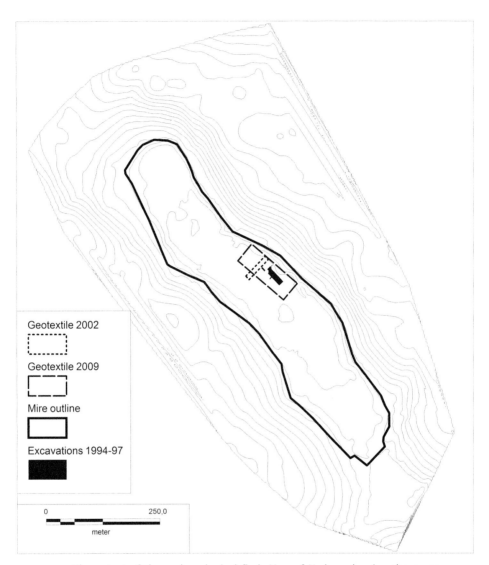

Geotextile 2002

Geotextile 2009

Mire outline

Excavations 1994-97

0   250,0
meter

FIGURE 2   The extent of the archaeological find. Map of Nydam showing the areas where archaeological excavations have taken place and where geotextiles has been used to cover areas where artefacts are known to be present.

corrosion was faster, prior to them being incorporated into the mire and often showed very different states of preservation based on these depositional formation processes (Matthiesen et al., 2004). On the contrary, those artefacts that appeared to be well preserved had been thrust into the lakebed and thus had been immediately deposited into a more preservative environment (Figure 3).

The physical, chemical, and biological nature of the environment around the site and the most significant threats to the site

Successful *in situ* preservation implies that the state of preservation of material is maintained, that is, that further decay does not take place or only at a very low rate.

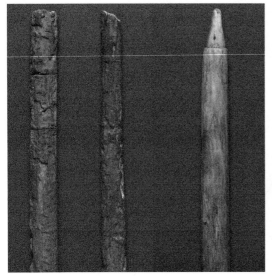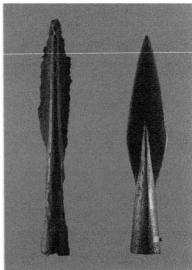

FIGURE 3   State of preservation of artefacts in Nydam. Wooden and metal artefacts showing the impotance of depositional process. Artefacts to the left had been deposited in oxic environments and were degraded/corroded prior to incorporation in the mire. Those on the right were deposited into anoxic environments.

Ongoing decay is difficult to measure directly, but we try to estimate it from a combination of studies of the archaeological objects, the environmental conditions at the site, and use of *in situ* decay studies with modern analogue materials (Gregory et al., 2008; Matthiesen et al., 2007).

Summarily, in Nydam the chemical/biological nature of the environment is seen to be conducive to the long-term preservation of wooden and metallic artefacts. The water level is consistently above the cultural layers. Levels of dissolved oxygen are considered to be anoxic, based on measurements with micro sensors, with only the upper few centimetres of the bog containing oxygen (Matthiesen et al., 2004a). pH is weakly acidic to neutral, with a rather high content of nutrient salts. Acidity in the soil is measured to be between pH 6.2 and 6.8 with it being buffered by high CO_2 and bicarbonate content (Matthiesen, 2004; Elberling and Matthiesen, 2007).

Under these conditions the wooden artefacts are resistant to further microbial attack as the conditions are unsuitable for the activity of those wood degrading fungi that could potentially degrade the lignin remaining in the artefacts (Helms et al., 2004). The only microbial deterioration of wood will be bacterial. However, as there is very little 'nutritious' material (cellulose) remaining for these organisms, deterioration rates are currently estimated to be infinitesimal. The iron artefacts are stable in the current environment, although they are vulnerable to even small decreases in pH, which could destabilize any protective corrosion products (Matthiesen et al., 2003). The studies from Nydam have led to a close collaboration with a French research group on corrosion of archaeological iron from waterlogged sites (Saheb et al., 2007; 2008; 2009; Remazeilles et al., 2010).

In Nydam the most significant threat is the presence of the horsetail plant, the rhizomes of which grow through the cultural layers penetrating wooden artefacts (Figure 4). The risk of the water table dropping below the layer of the cultural layers causing drying and irreversible damage to both wooden and metal artefacts was also deemed a potential threat (Björdal and Nilsson, 2002), and future excavations at the site should try to avoid excessive pumping (Matthiesen et al., 2004b).

Strategies to mitigate deterioration from cultural and natural impacts

Understanding the processes of deterioration and the effects of the physical, chemical, and biological nature of the environment on an archaeological site will enable a risk assessment of a site to be made. Based on this there are three options: passive preservation, that is, leave it as it is, the environment is safe; active preservation, that is, influencing environmental parameters; or, if these options are not possible, excavation of the site. In the case of Nydam, measures to prevent the growth of the horsetail were implemented by covering areas of the site with geotextile. Initial trials showed this to be effective at preventing the growth of the horsetail and relatively quickly became a natural-looking part of the landscape (Figure 5). A full-scale trial turned out less efficient due to a different quality of geotextile being used and is currently being reassessed.

Environmental Monitoring

The whole point of a systematic approach to *in situ* preservation is that we are safe-guarding the cultural heritage for the future. Therefore it is meaningless to implement

FIGURE 4   The rhizomes of the Horestail (Equisetum) are one of the major threats to the site as they can grow upward of 1.5 m into the mire and penetrate the degraded wooden artefacts.

FIGURE 5   Mitigation of horsetails with geotextile. Left to right: the site in 2001 before geotextile; 2002 after placing geotextile; and in 2007 where natural vegetation has covered the geotextile.

mitigation strategies if their efficacy is not to be checked periodically in the future by monitoring. This point leads back into points 2 and 3, whereby sacrificial examples of artefacts (or modern materials) can be placed on the site and periodically analysed to check their continued state of preservation, as has been done with both wooden and metal materials. Also, the environmental parameters deemed important for the site in question must be monitored to ensure they are not significantly changing.

Discussion

In situ preservation should not be a case of 'out of sight out of mind' and we think that the work at Nydam has demonstrated how *in situ* preservation is a viable option to sustainably manage cultural heritage. In a wider perspective it has also had a positive side effect in keeping the site in the public eye. The suggestion to preserve the site *in situ* was controversial when it was first mooted and was hotly debated by the public, archaeologists, and conservators. However, not only has the monitoring and research carried out over the past fifteen years resulted in a large number of scientific papers and reports, some of which may be found in the reference list, it has also kept the site in the public eye. Local newspapers, TV, and radio have always been interested in news from Nydam, for instance when field work is taking place. Furthermore, the local interest group (the Nydam Society[1]) has followed the work closely as it has a burning interest in the site, its history, and future preservation. Thus, both in terms of research and public interest, Nydam is still at work, despite no excavations having taken place in the last fifteen years.

Note

[1]   <www.nydam.nu>.

Bibliography

Björdal, C. G. and Nilsson, T. 2002. Waterlogged Archaeological Wood — A Substrate for White Rot During Drainage of Wetlands. *International Biodeterioration and Biodegradation*, 50(1): 17–23.

Remazeilles, C., Saheb, M., Neff, D., Guilminot, E., Tran, K., Bourdoiseau, J-A., Sabot, R., Jeannin, M., Matthiesen, H., Dillmann, P., and Refaita, P. 2010. Microbiologically Influenced Corrosion of Archaeological Artefacts: Characterization of Iron (II) Sulphides by Raman Spectroscopy. *Journal of Raman Spectroscopy*, DOI 10.1002/jrs.2717.

Dobson, S., Gregory, D., and Matthiesen, H. 2008. Geophysical and *In Situ* Preservation: Experiences at Nydam Mose, Denmark. In: H. Kars and R. M. van Heeringen. eds. *Preserving Archaeological Remains In Situ. Proceedings of the 3rd Conference 7–9 December 2006, Amsterdam*. Geoarchaeologiccal and Bioarchaeological Studies Volume 10, VU University, Amsterdam , pp. 123–30.

Elberling, B. and Matthiesen, H. 2007. Methodologically Controlled Variations in Laboratory and Field pH Measurements in Waterlogged Soils. *European Journal of Soil Science*, 58: 207–14.

Gregory, D., Helms, A. C., and Matthiesen, H. 2008. The Use and Deployment of Modern Wood Samples as a Proxy Indicator for Biogeochemical Processes on Archaeological Sites Preserved *In Situ* in a Variety of Environments of Differing Saturation Level. *Conservation and Management of Archaeological Sites*, 10(3): 204–22.

Gregory, D. J. and Matthiesen, H. 2007. *In Situ* Preservation of Waterlogged Archaeological Sites. In: E. May and M. Jones, eds. *Conservation Science*. London: Royal Society of Chemistry.

Gregory, D. and Jensen, P. 2006. The Importance of Analysing Waterlogged Wooden Artefacts and Environmental Conditions when Considering their *In Situ* Preservation. *Journal of Wetland Archaeology*, 6: 65–81.

Gregory, D., Matthiesen, H., and Björdal, C. 2002. *In Situ* Preservation of Artefacts in Nydam Mose: Studies into Environmental Monitoring and the Deterioration of Wooden Artefacts. In: P. Hoffman, T. Grant, and J. Spriggs, eds. *Proceedings of the 8th ICOM Group on Wet Organic Archaeological Materials Conference*. Stockholm. Bremerhaven, pp. 213–23.

Helms, A. C., Camillo Martiny, A. Hofman-Bang, J., Ahring, B., and Kilstrup, M. 2004. Identification Of Bacterial Cultures from Archaeological Wood using Molecular Biological Techniques. *International Biodeterioration and Biodegradation*, 53(2): 79–88.

Matthiesen, H., Hilbert, L. R., Gregory, D., and Sørensen, B. 2007. Long-term Corrosion of Iron at the Waterlogged Site of Nydam in Denmark: Studies of Environment, Archaeological Artefacts, and Modern Analogues. In: P. Dillmann, P. Piccardo, H. Matthiesen, and G. Beranger, eds. *Corrosion of Metallic Heritage Artefacts: Investigation, Conservation and Prediction for Long-Term Behaviour*. Cambridge: Woodhead Publishing Ltd, pp. 272–92.

Matthiesen, H. 2004. In Situ Measurement of Soil pH. *Journal of Archaeological Science*, 31: 1373–81.

Matthiesen, H., Gregory, D., Jensen, P., and Sørensen, B. 2004a. Environmental Monitoring at Nydam, a Waterlogged Site with Weapon Sacrifices from the Danish Iron Age. A Comparison of Methods Used and Results from Undisturbed Conditions. *Journal of Wetland Archaeology*, 4: 55–74.

Matthiesen, H., Gregory, D., Sørensen, B., Alstrøm, T., and Jensen, P. 2004b. Monitoring Methods in Mires and Meadows: Five Years of Studies at Nydam Mose, Denmark. In: T. Nixon, ed. *Preserving Archaeological Remains In Situ? Proceedings of the 2nd Conference 12–14 September 2001*. London: Museum of London Archaeology Service, pp. 91–97.

Matthiesen, H., Salomonsen, E., and Sørensen, B. 2004. The Use of Radiography and GIS to Assess the Deterioration of Archaeological Iron Objects from a Waterlogged Environment. *Journal of Archaeological Science*, 31: 1451–61.

Matthiesen, H., Hilbert, L. R., and Gregory, D. J. 2003. Siderite as a Corrosion Product on Archaeological Iron from a Waterlogged Environment. *Studies in Conservation*, 48(3): 183–94.

Rau, A. 2012. *Nydam mose — Die personengebundenen Gegenstände*. Carlsbergfondet, Nationalmuseet and Moesgård Museum in Denmark (part of the Project 'Jernalderen i Nordeuropa'). Jysk Arkæologisk Selskabs Skrifter 72.

Saheb, M., Neff, D., Dillmann, P., and Matthiesen, H. 2007. Long-term Corrosion Behaviour of Low Carbon Steel in Anoxic Soils. In: C. Degrigny, R. van Langh, I. Joosten, and B. Ankersmit, eds. *Metal 07. Chapter 2: Innovative Investigation of Metal Artefacts. Conference Proceedings from Metal07, Amsterdam, September 2007*. Rijksmuseum Amsterdam, pp. 69–75.

Saheb, M., Neff, D., Dillmann, P., Matthiesen, H. E., and Foy, E. 2008. Long-term Corrosion Behaviour of Low Carbon Steel in Anoxic Environment: Characterisation of Archaeological Artefacts. *Journal of Nuclear Materials*, 379: 118–23.

Saheb, M., Neff, D., Dillmann, P., Matthiesen, H., Foy, E., and Bellot-Gurlet, L. 2009. Multisecular Corrosion Behaviour of Low Carbon Steel in Anoxic Soils: Characterisation of Corrosion System on Archaeological Artefacts. *Materials and Corrosion*, 60: 99–105.

Notes on contributors

David Gregory is currently a senior scientist at the National Museum of Denmark's conservation department, where he is investigating the deterioration of waterlogged archaeological wood, assessment of its state of preservation and methods of *in situ* preservation of archaeological materials in underwater environments.

Correspondence to: David Gregory, National Museum of Denmark, Department of Conservation, Research, Analysis and Consultancy, I.C. Modewegs Vej, Brede Kongens Lyngby, DK-2800, Denmark. Email: david.john.gregory@natmus.dk

Henning Matthiesen is a senior researcher at the National Museum of Denmark, where he works with the *in situ* preservation of archaeological remains. His research is focused on wetlands, urban deposits, and permafrozen sites.